ESSENTIALS OF MANAGEMENT

ESSENTIALS OF MANAGEMENT

NINTH EDITION

Andrew J. DuBrin

Professor Emeritus of Management
College of Business
Rochester Institute of Technology

SOUTH-WESTERN
CENGAGE Learning

Australia • Brazil • Japan • Korea • Mexico • Singapore • Spain • United Kingdom • United States

SOUTH-WESTERN
CENGAGE Learning™

Essentials of Management, Ninth Edition
Andrew J. DuBrin

VP/Editorial Director: Jack W. Calhoun

Editor-in-Chief: Melissa Acuña

Executive Editor: Scott Person

Developmental Editor: Jennifer King

Senior Editorial Assistant: Ruth Belanger

Marketing Manager: Jonathan Monahan

Senior Marketing Communications
Manager: Jim Overly

Content Project Management:
PreMediaGlobal

Media Editor: Danny Bolan

Production Technology Analyst: Jeff
Weaver

Frontlist Buyer: Miranda Klapper

Production House/Compositor:
PreMediaGlobal

Senior Art Director: Tippy McIntosh

Permissions Acquisition Manager/Text:
Mardell Glinski-Schultz

Cover Designer: Stuart Kunkler, triartis
communications

Cover Image: Vance Vasu/Images.com

For product information and technology assistance, contact us at
Cengage Learning Customer & Sales Support, 1-800-354-9706.

For permission to use material from this text or product, submit all
requests online at **www.cengage.com/permissions**.
Further permissions questions can be emailed to
permissionrequest@cengage.com.

ExamView® is a registered trademark of eInstruction Corp. Windows is
a registered trademark of the Microsoft Corporation used herein under
license. Macintosh and Power Macintosh are registered trademarks of
Apple Computer, Inc. used herein under license.

Library of Congress Control Number: 2010938008

ISBN 13: 978-0-538-47823-6

ISBN 10: 0-538-47823-3

South-Western
5191 Natorp Boulevard
Mason, OH 45040
USA

Cengage Learning is a leading provider of customized learning solutions
with office locations around the globe, including Singapore, the United
Kingdom, Australia, Mexico, Brazil, and Japan. Locate your local office at
www.cengage.com/global.

Cengage Learning products are represented in Canada by Nelson
Education, Ltd.

To learn more about South-Western, visit www.cengage.com/
South-Western

Purchase any of our products at your local college store or at our
preferred online store **www.cengagebrain.com**.

Printed in the United States of America
1 2 3 4 5 6 7 14 13 12 11 10

Preface

Essentials of Management is written for newcomers to the field of management and for experienced managers seeking updated information and a review of the fundamentals. It is also written for the many professionals and technical people who work closely with managers and who take their turn at performing some management work. An example would be the member of a cross-functional team who is expected to have the perspective of a general manager.

Based on extensive research about curriculum needs, the design of *Essentials of Management* addresses itself to the needs of introductory management courses and supervision courses offered in educational and work settings. Previous editions of the text were used in the study of management in colleges and universities, as well as in career schools in such diverse programs as hospitality and tourism management and nursing. The book can also be used as a basic resource for management courses that rely heavily on lecture notes, PowerPoint presentations, and videos rather than an encyclopedia-like text.

Comments made by Jack and Suzy Welch support the intent and relevance of this text in both the present and previous editions. (Jack Welch was the long-time chairman and CEO of GE and Suzy Welch is a former *Harvard Business Review* editor.) Jack and Suzy Welch write,

> *In the past two years, we've visited 35 B-schools around the world and have been repeatedly surprised by how little classroom attention is paid to hiring, motivating, team-building, and firing. Instead B-schools seem far more invested in teaching brainiac-concepts—disruptive technologies, complexity modeling, and the like. Those may be useful, particularly if you join a consulting firm, but real managers need to know how to get the most out of people.*
>
> (*Business Week*, December 11, 2006, p. 112.)

ASSUMPTIONS UNDERLYING THE BOOK

The approach to synthesizing knowledge for this book is based on the following five assumptions:

1. A strong demand exists for practical and valid information about solutions to managerial problems. The information found in this text reflects the author's orientation toward translating research findings, theory, and experience into a form useful to both the student and the practitioner.

2. Managers and professionals need both interpersonal and analytical skills to meet their day-to-day responsibilities. Although this book concentrates on managing people, it also provides ample information about such topics as decision making, job design, organization structure, information technology, cost cutting, and inventory management.

3. The study of management should emphasize a variety of large, medium, and small work settings, as well as profit and not-for-profit organizations. Many students of management, for example, intend to become small business owners. Examples and cases in this book therefore reflect diverse work settings, including retail and service firms.

4. Introductory management textbooks tend to be unrealistically comprehensive. Many introductory texts today are more than 800 pages long. Such texts overwhelm students who attempt to assimilate this knowledge in a single quarter or semester. The goal with *Essentials of Management* was to develop a text that realistically—in terms of time and amount of information—introduces the study of management. This text is not merely a condensation of a larger text, but a concise and comprehensive treatment of management since the first edition.

FRAMEWORK OF THE BOOK

The first three chapters present an introduction to management. Chapter 1, "The Manager's Job," explains the nature of managerial work with a particular emphasis on managerial roles and tasks. Chapter 2, "International Management and Cultural Diversity," describes how managers and professionals work in a multicultural environment. Chapter 3, "Ethics and Corporate Social Responsibility," examines the moral aspects of management.

The next three chapters address the subject of planning. Chapter 4, "Essentials of Planning," presents a general framework for planning—the activity underlying almost any purposeful action taken by a manager. Chapter 5, "Problem Solving and Decision Making," explores the basics of decision making with an emphasis on creativity and other behavioral aspects. Chapter 6, "Quantitative Techniques for Planning and Decision Making," describes several adjuncts to planning and decision making such as break-even analysis, PERT, and production-scheduling methods used for both manufacturing and services.

Chapters 7–9 focus on organizing, culture, and staffing. Chapter 7, "Job Design and Work Schedules," explains how jobs are laid out and work schedules arranged to enhance productivity and customer satisfaction. Chapter 8, "Organization Structure, Culture, and Change," explains how work is organized from the standpoint of the organization, how culture profoundly influences an organization, and how to cope with and capitalize on change. Chapter 9, "Human Resource and Talent Management," explains the methods by which people are brought into the organization, trained, and evaluated.

The next three chapters, on leading, deal directly with the manager's role in influencing group members. Chapter 10, "Leadership," focuses on different approaches to leadership available to a manager and on the personal characteristics associated with leadership effectiveness. Chapter 11, "Motivation," describes what managers can do to increase or sustain employee effort toward achieving work goals. Chapter 12, "Communication," deals with the complex problems of accurately sending and receiving messages. Chapter 13, "Teams, Groups, and Teamwork," explains the nature of teams and how managers can foster group members' working together cooperatively. Chapter 14, "Information Technology and e-Commerce," describes how information technology, including the Internet and e-commerce, influences the manager's job,

The next two chapters, on controlling, deal with an important part of keeping performance in line with expectations. Chapter 15, "Essentials of Control," presents an overview of measuring and controlling performance and describes how managers work with a variety of financial measures to monitor performance. Chapter 16, "Managing Ineffective Performers," describes current approaches to dealing with substandard performers, with an emphasis on elevating performance.

The final chapter in the text, Chapter 17, "Enhancing Personal Productivity and Managing Stress," describes how personal effectiveness can be increased by developing better work habits and time management skills and keeping stress under control. A major theme of the chapter is that good work habits help prevent and manage stress.

PEDAGOGICAL FEATURES

Essentials of Management is designed to aid both students and instructors in expanding their interest in and knowledge of management. The book contains the following features:

- Learning objectives coordinate the contents of each chapter. They preview the major topics and are integrated into the text by indicating which major topics relate to the objectives. The end-of-chapter Summary of Key Points, based on the chapter learning objectives, pulls together the central ideas in each chapter.
- An opening case example illustrates a major topic to be covered in the chapter.
- The Management in Action feature presents a portrait of how specific individuals or organizations practice an aspect of management covered in the chapter.
- Concrete, real-world examples with which the reader can readily identify are found throughout the text. Some examples are original, while others relate research information from magazines, newspapers, journals, and Internet sources.
- Exhibits, which include figures, tables, and self-assessment quizzes, aid in the comprehension of information in the text.

- Key terms and phrases highlight the management vocabulary introduced in each chapter with definitions that appear in the margin.
- Questions at the end of each chapter assist learning by encouraging the reader to review and reflect on the chapter objectives.
- Skill-building exercises, including Internet activities, appear at the end of each chapter.
- Self-assessment quizzes appear throughout the text, designed to help students think through their standing on important dimensions of behavior that influence managerial and professional work.
- Case problems, also located at the end of each chapter, can be used to synthesize the chapter concepts and simulate the practice of management.
- Video selections are cued to places in the text where they have particular applicability.

NEW TO THE NINTH EDITION

A number of significant changes and additions have been incorporated into this edition. A brief listing of these changes here is followed by a more detailed look.

- All 17 chapters contain new information where appropriate; many older research findings and several topics of lesser interest today have been deleted.
- Twenty-three of the 34 end-of-chapter cases are new, and the Chapter 4 case about Dell has been updated.
- Fifteen of the chapter-opening cases are new.
- Nearly all of the many Management in Action boxes are new. The previous Management in Action stories about Wal-Mart and Hypertherm have been updated.
- There is a new end-of-chapter exercise called Management Now: Online Skill-Building Activities. These exercises will encourage students to use the Internet to obtain up-to-the-minute information, ideas, and applications directly related to each chapter's topic.
- Three of the skill-building exercises are new.

New Topics Added to the Text
- Coping with dangerous and defective products as a challenge for the manager involved in international trade (Chapter 2)
- Analysis of sources of unethical decisions in terms of characteristics of the individual, moral issues facing the person, and the organizational environment (Chapter 3)
- Extracting extraordinary compensation from the organization as a type of ethical temptation (Chapter 3)

- The preparation of fraudulent financial documents to deceive investors as a type of unethical behavior, with Bernard L. Madoff as an example (Chapter 3)
- The three components of corporate social responsibility: cognitive, linguistic, and conative (behavior) (Chapter 3)
- Expanded coverage of environmental protection as a form of social responsibility (Chapter 3)
- How decision making is influenced by emotional tagging, or the process by which emotional information attaches itself to our memories (Chapter 5)
- Engaging in physical exercise to enhance creativity (Chapter 5)
- Scenario planning for making good use of forecasts (Chapter 6)
- The Delphi technique for increasing the accuracy of forecasts (Chapter 6)
- Job design to help decrease back problems (Chapter 7)
- Social network analysis to understand the informal organization structure (Chapter 8)
- Resistance to change as a form of feedback (Chapter 8)
- Emphasis on concept of talent management instead of organizational staffing (Chapter 9)
- Situational judgment tests as a type of psychological test in employment (Chapter 9)
- Exhibit 10-2 about the measurement of three organizational influence tactics (Chapter 10)
- New section on leadership during adversity and crisis (Chapter 10)
- Four drives or needs hardwired into our brains (Chapter 11)
- The use of social media as a communication channel within the organization (Chapter 12)
- Reducing cross-cultural communication barriers by correctly pronouncing the names of people you interact with from other countries (Chapter 12)
- Ostracism of unwanted group member as a potential disadvantage of a group (Chapter 13)
- Section on social media and customer relationships (Chapter 14)
- Section on how cloud computing affects the internal operations of an organization (Chapter 14)
- Ethical problems associated with maintaining high cash flow by delaying payment of bills (Chapter 15)
- Section on potential hazards of cost reductions (Chapter 15)
- Relative standing against competition as a measure of a company's financial success (Chapter 15)
- The problem with controls limiting innovation (Chapter 15)
- Workplace harassment in general as a contributor to ineffective performance (Chapter 16)
- Avoiding surprises when terminating an employee (Chapter 16)
- Exhibit on causes of stress among the general population (Chapter 17)

New Skill-Building Exercises

Every chapter contains two skill-building exercises, with three new exercises added to the ninth edition, as follows:

- Conducting an Environmental Audit (Chapter 3)
- Stretching Your Imagination (Chapter 5)
- Learning from Failed Leadership (Chapter 10)

New Management Now: Online Skill-Building Exercises

Every chapter contains an Internet-based skill-building exercise designed to connect students to Web sites that will boost their knowledge of up-to-the-minute management topics and issues. Four new skill builders are:

- Finding the Best Jobs (Chapter 7)
- Analyzing a Motivational Program (Chapter 11)
- Sizing up an Executive on YouTube (Chapter 14)
- Finding a C-Level Manager Worthy of Being Terminated (Chapter 16)

Self-Quizzes

Not only will students enjoy taking the self-quizzes, they will also learn about their strengths and areas for improvement in the process. Your students will benefit from taking the following quizzes:

- My Managerial Role Analysis (Chapter 1)
- Cross-Cultural Skills and Attitudes (Chapter 2)
- The Ethical Reasoning Inventory (Chapter 3)
- How Involved Are You? (Chapter 7)
- Understanding Your Bureaucratic Orientation (Chapter 8)
- Behaviors and Attitudes of a Trustworthy Leader (Chapter 10)
- What Style of Leader Are You? (Chapter 10)
- My Approach to Motivating Others (Chapter 11)
- The Positive Organizational Politics Questionnaire (Chapter 12)
- Team Skills (Chapter 13)
- The Self-Sabotage Questionnaire (Chapter 16)
- Procrastination Tendencies (Chapter 17)
- The Stress Questionnaire (Chapter 17)

Brand-New Action Inserts

Students will find one Management in Action insert in every chapter. Fifteen inserts are completely new or an update of an insert from the eighth edition. A complete list follows:

- Brian O'Connor, the Chief Privacy Officer at Eastman Kodak Company (Chapter 1)
- Canadian Banks Open Doors for Employees with Disabilities (Chapter 2)

- Updating and Expansion of Wal-Mart Managers Take the High Road and the Low Road (Chapter 3)
- Mike's Carwash Puts People First (Chapter 4)
- Procter & Gamble and Google Swap Workers to Spur Innovation (Chapter 5)
- Data-Driven Decision Making at Hewlett-Packard (updated) (Chapter 6)
- Be Our Guest Hires Part-Time CFO (Chapter 7)
- Nokia Corp. Reorganizes (Chapter 8)
- Goodyear Tire Stretches Compensation Dollars (Chapter 9)
- Safety Coordinator Sherry Black Copes with a Tornado at a Caterpillar Plant (Chapter 10)
- Workers at Skyline Construction Choose Own Mix of Salary and Bonus (Chapter 11)
- Victor Gulas Draws a Map of Connections (Chapter 12)
- Hypertherm Chief Executive Organizes for Teamwork (Chapter 13)
- Companies Combat Online Insults (Chapter 14)
- Cash Doesn't Lie (Chapter 15)
- A Counseling Letter Sent to an Underperforming Employee (Chapter 16)
- Leading Banker Uses To-Do Lists to Keep Organized (Chapter 17)

New End-of-Chapter Cases

Twenty-three of the cases in the ninth edition are new and one is updated as follows:

- Big Hopes at Olive Garden, the Red Lobster, and LongHorn (Chapter 1)
- The Management Trainee Blues (Chapter 1)
- Aquarius Technologies is Caught in a Trade War (Chapter 2)
- Flippant Jessica (Chapter 2)
- Should We Launch Lightening Bolt? (Chapter 3)
- The Blue Ocean Strategy Team (Chapter 4)
- What Should Dell Do Next? (updated) (Chapter 4)
- What to Do with All these False Emergency Patients? (Chapter 5)
- Staple's Invention Quest (Chapter 5)
- Retro is Our Future (Chapter 6)
- Just-In-Time Worries at the University of Utah Hospital (Chapter 6)
- The Telecommuting Challenge at NewWest.Net (Chapter 7)
- Redesigning PepsiCo (Chapter 8)
- Performance Rankings at Portland Events Planners (Chapter 9)
- Michelle Rhee Makes Waves in D.C. (Chapter 10)
- Is Julia Too Empowering? (Chapter 10)
- Justin Tries a Little Recognition (Chapter 11)
- Networking Megan (Chapter 12)
- Team Player Jessica (Chapter 13)
- How Far Can MyGofer Go? (Chapter 14)
- The Adoring Bloggers (Chapter 14)

- Mr. Potato Head Visits Starbucks (Chapter 15)
- MySpace is Our Place (Chapter 15)
- "It Takes Me a Long Time to Get Here" (Chapter 16)
- Sean Struggles to Get Started (Chapter 17)
- Brittany Faces Reality (Chapter 17)

INSTRUCTIONAL RESOURCES

Essentials of Management is accompanied by comprehensive instructional support materials.

- *Instructor's Manual.* Available on the Instructor's Resource CD and online, the instructor's manual provides resources to increase the teaching and learning value of Essentials of Management. The Manual contains "Chapter Outline and Lecture Notes," which is of particular value to instructors whose time budget does not allow for extensive class preparation. For each chapter, the Manual provides a statement of purpose and scope, outline and lecture notes, lecture topics, comments on the end-of-chapter questions and activities, responses to case questions, an experiential activity, and video case notes.
- *Test Bank.* Also available on the IRCD or online, the Test Bank contains at least 25 multiple-choice questions, 25 true/false questions, and 3 essay questions. New to this edition are several critical thinking multiple-choice questions for each chapter.
- *Examview.* The Test Bank questions are also available on the Instructor's Resource CD with the test generator program, Examview. This versatile software package allows instructors to create new questions and edit or delete existing questions from the Test Bank.
- *PowerPoint Slides.* A set of 425 professionally prepared PowerPoint slides accompanies the text. This slide package is designed for easy classroom use and closely follows the Instructor's Manual to facilitate classroom presentation.
-  *Management CourseMate.* Cengage Learning's Management Course-Mate brings course concepts to life with interactive learning, study, and exam preparation tools that support the printed textbook. Through this website, available for an additional fee, students will have access to their own set of Powerpoint® slides, flashcards, and games, as well as the Learning Objectives, Opening Cases, and Glossary for quick reviews. A set of auto-gradable, interactive quizzes will allow students to instantly gauge their comprehension of the material.
- *Product Support Website.* The flashcards, Learning Objectives, and Glossary are available for quick reference on our complimentary student product support website.
- *Webtutor on BlackBoard® and Webtutor on WebCT™.* Available on two different platforms, Essentials of Management Webtutor enhances students' understanding of the material by featuring the Opening Cases,

Learning Objectives, key term flashcards, threaded discussion questions, puzzles and games, and quizzes that delve more deeply into key concepts presented in the book so that students can excel at all types of assessment.

A NOTE TO THE STUDENT

The information in the general preface is important for students as well as instructors. Here I offer additional comments that will enable you to increase the personal payoffs from studying management. My message can be organized around several key points.

- *Management is not simply common sense.* The number one trap for students studying management is to assume that the material is easy to master because many of the terms and ideas are familiar. For example, just because you have heard the word *teamwork* many times, it does not automatically follow that you are familiar with specific field-tested ideas for enhancing teamwork.
- *Managerial skills are vital.* The information in the course for which you are studying this text and in the text itself are vital in today's world. People with formal managerial job titles such as *supervisor*, *team leader*, *department head*, or *vice president* are obviously expected to possess managerial skills. But many other people in jobs without managerial titles also benefit from managerial skills. Among them are people with titles such as *administrative assistant*, *customer-service representative*, and *inventory-control specialist*.
- *The combination of managerial, interpersonal, and technical skills leads to outstanding career success.* A recurring myth is that it is better to study "technical" or "hard" subjects than management because the pay is better. In reality, the people in business making the higher salaries and other compensation are those who combine technical skills with managerial and interpersonal skills. Executives and business owners, for example, can earn incomes rivaled only by leading professional athletes and entertainment personalities.
- *Studying management, however, has its biggest payoff in the long run.* Entry-level management positions are in short supply. Management is a basic life process. To run a major corporation, manage a restaurant or a hair salon, organize a company picnic, plan a wedding, or run a good household, management skills are an asset. We all have some knowledge of management, but formally studying management can multiply one's effectiveness.

Take advantage of the many study aids in this text. You will enhance your learning of management by concentrating on such learning aids as the chapter objectives, summaries, discussion questions, self-quizzes, skill-development exercises, and the glossary. Carefully studying a glossary is an effective way of building a vocabulary in a new field. Studying the glossary will also serve as a reminder of important topics. Activities such as the cases, discussion questions, and skill-building exercises facilitate learning by creating the opportunity to think through the information. Thinking through information, in turn, leads to better comprehension and long-term retention of information.

ACKNOWLEDGMENTS

Any project as complex as this text requires a team of dedicated and talented people to see that it gets completed effectively. Many reviewers made valuable comments during the development of this new edition as well as the previous seven editions of the text. I appreciate the helpful suggestions of the following colleagues:

Jackie Armstrong
Hill College

Thelma Anderson
Montana State University–Northern

Zay Lynn Bailey
SUNY—Brockport

Kathy Baughman
Juniata College

Tom Birkenhead
Lane Community College

Genie Black
Arkansas Tech University

Thomas M. Bock
Baruch College

Brenda Britt
Fayetteville Technical Community College

Murray Brunton
Central Ohio Technical College

Michel Cardinale
Palomar College

Gary Clark
North Harris College

Glenn A. Compton
University of Maryland

Jose L. Curzet
Florida National College

Rex Cutshall
Vincennes University

Robert DeDominic
Montana Tech University

Robert Desman
Kennesaw State College

Kenneth Dreifus
Pace University

Ben Dunn
York Technical College

Karen A. Evans
Herkimer County Community College

Debra Farley
Ozark College

Thomas Fiock
Southern Illinois University at Carbondale

Renee T. Garcia
Luna Community College

Dan Geeding
Xavier University

Shirley Gilmore
Iowa State University

Philip C. Grant
Hussen College

Randall Greenwell
John Wood Community College

David R. Grimmett
Austin Peay State University

Robert Halliman
Austin Peay State University

Ed Hamer
George Mason University

Paul Hegele
Elgin Community College

Kermelle D. Hensley
Columbus Technical College

Thomas Heslin
Indiana University

Peter Hess
Western New England College

Melanie Hilburn
Lone Star College—North Harris

Nathan Himelstein
Essex County College

Kim T. Hinrichs
Minnesota State University—Mankato

Brad Hollaway
Ozarka College

Judith A. Horrath
Lehigh Corbon Community College

Margaret Huron
Lone Star College—North Harris

Lawrence H. Jaffe
Rutgers University

Steven Jennings
Highland Community College

B. R. Kirkland
Tarleton State University

Alecia N. Lawrence
Williamsburg Technical College

Donald Lee
Pitt Community College

Margaret S. Maguire
SUNY—Oneonta

Patrician Manninen
North Shore Community College

Noel Matthews
Front Range Community College

Ted Mattingly
George Mason University

Christopher J. Morris
Adirondack Community College

Ilona Motsiff
Trinity College of Vermont

David W. Murphy
University of Kentucky

Robert D. Nale
Coastal Carolina University

Christopher P. Neck
Virginia Tech

Ronald W. Olive
New Hampshire Technical College

George M. Padilla
New Mexico State University—Almogordo

J. E. Pearson
Dabney S. Lancaster Community College

Gregory F. Petranek
Eastern Connecticut State University

Joseph Platts
Miami-Dade Community College

Larry S. Potter
University of Maine—Presque Isle

Thomas Quirk
Webster University

Jane Rada
Western Wisconsin Technical College

James Riley
Oklahoma Junior College

Robert Scully
Barry University

William Searle
Asnuntuck Community Technical College

William Shepard
New Hampshire Technical College

Vladimir Simic
Missouri Valley College

Howard R. Stanger
Canisius College

Lynn Suksdorf
Salt Lake Community College

John J. Sullivan
Montreat College

Martin J. Suydam
George Mason University

Gary Tilley
Surry Community College

Bernard Weinrich
St. Louis Community College

Blaine Weller
Baker College

Mara Winick
University of Redlands

Alex Wittig
North Metro Technical College

Marybeth Kardatzke Zipperer
Montgomery College

Thanks also to the members of the Cengage Learning South-Western Team who worked with me on this edition: Editor-in-Chief Melissa Acuña; Executive Editor Scott Person; Developmental Editor Jennifer King; Senior Editorial Assistant Ruth Belanger; Senior Art Director Tippy McIntosh; Marketing Manager Jon Monahan; and Marketing Coordinator Julia Tucker. Writing without loved ones would be a lonely task. My thanks therefore go to my family: Drew, Rosie, Clare, Douglas, Gizella, Camila, Sofia, Eliana, Julian, Melanie, Will, and Carson. My thanks are also expressed to Stefanie, the woman in my life.

Andrew J. DuBrin

About the Author

Andrew J. DuBrin is Professor Emeritus of Management in the College of Business at the Rochester Institute of Technology, where he has taught courses and conducted research in management, organizational behavior, leadership, and career management. He also gives presentations at other colleges, career schools, and universities. He has served as department chairman and team leader in previous years. He received his Ph.D. in Industrial Psychology from Michigan State University. DuBrin has business experience in human resource management and consults with organizations and individuals. His specialties include career management leadership and management development. DuBrin is an established author of both textbooks and trade books, and he contributes to professional journals, magazines, newspapers, and online media. He has written textbooks on management, leadership, organizational behavior, human relations, and impression management. His trade books cover many management issues, including charisma, team play, office politics, overcoming career self-sabotage, and coaching and mentoring.

Brief Contents

PART 6 Managing for Personal Effectiveness

Contents

ESSENTIALS OF
MANAGEMENT

The Manager's Job

In November a few years ago, Nancy Jackson was able to hire a new full-time salesperson for the company she co-owns, Architectural Systems Inc. in New York, but found herself facing an angry 19-person staff. "I couldn't believe their reaction," she says. Just a few months earlier, some had seen their workweeks reduced or salaries scaled back; two colleagues had been laid off.

To mitigate the situation, Jackson quickly called a meeting to explain that beefing up the firm's sales force was a necessary first step for making a companywide recovery. Meanwhile, she has since gone about hiring differently, she says, bringing on a new marketing associate as a temporary part-time employee, rather than a full-time staff member, so as not to rile her team. "There's been a lot of emotional hand-holding here that we've never had to do before."[1]

The story about the manager and owner of the architectural firm illustrates, among other ideas, that a manager makes things happen, such as enabling the growth of the firm. Also illustrated is that managers often must deal with upset employees and resolve conflict. As will be described

[1]Sarah E. Needleman, "Business Owners Try to Motivate Employees," *The Wall Street Journal*, January 14, 2010, p. B5.

in this chapter, and throughout the book, the manager carries out a large number of demanding activities.

manager
A person responsible for the work performance of group members.

management
The process of using organizational resources to achieve organizational objectives through planning, organizing and staffing, leading, and controlling.

Go to www.cengage. com/management/ dubrin and view the video for Chapter 1. As you watch, think about the various types of managers shown in the video. What are some of the skills exhibited by the company founder? What are some of the skills exhibited by the other managers?

top-level managers
Managers at the top one or two levels in an organization.

WHO IS A MANAGER?

A **manager** is a person responsible for the work performance of group members. Approximately 10 percent of the U.S. workforce holds a managerial position of one type or another. A manager holds the formal authority to commit organizational resources, even if the approval of others is required. For example, the manager of a Jackson-Hewitt income tax and financial service outlet has the authority to order the repainting of the reception area. The income tax and financial services specialists reporting to that manager, however, do not have that authority.

The concepts of manager and managing are intertwined. The term **management** in this book refers to the process of using organizational resources to achieve organizational objectives through the functions of planning, organizing and staffing, leading, and controlling. These functions represent the broad framework for this book and will be described later. In addition to being a process, the term *management* is also used as a label for a specific discipline, for the people who manage, and for a career choice.

Levels of Management

Another way of understanding the nature of a manager's job is to examine the three levels of management shown in Exhibit 1-1. The pyramid in this figure illustrates progressively fewer employees at each higher managerial level. The largest number of people is at the bottom organizational level. (Note that the term *organizational level* is sometimes more precise than the term *managerial level*, particularly at the bottom organizational level, which has no managers.)

Top-Level Managers

Most people who enter the field of management aspire to become **top-level managers**—managers at the top one or two levels in an organization. **C-level manager** is a recent term used to describe a top-level manager; these managers usually have the word *chief* in their title, such as *chief operating officer*. Top-level managers are empowered to make major decisions affecting the present and future of the firm. Only a top-level manager, for example, would have the authority to purchase another company, initiate a new product line, or hire hundreds of employees. Top-level managers are the people who give the organization its general direction; they decide where it is going and how it will get there. The terms *executive, top-level manager*, and *c-level manager* can be used interchangeably.

Because management is an evolving field, new job titles for c-level managers continue to surface. Often these titles reflect a new emphasis on what

---

EXHIBIT 1-1   **Managerial Levels and Sample Job Titles**

Many job titles can be found at each level of management.

Top-Level Managers

Chairman of the board, CEO, president, vice president, COO (chief operating officer), CFO (chief financial officer), CIO (chief information officer)

Middle-Level Managers

Director, branch manager, department chairperson, chief of surgery, team leader

First-Level Managers

Supervisor, office manager, crew chief

Individual Contributors (Operatives and Specialists)

Tool-and-die maker, cook, word-processing technician, assembler

Note: Some individual contributors, such as financial analysts and administrative assistants, report directly to top-level managers or middle managers.

C-level manager
A recent term to describe top-level managers because they usually have *chief* in their title.

must be accomplished for an organization to run successfully. Here are a few of the recent c-level positions often found in large organizations:

- *Chief of staff.* High-level executives in politics and the military have long relied on the services of a chief of staff; this role has recently become a part of the executive suite in business. The chief of staff is a top level advisor who serves as a confidant, gatekeeper, and all-around strategic consultant. Three financial services firms with a chief of staff in the executive suite are Goldman Sachs, Aflac, and the global insurance business ING.[2]

- *Chief commercial officer.* A growing number of large business firms are designating a chief commercial officer who oversees growth and commercial success. The person in this position has major responsibility for customer relationships and for managing the company interface with the customer. The chief commercial officer position has been created because the many different sales channels, especially digital sales, has forced companies to think differently about their customers and how they interact with them. In some instances the CCO supplements the work of the head of marketing, and at other times replaces him or her. The biotech firm Cellular Dynamics International is one firm that employs a chief commercial officer.[3]

---

[2]"Latest CEO Accessory: A Chief of Staff," *Fortune*, January 18, 2010, p. 18.
[3]Ed Frauenheim, "'CCO' Becomes Hot Exec Title Amid Recession," *Workforce Management*, September 14, 2009, p. 4.

MANAGEMENT IN ACTION

As Rochester, New York-based Eastman Kodak struggles to transform from a film dinosaur to a digital powerhouse, it falls to Chief Privacy Officer Brian O'Connor to keep identity thieves away from EasyShare, Kodak's photo-sharing Web site. It's also his job to ensure that HR (human resources) and line managers don't put the company at risk by overzealously investigating job applicants. Welcome to the world of chief privacy officer (CPO), a young profession with a complicated mandate: protecting the privacy of consumer and employment data.

At Kodak, where O'Connor has served as CPO since 2005, safeguarding customer information—including the millions of digital photos shutterbugs add to EasyShare each day—is key to survival. But it is also at the heart of a complex tangle of federal, state, and international rules governing how organizations handle personal information.

Questions
1. After studying the section about managerial roles later in this chapter, identify which roles O'Connor is carrying out.
2. Explain whether you think a company really needs a "chief privacy officer."
3. Assuming you had the necessary knowledge and skills, to what extent would the position of chief privacy officer appeal to you?
4. Do you worry about identity theft when you post photos on the Internet?

Source: Rita Zeidner, "New Face in the C-Suite," *HR Magazine*, January 2010, p. 39.

- *Chief privacy officer.* As illustrated in the accompanying Management in Action, the chief privacy officer works on such problems as safeguarding customer information in the digital world.

Middle-Level Managers

middle-level managers

Managers who are neither executives nor first-level supervisors, but who serve as a link between the two groups.

Middle-level managers are managers who are neither executives nor first-level supervisors, but who serve as a link between the two groups. Middle-level managers conduct most of the coordination activities within the firm, and they are responsible for implementing programs and policies formulated by top-level management. The jobs of middle-level managers vary substantially in terms of responsibility and income. A branch manager in a large firm might be responsible for more than 100 workers. In contrast, a general supervisor in a small manufacturing firm might have 20 people reporting to him or her. Other important tasks for many middle-level managers include helping the company undertake profitable new ventures and finding creative ways to reach goals. A major part of a middle manager's job is working with teams to accomplish work. Middle-level managers play a major role in operating an organization, and therefore continue to be in demand.

Although advances in information technology have reduced the communication requirement of the middle manager positions, the need for middle managers is still strong. Paul Osterman, a management scholar at the MIT Sloan School of Management, conducted an interview and survey study of a group of middle managers. One of the conclusions he reached was as follows: "They are responsible for making many of the judgment calls and trade-offs that shape the firm's success. They are also the key communication channel from senior management down through the ranks."[4]

First-Level Managers

first-level managers
Managers who supervise operatives (also known as first-line managers or supervisors).

Managers who supervise operatives are referred to as **first-level managers**, first-line managers, or supervisors. Historically, first-level managers were promoted from production or clerical (now called staff support) positions into supervisory positions. Rarely did they have formal education beyond high school. A dramatic shift has taken place in recent years, however. Many of today's first-level managers are career school graduates and four-year college graduates who are familiar with modern management techniques. The current emphasis on productivity and cost control has elevated the status of many supervisors.

To understand the work performed by first-level managers, reflect back on your first job. Like most employees in entry-level positions, you probably reported to a first-level manager. Such a manager might be supervisor of newspaper carriers, dining room manager, service station manager, maintenance supervisor, or department manager in a retail store. Supervisors help shape the attitudes of new employees toward the firm. Newcomers who like and respect their first-level manager tend to stay with the firm longer. Conversely, new workers who dislike and disrespect their first supervisor tend to leave the firm early.

TYPES OF MANAGERS

The functions performed by managers can also be understood by describing different types of management jobs. The management jobs discussed here are functional and general managers, administrators, entrepreneurs and small-business owners, and team leaders. (The distinction between line and staff managers will be described in Chapter 8 about organization structure.)

Functional and General Managers

Another way of classifying managers is to distinguish between those who manage people who do one type of specialized work and those who manage people who engage in different specialties. *Functional managers* supervise the work of employees engaged in specialized activities such as accounting, engineering, information systems, food preparation, marketing, and sales. A functional manager is a manager of specialists and of their support team, such as office assistants.

---

[4]Paul Osterman, *The Truth About Middle Managers: Who They Are, How They Work, Why They Matter* (Boston: Harvard Business School Press, 2009). Quoted in Dean Foust, "Speaking Up for the Organization Man," *Business Week*, March 9, 2009, p. 78.

General managers are responsible for the work of several different groups that perform a variety of functions. The job title "plant general manager" offers insight into the meaning of general management. Reporting to the plant general manager are various departments engaged in both specialized and generalized work such as manufacturing, engineering, labor relations, quality control, safety, and information systems. Company presidents are general managers. Branch managers also are general managers if employees from different disciplines report to them. The responsibilities and tasks of a general manager highlight many of the topics contained in the study of management. These tasks will be introduced at various places in this book.

Administrators

An *administrator* is typically a manager who works in a public (government) or nonprofit organization, including educational institutions, rather than in a business firm. Among these managerial positions are hospital administrator and housing administrator. Managers in all types of educational institutions are referred to as administrators. The fact that individual contributors in nonprofit organizations are sometimes referred to as administrators often causes confusion. An employee is not an administrator in the managerial sense unless he or she supervises others.

Entrepreneurs and Small-Business Owners

Millions of students and employees dream of turning an exciting idea into a successful business. Many people think, "If Michael Dell started Dell computers from his dormitory room and he is the wealthiest man in Texas today, why can't I do something similar?" Success stories such as Dell's kindle the entrepreneurial spirit. By a strict definition, an **entrepreneur** is a person who founds and operates an innovative business. After the entrepreneur develops the business into something bigger than he or she can handle alone or with the help of only a few people, that person becomes a general manager.

Similar to an entrepreneur, the owner and operator of a small business becomes a manager when the firm grows to include several employees. **Small-business owners** typically invest considerable emotional and physical energy into their firms. Note that entrepreneurs are (or start as) small-business owners, but that the reverse is not necessarily true. You need an innovative idea to fit the strict definition of an entrepreneur. Simply running a franchise that sells sub sandwiches does not make a person an entrepreneur, according to the definition presented here. Also, an entrepreneur may found a business that becomes so big it is no longer a small business.

A major characteristic of both entrepreneurs and small-business owners is their passion for the work. These types of managers will usually have a single-minded drive to solve a problem. Recent research has identified three roles, or activities, within entrepreneurial work that arouse passion. The first is *opportunity recognition*, the inventor role. Second is *venture creation*, the

entrepreneur
A person who founds and operates an innovative business.

small-business owner
An individual who owns and operates a small business.

founder role. Third is *venture growth*, the developer role.[5] A person might invent a small turbine the size of a garbage can to replace the large turbines (or wind mills) used to generate renewable energy. The person becomes exited about creating a business to manufacture and market these small turbines. Passion would then be invested in growing the business. If being an inventor fits the person's self-image best, he or she is likely to be the most passionate about the first role and then lose some passion in the second and third roles.

Team Leaders

team leader
A manager who coordinates the work of a small group of people, while acting as a facilitator and catalyst.

A major development in types of managerial positions during the last 25 years is the emergence of the **team leader**. A manager in such a position coordinates the work of a small group of people while acting as a facilitator or catalyst. Team leaders are found at several organizational levels and are sometimes referred to as project managers, program managers, process managers, and task force leaders. Note that the term *team* could also refer to an executive team, yet a top executive almost never carries the title *team leader*. You will be reading about team leaders throughout this text.

All of the managerial jobs described above vary considerably as to the demands placed on the job holder. All workers carrying the job title *chief executive officer* may perform similar work, yet the position may be much more demanding and stressful in a particular organization.[6] Imagine being the CEO of an American auto parts manufacturer that is facing extinction because of overseas competition. His or her job is more demanding than that of the CEO of a company like Binney & Smith, the subsidiary of Hallmark Cards, which produces Crayola crayons among other popular products. With more than three billion crayons produced each year, and a fan base in the millions, Binney & Smith is not threatened with extinction. The CEO can enjoy his or her golf outings while the auto parts CEO worries about losing customers and laying off employees.

LEARNING OBJECTIVE 2
Describe the process of management including the functions of management.

THE PROCESS OF MANAGEMENT

A helpful approach to understanding what managers do is to regard their work as a process. A process is a series of actions that achieves something—making a profit or providing a service, for example. To achieve an objective, the manager uses resources and carries out four major managerial functions. These functions are planning, organizing and staffing, leading, and controlling. Exhibit 1-2 illustrates the process of management.

---

[5]Melissa S. Cardon, Joakim Wincent, Jagdip Singh, and Mateja Drnovsek, "The Nature and Experience of Entrepreneurial Passion," *Academy of Management Review*, July 2009, pp. 511–532.

[6]Donald C. Hambrick, Sydney Finkelstein, and Ann C. Mooney, "Executive Job Demands: New Insights for Explaining Strategic Decisions and Leader Behavior," *Academy of Management Review*, July 2005, pp. 472–491.

EXHIBIT 1-2	The Process of Management

The manager uses resources and carries out functions to achieve goals.

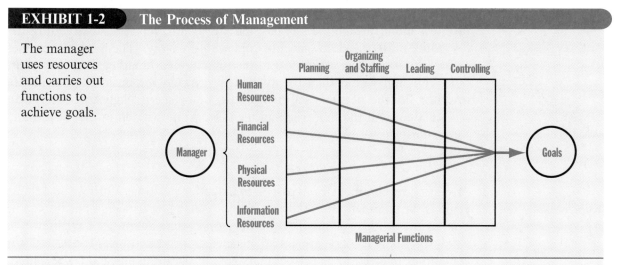

Resources Used by Managers

Managers use resources to accomplish their purposes, just as a carpenter uses resources to build a terrace. A manager's resources can be divided into four types: human, financial, physical, and informational.

Human resources are the people needed to get the job done. Managers' goals influence which employees they choose. A manager might set the goal of delivering automotive supplies and tools to auto and truck manufacturers. Among the human resources he or she chooses are manufacturing technicians, sales representatives, information technology specialists, and a network of dealers.

Financial resources are the money the manager and the organization use to reach organizational goals. The financial resources of a business organization are profits and investments from stockholders. A business must occasionally borrow cash to meet payroll or to pay for supplies. The financial resources of community agencies come from tax revenues, charitable contributions, and government grants.

Physical resources are a firm's tangible goods and real estate, including raw materials, office space, production facilities, office equipment, and vehicles. Vendors supply many of the physical resources needed to achieve organizational goals.

Information resources are the data that the manager and the organization use to get the job done. For example, to supply leads to the firm's sales representatives, the sales manager of an office-supply company reads local business newspapers and Internet postings to learn about new firms in town. These newspapers and Web sites are information resources. Jeffrey R. Immelt, the chairman and CEO of General Electric Corp., surfs the Internet regularly to learn about developments in the industry, thus using the Internet as an information resource.

As originally designated by the famous management thinker Peter Drucker, managers are *knowledge workers*. As knowledge workers, managers rely heavily on information resources. Drucker also observed that managers are quite skilled at obtaining data, but less skilled at converting these data into useful information. According to Drucker, few executives will ask, "What new tasks can I tackle, now that I have all these data? Which old tasks should I abandon?"[7] Imagine that a middle manager is wondering about how to best motivate workers. She inserts into Ask.com the question, "How do you motivate workers?" She receives close to two million entries. She must then understand how to sort out the most useful of these entries. (Or, she could study the motivational chapter of a management textbook.)

THE FOUR MANAGERIAL FUNCTIONS

Exhibit 1-2 shows the four major resources in the context of the management process. To accomplish goals, the manager performs four managerial functions. These functions are planning, organizing and staffing, leading, and controlling.

Planning

Planning involves setting goals and figuring out ways of reaching them. Planning, considered the central function of management, pervades everything a manager does. In planning, a manager looks to the future, saying, "Here is what we want to achieve, and here is how we are going to do it." Decision making is usually a component of planning, because choices must be made in the process of finalizing plans. The importance of planning expands as it contributes heavily to performing the other management functions. For example, managers must make plans to do an effective job of staffing the organization. Planning is also part of marketing. For example, cereal maker Kellogg Corp. established plans to diversify further into the snack-food business to reach its goal of expanding market share.

Organizing and Staffing

Organizing is the process of making sure the necessary human and physical resources are available to carry out a plan and achieve organizational goals. Organizing also involves assigning activities, dividing work into specific jobs and tasks, and specifying who has the authority to accomplish certain tasks. Another major aspect of organizing is grouping activities into departments or some other logical subdivision. The staffing function ensures the availability of necessary human resources to achieve organizational goals. Hiring people for jobs is a typical staffing activity. Staffing is such a major activity that it is sometimes classified as a function separate from organizing.

---

[7]"An American Sage," *The Wall Street Journal*, November 14, 2005, p. A22.

Leading

Leading means influencing others to achieve organizational objectives. As a consequence, it involves energizing, directing, persuading others, and creating a vision. Leadership involves dozens of interpersonal processes: motivating, communicating, coaching, and showing group members how they can reach their goals. Leadership is such a key component of managerial work that management is sometimes seen as accomplishing results through people. The leadership aspect of management focuses on inspiring people and bringing about change, whereas the other three functions focus more on maintaining a stable system. According to management guru Henry Mintzberg, effective leaders develop the sense of community or shared purpose that is essential for cooperative effort in all organizations.[8]

Although leadership deals heavily with persuasion and inspiration, the leader also executes the visions and other ideas for change he or she formulates. As explained by business executive Larry Bossidy and consultant Ram Charan, visionaries often fail because they do not translate their strategies (master plans) into results.[9] It has been said that *execution* has become an important new buzzword in business because leaders in the past placed too much emphasis on spinning grand visions without really taking care of business.

Controlling

Controlling generally involves comparing actual performance to a predetermined standard. Any significant difference between actual and desired performance would prompt a manager to take corrective action. He or she might, for example, increase advertising to boost lower-than-anticipated sales.

A secondary aspect of controlling is determining whether the original plan needs revision, given the realities of the day. The controlling function sometimes causes a manager to return to the planning function temporarily to fine-tune the original plan. For example, many retailers in recent years have found that the sales volume in stores was not enough to earn the company a profit. They closed the stores, shifted sales to online, and sold their product in other retailers.

One important way in which the jobs of managers differ is in the relative amounts of time spent on planning, organizing and staffing, leading, and controlling. Executives ordinarily spend much more time on strategic (high-level and long-range) planning than do middle- or first-level managers. Lower-level managers are more involved with day-by-day and other short-range planning. Also, lower-level managers spend the most time in face-to-face leadership such as coaching and disciplining workers. This is true because entry-level workers are likely to need more assistance than those workers who have advanced higher in the organization.

---

[8]Henry Mintzberg, *Managing* (San Francisco: Berrett-Koehler, 2009), p. 9.

[9]Larry Bossidy and Ram Charan, *The Discipline of Getting Things Done* (New York: Crown, 2002).

LEARNING
OBJECTIVE **3**
Describe the
various managerial
roles.

role
An expected set of
activities or behaviors
stemming from a job.

THE SEVENTEEN MANAGERIAL ROLES

To further understand the manager's job, it is worthwhile to examine the various roles managers play. A **role**, in the business context, is an expected set of activities or behaviors stemming from a job. Mintzberg conducted several landmark studies of managerial roles. Other researchers extended his findings.[10] In the sections that follow, the roles delineated by these researchers are associated with the major managerial functions to which they most closely pertain. (Roles and functions are closely related. They are both activities carried out by people.) The description of the 17 roles should help you appreciate the richness and complexity of managerial work, and also serve as a generic job description for a manager's position. These roles are described next and listed in Exhibit 1-3.[11]

Planning

Two managerial roles—strategic planner and operational planner—relate to the planning function.

1. *Strategic Planner.* Top-level managers engage in strategic planning, usually assisted by input from others throughout the organization. Specific activities in this role include (a) setting a direction for the organization,

---

EXHIBIT 1-3	The Seventeen Managerial Roles

Planning
1. Strategic planner
2. Operational planner

Organizing and Staffing
3. Organizer
4. Liaison
5. Staffing coordinator
6. Resource allocator
7. Task delegator

Leading
8. Figurehead
9. Spokesperson

10. Negotiator
11. Motivator and coach
12. Team builder
13. Team player
14. Technical problem solver
15. Entrepreneur

Controlling
16. Monitor
17. Disturbance handler

---

[10]This research is reported in Henry Mintzberg, *The Nature of Managerial Work* (New York: Harper & Row, 1973); Mintzberg, *Managing,* pp. 44–45.

[11]Kenneth Graham Jr. and William L. Mihal, *The CMI Managerial Job Analysis Inventory* (Rochester, NY: Rochester Institute of Technology, 1987); Jeffrey S. Shippman, Erich Prien, and Gary L. Hughes, "The Content of Management Work: Formation of Task and Job Skill Composite Classifications," *Journal of Business and Psychology,* Spring 1991, pp. 325–354.

(b) helping the firm deal with the external environment, and (c) developing corporate policies.

2. *Operational Planner.* Operational plans relate to the day-to-day operation of a company or unit. Two such activities are (a) formulating operating budgets and (b) developing work schedules for the unit supervised. Middle-level managers are heavily involved in operational planning; first-level managers are involved to a lesser extent.

Organizing and Staffing

Five roles that relate to the organizing and staffing function are organizer, liaison, staffing coordinator, resource allocator, and task delegator.

3. *Organizer.* As a pure organizer, the manager engages in activities such as (a) designing the jobs of group members; (b) clarifying group members' assignments; (c) explaining organizational policies, rules, and procedures; and (d) establishing policies, rules, and procedures to coordinate the flow of work and information within the unit.

4. *Liaison.* The purpose of the liaison role is to develop and maintain a network of work-related contacts with people. To achieve this end, the manager (a) cultivates relationships with clients or customers; (b) maintains relationships with suppliers, customers, and other persons or groups important to the unit or organization; (c) joins boards, organizations, or public service clubs that might provide useful, work-related contacts; and (d) cultivates and maintains a personal network of in-house contacts through visits, telephone calls, e-mail, text messages, and participation in company-sponsored events.

5. *Staffing Coordinator.* In the staffing role, the manager tries to make sure that competent people fill positions. Specific activities include (a) recruiting and hiring staff; (b) explaining to group members how their work performance will be evaluated; (c) formally evaluating group members' overall job performance; (d) compensating group members within the limits of organizational policy; (e) ensuring that group members are properly trained; (f) promoting group members or recommending them for promotion; and (g) terminating or demoting group members.

6. *Resource Allocator.* An important part of a manager's job is to divide resources in the manner that best helps the organization. Specific activities to this end include (a) authorizing the use of physical resources (facilities, furnishings, and equipment); (b) authorizing the expenditure of financial resources; and (c) discontinuing the use of unnecessary, inappropriate, or ineffective equipment or services.

7. *Task Delegator.* A standard part of any manager's job is assigning tasks to group members. Among these task-delegation activities are (a) assigning projects or tasks to group members; (b) clarifying priorities and performance standards for task completion; and (c) ensuring that group members are properly committed to effective task performance.

Leading

Eight identified managerial roles relate to the leadership function. These roles are motivator and coach, figurehead, spokesperson, negotiator, team builder, team player, technical problem solver, and entrepreneur.

8. *Motivator and Coach.* An effective manager takes time to motivate and coach group members. Specific behaviors in this role include (a) informally recognizing employee achievements; (b) offering encouragement and reassurance, thereby showing active concern about the professional growth of group members; (c) providing feedback about both effective and ineffective performance; and (d) giving group members advice on steps to improve their performance.

9. *Figurehead.* Figurehead managers, particularly high-ranking ones, spend some of their time engaging in ceremonial activities or acting as a figurehead. Such activities include (a) entertaining clients or customers as an official representative of the organization, (b) serving as an official representative of the organization at gatherings outside the organization, and (c) escorting official visitors.

10. *Spokesperson.* When a manager acts as a spokesperson, the emphasis is on answering inquiries and formally reporting to individuals and groups outside the manager's organizational unit. As a spokesperson, the manager keeps five groups of people informed about the unit's activities, plans, and capabilities. These groups are (a) upper-level management, (b) clients and customers, (c) other important outsiders (such as labor unions), (d) professional colleagues, and (e) the general public. Usually, top-level managers take responsibility for keeping outside groups informed.

11. *Negotiator.* Part of almost any manager's job is trying to make deals with others for needed resources. Three specific negotiating activities are (a) bargaining with supervisors for funds, facilities, equipment, or other forms of support; (b) bargaining with other units in the organization for the use of staff, facilities, and other forms of support; and (c) bargaining with suppliers and vendors about services, schedules, and delivery times.

12. *Team Builder.* A key aspect of a manager's role is to build an effective team. Activities contributing to this role include (a) ensuring that group members are recognized for their accomplishments (by issuing letters of appreciation, for example); (b) initiating activities that contribute to group morale, such as giving parties and sponsoring sports teams; and (c) holding periodic staff meetings to encourage group members to talk about their accomplishments, problems, and concerns.

13. *Team Player.* Three behaviors of the team player are (a) displaying appropriate personal conduct, (b) cooperating with other units in the organization, and (c) displaying loyalty to superiors by fully supporting their plans and decisions.

14. *Technical Problem Solver.* It is particularly important for first- and middle-level managers to help group members solve technical problems. Two such specific activities related to problem solving are (a) serving as

a technical expert or advisor and (b) performing individual contributor tasks such as making sales calls or fixing software problems on a regular basis. The managers most in demand today are those who combine leadership skill with a technical or business specialty.

15. *Entrepreneur.* Managers who work in large organizations have some responsibility for suggesting innovative ideas or furthering the business aspects of the firm. Three entrepreneurial role activities are (a) reading trade publications and professional journals and searching the Internet to remain up-to-date; (b) talking with customers or others in the organization to remain abreast of changing needs and requirements; and (c) becoming involved in activities outside the unit that could result in performance improvements within the manager's unit. These activities might include visiting other firms, attending professional meetings or trade shows, and participating in educational programs.

Controlling

The monitor role mentioned next fits the controlling function precisely, because the term *monitoring* is often used as a synonym for *controlling*. The role of disturbance handler is categorized under controlling because it involves changing an unacceptable condition to an acceptable stable condition.

16. *Monitor.* The activities of a monitor are (a) developing systems that measure or monitor the unit's overall performance, (b) using information systems to measure productivity and cost, (c) talking with group members about progress on assigned tasks, and (d) overseeing the use of equipment and facilities (for example, vehicles and office space) to ensure that they are properly used and maintained.

17. *Disturbance Handler.* Four typical activities of a disturbance handler are (a) participating in grievance resolution within the unit (working out a problem with a labor union, for example); (b) resolving complaints from customers, other units, and superiors; (c) resolving conflicts among group members; and (d) resolving problems about work flow and information exchange with other units. Disturbance handling might also be considered a leadership role.

Managerial Roles Currently Emphasized

Managerial work has shifted substantially away from the controller and director role to that of motivator and coach, facilitator, and supporter. As reflected in the position of team leader, many managers today deemphasize formal authority and rank. Instead, they work as partners with team members to jointly achieve results. Managers today emphasize horizontal relationships and deemphasize vertical (top-down) relationships. We encourage you not to think that traditional (old) managers are evil, while new managers are good.

Exhibit 1-4 gives you the opportunity to relate managerial roles to yourself, even if you are not presently working as a manager.

EXHIBIT 1-4   My Managerial Role Analysis

Here is an opportunity for you to think through your current level of skill or potential ability to carry out successfully the 17 managerial roles already described. Each role will be listed with a few-word reminder of one of its key aspects. Check next to each role whether it is an activity you could carry out now, or something for which you will need more experience and preparation. For those activities you check as "capable of doing it now," jot down an example of your success in this area. For example, a person who checked "capable of doing it now" for Role 5, staffing coordinator, might have written, "I recruited three part-time servers to work in the restaurant where I worked as an assistant manager."

Few readers of this book will have had experience in carrying out most of these roles. So relate the specific roles to any management experience you may have had, including full-time work, part-time work, volunteer work, clubs, committees, and sports.

Managerial Role	Capable of Doing It Now	Need Preparation and Experience
1. Strategic planner (Set direction for others based on external environment.)	_____	_____
2. Operational planner (Plan for running the organization or the unit.)	_____	_____
3. Organizer (Design jobs for group members and clarify assignments.)	_____	_____
4. Liaison (Develop and maintain network of work-related contacts.)	_____	_____
5. Staffing coordinator (Recruit, hire, train, evaluate, and fire group members.)	_____	_____
6. Resource allocator (Divide resources to help get job done.)	_____	_____
7. Task delegator (Assign tasks to group members.)	_____	_____
8. Figurehead (Engage in ceremonial activities, and represent the group to outsiders.)	_____	_____
9. Spokesperson (Answer inquiries and report information about the group to outsiders.)	_____	_____
10. Negotiator (Make deals with others for needed resources.)	_____	_____
11. Motivator and coach (Recognize achievements, encourage, give feedback and advice.)	_____	_____
12. Team builder (Contribute to group morale, hold meetings to encourage members to talk about accomplishments and concerns.)	_____	_____
13. Team player (Correct conduct, cooperate with others, and be loyal.)	_____	_____
14. Technical problem solver (Help group members solve technical problems; perform individual contributor tasks.)	_____	_____
15. Entrepreneur (Suggest innovative ideas and further business activity of the group; search for new undertakings for the group.)	_____	_____
16. Monitor (Measure performance and productivity, and review progress on tasks.)	_____	_____
17. Disturbance handler (Resolve problems and complaints.)	_____	_____

Interpretation: The more of the 17 roles you are ready to perform, the more ready you are to function as a manager or to perform managerial work. Your study of management will facilitate carrying out more of these roles effectively.

The Influence of Management Level on Managerial Roles

A manager's level of responsibility influences which roles he or she is likely to engage in most frequently. Information about the influence of level on roles comes from research conducted with 228 managers in a variety of private-sector service firms (such as banks and insurance companies) and manufacturing firms. The roles studied were basically those described in this chapter. One clear-cut finding was that, at the higher levels of management, four roles were the most important: liaison, spokesperson, figurehead, and strategic planner. Another finding was that the role of leader is critical at the first level of management.[12] Although the study in question is 30 years old, it is consistent with current management practice. For example, in organizations of today first-level managers are expected to be effective leaders who motivate and coach subordinates.

Management as a Practice

A useful perspective on the nature of management is that it is a practice, rather than a science or a profession. Managers learn through both experience and study. As Mintzberg explains, science is about the development of systematic knowledge through research. In contrast, the major purpose of management is to help get things done in organizations.[13] Managers sometimes make use of systematic knowledge, yet they also rely on the intuition that stems from experience.

Management is not a profession in the sense of being a licensed occupation such as law, medicine, psychology, veterinary medicine, or electrician. If management were a profession in this strict sense, you would be forbidden to work as a middle manager or start a software firm without being licensed by your state or province. The fact that managerial work is not defined as a profession does not downgrade its importance. You don't need a license to be the President of the United States.

Another point of view is advanced by Harvard Business School professors Rakesh Khurana and Nitin Nohria, who claim that it is time to make management a true profession. In their opinion, to regain public trust, management must become a profession that follows an ethical code. Managers should have appropriate education, as with other professions.[14] (These authors appear to be referring to top-level executives).

One way in which the occupation of management can become more professionalized is for managers to base more of their decisions on systematically

---

[12]Cynthia M. Pavett and Alan W. Lau, "Managerial Work: The Influence of Hierarchical Level and Functional Specialty," *Academy of Management Journal*, March 1983, pp. 170–177.

[13]Mintzberg, *Managing*, p. 10.

[14]Rakesh Khurana and Nitin Nohria, "It's Time to Make Management a True Profession," *Harvard Business Review*, October 2008, pp. 70–77.

evidence-based management

The systematic use of the best available evidence to improve management practice.

gathered evidence such as surveys and experiments. **Evidence-based management** is the systematic use of the best available evidence to improve management practice.[15] To use this approach, managers would rely on both scientific evidence and local business evidence. To illustrate, there are hundreds of articles published in professional journals about the usefulness of goals for improving performance, and how best to use goals. (Chapter 11 contains information about goals and motivation.) The manager might also check out how well goals worked in local business firms. A manager who used some of this information would be working more professionally than a manager who relied only on common sense to boost motivation and performance.

LEARNING OBJECTIVE **4**

Identify the basic managerial skills and understand how they can be developed.

FIVE KEY MANAGERIAL SKILLS

To be effective, managers must possess technical, interpersonal, conceptual, diagnostic, and political skills. The sections that follow will first define these skills and then comment on how they are developed. Whatever the level of management, a manager needs a combination of all five skills.

Technical Skill

Technical skill involves an understanding of and proficiency in a specific activity that involves methods, processes, procedures, or techniques. Technical skills include the ability to prepare a budget, lay out a production schedule, prepare a spreadsheet analysis, upload information onto a social networking site, and demonstrate a piece of electronic equipment. Intricate knowledge of the business, such as developing a marketing campaign for a product, can also be regarded as a technical skill. Technical skills are frequently referred to as *hard skills*. A well-developed technical skill can facilitate the rise into management. For example, Bill Gates of Microsoft Corp. launched his career by being a competent programmer.

Interpersonal Skill

Interpersonal (or human relations) skill is a manager's ability to work effectively as a team member and to build cooperative effort in the unit. Communication skills are an important component of interpersonal skills. They form the basis for sending and receiving messages on the job. Although interpersonal skills are often referred to as *soft skills*, it does not mean these skills are easy to learn or insignificant. Interpersonal skills are more important than technical skills in getting to the top and providing leadership to people. Many managers at all levels ultimately fail because their interpersonal skills do not match the demands of the job. For example, some managers

---

[15]Trish Reay, Whitney Berta, and Melanie Kazman Kohn, "What's the Evidence on Evidence-Based Management?" *Academy of Management Perspectives*, November 2009, p. 5; Jeffrey Pfeffer and Robert I. Sutton, "Evidence-Based Management," *Harvard Business Review*, January 2006, pp. 62–74.

intimidate, bully, and swear at group members. In the process, they develop such a poor reputation that it may lead to their being replaced. Have you ever worked for a manager who was so rude and insensitive that he or she damaged morale and productivity?

multiculturalism
The ability to work effectively and conduct business with people from different cultures.

An important subset of interpersonal skills for managers is **multiculturalism**, the ability to work effectively and conduct business with people from different cultures. Closely related is the importance of bilingualism for managers as well as other workers. Being able to converse in a second language represents an important asset in today's global and multicultural work environment.

Conceptual Skill

Conceptual skill is the ability to see the organization as a total entity. It includes recognizing how the various units of the organization depend on one another and how changes in any one part affect all the others. It also includes visualizing the relationship of the individual business to the industry; the community; and the political, social, and economic forces of the nation as a whole. For top-level management, conceptual skill is a priority because executive managers have the most contact with the outside world.

Drucker emphasized that the only comparative advantage of the developed countries is in the number of knowledge workers (people who work primarily with concepts). Educated workers in underdeveloped countries are just as smart as those in developed countries, but their numbers are smaller. According to Drucker and many other authorities, the need for knowledge workers and conceptual knowledge will continue to grow.[16]

Diagnostic Skill

Managers are frequently called on to investigate a problem and then to decide on and implement a remedy. Diagnostic skill often requires other skills, because managers must use technical, human, conceptual, or political skills to solve the problems they diagnose. Much of the potential excitement in a manager's job centers on getting to the root of problems and recommending solutions. An office supervisor, for example, might attempt to understand why productivity has not increased in his office despite the installation of the latest office technology.

Political Skill

An important part of being effective is the ability to obtain power and prevent others from taking it away. Managers use political skill to acquire the power necessary to reach objectives. Other political skills include establishing the right connections and impressing the right people. Furthermore, managers high in political skill possess an astute understanding of people, along

---

[16]Peter F. Drucker, "The Future Has Already Happened," *Harvard Business Review*, September–October 1997, p. 22; "An American Sage," p. 22.

with a fundamental belief that they can control the outcomes of their interactions with people. This feeling of mastery often reduces the stress associated with interacting with people.[17]

Political skill should be regarded as a supplement to job competence and the other basic skills. Managers who overemphasize political skill at the expense of doing work of substance focus too much on pleasing company insiders and advancing their own careers. Too much time invested in office politics takes time away from dealing with customer problems and improving productivity.

DEVELOPMENT OF MANAGERIAL SKILLS

This text is based on the assumption that managerial skills can be learned. Education for management begins in school and continues in the form of training and development programs throughout a career. Examples of such programs include a seminar about how to be an effective leader or a workshop about e-commerce.

Developing most managerial skills is more complex than developing structured skills such as computing a return on investment ratio or transferring images from a camcorder to a projector. Nevertheless, you can develop managerial skills by studying this text and doing the exercises, which follow a general learning model:

1. *Conceptual knowledge and behavioral guidelines.* Each chapter in this text presents useful information about the practice of management, including step-by-step procedures for a method of group decision making called the nominal group technique.

2. *Conceptual knowledge demonstrated by examples.* Brief descriptions of managers and professionals in action, including small-business owners, are presented throughout the text.

3. *Skill-development exercises.* The text provides an opportunity for practice and personalization through cases and self-assessment exercises. Self-quizzes are included because they are an effective method of helping you personalize the information.

4. *Feedback on skill utilization, or performance, from others.* Feedback exercises appear at several places in the text. Implementing some of these managerial skills outside of the classroom will provide additional opportunities for feedback.

5. *Frequent practice of what you have learned, including making adjustments from the feedback.* Both soft skills and technical skills must be practiced frequently to develop expertise. If you also make the adjustments that feedback has suggested, the level of expertise is likely to be higher. Suppose you wanted to develop the managerial skill of giving praise and recognition to others. Not everybody is naturally good at giving praise and

---

[17]Pamela L. Perrewé et al., "Political Skill: An Antidote for Workplace Stressors," *Academy of Management Executive*, August 2000, p. 120.

recognition; you might have to practice frequently. If several people told you that your praise was too heavy, you might diminish the amount of praise you were heaping upon others.

Experience is obviously important in developing management skills. Yet experience is likely to be more valuable if it is enhanced with education. Consider an analogy to soccer. A person learning soccer might read and watch a video about the proper way to kick a soccer ball. With this education behind her, she now kicks the ball with the side of her foot instead of toe first. She becomes a competent kicker by combining education and experience. People often make such statements as, "You can't learn to be a manager (or leader) from a book." However, you can learn managerial concepts from a book or lecture and then apply them. People who move vertically in their careers usually have both education and experience in management techniques.

A key reason for continuing to develop managerial skills is that the manager's job is more demanding than ever, and the workplace keeps changing. A manager is likely to work in an intense, pressure-filled environment requiring many skills. Companies forced to keep up with competition are driving the demand for managers with updated skills. Rapid changes, such as the need for e-commerce and a social networking presence, require managers to continually develop new skills.

LEARNING
OBJECTIVE **5**
Identify the major
developments in
the evolution of
management
thought.

THE EVOLUTION OF MANAGEMENT THOUGHT

Management as a practice has an almost unlimited history. Visualize a group of prehistoric people attempting to develop a device that would help transport heavy objects. Given a modern label, the caveperson suggesting this development is the head of product research and development. The project of building the curious new circular device was turned over to a group of people who had hands-on access to raw material. Because the developers of the wheel did not constitute a business enterprise, they handed over the technology of the wheel to all interested parties (in prehistoric times, patents were not available).

Management as a formal study, in comparison to a practice, began in the 1700s as part of the Industrial Revolution. Here we take a brief look at management, covering both historical developments and various approaches to understanding it. The anchor points to our discussion are as follows:

1. The classical approach (scientific management and administrative management)
2. The behavioral approach
3. Quantitative approaches
4. The systems perspective
5. The contingency approach
6. The information technology approach and beyond

All of these approaches mentioned here also appear in later sections of the book. For example, the study of leadership and motivation stems from both the classical and behavioral approaches. The historical approaches laid the foundation for understanding and practicing management.

Classical Approach to Management

The study of management became more systematized and formal as a by-product of the Industrial Revolution that took place from the 1700s through the 1900s. It was necessary to develop approaches to managing work and people in order to manage all the new factories that were a central part of the Industrial Revolution. The classical approach to management encompasses scientific management and administrative management.

scientific management

The application of scientific methods to increase individual workers' productivity.

The focus of **scientific management** was the application of scientific methods to increase individual workers' productivity. An example would be assembling a washing machine with the least number of wasted motions and steps. Frederick W. Taylor, considered the father of scientific management, was an engineer by background. He used scientific analysis and experiments to increase worker output. Other key contributors to scientific management were Henry Gantt and Frank and Lillian Gilbreth. (Gantt charts for scheduling activities are still used today.)

administrative management

The use of management principles in the structuring and managing of an organization.

Administrative management was concerned primarily with how organizations should be managed and structured. The French businessman Henri Fayol and the German scholar Max Weber were the main contributors to administrative management. Based on his practical experience, Fayol developed 14 management principles through which management engaged in planning, organizing, commanding, coordinating, and controlling. Two examples of his principles are (1) *unity of command*—for any tasks, each worker should receive orders from only one supervisor, and (2) *esprit de corps*—promoting team spirit builds harmony and creates organizational unity. Weber proposed an ideal form of bureaucracy to improve upon inefficient forms of organization that included using favoritism to promote workers.[18] Among Weber's recommendations was the idea of breaking down each job into simple, routine, and well-defined tasks.

Alfred D. Chandler, Jr., the Harvard University business historian, was a key figure in promoting the importance of the classical approach to management. He championed the study of modern bureaucratic administration and influenced the thinking of executives about organizing large business firms. Many of the insights Chandler developed were based on the individual histories he gathered of Du Pont, General Motors, Standard Oil (now ExxonMobil), and Sears, Roebuck & Co. The time period he chose for studying these organizations was between 1850 and 1920; the most comprehensive version of his conclusions about major business firms was published in *Strategy and Structure* in 1962.

---

[18]"Theory of Social and Economic Organization: Max Weber," in *Business: The Ultimate Resource* (Cambridge, MA: Perseus Publishing, 2002), p. 950.

Chandler's book demonstrates the essential link between a company's strategy (master plan) and its structure (layout or division of work). His famous thesis is that a firm's structure is determined or chosen by its strategy—and unless structure follows strategy, inefficiency results. In other words, what a firm wants to accomplish determines how the company is organized. Chandler's insights contributed to the decentralization of many modern organizations.[19]

Consider today's Colgate-Palmolive Company, whose strategy might be stated as responding to the personal-care needs of people and animals throughout the world. To achieve this lofty goal, the company is divided into four mammoth divisions: Oral Care, Personal Care, Home Care, and Pet Nutrition. Each division is subdivided into products groups of its own, such as Personal Care including Men's Antiperspirant and Deodorant, Women's Antiperspirant and Deodorant, Body Wash, and Liquid Hand Soap. If Colgate-Palmolive were not organized by divisions, the company would consist of major groups such as manufacturing, engineering, research and development, finance, and information systems.

The core of management knowledge lies within the classical school. As its key contributions, it studies management from the framework of planning, organizing, leading, and controlling—the framework chosen in this text. Many major historical developments in organizations, such as the decentralization of General Electric (GE) in the 1950s, were based on classical principles. The classical school provides a systematic way of managing people and work that has proven useful over time and represents its major strength. Its major limitation is that it sometimes ignores differences among people and situations. For example, some of the classical principles for developing an organization are not well suited to fast-changing situations.

The Behavioral Approach

behavioral approach to management
An approach to management that emphasizes improving management through an understanding of the psychological makeup of people.

The **behavioral approach to management** emphasizes improving management through the psychological makeup of people. In contrast to the largely technical emphasis of scientific management, a common theme of the behavioral approach focuses on the need to understand people. The behavioral approach is sometimes referred to as the human resources approach because of the focus on making optimum use of workers in a positive way, such as making jobs motivational. One hope of the behavioral approach was to reduce some of the labor-management conflict so prevalent under the classical approach to management. The behavioral approach has profoundly influenced management, and a portion of this book is based on behavioral theory. Typical behavior and human resource topics include leadership, motivation, communication, teamwork, and conflict.

[19]Alfred Chandler, *Strategy and Structure* (New York: Doubleday, 1962); Albert Chandler, "Strategy and Structure: Albert Chandler," in *Business: The Ultimate Resource* (Cambridge, MA: Perseus Publishing, 2002), p. 950.

The most direct origins of the behavioral approach are set in the 1930s through the 1950s. Yet earlier scholars such as Robert Owen and Mary Parker Follett also wrote about the importance of the human element. Working in the textile industry in Scotland in the early 1800s, Owen criticized fellow managers for failing to understand the human element in the mills. He contended that showing concern for workers resulted in greater profitability while at the same time reducing hardship for workers. Owen reported that efforts to pay careful attention to the human element often resulted in a 50 percent return on his investment.[20]

Follett focused her attention on the importance of groups in managing people. Although she published her works during the period of scientific management, Follett did not share Taylor's view that organizations should be framed around the work of individuals. In contrast, she argued that groups were the basis on which organizations should be formed. Follett explained that to enhance productivity and morale, managers should coordinate and aid the efforts of work groups.[21]

Three cornerstones of the behavioral approach are the Hawthorne studies, Theory X and Theory Y, and Maslow's need hierarchy. These developments contributed directly to managers' understanding of the importance of human relations on the job. Yet again, practicing managers have probably always known about the importance of human relations. The prehistoric person who developed the wheel probably received a congratulatory pat on the back from another member of the tribe!

The Hawthorne Studies

The purpose of the first study conducted at the Hawthorne plant of Western Electric (an AT&T subsidiary located in Cicero, Illinois) was to determine the effects of changes in lighting on productivity.[22] In this study, workers were divided into an experimental group and a control group. Lighting conditions for the experimental group varied in intensity from 24 to 46 to 70 foot-candles. The lighting for the control group remained constant.

As expected, the experimental group's output increased with each increase in light intensity. But unexpectedly, the performance of the control group also changed. The production of the control group increased at about the same rate as that of the experimental group. Later, the lighting in the experimental group's area was reduced. The group's output continued to increase, as did that of the control group. A decline in the productivity of the control group finally did occur, but only when the intensity of the light was roughly the same as moonlight. Clearly, the researchers reasoned, something other than illumination caused the changes in productivity.

---

[20]Robert Owen, *A New View of Society* (New York: E. Bliss and F. White, 1825), p. 57.

[21]Mary Parker Follett, *The New State: Group Organization of the Solution of Popular Government* (New York: Longmans Green, 1918), p. 28.

[22]E. J. Roethlisberger and W. J. Dickson, *Management and the Worker* (Cambridge, MA: Harvard University Press, 1939).

An experiment was then conducted in the relay-assembly test room over a period of six years, with similar results. In this case, relationships among rest, fatigue, and productivity were examined. First, normal productivity was established with a 48-hour week and no formal rest periods. Rest periods of varying length and frequency were then introduced. Productivity increased as the frequency and length of rest periods increased. Finally, the original conditions were reinstated. The return to the original conditions, however, did not result in the expected productivity drop. Instead, productivity remained at the same high level.

Hawthorne effect

The phenomenon in which people behave differently in response to perceived attention from evaluators.

One interpretation of these results was that the workers involved in the experiment enjoyed being the center of attention. Workers reacted positively because management cared about them. The phenomenon is referred to as the **Hawthorne effect**. It is the tendency of people to behave differently when they receive attention because they respond to the demands of the situation. In a work setting, employees perform better when they are part of any program, whether or not that program is valuable. Another useful lesson learned from the Hawthorne studies is that effective communication with workers is critical to managerial success.

Theory X and Theory Y of Douglas McGregor

A widely quoted development of the behavioral approach is Douglas McGregor's analysis of the assumptions managers make about human nature.[23] Theory X is a set of traditional assumptions about people. Managers who hold these assumptions are pessimistic about workers' capabilities. They believe that workers dislike work, seek to avoid responsibility, are not ambitious, and must be supervised closely. McGregor urged managers to challenge these assumptions about human nature because they are untrue in most circumstances.

Theory Y, the alternative, poses an optimistic set of assumptions. These assumptions include the idea that people do accept responsibility, can exercise self-control, possess the capacity to innovate, and consider work to be as natural as rest or play. McGregor argued that these assumptions accurately describe human nature in far more situations than most managers believe. He therefore proposed that these assumptions should guide managerial practice.

Maslow's Need Hierarchy

Most readers are already familiar with the need hierarchy developed by psychologist Abraham Maslow. This topic will be presented in Chapter 11 in discussions about motivation. Maslow suggested that humans are motivated by efforts to satisfy a hierarchy of needs ranging from basic needs to those for self-actualization, or reaching one's potential. The need hierarchy

---

[23]Douglas McGregor, *The Human Side of Enterprise* (New York: McGraw-Hill, 1960), pp. 33–57.

prompted managers to think about ways of satisfying a wide range of worker needs to keep them motivated.

The primary strength of the behavioral (or human resources) approach is that it encourages managers to take into account the human element. Many valuable methods of motivating employees are based on behavioral research. The primary weakness of the behavioral approach is that it sometimes leads to an oversimplified view of managing people. Managers sometimes adopt one behavioral theory and ignore other relevant information. For example, several theories of motivation pay too little attention to the importance of money in people's thinking.

Quantitative Approaches to Management

quantitative approach to management

A perspective on management that emphasizes use of a group of methods in managerial decision making, based on the scientific method.

The **quantitative approach to management** is a perspective on management that emphasizes the use of a group of methods in managerial decision making, based on the scientific method. Today, the quantitative approach is often referred to as management science or operations research (OR). Frequently used quantitative tools and techniques include statistics, linear programming, network analysis, decision trees, and computer simulations. These tools and techniques can be used when making decisions regarding inventory control, plant-site locations, quality control, and a range of other decisions where objective information is important. Several quantitative approaches to decision making are found in Chapter 6 (quantitative techniques for planning and decision making).

Frederick Taylor's work provided the foundation for the quantitative approach to management. However, the impetus for the modern-day quantitative approach was the formation of OR teams to solve a range of problems faced by the Allied forces during World War II. Examples of the problems considered by the OR team included the bombing of enemy targets, the effective conduct of submarine warfare, and the efficient movement of troops from one location to another. Following World War II, many industrial applications were found for quantitative approaches to management. The approach was facilitated by the increasing use of computers. A representative problem tackled by a quantitative approach to management would be to estimate the effect of a change in the price of a product on the product's market share.

The primary strength of the quantitative approach to management is that it enables managers to solve complex problems that cannot be solved by common sense alone. For example, management science techniques are used to make forecasts that take into account hundreds of factors simultaneously. A weakness of management science is that the answers it produces are often less precise than they appear. Although quantitative approaches use precise methods, much of the data is based on human estimates, which can be unreliable.

The Systems Perspective

systems perspective
A way of viewing aspects of an organization as an interrelated system.

The **systems perspective** is a way of viewing problems more than it is a specific approach to management. It is based on the concept that an organization is a system, or an entity of interrelated parts. If you adjust one part of the system, other parts will be affected automatically. For example, suppose you offer low compensation to job candidates. According to the systems approach, your action will influence your product quality. The "low-quality" employees who are willing to accept low wages will produce low-quality goods. Exhibit 1-2, which showed the process of management, reflected a systems viewpoint.

Another aspect of systems theory is to regard the organization as an open system, one that interacts with the environment. As illustrated in Exhibit 1-5, the organization transforms inputs into outputs and supplies them to the outside world. If these outputs are perceived as valuable, the organization will survive and prosper. The feedback loop indicates that the acceptance of outputs by society gives the organization new inputs for revitalization and expansion. Managers can benefit from this diagram by recognizing that whatever work they undertake should contribute something of value to external customers and clients.

entropy
A concept of the systems approach to management that states that an organization will die without continuous input from the outside environment.

synergy
A concept of the systems approach to management that states that the whole organization working together will produce more than the parts working independently.

Two other influential concepts from the systems perspective are entropy and synergy. **Entropy** is the tendency of a system to run down and die if it does not receive fresh inputs from its environment. As indicated in Exhibit 1-5, the organization must continually receive inputs from the outside world to make sure it stays in tune with, or ahead of, the environment. **Synergy** means that the whole is greater than the sum of the parts. When the various parts of an organization work together, they can produce much more than they could by working independently. For example, a few years ago product developers at Apple Corp. thought about building a stylish new smart phone called iPhone. The developers consulted immediately with manufacturing, engineering, purchasing, and dealers to discuss the feasibility of their idea. Working together,

---

EXHIBIT 1-5   A Systems View of Organization

A systems perspective keeps the manager focused on the external environment.

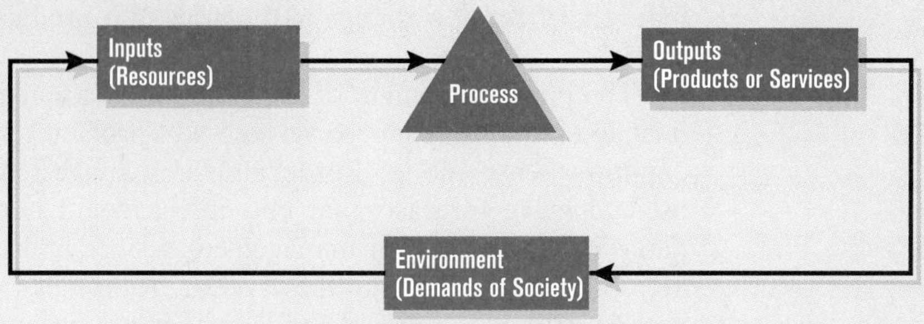

Inputs (Resources) → Process → Outputs (Products or Services) → Environment (Demands of Society)

the units of the organization produced a highly successful product launch in a tightly competitive market.

The Contingency Approach

contingency approach to management

A perspective on management that emphasizes that no single way to manage people or work is best in every situation. It encourages managers to study individual and situational differences before deciding on a course of action.

The **contingency approach to management** emphasizes that there is no single best way to manage people or work in every situation. A method that leads to high productivity or morale under one set of circumstances may not achieve the same results in another. The contingency approach is derived from the study of leadership and organization structures. With respect to leadership, psychologists developed detailed explanations of which style of leadership would work best in which situation. An example would be for the manager to give more leeway to competent group members. Also, the study of organization structure suggests that some structures work better in different environments. For example, a team structure is often best for a rapidly changing environment. Common sense also contributes heavily to the contingency approach. Experienced managers know that not all people and situations respond in the same way to identical situations. The contingency approach is emphasized throughout this book.

The strength of the contingency approach is that it encourages managers to examine individual and situational differences before deciding on a course of action. Its major problem is that it is often used as an excuse for not acquiring formal knowledge about management. If management is determined by the situation, why study management theory? The answer is because a formal study of management helps a manager decide which factors are relevant in a given situation.

The Information Technology Era and Beyond

The information technology era had relatively modest beginnings in the 1950s with the use of electronic data processing to take over the manual processing of large batches of data and numbers. By the late 1980s, the impact of information technology and the Internet began to influence how managers manage work and people. A report by two economists concluded that the impact of the Internet on business is similar to the impact of electricity at the beginning of the twentieth century.[24] Can you visualize what it must have been like to work in an office or factory without electricity?

The impact of information technology and the Internet on the work of managers is so vast that it receives separate attention in Chapter 14. Information technology modified managerial work in the following ways:

* Managers often communicate with people, even sending layoff notices, by e-mail rather than by telephone or in person. Managers send and

---

[24]Martin Brooks and Zakhi Wahhaj, "Is the Internet Better Than Electricity?" Goldman Sachs report cited in Gary Hamel, "Inside the Revolution—Edison's Curse," *Fortune*, March 5, 2001, p. 176.

receive messages more frequently than in the past because they are in frequent contact with the office through a BlackBerry or some other brand of personal digital assistant or smart phone.

- Many managers organize their sales and marketing efforts differently by using the Internet to conduct most transactions. Similarly, much purchasing of supplies and materials is conducted through the Internet. Almost every consumer-oriented business today has been drawn into using social networking sites such as Twitter and Facebook to market its products.
- Managers run their organizations more democratically because they receive input from so many workers at different levels in the organization through e-mail and intranets.

Be careful not to dismiss the evolution of management thought with historical information that is no longer relevant. Practicing managers can use all six major developments in management thought. An astute manager selects information from the various schools of thought to achieve good results in a given situation. Visualize an executive making a large financial services firm more efficient and effective. The manager might rely on the classical school of management in restructuring company divisions. At the same time the executive uses site visits and town hall meetings to communicate with employees, reflecting the behavioral approach to management.

The history of management is being written each year in the sense that the practice of management continues to evolve. As you study this book and listen to associated lectures you will learn about the new era in management, such as more emphasis on employee empowerment, outsourcing, and helping employees manage stress. An example of a leading-edge approach to management is evidence-based management whereby managers translate principles (based on the most reliable evidence at the time) into organizational practices, as already mentioned. Quite often the best evidence is empirical (based on experience) and recent, yet old principles can still be useful. The alternative to evidence-based management is to rely heavily on common sense and adopting practices used by other companies whether or not they fit a particular situation. Many of the principles and suggestions presented throughout this text would help a manager practice evidence-based management.

Evidence-based management is not yet widely practiced, but taking the study of management seriously will have moved managers and organizations toward basing their practices and decisions on valid evidence. The results are likely to be higher productivity and employee morale.

Summary of Key Points

To facilitate your study and review of this and the remaining chapters, the summaries are organized around the learning objectives.

1 Explain what the term *manager* means, and identify different types of managers.

A manager is a person responsible for work performance of other people. Management is the process of using organizational resources to achieve specific objectives through the functions of planning, organizing and staffing, leading, and controlling. Organizational levels consist of top-level managers, middle-level managers, first-level managers, and individual contributors. New types of C-level managers continue to emerge, such as chief of staff and chief commercial officer. Categories of managers include functional managers (who deal with specialties within the firm), general managers, administrators (typically managers in nonprofit firms), entrepreneurs (those who start innovative businesses), small-business owners, and team leaders. Entrepreneurs and small-business owners are particularly passionate about their work.

2 Describe the process of management, including the functions of management.

To accomplish organizational goals, managers use resources and carry out the basic management functions. Resources are divided into four categories: human, financial, physical, and informational. The four managerial functions are planning, organizing and staffing, leading, and controlling.

3 Describe the various managerial roles.

The work of a manager can be divided into 17 roles that relate to the four major functions. Planning roles include strategic planner and operational planner. Organizing and staffing calls for the organizer, liaison, staffing coordinator, resource allocator, and task delegator roles. Leading roles include figurehead, spokesperson, negotiator, motivator and coach, team builder, team player, technical problem solver, and entrepreneur. Controlling involves the monitor and disturbance handling roles. Managerial work has shifted substantially away from the controller and director role to that of coach, facilitator, and supporter. Top-level managers occupy more external roles than do lower-ranking managers. A useful perspective on the nature of management is that it is a practice, rather than a science or profession. The use of evidence-based management helps professionalize the work of managers.

4 Identify the basic managerial skills and understand how they can be developed.

Managers need interpersonal, conceptual, diagnostic, and political skills to accomplish their jobs. An effective way of developing managerial skills is to follow a general learning model. The model involves conceptual knowledge, behavioral guidelines, examples, skill-development exercises, feedback, and frequent practice. Management skills are acquired through a combination of education and experience.

5 Identify the major developments in the evolution of management thought.

Management practice has an almost unlimited history, whereas the formal study of management began as part of the Industrial Revolution. The major developments in management thought and the history of management are (1) the classical approach (scientific management and administrative management); (2) the behavioral or human resources approach; (3) quantitative approaches; (4) the systems approach; (5) the contingency approach; and (6) the information technology era and beyond.

The best practices of managers today include elements of the six major developments in management thought. Management thought continues to evolve. A leading-edge trend is evidence-based management in which managers base their decisions and practices on principles derived from good evidence.

Key Terms and Phrases

Manager, 2
Management, 2
Top-level managers, 2
C-level manager, 3
Middle-level managers, 4
First-level managers, 5
Entrepreneur, 6
Small-business owners, 6
Team leader, 7
Role, 11
Evidence-based management, 17

Multiculturalism, 18
Scientific management, 21
Administrative management, 21
Behavioral approach to management, 22
Hawthorne effect, 24
Quantitative approach to management, 25
Systems perspective, 26
Entropy, 26
Synergy, 26
Contingency approach to management, 27

Questions

Here, as in other chapters, groups or individuals can analyze the questions and cases. We strongly recommend using some small-group discussion to enhance learning.

1. In addition to a paid job, where else might a person develop managerial experience?
2. In recent years, many employers seek out technically trained job candidates who also have studied management. What advantages do you think employers see in a technical person studying management?
3. Why do large companies encourage many of their employees to "think like entrepreneurs"?

4. During weather emergencies such as a severe ice storm, some companies send out an alert that only "essential" employees should report to work. Explain why managers should or should not stay home on such emergency days.
5. What do you think might be advantages of making business executives adhere to a code of ethics as do physicians and lawyers?
6. Why might evidence-based management make an organization more competitive?
7. Why is "management" regarded by some people as an essential life skill?

Skill-Building Exercise 1-A: Identifying Managerial Roles

Interview a manager at any level in any organization, including a retail store or restaurant. Determine which of the 17 managerial roles the manager you interview thinks apply to his or her job. Find out which one or two roles the manager thinks are the most important. Be ready to discuss your findings in class. You can often gain insight into which roles the manager emphasizes by asking about challenges the manager faces. For example, when asked about the biggest challenges in her job, a restaurant manager might say, "Turnover is a bear. It's so hard to find good servers who stick around for at least a year." The manager's comments indicate the organizing function.

Skill-Building Exercise 1-B: Managerial Skills of Athletic Coaches

The key managerial skills described in this chapter apply to managers in all fields. To help visualize these skills in action, individually or as a group, identify these skills as used by a coach during the next week. Watch a coach in person or on television or read a newspaper report. Find a good example for each of the five skills, and jot down the basis for your answer. To help point you in the right direction, consider the following example a student might furnish: "Last night I was watching a college basketball game on television. The score was tied with ten seconds to go, and a timeout was called. With the five players in the game in a huddle, the coach got out his clipboard and diagrammed a play using Xs, Os, and a marker. The play worked, and the team won in the final second. I would say the coach was using technical skill because he dug into the details of how to win."

For which skills was it easiest to find an example? For which skill was it the most difficult? What conclusions can you draw about the managerial skills of athletic coaches?

Technical skill _____

Interpersonal skill _____

Conceptual skill _____

Diagnostic skill _____

Political skill _____

Management Now: Online Skill-Building Exercise: Hard Skills and Soft Skills for Managers

As explained in the chapter section Five Key Managerial Skills, managers need a combination of hard skills and soft skills to be effective. However, it is not so easy to find a specific list of both types of skills, and perhaps what constitutes an effective combination of these skills. Use one or two of your favorite search engines to compose a list of at least five hard skills and five soft skills that will help you in your managerial career. A starting point in your search might be to enter into your search engine the phrase "hard skills and soft skills for managers." You will most likely have to dig further to get the information you need to complete this assignment. Restrict your analysis to articles about managerial skills published within the last two years so that you become familiar with current trends.

1-A Case Problem

Big Hopes at Olive Garden, Red Lobster, and LongHorn Steakhouse

Clarence Otis, chairman and chief executive of Darden Restaurants Inc., sees better days ahead for an industry that took a beating during the Great Recession of the recent past. Otis, whose company owns Olive Garden, Red Lobster, LongHorn Steakhouse, and other casual-dining chains, expected the job losses that cut consumer spending to abate in the first quarter of 2010.

"Restaurants, historically, are one of the first industries to benefit coming out of a recession. People have deferred big-ticket items like cars, appliances and vacations, and a meal out is a low-ticket treat," said Otis.

Darden planned to capitalize on the recovery by doing the things it had been planning to do prior to the recession, such as investing in menu development and employee training, remodelling restaurants, and preserving cash.

Unlike many restaurant chains that turned to heavy discounting to lure customers, Darden avoided that. Buy-one-get-one-free or half-off promotions "run the risk of communicating to consumers that price is the primary attribute of your brand and it overwhelms all the other things that go into developing a strong brand," Otis said. Instead, Darden introduced new menu items at lower prices; that helped restaurants keep the same profit.

At its upscale Capital Grille chain the company offered, for $40 per person, new seafood entrées paired with appetizers and wine from regions of the world where prices are lower or from newer vineyards that charge less than more established ones. Darden also reduced the pace at which it opened new restaurants.

The biggest lesson that was reinforced for him during the downturn, Otis said, was to spend conservatively and to keep debt low even when times are good.

Discussion Questions

1. What managerial roles is Clarence Otis emphasizing in the case just presented?
2. What challenges would restaurant managers face in implementing Otis's approach to keeping the restaurants performing well during a slow period in the economy?
3. If you have visited a Darden restaurant lately, what suggestions can you offer top-level management for attracting even more customers?
4. Based on media reports, how successful do you think Clarence Otis has been in helping the Darden chain become a continuing success?
5. What financial management practices of the Darden chain might be useful to you in managing your personal finances?

Source: Julie Jargon, "Darden Runs Lean, Keeps Pricing Firm at Restaurant Chains," *The Wall Street Journal*, December 28, 2009, p. B5.

1-B Case Problem

The Management Trainee Blues

Sara Fenton was excited about having been recruited into the restaurant manager training program at a national restaurant chain. As an assistant manager to Johnny Sanchez, she would perform a variety of managerial duties at a busy restaurant in suburban Cleveland, Ohio. If she performed well in her responsibilities for two years, she would be assigned to manage her own restaurant within the chain.

Before shifting into her job as assistant manager, first Sara had to spend six weeks on the wait staff. "This assignment was a natural for me because I had worked part-time as a server for several years in high school and college," Sara said. "Working in the dining room was also a good way to learn more about the restaurant where I would be an assistant manager." After performing well as a server, and earning wonderful tips, Sara was appointed to the assistant manager position as promised.

Influenced by a workshop on the topic of time management Sara took at school, she decided to maintain a log of her activities as manager. Among the entries were as follows:

September 2:   Bill, one of the wait staff, sent me an e-mail saying that he could not work today because his uncle shot himself in a hunting accident, and Bill had to wait at the hospital. What a mess, because we are short-handed in the dining room this busy Labor Day weekend anyway.

September 6:   Jen, one of the best servers on the staff, said she needs a week off to take care of a personal problem. After 25 years of marriage, her mother and father announced their plans to divorce and Jen just can't take the emotional pain. It will be tough replacing Jen until she returns.

September 25:   Chuck, a member of the wait staff, accidentally spilled hot coffee on one of the customers. The customer demanded to see the manager, so I tried to take care of the problem. The man was irate, and talked about suing the restaurant. I tried to calm him down, and offered to pay for his meal as well as for dry cleaning his trousers. I don't know the final outcome of this problem, but it looks ugly.

October 5:   Johnny informs me that the restaurant chain is concerned that some of the spinach it bought this week contained E. coli bacteria. We are getting rid of all the spinach we can find in the restaurant, but some of the salads we served the last few days may have been contaminated. Johnny wants me to investigate. Does he think I'm a chemist and detective as well as a management trainee?

Sara is scheduled to meet with Johnny Sanchez later this week to discuss her impressions of her work as the assistant restaurant manager. Sara reflected, "What can I say that is positive? The problems I'm dealing with so far don't seem like the job of a real manager. I wonder if I've chosen the right field? These day-by-day headaches are a lot to cope with."

1-B   Case Problem

Discussion Questions

1. Advise Sara on whether she is really learning some valuable lessons as a potential manager.

2. What should Sara tell Johnny on her review of her experiences?

3. Which managerial roles has Sara been carrying out as indicated by her activity log?

CHAPTER 2

International Management and Cultural Diversity

OBJECTIVES

After studying this chapter and doing the exercises, you should be able to:

1 Describe the importance of multinational corporations and outsourcing in international business.

2 Recognize the importance of sensitivity to cultural differences in international enterprise.

3 Identify major challenges facing the global managerial worker.

4 Explain various methods of entry into world markets.

5 Pinpoint success factors in the global marketplace, and several positive and negative aspects of globalization.

6 Describe the scope of diversity and the competitive advantage and potential problems of a culturally diverse workforce.

7 Summarize organizational practices to encourage diversity.

Tom Bonkenburg is the director of European operations for a small supply-chain consulting firm, the St. Onge Company, Inc., located in York, Pennsylvania. Several years ago Bonkenburg traveled to Moscow to develop a working relationship with a large Russian firm. Yet when he met the company's Russian branch director, something unusual happened. "I gave my best smile, handshake, and friendly joke…only to be met with a dreary and unhappy look," says Bonkenburg.

Later, Bonkenburg received an e-mail from the Russian that appeared to clarify what took place. The Russian gentleman thanked him for a great meeting. To his surprise Bonkenburg later learned that Russian culture fosters smiling in private settings and seriousness in business settings. "He was working as hard to impress me as I was to impress him," Bonkenburg says.[1]

The anecdote about the supply-chain consulting firm illustrates two major themes about today's business world. First, even small companies are likely to be engaged in international commerce in order to be successful. Second, to be successful in business it is necessary to understand key

[1]Emily Maltby, "Expanding Abroad? Avoid Cultural Gaffes," *The Wall Street Journal*, January 19, 2010, p. B5.

cultural differences between you and the person you are dealing with. In this chapter we describe major aspects of the international and culturally diverse environment facing managers. Among the topics covered are methods of entry into the global marketplace, success factors in globalization, and the advantages and disadvantages of going global. We also highlight cultural diversity, including its competitive advantage and the skills required to become a multicultural manager. Globalization and cultural diversity are such major forces in the workplace that they receive some attention throughout our study of management.

LEARNING OBJECTIVE ①

Describe the importance of multinational corporations and outsourcing in international business.

INTERNATIONAL MANAGEMENT

The internationalization (or global integration) of business and management exerts an important influence on the manager's job. Approximately 10 to 15 percent of all jobs in the United States are dependent upon trade with other countries. Another way of understanding the impact of global integration is to recognize that many complex manufactured products are built with components from several countries. The mix of components can sometimes confuse the national identity of a product, with automobiles being a prime example. The Ford Mustang, identified as an American vehicle, is manufactured in Michigan and Ontario; it contains 65 percent U.S. and Canadian parts. The Toyota Sienna XLE, identified as a Japanese vehicle, is manufactured in Indiana; it contains 90 percent U.S. and Canadian parts.[2]

The internationalization of management is part of the entire world becoming more global, representing challenges for workers at every level. For example, a financial analyst in Bangalore, India, can perform the work of a financial analyst in Columbus, Ohio, at a lower wage rate. A counterforce to the global economy is that jobs involving personal contacts and relationships are less subject to competition from another country.

As business becomes more global, the manager must adapt to the challenges of working with organizations and people from other countries. Keeping time zone differences clearly in mind and converting back and forth between the metric and decimal (American) system is a challenge for many people.

The Multinational Corporation

multinational corporation (MNC)

A firm with operating units in two or more countries in addition to its own.

The heart of international trade is the **multinational corporation (MNC)**, a firm with units in two or more countries in addition to its own. An MNC has headquarters in one country and subsidiaries in others. However, it is more than a collection of subsidiaries that carry out decisions made at headquarters. A multinational corporation sometimes hires people from its country of origin (expatriates) for key positions in facilities in other countries. At other

---

[2]Jathon Sapsford and Norihiko Shirouzu, "Mom, Apple Pie and... Toyota?" *The Wall Street Journal*, May 11, 2006, pp. B1–B2.

times, the MNC will hire citizens of the country in which the division is located (host-country nationals) for key positions. Most of the best-known companies are MNCs, including PepsiCo, IBM, and Microsoft among hundreds of others.

transnational corporation

A special type of MNC that operates worldwide without having a single national headquarters.

The **transnational corporation** is a special type of MNC that operates worldwide without having one national headquarters. The transnational executive thinks in terms of the entire world, rather than looking upon operations in other countries as being "foreign operations." Components of the company located in different parts of the world sometimes provide continuous service as the workers from different time zones begin their contribution when work ends in another time zone. Tokyo-based Trend Micro, a specialist in combating computer viruses, is a highly developed transnational company. Trend Micro is able to respond quickly because it spreads the top executives, engineers, and support staff around the world to enhance its response to new virus threats. The main virus response center is in the Philippines, yet six other labs are spread out from Munich to Tokyo. "With the Internet, viruses became global. To fight them, we had to become a global company," says Chairman Steve Chang, a Taiwanese who launched the company.[3]

Two key issues in international business and management are government agreements about trade and outsourcing, or "offshoring." Both issues have been highly challenging for many companies, workers, and countries.

Trade Agreements Among Countries

Trade agreements are important for understanding international management because these agreements facilitate business in exporting, importing, and building goods in other countries. The agreements have triggered considerable controversy, often leading to anti–trade-agreement demonstrations.

The North American Free Trade Agreement (NAFTA)

NAFTA establishes liberal trading relationships among the United States, Canada, and Mexico. The pact also calls for the gradual removal of tariffs and other trade barriers on most goods produced and sold in the United States. NAFTA became effective in Canada, Mexico, and the United States as of January 1, 1994. The agreement creates a giant trading zone extending from the Arctic Ocean to the Gulf of Mexico. NAFTA forms the world's second largest free trade zone, bringing together 450 million consumers in the three countries. The largest free trade zone is the European Union.

Many companies benefit from NAFTA because of better access to the two other countries in the pact. Consequently, U.S. trade with Mexico and Canada has increased dramatically. Many U.S. companies have expanded sales of industrial and consumer products to Canada and Mexico. These products include computers, DVDs, and machine tools. As a result of NAFTA, Canadian and Mexican firms have sold more products to the United States.

---

[3]Quoted in Steve Hamm, "Borders Are So 20th Century," *Business Week*, September 22, 2003, p. 68; www.TrendMicro.com, accessed January 29, 2010.

More Canadian and Mexican beer now flows in the United States, and the sale of electronic products and furniture has increased. Much of the surge in the Mexican auto industry can be attributed to the substantial drop in tariffs between the United States and Mexico. (Mexico assembles autos for the U.S. market.)

Large American manufacturers benefited from NAFTA as they slashed production costs and boosted profits by opening factories in Mexico, where workers are paid about $3 an hour. In addition to auto manufacturers, computer and electronic companies have used Mexico as a platform for fast, inexpensive, and flexible production facilities.[4]

A number of critics perceive NAFTA to be a miserable failure. Many labor union representatives argue that NAFTA threatens jobs of American workers. For example, workers in Ohio claim that NAFTA has devastated lives in their part of the country. Many Mexican farm workers lost out economically when subsidies and import quotas were lifted. Illegal immigration to the United States surged as millions of rural Mexican citizens left Mexican farms in search of opportunity. Critics of NAFTA point out that the agreement does not maintain labor or environmental standards.[5]

Central American Free Trade Agreement (CAFTA)

The United States–Dominican Republic–Central American Free Trade Agreement (CAFTA) is another free-trade agreement that the United States has joined with other countries in the Western Hemisphere. ("United States–Dominican Republic" is included in the official name of CAFTA.) U.S. government policies have granted the six countries already in the agreement relatively open access to American markets for their goods, while at the same time facilitating U.S. entry into their markets. CAFTA has eliminated all tariffs on 80 percent of U.S. manufactured goods, with further reductions in tariffs planned. Agricultural products, professional services, and investments are included in CAFTA. The agreement also strengthens regulatory standards and environmental protection in Central America and the Dominican Republic. Independent, outside monitoring is permitted.[6]

The ultimate hope of proponents of the agreement is a 34-nation Free Trade Agreement covering all countries in the Western Hemisphere except Cuba. Critics of the proposed agreements contend that thousands of textile and apparel jobs will be lost in the United States.[7]

---

[4]"Obama Continues NAFTA Criticism," *msnbc* (http://firstread.msnbc.com), February 24, 2008.

[5]"Trade: What Exactly Is A Free Trader, Anyway," *The Wall Street Journal*, August 25, 2008, p. R7.

[6]"What is CAFTA?" *The CAFTA Intelligence Center* (www.caftaintelligencecenter.com), 2010.

[7]Tom Ricker and Burke Stansbury, "CAFTA Chronicles: Strong-Arming Central America, Mocking Democracy," *Multinational Monitor*, Volume 27, Number 1, January/February 2006, pp. 1–7.

The European Union (EU)

The European Union is a 27-nation alliance that virtually turns member countries into a single marketplace for ideas, goods, services, and investment strategies. The EU was a 15-nation alliance for many years; it continues to incorporate new nations and has become the world's largest economic entity. The EU trades with member nations, the United States, Canada, and other countries throughout the world. Japanese firms are now investing extensively in Europe. An example of the unity created among nations is the Schengen Agreement. The agreement ended passport control and customs checks at many borders, creating a single space where EU citizens can travel, work, and invest. A major step for the European Union is its monetary union in which 11 countries traded their national money for currency called the Euro. The Euro fluctuates in value; in 2010 one Euro was worth about $1.40.

The World Trade Organization (WTO)

The World Trade Organization is the only international agency overseeing the rules of international trade; it liberalizes trade among many nations throughout the world. The idea is to lower trade barriers, thereby facilitating international trade, with the ultimate goal of moving the world toward free trade and open markets. According to the *most favored nation* clause, each member country is supposed to grant all other member countries the most favorable treatment it grants any country with respect to imports and exports. As a result, all countries are supposed to make trade with other member countries quite easy.

An important function of the World Trade Organization is to settle trade disputes between two countries. The decisions of the WTO are absolute, and all members must abide by its rulings. For example, when the U.S. and the European Union are in conflict over imports and exports of beef and lumber, the WTO acts as judge and jury. Countries that violate trade rules are subject to sanctions such as substantial fines.[8]

The WTO now has about 153 member countries, which account for about 95 percent of world trade. Lower trade barriers eliminate the artificially high prices consumers previously paid for imported goods. A continuing problem for the WTO is the distrust of developing countries that claim they are bullied by rich countries. Instead the developing countries want trade agreements that will also help poor nations. Another concern is that the WTO exerts too much authority, such as ruling that the EU law banning hormone-treated beef is illegal.[9]

One issue in facilitating trade is that global trade liberalization leads to continuous job cuts and downward pressures on wages in industrialized nations. The concern about global trade contributing to worker exploitation is so strong that riots frequently take place outside the meetings of the WTO.

---

[8]"Profile: World Trade Organization," *BBC NEWS* (http://newsvote.bbc.co.uk), January 21, 2010.

[9]"World Trade Organization," http://www.globalexchange.org, Updated November 5, 2009.

Rioters regularly pelt security workers with rocks and smash the windows of American-owned stores and U.S. franchises abroad. McDonald's restaurants are a frequent target because McDonald's symbolizes American trade overseas.

The counterargument to objections to overseas trade is that free trade, in the long run, creates more job opportunities by making it possible to export more freely. For example, the United States has more recycled paper than it needs. At the same time, China and other developing countries, such as India, are building paper plants but have a shortage of forests. As a result, these countries are big purchasers of cellulose fiber. A related argument is that when companies shift manufacturing to low-wage countries, the companies can remain more cost competitive. As a consequence of globalizing production, the companies stay in business and keep more domestic workers employed.

Global Outsourcing as Part of International Trade

The trade agreements described above have made it much easier for companies to have manufacturing and many services performed in other countries. In general, **outsourcing** refers to the practice of hiring an individual or another company outside the organization to perform work. Here we are concerned with global outsourcing, sometimes referred to as **offshoring**. We will visit outsourcing again in Chapter 8, as part of the discussion of organization structure.

outsourcing
The practice of hiring an individual or another company outside the organization to perform work.

offshoring
Global outsourcing.

Outsourcing continues to grow in scope, thereby increasing trade among countries. The number of industries immune to outsourcing is shrinking. A case in point is the U.S. construction industry, particularly because construction is thought to be a local or regional activity. Today major components, such as panels for buildings, might be imported from another country. Some knowledge work, including financial analysis and legal work, is globally outsourced. In Gurgaon, India, for example, Copal partners conduct equity, fixed income, and trading research for big name banks such as Goldman Sachs and JP Morgan.[10] Legal outsourcing to firms of lawyers in India has also grown considerably in recent years to help hold down legal fees in the United States.[11]

A major force behind global outsourcing is the pressure discount retailers such as Wal-Mart, Target, and Dollar General exert on manufacturers to keep their prices low. Visualize a mermaid doll being sold for $1.00 at a discount store in the United States. The distributor of these dolls must rely on an extremely low-priced manufacturer to be able to sell the doll to the retailer for about 50 cents. The doll is made in China, where the cost of production is extremely low. Sending so much manufacturing and service work

---

[10]Heather Timmons, "Cost-Cutting in New York, but a Boom in India," *The New York Times* (nytimes.com), August 12, 2008, p. 1.

[11]Niraj Sheth and Nathan Koppel, "With Times Tight, Even Lawyers Get Outsourced," *The Wall Street Journal*, November 26, 2008, p. B1.

(such as computer programming and call centers) continues to create heated controversy. Here we look briefly at the major arguments for and against outsourcing. Some of these arguments are included in the discussion later of the pros and cons of globalization.

The Case for Global Outsourcing

Sending jobs overseas can create new demand for the lower-priced goods, ultimately leading to new jobs in the United States. Consumer electronics is a germane example. In the United States and Canada, people consume an enormous number of electronic products such as cell phones, video games, and laptop computers made overseas. As a result, many retail stores and jobs are created and technicians must be trained to service all the equipment. If these products were manufactured domestically, their high price might limit demand.

The arguments in favor of global outsourcing are part of the argument for free trade. Slashing costs of production through global outsourcing can help a company become more competitive and win new orders. An example is the Paper Converting Machine Company (PCMC) in Green Bay, Wisconsin. Part of the parent company's turnaround strategy for PCMC was to shift some design work to its 160-engineer center in Chennai, India. By having U.S. and Indian designers collaborate around the clock, the company was able to slash development costs and time and win orders—and keep production in Green Bay. The same strategy boosted profits at many other midsize U.S. machinery makers the parent company bought. "We can compete and create great American jobs," vows CEO Robert Chapman. "But not without offshoring."[12]

Outsourcing to other countries sometimes creates a favorable climate for reciprocity on the part of companies that are the major beneficiaries of global outsourcing, such as India. A case in point is the Tata Group conglomerate from India. The Tata Consultancy Services unit has hired 1,300 employees who are American, among its 13,000 employees in the U.S.[13]

The Case Against Global Outsourcing

Many Americans believe that offshoring is responsible for the permanent loss of jobs in the United States and for slow job creation. Yet, increased productivity through information technology is responsible for the vast majority of the lost jobs.[14] Another problem tied with global outsourcing is that American employers can offer low wages to domestic employees backed by the threat that their work could be sent offshore.

---

[12]Pete Engardio, "The Future of Outsourcing: How It's Transforming Whole Industries and the Way We Work," *Business Week*, January 30, 2006, p. 50.

[13]Mehul Srivastava and Moira Herbst, "The Return of the Outsourced Job," *Bloomberg Business Week*, January 11, 2010, p. 16.

[14]"Where Are the Jobs?" *Business Week*, March 22, 2004, p. 37.

A notable problem some American companies have with outsourcing call centers to foreign countries is that language barriers sometimes make it difficult to resolve customer problems. Although the call center workers in the other country are fluent in English, some Americans have difficulty understanding English as spoken in other countries. Art O'Donnell, the executive vice president of customer service at Monster, offers this explanation: "We're really dealing with people putting together a résumé or posting a job; you need to be able to do troubleshooting and problem analysis and provide directions. And you can't do that if there is a language barrier."[15]

A financial problem with global outsourcing is that the cost savings may be elusive. One factor is when the currency of your own country is weak, global outsourcing is more expensive. During 2010, for example, when the U.S. currency was relatively weak, many U. S. firms began an *onshoring* or *reshoring* trend in which some manufacturing was brought back to the United States. Another contributing factor to onshoring was that many U.S. suppliers were hurting for business and were therefore willing to negotiate lower prices. Manufacturing domestically also saves the costs of shipping raw materials overseas, and shipping back the finished product. For instance, U.S. Block Windows Inc. found that it was less expensive to manufacture in Florida rather than China after taking into account shipping costs and complexities of the inventory and lead times.[16]

Sensitivity to Cultural Differences

LEARNING OBJECTIVE 2
Recognize the importance of sensitivity to cultural differences in international trade.

cultural sensitivity
Awareness of local and national customs and their importance in effective interpersonal relationships.

The guiding principle for people involved in international enterprise is sensitivity to cultural differences. **Cultural sensitivity** is awareness of local and national customs and their importance in effective interpersonal relationships. Ignoring the customs of other people creates a communications block that can impede business and create ill will. For example, Americans tend to be impatient to close a deal while businesspeople in many other cultures prefer to build a relationship slowly before consummating an agreement. Exhibit 2-1 presents a sampling of cultural differences that can affect business.

Cultural sensitivity can take the form of adapting your behavior to meet the requirements of people from another culture. A frequent challenge in international business is speaking slowly in your own language, so workers for whom your language is not their native tongue can understand you readily. Failing to adapt your rate of speech can be a sign of cultural insensitivity.

multicultural worker
An individual who is aware of and values other cultures.

Cultural sensitivity is also important because it helps a person become a **multicultural worker**. Such an individual is convinced that all cultures are equally good, and enjoys learning about other cultures. Multicultural

---

[15]Jeremy Smerd, "India on the Outs?" *Workforce Management*, May 18, 2009, p. 32.

[16]Kris Maher and Bob Tita, "Caterpillar Joins 'Onshoring Trend,'" *The Wall Street Journal*, March 12, 2010, p. B1.

workers are usually people who were exposed to more than one culture in childhood. A person from another culture is likely to accept a multicultural person. A theoretical analysis concludes that multiculturalism is the virtue of being open to others.[17] The multicultural worker is open to people who harbor different beliefs and customs.

Being culturally sensitive and multicultural is important; it is challenging to manage employees with dissimilar backgrounds and cultures and attain business goals while adapting to these differences. According to the research of Development Dimensions International, *how* a manager manages people in different cultures can influence results. One potential area for culture conflict occurs between East and West. In Japan, communication about change tends to be more subtle and indirect than in the United States. Japanese managers often use consensus-building techniques to bring about acceptance of change before executing the change. An American manager in Japan might fall back on his or her natural pattern of being much more authoritarian and direct as a way of bringing about change.[18]

Candidates for foreign assignments generally receive training in the language and customs of the country they will work in. The accompanying Management in Action provides more information about the business use of cultural training. Intercultural training exercises include playing the roles of businesspeople from different cultures. International workers are made aware of cultural mistakes to avoid, as shown in Exhibit 2-1.

A large-scale research study has demonstrated that personality factors as well as cultural understanding contribute to the effectiveness of expatriate (sent to another country) managers. The participants in the study included a diverse sample of expatriates in Hong Kong as well as expatriate managers from Japan and Korea working throughout the world. Substantial individual differences were found in terms of performing well in another country, including getting the job done and adjusting well to the new culture. In terms of personality factors, expatriates who function better than others are emotionally stable, extraverted (outgoing), and open to new experiences. Several cross-cultural competencies are also important. Being able to focus on the task to be done as well as the attitudes and feelings of people is important, as is not being ethnocentric.[19](Ethnocentrism is the belief that the ways of one's culture are the best ways of doing things.) Although the previous findings might not be surprising, they contribute to management knowledge because the findings stem from research with hundreds of managers in dozens of countries.

---

[17]Blaine J. Fowers and Barbara J. Davidov, "The Virtue of Multiculturalism," *American Psychologist*, September 2006, pp. 581–594.

[18]Dianne Nilsen, Brenda Kowske, and Kshanika Anthony, "Managing Globally," *HR Magazine*, August 2005, pp. 111–115.

[19]Margaret A. Shaffer et al., "You Can Take It With You: Individual Differences and Expatriate Effectiveness," *Journal of Applied Psychology*, January 2006, pp. 109–125.

EXHIBIT 2-1   Cultural Mistakes to Avoid in Selected Regions and Countries

EUROPE

Great Britain	• Asking personal questions. The British protect their privacy. • Thinking that a businessperson from England is unenthusiastic when he or she says, "Not bad at all." English people understate positive emotion. • Gossiping about royalty	Spain	• Expecting punctuality. Your appointments will usually arrive 20 to 30 minutes late. • Making the American sign of "okay" with your thumb and forefinger. In Spain (and many other countries) this is vulgar.
France	• Expecting to complete work during the French two-hour lunch. • Attempting to conduct significant business during August—les vacances (vacation time).	Scandinavia (Denmark, Sweden, Norway)	• Being overly rank conscious. Scandinavians pay relatively little attention to a person's place in the hierarchy.
Italy	• Eating too much pasta, as it is not the main course. • Handing out business cards freely. Italians use them infrequently.		

ASIA

All Asian countries	• Pressuring an Asian job applicant or employee to brag about his or her accomplishments. Asians feel self-conscious when boasting about individual accomplishments, and prefer to let the record speak for itself. In addition, they prefer to talk about group rather than individual accomplishment.		• Avoid giving expensive gifts because this may obligate the person to reciprocate with something of equal value to you.
Japan	• Shaking hands or hugging Japanese (as well as other Asians) in public. Japanese consider the practices to be offensive. • Not interpreting "We'll consider it" as a no when spoken by a Japanese businessperson. Japanese negotiators mean no when they say, "We'll consider it." • Not giving small gifts to Japanese when conducting business. Japanese are offended by not receiving these gifts.	Korea India Thailand	• Saying "no." Koreans feel it is important to have visitors leave with good feelings. • Telling Indians you prefer not to eat with your hands. If the Indians are not using cutlery when eating, they expect you to do likewise. • Pointing the soles of your shoes toward another person. Be aware of this potential mistake when sitting.
China	• Using black borders on stationary and business cards. Black is associated with death.		

MEXICO AND LATIN AMERICA

Mexico	• Flying into a Mexican city in the morning and expecting to close a deal by lunch. Mexicans build business relationships slowly.	Most of Latin America	• Wearing elegant and expensive jewelry during a business meeting. Most Latin Americans think people should appear more conservative during a business meeting.
Brazil	• Attempting to impress Brazilians by speaking a few words of Spanish. Portuguese is the official language of Brazil.		

Note: A cultural mistake for Americans to avoid when conducting business in most countries outside the United States and Canada is to insist on getting down to new business quickly. North Americans in small towns also like to build a relationship before getting down to business.

LEARNING OBJECTIVE 3

Identify major challenges facing the global managerial worker.

CHALLENGES FACING THE GLOBAL MANAGERIAL WORKER

Managerial workers on assignment in other countries, as well as domestic managers working on international dealings, face a variety of challenges. Rising to these challenges can be the difference between success and failure. Among the heaviest challenges are the development of global leadership skills, economic crises, balance of trade problems, human rights violations, culture shock, differences in negotiating style, piracy, and dangerous and defective products (see Exhibit 2-2).

Developing Global Leadership Skills

global leadership skills

The ability to effectively lead people of other cultures.

Managerial workers occupying leadership positions must develop **global leadership skills**, the ability to effectively lead people from other cultures. Global leadership skills are a combination of cultural sensitivity and general leadership skills. A welcoming attitude toward other cultures is perhaps more important than overseas experience itself in becoming an effective global leader. The global leader manages across distance, countries, and cultures. To be effective as a global leader, the manager must inspire others and excite workers in another country about the future of the multinational corporation. Good interpersonal relationships are required, as they are of all leaders. Similar to leaders in general, the global leader must show initiative and be oriented toward success.[20]

Another aspect of global leadership skills is understanding how well management principles from one's own culture transfer to another. The point about understanding cultural differences as part of cultural sensitivity made in Figure 2-2 is a variation on the same theme. A specific example is supply-chain management. According to Kim Tae Woo, a management advisor from South Korea, most Western companies are quite willing to

---

[20]Maxine Dalton, Chris Ernst, Jennifer Deal, and Jean Leslie, *Success for the New Global Manager: How to Work Across Distances, Countries, and Cultures* (San Francisco: Jossey-Bass, 2002).

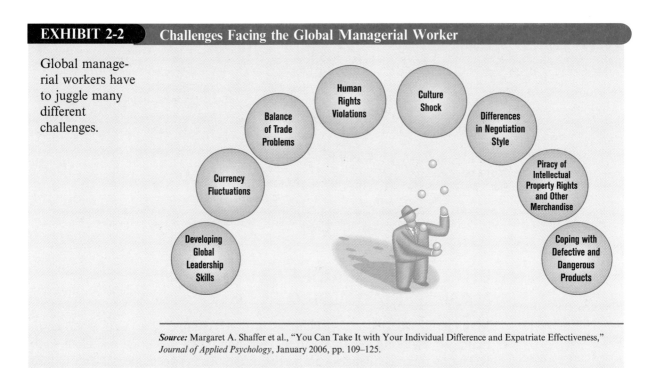

EXHIBIT 2-2 Challenges Facing the Global Managerial Worker

Global managerial workers have to juggle many different challenges.

- Human Rights Violations
- Culture Shock
- Balance of Trade Problems
- Differences in Negotiation Style
- Currency Fluctuations
- Piracy of Intellectual Property Rights and Other Merchandise
- Developing Global Leadership Skills
- Coping with Defective and Dangerous Products

Source: Margaret A. Shaffer et al., "You Can Take It with Your Individual Difference and Expatriate Effectiveness," *Journal of Applied Psychology*, January 2006, pp. 109–125.

switch parts suppliers to cut costs. Switching suppliers is a tougher sell in Japan, where executives frequently have long-term or personal relationships with key people at their suppliers.[21]

The nature of what constitutes global leadership skills is a vast topic, yet consider this example: You are the manager of a unit of a company that expects employees to give utmost attention to meeting customer deadlines, even if it means working 70 hours per week. In your group are several workers from overseas who are from a culture that gives family life much higher priority than work life; they are not disposed to work more than 37 and one-half hours per week. Before crunch time arrives, it is your job to cultivate the overseas worker to become more work oriented.

Currency Fluctuations

A frequent challenge to the international manager is adjusting business practices in response to changes in the value of currencies in the home country and elsewhere. If the currency of a country suddenly *gains* in value, it may be difficult to export products made in that country. When a country's currency *weakens* versus the currency of other countries, it is easier to export goods because the goods are significantly less expensive and more competitive in other countries. The weakening of the U.S. dollar during the 2000s made it more difficult for U.S. citizens to purchase foreign goods. For example, the U.S. dollar fell to about 71 cents against the euro (€) in 2010.

---

[21]Phred Dvorak, "Making U.S. Management Ideas Work Elsewhere," *The Wall Street Journal*, May 22, 2006, p. B3.

(A handbag for 100€ would cost $141 U.S. In contrast, a handbag priced at $100 U.S. would cost 71€, excluding differences in sales taxes). Europeans would find U.S. handbags to be a relative bargain.

An example of the impact on business of a falling currency took place in Iceland several years ago. The three McDonald's restaurants closed as the collapse of the Icelandic krona made operating the business too expensive. In that region of the world, McDonald's requires that franchises import from Germany all the goods required for its restaurants. High tariffs on imported goods contributed to the high costs of operating the McDonald's restaurants.[22]

In overview, a falling U.S. dollar invigorates the market for U.S. exports and helps close the trade gap. The weaker dollar makes foreign goods more expensive in the United States and gives domestic companies more leeway to raise their prices. However, as described later, the United States remains a much bigger importer than exporter of goods. It is often argued that one of the reasons China can export so freely to the United States is that the Chinese government keeps the yuan (the Chinese currency) at an artificially low rate, approximately 6.83 per dollar.

Despite the short-term exporting advantage of the lowering of the value of currency in one's country, a long-term risk exists. For example, a precipitous U.S. dollar decline could lead to high inflation and higher interest rates as foreign creditors demand greater returns for lending to the United States.[23]

Currency fluctuations are of obvious concern for workers in marketing. Managers in manufacturing and in services must also be concerned. For example, the manufacturing manager might be forced to find ways to lower the manufacturing cost of a product in order to compete better against imports. As a country's currency rises in value, exporting companies must become more and more efficient to lower costs.

Balance of Trade Problems

balance of trade
The difference between exports and imports in both goods and services.

A concern at the broadest level to an international manager is a country's **balance of trade**, the difference between exports and imports in both goods and services. Many people believe that it is to a country's advantage to export more than it imports. Yet in 2009, the total international deficit in goods and services for the United States was $375 billion. For goods, the deficit was $507 billion, the highest on record. For services, the surplus was $132 billion. It marked a slowing down of the deficit from the previous five years.

The trade deficit can be attributed to many factors, such as the preference for Americans to purchase lower-priced goods and to take vacations in foreign countries rather than the United States and deficit spending by the U.S. government. The sharp increase in the price of imported petroleum products has also contributed to the deficit. Exhibit 2-3 presents some interesting facts about the trade deficit.

---

[22]"Iceland's Three McDonald's Restaurants to Close," Associated Press, October 27, 2009.

[23]Mark Gongloff, "The Case for the Weak Dollar Isn't Strong," *The Wall Street Journal*, November 13, 2009, p. C1.

EXHIBIT 2-3   U.S. International Trade in Goods and Services Highlights May 12, 2010

Goods and Services Deficit Increases in March 2010

The Nation's international trade deficit in goods and services increased to $40.4 billion in March from $39.4 billion (revised) in February, as imports increased more than exports.

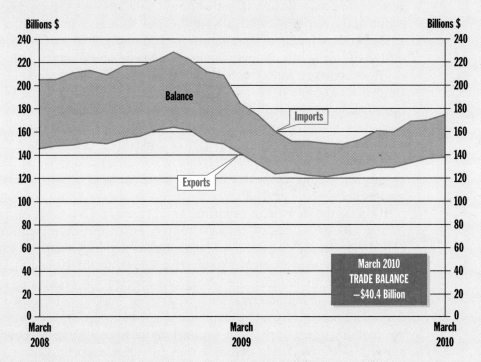

Goods and Services

- Exports increased to $147.9 billion in March from $143.3 billion in February. Goods were $102.7 billion in March, up from $98.5 billion in February, and services were $45.2 billion in March, up from $44.8 billion in February.
- Imports increased to $188.3 billion in March from $182.7 billion in February. Goods were $155.6 billion in March, up from $149.6 billion in February, and services were $32.7 billion in March, down from $33.1 billion in February.
- For goods, the deficit was $52.9 billion in March, up from $51.1 billion in February. For services, the surplus was $12.5 billion in March, up from $11.7 billion in February.

Goods by Geographic Area (Not Seasonally Adjusted)

- The goods deficit with Canada decreased from $2.8 billion in February to $2.3 billion in March.

Exports increased $3.4 billion (primarily automotive parts and accessories; iron and steel mill products; and toys, games, and sporting goods) to $22.0 billion, while imports increased $3.0 billion (primarily passenger cars and crude oil) to $24.3 billion.

- The deficit with the European Union increased from $5.3 billion in February to $7.1 billion in March. Exports increased $3.1 billion (primarily pharmaceutical preparations and civilian aircraft, engines, equipment, and parts) to $21.0 billion, while imports increased $4.8 billion (primarily pharmaceutical preparations, civilian aircraft, and passenger cars) to $28.0 billion.
- The goods deficit with Mexico increased from $4.8 billion in February to $6.0 billion in March. Exports increased $2.4 billion (primarily petroleum products) to $14.1 billion, while imports increased $3.7 billion (primarily crude oil; TVs and VCRs; and automobiles, parts, and accessories) to $20.1 billion.

Note: Total goods data are reported on a Balance of Payments basis; commodity and country detail data for goods are on a Census basis.

Source: www.census.gov/indicator/www/ustrade.html

An individual manager might want to contribute to the national economy by exporting more than importing. In an effort to accomplish this goal, the manager might have to find ways to cut costs on products or services offered for export. An alternative would be to design products or services so attractive they would sell well despite their relatively high price in foreign markets. Examples include American movies, the iPhone, and NFL sweatshirts and T-shirts.

A concern about the U.S. trade deficit is that it contributes to the loss of domestic manufacturing jobs as U.S. companies shifted production to nations that pay lower wages. Yet free traders contend that American consumers benefit from the flood of imports from low-cost producers by being able to purchase goods at low prices. For example, electric alarm clocks made in China retail for about $4.00 at discount stores in the United States.

Human Rights Violations, Corruption, and Violence

International managers face potential ethical problems when their customers and suppliers reside in countries where human rights are violated. Should a U.S. rug distributor purchase carpets from a supplier that employs ten-year-old children who work 11 hours a day for the equivalent of $4 U.S.? Should a U.S. shoe manufacturer buy components from a country that uses political prisoners as free labor? Ethical issues require careful thought, especially because they are not always clear-cut. To a child in an underdeveloped country, receiving $4 per day can mean the difference between malnutrition and adequate food.

The subject of human rights violations is complicated and touchy. Multinational corporations based in the United States are often accused of profiting from the labor of employees exploited in less-developed countries. Many U.S. companies hire undocumented aliens at below minimum wage and maintain substandard and dangerous working conditions. The United States sets high standards when it comes to human rights in other countries. Yet, according to Amnesty International, these standards are sometimes violated at home. Examples include unfair treatment of indigenous people (Eskimos and Native Americans) and capital punishment.[24]

Another ethical and legal problem the international manager faces is corruption by foreign officials. In some countries, a string of officials demand payments before allowing foreigners to conduct business or to speed approval of an operating license. Mexican officials have estimated that as much as 9 percent of Mexico's gross domestic product goes for corruption, more than the nation invests in education and defense combined. The United States is not immune to corruption, as evidenced by the billions in waste and fraud surrounding federal payouts resulting from Hurricane Katrina.[25]

---

[24]"Americas: Solutions to the Historic Violation of Indigenous Rights Will Only Be Found through Respectful Dialogue, In Good Faith, with Indigenous People," Amnesty International Press Release, http://www.amnesty.org, August 7, 2009.

[25]Marla Dickerson, "The Bite of Corruption," *The Los Angeles Times* (http://www.latimes.com), August 6, 2006.

A life-threatening risk for U.S. multinational companies occurs when its employees are trapped in violent acts in another country. Among these violent uprisings were the terrorist attacks in Mumbai, India, in 2009 and the repeated Somali pirate attacks. Of even greater threat is the large number of people killed in the drug-fueled wars gripping cities that are home to U.S. factories in Mexico.[26] Civil unrest, such as in Iran, can create loss of life and severely disrupt the business.

Culture Shock

culture shock

A group of physical and psychological symptoms that may develop when a person is abruptly placed in a foreign culture.

Many managers and professionals on overseas assignments face **culture shock**. The condition refers to a group of physical and psychological symptoms that may develop when a person is abruptly placed in a foreign culture. Among them are excessive hand washing and concern for sanitation, fear of physical contact with others, fear of being mugged, and strong feelings of homesickness.[27] Another potential contributor to culture shock is that the expatriate may work in one time zone while contacts in company headquarters work in a time zone with a difference of six hours or more. As a result, the expatriate is often expected to answer e-mails and respond to phone calls during his or her typical evening or sleeping hours. For example, a person from headquarters in Los Angeles might place an urgent phone call at 5 p.m. his time to a worker in London whose time is 3 a.m. Frequent disruptions to personal life of this nature contribute to making the international assignment uncomfortable for the expatriate.

As an expatriate working in Amsterdam, Holland, said, "People never remember what time zone you're in. I decided that I was going to make my own schedule. I wanted to be available to our European clients and have meetings in Europe, but I didn't want to be in a position where I missed the West Coast." Her own schedule involved working from noon to 8:30 p.m. on Mondays and Fridays.[28] On other workdays, she worked from 9 a.m. to noon, then restarted at 5 p.m. and stayed until late in the evening.

Differences in Negotiating Style

A recurring challenge in other countries, as indicated in Exhibit 2-1, is that the international managerial worker may have to use a different negotiation style. A do-or-die attitude is often self-defeating. American negotiators, for example, often find that they must be more patient, use a team approach, and avoid being too informal. Patience is a major factor in negotiating outside the United States. Asian negotiators are willing to spend many days negotiating a deal. Much of their negotiating activity seems to be ceremonial (including elaborate dining)

---

[26]Fay Hansen, "Skirting Danger," *Workforce Management*, January 19, 2009, pp. 1, 3.

[27]Harry C. Triandis, *Culture Shock and Social Behavior* (New York: McGraw-Hill, 1994), p. 263.

[28]Mary Kissel, "The Jungle: Focus on Recruitment, Pay and Getting Ahead," *The Wall Street Journal*, January 25, 2005, p. B6.

and unrelated to the task. This protracted process can frustrate many Americans. Although members of another culture spend a long time working a deal, they may still take a tough stance, such as insisting on a reasonable profit.

An experiment conducted by Jeanne Brett and Tetsushi Okumura provides more evidence about the challenges of cross-cultural negotiation. The researchers demonstrated that people negotiating with others from their own culture were more likely to achieve mutual gains, as when Americans negotiated with Americans or Japanese negotiated with Japanese. Mutual gains were less likely when negotiating across cultures—when Americans negotiated with Japanese.[29]

Piracy of Intellectual Property Rights and Other Merchandise

In international business, considerable revenue is lost when firms in other countries illegally copy and sell products. These imitations (or "knock-offs") might be sold in the domestic market as well, depriving the firm of additional revenue. Managers must address the reality of unauthorized third-party sales of imitations of their product. Products widely reproduced illegally include fine watches, perfume, videos and CDs, clothing with high-status brand names, and software. The movie industry is another major victim of piracy, with unauthorized copies of films sometimes surfacing even before the formal release date of a film.

The global cost of software piracy was estimated to be $40 billion in 2007, according to data provided by Symantec. Software piracy occurs in two primary ways: physical counterfeiting and file sharing. Approximately 50 percent of the software piracy observed was of desktop games. The dollar volume of piracy, however, is greater for multimedia applications such as photo editors.[30] Microsoft is working hard to reduce software piracy. One tactic was to make China part of an effort to improve communications with government worldwide. Part of the Microsoft message was that stronger intellectual property protection would help China build its own economy in addition to protecting foreign developers of technology products.[31]

In recent years, the Chinese government itself has invested resources in protecting intellectual property rights, which includes forbidding software piracy. The Outline of National Intellectual Property Rights is a strategy to tackle many of the issues surrounding the violation of intellectual property rights. According to Wang Qishan, the vice premier of the State Council of the People's Republic of China, the IPR protection is working. For example,

---

[29]Jeanne Brett and Tetsushi Okumura, "Inter- and Intracultural Negotiations: U.S. and Japanese Negotiators," *Academy of Management Journal*, October 1998, pp. 495–510.

[30]Téo Adams, "The Cost of Software Piracy," www.symtec.com, November 25, 2008.

[31]Jason Dean and Ron Guth, "How Microsoft, Boeing Manage Business in China," *The Wall Street Journal*, April 17, 2006, p. A4.

a growing number of Chinese are refusing to purchase counterfeit products, and a market known for selling replicas of brand products has been closed.[32]

Coping with Dangerous and Defective Products

Yet another potential risk for the international worker is the need to cope with dangerous and defective imported products. Based on these problems, the international manager may be involved in such activities as assisting with a product recall and dealing with angry customers, government agencies, and attorneys. The manager may have to help employees cope with the confusion and uncertainty surrounding negative publicity about the company. Imagine yourself as a purchasing manager at a supermarket, responsible for purchasing contaminated products.

A highly publicized situation involving melamine-contaminated products from China took place during 2007 and 2008. The Food and Drug Administration issued a national alert, warning Americans not to consume imported Chinese foods and beverages that contained milk. Chinese baby formulas and various pet foods made in China were recalled because of melamine contamination. The adverse effects of melamine include kidney stones, kidney failure, reproductive disorders, and death.[33]

A more widespread problem involving dangerous and defective products is the unintentional importation of infected bugs and plants. As global trade increases, more goods arrive from overseas, sometimes bringing with them destructive bugs and plants. About 30 new invasive insects arrive annually in the United States. Among the associated costs of control and prevention are pesticides, inspection programs, and danger to crops. Dangerous plants include weeds that affect crops or animal habitats. Among the dangerous plants is the Asian purple loosestrife, which crowds out native plant species that help support duck, geese, and muskrat.[34]

LEARNING OBJECTIVE **4**

Explain various methods of entry into world markets.

METHODS OF ENTRY INTO WORLD MARKETS

Firms enter the global market in several different ways, and new approaches continue to evolve. At one time a small firm relied on importer-exporters or distributors to enter the world market. Now many home-based businesses sell worldwide through an established Web site. Two broad purposes of foreign commerce are to enhance sales and to produce goods and services. A physical presence in another country might enhance sales; goods and services, such as a call center, might be produced less expensively in another country. The reference to *markets,* however, implies that the company is

---

[32]Wang Qishan, "No More Chinese Knock-Offs," *The Wall Street Journal*, June 17, 2008, p. A23.

[33]"Melamine-Contaminated Chinese Products," www.adrugrecall.com, November 14, 2008.

[34]Kris Maher, "The Vexing Bugs in the Global Trading System," *The Wall Street Journal*, January 15, 2010, p. A15.

looking to sell goods and services in another country rather than manufacture in or provide services from the new location.

The initial entry mode used to penetrate a foreign market must be chosen carefully because of its potential effects on the success of the venture. Another factor is the difficulty of changing the mode without considerable loss of time and money. Six methods of entry into world markets are described next.

1. *Exporting.* Goods produced in one country are sold for direct use or resale to one or more companies in foreign countries. Many small firms specialize in helping companies gain entry into foreign markets through exporting. An overseas distributor can be quite helpful, but must be evaluated carefully to determine compatibility and perhaps the integrity of the proposed partner.

2. *Licensing and franchising.* Companies operating in foreign countries are authorized to produce and market products or services with specific territories on a fee basis. A franchise arrangement, such as a U.S. citizen operating a Subway store in Madrid, Spain, would fit this category.

3. *Local assembly and packaging.* In this arrangement, components rather than finished products are shipped to company-owned facilities in other countries. There assembly is completed and the goods are marketed. Trade regulations sometimes require that a large product, such as a computer server or an automobile, be assembled locally rather than shipped from the exporting country as a finished product.

4. *Strategic alliance and joint ventures.* Instead of merging formally with a firm of mutual interest, a company in one country pools resources with one or more foreign companies. A major reason for the willingness of so many firms to form alliances is the enormous expense and effort necessary for a single organization to accomplish a full range of business activities. In a joint venture, the companies in alliance produce, warehouse, transport, and market products. A joint venture is thus a special type of strategic alliance. Profits or losses from these operations are shared in some predetermined proportion. Many digital products, including digital cameras, result from strategic alliances and joint ventures. Alliances are becoming more frequent with consumer vehicles; Fiat of Italy and Chrysler of the United States have pooled resources to make small cars for the American market.

5. *Direct foreign investment.* The most advanced stage of multinational business activity takes place when a company in one country produces and markets products through wholly owned facilities in foreign countries. Toyota Motor Co. and Ford Motor Co., two well-known multinational corporations, conduct business in this manner. A positive perspective on direct foreign investment is that the multinational corporation exports jobs to other countries, such as the substantial manufacturing facilities of Honda, Toyota, Hyundai, and Mercedes-Benz in the United States. These overseas companies have helped turn the United States into the center of a global industry. Foreign players are said to have reinvigorated the U.S. auto industry. A merger of business firms from different countries, such

as Fiat acquiring Chrysler and its Jeep brand, is a similar way of gaining entry into the international marketplace.

global start-up
A small firm that comes into existence by serving an international market.

6. *Global start-up.* A **global start-up** is a small firm that comes into existence by serving an international market. By so doing, the firm circumvents the previous methods. Logitech Inc., the leading manufacturer of the computer mouse, is one of the most successful global start-ups. A Swiss and two Italians who wanted to have an international company from the start founded the company in 1982. Logitech began with headquarters, manufacturing, and engineering in California and Switzerland and then established facilities in Taiwan and Ireland. Founders of global start-ups have one key characteristic in common: some international experience before going global.[35] Selling through the Internet facilitates creating a global start-up because customers can be reached directly without a distributor. Trade restrictions such as tariffs and the need to obtain approval from the foreign government usually apply.

Of the methods of entry into the global marketplace, exporting offers the least protection for the company doing business in another country. Multinational firms run the risk that the firm in the other country may drop its affiliation and sell the product on its own. The affiliate thus becomes a competitor. To avoid this risk, direct foreign investment is recommended as the best way to protect the company's competitive advantage. The advantage is protected because the manager of a foreign subsidiary can control its operation.

LEARNING OBJECTIVE 5
Pinpoint success factors in the global marketplace and several positive and negative aspects of globalization.

SUCCESS FACTORS IN THE GLOBAL MARKETPLACE

Success in international business stems from the same factors that lead to success at home. The ultimate reason for the success of any product or service is its ability to satisfy customer needs. Additional strategies and tactics, however, are required for success in the global marketplace. It is important to recognize that internationalization of business is not always successful. Most of these strategies and tactics logically extend the topics discussed previously in this chapter.

Think Globally, Act Locally

A competitive enterprise combines global scale and world-class technology with deep roots in local markets. Local representatives of the firm behave as though their primary mission is to serve the local customer. Multinational corporations implementing a local market focus face the challenge of adapting a product to local trends and preferences. Often the differences are subtle, and require a careful study of the local market. For example, the direct seller of cosmetics, Mary Kay, has adapted its products to Chinese culture,

---

[35]Benjamin M. Oviatt and Patricia Phillips McDougal, "Global Start-Ups: Entrepreneurs on a Worldwide Stage," *The Academy of Management Executive*, May 1995, p. 30.

which perceives smooth white skin as the essence of beauty, said Paul Mak, president of Mary Kay China. As a result, sunless tanners or bronzers are not distributed in China. Instead, Mary Kay markets skin whiteners and is developing a line of botanical lotions that include traditional Chinese herbs.[36]

Part of acting locally is close familiarity with the local scene. U.S. companies with established maquiladoras (assembly factories) have discovered the importance of this principle. For example, a unique aspect of Mexican law comes into play when an officially recognized labor union declares a strike. All employees, including managers, must leave the building, and red and black flags are hung at entrances to the plant. Employees receive full pay for all the time they are out on a legal strike.

A major aspect of thinking globally, yet acting locally is for the multinational corporation to compete successfully against well-established, well-managed domestic (local) companies. Two members of the Boston Consulting Group studied this challenge. One of the key principles is that the multinational company must create customized products and services for the local market—as does Mary Kay. An Indian company, CavinKare, has been quite successful with its single-use plastic sachets of shampoo. To compete successfully against CavinKare, Hindustan Unilever and Procter & Gamble package shampoos in sachets as well.[37]

Recruit and Select Talented Nationals

A major success factor in building a business in another country is to hire talented citizens of that country to fill important positions. After the host-company nationals are hired, they must be taught the culture of the parent company. By teaching the overseas managers the values and traditions of the firm, you enable those managers to better achieve corporate objectives. Networking with contacts in the other country is important. One way to network would be to seek out contacts within other companies from your country already established in your destination country. These people might include bankers, lawyers, suppliers, and distributors.

Staffing in other countries may require a modification of U.S. ideas about good candidates. An international human resources manager observes that "One of the most common mistakes companies make when hiring and recruiting employees in China is to judge candidates based on U.S. perceptions and criteria. Chinese employees often have different ways of communicating their interests and skills during an interview, and they consider it unbecoming to place too much emphasis on their skills and experience."

---

[36]Julia Glick, "China Market Helps Mary Kay Stay in the Pink," Associated Press, August 6, 2006.

[37]Arindam K. Bhattacharya and David C. Michael, "How Local Companies Keep Multinationals at Bay," *Harvard Business Review*, March 2008, p. 90.

An interviewer not familiar with this mind-set could miss hiring an excellent candidate.[38]

Hire or Develop Multicultural Workers

A contributing factor to success in global markets is to hire multicultural workers. Multiculturalism enhances acceptance of a firm by overseas personnel and customers. Included in multiculturalism is the ability to speak the language of the target (or host) country. Even though English is the official language of business and technology, overseas employees should develop the right foreign language skill. Being able to listen to and understand foreign customers speaking in their native language about their requirements may reveal nuances that would be missed by expecting them to speak in English. Showing that one has made an effort to learn the native language can earn big dividends with employees, customers, prospective customers, bankers, and government officials. To be impressive, however, it is important to go beyond the most basic skill level.

To help workers and their family members become multicultural, many companies offer cultural training. Joerg Schmitz, a global management training expert, shares an illuminating insight about the impact of culture on an employee's job performance: "The U.S. culture is extraordinarily task oriented. Northern Europe is perhaps the closest to the type of task orientation you'll find in the United States. But about every other country in the world is relationship oriented."[39] Expatriates must understand this observation as they work hard to build rapport and gain credibility with business colleagues in other cultures.

Research and Assess Potential Markets

Another basic success strategy in international markets is to acquire valid information about the firm's target market. Trade statistics usually provide a good starting point. If the company manufactures energy-saving light bulbs, it must find out where such bulbs sell the best. Basic trade data are often available at foreign embassies, banks with international operations, and departments of commerce. Wal-Mart invests enormous energy and money into researching which overseas markets—and consumer reaction—would fit its retailing model. In general, the planning has worked well. For example, Wal-Mart has been highly successful in Mexico and Canada, and has stayed out of Paris (as well as New York City!). The company, however, stumbled in Germany and eventually sold its stores in that country.

The Advantages and Disadvantages of Globalization

Many managers and scholars believe that globalization of business is both inevitable and highly desirable. Yet for other managers, business owners, and individual workers, the internationalization of the workplace has created

---

[38]Mary E. Medland, "Setting Up Overseas," *HR Magazine*, January 2004, p. 72.
[39]Andrea C. Poe, "Selection Savvy," *HR Magazine*, April 2002, p. 78.

more problems than opportunities. Many of the advantages and disadvantages of globalization depend upon an individual's vantage point. An executive in an MNC might receive a generous bonus because shifting a call center to India saves the company $5 million per year in labor costs. As a consequence, she welcomes globalization. The middle-aged call center supervisor who lost his enjoyable, well-paying job and is now a greeter at a discount department store would view globalization more negatively. Exhibit 2-4 outlines the major pros and cons of globalization.

EXHIBIT 2-4   **The Pros and Cons of Globalization**

Advantages

- By sending jobs overseas, a country such as the United States is better able to compete globally, thus saving jobs in the long run. A company frequently cannot get the contracts it needs to survive if it cannot reduce prices, so global outsourcing becomes a necessity.
- Productivity grows more quickly when countries produce goods and services in which they have a comparative advantage. Living standards go up faster. Productivity in high-wage companies also increases because they are forced to reduce the cost of production to survive world-wide competition.
- Global integration helps reduce world-wide poverty, as poorer countries become wealthier because of new employment and exports. At the same time, economic growth around the world contributes to economic stability and peace because impoverished people are more likely to revolt and attack wealthier people and institutions.
- Global competition and inexpensive imports set a ceiling on prices, so inflation is less likely to be too high.
- When one country buys goods from and sends jobs to another country, the second country is better able to purchase goods from the first country. For example, India furnishes its call centers for U.S firms with U.S. computers and software.
- An open economy spurs innovation with fresh ideas from abroad. Innovation at home

Disadvantages

- Millions of Americans have lost jobs due to imports or production shifts abroad. Most find lower-paying jobs. One-quarter of laid-off workers are still job-hunting three years later. Most of the jobs sent overseas from the United States are permanent losses. Many service and professional jobs, such financial analysis and design engineering, are now sent to other countries.
- Millions of others fear losing their jobs, especially at companies operating under competitive pressure. Workers are forced to compete against foreign workers in countries such as Pakistan and Malaysia, where workers are paid on average one-tenth as much as their American counterparts.
- To stay competitive in a global economy, many companies reduce wages, close plants rather than have a unionized workforce, reduce health and retirement benefits, and eliminate some pension plans.
- Profits and executive salaries increase while workers toil in overseas sweatshops. Many of these workers are vulnerable to human rights violations.

(continued)

EXHIBIT 2-4	The Pros and Cons of Globalization *(continued)*

Advantages

receives a boost because the domestic company must become more specialized and creative to compete against international rivals.

- When research and development jobs are moved overseas, products reach the market faster because work can be done 24/7 as scientists and engineers in one part of the world pass off projects at the end of the day to research workers just starting the workday overseas.
- Workers become broader in their outlook and profit from the opportunity to become multicultural, resulting from foreign travel.
- With many jobs shipped overseas, talent within the United States is freed up to be re-skilled and used elsewhere during a tight labor market. At the same time, many people whose jobs are outsourced, or who fear being outsourced, start small enterprises that help revitalize the economy.
- It is possible for an American company, such as online store Fair Indigo, to promote fair trade around the world by choosing foreign vendors who pay beyond the minimum wage and offer workers bonuses and medical benefits.
- To stave off foreign competition, domestic companies are forced to increase the quality of their goods and services.
- Taxes are lower and financial incentives for establishing manufacturing are often higher in countries such as Malaysia and Singapore than they are in the U.S., making it easier for American firms to operate profitably. It is often easier for U.S. companies to find inexpensive funding overseas.

Disadvantages

- National pride is hurt as many Americans lament, "Nothing is 'made in the USA' any longer. We used to be such a great country." At the same time, many American consumers resent call center workers from 6,000 miles away responding to their requests for information and service. Many Americans have a difficult time understanding workers who speak English with a foreign accent.

Source: Brian Blackstone, "Fed Chairman Expects Globalization to Enhance Living Standards," *The Wall Street Journal,* August 26–27, 2006, p. A3; Bob Tedeschi, "A Click on Clothes to Support Fair Trade," *The New York Times* (www.nytimes.com), September 25, 2006; "Don't Discount the Positive Side of Globalization," *Toronto Star* (www.thestar.com); Douglas A. Irwin, "Outsourcing Is Good for America," January 28, 2004, *The Wall Street Journal,* p. A16; Pete Engardio, "Can the Future Be Built in America?" *Business Week,* September 21, 2009, pp. 46–51.

LEARNING OBJECTIVE 6

Describe the scope of diversity and the competitive advantage and potential problems of a culturally diverse workforce.

diversity
A mixture of people with different group identities within the same work environment.

PLAY VIDEO

Go to www.cengage.com/management/dubrin and view the video for Chapter 2. As you view the video, study how the leaders at this company decided to deal with issues of diversity and discrimination. What practices and policies did they set in place?

THE SCOPE, COMPETITIVE ADVANTAGE, AND POTENTIAL PROBLEMS OF MANAGING DIVERSITY

The globalization of business means that managerial workers must be able to deal effectively with people from other countries. At the same time, it is important to deal effectively with different cultural groups within one's own country and company. Both international and domestic workforces are diverse. In the present context, **diversity** refers to a mixture of people with different group identities within the same work environment. Workplace diversity is not prized simply because it is pleasant to have different groups working next to each other, but because these groups work *together* as a team to serve a variety of customers and to generate a wide variety of useful ideas.[40] The term *diversity* includes two subtypes, demographic and cultural.

Demographic diversity refers to the mix of group characteristics of the organization's workforce. Demographic characteristics include such factors as age, sex, religion, physical status, and sexual orientation. *Cultural diversity* refers to the mix of cultures and subcultures to which the organization's workforce belongs. Among these cultures are the Hispanic culture, the deaf culture, the Muslim culture, the Jewish culture, the Native American culture, and the Inuit (Eskimo) culture. It is possible for people with the same demographic characteristics not to share the same cultural characteristics. A deaf person who went to school with hearing people, whose parents are hearing, and most of whose friends can hear, may be deaf from a demographic standpoint, yet the person does not identify with the deaf culture. Following common practice, in this text the term *diversity* is used to reflect both demographic and cultural diversity.

Here and in the next section, we study diversity in the workplace from five perspectives: (1) the scope of diversity, (2) its competitive advantage, (3) potential disadvantages, (4) organizational practices for capitalizing on diversity, and (5) an analysis of how the English language is used to unify people in business. Before reading further, take the self-quiz about cross-cultural skills and attitudes presented in Exhibit 2-5.

The Scope of Diversity

Improving cross-cultural relations includes appreciating the true meaning of diversity. To appreciate diversity, a person must go beyond tolerating to treating people from different racial and ethnic groups fairly. Valuing diversity means to respect and enjoy a wide range of cultural, demographic, and individual differences. To be diverse is to embrace measurable differences. Although the diversity factor is measurable in a scientific sense, it may not be visible on the surface. Upon meeting a team member, it may not be

---

[40]Jennifer Schramm, "Acting Affirmatively," *HR Magazine*, September 2003, p. 192.

EXHIBIT 2-5	Cross-Cultural Skills and Attitudes

Various employers and cross-cultural experts believe the following skills and attitudes are important for relating effectively to coworkers in a culturally diverse environment.

	Applies to Me Now	Not There Yet
1. I have spent some time in another country.	_____	_____
2. At least one of my friends is deaf, blind, or uses a wheelchair.	_____	_____
3. I know how much at least two foreign currencies are worth in comparison to the money of my country	_____	_____
4. I can read in a language other than my native tongue.	_____	_____
5. I can speak in a language other than my native tongue.	_____	_____
6. I can write in a language other than my own.	_____	_____
7. I can understand people speaking in a language other than my own.	_____	_____
8. I use my second language regularly.	_____	_____
9. My friends include people of races different from my own.	_____	_____
10. My friends include people of different ages.	_____	_____
11. I feel (or would feel) comfortable having friends with a sexual orientation different from mine.	_____	_____
12. My attitude is that although another culture may be different from mine, that culture is equally good.	_____	_____
13. I would be willing to (or already do) hang art from various countries in my home.	_____	_____
14. I would accept (or have already accepted) a work assignment of more than several months in another country.	_____	_____
15. I have a passport.	_____	_____
16. I sometimes eat in restaurants that serve the food of a country quite different from mine, and/or I prepare such food at home.	_____	_____

Interpretation: If you answered "Applies to Me Now" to ten or more of the questions, you most likely function well in a multicultural work environment. If you answered "Not There Yet" to ten or more of the questions, you need to develop more cross-cultural awareness and skills to work effectively in a multicultural work environment. You will notice that being bilingual gives you at least five points on this quiz.

Source: Several of the statements are based on Ruthann Dirks and Janet Buzzard, "What CEOs Expect of Employees Hired for International Work," *Business Education Forum*, April 1997, pp. 3–7; Gunnar Beeth, "Multicultural Managers Wanted," *Management Review*, May 1997, pp. 17–21.

apparent that the person is dyslexic, color-blind, gay, lesbian, or vegetarian. However, all these factors are measurable.

As just implied, some people are more visibly different from others because of physical features or disabilities. Yet the diversity umbrella is supposed to include everybody in an organization. The goal of a diverse organization, then, is for persons of all cultural backgrounds to achieve their full potential, not restrained by group identification such as sex, nationality, race, physical status, or sexual orientation. A diverse organization is also thought to be inclusive, valuing and appreciating the contributions of every employee and leveraging those contributions for the good of the company.[41]

Integrating generations has become an important part of both cultural and demographic diversity in organizations; the goal is to have people of all ages working well together. The two extremes are traditionalists (or veterans) born 1922–1945, and millennials born 1981–2000. One cultural difference between the groups is that traditionalists are likely to prefer to communicate by telephone and e-mail; millennials prefer to send text mesages.[42] Considerable attention has been paid in recent years to integrating people with physical disabilities into the workforce, as illustrated in the accompanying Management in Action.

Another cultural and demographic group being emphasized for full inclusion in the work force is made up of people who are gay, lesbian, bisexual, and transgender (GLBT). Janis Walworth, co-founder of the Center for Gender Sanity says, "The country is on a path of increasing respect for gays and lesbians as well, and transgender people are riding the coattails."[43] For example, more people in key managerial positions now openly announce that they are gay or lesbian. Some transgender people return to work one day announcing that they have changed their sexual identification. For example, Sam in customer service returns from his summer vacation as Sally, and now wears women's clothing to work.

The Competitive Advantage of Diversity

Encouraging diversity within an organization helps an organization achieve social responsibility goals. Diversity brings a competitive advantage to a firm, but before diversity can offer that competitive advantage it must be woven into the fabric of the organization. This stands in contrast to simply having a "diversity program" offered by the human resources department. Instead, the human resource efforts toward accomplishing diversity become part of organizational strategy. The potential competitive (or bottom-line)

---

[41]Susan Meisinger, "Diversity: More Than Just Representation," *HR Magazine*, January 2008, p. 8.

[42]"The Multigenerational Workforce: Opportunity for Competitive Success," *SHRM Research Quarterly*, First Quarter 2009, p. 2.

[43]Quoted in Diane Cadrain, "Accommodating Sex Transformations," *HR Magazine*, October 2009, p. 59.

MANAGEMENT IN ACTION

Canadian Banks Open Doors for Employees with Disabilities

Tom Proszowski, age 56, director of employment equity and diversity at CIBC, is more than just another mid-level banking executive. As he rolls his wheelchair through the bank's Toronto headquarters, he is a symbol of the progress Canadian banks have made when it comes to hiring people with disabilities and not just in the low or mid-level ranks.

"We did an informal survey recently and it showed that 5 percent of all those men and women in the executive levels of the bank report they have a disability," he says. Overall, about 4 percent of CIBC's 40,000-plus Canadian employees have a disability, says Sharon Wingfelder, vice-president, human resources.

The goal of the CIBC diversity programs, says Wingfelder, is to identify men and women from any background, any culture, any lifestyle preference, and with any disability in order to see what they might bring in the long term to the bank and then follow up by providing the skills and tools they need to achieve that potential.

Martha Johnson, age 43, an IT specialist at TD Bank, provides another reflection of the progress people with disabilities have made in gaining acceptance in the workplace. She has cerebral palsy. In recent years this meant she must depend on a walker to get around. Juggling a walker and opening doors at the same time proved a challenge, so TD bank installed an automatic door on her floor. "That is just one very visible example of how this bank is always working to create an equitable workplace for those with disabilities," she says.

Beth Grudzinski, TD's vice-president of corporate diversity, says 3.8 percent of TD's 49,000 Canadian employees have disabilities; the bank has dedicated $1 million to take the steps necessary to make them effective, productive, and welcome. That percentage almost triples the 1.3 percent reported in 2003, she adds.

TD also provides 25 internships through a partnership with Ability Edge and recently joined with companies in the United Kingdom in a program that benchmarks how corporations compare when it comes to treating those with disabilities.

Wingfelder says 86 percent of the people with disabilities hired by CIBC are still there after a year and 79 percent after three years. "At CIBC we start by looking at what people can do regardless of their race, culture, lifestyle choice, or disability and then help them develop the skills and create an environment where they can do it," says Proszowski.

Questions

1. In what way are the banks in question managing cultural diversity?
2. Given that a bank is supposed to earn a profit, what impact might these diversity programs have on customer relationships?

Source: Terrence Belford, "Opening Doors for Employees with Disabilities," *www.thestar.com* (*The Toronto Star*), June 13, 2008. Reprinted with permission.

benefits of cultural diversity, as revealed by research and observations, are described next:

1. *Managing diversity well offers a marketing advantage, resulting in increased sales and profits.* A representational workforce facilitates reaching a multicultural market. Allstate Insurance Company invests considerable effort

into being a culturally diverse business firm. More than coincidentally, Allstate is now recognized as the nation's leading insurer of African Americans and Hispanics. The financial advantage resulting from diversity is the most likely to take place when employees perceive a positive diversity climate to exist. A study at JC Penney Inc. found that the largest sales growth was found in stores during one year when managers and subordinates perceived a highly pro-diversity climate. In contrast, the lowest sales growth took place for stores in which both managers and subordinates perceived a less hospitable diversity climate.[44]

2. *Effective management of diversity can reduce costs.* More effective management of diversity may increase job satisfaction of diverse groups, thus decreasing turnover and absenteeism and their associated costs. A diverse organization that welcomes and fosters the growth of a wide variety of employees will retain more of its minority and multicultural employees. A study of 250,000 crew members from 3,400 quick-service restaurants indicated that diversity helps reduce turnover. It was noted that crew workers were more likely to quit when they were the only member of their demographic group within the crew.[45] Effective management of diversity can also help avoid costly lawsuits over discrimination based on age, race, or sex.

3. *Companies with a favorable record in managing diversity are at a distinct advantage in recruiting talented people.* Those companies with a favorable reputation for welcoming diversity attract the strongest job candidates among women and racial and ethnic minorities. A shortage of workers gives extra impetus to diversity. During a tight labor market, companies cannot afford to be seen as not welcoming any particular group.

4. *Workforce diversity can provide a company with useful ideas for favorable publicity and advertising.* A culturally diverse workforce, or advertising agency, can help a firm place itself in a favorable light to targeted cultural groups. During Kwanzaa, the late-December holiday celebrated by many African Americans, McDonald's Corp. has run ads aimed at showing its understanding of and respect for African Americans' sense of family and community. For such ads to be effective, however, the company must also have a customer-contact workforce that is culturally diverse. Otherwise the ads would lack credibility.

5. *Workforce diversity, including the services of a culturally diverse advertising agency, can help reduce cultural bloopers and hidden biases.* Companies still make the occasional advertising bloopers that might offend a particular consumer group, leading to lost sales or potential. For example, an extra pair of eyes helped PNC bank avoid what could have been

---

[44]Patrick F. McKay, Derek R. Avery, and Mark A. Morris, "A Tale of Two Climates: Diversity Climate from Subordinates' and Managers' Perspectives and their Role in Store Unit Sales Performance," *Personnel Psychology*, Winter 2009, pp. 767–791.

[45]Joshua M. Sacco and Neal Schmitt, "A Dynamic Multilevel Model of Demographic Diversity and Misfit Effects," *Journal of Applied Psychology*, March 2005, pp. 203–231.

a painful error. A PNC branch employee noticed that the brochures for low-income people showed far more photos of people of color than did brochures developed for higher-income customers. The employee contacted the worker responsible for developing the brochures, who quickly pulled the materials and developed more inclusive replacements.[46]

6. *Workforce heterogeneity may offer a company a creativity advantage.* Creative solutions to problems are more likely when a diverse group with a variety of perspectives attacks a problem and contributes to creative alternatives. For example, if a company wishes to launch products that fit the needs of young people, it is best to include young people in generating ideas for these products.

The implication for managers is that diversity initiatives should be explained in terms of tangible business purposes to achieve the best results. Yet managers must also recognize that diversity within the organization can also create problems.

Potential Problems Associated with Diversity

In addition to understanding the competitive advantages of diversity within an organization, it's helpful to look at some of the potential problems. Cultural diversity initiatives are usually successful in assembling heterogeneous groups, but the group members do not necessarily work harmoniously. The potential for conflict is high. In general, if the demographically different work group members are supportive toward each other, the benefits of group diversity, such as more creative problem solving, will be forthcoming. If the heterogeneous group is to be successful, group members must be willing to share knowledge with each other. Another problem is that diverse groups may be less cohesive than those with a more homogeneous composition.

A problem with diversity from a business standpoint is that having a diverse workforce does not always translate into profits. General Motors, for example, has had a diverse workforce and a diverse dealer network for many years, but the company still lost billions of dollars, went bankrupt, and had to be rescued by the federal government.

LEARNING OBJECTIVE 7

Summarize organizational practices to encourage diversity.

ORGANIZATIONAL PRACTICES TO ENCOURAGE DIVERSITY

The combined forces of the spirit of the times and the advantages of valuing diversity spark management initiatives to manage diversity well. Three representative practices that enhance diversity management are (1) corporate policies about diversity, (2) the establishment of employee network groups, and (3) diversity training.

---

[46]Indra Lahiri, "Avoid Bloopers in Multicultural Marketing," http://www.workforcedevelopmentgroup.com/news_seven.html.

Corporate Policies Favoring Diversity

Many companies formulate policies that encourage and foster diversity. A typical policy: "We are committed to recruiting, selecting, training, and promoting individuals based solely on their capabilities and performance. To accomplish this goal, we value all differences among our workforce." To create a culturally and demographically diverse organization, some companies monitor recruitment and promotions to assure that people from various groups are promoted into key jobs. After they are promoted, minority group members are eligible for coaching by leadership consultants—as is frequently done with majority group members.

MGM Mirage, the hotel, entertainment, and gambling giant, is a leading example of a company with corporate policy favoring diversity. The company's Bellagio resort unit runs a nine-month executive mentoring program designed to prepare high-potential minority employees in management positions for advancement into the executive level.[47]

Employee Network Groups

employee network group
Employees throughout the company who affiliate on the basis of group characteristics such as race, ethnicity, gender, sexual orientation, or physical ability status.

A common approach to recognizing cultural differences is to permit and encourage employees to form **employee network groups**. The network group is composed of employees throughout the company who affiliate on the basis of group characteristics such as race, ethnicity, gender, sexual orientation, or physical ability status. Group members typically have similar interests, and look to groups as a way of sharing information about succeeding in the organization. Although some human resource specialists are concerned that network groups can lead to divisiveness, others believe they play a positive role.

The Latino Employee Network at Frito-Lay, the snack food division of PepsiCo, illustrates how such a network group can contribute to the bottom line. The Latino group proved invaluable during the development of Doritos Guacamole Flavored Tortilla Chips. Members of the network group, called Adelante, gave management feedback on the taste and packaging to help ensure that the product would have authenticity in the Latino community. The guacamole-flavored Doritos became one of the most successful new-product launches in the company's history, with sales of more than $100 million in its first year. PepsiCo management notes that the Doritos experience is one example of how the company leverages diversity to drive business results.[48]

Diversity Training

diversity training
Training that attempts to bring about workplace harmony by teaching people how to get along better with diverse work associates.

Cultural training, as described in the section about international business, aims to help workers understand people from another culture. **Diversity training** has a slightly different purpose. It attempts to bring about workplace harmony by teaching people how to get along better with diverse work

---

[47]Janet Perez, "A Fresh Deck: Publicly Traded MGM Mirage Begins Dealing Diversity," *Hispanic Business*, January/February 2006, p. 62.
[48]Robert Rodriguez, "Diversity Finds Its Place," *HR Magazine*, August 2006, pp. 57–58.

associates. A more strategic goal of diversity training is to gain acceptance on all types of diversity with the belief that enhanced business performance will result.[49] Quite often the program is aimed at minimizing open expressions of racism and sexism. All forms of diversity training center on increasing people's awareness of and empathy for people who are different from themselves.

Diversity training sessions focus on the ways that men and women, or people of different races, reflect different values, attitudes, and cultural background. These sessions can vary from several hours to several days. Sometimes the program is confrontational, sometimes not.

An essential part of relating more effectively to diverse groups is to empathize with their point of view. To help training participants develop empathy, representatives of various groups explain their feelings related to workplace issues. During one of these training sessions, a Chinese woman said she wished people would not act so shocked when she is assertive about her demands. She claimed that many people she meets at work expect her to fit the stereotype of the polite, compliant Chinese woman.

Many other exercises are used in diversity training. In one exercise, the discussion focuses on nationalities. Group members are asked to describe what comes to mind when the nationality is mentioned, for example, "Italian." Later, the group discusses how their stereotypes help and hinder diversity. Another type of training focuses on cross-generational diversity, relating effectively to workers much older or younger.

A study demonstrated that diversity training is most likely to lead to more promotions for women and minorities when it is combined with a person or committee to oversee diversity, and to ensure direct accountability for results.[50] Another study found that diversity training is likely to have a strong impact on retaining people of color when the program is tied to business strategy and the CEO is committed to the program.[51] Nevertheless, diversity training can still make a contribution in terms of better understanding among diverse workers.

The English Language as a Force for Unity

Although differences among people are important to businesses everywhere, international workers must communicate effectively with each other. To compete globally, more and more European businesses are making English their official language. In this way, workers of different European nationalities can communicate with each other. In many Asian countries, English is

---

[49]Rohini Ahand and Mary-Frances Winters, "A Retrospective View of Corporate Diversity Training From 1964 to Present," *Academy of Management Learning & Education*, September 2008, p. 356.

[50]Research synthesized in Lisa Takeuchi Cullen, "The Diversity Delusion," *Time*, May 7, 2007, p. 74.

[51]Research cited in Ahand and Winters, "A Retrospective View of Corporate Diversity," p. 367.

widely used in business. The majority of managerial, professional, technical, and support positions in Europe require a good command of English.

One reason English maintains the edge as the official language of business in so many countries is that English grammar is less complex than that of many other languages. The Internet, and information technology in general, with its heavy emphasis on English, is another force for making English the language of business. A cartoon in *Fortune* summarizes the heavy presence of English in the e-world. Two men wearing business suits and carrying brief-cases are talking to each other with the Eiffel Tower in the background. One man says to the other, "*Oui, j'adore* [French for 'Yes, I love'] e-commerce start-ups!"[52]

Although English may have emerged as the official language of business, the successful international manager must be multicultural. Because business associates throughout the world are fluent in their native tongue as well as English, command of a second language remains an asset for North Americans. In many situations it can be helpful for American companies to communicate with workers in their native language. One example is the need to advise workers of dangerous circumstances on construction sites and on oil rigs. Some employers provide banking, health care, and retirement information in Spanish to help Hispanic workers become more knowledgeable about money matters.[53] The perceptive manager knows when being bicultural and bilingual is helpful.

---

[52]Justin Fox, "The Triumph of English," *Fortune*, September 18, 2000, pp. 209–212.
[53]Kathryn Tyler, "Financial Fluency," *HR Magazine*, July 2006, pp. 76–81.

Summary of Key Points

Appreciate the importance of multinational corporations in international business.

Multinational corporations (MNCs) are the heart of international business. The continued growth of the MNC has been facilitated by the North American Free Trade Agreement, the Central America Free Trade Agreement, the World Trade Organization, and the European Union. Concern has been expressed that free trade agreements have shrunk the number of middle-class jobs in the United States, and that they lead to downward pressures on wages in industrialized nations. Sending work offshore, or global outsourcing, has become a key part of international trade. Global outsourcing has both advantages and disadvantages.

Recognize the importance of sensitivity to cultural differences in international enterprise.

The guiding principle for people involved in international enterprise is sensitivity to cultural differences. Cultural sensitivity can take the form of adapting your behavior (such as speaking more slowly) to meet the requirements of people from another culture. Candidates for foreign assignments generally receive training in the language and customs of the country in which they will work. Another approach to developing cross-cultural sensitivity is to learn cultural mistakes to avoid in the region in which you will be working.

Identify major challenges facing the global managerial worker.

Challenges facing global managerial workers include the following: the development of global leadership skills; currency fluctuations; balance of trade problems; human rights violations, corruption, and violence; culture shock; differences in negotiating style; piracy of intellectual property rights and other merchandise; and coping with dangerous and defective products.

Explain various methods of entry into world markets.

Firms enter global markets via the following methods: exporting, licensing and franchising, local assembly

and packaging, strategic alliance and joint ventures, direct foreign investment, and global start-up.

Pinpoint success factors in the global marketplace and several positive and negative aspects of globalization.

Success factors for the global marketplace include (a) think globally, act locally, (b) recruit talented nationals, (c) hire or develop multicultural workers, and (d) research and assess local markets. Many of the advantages and disadvantages of globalization depend upon an individual's point of view. For example, profits may increase at the cost of many workers' jobs.

Describe the scope of diversity and the competitive advantage and potential problems of a culturally diverse workforce.

To be diverse is to be made up of components that are different in some measurable, but not necessarily visible, way. The diversity umbrella is meant to encompass everybody in the organization. Diversity often brings a competitive advantage to a firm, including the following: marketing advantage, lowered costs due to reduced turnover and absenteeism, improved recruitment, useful ideas for publicity and advertising, a reduction of cultural bloopers and hidden biases, and a creativity advantage. A potential problem is that group members may not get along well with each other, and sometimes diversity does not translate into profits.

Summarize organizational practices to encourage diversity.

Three representative practices that enhance diversity management are corporate policies about diversity, the establishment of employee network groups, and diversity training. Although cultural diversity is welcomed, the English language has become a force for unity throughout the world of business.

Key Terms and Phrases

Multinational corporation (MNC), 36
Transnational corporation, 37
Outsourcing, 40
Offshoring, 40
Cultural sensitivity, 42
Multicultural worker, 42
Global leadership skills, 45

Balance of trade, 47
Culture shock, 50
Global start-up, 54
Diversity, 59
Employee network groups, 65
Diversity training, 65

Questions

1. Assume that a person living in the United States thinks that international trade is important for the economy, yet still believes that U. S. manufacturers of consumer goods must survive. What percent of that person's purchases should therefore be of goods made in the U.S.?
2. Identify a profit-making enterprise that need not be bothered with international trade, and for whom international competition is not a threat.
3. What can you do in your career to help reduce the threat that your job will be outsourced to another country?
4. How can a management team justify dealing with a subcontractor based in a country in which human rights are being widely violated?
5. What steps can you take, starting this week, to ready yourself to become a multicultural worker?
6. Suppose an African American couple opens a restaurant that serves African cuisine, hoping to appeal mostly to people of African descent. The restaurant is a big success, and the couple finds that about 50 percent of its clientele is Caucasian or Asian. Should the restaurant owners hire several Caucasians and Asians so the employee mix will match the customer mix?
7. In what ways does playing on a sports team in high school or college help a person develop cross-cultural skills?

Skill-Building Exercise 2-A: Coping with Cultural Values and Traditions

The purpose of this exercise is to develop sensitivity to how cultural values and traditions create problems for people from other countries. Find three fellow students, coworkers, friends, or acquaintances from another country who are willing to be interviewed briefly on the subject of adapting to a new culture. Or interview people from a far-away region in the same country; for example, if you are taking this course in Salt Lake City, interview somebody from New York. Dig for answers to the following questions:

1. Which cultural values in this country (the country or region in which you are taking this course) do you find the most unusual?
2. In what way are these values unusual?
3. What adaptations have you had to make to cope with these values?

Be prepared to have a class discussion of your findings and conclusions. Identify any lesson you have learned that will help you be more effective as a multicultural worker.

Skill-Building Exercise 2-B: Evaluating a Multicultural Digital Assistant

You and several of your classmates are part of a task force to help develop the multicultural skills of your workforce. Your transnational corporation conducts business in 17 different countries, with a total of six different languages. Today you are asked to evaluate the feasibility of developing a digital device to enhance the multicultural and foreign language skills of your workforce. The product description is as follows:

*Next time you find yourself linguistically challenged, whip out the **Universal Translator UT 106 from Ectaco Inc.** Here's how it works: Simply speak the desired phrase into the unit's built-in microphone. The palm-size machine uses speech-to-speech technology to translate the phrase into one of six languages. Then the translator talks back, providing the correct pronunciation via a built-in speaker. Easy to use, the unit can store 2,000 sentences in French, German, Italian, Portuguese, Russian, and Spanish. And you can go to the Web to download additional phrases. Bravo! The Universal Translator UT 106 retails for about $200. Visit Ectaco on the Web (http://www.ectaco.com).*

Discuss the merits of the Universal Translator (or competitive product) for helping your workforce become more multicultural, and reach a conclusion about equipping your international workers with the Translator. As part of your evaluation, visit the company Web site. See whether you can obtain a demonstration that can be played through the speakers connected to your computer and monitor.

Management Now: Online Skill-Building Exercise: Becoming Multicultural

A useful way of developing skills in a second language and learning more about another culture is to use a foreign-language Web site as your homepage. Each time you go to the Internet on your own computer, your homepage will contain fresh information in the language you want to develop. Or, simply make the foreign language site a favorite or bookmark so you can easily and routinely access it.

To get started, use a search engine that offers choices in several languages. Enter a keyword such as "newspaper" or "current events" in the search field. Once you find a suitable choice, enter the edit function for "Favorites" or "Bookmarks" and insert that newspaper as your homepage or cover page.

If French is your choice, your search might bring you to http://www.france2.fr or http://www.cyberpresse.ca. These Web sites keep you abreast of French (or Canadian) international news, sports, and cultural events—written in French. Another option is to find a Spanish-language version of a U.S. newspaper such as found on http://www.elpasotimes.com.

Typically these Web sites have accompanying videos in your target language. Now every time you access the Internet, you can spend five minutes becoming multicultural. You can save a lot of travel costs and time using the Internet to find a daily, up-to-date source of information about your target language and culture.

2-A Case Problem

Ambitious Volkswagen

Although Volkswagen had weak performance in the United States market for many years, the company announced its goal of doubling the number of vehicles it sells in the US by 2012 or 2013. VW wants to move from its niche status and become part of the mass market. At the 2010 Detroit Auto Show, Stefan Jacoby, head of Volkswagen of Americas said: "We will sell 400,000 to 450,000 vehicles in 2012/13." He added that the U.S. business could be profitable by 2013. A few years before the Detroit Auto Show, Jacoby established the goal of selling 1 million vehicles annually by 2018, with 800,000 sales from the Volkswagen brand, and 200,000 from the Audi brand.

Volkswagen is Europe's largest automobile manufacturer. VW's mediocre performance in the U.S. market had been attributed in part to its product line which does not fit well with the American auto preferences. "Volkswagen has neither a premium brand like Mercedes, nor a mass-market brand," said Marc Tonn, a senior automobile analyst. "The company was kind of stuck in the middle."

Volkswagen's ambitious goals were made public in 2008 when CEO Martin Winterkorn said that he was determined to surpass Toyota to become the world's biggest automaker. At the time, the German automaker sold 3 million fewer vehicles that Toyota, was losing market share in the U.S., and had a reputation for variable quality. Toyota, then poised to pass General Motors as the best-selling car maker on the planet, appeared invincible.

Toyota became vulnerable in 2010 because of massive recalls about safety features. At that point Winterkorn's ambitions seemed less preposterous. November 2009 was a milestone for VW, because for the first time the German automaker built more cars than its Japanese rival.

Winterkorn sees a history-making opportunity. Winterkorn contends that by 2018 Volkswagen will pass Toyota. "VW saw a chink in Toyota's armor and realized they could act out their ambitions," says automobile analyst Stephen Pope. "They went for it straightaway."

Throughout the world, Winterkorn, 62, is pressing the accelerator. VW has agreed to buy a 20 percent stake in Suzuki Motors to capitalize on the rapidly growing markets of Southeast Asia and India. Winterkorn is hoping to gain potential sales from BMW and Mercedes, committing $11 billion over the next three yeas to the development and manufacture of Audi, the luxury brand of Volkswagen.

In terms of doubling U.S. sales, Winterkorn predicts that Volkswagen can entice customers from Toyota, Honda, Ford, and others by selling Americans on German engineering and style at reasonable prices. In 2010, VW introduced a compact sedan priced to compete with cars such as the $16,000 Toyota Corolla. "We have to bring the masses to VW," says Mark Barnes, VW's U. S. chief operating officer.

Competing against Toyota won't be easy despite the company's embarrassing recalls in 2010. Above all, Volkswagen sells fewer vehicles in the U.S. than Subaru or Kia and has a reputation for making undependable, pricey vehicles. In Southeast Asia where Toyota dominates, the VW brand has very little recognition. The same problem exists in India. Winterkorn's goal to double Audi sales in the U. S. by 2018, meanwhile, isn't troubling BMW. "They have been saying that for years," says Jim O'Donnell, president of BMW of North America.

In the summer of 2007, Winterkorn and the Volkswagen board met to brainstorm ways to become the world's largest automaker. A key agenda-item was repairing VW's American

2-A Case Problem

problem. That year, VW forecast sales of 200,000 cars in the U.S., a 40 percent drop from 2000. Even worse the sales forecast was a third of what VW sold in 1970 when the Bug and Bus were Hippie favorites. Jacoby says executives at the meeting laid out three choices: They could continue to lose considerable money selling cars that were too small and too expensive, they could surrender, or they could take the offensive. They chose option No. 3.

Discussion Questions

1. What suggestions might you offer Volkswagen for gaining more market share in the United States?

2. Which success factors for international commerce does VW appear to be following?

3. Which success factors for international commerce does VW appear to need to strengthen?

Source: David Welch, "The Transformer: Why VW Is the Car Giant to Watch," *Business Week*, January 28, 2010, pp. 44–46; Kyle James, "VW Announces Big Expansion Plans for US Market," *Deutsche Welle* (www.dw-World.de), January 1, 2010, pp. 1–2; Matthew Barakat, "Volkswagen Outlines Plans for Growth in U.S., Sees Opportunities in Clean Diesel," The Associated Press, March 7, 2008.

2-B **Case Problem**

Flippant Jessica

Jessica, age 26, is a consumer loan associate at a large downtown branch of First Street Trust. Her expertise centers on processing loans for vehicles, boats, large home appliances, and furniture. Jessica hopes to soon be promoted to a loan officer and then perhaps a bank manager several years later. The loan applications she works with come through hand-written forms at the bank as well as in digital form from the bank's many retail partners.

First Street Trust is almost 100 years old, but it is thoroughly modern in its business processes and human resource management policies. For more than ten years First Street has been working hard to achieve a diverse workforce that matches its customer base. First Street management has placed considerable emphasis on hiring older people and men and women of different races and ethnic groups because the majority of its customers are 50 years or older.

During a recent performance evaluation, Jessica's manager Cindy informed her that she was doing an above-average job in terms of carrying out her duties as a loan associate, including the evaluation of loan risks. Cindy, however, expressed concern about how well Jessica was working smoothly and cooperatively with older coworkers and customers.

"Are you serious?" said Jessica. "I get along great with baby boomers and people who are even older. It's just that I have a great sense of humor."

"I think that perhaps your sense of humor could be interpreted as sarcasm and flippancy at times," said Cindy.

"No way," said Jessica. "I've got a kind heart."

Cindy then proceeded to present four examples of complaints she had heard about Jessica in recent months with respect to her dealings with people 50 and older, as follows:

- I received an e-mail from a retired customer who said you referred to her as 'Granny' about four times while she was completing a loan application.
- Bill Gordon, our head teller, told me that you said he should receive a Silver Dinosaur award because he reads a newspaper at lunch and during breaks.
- Nancy Mets, our office supervisor, informed my by e-mail that you refer to her as Ms. Depends because she prefers e-mail over IM or texting.
- Nick Jackson, our head custodian, came to me one day shaking his head because you asked him if he had any stories he could share with you from his combat days in World War II.

Looking bewildered, Jessica said, "I'm sorry if I hurt anybody's feelings. It's like some of these older people can't take a joke. I never complained when Bill or Nick call me 'young lady.'"

Cindy then said, "You need to change your attitude. Or maybe we should send you to diversity training. I'll let you know my decision soon."

Discussion Questions

1. What actions do you recommend that Cindy take to help Jessica relate more effectively to baby boomers and older coworkers and customers?
2. What steps do you recommend that Jessica take to modify her age-related jokes? (Or, is Cindy being too picky?)
3. What impact might Jessica's behavior have on the diversity climate at this branch of First Street Trust?

CHAPTER 3

Ethics and Corporate Social Responsibility

Nestlé India has a vested interest in solving that nation's water problems. It, too, wants to be sure it can produce its products locally. About half of Nestlé's 480 factories are located in developing countries. In India, the company doesn't just make chocolate. It produces milk products, prepared dishes, cooking aids, and a host of beverages that are staples to Indian consumers. The company has introduced a water education program, has bored wells for nearly 100 village schools for children, and teaches hygiene programs.

"Water is, of course, critical for a global food and beverage company like Nestlé," says Christian Frutiger, the company's public affairs manager. "Our village school wells project in India is probably the most telling example. So far, 96 such village school wells have been completed. The program started in the villages around the Nestlé factories and gradually expanded to the entire milk district."

Nestlé wants to create value for its shareholders and generate long-term values for society, Frutiger says. To that end, the company has a vested interest in making sure clean water is available for its operations.[1]

---

[1]Aliah D. Wright, "Dive Into Clean Water," *HR Magazine,* June 2009, p. 78.

OBJECTIVES

After studying this chapter and doing the exercises, you should be able to:

1. Identify the philosophical principles behind business ethics.

2. Explain how values relate to ethics.

3. Identify factors contributing to lax ethics and common ethical temptations and violations.

4. Apply a guide to ethical decision making.

5. Describe the stakeholder viewpoint of social responsibility and corporate social performance.

6. Present an overview of corporate social responsibility initiatives.

7. Describe social responsibility initiatives aimed specifically at building a sustainable environment.

8. Summarize how managers can create an environment that fosters ethically and socially responsible behavior and the benefits of such activity.

The initiatives by Nestlé India to create clean water supplies can be considered socially responsible; they are looking out for the welfare of society. At the same time, Nestlé makes a point that being socially responsible can also lead to increased profits for a company. Without clean water available locally, the company cannot operate successfully. If a high proportion of the local school children are ill from contaminated water, they cannot consume Nestlé products. The purpose of this chapter is to explain the importance of and provide insights into ethics and social responsibility. To accomplish this purpose we present various aspects of ethics and social responsibility, including organizational activities to help create a sustainable (green) environment. We also present guidelines to help managerial workers make ethical decisions and to conduct socially responsible acts.

LEARNING OBJECTIVE **1**

Identify the philosophical principles behind business ethics.

PLAY VIDEO

Go to www.cengage. com/management/ dubrin and view the video for Chapter 3. In this case, ethical issues and corporate social responsibility extend far beyond the reaches of the company, Numi Teas. Why was this issue important, and how did it affect the company?

Ethics

The study of moral obligation, or separating right from wrong.

BUSINESS ETHICS

Understanding and practicing good business ethics is an important part of a manager's job. **Ethics** is the study of moral obligation, or separating right from wrong. Although many unethical acts are illegal, others are legal and issues of legality vary by nation. An example of an illegal unethical act in the United States is giving a government official a kickback for placing a contract with a specific firm. An example of an unethical yet legal practice is making companies more profitable by eliminating their pension plans. A master of this approach was turnaround artist Robert S. Miller. As chief executive of Bethlehem Steel in 2002, Miller closed the pension plan, leaving a federal program to take care of the company's $3.7 billion in unfunded obligations to retirees. Several years later at Delphi, the auto parts maker spun off by General Motors, Miller succeeded in reducing health-care payments to retirees and was working on ditching the pension plan. Nasty but legal if you are a retiree; an astute move if you are a stockholder.[2]

One of the many reasons ethics are important is that customers, suppliers, and employees prefer to deal with ethical companies. According to an LRN ethics study, corporate ethics have an impact on the company's ability to attract, retain, and ensure productivity. Specifically, among a sample of 834 U.S. workers, it was found that

• A majority of full-time workers say it is critical to work for a company that is ethical.
• More than one in three workers say they have left a job because of ethical misconduct by fellow employees or managers.

---

[2]Mary Williams Walsh, "Whoops! There Goes Another Pension Plan," *The New York Times* (http://www.nytimes.com), September 18, 2005.

• Eighty-two percent of workers would be willing to receive less pay if they worked for an ethical company.
• Only 11 percent claim not to be negatively affected by unethical behavior in the workplace.[3]

Moral intensity
The magnitude of an unethical act.

A useful perspective in understanding business ethics emphasizes **moral intensity**, or the magnitude of an unethical act.[4] When an unethical act is not of large consequence, a person might behave unethically without much thought. However, if the act is of large consequence, the person might refrain from unethical or illegal behavior. For example, a manager might plagiarize someone else's speech or make an unauthorized copy of software (both unethical and illegal acts). The same manager, however, might hesitate to dump toxins into a river or sexually harass a business intern. Another component of moral intensity is social consensus, the degree of peer agreement that the action is wrong. If you know that most of your peers think an act is unethical, you would be hesitant to engage in that action.

Business ethics will be mentioned at various places in this text. Here we approach the subject from several perspectives: philosophical principles, values, contributing factors to ethical problems, common ethical problems, and a guide to ethical decision making. To better relate the study of ethics to you, take the self-quiz presented in Exhibit 3-1.

Philosophical Principles Underlying Business Ethics

A standard way of understanding ethical decision making is to know the philosophical basis for making these decisions. When attempting to decide what is right and wrong, managerial workers can focus on (1) consequences, (2) duties, obligations, and principles, or (3) integrity.[5]

Focus on Consequences and Pragmatism

When attempting to decide what is right or wrong, people can sometimes focus on the consequences of their decision or action. According to this criterion, if no one gets hurt, the decision is ethical. Focusing on consequences is often referred to as *utilitarianism*. The decision maker is concerned with the utility of the decision. What really counts is the net balance of good consequences versus bad. An automotive body-shop manager, for example, might decide that using low-quality replacement fenders is ethically wrong because the fender will rust quickly. To focus on consequences, the decision

---

[3]"New Report Details Findings of LRN Ethics Study," http://www.lrn.com, August 14, 2006.
[4]Thomas M. Jones, "Ethical Decision Making by Individuals in Organizations," *Academy of Management Review*, April 1991, p. 391.
[5]Linda K. Treviño and Katherine A. Nelson, *Managing Business Ethics: Straight Talk About How to Do It Right* (New York: Wiley, 1995), pp. 66–70; O. C. Ferrell, John Fraedrich, and Linda Ferrell, *Business Ethics: Ethical Decision Making and Cases* (Boston: Houghton Mifflin Company, 2000), pp. 54–60.

EXHIBIT 3-1   The Ethical Reasoning Inventory

Describe how much you agree with each of the following statements, using the following scale: disagree strongly (DS); disagree (D); neutral (N); agree (A); agree strongly (AS). Circle the answer that best fits your level of agreement.

		DS	D	N	A	AS
1.	When applying for a job, I would cover up the fact that I had been fired from my most recent job.	5	(4)	3	2	1
2.	Cheating just a few dollars in one's favor on an expense account is okay if the person needed the money.	(5)	4	3	2	1
3.	Employees should inform on each other for wrongdoing.	1	2	3	(4)	5
4.	It is acceptable to give approximate figures for expense account items when one does not have all the receipts.	(5)	4	3	2	1
5.	I see no problem with conducting a little personal business, such as shopping online, on company time.	5	(4)	3	2	1
6.	A business owner has the right to take family members on a business trip and claim the cost as a business expense.	(5)	4	3	2	1
7.	To make a sale, I would stretch the truth about a delivery date.	(5)	4	3	2	1
8.	I would flirt with my boss just to get a bigger salary increase.	(5)	4	3	2	1
9.	If I received $200 for doing some odd jobs, I would report it on my income tax returns.	(1)	2	3	4	5
10.	I see no harm in taking home a few office supplies.	5	(4)	3	2	1
11.	It is acceptable to read the e-mail and instant messages of coworkers even when not invited to do so.	(5)	4	3	2	1
12.	It is unacceptable to call in sick to take a day off, even if only done once or twice a year.	1	2	3	(4)	5
13.	I would accept a permanent, full-time job even if I knew I wanted the job for only six months.	5	4	3	2	(1)
14.	I would check company policy before accepting an expensive gift from a supplier.	1	2	3	(4)	5
15.	To be successful in business, a person usually has to ignore ethics.	(5)	4	3	2	1
16.	If I were physically attracted to a job candidate, I would hire him or her over another better qualified candidate.	(5)	4	3	2	1
17.	I tell the truth all the time on the job.	1	2	3	(4)	5
18.	Software should never be copied, except as authorized by the publisher.	1	2	3	4	(5)
19.	I would authorize accepting an office machine on a 30-day trial period, even if I knew I had no intention of making a purchase.	5	(4)	3	2	1
20.	I would never accept credit for a coworker's ideas.	1	2	3	4	(5)
21.	I would park my car in the parking lot of another company just to make use of that company's wi-fi for my laptop computer.	5	4	3	(2)	1
22.	I would see no problem in taking debris from our company and placing it in another company's dumpster just to save us hauling fees.	(5)	4	3	2	1

91

Scoring and interpretation: Add the numbers you have circled to obtain your score.

90–100   You are a strongly ethical person who may take a little ribbing from coworkers for being too straightlaced.

60–89   You show an average degree of ethical awareness, and therefore should become more sensitive to ethical issues.

41–59   Your ethics are underdeveloped, but you have at least some awareness of ethical issues. You need to raise your level of awareness about ethical issues.

20–40   Your ethical values are far below contemporary standards in business. Begin a serious study of business ethics.

maker would have to be aware of all the good and bad consequences of a given decision. The body-shop manager would have to estimate such factors as how angry customers would be if their cars were repaired with inferior parts, and how much negative publicity would result.

Closely related to focusing on consequences is *pragmatism*, the belief that there are no absolute principles or standards, no objective truth, and no objective reality. "Truth" is whatever works, or helps you attain the goals you want. Edwin A. Locke, professor of leadership and management at the University of Maryland, believes that pragmatism is the most prevalent ethical theory in use.[6] Unfortunately, being a pragmatist can land an executive in prison. An example is Bernard L. Madoff, the former Nasdaq chairman and later head of his own investment company, who pretended to customers that he was making actual investments with their money. Madoff apparently thought that lying to customers was pragmatic.

Focus on the Rights of Individuals (Deontology)

Another approach to making an ethical decision is to examine one's duties in making the decision. The theories underlying this approach are referred to as *deontology*, from the Greek word *deon*, or duty. Deontology also refers to moral philosophies that center on the rights of individuals and the intentions associated with a particular behavior. A fundamental idea of deontology is that equal respect must be given to all persons. The deontological approach is based on universal principles based on moral philosophies such as honesty, fairness, justice, and respect for persons and property.

Rights, such as the rights for privacy and safety, are the key aspect of deontology. From a deontological perspective, the principles are more important than the consequences. If a given decision violates one of these universal principles, it is automatically unethical even if nobody gets hurt. An ethical body-shop manager might think, "It just isn't right to use replacement fenders that are not authorized by the automobile manufacturer. Whether or not these parts rust quickly is a secondary consideration."

Focus on Integrity (Virtue Ethics)

The third criterion for determining the ethics of behavior focuses on the character of the person involved in the decision or action. If the person in question has good character, and genuine motivation and intentions, he or she is behaving ethically. The ingredients making up character will often include the two other ethical criteria. One might judge a person to have good character if she or he follows the right principles and respects the rights of others.

The decision maker's environment, or community, helps define what integrity means. You might have more lenient ethical standards for a person

---

[6]Edwin A. Locke, "Business Ethics: A Way Out of the Morass," *Academy of Management Learning & Education*, September 2006, pp. 324–332.

selling you a speculative investment than you would for a bank vice president who accepted your cash deposit.

The virtue ethics of managers and professionals who belong to professional societies can be judged readily. Business-related professions having codes of ethics include accountants, purchasing managers, and certified financial planners. To the extent that the person abides by the tenets of the stated code, he or she is behaving ethically. An example of such a tenet would be for a financial planner to be explicit about any commissions gained from a client accepting the advice.

When faced with a complex ethical decision, you are best advised to incorporate all three philosophical approaches. You might think through the consequences of a decision, along with an analysis of duties, rights, principles, and intentions. Tim Berry, the president of Palo Alto Software in Eugene, Oregon, exemplifies a manager who believes that integrity contributes to his success. Part of his integrity is expressed in refusing to lie. "There were times I felt at a disadvantage with people who lacked integrity," he admits. "But I've found the truth always pays off in the long term, even if it hurts in the short term." Berry learned to appreciate the power of integrity while working as a consultant for Apple Computer, early in his career. He observed as other consultants made generous promises, only to back out or fail to deliver. Berry says that clients might be fooled temporarily, but dishonest consultants lost clients quickly. Today, Berry is active as an executive, writer, and teacher.[7]

<table>
<tr><td>LEARNING OBJECTIVE **2**
Explain how values relate to ethics.</td><td>

Values and Ethics

Values are closely related to ethics. Values can be considered clear statements of what is critically important. Ethics become the vehicle for converting values into actions, or doing the right thing. For example, a clean environment is a value, whereas not littering is practicing ethics. Many firms contend that they "put people before profits" (a value). If this assertion were true, a manager would avoid actions such as delaying payments to a vendor just to hold on to money longer or firing a group member for having negotiated a deal that lost money.

</td></tr>
</table>

A person's values also influence which kind of behaviors he or she believes are ethical. An executive who strongly values profits might not find it unethical to raise prices more than is needed to cover additional costs. Another executive who strongly values family life might suggest that the company invest money in an on-premises child-care center.

Values are important because the right values can lead to a competitive advantage. An example of a winning value is building relationships with customers. A major contributor to the success of Mary Kay is that associates are taught to build relationships with their direct customers and try extra hard to please them.

---

[7]"Software Executive Puts Integrity First," *Executive Leadership*, April 2001, p. 3; www.timberry.com, accessed February 1, 2010.

ethically centered management

An approach to management that emphasizes that the high quality of an end product takes precedence over its scheduled completion.

The concept of **ethically centered management** helps put some teeth into an abstract discussion of how values relate to ethics. Ethically centered management emphasizes that the high quality of an end product takes precedence over its scheduled completion. At the same time, it sets high quality standards for dealing with employees and managing production. The concept of ethically centered management is helpful in understanding what went wrong in the many product recalls. A product such as a baby crib is shipped to distributors before all the possible hazards are removed. The product developers and the manufacturers might have been given such a tight deadline for product delivery that a thorough, field-tested inspection was not possible.

Sources of Unethical Decisions and Behavior

LEARNING OBJECTIVE **3**

Identify factors contributing to lax ethics and to common temptations and violations.

Ethical problems remain a major concern in the workplace. Despite a heightened emphasis on business ethics following scandals earlier this decade, a significant number of employees say they still witness questionable workplace behavior. Here is the percentage of employees who say they observed certain behaviors in the previous year, according to a survey of 2,852 workers by the Ethics Resource Center:[8]

- Lying to employees (19%)
- Engaging in conflicts of interest (16%)
- Lying to outside stakeholders (12%)
- Engaging in health and safety violations (11%)
- Producing poor product quality (9%)
- Stealing (9%)
- Sexual harassment (7%)

Many factors contribute to these types of unethical behavior. A team of researchers pulled together 30 years of research to conclude that drivers of unethical behavior fall into characteristics of the (a) individual, (b) moral issue facing the person, and (c) organizational environment.[9] Here we will present several of the possibilities under each source of unethical decisions and behavior.

Individual Characteristics

Self-interest continues to be a factor that influences ethics, often taking the form of greed and gluttony or the desire to maximize self-gain at the expense of others. For example, when a company is losing money, is the CEO justified in maneuvering his or her way into a $20 million compensation package for that year? Greed and gluttony are sometimes attributed to a Machiavellian personality that relates to a desire to manipulate others for personal

---

[8]"Questionable Workplace Behavior as Reported by Employees," National Business Ethics Survey, Ethics Resource Center, Arlington, VA, 2009 survey. (www.ethics.org).

[9]Jennifer J. Kish-Gephart, David A. Harrison, and Linda Klebe Treviño, "Bad Apples, Bad Cases, and Bad Barrels: Meta-Analytic Evidence About Sources of Unethical Decisions at Work," *Journal of Applied Psychology*, January 2010, pp. 1–31.

gain. For example, a person with strong Machiavellian tendencies would be willing to claim that somebody else was responsible for his or her spreadsheet analysis containing serious errors.

Another individual driver of unethical behavior is *unconscious biases that lead us to behave in unjust ways toward others*. More than two decades of psychological research indicates that most of us harbor unconscious biases that differ from our consciously held beliefs. The flawed judgments from these biases create ethical problems and can interfere with a manager's intention to recruit and retain high-level talent, among other problems. Suppose a real-estate manager holds the common stereotype that women are more suited to real-estate sales because they are more home oriented and more responsive to the needs of customers. When the manager is recruiting new agents, he or she might unjustly exclude a qualified male for the position. If the male candidate is equally or better qualified than a given female candidate, the real-estate manager is behaving unethically.

It is difficult to overcome an unconscious bias because it is below the level of awareness. However, if you carefully analyze the decisions you have made recently, you might find a pattern of slightly unethical behavior.[10] For example, a worker might say, "Of the last six people I recommended to work for our company, all are the same nationality and race as mine. Have I been excluding other good candidates without meaning to do so?"

Perhaps the most pervasive reason for unethical behavior is *rationalization,* or making up a good excuse for poor ethics. In this context, a rationalization can be regarded as a mental strategy that enables employees, and others around them, to view their corrupt acts as justified.[11] Many of the reasons already presented for unethical behavior involve an element of rationalization, such as blaming the organizational culture for a personal misdeed.

The person who commits an unethical act might dismiss its significance by observing that other people in comparable positions are doing the same thing, such as cheating on an expense account. At the top of the organization, a CEO and CFO might team together to lie to outside analysts about accumulating debt and plunging sales with the rationalization that they are trying to save the company. Bernie Ebbers, the now imprisoned former top executive at MCI/Worldcom, was at the center of the biggest accounting fraud of all time. One of his courtroom pleas was that he was only trying to save the company and jobs.

Job dissatisfaction can also contribute to unethical behavior. A worker who is strongly dissatisfied might behave unethically as a way of getting revenge on the employer. For example, a manager who is strongly

---

[10]Mahzarin R. Banaji, Max H. Bazerman, and Dolly Chugh, "How (Un)ethical Are You?" *Harvard Business Review*, December 2003, pp. 56–64.

[11]Vikas Anand, Blake E. Ashforth, and Mahendra Joshi, "Business as Usual: The Acceptance and Perpetuation of Corruption in Organizations," *Academy of Management Executive*, November 2005, p. 9. Reprinted from 2004, Vol. 18, No. 3.

dissatisfied with his pay might use his company-paid smart phone to make a series of personal calls.

The Nature of the Moral Issue

The moral intensity of the issue is a driver of unethical behavior; many people are willing to behave unethically when the issue does not appear serious. Visualize Gus, preparing a vat of soup at a food company. If one mosquito flies into the vat, Gus might go ahead and send the soup off for placement into cans. However, if a swarm of hornets flew into the soup, Gus might blow the whistle even if he knew his supervisor would not be happy about stopping the line.

moral laxity

A slippage in moral behavior because other issues seem more important at the time.

Another issue-related driver of unethical behavior is ***moral laxity***, *a slippage in moral behavior because other issues seem more important at the time*. The implication is that the businessperson who behaves unethically has not carefully planned the immoral behavior but lets it occur by not exercising good judgment. For example, many deaths from fires in nightclubs result from management not paying careful attention to fire regulations calling for fireproofing and the availability of adequate escape exits.

The Ethical Climate in the Organization

Another major contributor to unethical behavior is an *organizational atmosphere that condones such behavior*. A group of case histories of unethical behavior in business detected an underlying theme, a management culture that fostered ethical misdoing—or at least permitted it to happen—even when the organization espoused a code of ethics. One such ethical lapse involved hiring undocumented immigrant workers.[12]

The financial scandals at the now bankrupt Enron Corporation illustrate how a culture of lawless behavior and high risk-taking directly feeds unethical, and even criminal, behavior. One of the many scandals involved company officials hiding $25 billion in debt to help inflate the stock price so a handful of executives could sell their stock at a high price before declaring bankruptcy. Enron's culture supported risk-taking and entrepreneurial thinking and behavior. It also valued personal ambition over teamwork, youth over wisdom, and earnings growth no matter the cost. The preoccupation with earnings, without a system of checks and balances, resulted in ethical lapses that led to the company's downfall.[13]

Unethical behavior is often triggered by *pressure from higher management to achieve goals*. Too much emphasis on meeting financial targets can push workers toward meeting those targets in questionable ways. Visualize a chain of hearing centers for which management sets difficult-to-attain sales goals on each unit. Some associates might be inclined to exaggerate the necessity for hearing aids for potential customers who visit the center to learn whether their hearing needs improvement.

---

[12]Ann Pomeroy, "The Ethics Squeeze," *HR Magazine*, March 2006, p. 48.

[13]John A. Byrne, "How to Fix Corporate Governance," *Business Week*, May 6, 2002, p. 78.

An unethical decision or behavior can sometimes stem from a combination of individual, issue-related, and organizational factors. In 2010 eight Toyota models were experiencing accelerators that stuck while the vehicles were being driven. Toyota recalled millions of vehicles worldwide for repair. A related problem was that accelerators were sometimes catching on floor mats. The company had received more than 2,000 complaints of unintended acceleration during an eight-year period. Toyota management discounted early reports of the problem and was not entirely truthful about supporting evidence from the National Highway Traffic Safety Administration regarding the gravity of the problem. An ethical issue here might be that Toyota management did not pay enough attention to the seriousness of the sticking accelerator problem.[14]

An individual factor contributing to this unethical behavior might have been that Toyota executives wanted to escape blame. An issue factor is that at first it appeared that the number of problem accelerators was quite small compared to the total number of Toyota vehicles on the road. An organizational climate factor is that Toyota had developed such a great reputation for its meticulous approach to building cars and servicing customers. It might therefore have seemed unbelievable to Toyota top-level managers that the company was facing a true safety and quality issue. An organization can develop a climate or culture of smugness.

Ethical Temptations and Violations

Certain ethical mistakes, including illegal actions, recur in the workplace. Familiarizing oneself with these behaviors can be helpful in managing the ethical behavior of others as well as monitoring one's own behavior. A list of commonly found ethical temptations and violations, including criminal acts, follows:[15]

1. *Stealing from employers and customers.* Employee theft costs U.S. companies about $50 billion annually. Retail employees steal goods from their employers and financial service employees steal money. Examples of theft from customers include airport baggage handlers who steal from passenger suitcases and bank employees, stockbrokers, and attorneys who siphon money from customer accounts. Many corporate security specialists estimate that 25 to 40 percent of all employees steal from their employers.

2. *Illegally copying software.* A rampant problem in the workplace is making unauthorized copies of software for either company or personal use, as described in Chapter 2 in relation to piracy. The penalties for violating

---

[14]Bill Vlasic, "Toyota's Slow Awakening to a Deadly Problem," *The New York Times* (nytimes.com) February 1, 2010.

[15]The first seven items on the list are from Treviño and Nelson, pp. 47–57; *Reference for Business,* 2nd ed. "Employee Theft" (www.referenceforbusiness.com), 2010. "Cyber ethics: Teaching Internet Ethics," *Keying In,* November 2000, pp. 1, 3, 5–7; Matt Villano, "Sticky Fingers in the Supply Closet," *The New York Times* (http://www.nytimes.com), April 30, 2006.

software licensing agreements can be stiff, reaching over $500,000. Similarly, many employees make illegal copies of videos, books, and magazine articles instead of purchasing these products.

3. *Treating people unfairly*. Being fair to people includes equity, reciprocity, and impartiality. Fairness revolves around the issue of giving people equal rewards for accomplishing the same amount of work. The goal of human resource legislation is to make decisions about people based on their qualifications and performance—not on the basis of demographic factors such as gender, race, or age. A fair working environment is one in which performance is the only factor that counts (equity). Employer-employee expectations must be understood and met (reciprocity). Prejudice and bias must be eliminated (impartiality).

4. *Sexual harassment*. Sexual harassment involves making compliance with sexual favors a condition of employment or creating a hostile, intimidating environment related to sexual topics. Harassment violates the law; it is also an ethical issue because it is morally wrong and unfair. Sexual harassment is widespread in U.S. workplaces and in other countries as well. According to one large-scale study, when conclusions are based on more scientific studies, 58 percent of women report having experienced potential harassment behaviors and 24 percent report having experienced sexual harassment on the job.[16] More recent data suggest that sexual harassment directed at professional women by clients and customers is more frequent than harassment within the company. Sexist hostility, such as putting a person down because of his or her sex, was the most frequently noted type of harassment.[17] A study of 35 teams in the food-service industry found that when sexual harassment is frequent within a team, cohesiveness and financial performance tend to be lower.[18]

   Sexual harassment is such a widespread problem that most employers take steps to prevent it. Exhibit 3-2 describes actions employers can take to protect themselves against harassment charges.

5. *Conflict of interest*. Part of being ethical is making business judgments only on the basis of the merits in a situation. Imagine you are a supervisor who is romantically involved with a worker within the group. When it comes time to assigning raises, it will be difficult for you to be objective. A **conflict of interest** occurs when your judgment or objectivity is compromised. Most of the major financial scandals in brokerage firms

conflict of interest
A situation that occurs when one's judgment or objective is compromised.

[16]Remus Ilies, Nancy Hauserman, Susan Schwochau, and John Stibal, "Reported Incidence Rates of Work-Related Sexual Harassment in the United States: Using Meta-Analysis to Explain Rate Disparities," *Personnel Psychology,* Autumn 2003, pp. 607–631.

[17]Hilary J. Gettman and Michele J. Gelfand, "When the Customer Shouldn't Be King: Antecedents and Consequences of Sexual Harassment by Clients and Customers," *Journal of Applied Psychology*, May 2007, pp. 757–770.

[18]Jana L. Raver and Michele J. Gelfand, "Beyond the Individual Victim: Linking Sexual Harassment, Team Processes and Team Performance," *Academy of Management Journal,* June 2005, pp. 387–400.

| EXHIBIT 3-2 | A Corporate Tip Sheet on Sexual Harassment |

The U.S. Supreme Court has given companies guidelines on how to protect themselves against sexual harassment charges. Most of these suggestions reflect actions that many companies already employ to prevent and control sexual harassment.

- Develop a zero-tolerance policy on harassment, and communicate it to employees.
- Ensure that victims can report abuses without fear of retaliation.
- Take reasonable care to prevent and promptly report any sexually harassing behavior.
- When defending against a charge of sexual harassment, show that an employee failed to use internal procedures for reporting abusive behavior.
- Publicize antiharassment policies aggressively and regularly—in handbooks, on posters, in training sessions, and in reminders in paychecks.
- Give supervisors and employees real-life examples of what could constitute offensive conduct.
- Ensure that workers do not face reprisals if they report offending behavior. Designate several managers to take these complaints so that employees do not have to report the problem to their supervisor, who may be the abuser.
- Train managers at all levels in sexual harassment issues.
- Provide guidelines to senior managers explaining how to conduct investigations that recognize the rights of all parties involved.
- Punishment against harassers should be swift and sure.

Source: Adapted from information in Susan B. Garland, "Finally, a Corporate Tip Sheet on Sexual Harassment," *Business Week*, July 13, 1998, p. 39; Jonathan A. Segal, "Prevent Now or Pay Later," *HR Magazine*, October 1998, pp. 145–149.

in recent years stemmed from blatant conflicts of interest. An example would be a research analyst from an investment firm recommending a stock purchase from a company that is an investment banking client of the analyst's firm. If the analyst makes "buy" recommendations about the company's stock, that company will more likely continue to be a lucrative client of the analyst's firm.

The Sarbanes–Oxley Act of 2002 attempted to reduce many conflicts of interest in business. For example, a company auditing a firm must not receive money for other services from that firm. Companies are now required to assign certain consulting and auditing work to different firms. Sun Microsystems Inc., for example, spreads its business among the four major accounting firms for auditing, tax, and internal-control assignments.

6. *Accepting kickbacks and bribes for doing business with another company.* Also referred to as "payola," accepting cash payments, special deals on stock purchases, and lavish gifts from industrial customers is a perennial temptation in business. Sending a manager and his or her family on a week's vacation after the manager closes a deal with a vendor is an example of a kickback. In the high-tech industry, kickbacks often take the form of stock options granted to managers by companies with which their employers do business. The kickbacks extend to stock

analysts who are inclined to give favorable recommendations to companies that grant them stock options. Giving gifts to curry favor in business has long been standard practice, yet is unethical because it creates a conflict of interest.

7. *Divulging confidential information.* Other people can trust an ethical person not to divulge confidential information unless the welfare of others is at stake. The challenge of dealing with confidential information arises in many areas of business, including information about performance-evaluation results, compensation, personal problems of employees, disease status of employees, and coworker bankruptcies. A serious betrayal of confidence took place when Anil Kumar, a former senior partner at the consulting firm McKinsey & Co., was paid more than $1 million to provide tips on McKinsey's clients to the hedge fund firm, Galleon Group. The tips were useful to the hedge fund firm (one that deals in complex investments) because it could make profitable trades based on that information.[19]

8. *Misuse of corporate resources.* A corporate resource is anything the company owns, including its name and reputation. Assume that a woman named Jennifer Yang worked as a financial consultant at Bank of America, Merrill Lynch. It would be unethical for her to establish a financial advisory service and put on her Web site "Jennifer Yang, financial consultant, Bank of America, Merrill Lynch." Using corporate resources can fall into the gray area, such as whether it's acceptable for an employee to borrow a company's notebook computer to prepare income taxes for a fee in a personal business.

   An ethical temptation, particularly among top-level executives, is to misuse corporate resources in an extravagant, greedy manner. The temptation is greater for top executives because they have more control over resources. Examples of the greedy use of corporate resources include using the corporate jet for personal vacations for oneself, friends, and family members; paying for personal items with a company expense account; and paying exorbitant consulting fees to friends and family members. Misusing resources is an ethical temptation; greed can be a cause of additional ethical problems.

9. *Extracting extraordinary compensation from the organization.* Related to the misuse of corporate resources is the extraction of a disproportionate share of compensation from a company. A person usually has to be a CEO to engage in this type of ethical violation. An extreme example is that of Citigroup, which paid Andrew J. Hall, the chief of its Phibro energy-trading unit, $100 million in 2008. The Obama administration thought that such high pay encouraged undue risk taking, and pressured Citigroup to sell Phibro to Occidental Petroleum Corp.[20] Some

---

[19]Chad Bray, "Kumar Said He Was Paid for Tips," *The Wall Street Journal*, January 8, 2010, p. C3.

[20]Julianna Goldman and Bradley Keoun, "Citi Sold Phibro to Shed Risk-Taking on CEO's Payout Plan," *Bloomberg.com*, October 10, 2009.

management writers, however, do not regard such payouts as unethical. One argument for the high compensation is that unless a talented executive is highly paid, he or she will join the competition. Another argument is that some of these high executive payouts are in stock, and the stock can lose value rapidly.

10. *Corporate espionage.* An entrenched unethical practice is to collect competitive information to the extent that it constitutes spying. Among the common forms of spying are computer hacking, bribing present employees to turn over trade secrets, and prying useful information from relatives of workers. Outright stealing of information about rivals is obviously unethical. A less obvious form of espionage occurs when an employee leaves to join a competitor and reveals key insider information about the original employer.

11. *Poor cyberethics.* Because the Internet creates considerable potential for unethical behavior, it's important for all employees to resist the temptation of poor cyberethics. One example of questionable ethics would be to send an e-mail with large attachments to everyone in your company. If attachments are not work related and many people send them, blocked servers could impede legitimate company business. An ethical breach of greater consequences would be to steal personal identities from job résumés online. A scam in this area involves contacting the author of a résumé claiming to be an employer. The scam artist then asks for additional personal information such as the person's social security number and bank account number. Exhibit 3-3 presents suggestions for good cyberethics and netiquette. (Etiquette is related to ethics; for example, distributing racist or sexist jokes borders on unethical and could create a climate of hostility within a work environment.)

Business Scandals as Ethical Violations

Major ethical and legal violations have long been a part of the business world. The best-known scandals are associated with infamous executives. Yet scandals including Internet fraud, identity theft, and work-at-home scams (such as making you an agent for transferring funds received from customers) are perpetuated by players everywhere. Identity theft and virus spreading are rampant on Facebook and Twitter.

Among the consequences of major financial scandals have been mammoth job losses, the wiping out of pension funds, huge investment losses by individuals, and the bankruptcy of vendors who supplied the companies that went bankrupt. The families of unethical executives were badly hurt when the primary breadwinner consumed family resources on legal fees and then went to prison. People who worked for a scandal-plagued company sometimes have difficulty finding work elsewhere. Another problem is that distrust of managers could lead to fewer talented people wanting to enter the field of business. Sometimes scandals are embarrassing but do not have

EXHIBIT 3-3   Netiquette Tips

- Observe the Golden Rule in cyberspace: Treat others as you would like to be treated.
- Act responsibly when sending e-mail, instant messages, or posting messages to a discussion group. Do not use language or photographs that are racist, sexist, or offensive.
- Respect the privacy of others. Do not read other individuals' e-mail or access their personal files without permission.
- Help maintain the security of your local system and the Internet by taking precautions when downloading files to avoid introducing a virus. Also, watch out for opening e-mail attachments from unknown sources. Protect your account number, password, and access codes.
- Respect intellectual property rights. Do not use or copy software you have not paid for.

- Give proper credit for other people's work—do not plagiarize work from the Internet.
- Observe the rules of your school or employer. Most schools and companies have Acceptable Use Policies that outline responsible behavior on the Internet.
- Conserve resources. Do not add to network congestion by downloading huge files, sending long-winded e-mail messages, or spamming.
- Protect your personal safety. Never give personal information, such as your phone number or address, to strangers on the Internet. Report any concerns to a network administrator.
- Do not engage in hacking.

Source: Adapted from "Netiquette Tips," *Keying In*, November 2000, p. 4.

huge negative financial consequences. A brief description of four well-publicized scandals follows.

- *Click Fraud.* An individual or dozens of people click on Internet advertising solely to generate illegitimate revenue for the Web site carrying those ads. (Search engines charge the advertiser by the number of mouse clicks in response to an ad.) The people doing the clicking receive a small payment also. Major search engines such as Google and Yahoo! attempt to minimize click fraud, and the scandal usually focuses on a *parked* Web site. Nevertheless, a major search engine benefits from click fraud. A parked Web site usually has little or no content except for lists of Internet ads. Because Google and Yahoo! have distributed these ads to the parked sites, the scam artists receive a small cut of the money Google and Yahoo! receive from the advertiser. The owner of the parked Web site might use live people or software to generate an enormous number of useless clicks on the Web sites of advertisers. About 10 percent to 15 percent of ad clicks are estimated to be fake.[21]
- *Enron Corporation.* One of the most famous business frauds of all time was the collapse of Enron Corporation in 2001. Jeffrey Skilling was the last Enron executive to be punished; he was sent to prison for 24 years and four months. Accounting tricks and dishonest deals cost thousands of jobs, along

---

[21]Brian Grow and Ben Elgin, "Click Fraud: The Dark Side of Online Advertising," *Business Week*, October 2, 2006, pp. 46–56.

with $60 billion in shareholder value and more than $2 billion in employee pension assets. Dawn Powers Martin, a 22-year Enron employee summed up years of testimony in these words: "Mr. Skilling has proved to be a liar, a thief and a drunk, flaunting an attitude above the law. He has betrayed everyone who trusted him."[22] When Enron was on the rise, Skilling was considered to be a brilliant business strategist who had found new ways of making money for a corporation. He professed his innocence throughout the trial, and blamed market forces and bad press for the demise of Enron.

• *The Preparation of Fraudulent Financial Documents to Deceive Investors.* One of the most widely publicized financial frauds in history was carried out by Bernard L. Madoff; investors lost as much as $50 billion. Using a Ponzi scheme, Madoff took money from investors but did not make true investments in stocks or mutual funds. Instead, he pocketed most of the money after paying out investment returns to new investors with money collected from previous investors. (Although we can assume one person alone cannot conduct a fraud of this magnitude, only one other Madoff associate was convicted—his auditor.) David Friehling, the Madoff auditor in question, was an accountant from a storefront accounting firm in New York. He was later arrested because he conducted sham audits that enabled Madoff to perpetuate the fraud. Friehling was accused specifically of helping to foster the illusion that Madoff legitimately invested his client's money.[23]

• *Backdating Stock Options at Silicon Valley Companies.* One way of compensating managers and other employees is to grant them the opportunity some time in the future to purchase stock at today's price. If the price goes up, the recipient profits; if the price goes down, the recipient is not obliged to purchase the stock. In 2006, Apple Inc. executives and senior officers of many other Silicon Valley (high-tech area of California) companies were accused of sliding the stock-price date back to a time when the stock was lower than the true date of the option. In this way, the company pretends the stock-option date was earlier than reality. Backdating usually involves accounting and disclosure violations; it can constitute fraud. Apple said that CEO Steve Jobs was aware of the "favorable grant dates," but that he didn't profit from them personally and he was not aware of the accounting implications. Nevertheless, Jobs along with several other Apple executives reached a tentative settlement with shareholders to pay $14 million through liability insurance to settle claims about their alleged involvement to select favorable option grant dates.[24]

---

[22]Juan A. Lozano, "Former Enron CEO Gets 24 Years in Federal Prison," Associated Press, October 24, 2006.

[23]Amir Efrati, "Accountant Arrested for Sham Audits," *The Wall Street Journal*, March 9, 2009, pp. C1, C4; "As If a Credit Tsunami Weren't Enough: The Case of Accused Ponzi Schemer Bernard L. Madoff," January 19, 2009, p. 61.

[24]Charles Forrelle and James Bandler, "As Companies Probe Backdating, More Top Officials Take a Fall," *The Wall Street Journal*, October 12, 2006; Nick Wingfield and Justin Scheck, "Jobs, Other Apple Executives Settle Options Suit," *The Wall Street Journal*, September 11, 2008, p. B7.

Whether or not backdating stock options is unethical depends on one's point of view. Defenders of the practice claim that stockholders are not really harmed and that backdated options are simply another way of rewarding good performance.[25]

A person reading these examples of unethical manager behavior might wonder how wealthy, intelligent people could exercise such poor judgment. The answer lies partially in the explanations for unethical behavior presented earlier, with particular attention to greed, gluttony, and avarice. A small number of senior officers believe they are entitled to extraordinary perks such as penthouse apartments and stock options guaranteed to be profitable. For a deeper explanation, recognize that emotion can cloud anybody's judgment. Think of all the young professional football players who ruin careers by drunk driving or illegal use of handguns.

LEARNING
OBJECTIVE **4**

Apply a guide to
ethical decision
making.

A Guide to Ethical Decision Making

A practical way of improving ethical decision making is to run contemplated decisions through an ethics test when any doubt exists. The ethics test presented next is used at the Center for Business Ethics at Bentley College as part of corporate training programs. Decision makers are taught to ask themselves six things:[26]

1. *Is it right?* This question is based on the deontological theory of ethics, which says that there are certain universally accepted guiding principles of rightness and wrongness; for example, "thou shall not steal."
2. *Is it fair?* This question is based on the deontological theory of justice, implying that certain actions are inherently just or unjust. For example, it is unjust to fire a high-performing employee to make room for a less competent person who is a personal friend.
3. *Who gets hurt?* This question is based on the utilitarian notion of attempting to do the greatest good for the greatest number of people.
4. *Would you be comfortable if the details of your decision were reported on the front page of your local newspaper, on a popular Web site or blog, or through your company's e-mail system?* This question is based on the universalist principle of disclosure.
5. *Would you tell your child (or young relative) to do it?* This question is based on the deontological principle of reversibility, referring to reversing who carries out the decision.
6. *How does it smell?* This question is based on a person's intuition and common sense. For example, underpaying many accounts payable by a few dollars to save money would "smell" bad to a sensible person.

A decision that was obviously ethical, such as donating managerial time for charitable organizations, need not be run through the six-question test. Neither

---

[25]Holman W. Jenkins, Jr., "One Last Backdating Whipping Boy?" *The Wall Street Journal,* April 30, 2008, p. A15.

[26]James L. Bowditch and Anthony F. Buono, *A Primer on Organizational behavior,* 5th ed. (New York: Wiley, 2001), p. 4.

would a blatantly illegal act, such as not paying employees for work performed. But the test is useful for decisions that are neither obviously ethical nor obviously unethical. Among such gray areas would be charging clients based on their ability to pay and developing a clone of a successful competitive product.

Another type of decision that often requires an ethics test is choosing between two rights (rather than right versus wrong).[27] Suppose a blind worker in the group has personal problems so great that her job performance suffers. She is offered counseling but does not follow through seriously. Other members of the team complain about the blind worker's performance because she is interfering with the group achieving its goals. If the manager dismisses the blind worker, she might suffer severe financial consequences. (She is the only wage earner in her family.) However, if she is retained the group will suffer consequences of its own. The manager must now choose between two rights, or the lesser of two evils.

LEARNING OBJECTIVE **5**
Describe the stakeholder viewpoint of social responsibility and corporate social performance.

Corporate social responsibility
The idea that firms have obligations to society beyond their economic obligations to owners or stockholders and also beyond those prescribed by law or contract.

CORPORATE SOCIAL RESPONSIBILITY

Many people believe that firms have an obligation to be concerned about outside groups affected by an organization. **Corporate social responsibility** is the idea that firms have obligations to society beyond their economic obligations to owners or stockholders and also beyond those prescribed by law or contract. Both ethics and social responsibility relate to the goodness or morality of organizations. Business ethics is a narrower concept that applies to the morality of an individual's decisions and behaviors. Corporate social responsibility is a broader concept that relates to an organization's impact on society, beyond doing what is ethical.[28] To behave in a socially responsible way, managers must be aware of how their actions influence the environment.

Corporate social responsibility has three components, according to professors Kunal Basu of the University of Oxford and Guido Palazzo of the University of Lausanne.[29] First is the *cognitive,* which implies thinking about the organization's relationships with its parties at interest. Also included here is the firm's rationale for engaging in specific activities that might have an impact on key relationships. For example, Nestlé might think about how providing clean water for school children in India could help its reputation.

Second is the *linguistic* component, which involves explaining the organization's reasons for engaging in certain activities and how it goes about sharing these explanations with others. The corporate communications (or public relations) group assists with the linguistic component.

Third is the *conative* component, which involves what the firm actually does, along with the commitment and consistency it shows in conducting its

---

[27]Joseph L. Badaracco Jr., *Defining Moments: When Managers Must Choose Between Right and Wrong* (Boston: Harvard Business School Press, 1997).

[28]"Corporate Social Responsibility: Good Citizenship or Investor Rip-off?" The *Wall Street Journal*, January 9, 2006, p. R6.

[29]Kunal Basu and Guido Palazzo, "Corporate Social Responsibility: A Process Model of Sensemaking," *Academy of Management Review*, January 2008. pp. 122–136.

acts of social responsibility. The consistent behavior of Nestlé in using clean water for its products in India, as well as furnishing clean water to the school children, is part of the conative component.

A continuing debate concerns what obligations companies have for social responsibility. One position is that businesses should take action on issues ranging from pollution and global warming to AIDS, illiteracy, and poverty. The other position is that investors want companies in which they invest to focus on the bottom line in order to maximize their returns. In reality, these positions can be mutually supportive. Many socially responsible actions are the by-products of sensible business decisions. For instance, it is both socially responsible and profitable for a company to improve the language and math skills of entry-level workers and invest in local schooling. Literate and numerate entry-level workers for some jobs may be in short supply, and employees who cannot follow written instructions and do basic math may be unproductive. A firm that is environmentally friendly might attract workers who are talented enough to help the firm become more profitable.

A practical problem in practicing corporate social responsibility is that sometimes interested parties do not agree on what constitutes responsible behavior. Target stores might have customers who believe that citizens have a Constitutional right to defend their homes against intruders with handguns. To this group of customers, a retailer selling handguns to the public would reflect corporate social responsibility. Another customer group might believe strongly in tight gun controls. To this group, Target would reflect corporate social responsibility by not selling handguns to the public.

This section will examine three aspects of corporate social responsibility: (1) stockholder versus stakeholder viewpoints, (2) corporate social performance, and (3) a sampling of social responsibility initiatives.

Stockholder versus Stakeholder Viewpoints

stockholder viewpoint
The traditional perspective on social responsibility that a business organization is responsible only to its owners and stockholders.

The **stockholder viewpoint** of social responsibility is the traditional perspective. It holds that business firms are responsible only to their owners and stockholders. The job of managers is therefore to satisfy the financial interests of the stockholders. By so doing, says the stockholder view, the interests of society will be served in the long run. Socially irresponsible acts ultimately result in poor sales. According to the stockholder viewpoint, corporate social responsibility is a by-product of profit seeking.

stakeholder viewpoint
The viewpoint on social responsibility contending that firms must hold themselves responsible for the quality of life of the many groups affected by the firm's actions.

The **stakeholder viewpoint** of social responsibility contends that firms must hold themselves responsible for the quality of life of the many groups affected by the firm's actions. These interested parties, or stakeholders, include groups within the firm's general environment. Two categories of stakeholders exist. Internal stakeholders include owners, employees, and stockholders; external stakeholders include customers, labor unions, consumer groups, and financial institutions. The stakeholder viewpoint reflects the modern viewpoint of the corporation. Today, a company's assets are likely to include the employees who contribute their time and talents, not just stockholders' investments. The modern company should be a wealth-creating community

EXHIBIT 3-4

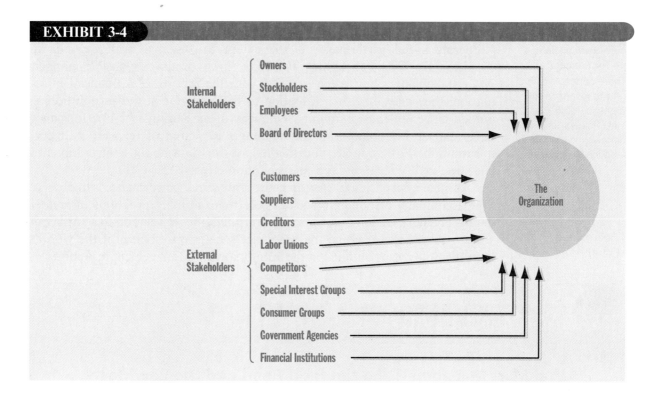

Internal Stakeholders
- Owners
- Stockholders
- Employees
- Board of Directors

External Stakeholders
- Customers
- Suppliers
- Creditors
- Labor Unions
- Competitors
- Special Interest Groups
- Consumer Groups
- Government Agencies
- Financial Institutions

The Organization

whose members have certain rights. In this way, the various stakeholders will be more willing to cooperate with each other.[30] Exhibit 3-4 depicts the stakeholder viewpoint of social responsibility.

Many organizations regard their various stakeholders as partners in achieving success, rather than as adversaries. The organizations and the stakeholders work together for their mutual success. An example of a company partnership with a labor union is the establishment of joint committees on safety and other issues of concern to employees.

Part of understanding the stakeholder viewpoint is recognizing that stakeholders are not all the same. They can be differentiated along three dimensions. Some stakeholders are more powerful than others; for example, the United Auto Workers (UAW) union is more powerful than a small group of protesters. Some stakeholders are more legitimate than others; for example, the UAW is a well-established and legal entity. Some stakeholders are more urgent than others because they require immediate attention. A group of protesters chaining themselves to a company fence because they believe the company is polluting the soil would require immediate attention.[31]

---

[30]Charles Handy, "What's Business For?" *Harvard Business Review*, December 2002, pp. 49–55. For an expansion on this point of view, see Stuart Cooper, *Corporate Social Performance: A Stakeholder Approach* (Burlington, VT: Ashgate, 2004).

[31]Ronald K. Mitchell, Bradly R. Agle, and Dona J. Wood, "Toward a Theory of Stakeholder Identification and Salience: Defining the Principle of Who and What Really Counts," *Academy of Management Review*, October 1997, p. 869.

Corporate Social Performance

Corporate social performance is the extent to which a firm responds to the demands of its stakeholders to behave in a socially responsible manner. After stakeholders have been satisfied with the reporting of financial information, they may turn their attention to the behavior of the corporation as a good citizen in the community. One way of measuring social performance is to analyze the company's annual report in search of relevant statistical information. For example, you might look for data about contributions to charities, arts, education, and anti-pollution efforts.

Another approach to measuring corporate social performance is to observe how a company responds to social issues by examining programs in greater detail. The next section describes corporate activities in relation to a variety of social issues. First examine the corporate social performance of the world's largest employer, as outlined in the accompanying Management in Action.

MANAGEMENT IN ACTION

Wal-Mart Managers Take the High Road and the Low Road

Wal-Mart Stores Inc. is the world's largest retailer and one of the best-known, with annual sales of more than $400 billion and a payroll of 2.1 million associates worldwide. About 1.4 million are U.S. employees—1 percent of the U.S. workforce. Every week, 200 million shoppers visit Wal-Mart's 8,000 stores in 15 countries. About 8.2% of all money spent on goods other than vehicles goes to a Wal-Mart or Sam's Club store. (All of these figures trend upward each year.) Company management, as well as many employees and outside observers, perceive Wal-Mart to be a wonderful corporate citizen because of the jobs it creates, the suppliers it helps keep in business, its endless amount of site construction and real-estate purchases, its corporate philanthropy, and its responsiveness to natural disasters. The many critics of Wal-Mart, however, regard the super-giant as an unethical and evil force that suppresses wages and health benefits and combats labor unions; they believe it should be dismantled. Here we present a sampling of some of the evidence and opinion on the positive and negative aspects of Wal-Mart's ethics and social responsibility.

The Ethical and Socially Responsible Side of Wal-Mart

Wal-Mart is a great boon for low-income and middle-income people in every location it serves. The purpose of Wal-Mart is to save people money so they can live better. Customers can stretch their dollars at Wal-Mart and afford things they could not without the megaretailer. Wal-Mart has wrung tens of billions of dollars in cost efficiencies out of the retail supply chain, passing many of these savings on to shoppers. Wal-Mart's low prices save the average American household $2,500 per year. The company's low prices on generic drugs have forced other chain stores to follow suit.

During a recession when consumers are trying to conserve money, shopping at Wal-Mart provides an opportunity for even middle-class and upper-middle class families to spend less money on goods and services they need (such as eye exams).

(continued)

MANAGEMENT IN ACTION (Continued)

Wal-Mart is an excellent corporate citizen, as evidenced by its quest to help build a green (environmentally friendly) environment. The company strives to be supplied 100 percent by renewable energy, to minimize waste, and to sell products that sustain resources and the environment. The chain encourages customers to purchase energy-saving light bulbs, thereby helping to fight global warming. Wal-Mart has taken many steps to reduce excess packaging.

Wal-Mart has established an emergency relief team that responds quickly and more effectively than the U.S. government to natural disasters. In response to Hurricane Katrina, Wal-Mart contributed $20 million in cash donations, 1,500 truckloads of free merchandise, food for 100,000 meals, and the promise of a job for each one of its displaced workers. Wal-Mart was one of the first corporate responders to the crisis in Haiti caused by an earthquake. The company donated $1 million directly including packaged food kits, blankets, and face masks. In addition, store associates and customers contributed another $2.8 million to relief in Haiti.

Wal-Mart has taken the initiative to help small businesses in the communities it serves. The Jobs and Opportunity Zones assist nearby small business enterprises, sponsor local training programs, and support the local chamber of commerce. Most of the company's charitable donations are made at the local level.

Wal-Mart provides one-stop shopping, including groceries, furniture, digital image and film processing, and pharmaceuticals, for individuals whose busy lives make it difficult to visit several stores during a shopping trip. Wal-Mart thereby saves consumers time, a precious resource for many.

The "Wal-Mart Effect" has suppressed inflation and rippled productivity gains through the economy year after year.

Wal-Mart encourages free trade because it forces suppliers to go offshore for its products, and Wal-Mart buys directly from many overseas suppliers.

Wal-Mart forces the companies it does business with to become more efficient and focused, leaner, and faster. The suppliers learn the art of continuous improvement.

Wal-Mart provides stable employment for many members of the workforce who might not qualify for jobs in higher-end retail stores or offices. Wal-Mart creates jobs for people who need them the most and offers them mobility. About 70 percent of Wal-Mart managers worked their way up from the company frontlines.

During a recession, Wal-Mart will often increase hiring because it typically does well during hard times, therefore creating much needed job opportunities.

The wages, benefits, and job security offered by Wal-Mart surpass those typically offered by smaller enterprises such as mom-and-pop stores and many large retailers. Wal-Mart provides health insurance to more than 1 million associates and family members. Leadership at Wal-Mart advocates a higher federal minimum wage, thus championing the cause of low-paid workers.

Wal-Mart welcomes diversity, as evidenced by it joining the corporate council of the National Gay and Lesbian Chamber of Commerce. The company conducts workshops for gay and lesbian business owners on how to become a Wal-Mart supplier.

The Unethical and Socially Irresponsible Side of Wal-Mart

Wal-Mart encourages its suppliers to rely on low-paid offshore workers so it can make large profits on its general merchandise, allowing it to give away toys at below cost. As a result, several toy stores, including FAO and Zany Brainy, have gone bankrupt. To remain a Wal-Mart supplier, many companies are forced to lay off employees, close U.S. plants, and send production offshore.

Many Wal-Mart suppliers face such a price squeeze that they are forced to produce goods of lower quality. As a mother told the **Denver Post**, "When you buy a kid a swimsuit that falls apart after they wear it, was it worth the $10?"

Wal-Mart is a poor corporate citizen because its presence leads to the deterioration of many small downtown areas. The company often abandons stores to pursue lower taxes in another county, leaving behind an ugly, limited-use big box building. The presence of a Wal-Mart store cheapens the image of a city or village.

Wal-Mart keeps hundreds of thousands of employees in low-wage jobs with meager health benefits, making it difficult for them to move up the economic ladder. Wal-Mart pay practices depress wages beyond the retail sector. The antiunion stance of the company has contributed to the low wages in retailing throughout North America.

The company forces out of business many supermarkets as well as other merchants. The failures of so many stores forces thousands of store owners and employees out of work. As Wal-Mart takes away business from traditional grocery chains, more and more union workers will lose jobs paying decent wages.

During a recession, Wal-Mart places even more pressure on suppliers to reduce prices. Competitors to Wal-Mart often fold during a recession, giving suppliers few alternatives other than to sell to Wal-Mart.

Wal-Mart faces a continuing stream of lawsuits for mistreating employees, including sex discrimination and forced unpaid overtime.

Wal-Mart acts as a cultural gatekeeper by choosing which magazines, books, and music it will sell. Its preferences tend to be conservative, thus presenting a one-sided viewpoint to the public.

Wal-Mart has capped wages, increased the percentage of part-time employees, and schedules more workers on nights and on weekends, making it difficult on families.

Despite its impressive financial resources, Wal-Mart engages in corporate downsizings. In early 2010, the company cut about 11,200 jobs at its Sam's Clubs warehouses. The layoffs included 10,000 product demonstrators who were eligible to apply for positions at Shopper Events, a company to which the jobs would be outsourced.

The American Family Association believes that Wal-Mart is shifting away from its "pro-family" stance. Pride at Work, a group that represents gay and lesbian workers, claims that the company is just taking advantage of a shameless marketing opportunity.

Questions

1. If many of these charges about Wal-Mart being unethical and socially irresponsible are true, why does the company keep growing in size and profits?

2. Recommend several additional actions Wal-Mart might take to develop a better reputation for ethics and social responsibility.

3. Has the information just presented had any impact on your propensity to shop or *not* shop at Wal-Mart? Explain.

Source: Charles Fishman, "The Wal-Mart Effect and a Decent Society: Who Knew Shopping Was So Important?" *Academy of Management Perspectives*, August 2006, pp. 6–25; Fishman, "The Wal-Mart You Don't Know: Why Low Prices Have Such a High Cost," *Fast Company*, December 2003, pp. 68–80; Marc Gunther, "The Green Machine," *Fortune*, August 7, 2006, pp. 42–57; Kris Hudson and Gary McWilliams, "Seeking Growth in Urban Areas, Wal-Mart Gets Cold Shoulder," *The Wall Street Journal*, September 25, 2006, pp. A1, A8; Ylan Q. Mui and Amy Joyce, "Wal-Mart to Shrink Options for New Hires' Health Care," *Washington Post* (http://www.washingtonpost.com), September 27, 2006, p. D3; Abigail Goldman, "Wal-Mart Seeks Unbiased Research—and Gets It," *Los Angeles Times*, November 3, 2005; Steven Greenhouse and Michael Barbara, "Wal-Mart's Shift Changes Irk Workers," *The New York Times* syndicated story, October 3, 2006; Abigail Goldman, "Wal-Mart Can't Seem to Win," *Chicago Tribune*, August 27, 2006; Holman W. Jenkins Jr., "Propaganda Clean-Up in Aisle Six," *The Wall Street Journal*, November 9, 2005, p. A17; http://www.walmartfacts.com/FactSheets/, accessed October 22, 2006.

LEARNING OBJECTIVE 6

Present an overview of social responsibility initiatives.

Corporate Social Responsibility Initiatives

Creating opportunities for a diverse workforce, as described in Chapter 2, is an important social responsibility initiative. Here we describe positive corporate responses to other important social issues. A firm that takes initiatives in these areas can be considered socially responsible. The five social responsibility initiatives described here are: environmental protection, work/life programs, community redevelopment projects, acceptance of whistle-blowers, and compassionate downsizing. Environmental protection, the new thrust in corporate social responsibility, is described in a separate section.

Philanthropy

A standard approach to social responsibility is to donate money to charity and various other causes. Most charities are heavily dependent on corporate support. Colleges, universities, and career schools also benefit from corporate donations. Many corporate donors want their charitable investments to benefit the end consumer, not get lost in red tape and overhead, and they want them to show measurable results. The new breed of philanthropist studies each charitable cause as he or she would a potential business investment, seeking maximum return in terms of social impact. This philanthropist might also seek follow-up data, for example, on how many children were taught to read or by what percentage new cases of AIDS declined. The type of corporate response to natural disasters shown by Wal-Mart, as well as many other large firms, might also be classified as philanthropy.

Work/Life Programs

Organizations take a major social responsibility initiative when they establish programs that help employees balance the demands of work and personal life. The intent of a work-life program is to help employees lead a more balanced life and be more satisfied and productive on the job. Exhibit 3-5 lists a variety of work/life programs. The most popular of these programs continues to be flextime, or flexible work schedules. Flextime has grown in popularity because evidence suggests that it reduces turnover, improves morale, and helps recruit talent.

Community Redevelopment Projects

As a large-scale social responsibility initiative, business firms invest resources in helping rebuild distressed communities. Investing in a community is but one aspect of philanthropy. Investment could mean constructing offices or factories in an impoverished section of town, or offering job training for residents from these areas. A specific goal of some community redevelopment projects is to replace a crime-ridden development with new housing that is associated with less crime and more community pride.

A notable example of community redevelopment is the Prudential Foundation established by Prudential Financial. The Foundation provides support to innovative direct-service programs that address the needs of the

EXHIBIT 3-5	A Variety of Work/Life Programs

- Flexible work schedules
- Child-care resource and referral
- Part-time options
- Compressed workweek
- Telecommuting
- Job sharing among two or more employees
- Eldercare resource and referrals
- Eldercare case management and assessment
- Subsidy for emergency care for dependents
- "Family sick days" that permit employees to stay home and care for sick children or relatives
- Arrangements for school counselors to meet with parents on-site during regular working hours
- Electric breast pumps for mothers of young children who want to return to work and continue breast-feeding

- Maintenance worker on company payroll whom employees can hire for household tasks, by paying only for supplies
- Laundry service, including ironing, on company premises
- Concierge service in which company employee runs a variety of errands for employees
- Postal service
- Automatic teller machines
- On-site fitness centers, including massages at workplace

Note: During a business downturn, the least essential of these work/life programs are likely to be abandoned, such as maintenance workers for household tasks and concierge service.

community in three areas: Ready to Learn, Ready to Work, and Ready to Live. Community housing development is included in the Ready to Work initiative that helps rebuild inner cities by investing money in ventures such as grocery stores, housing, and entertainment. The New Jersey Performing Arts Center is one of their investment projects. The Ready to Work program concentrates on initiatives that increase employment opportunities by strengthening job skills and opportunities and promoting neighborhood development activities. Encouraging entrepreneurship is also emphasized. The program also aims to create decent, affordable housing by working in partnership with Community Housing Development Corporations and community development financial institutions.[32]

Despite the contribution of community redevelopment, this social responsibility initiative does have its drawbacks. Tenants may be forced out of their homes to make way for new development, which cannot accommodate all previous tenants.

Acceptance of Whistle-Blowers

whistle-blower

An employee who discloses organizational wrongdoing to parties who can take action.

A **whistle-blower** is an employee who discloses organizational wrongdoing to parties who can take action. It was a whistle-blower who began the process of exposing the scandalous financial practices at Enron Corp., such as hiding losses. Sherron Watkins, a vice president, wrote a one-page anonymous letter exposing unsound, if not dishonest, financial reporting. Enron had booked

---

[32]http://www.prudential.com, accessed October 26, 2006.

profits for two entities that had no assets. She dropped the letter off at company headquarters the next day. At the same time, the CEO announced to employees that Enron's financial liquidity had never been stronger, while exercising his own $1.5 billion in stock options just ahead of the company's announcement of a $618 million quarterly loss.[33] Watkins later became a public heroine and celebrity because of her role in exposing the Enron scandal. A whistle-blower may also have been involved in bringing the illegal and unethical behavior of Bernard Madoff to the attention of authorities, although this person's name has not been publicized.

A whistle-blower must be patient because it usually takes years to resolve a claim, including an agonizing court procedure. Another problem is that whistle-blowers are often ostracized and humiliated by the companies they hope to improve. They may be given poor performance evaluations and denied further promotions. More than half the time, the pleas of whistle-blowers are ignored. It is important for leaders at all levels to create a comfortable climate for legitimate whistle-blowing.

The manager needs the insight to sort out the difference between a troublemaker and a true whistle-blower. Careful investigation is required. Only an organization with a strong social conscience would embrace employees who inform the public about its misdeeds. Yet some companies are becoming more tolerant of employees who help keep the firm socially responsible by exposing actions that could harm society.

Compassionate Downsizing

downsizing
The slimming down of operations to focus resources and boost profits or decrease expenses.

To remain competitive and provide shareholders with a suitable return on investment, about 80 percent of large organizations have undergone downsizing. **Downsizing** is the slimming down of operations to focus resources and boost profits or decrease expenses. Downsizings occur regularly worldwide among companies of all sizes, and the size of layoffs is more substantial during business downturns. Laid-off employees suffer from downsizing when they cannot readily find comparable employment or are forced to leave their communities.

Lincoln Electxric Co., a Cleveland-based manufacturer of welding equipment, has become the model of a company whose management has avoided downsizing. Compassion is involved because an implicit goal at Lincoln has been to spare employees the pain and suffering usually associated with job loss. Spanning a 65-year period, the company has avoided downsizing despite several major downturns in profits. Lincoln management believes that layoffs deprive companies of talent that can generate profit, and leave the remaining employees distrustful of management and eager to find employment elsewhere.[34]

---

[33]Erin McClam, "*Time* Names Whistle-blowers Persons of Year," Associated Press, December 2002; "Former Enron Vice President Sherron Watkins on the Enron Collapse," *Academy of Management Executive*, November 2003, p. 119.

[34]Frank Koller, *Spark* (Cambridge, MA: PublicAffairs, 2010).

The community also suffers from mammoth downsizings. For example, in the aftermath of the many cutbacks in the Michigan-based automotive industry, other entities suffered significant collateral damage. Retailers, restaurants, the housing market, charitable organizations, and community tax bases were all hurt as the state lost an estimated 158,000 manufacturing jobs between 2003 and 2008, according to a University of Michigan study. A total of 700,000 jobs were lost between 1999 and 2009.[35] The loss of jobs continued several years later, even as business and government leaders attempted to revitalize the Michigan economy by attempting to become a center of companies providing products and services for protecting the environment.

The focus here is on the social responsibility aspects of downsizing. Chapter 8 views downsizing as a strategy for improving organizational effectiveness. To begin, a company might challenge the need for downsizing. An ideal alternative is to expand sales rather than downsize. Quite often a company sees no way out of financial trouble other than downsizing. In these circumstances, compassionate downsizing would include the following considerations:

- Redeploy as many workers as possible by placing them in full-time or temporary jobs throughout the organization where their skills and personality fit. When possible, shift workers to sales positions to help generate sales. Luxury Retreats, a villa rental agency in Montreal, shifted 8 of its 75 employees from areas such as product development to sales.
- Several companies in financial difficulty have sent workers on temporary assignment to help another company in need of an expanded workforce. For example, Vermont's Rhino Foods sent 15 factory workers to nearby lip balm manufacturer Autumn Harp for one week to help it respond to a holiday rush. The employees were paid by Rhino, which then sent an invoice to its neighbor for the hours worked.
- Reduce the pay of all workers by a small amount rather than have a layoff. Peter Cappelli, director of the Center for Human Resource Management at the Wharton School of Business, calculates that a 5 percent salary cut costs less than a 5 percent layoff because there are no severance payments.[36]
- Provide outplacement services to laid-off employees, thereby giving them professional assistance in finding a new position or redirecting their careers. (The vast majority of employers do provide outplacement services to laid-off workers.) A related approach is for a company that has laid off a large number of employees to organize a job fair, assisting

---

[35]Study cited in Louis Aguilar, "Cutbacks to Ripple through Economy," *The Detroit News* (http://www.detnews.com), September 16, 2006; "Labor Day 2009: Dreams Downsized in Michigan as Jobs, Wages May Be Crippled Long-Term by Recession," *The Grand Rapids Press*, September 07, 2009.

[36]The first two examples and the citation are from Matthew Boyle, "Cutting Costs Without Cutting Jobs," *Business Week*, March 9, 2009, p. 55.

other employers to hire the workers who were downsized. Home Depot found this approach to be promising after it closed its Expo stores and laid off 7,000 workers.[37]

- Provide financial and emotional support to the downsized worker. Included here are behaviors such as treating employees with respect and dignity rather than escorting them out the door immediately after the downsizing announcement. Many companies already provide severance pay and extended health benefits to the laid-off workers. Financial assistance with retraining is also helpful.

LEARNING
OBJECTIVE **7**
Describe social responsibility initiatives aimed specifically at building a sustainable environment.

ENVIRONMENTAL PROTECTION

A major corporate thrust toward ethical and socially responsible behavior calls for business firms and not-for-profit organizations to *go green*, to make a deliberate attempt to create a sustainable environment. In more technical detail, going green is an approach to defining and creating processes that are (1) environmentally friendly, (2) economically viable, and (3) pragmatic in the long term. *Environmentally friendly* refers to reducing the generation of pollution at its source and minimizing life risks to humans, animals, plants, and the planet. *Economically viable* refers to such financial benefits as attaining reduced costs from energy savings, gaining governmental subsidies, and avoiding penalties. A *pragmatic* approach to sustainability affects the global or local environment, community, society, or economy by means of a practical and realistic approach, rather than seeking an impossible ideal.[38]

People often disagree vehemently about whether global warming exists, but almost nobody disagrees that a clean, safe environment is desirable. Here we highlight seven illustrative approaches to environmental protection. You will notice that many of the approaches to being green overlap and support others. For example, a lawn mower manufacturer might produce a lawn mower that increases fuel efficiency and at the same time reduces carbon dioxide emissions in its plant by using solar energy. In other words, various approaches to reducing a carbon footprint overlap. You can walk to the grocery store, purchase products that use minimal plastic packaging, and carry a re-usable shopping bag.

1. *Commit to lowering carbon dioxide and other hazardous emissions.* A major thrust in going green is to emit fewer toxins into the atmosphere. In one initiative, 67 companies including General Electric and Siemens agreed to create a "low emitting society." CSA, an architecture and engineering company in Miami, frames sustainability in terms of different types of low-emissions power including wind, solar, geothermal, and even tidal. In response to criticism of the amount of petroleum consumed

---

[37]Jia Lynn Yang, "For Hire: Old Staff," *Fortune*, May 4, 2009, p. 34.
[38]Probal DasGupta, "A Practical Inquiry Into the New Green Revolution," *Newark Business Strategies Examiner* (www.examiner.com) January 30, 2010.

in plastic bottles, Coca Cola unveiled a new plastic bottle made partially from plants. Pepsi, also, now has bottles containing less plastic. DuPont has a new line of polymers called Sonora. Similar to nylon and Lycra, Sonora is produced using fermented corn sugar, a renewable resource, rather then the petrochemical-derived materials it replaces. Another commitment to low carbon dioxide emissions is the development and use of biofuels such as ethanol derived from agribusiness waste and plants. Making existing fuels burn cleaner is a related green initiative.[39]

2. *Develop a green supply chain.* In addition to management reducing emissions from its own company, pressure can be placed on supply-chain members to reduce their emissions. A few years ago a Supply Chain Leadership Collaboration was formed by a group of companies to pressure suppliers to disclose greenhouse gas emissions and to reduce them. About 60 percent of the 500 largest companies participate in this voluntary emissions-disclosure program, with more companies joining regularly. For example, Nestlé places strict quality control on it suppliers that includes limiting potential contaminants.[40]

3. *Make sustainability and eco-friendly policies part of your business plan.* A strategic approach to becoming a green company is to build sustainability into the company's business plan or strategy. Xerox Corp. has followed this approach for many years. Anne Mulcahy, former chairman of Xerox, notes that the company was an early adopter of eco-friendly policies long before it was about economics or regulation or remanufacturing. Her company invented two-sided copying and focused on forestry standards. Eco-friendly policies are perceived by company management as a way of taking care of employees, customers, and the community.[41]

An advanced approach to building sustainability into a business plan is to create the executive position of chief sustainability officer. The responsibilities of this *eco-officer* include making the firm and its projects more energy efficient and environmentally conscious. At Coca-Cola Co. and Mitsubishi Motors North America Inc., the chief executives have adopted the sustainability title as well.[42] Linda Fisher is the chief sustainability officer at DuPont. She explains that one of her specific responsibilities is to help tie business strategies into megatrends. One such trend is a growing population

---

[39]Guy Chazan, "Arguing from the Inside," *The Wall Street Journal*, September 8, 2009, p. R7; David Hoybal, "Planting the Seeds for More Green Jobs," *Hispanic Business*, May 2009, p. 16; Jeremiah McWilliams, "Companies Producing Lighter, Greener Water Bottles," *The Atlanta-Journal Constitution* (www.ajc.com), January 20, 2010; Peter A. Heslin and Jenna D. Ochoa, "Understanding and Developing Strategic Corporate Responsibility," *Organizational Dynamics*, April-June 2008, p. 135; José Sergio Gabrielli de Asevedo, "The Greening of Petrobas," *Harvard Business Review*, March 2009, p. 46.

[40]David Roberts, "Carbon Copy," *Fact Company*, December 2007/January 2008, p. 78; Heslin and Ochoa, "Understanding and Developing Strategic Corporate Responsibility," p. 138.

[41]"Paper Trail," *The Wall Street Journal*, March 9, 2009, p. R7.

[42]Tiffany Hsu, "Eco-Officers Are Moving Into Executive Suites," *latimes.com*, December 30, 2009.

that will require that more crops be produced from limited acreage. (DuPont has a large agricultural seeds and crop-protection business.)[43]

4. *Implement a four-day workweek.* The less time employees spend driving to work in their own vehicles, the more energy is saved and the less air is polluted with carbon dioxide emissions. When offices are closed, less energy is required to heat or cool the building. In 2008, Utah became the first state to mandate a four-day workweek for most state employees. To save energy, offices are closed on Fridays; staff work ten-hour days Monday through Thursday. The program involves 17,000 employees in executive offices. State officials calculated that the compressed workweek reduced energy consumption 13 percent. Employees saved as much as $6 million in gasoline costs (assuming that they did not drive much on Friday).[44] Many business firms offer a four-day workweek option to employees, and other states have been closely following the Utah experience.

5. *Manufacture and sell products made with recycled materials.* At age 24, Tom Szaky founded TerraCycle. It began as a plant-food manufacturer, but now also sells household items such as bathroom cleaners and notebooks. The plant food is a ready-to-use organic product fabricated from the droppings of worms fed on compost. It is packed as a spray in repurposed soda bottles. (Okay, it's not a glamour industry but it is green.) Other products are made entirely from waste: reduced plastic bottles, empty juice pouches, and worm castings. The company's furniture is manufactured from recycled trash. Szaky defines garbage as any commodity with a negative value—something you are willing to pay to discard.[45]

6. *Invest heavily in recycling.* Another way to sustain the environment also involves recycling, but on a grander scale. Waste Management, the trash hauler, combined with its wholly owned subsidiary, Recycle America, is North America's largest recycler. Management estimates that the company recycles enough paper to save more than 41 million trees annually. The landfills of Waste Management provide more than 17,000 acres of protected habitat for wildlife. This activity fits into the green movement because many people believe that protecting wildlife is an important component of building a sustainable environment.

7. *Plant a rooftop garden on your office building or factory.* An esthetically pleasant approach to being green is to be literally green. Rooftop gardens are powerful insulators and such gardens have caught on as a way of conserving energy. Ten years ago Chicago began overhauling 15 million square feet of municipal buildings to reduce power consumption.

[43]"Linda Fisher: Chief Sustainability Officer, DuPont," *Fortune*, November 23, 2009, pp. 45–46.

[44]Jessica Marquez, "Utah: Closed Fridays," *Workforce Management*, July 14, 2008, pp. 1, 3; Bryan Walsh, "Thank God Its' Thursday," *Time*, September 7, 2009, p. 58.

[45]Tom Szaky, *Revolution in a Bottle* (New York: Portfolio, 2009); Laura Blue, "Let's Talk Trash," *The Wall Street Journal*, June 14, 2006, p. B1.

Because the gardens can keep a roof as much as 70 F degrees cooler, planting rooftop gardens became a major initiative. On a hot day, an office building roof can soar to 160 degrees. Greenery deflects heat and provides shade. Lightweight permeable soils are used for the gardens to prevent the roofs from caving.[46]

In addition to top-level management taking the initiative to protect the environment, companies often motivate employees to think about environmental protection by means of carpooling, recycling, and not littering.

LEARNING OBJECTIVE **8**
Summarize how managers can create an environment that fosters ethical and socially responsible behavior and the benefits of such activity.

CREATING AN ETHICAL AND SOCIALLY RESPONSIBLE WORKPLACE

Establishing an ethical and socially responsible workplace is not simply a matter of luck and common sense. Top-level managers, assisted by other managers and professionals, can develop strategies and programs to enhance ethical and socially responsible attitudes and behavior. We turn now to a description of several of these initiatives.

Formal Mechanisms for Monitoring Ethics

Most companies with 500 or more employees have ethics programs of various types. Large organizations frequently set up ethics committees to help ensure ethical and socially responsible behavior. Committee members include a top management representative and other managers throughout the organization. An ethics and social responsibility specialist from the human resources department might also join the group. The committee establishes policies about ethics and social responsibility and may conduct an ethics audit of the firm's activities. In addition, committee members might review complaints about ethics violations.

The Lockheed Martin Corporation's ethics and compliance program has received much favorable publicity. A contributing factor to its formation was a series of ethics scandals in the mid-1980s regarding its role as a defense contractor to the U.S. government. (Among the problems was a product substitution not in agreement with the contract.) Elements of the Lockheed Martin program include the following:

- *Make ethics training mandatory*. Mandatory means for every employee, the CEO included.
- *Develop multiple channels for raising questions and voicing concerns*. These mechanisms include a toll-free hotline, a formal ethics office at the corporate level, and a culture that welcomes discussion of ethics issues.
- *Allow for voicing concerns anonymously*. Many employees fear reprisals if they identify ethics problems in their company.

---

[46]Jim Carlton, "Nine Cities, Nine Ideas" *The Wall Street Journal,* February 11, 2008, pp. R1, R4.

• *Act decisively on legitimate ethics problems reported by employees.* Demonstrate to employees that the company's commitment to good ethics is serious.[47]

The point of these suggestions is that they should be incorporated into a manager's way of thinking and behaving. To facilitate making use of these ideas, Lockheed Martin managers have ethics discussion with their direct reports annually. The same approach to thinking through ethics issues apply to you. Being aware of laws and regulations about unethical behavior is not enough. An individual must personalize ideas about unethical behavior.

Written Organizational Codes of Conduct

About 75 percent of large organizations use written codes of conduct as guidelines for ethical and socially responsible behavior. These codes require people to conduct themselves with integrity and candor. Here is a statement of this type from the Johnson & Johnson (medical and health supplies) code of ethics: "We believe our first responsibility is to the doctors, nurses, and patients, to mothers and fathers and all others who use our products and services. In meeting these needs everything we do must be of high quality."

Other aspects of the codes might be specific, such as indicating the maximum gift that can be accepted from a vendor. In many organizations, known code violators are disciplined.

Widespread Communication about Ethics and Social Responsibility

Extensive communication about the topic reinforces ethical and socially responsible behavior. Top management can speak widely about the competitive advantages of being ethical and socially responsible. Another effective method is to discuss ethics and social responsibility issues in small groups. In this way the issues stay fresh in the minds of workers. A few minutes of a team meeting might be invested in a topic such as "What can we do to help the homeless people who live in the streets surrounding our office?"

Leadership by Example and Ethical Role Models

A high-powered approach to enhancing ethics and social responsibility is for members of top management to model the behavior. If people throughout the firm believe that behaving ethically is "in" and behaving unethically is "out," ethical behavior will prevail. Visualize a scenario in which key people in an investment-banking firm vote themselves a $3 million year-end bonus.

---

[47]Barbara Ley Toffler, "Five Ways to Jump-Start Your Company's Ethics," *Fast Company*, October 2003, p. 36; Erin White, "What Would You Do? Ethics Courses Get Context," *The Wall Street Journal*, June 12, 2006, p. B2.

To save money, entry-level clerical workers earning $10 an hour are denied raises. Many employees might feel that top management has a low sense of ethics, and therefore that being ethical and socially responsible is not important.

Leading by example is particularly useful in encouraging ethical behavior because it provides useful role models. Employees are often influenced by the people they work with every day, by supervisors and team leaders. In contrast, top executives are distant figures who most workers rarely observe directly. Role modeling might proceed in this manner: A worker observes a manager who consistently treats others fairly (and does not play favorites). In future dealings with people, the worker treats people fairly, modeling the behavior of his or her manager.

One way of encouraging managers to lead by example and act as a good role model is to tie compensation to ethical behavior. A year after Jim McNerney was appointed CEO of Boeing Co., he developed a plan to facilitate strong ethical behavior at the aerospace giant—a company that had major ethics problems in the past. Executive compensation would be tied in part to ethical leadership, McNerney included. The CEO said, "The message is that there is no compromise between doing things the right way and performance."[48]

Encouragement of Confrontation about Ethical Deviations

Unethical behavior may be minimized if every employee confronts anyone seen behaving unethically. For example, if you spotted someone making an unauthorized copy of software, you would ask the software pirate, "How would you like it if you owned a business and people stole from your company?" The same approach encourages workers to ask about the ethical implications of decisions made by others in the firm.

Training Programs in Ethics and Social Responsibility

Training about ethics and responsibility typically includes messages about ethics from executives, classes on ethics at colleges, and exercises in ethics. The company's code of ethics is usually incorporated into the training. Knowledge of relevant legislation, such as antidiscrimination laws, is essential. A recent approach is to address ethics issues through e-learning (over the computer), videos, and small-group discussion led by managers.

Ethics training programs reinforce the idea that ethical and socially responsible behavior is both morally right and good for business. A discussion of ethics issues combined with factual knowledge helps raise workers' level of awareness. Much of the content of this chapter reflects the type of information communicated in such programs. In addition, Skill-Building

---

[48]J. Lynn Lunsford, "Piloting Boeing's New Course," *The Wall Street Journal*, June 13, 2006, p. B1.

Exercise 3-A represents the type of activity included in ethical training programs in many companies.

Benefits Derived from Ethics and Social Responsibility

Highly ethical behavior and socially responsible acts are not always free. Initiatives such as work/life programs and community redevelopment may not have an immediate return on investment. Here we look at evidence and opinions about the advantages of ethics and social responsibility.

Profits and social responsibility sometimes have a reciprocal influence on each other. More profitable firms can better afford to invest in social responsibility initiatives, and these initiatives in turn lead to more profits. A pioneering study by Sandra A. Waddock and Samuel B. Graves found that levels of corporate social performance were influenced by prior financial success. This result suggests that financial success creates enough money left over to invest in corporate social performance. The study also found that good corporate social performance contributes to improved financial performance as measured by return on assets and return on sales. The researchers concluded that the relationship between social and financial performance may be a **virtuous circle**, meaning that corporate social performance and corporate financial performance feed and reinforce each other.[49]

virtuous circle
The relationship between social and financial performance where corporate social performance and corporate financial performance feed and reinforce each other.

The overall argument for green management is that it matters; people expect managers to use resources prudently and responsibly and protect the environment. Another expectation is for managers to minimize the amounts of air, water, energy, and materials used to produce consumer products. Many people also want companies to eliminate toxins that harm people in the workplace and in communities.[50]

The experience of London-based Radio Taxi Cabs illustrates how being environmentally conscious can be profitable. Several years ago the largest cab company in the U.K. started a project to reduce and offset carbon emissions from its fleet of 3,000 cabs. The project included developing a long-term carbon management plan and prioritizing and scheduling carbon reductions. Today, Radio Taxi saves 24,000 tons of carbon dioxide annually at the cost of £100,000 ($163,000) per year and calculates that the project has yielded £1.2 million ($1.96 million).[51]

Another potential benefit of corporate social responsibility is enhanced organizational efficiency. Green practices such as recycling, reusing, and reducing waste can reduce costs. At the Subaru plant in Indiana, workers

---

[49]Sandra A. Waddock and Samuel B. Graves, "The Corporate Social Performance–Financial Performance Link," *Strategic Management Journal*, Spring 1997, pp. 303–319.

[50]Alfred A. Marcus and Adam R. Fremeth, "Green Management Matters Regardless," *Academy of Management Perspective*, August 2009, p. 17.

[51]Cara Cannella, "A Green Formula," *2008 Leadership in Project Management*, p. 36.

regularly devise and revise green initiatives. The factory has substantially reduced waste per vehicle and places no garbage in landfills.[52]

Being ethical also helps avoid huge fines for unethical behavior, including charges of discrimination and class action lawsuits because of improper financial reporting. Charges of age discrimination and sex discrimination are two leading sources of lawsuits against companies.

Finally, an organization with a strong reputation for social responsibility will attract people who want to work for the firm. Business firms high on the *Fortune* list of best companies to work for are flooded with résumés of job applicants.

---

[52]Alan G. Robinson and Dean M. Schroeder, "Greener and Cheaper," *The Wall Street Journal*, March 23, 2009, p. R4.

Summary of Key Points

1 **Identify the philosophical principles behind business ethics.**

When deciding on what is right and wrong, people can focus on consequences, duties, rights of individuals, or integrity. Focusing on consequences is called utilitarianism; the decision maker is concerned with the utility of the decision. Examining the rights of individuals in making a decision is the deontological approach; it is based on universal principles such as honesty and fairness. According to the integrity (or virtue) approach, if the decision maker has good character and genuine motivation and intentions, he or she is behaving ethically. Pragmatism (whatever works) is closely related to focusing on the consequences.

2 **Explain how values relate to ethics.**

Ethics become the vehicle for converting values into action and doing the right thing. A firm's moral standards and values influence which kind of behaviors managers believe are ethical. According to ethically centered management, the high quality of an end product takes precedence over meeting a delivery schedule. Catastrophes can result when management is not ethically centered.

3 **Identify factors contributing to lax ethics and to common temptations and violations.**

Drivers, or sources, of unethical behavior fall into several general areas: the characteristics of specific moral issues facing an individual and the organizational environment. Factors contributing to unethical behavior include greed and avarice, a Machiavellian personality, unconscious biases, and rationalization. Moral issue factors include the gravity of the issue and moral laxity (other issues seem more important at the time). Organizational factors includes an atmosphere that condones unethical behavior and pressure from higher management to achieve goals.

Recurring ethics temptations, violations, and criminal acts include the following: stealing from employers and customers, illegally copying software, treating people unfairly, sexual harassment, conflict of interest, accepting kickbacks and bribes, divulging confidential information, and misusing corporate resources. Three other problems are corporate espionage, poor cyberethics, and executives who extract extraordinary compensation. Business scandals are ethical and legal violations that create mammoth job losses, wipe out pension funds, cause investment losses, and bankrupt vendors. Backdating of stock options is scandalous but so far has not brought down companies.

4 **Apply a guide to ethical decision making.**

When faced with an ethics dilemma, ask yourself: Is it right? Is it fair? Who gets hurt? Would you be comfortable with the deed exposed? Would you tell your child to do it? How does it smell?

5 **Describe the stakeholder viewpoint of social responsibility and corporate social performance.**

Social responsibility refers to a firm's obligations to society. Corporate consciousness expands this view by referring to values that guide and motivate individuals to act responsibly. The stakeholder viewpoint of social responsibility contends that firms must hold themselves accountable for the quality of life of the many groups affected by the firm's actions. Corporate social performance is the extent to which a firm responds to the demands of its stakeholders for behaving in a socially responsible way. Wal-Mart makes an excellent case study of corporate social performance.

6 **Present an overview of social responsibility initiatives.**

Creating opportunities for a diverse workforce is a major social responsibility initiative. Also important are philanthropy, work/life programs, community redevelopment projects, acceptance of whistle-blowers, and compassionate downsizing.

7 **Describe social responsibility initiatives aimed specifically at building a sustainable environment.**

A major corporate thrust toward ethical and socially responsible behavior is to go green. Seven such initiatives include (a) commit to low hazardous emissions, (b) develop a green supply chain, (c) make sustainability part of the business plan, (d) implement a four-day workweek, (e) make and sell products with recycled materials, (f) invest heavily in recycling, and (7) plant a rooftop garden.

8 **Summarize how managers can create an environment that fosters ethical and socially responsible behavior and the benefits of such activity.**

Initiatives for creating an ethical and socially responsible workplace include (a) formal mechanisms for monitoring ethics, (b) written organizational codes of conduct, (c) communicating about the topic, (d) leadership by example and ethical role models, (e) confrontation about ethics deviations, and (f) training programs.

Profitable firms can invest in good corporate social performance. Green management matters because people expect managers to use resources prudently. Being environmentally conscious can be profitable; it can also enhance organizational efficiency. Being ethical avoids fines, and ethical organizations attract employees.

Key Terms and Phrases

Ethics, 75
Moral intensity, 76
Ethically centered management, 80
Moral laxity, 82
Conflict of interest, 84
Corporate social responsibility, 91

Stockholder viewpoint, 92
Stakeholder viewpoint, 92
Corporate social performance, 94
Whistle-blower, 98
Downsizing, 99
Virtuous circle, 107

Questions

1. What is your reaction to the following statement made by many business graduates? "It may be nice to study ethics, but in the real world the only thing that counts is money."
2. Give examples of rights that you think every employee is entitled to.
3. The Vice Fund (http://www.USAMutuals.com) is a mutual fund that favors "products or services often considered socially irresponsible," including tobacco, alcoholic beverages, gambling companies, and defense contractors. Discuss whether you would be willing to invest in this fund (its returns vary considerably).
4. According to several religious and community leaders, companies can become more socially responsible by allowing homeless people to stay overnight in the office lobby. The need is particularly urgent in extremely cold weather. The companies are also urged to serve basic meals. What is your opinion about sheltering the homeless in office lobbies during extreme weather conditions?
5. During the Great Recession, many employees avoided asking for work/life benefits because they wanted to appear completely dedicated to the company. To what extent do you think their concerns were justified?
6. Get together with a group of people and rank the occupations listed next in terms of your perception of their reputation. The most ethical occupation receives a rank of one. (The list that follows is presented in random order.) Use the average rank of the group members if consensus is not reached.

___ Cosmetic (plastic) surgeon
___ Computer programmer
___ Business executive, major firm
___ Criminal lawyer
___ Veterinarian for domestic animals
___ Business school professor
___ Family court judge
___ Small-business owner
___ New-car sales representative
___ Stockbroker/financial consultant

7. To avoid becoming trapped in the politically charged argument of whether global warming really exists, a company might defend its initiatives for reducing carbon dioxide emission by saying, "Cleaning up the environment is a good idea in its own right, whether or not we truly have global warming." What do you think of this argument?

Skill-Building Exercise 3-A: Ethical Decision Making

Working in small groups, take the following two ethical dilemmas through the six steps for screening contemplated decisions. You might also want to use various ethical principles in helping you reach a decision.

Scenario 1: The Budget Furniture

You are the office manager for a company that does considerable business with the federal government. You put together a proposal for purchasing $20,000 of new furniture for the office, including desks, chairs, sofas, and filing cabinets. You have asked for several bids and investigated several business-to-business portals. You have identified a supplier whom you think offers the best combination of price and quality. You submit your proposal to your manager for final approval. He says, "I have studied your proposal, and I think we can do much better. Through our contacts with the government, we can purchase the same furniture for about $6,000 through Unicor. All their goods are manufactured with prison labor. The inmates are paid about $1.00 per hour, so a lot of the cost savings would go directly to us. Besides, these jobs keep the inmates out of trouble and teach them valuable skills they can use in the future."

You begin to reflect: "Yes, Unicor furniture may be a bargain, but what about the honest furniture-company employees who are losing their jobs? Their employers cannot compete with Unicor."

What do you do now? Do you fight for your proposal to spend $20,000 for furniture manufactured by workers not in the prison system? Or do you go along with the idea of purchasing from Unicor? Explain your position.

Scenario 2: The Enormous Omelet Sandwich

You and three other students are placed on an ethics task force at Burger King and you are asked to investigate ethical issues related to selling the Enormous Omelet Sandwich. The sandwich is composed of one sausage patty, two eggs, two American cheese slices, and three strips of bacon on a bun; it contains 730 calories and 47 grams of fat. The Enormous Omelet sells particularly well with males between the ages of 18 and 35. "Food police" outside the company claim that the Enormous Omelet Sandwich is so loaded with fat and bad cholesterol that it could lead to heart disease. The position of company management is that there are plenty of options on the Burger King menu for customers who want to make healthy choices. The Enormous Omelet Sandwich has been a major financial success for the restaurant chain. You and your teammates are asked to present top management with an evaluation of the ethics of continuing the Enormous Omelet Sandwich.

Skill-Building Exercise 3-B: Conducting an Environmental Audit

To create an environmentally friendly workplace, somebody must take the initiative to spot opportunities for change. Organize the class into groups of about five and appoint one person to be the team leader. Your assignment is to perform an environmental audit of a workplace in a nonprofit setting such as a place of worship, a school, or an athletic facility (you might have to do the work outside of class). If the audit is to be done during class time, evaluate a portion of your school (for example, a classroom, an athletic facility, or the cafeteria). Your task is to conduct an environmental audit with respect to the energy efficiency and healthfulness of the workplace. Make judgments, perhaps on a scale of 1 to 10, and add comments about the following factors:

1. How energy efficient is the workplace in terms of such factors as building insulation, fluorescent lighting, heating and cooling, and solar panels?
2. How safe is the environment in terms of pollutants and steps to prevent physical accidents?

3. How esthetic is the environment in terms of protecting against sight and sound pollution?

Summarize your findings and suggestions in a bulleted list of less than one page. Present your findings to classmates and perhaps to a manager of the workplace. Ask classmates to comment on whether your findings will really improve the planet from an ecology standpoint.

Management Now: Online Skill-Building Exercise: Ethical Product Promotion

Search the Internet for an advertisement or similar promotional information about a food supplement or beauty product such as wrinkle remover. An example of such a product would be a bottle of pine-tree resin to help ward off colds. Note carefully whether the information is provided by the company that manufactures or sells the product or by an objective third party. Give your opinion about the ethics of the claim. Attempt to evaluate the honesty of the claims. Use the six-step guide to ethical decision making to help you in your evaluation.

3-A Case Problem

Should We Launch Lightening Bolt?

Nancy Reid is the marketing and new product director at Katona Beverages, a small niche player in the beverage industry. Among Katona's products are iced tea in a can, vitamin water, fruit drinks made from natural ingredients, and bottled water pumped from underground springs.

Despite some success, sales and profits at Katona are barely enough for the 65-employee company to survive. Today Reid is meeting with the owner, Al Trout, and the sales director, Louise Garcia.

"The bad news," said Nancy, "is that we are barely surviving. Even big players like Coca Cola, Pepsi, and Cadbury are invading our niches. But the good news is that I have a product in mind that should vastly improve our business outlook.

"My new product idea will be called Lightening Bolt. It's a caffeinated alcoholic drink. As you know, this category is a small but fast-growing beverage popular among people under age 30. Because of the caffeine, and a high dose of sugar, we can call it an energy drink. The alcohol will give the consumer the same good feeling as beer or wine, and we will capture a little of their spending on beer, wine, and liquor.

"My tentative design for the can will pull no punches. We'll have a drawing of yellow lightening bolt and show young people having a great celebration."

Scratching his head, Al commented, "I recently read scientific research reported in a trade journal that people who consume caffeine and alcohol at the same time increase their risk of alcohol-related injuries or other problems. Suppose a few of our customers downed a six pack of Lightening Bolt and then had a multiple-vehicular accident? Would we be liable?

"I have also read that the Food and Drug Administration and the Federal Trade Commission might be cracking down on beverages that combine alcohol and caffeine."

Louise said, "I kind of like the idea of Lightening Bolt. It will be years before the government agencies get around to placing any real restrictions on this product. We can post a warning on the label about the potential dangers, like they do with medicine. Consumers have to act responsibly with whatever product they use. Look, peanut butter is about 50% fat; that can do more harm to the body than an occasional drink of caffeine and alcohol."

Nancy said, "I'm glad you two are at least listening."

Al said, "Before we move forward, we should study the pros and cons more carefully. But by the way, Nancy, how long do you think it would take to launch Lightening Bolt?"

Discussion Questions

1. What is your evaluation of the ethics of introducing Lightening Bolt to the market?
2. How socially responsible would it be of Katona Beverages to launch Lightening Bolt?
3. From a management perspective, what do you see as the pros and cons of launching Lightening Bolt?

Source: A few of the facts used in this case are from David Kesmodel, "Buzz Kill? Critics Target Alcohol-Caffeine Drinks," *The Wall Street Journal*, August 4, 2009, pp. D1, D4.

3-B Case Problem

Is it Fair That Anyone Owns the Rights to Asthmahelp.com?

The Web site http://www.flashgames.com has no staff, spends no money on marketing its name, and offers no games. All it offers is a list of links to other game sites. Yet it earns revenue of more than $150,000 a year selling online ads. Flashgames.com is just one of thousands of Web sites that are cashing in on the online advertising boom in an unusual way—by piggybacking on the ad-sales efforts of giant search engines Google Inc. and Yahoo! Inc.

These sites' ability to make lots of money for little investment is now attracting attention from big players. A group of investors led by former MySpace.com chairman Richard Rosenblatt has raised $120 million from investors to build a new company, Demand Media Inc., centered on generic domain names like these. The venture has already acquired 150,000 domain names—including flashgames.com—and plans to aggressively acquire more. Conscious of the limitations of these bare-bones sites, it plans to add some low-cost content in hopes of making the business even stronger. "We will be taking billboards and turning them into content Web sites," says Rosenblatt.

Sites like flashgames.com used to be considered "cybersquatting," a long-standing Internet tactic where entrepreneurs register domain names associated with a particular subject or company and then sell the name for a quick profit. These new generation sites go a little further, reaping ad revenue. Demand Media says it will not buy trademarked domain names.

Owned until recently by two Australian entrepreneurs, flashgames.com draws people—about 250,000 per month—looking for a Web-based game that uses flash-animation technology. The links that the would-be gamers find on flashgames.com are actually paid ads placed by Google or Yahoo!, both of which sprinkle ad links all over the Web, paying the host sites a cut of the revenue they receive when anyone clicks on one of their links. When someone finds flashgmes.com and then clicks on a link to another games site, flashgames.com gets paid.

Analysts estimate these types of sites, known as "domain parking," generate about 5 percent to 10 percent of search-engine revenue, putting the industry's annual revenue at about $600 million. "The profit margins are extraordinary," says RBC Capital Markets' Jordan Rohan. He predicts industry revenue could double to $1.2 billion in three years.

Given the sites' meager offerings, some in the industry worry that these domains may not have staying power. Even finding one of these sites is a matter of luck. Web surfers must type its full name into the address line of a Web browser, although some browsers automatically add a dot-com to the end of something they type. Most parked domains don't generate enough traffic to show up at the top of search-engine rankings.

"This is grandma-type navigation," says Matt Bentley, chief strategy officer of Sedo.com LLC, a domain-name parking business. "It's probably not currently being done by a lot of sophisticated people."

A critic of the domain-game business commented, "How crazy has the world become? A handful of people are getting rich when people with poor Internet search skills type into their browser, phrases like *dogfood.com, helpwitharthritis.com, asthmahelp.com,* and *carloan.com.* What really drives me up the wall is that somebody is getting a cut when a person enters *alzheimersdisease.com* into the browser."

3-B Case Problem

Discussion Questions

1. What is your evaluation of the ethics of domain-name companies earning commissions when people insert ordinary names into their Internet browser?

2. What about the ethics of Google and Yahoo! becoming involved by paying ad revenues to the domain-name companies?

3. What possible links are there between domain-name companies and click fraud? (Click fraud occurs when someone clicks on an online ad multiple times, perhaps with a robot, in order to receive pay-per-click commissions from a bigger and better-known Web site.)

Source: All but the last paragraph are from Julia Angwin, "For These Sites, Their Best Asset Is a Good Name," *The Wall Street Journal*, May 1, 2006, p. B1.

CHAPTER 4

Essentials of Planning

At a time when many large restaurant chains are struggling, Burger King Holdings Inc. CEO John Chidsey has managed to sustain the once-floundering fast-food company's turnaround. The world's No. 2 hamburger chain by location behind McDonald's Corp. is using what it calls a "barbell" menu strategy that pushes upscale products such as its new Steakhouse Burger with Angus beef alongside $1 sandwiches to appeal to cash strapped customers. Chidsey, a 45-year-old certified public accountant and member of the Georgia Bar Association, sat down for an interview with the *Wall Street Journal*, excerpted as follows:

- **WSJ:** Just six years ago, people were writing the obituary for fast food as "fast-casual" restaurants like Panera Bread were on the rise. Now fast-food companies are among the few restaurant chains doing well. How did that happen?
- **Chidsey:** I think that fast-casual really did a great job of scaring quick-service restaurants into getting their act back together. I think the whole industry has done a much better job over the last four or five years in terms of improving the quality of the products, improving the breadth of the offering.

If you look in the fast-food hamburger space, it is unfortunate for the greater economy as a whole, but we benefit from

OBJECTIVES

After studying this chapter and doing the exercises, you should be able to:

1. Summarize a general framework for planning and apply it to enhance your planning skills.

2. Describe the nature of business strategy.

3. Explain how business strategy is developed, including SWOT analysis.

4. Identify levels of business strategy, competitive forces, and types of business strategies.

5. Explain the use of operating plans, policies, procedures, and rules.

6. Present an overview of management by objectives.

the pressure people feel from a disposable-income standpoint. People who cannot afford to go to Applebee's, cannot afford to go to Chili's, we are the beneficiaries of that squeeze. It's very hard for me to imagine that the economy could ever get so bad that somebody could not afford to buy a double Cheeseburger from McDonald's or a Whopper Jr. from us for $1. Off you go to the grocery store, I really challenge you to find something for under $1.

- **WSJ:** What were the keys to your company's turnaround?
- **Chidsey:** Most importantly, I'd say it was finding who our target customer was, figuring out who was the superfan and not wasting our time trying to be all things to all people.
- **WSJ:** When you looked more closely at your core customer base, you learned that it's almost split evenly between males and females. Did that surprise you?
- **Chidsey:** It was a little bit surprising.
- **WSJ:** But your marketing is more targeted at males, isn't it?
- **Chidsey:** If you think about sports like the NFL or Nascar, believe it or not, if you rip the demographics apart, women are humongous NFL fans. Nascar has an enormous female following.[1]

The interview with the Burger King CEO illustrates how formulating and carrying out a strategy can catapult a business to success. Chidsey and his executive team were in the right business at the right time, but they also focused on identifying and satisfying a niche (a particular group of customers) they can serve best. Finding a focus or developing a niche is one of the business strategies covered in this chapter. By virtue of planning, including using a basic strategy, businesspeople manage the future instead of being guided by fate. Planning often leads to improvement in productivity, quality, and financial results.

The purpose of this chapter is to describe the planning function in such a way that you can use what you learn to plan more effectively as a manager or individual contributor. First the chapter looks at a framework for the application of planning. You will also learn about high-level, or strategic, planning including how strategy is developed and the types of strategy that result from strategic planning. We then describe operating plans, policies, procedures, and rules and a widely used method for getting large

---

[1]Excerpted from Janet Adamy, "Man Behind Burger King Turnaround," *The Wall Street Journal*, April 2, 2008, pp. B1, B7.

numbers of people involved in implementing plans: management by objectives.

A GENERAL FRAMEWORK FOR PLANNING

Planning is a complex and comprehensive process involving a series of overlapping and interrelated elements or stages, including strategic, tactical, and operational planning. **Strategic planning** establishes master plans that shape the destiny of the firm. An example of strategic planning is when the executive team at Harley-Davidson Inc. planned how to deal with the demographic shift of their customer base becoming much older. The strategic issue it faced was whether to change its iconic product line to win over young buyers. A second type of planning is needed to support strategic planning, such as how to build motorcycles that fit the preferences of younger motorcyclists. **Tactical planning** translates strategic plans into specific goals and plans that are most relevant to a particular organizational unit. The tactical plans also provide details of how the company or business unit will compete within its chosen business area. Middle managers have the primary responsibility for formulating and executing tactical plans. These plans are based on marketplace realities when developed for a business. Conditions can change rapidly in competitive fields such as a Korean company suddenly developing a substantially lower-priced sports bike. The scope of tactical plans is broader than operational plans (described next), but not as broad as that of strategic plans.

A third type of planning is aimed more at day-to-day operations or the nuts and bolts of doing business. **Operational planning** identifies the specific procedures and actions required at lower levels in the organization. If Harley-Davidson wants to revamp an assembly line to produce more sports bikes, operational plans would have to be drawn. In practice, the distinction between tactical planning and operational planning is not clear-cut. However, both tactical plans and operational plans must support the strategic plan such as revamping manufacturing and marketing to capture a larger group of young cyclists.

The framework presented in Exhibit 4-1 summarizes the elements of planning. With slight modification the model could be applied to strategic, tactical, and operational planning. A planner must define the present situation, establish goals and objectives, and analyze the environment in terms of aids and barriers to goals and objectives. The planner must also develop action plans to reach goals and objectives, develop budgets, implement the plans, and control the plans.

This chapter examines each element separately. In practice, however, several of these stages often overlap. For example, a manager might be implementing and controlling the same plan simultaneously. Also, the planning steps are not always followed in the order presented in Exhibit 4-1. Planners frequently start in the middle of the process, proceed forward, and then return to an earlier step. This change of sequence frequently happens because the planner discovers new information or because objectives change. Also, many managers set goals before first examining their current position.

To illustrate the general framework for planning we turn to Harley-Davidson, which is dealing with the planning challenge presented by its aging

EXHIBIT 4-1	A Framework for Planning

Planning at its best is a systematic process.

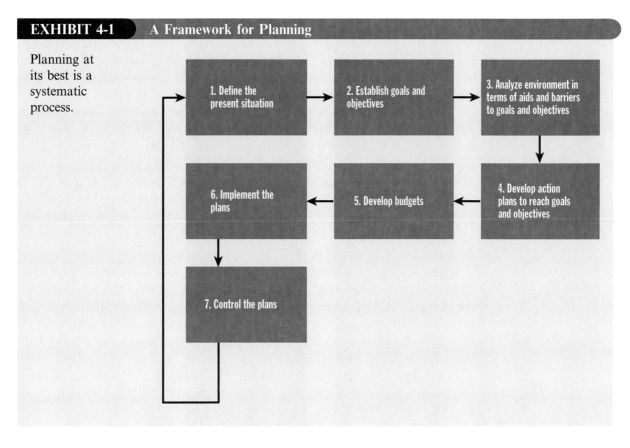

customer base. The challenge was expressed by Joe Mammolito, a tow-truck company owner from Dix Hills, N.Y., and Harley devotee for 30 years: "I have about 14 guys driving trucks for me. The younger guys ride sports bikes, the older fellows like a big bike. I think they should get guys in their 20s and 30s accustomed to riding Harleys. They need to get the younger guys accustomed to the name, the products, and the dealership network."[2]

Define the Present Situation

Knowing where you are is critical to establishing goals for change. Defining the present situation includes measuring success and examining internal capabilities and external threats. Harley-Davidson has had a long tradition of success. At one time the motorcycle has a youth-oriented counterculture mystique. By the mid-2000s, Harley had become a middle-aged nostalgia brand. Because of so many loyal customers, Harley has been able to turn small product improvements into sustained growth. Many Harley-Davidson customers own multiple—sometimes even 12—Harley motorcycles. At the moment the new, bigger

[2]The facts about Harley-Davidson and the quotes are from Joseph Weber, "Harley Just Keeps on Cruisin'," *Business Week*, November 6, 2006, pp. 71–72; "Harley-Davidson Reports 2008 Results, Plans Lower 2009 Shipments and Unveils Strategy for Current Environment," **www.harley-davidson.com.**, 2009. Mike Ramsey and Anjali Athavaley, "Harley-Davidson Profit, Sales, Fall, *The Wall Street Journal*, April 21, 2010, p. B2.

Twin Cam engine and six-speed transmission was announced in July 2006, orders began pouring into dealers. Annual sales of $6 billion were forecast. Another capability of Harley is a fast-growing overseas fan base that perceives the Harley-Davidson in the best possible sense, referring to being powerful and free. Over one-fifth of Harleys are sold outside the United States.

A major external threat facing Harley-Davidson was the long-time prediction that a demographic time bomb would blow up the company. The median age of a Harley buyer had leapt from 35 in 1987 to nearly 47 in 2010. The company has done little to shake its image with people in their twenties as Granddad's or Grandma's bike. "They haven't kept up with the younger riders," says a 44-year-old business analyst who owns two Harleys.

Establish Goals and Objectives

The second step in planning is to establish goals and identify objectives that contribute to the attainment of goals. (Goals are broader than objectives, whereas objectives function as smaller goals that support the bigger goals.) A major goal Harley management might establish is to continue to cultivate people over 30 who prefer the big, loud bikes that allow for smooth rides on long trips. Another goal would be to promote the Harley as a retirement treat, especially for young retirees.

Genevieve Schmitt, founding editor of *WomenRidersNow.com*, believes Harley should establish the goal of continuing to focus on what they do best. She says, "They've responded to the needs of smaller, less muscular riders by offering motorcycles with lower motors. They realize women are an up-and-coming segment and that they need to accommodate them. They don't market to a specific gender, but are gender-neutral. They market a lifestyle, with daughters and moms, dads and sons." Following this thought Harley might establish the goal of making their marketing more gender neutral.

Analyze the Environment to Forecast Aids and Barriers to Goals and Objectives

As an extension of defining the present situation, the manager or other planner attempts to predict which internal and external factors will foster or hinder attainment of the desired ends. A key strength of Harley being able to retain its prominence in the motorcycle business is that its brand is so well established. The loyal and talented Harley-Davidson workforce will be able to adapt to any shift toward smaller, sportier bikes.

A potential barrier in the environment to the continued success of Harley is that the Japanese bike makers quickly change to suit the shifting taste of customers. In contrast, Harley is over 100 years old and much more conservative. Company management is less than eager to mess with its iconic image. Kent Grayson, a marketing professor at Northwestern University says, "It's more than a brand. It's a culture." Another barrier to attaining goals is that European and Japanese motorcycle manufacturers dominate sales of smaller bikes in the United States.

Another external threat is that many individuals are concerned about motorcycle safety and the disturbance to the environment from the loud exhaust blast. The Hell's Angels image of motorcyclists is a potential barrier. Yet the barrier is offset somewhat by the fact that many would-be drivers are attracted to the rebellious image.

Develop Action Plans to Reach Goals and Objectives

Goals and objectives are only wishful thinking until action plans are drawn. An **action plan** consists of the specific steps necessary to achieve a goal or objective. The planners must figure out specifically how they will accomplish such ends as encouraging Harley users to keep motorcycling until later in life. Other action plans might include more advertising aimed at women, including the objective of featuring women celebrities in advertisements for Harley-Davidson. Another action plan might include free seminars for seniors about the joy of motorcycles. By 2008, Harley-Davidson began purposely reaching out to younger drivers in its marketing campaigns. The recession that continued for a couple of years made it difficult to evaluate how successful this program would prove to be.

In mid-2000, Harley-Davidson acquired two manufacturers of sports bikes, Buell and MV Augusta. (Sport bikes are lightweight, can accelerate quickly, and turn corners at high speeds.) Company management dropped the Buell lines in 2009, and was looking to sell MV Augusta in 2010 because neither motorcycle was really bringing in young riders. As a result, the company was thinking of de-emphasizing going after younger motorcycle riders, and concentrating on global expansion, including the Mexican and Indian markets. (The take-away lesson here is that if a strategic plan is not working, a backup strategy must be developed quickly.)

Develop Budgets

Planning usually results in action plans that require money to implement. Among the expenses would be larger advertising and promotion budgets geared to younger people and women. Another budget item would include safe-driving campaigns to help soften the image of motorcycling being so dangerous. If the international expansion plan is pursued heavily, that too would involve expenses in establishing dealers in other countries.

Implement the Plans

If the plans developed in the previous five steps are to benefit the firm, they must be put to use. A frequent criticism of planners is that they develop elaborate plans and then abandon them in favor of conducting business as usual. One estimate is that 70 percent of the time when CEOs fail, the major cause of failure is poor execution, not poor planning. Poor execution in this study included not getting things done, being indecisive, and not delivering on commitments.[3] Furthermore, execution is considered to be a specific set of

action plan

The specific steps necessary to achieve a goal or an objective.

---

[3]Ram Charan and Geoffrey Colvin, "Why CEOs Fail," *Fortune*, June 21, 1999, p. 70.

behaviors and techniques that companies need to master in order to maintain a competitive advantage.[4] When the CEO of Yahoo, Carol Bartz, appointed Timothy Morse as the new chief financial officer, she offered this compliment: "Tim has a proven ability to translate strategy into structure, process, and execution, and I am delighted that he will be joining my leadership team to help drive Yahoo's growth."[5]

Harley managers and specialists seem poised to execute because their planning sessions heavily emphasize turning plans into action. Harley-Davidson management desperately wants the success of the Harley line of motorcycles to continue into the future.

Control the Plans

Planning does not end with implementation, because plans may not always proceed as conceived. The control process measures progress toward goal attainment and indicates corrective action if too much deviation is detected. The deviation from expected performance can be negative or positive. Progress against all of the goals and objectives mentioned above must be measured. One goal was to hold on to much of the existing customer base. Mark Barnett, an El Paso, Texas, Harley dealer believes that Harley is attaining this goal. He observes: "When they get into their 30s and 40s, people slow down and get tired of sports bikes. If you look at the sport bike demographics, the number on them over 40 is pretty low. As long as people don't quit riding motorcycles altogether, they're going to be our customer when they turn 40." Company management needs more time to know if the goal for getting more young riders and riders from other countries to purchase Harley bikes has been successful.

In Exhibit 4-1, note the phrase "Evaluation and Feedback" on the left. The phrase indicates that the control process allows for the fine-tuning of plans after implementation. One common example of the need for fine-tuning is a budget that has been set too high or too low in the first attempt at implementing a plan. A manager controls by making the right adjustment.

Make Contingency Plans

contingency plan
An alternative plan to be used if the original plan cannot be implemented or a crisis develops.

Many planners develop a set of backup plans to be used in case things do not proceed as hoped. A **contingency plan** is an alternative plan to be used if the original plan cannot be implemented or a crisis develops. (The familiar expression "Let's try plan B" gets at the essence of contingency planning.) One potential crisis for Harley management would be substantial climate changes in the form of rain, snow, and ice that would make motorcycle riding less feasible in many parts of the world. Another crisis would be the

---

[4]Larry Bossidy and Ram Charan with Charles Burck, *Execution: The Discipline of Getting Things Done* (New York: Crown Business, 2002).

[5]Jessica E. Vascellaro and Joann S. Lublin, "Yahoo's Bartz Taps Outsider as CFO," *The Wall Street Journal*, June 12, 2009, p. B1.

escalation of motorcycle insurance premiums to the point that the demand for motorcycles would decline sharply.

Contingency plans are often developed from objectives defined in earlier steps in planning. The plans are triggered into action when the planner detects, however early in the planning process, deviations from objectives. Construction projects, such as building an airport hangar, are particularly prone to deviations from completion dates because so many different contractors and subcontractors are involved.

An *exit strategy* might be part of the contingency plan. For example, if the demand for bikes declined to the point of major losses, the Harley facilities might be sold to Suzuki. Harley management, of course, does not envision this crisis.

Another example of making strategic plans is to prepare for volatility that might have a serious impact on the firm. Factors leading to volatility include sudden changes in commodity prices, terrorism, pandemics, and changes in consumer sentiment, such as going green. Strategy professor C. K. Prahalad explains that one element of managing a volatile environment is the ability to scale up and down and reconfigure resources rapidly. A basic example would be using temporary workers as necessary to meet surges and plunges in demands for the company's products and services. A more complex example would be a telecom carrier leasing network capacity as needed to meet changes in demand for telephone and Internet service.[6]

<table>
<tr><td>LEARNING
OBJECTIVE ②
Describe the
nature of business
strategy.</td></tr>
</table>

THE NATURE OF BUSINESS STRATEGY

What constitutes business strategy has been described in dozens of ways. A **strategy** is an integrated overall concept and plan of how the organization will achieve its goals and objectives.[7] For many managers, strategy simply refers to the direction in which the firm is pointed. For example, a paycheck loan company might decide to set up shop in poor neighborhoods where many of the residents lack a bank account. An explanation of business strategy developed by Michael Porter, a leading authority, provides useful guidelines for managers who need to develop strategy. According to Porter, true business strategy has four components as outlined in Exhibit 4-2 and described next.[8]

strategy
The organization's plan, or comprehensive program, for achieving its vision, mission, and goals in its environment.

Strategy Involves More Than Operational Effectiveness

A starting point in understanding the nature of business strategy is to understand that it involves more than operational effectiveness or being efficient.

---

[6]C. K. Prahalad, "In Volatile Times, Agility Rules," *Business Week*, September 21, 2009, p. 080.

[7]Donald C. Hambrick and James W. Frederickson, "Are You Sure You Have a Business Strategy?" *Academy of Management Executive*, November 2005, p. 51.

[8]Michael E. Porter, "What Is Strategy?" *Harvard Business Review*, November–December 1996, pp. 61–78; John W. Bachmann, "Competitive Strategy: It's O.K. to be Different," *Academy of Management Executive*, May 2002, pp. 61–65.

EXHIBIT 4-2　　The Nature of Strategy

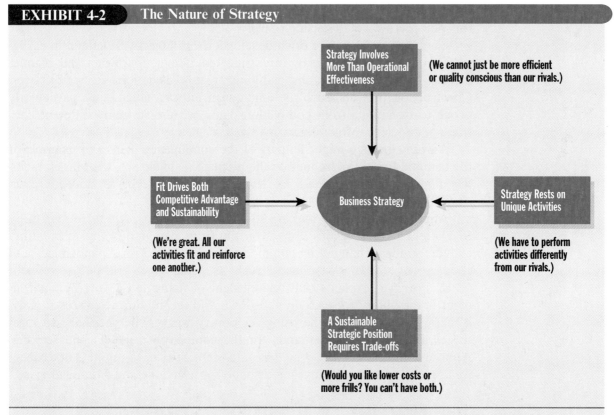

Source: Developed from Michael E. Porter, "What Is Strategy?" *Harvard Business Review*, November–December 1998, pp. 61–78.

In recent years many firms in the private and public sectors have become more efficient through such means as downsizing, performing work more efficiently, and outsourcing. Although improvements in operations may often be dramatic, they rarely lead to sustainable improvements in profitability. As many top-level executives have said, "You can't cost-cut your way to growth." Strategy essentially involves performing activities differently, as does 1-800-MATTRESS, the company that pioneered selling mattresses over the phone. Being able to purchase a mattress over the phone is a convenience that adds value to the purchase of a mattress.

Strategy Rests on Unique Activities

Competitive strategy means deliberately choosing a different set of activities to deliver a unique value. An often-cited example is Southwest Airlines. They offer short-haul, low-cost, direct service between midsized cities and secondary airports in large cities. Southwest's frequent departures and low fares attract price-conscious customers who would otherwise travel by car or bus. Southwest customers willingly forego frills such as in-flight meals to save money and have a wide choice of flight departures. All Southwest activities focus on delivering low-cost, convenient service on its routes. By doing away with added features such as meals and interline transfer of baggage, the airline can achieve gate turnarounds in about 15 minutes. Planes can then be airborne more of the time, allowing for more frequent flights. By using automated ticketing, passengers can bypass travel agents, saving Southwest money on commissions. Another unique activity practiced by Southwest is flying only 737 aircraft, which boosts the efficiency of maintenance.

Southwest has been so successful with its business model that several competitors have surfaced to implement the same strategy. Among these direct competitors are JetBlue and Ted (of United Airlines) in situations where these two carriers fly the same routes as Southwest. Despite this winning strategy, Southwest and its direct competitors are not immune to recessionary forces and the reluctance of some people to fly based on fears of terrorism.

A Sustainable Strategic Position Requires Trade-Offs

After a firm finds a strategic position (or place in the market), it can best sustain it by making trade-offs with other positions. Trade-offs are necessary when activities are incompatible. A good example is shopping through the Internet. If you want the convenience of shopping anytime from your home or office, you sacrifice interacting with a sales associate who can answer your questions. Another trade-off with e-commerce (and shopping by phone) is that defective or ill-fitting merchandise must be repacked and shipped back to the merchant. For many people, repacking and reshipping is more inconvenient than driving back to the merchant with a product that doesn't work.

Fit Drives Both Competitive Advantage and Sustainability

Strategy includes efficiently combining activities related to making a product or service. Company activities fit and support each other to form an effective system. Bic Corporation is an example of the fit aspect of strategy. The company sells a narrow line of standard, low-priced ballpoint pens to the major customer markets (retail, commercial, promotional) through practically every available channel. Bic targets the common need for a low-price, acceptable pens throughout the markets it serves. The company gains the benefit of consistency across nearly all activities, meaning that they do not need different equipment or staff to conduct their business with different customer groups. Bic achieves fit by means of a product design that emphasizes ease of manufacturing; manufacturing plants designed for low-cost, large-scale purchasing to minimize material costs; and in-house parts production whenever cost effective.

As mentioned in passing at the outset of this section, business strategy also involves "thinking big," or taking an overall perspective even when it means glossing over some worrisome details. For example, business strategists never seem to mention that many customers fail to pay their bills or attempt to defraud companies.

LEARNING
OBJECTIVE ❸
Explain how
business strategy
is developed,
including SWOT
analysis.

THE DEVELOPMENT OF BUSINESS STRATEGY

Elaborate methods of planning are often used to help develop business strategy. The planning model presented earlier in the chapter contains the foundation of these tools; SWOT analysis presented later is another planning tool. In the opinion of some management, the best strategy emerges when an organization has a grand purpose.[9] The effective leader, and often the founder, sets the purpose of the firm. Coca Cola began this way, and so did the Boeing Corp. and the Sloan Kettering Cancer Institute. After the firm's purpose is established, the leader becomes the steward of the strategy. Mintzberg argues that if you want good strategy, skip all the elaborate planning and focus on having a great vision.[10]

Strategic planning and setting the vision without planning share an important purpose. Both strive to motivate managerial workers throughout the organization to think strategically about how the firm adapts to its environment and how it will cope with its future. One of the central challenges of modern organizations is motivating leaders at all levels of the firm to think strategically—including seeing the overall picture as they go about their work.[11]

A strategically minded worker at any level would think, "How does what I am doing right now support corporate strategy?" The call-center worker at Hewlett-Packard might say to himself, "Each time I help a customer solve a problem, I am contributing to the strategy of achieving the highest-quality products in all the markets we serve."

Strategic planning encompasses those activities that lead to the statement of goals and objectives and the choice of strategies to achieve them. The final outcomes of strategic planning are statements of vision, mission, strategy, and policy. A **vision** is an idealized picture of the future of the organization. The **mission** identifies the firm's purpose and where it fits into the world. Specifying a mission answers the question "What business are we really in?" A mission is more grounded in present-day realities than is a vision, but some companies use the terms interchangeably. A firm's mission may not be apparent to the casual observer. For example, Godiva Chocolates (producer of high-priced chocolate sold in separate displays in retail outlets) would appear to be in the candy business. In reality, their real mission places them in the luxury and pampering business. Exhibit 4-3 presents a few examples of company vision and mission statements. You will observe that companies vary considerably in what should be included in a mission or vision statement.

vision
An idealized picture
of the future of an
organization.

mission
The firm's purpose
and where it fits into
the world.

---

[9]Cynthia A. Montgomery, "Putting Leadership Back Into Strategy," *Harvard Business Review*, January 2008, pp. 54–60.

[10]Henry Mintzberg, *Managing* (Berrett-Koehler, 2009), pp. 162–163.

[11]James R. Bailey, "The Mind of the Strategist," *Academy of Management Learning and Education*, December 2003, p. 385.

EXHIBIT 4-3	Sample Vision and Mission Statements

Microsoft: "Innovation is the core of providing opportunity."

Starfire Systems:

Vision: "Starfire Systems will pioneer the creation of new advanced materials through enabling technology based on a wide range of ceramic-forming polymers that meet the needs of customers."

Mission: "Starfire Systems invents, manufactures high-performance ceramic-forming polymers and provides the engineered material systems that will allow our customers to break through cost, performance and design barriers."

Bombardier: "Bombardier's mission is to be the leader in all the markets in which it operates. This objective will be achieved through excellence in design, manufacturing, and marketing in the fields of transportation equipment, aerospace, recreational products, financial services, and services related to its products and core competencies."

Roth Staffing Companies: "We are the preeminent staffing-services company, recognized as a creative industry leader, equally fulfilling the diverse needs of our customers, staffing associates, and coworkers."

Mrs. Fields Cookies: "I've always been in a feel good feeling business. My job was to sell joy, happiness, an experience, and my mission was to take my product to the extreme. You've got to strive to be the best in whatever you can." (As articulated by Debbi Fields, company founder)

As mentioned above, planning alone does not create strategy; strategy can stem from inspired thinking. Corporate values also influence strategy; well-managed organizations tend to develop strategy to fit what the people in power think is important. If the company values innovation, it will not adopt a strategy that involves imitating (or benchmarking) other successful products. Piaget, for example, has remained successful for more than 200 years by staying with its own high-quality watches and not imitating trends in the watch industry.

Strategy often stems from planning, yet many firms choose a strategy prior to strategic planning. Once the firm has the strategy, a plan is developed to implement it. A chief executive might say, "Let's compete by becoming the most recognizable company in our field." The executive team would then develop specific plans to implement that strategy rather than allowing the strategic planning process to lead to the conclusion that brand recognition would be an effective strategy. For many medium-sized and small organizations it is strategy first, followed by planning.

Three major approaches to developing strategy are gathering multiple inputs, analyzing the realities of the business situation, and performing a SWOT analysis. All three of these approaches are consistent with, and extensions of, the basic planning model presented in Exhibit 4-1.

Gathering Multiple Inputs to Formulate Strategy

Strategic managers and leaders are often thought of as mystics who work independently and conjure up great schemes for the future. In reality, many strategic leaders arrive at their ideas for the organization's future by consulting with a wide range of parties at interest. Strategy theorist Gary Hamel advises executives to make the strategy-creation process more democratic. He reasons that imagination is scarcer than resources. As a consequence, "We have to involve hundreds, if not thousands, of new voices in the strategy process if we want to increase the odds of seeing the future."[12]

An extreme approach to gathering multiple inputs for strategy is a development termed *crowdcasting*. A consultancy, such as Idea Crossing, holds an online contest with 3,500 MBA students to solve strategic dilemmas. Companies pay Idea Crossing to obtain the input from the students. The payoff from crowdcasting is the opportunity to penetrate a closed-circuit corporate culture and profit from the fresh insights of a large group of smart and motivated outsiders. Contestants sign confidentiality agreements and their strategic solutions become the property of the corporate sponsors. An example of a strategic problem tackled by the business students was to devise new services featuring high-speed wireless technologies for Sprint. Many strategy experts might label the students' activities problem solving rather than true strategy. Nevertheless, the consulting firm involved and the participating companies regard the activity as resolving strategic dilemmas.[13]

Analyzing the Realities of the Business Situation

To develop an effective business strategy, the strategist must make valid assumptions about the environment. When the assumptions are incorrect, the strategy might backfire. Let's be preposterous for a moment. Assume that Krispy Kreme regards e-commerce as the wave of the future and therefore halts its plans to vend donuts through stores of its own and in grocery stores and service stations. Instead, Krispy Kreme develops Web sites so people can purchase donuts and coffee online and pay for quick delivery service. The wrong assumption is that potential Krispy Kreme customers throughout the world own computers, are online, have credit cards, and are willing to pay a premium to have donuts and coffee delivered to their home or office. The e-tailing strategy fails because assumptions about the potential customer base were flawed.

The general point here is that firms must constantly change in order to be aligned with their key environments.[14] Sometimes management can shape the nature of the business to match the external environment, such as Harley-Davidson does by crafting motorcycles that its aging customer base can continue to ride. (What about trikes and motorcycles with a side-car?) The assumption Harley would be making here is that motorcyclists want to continue riding as late in life as possible.

---

[12]Cited in John A. Byrne, "Three of the Busiest New Strategists," *Business Week*, August 26, 1996, p. 50.

[13]Melanie Haiken, "Tuning Into Crowdcasting," *Business 2.0*, November 2006, p. 68.

[14]Bob De Wit and Ron Meyer, *Strategy Synthesis: Resolving Strategy Paradoxes to Create Competitive Advantage* (London, UK: Thomson Learning, 2005).

Accurately analyzing the environment to understand customers, potential customers, production capability, and the relevant technology is a time-consuming and comprehensive activity. Yet for strategy to work well, the manager must understand both the external environment and the capabilities of the firm, as already implied from the basic planning model. Exhibit 4-4

EXHIBIT 4-4   **A Strategic Inventory**

The purpose of the *strategic inventory* is to help a manager relate ideas about strategy to his or her own organization. By finding answers to these questions, the manager is likely to do a better job of sizing up the competition, the customers, and the technology necessary to compete effectively. The manager will often need the assistance of others in finding answers to these challenging questions.

Defining the Boundaries of the Competitive Environment

- What are the boundaries of our industry? What market do we serve? What products or services do we provide?
- Who are our customers? Who has chosen not to buy from us? What is the difference between these two groups?
- Who are our competitors? Which firms do not compete with us? What makes one firm a competitor and not the other?

Defining the Key Assumptions Made About the Environment, Customers, Competition, and the Capabilities of the Firm

- Who is our customer? What product or service features are important to that customer? How does the customer perceive us? What kind of relationship do we have with the customer?
- Who are our competitors? What are their strengths and weaknesses? How do they perceive us? What can we learn from our competitors?
- Who are our potential competitors? New entrants? What changes in the environment or their behavior would make them competitors?

- What is the industry's value chain (points along the way in which value is added)? Where is value added? What is the industry's cost structure? How does our firm compare? How about the cost structure of our competitors?
- What technologies are important in our industry? Product technologies? Delivery and service technologies? How does our firm compare? How about our competitors?
- What are the key factors of production? Who are the suppliers? Do we rely on just a few suppliers and sources? How critical are these relationships to our success? How solid are these relationships?
- What are the bases for competition in our industry? What are the key success factors? How do we measure up on these success factors? How do our competitors measure up?
- What trends and factors in the external environment are important in our industry? How are they likely to change? What is likely to be the time period for the changes?
- Are we able, in assessing our knowledge and assumptions, to clearly separate fact from assumption?
- Which of the preceding assumptions are the most important in terms of the impact on our business?

Examining the Process for Reviewing and Validating Our Key Assumptions and Premises

- Do we have a process already established? Have responsibilities been assigned? Are periodic reviews planned and scheduled?

Source: Adapted from Joseph C. Picken and Gregory G. Dess, "Right Strategy—Wrong Problem," *Organizational Dynamics*, Summer 1998, p. 47.

presents a series of questions the strategist must answer to accurately size up the environment. Finding valid answers to these questions will often require considerable interviewing, including interviewing groups of consumers, and information gathering.

To help demystify what the development of strategy means in practice, we present the strategy statement of investment broker Edward Jones, which was developed using a process similar to the one described in the preceding paragraphs:

To grow to 17,000 financial advisors by 2012 by offering trusted and face-to-face financial advice to conservative individual investors who delegate their financial decisions through a national network of one-financial-advisor offices.[15]

Performing a SWOT Analysis

SWOT analysis
A method of considering the strengths, weaknesses, opportunities, and threats in a given situation.

Quite often strategic planning takes the form of a **SWOT analysis**, a method of considering the strengths, weaknesses, opportunities, and threats in a given situation. The strengths and weaknesses take into account internal resources and capabilities; opportunities and threats refer to factors external to the organization. SWOT is considered the most applicable to the early stages of strategic and marketing planning. Elements of a SWOT analysis are included in the general planning model and in the strategic inventory used to size up the environment. Because of SWOT's straightforward appeal, it has become a popular framework for strategic planning. The framework, or technique, can identify a niche the company has not already exploited.

Preparing for the Analysis Four steps are recommended to bring about a successful SWOT analysis.[16] First, it is important to be clear about what you are doing and why. The purpose might be to fine-tune a present strategy or to point the business in a new direction. Second, it is important to select appropriate contributors. Select people with appropriate experience, talent, and enthusiasm. Imaginative people are particularly useful for a SWOT analysis. Usually six to ten people are enough, but involving more people can be helpful to involve more people in the changes SWOT might trigger. Third, allocate research and information-gathering tasks. Several members of the team might concentrate on analyzing the firm; others might concentrate on analyzing the outside environment. Step four is to create a workshop environment by encouraging open communication among participants. All present should feel free to criticize the status quo, even questioning what most people think is a company strength. A SWOT team member of a group at Starbucks might say, "Is having so many stores such a great strength? Could we be losing out to the coffee lovers who want a more unique, intimate experience?"

---

[15]David J. Collis and Michael G. Rukstad, "Cay You Say What Your Strategy Is?" *Harvard Business Review*, April 2008, p. 90.

[16]"Performing a SWOT Analysis," in *Business: The Ultimate Resource* (Cambridge, MA: Perseus Publishing, 2002), pp. 468–469.

Conducting the Analysis

To illustrate the use of the model, we turn to Ulysse Nardin, a Swiss manufacturer of fine watches founded in 1846. The price range of Ulysse Nardin watches is between $6,000 and $38,000. Assume that top executives at Ulysse Nardin are thinking about finding another niche by manufacturing luxury pens in the $200 to $500 range. Some of their thinking in regard to a SWOT analysis might proceed as follows:

> ***Strengths.*** *What are the good points about a particular alternative? Use your judgment and intuition; ask knowledgeable people.* Selling luxury pens appears to be a reasonable fit with the watch line because a luxury pen is often worn as jewelry. We are great at making small-size luxury items. People who just want a writing instrument could settle for a Bic or competitive brand. The profit margins on luxury pens are quite good and they are not likely to be deeply discounted in department stores or discount stores. We can also maintain low inventories until we assess the true demand. As our sales representatives and distributors receive orders, we can manufacture pens quickly. Our beautiful Web site, http://www.ulysse-nardin.com, could easily incorporate a line of luxury pens.

> ***Weaknesses.*** *Consider the risks of pursuing a particular course of action, such as getting into a business you do not understand.* We are watchmakers, pure and simple. We would need to train our skilled craftspeople to make pens or hire new workers. If only a handful of companies manufacture luxury pens, it could be because it is a tough market to crack. We are so well known for watches that our clientele might not perceive us to be a crafter of fountain pens. (We will need to do some market research here.) Another risk is that we will cheapen the Ulysse Nardin name. The average price of a Ulysse Nardin product is now about $12,000. With a brand of luxury pens, a person could take home a Ulysse Nardin brand product for about $400, which could result in a scaling down of our image. Another problem is that we are not presently linked to office supply stores and the distribution channels that sell luxury pens. We might have to rely on new distributors to get us into that channel. We do not sell over the Internet, and selling pens might move us in this direction.

> ***Opportunities.*** *Think of the opportunities that welcome you if you choose a promising strategic alternative. Use your imagination and visualize the opportunities.* The opportunities could be quite good in terms of snob appeal. Maybe large numbers of consumers would welcome the opportunity to carry a Ulysse Nardin anything in a shirt pocket, handbag, or attaché case. Many of the people who become Ulysse Nardin luxury pen customers might want to step up to become a Ulysse Nardin watch owner.

> ***Threats.*** *Every alternative has its downside, so it is important to think ahead to allow for contingency planning. Ask people who have tried in the past what you are attempting now. But don't be dissuaded by the naysayers, heel draggers, and pessimists. Just take action.* Several manufacturers of high-end products in jewelry, clothing, and automobiles have cheapened

their image and lost market share when they spread their brand name too thin. Following this approach, we could wind up having not only Ulysse Nardin pens but also wallets and handbags. At that point the high prestige of the Ulysse Nardin brand would be at risk.

As a result of this SWOT analysis, Ulysse Nardin sticks to its knitting (or watch making) and continues to make world-class watches. Do you think they are making the right decision? Or do you think the brand equity (value of the brand name) warrants putting the Ulysse Nardin label on another product?

A caution about the SWOT analysis is needed. It is sometimes viewed as too superficial because it relies on description instead of analysis and ignores prioritizing the alternatives it generates.

<table>
<tr><td>LEARNING
OBJECTIVE **4**
Identify levels of
business strategy,
competitive forces,
and types of
business
strategies.</td></tr>
</table>

Levels of Strategy, Competitive Forces, and Types of Strategies

The nature of strategy and how it is developed may appear complex. Yet strategy statements themselves, as expressed by managers and planners, are usually straightforward and expressed in a few words: "We will be cost leaders" or "We will be competitive by offering superior service." Keep in mind that businesspeople are likely to have a less precise and less scientific meaning of strategy than do strategy researchers. A variety of business strategies have already been mentioned in this chapter. Here we look at levels, competitive forces, and types of business strategies.

Levels of Business Strategies

A strategy chosen to reach an important goal depends considerably on the level it serves within the organization. At the level of the overall firm, Amazon.com might decide that its strategy is to allow people throughout the world to purchase as many products online as they wish. At the level of the distribution centers, the managers must develop a strategy for enabling world-wide distribution of products at a reasonable cost. Exhibit 4-5 provides a few details about strategy levels.

Two major concerns of *corporate-level strategy* are the total direction of the enterprise and the selection of specific businesses. Usually the total direction of the enterprise begins with the founding of the company. For example, Boeing Co. was founded as an aerospace company. Later, a variety of businesses emerged, such as a commercial division, a military division, and a service division. Executives in large, diversified firms invest considerable time in deciding which businesses to enter; for example, Yahoo! has moved into various types of entertainment.

The *business-level strategy* focuses on the question of how to compete in each of our businesses. Several of these strategies will be mentioned in the next section.

Functional-level strategies are formulated to specify actions required to successfully implement strategies at the corporate and business levels. An

| EXHIBIT 4-5 | Strategy Levels for Diversified and Single-Business Firms |

Diversified Business Firms

Corporate-Level Strategy

What direction do we pursue for the total enterprise?

Which businesses should be we enter?

Business-Level Strategy

How do we compete within each of the businesses we have chosen?

Functional-Level Strategy

How can each function best support each of our businesses?

How do we get the various functions working together smoothly?

Single-Business Firms

Corporate-Level Strategy

Which business should we be in?

How do we compete within the market we have chosen?

Functional-Level Strategy

How can each function best support each of our businesses?

How do we get the various functions working together smoothly?

example is the corporate-level strategy of Google to be a leading innovator in any business it enters. The human resources function must then assist in attracting, selecting, and retaining imaginative workers. Fit among the various functions is another major consideration. If the human resources department at Google recruits imaginative workers, these workers must be placed in functions such as marketing and finance that provide them with stimulating work.

Under ideal circumstances, the activities of managers and other workers at the functional level support the business-level and corporate-level strategies. For example, if top-level management wants the firm to be world recognized for its quality products and services (such as IBM), business units would not engage in activities such as selling refurbished office furniture). At the functional level, all IBM departments would hire talented people who can help deliver quality goods and services.

Five Competitive Forces

Before choosing the most appropriate strategy or strategies for the business, it is helpful to examine the relevant competitive forces. Michael E. Porter studied many business firms, which led him to conclude that business-level strategies are the result of five competitive forces in the company's environment.[17] The same five forces can also influence enterprise-level strategy. For example, strategists at PepsiCo might say, "Why bother going into the wine business? The market is already flooded." The competitive forces the organization must take into account are as follows:

1. *The power of customers to affect pricing and reduce profit margins.* Informed customers become empowered customers. If customers can readily purchase your product or service from a competitor, you must keep costs low. A telecommunications company, for example, might shop worldwide for the least expensive fiber-optic cables.

2. *The power of suppliers to influence the company's pricing.* Manufacturing companies are dependent on suppliers for raw materials and components. With the growth of outsourcing, companies are sometimes dependent on suppliers for marketing, research and development, and even staffing. High-price suppliers could drive up costs, forcing a company to think of better ways of attracting customers other than low prices.

3. *The threat of similar or substitute products to limit market freedom and reduce prices and thus profits.* Alternatives to a company's products are a constant menace even for stable products and services. The Internet has accelerated the power of this competitive force; people now purchase investments online, thus decreasing the perceived need for personal advice from a stockbroker. The in-person travel agency business has been severely reduced because of online travel agencies and direct purchases of airplane tickets and hotel rooms.

4. *The level of existing competition that affects investment in marketing and research and thus erodes profits.* Every shopper knows it; the greater the competition, the lower the price. A few years ago Wal-Mart priced more than 300 generic drugs at $4 per prescription in 14 states. Within a couple of weeks many supermarkets and pharmacy chains followed suit, lowering profits for all.

5. *The threat of new market entrants to intensify competition and further affect pricing and profitability.* Some businesses are more difficult to enter than others, often depending on the amount of investment and time required both in the home country and elsewhere. Relatively few new tire manufacturers emerge, but new online shopping sites emerge daily. Complexity and bigness tend to lower the competitive threat of

---

[17]Michael E. Porter, "The Five Competitive Forces That Shape Business Strategy," *Harvard Business Review*, January 2008, pp. 78–93 (Updating of 1979 article in *Harvard Business Review*.); Porter, "What Is Strategy?" *Business: The Ultimate Resource* (Cambridge, MA: Perseus Publishing, 2002), pp. 1038–1039.

new entrants. Yet the existence of even great enterprises such as Ford Motor has been threatened by companies such as Honda and Kia.

According to Porter's analysis, strategy can be viewed as positioning against competitive forces or as finding a position in an industry where the forces are weaker. If Apple Inc. can deliver downloaded songs for 99 cents and your company wants to stay competitive, you must develop a plan to sell music for about the same price.

Types of Business Strategies

Companies use a variety of strategies to survive and prosper, and these strategies have been classified in several ways. For convenience in integrating our discussion of strategy, we present eight types of strategy placed under the level in which they most nearly fit. Managers tend to think in terms of the strategy type rather than worrying about which competitive force it best meets.

Corporate-level Strategies Three examples of corporate-level strategies are strategic alliances, diversification, and sticking to core competencies.

1. *Strategic alliances.* A widely used business strategy calls for forming alliances or sharing resources with other companies to exploit a market opportunity. A major factor contributing to the growth of alliances is the enormous costs and time involved in developing and distributing products when a company starts from zero. According to the consultancy Booz-Allen & Hamilton, strategic alliances are sweeping through nearly every industry and are a driver of superior growth.[18] In 2010, Hewlett-Packard Co. and Microsoft Corp. invested $250 million to more tightly couple their software and hardware products to compete successfully in the market for one-stop technology. All the initiatives in the alliance were aimed at helping business organizations reduce some of the difficulties of establishing and operating data centers, the backroom operations that house corporate software and computer equipment.[19]

2. *Diversification of goods and services.* "Don't put all your eggs in one basket" is a standard business strategy. One of the many reasons that diversification is an effective strategy is that it serves as a hedge in case the market for one group of products or services softens. Another advantage of diversification is that it can lead to immediate growth at the same time. A few years ago, Xerox Corp was seeking to enhance its revenue and offer more services at the same time. The solution to the challenge was to purchase Affiliated Computer Services (ACS), a major player in the business process outsourcing industry. Immediately, the revenues of Xerox increased by one-third. The acquisition of ACS meant

---

[18]"Strategic Alliances," *Small Business Notes* (http://www.smallbusinessnotes.com), October 3, 2006.

[19]Nick Wingfield and Justin Scheck, "H-P, Microsoft Partner Against Rivals," *The Wall Street Journal*, January 14, 2010, p. B1.

that Xerox now provided such diverse services as processing health claims, electronic toll collection, and the design of defined employee benefit plans.[20]

3. *Sticking to core competencies.* It may be valuable not only to avoid putting all your eggs in one basket, but also to guard against spreading yourself too thin. Many firms of all sizes believe they will prosper if they confine their efforts to business activities they perform best—their core competencies. At one time Wal-Mart attempted to lure higher-income shoppers with trendier fashions; the experiment flopped, eroding profit. The company then returned to its low-price roots, which helped it prosper during the Great Recession. As Wal-Mart re-strengthened its reputation for very low prices, many higher-than-average income shoppers traded down.[21]

Business-Level Strategies Three examples of business-level strategies are product differentiation, focus, and cost leadership.

1. *Product Differentiation.* A differentiation strategy attempts to find a niche or offer a product or service perceived by the customer as different from available alternatives. Most companies believe they have a differentiated product unless their strategy is to imitate another product or service or produce *knock off* merchandise. Luxury brands often stem from a differentiation strategy. An example of a low-price luxury brand that has honed a differentiation strategy is Etón Corporation of Palo Alto, California. The Etón® AM/FM/Shortwave radio retails for about $100; it receives AM and FM stations from several hundred miles away. The radio is advertised in such elite places as *The Wall Street Journal.* The radios are also advertised under the Grundig brand, and the corporate Web site (http://www.etoncorp.com) has a differentiated, exciting appeal.

   An extension of the product differentiation strategy is to create a new market in which competition does not exist, referred to as a *blue ocean strategy.* A prime example is Cirque du Soleil, which increased revenue 22-fold in a ten-year period by reinventing the circus with extravagant shows that combine several forms of entertainment at once. The 1984 Chrysler minivan, which created a new class of automobile, is another example of blue ocean strategy.[22]

2. *Focus.* In a focus strategy, the organization concentrates on a specific regional or buyer market. To gain market share, the company uses either a differentiation or a low-cost approach in a targeted market. Some

---

[20]Matthew Daneman, "Xerox, ACS Say 'Yes' to Deal," *Democrat and Chronicle*, February 6, 2010, p. 5B.

[21]Ann Zimmerman, "Engineering a Change at Wal-Mart," *The Wall Street Journal*, August 12, 2008, p. B1; Zimmerman and Miguel Bustillo, "Wal-Mart Angles to Keep Those Who Traded Down," *The Wall Street Journal*, October 2, 2009, p. B1.

[22]W. Chan Kim and Renée Mauborgne, "Blue Ocean Strategy," *Harvard Business Review*, October 2004, pp. 76–84.

companies have several products or services catering to a buyer market, such as vitamins for seniors, but this does not constitute a full focus strategy. Specialized medical products, such as leg and arm prostheses, are based on a focus or niche strategy. Payday-loan stores are based on a focus strategy. Typically these stores, such as Advance America, focus on the working poor who live paycheck to paycheck. Yet in recent years, these payday-loan stores have developed a presence in affluent neighborhoods. The real focus of payday-loan stores is people in financial need, people who have already used up their credit or who have poor credit.

3. *Cost leadership.* The cost leader provides a product or service at a low price in order to gain market share. Save-A-Lot has become one of the most successful grocery chains in the United States by serving a demographic that most supermarkets have long ignored—the poor. The Earth City, Missouri, chain is covering the country with small, cheap stores catering to households earning less than $35,000 a year. Many Save-A-Lot stores are located in poor sections of the inner city; they offer prices lower than those of Wal-Mart.[23] Note that Save-A-Lot uses the focus and cost leadership strategy simultaneously, illustrating the point that business strategies sometimes overlap. Dollar stores, such as Dollar General and Family Dollar, follow the same strategy. A cost leadership strategy can create ethical problems because of what suppliers must do to cut costs, such as having goods manufactured at sweatshops.

Functional-Level Strategy Two examples of functional-level strategy are finding and retaining the best people and moving at high speed.

1. *Find and retain the best people.* A foundation strategy for becoming and remaining a successful organization is to find and retain competent people. Such people will help the organization develop products and services that are in demand, and they will find ways to reduce costs and behave ethically. Concentrating on hiring talent can be considered a functional-level strategy because people are usually hired into specific departments. Top management at Microsoft and Amazon.com attribute most of their success to hiring only intelligent, motivated job candidates. *Fast Company* magazine offers this advice to modern business executives:

   Yes, you need an Internet strategy. Sure, you've got to stay on the good side of Wall Street. But when it comes to building great companies, the most urgent business charge is finding and keeping great people. In an economy driven by ideas and charged by the Web, brainpower is the real source of competitive advantage.[24]

---

[23]Janet Adamy, "To Find Growth, No-Frills Grocer Goes Where Other Chains Won't," August 30, 2005, *The Wall Street Journal* p. A1.

[24]Bill Breen and Anna Mudio, "Peoplepalooza," *Fast Company*, January 2001, pp. 80–81.

2. *High speed.* Satisfy customer needs more quickly and you will make more money. High-speed managers focus on speed in all of their business activities, including product development, sales response, and customer service. Knowing that "time is money," they use time as a competitive resource. It is important to get products to market quickly to prevent the competition from being there first. Part of Domino's Pizza's original success was based on getting pizzas delivered more quickly than competitors could. The strategy had to be modified slightly when too many deliverers sacrificed auto safety to enhance delivery speed. Dell Computer relies on high speed as part of its strategy. A custom order placed at 9 a.m. Wednesday can *often* be on a delivery truck by 9 p.m. on Thursday. Not every customer has the same good fortune. Porter notes that speed is not good for its own sake. The effectiveness of speed depends on what the speed allows you to do that creates lower cost or differentiation. In Dell's case, the rapid delivery eliminates the need to keep loads of products in inventory and it appeals to users who want equipment in a hurry.[25]

So now that you are a top executive, or an advisor to a top executive, which combination of strategies should you choose to help you triumph? Strategies must be selected carefully and given a chance to work. When a strategy is agreed upon, it must be executed carefully. Jumping from strategy to strategy in the hopes of revitalizing a company has been cited as a major reason why companies fail.

Although strategies should be given a reasonable chance to work, current thinking suggests that strategic plans and strategy must remain flexible to adapt to changing circumstances. Most strategies are only effective for about five years, and adverse circumstances can shorten their useful cycle. A few companies in recent years have gone to the extreme of establishing "situation rooms" in which staffers glued to computer screens monitor developments affecting sales and finance. In this way, the implementation of the strategy can change rapidly even when the basic strategy remains stable.

A few years ago, J.C. Penney put its long-term strategy on hold and called in a substitute because of the Great Recession. The company had launched an ambitious five-year plan in 2007, but the recession created a need to slow down expansion. The company successfully shifted to a marketing strategy that called for the use of social-networking sites to cultivate customers in fresh ways.[26] J.C. Penney management implemented the new

---

[25]Cited in Nicholas Argyres and Anita M. McGahan, "Introduction: Michael Porter's, *Competitive Strategy, Academy of Management Executive*, May 2002, p. 47.

[26]Joann S. Lublin and Dana Mattioli, "Strategic Plans Lose Favor," *The Wall Street Journal*, January 25, 2010, p. B7.

MANAGEMENT IN ACTION

Mike's Carwash Puts People First

Mike's Carwash, with 37 locations in Indiana and Ohio, has earned a reputation for stellar service by rigorously vetting even entry-level job candidates and then reducing turnover through heavy training and incentives. About two-thirds of the company's employees work part time.

"If there's anything we've learned the hard way, it's that turnover hurts profits and customer service," says Bill Dahm, chief executive and co-owner of the second-generation family business. The company hires roughly one of every 100 applicants. All candidates are interviewed by at least two people. Applicants take computerized tests, one gauging personality and one testing basic math skills. Managers seek candidates with strong social and reasoning skills, viewed as key to good customer service. The company also conducts drug testing and trains hiring managers to spot "red flags" such as a history of bounding from job to job.

Once hired, Mike's employees get many incentives to stay. The company offers tuition reimbursement of up to $2,500 annually to everyone working at least 20 hours a week—a benefit about 100 employees claimed in a recent year. Amanda Heim, 21, who has worked at Mike's 4 ½ years as a part-time wash associate, says the company has reimbursed about $2,000 of her tuition at Indiana-Purdue University Indianapolis, where she is pursuing her nursing degree. "They make it easy for us to do both college and work," says Heim.

Mike's also shares profits with all employees, even the part-timers. Its gain sharing program sets target labor costs at each car wash.

(Gain sharing is a type of profit sharing based on labor costs.) Locations that beat those targets each month split the difference among all non-managerial employees there based on how many hours they worked. During a recent year, Mike's gave out about $569,000 in gain-sharing, averaging about $1.25 per hour extra per employee. Front-line workers also earn points for providing strong customer service. Each month, staffers at each location can be named "associate of the month" and win prizes of $25 or $50.

The company spends a lot of time training employees on customer service: All Mike's employees are required to watch a weekly 10-minute video with updates on company news and customer service practices and other on-the-job education.

Questions

1. Why is this story about how a successful carwash chain treats its employees in a chapter about business strategy?
2. To what extent do you think Mike's would be more profitable if it stopped benefits such as tuition reimbursement and gain sharing for part-time carwash associates?
3. Based on your own direct observations, describe an example of what might constitute good customer service at a carwash. How about poor customer service?

Source: Kelly K. Spors, "Top Small Workplaces 2009: Mike's Carwash," *The Wall Street Journal*, September 28, 2009, p. R5.

strategy but did not abandon their core strategy of appealing to the middle group of consumers. Management did not shift strategy to compete directly with Dollar Stores or Bloomingdales.

The accompanying Management in Action illustrates how a company in a basic industry carries out a functional-level business strategy.

LEARNING
OBJECTIVE **5**
Explain the use
of operating
plans, policies,
procedures, and
rules.

OPERATING PLANS, POLICIES, PROCEDURES, AND RULES

Strategic plans are formulated at the top of the organization, often with the input of many people throughout the organization. Four of the vehicles through which strategic plans and strategy are converted into action are operating plans, policies, procedures, and rules.

Operating Plans

operating plans
The means through which strategic plans alter the destiny of the firm.

Operating plans are the means through which strategic plans alter the destiny of the firm. Operating plans involve organizational efficiency (doing things right), whereas strategic plans involve effectiveness (doing the right things). Both strategic and operational plans involve such things as exploring alternatives and evaluating the effectiveness of the plan. In a well-planned organization, all managers take responsibility for making operating plans that mesh with the strategic plans of the business. Operating plans provide the details of how strategic plans will be accomplished. In many firms, suggestions to be incorporated into operating plans stem from employees at lower levels.

Operating plans focus more on the firm than on the external environment. To illustrate, the strategic plan of a local government might be to encourage the private sector to take over government functions. One operating unit within the local government might then formulate a plan for subcontracting refuse removal to private contractors and phasing out positions for civil-service sanitation workers.

Operating plans tend to be drawn for a shorter period than strategic plans. The plan for increasing the private sector's involvement in activities conducted by the local government might be a ten-year plan. The phasing out of government sanitation workers might take two years.

Policies

policies
General guidelines to follow in making decisions and taking action.

Policies are general guidelines to follow when making decisions and taking action; as such, they are plans. Many policies are written; some are unwritten, or implied. Policies, designed to be consistent with strategic plans, must allow room for interpretation by the individual manager. An important managerial role is interpreting policies for employees. Here is an example of a policy and an analysis of how it might require interpretations.

> *Policy: When hiring employees from the outside, consider only those candidates who are technically competent or show promise of becoming technically competent and who show good personal character and motivation.*

A manager attempting to implement this policy with respect to a given job candidate would have to ask the following questions:

* What do we mean by "technical competence"?
* How do I measure technical competence?

- What do we mean by "show promise of becoming technically competent"?
- How do I rate the promise of technical competence?
- What do we mean by "good personal character and motivation"?
- How do I assess good personal character and motivation?

Policies are developed to support strategic plans in every area of the firm. Many firms have strict policies against employees accepting gifts and favors from vendors or potential vendors. For example, many schools endorse the Code of Ethics and Principles advocated by the National Association of Educational Buyers. One of the specific policies states that buyers should "decline personal gifts or gratuities which might in any way influence the purchase of materials."

Procedures

procedures
A customary method for handling an activity. It guides action rather than thinking.

Procedures are considered plans because they establish a customary method of handling future activities. They guide action rather than thinking, in that they state the specific manner in which a certain activity must be accomplished. Procedures exist at every level in the organization, but they tend to be more complex and specific at lower levels. For instance, strict procedures may apply to the handling of checks by store associates. The procedures for check handling by managers may be much less strict. Procedures, such as in security screening of airport passengers, are very important,

Rules

rule
A specific course of action or conduct that must be followed. It is the simplest type of plan.

A **rule** is a specific course of action or conduct that must be followed; it is the simplest type of plan. Ideally, each rule fits a strategic plan. In practice, however, many rules are not related to organizational strategy. When rules are violated, corrective action should be taken. Two examples of rules follow:

- Any employee engaged in an accident while in a company vehicle must report that accident immediately to his or her supervisor.
- No employee is authorized to use company photocopying machines for personal use, even if he or she reimburses the company for the cost of the copies.

Some workers think that policies, procedures, and rules are rigid, bothersome, and old-fashioned. The other point of view is that policies and procedures protect company assets and provide a guide for employee actions. Business consultant Susan Kastan provides this example:

Several laptops were stolen from an office by a group of people pretending to be part of the cleaning company. Every laptop stolen contained sensitive client data. After the theft, all clients had to be notified that their personal information may have been compromised. The breach of security prompted 25 percent of the company's clients to close their accounts.

One laptop had the company's identifications and passwords taped to the bottom, which the thieves used to gain access to the plans for an upcoming product. The information was then sold to a competitor.

If the company had policies on how computer ID and passwords should be stored, and how laptops should be secured, these problems would most likely have been avoided.[27]

MANAGEMENT BY OBJECTIVES: A SYSTEM OF PLANNING AND REVIEW

Management by objectives (MBO) is a systematic application of goal setting and planning to help individuals and firms be more productive. The system began in the 1950s and continues to contribute to organizational effectiveness. An MBO program typically involves people setting many objectives for themselves. However, management frequently imposes key organizational objectives upon people. An MBO program usually involves sequential steps, which are cited in the following list. (Note that these steps are related to those in the basic planning model shown in Exhibit 4-1.)

1. *Establishing organizational goals.* Top-level managers set organizational goals to begin the entire MBO process. Quite often these goals are strategic. A group of hospital administrators, for example, might decide upon the strategic goal of improving health care to poor people in the community. After these broad goals are established, managers determine what the organizational units must accomplish to meet these goals.

2. *Establishing unit objectives.* Unit heads then establish objectives for their units. A cascading of objectives takes place as the process moves down the line. Objectives set at lower levels of the firm must be designed to meet the general goals established by top management. Because a general goal usually leaves considerable latitude for setting individual objectives to meet that goal, lower-level managers and operatives provide input. The head of inpatient admissions might decide that working more closely with the county welfare department must be accomplished if the health-care goal cited earlier in this list is to be met. Exhibit 4-6 suggests ways to set effective goals.

3. *Reviewing group members' proposals.* At this point, group members make proposals about how they will contribute to unit objectives. For example, the assistant to the manager of inpatient admissions might agree to set up a task force to work with the welfare department. Each team member is given the opportunity to set objectives in addition to those that meet the strategic goals.

4. *Negotiating or agreeing.* Managers and team members confer together at this stage to either agree on the objectives set by the team members or negotiate further. In the hospital example, one department head might state that he or she wants to reserve ten beds on the ward for the exclusive use of indigent people. The supervisor might welcome the suggestion

---

[27]Susan Kastan, "Policies, Procedures Serve Real Purpose," *Democrat and Chronicle*, December 27, 2009, p. 2E.

EXHIBIT 4-6   Guide to Establishing Goals and Objectives

Effective goals and objectives have certain characteristics in common. Effective goals and objectives

- **Are clear, concise, and unambiguous.** An example of such an objective is "Reduce damaged boxes of printer paper during April 27 to April 30 of this year."
- **Are accurate in terms of the true end state or condition sought.** An accurate objective might state, "The factory will be as neat and organized as the front office after the cleanup is completed."
- **Are achievable by competent workers.** Goals and objectives should not be so high or rigid that the majority of competent team members become frustrated and stressed by attempting to achieve them.
- **Include three difficulty levels: routine, challenging, and innovative.** Most

objectives deal with routine aspects of a job, but they should also challenge workers to loftier goals.

- **Are achieved through team-member participation.** Subordinates should participate actively in setting objectives.
- **Relate to small chunks of accomplishment.** Many objectives should concern small, achievable activities, such as un-cluttering a work area. Accomplishing small objectives is the building block for achieving larger goals.
- **Specify what is going to be accomplished, who is going to accomplish it, when it is going to be accomplished, and how it is going to be accomplished.** Answering the what, who, when, and how questions reduces the chance for misinterpretation.

but point out that only five beds could be spared for such a purpose. They might settle for setting aside seven beds for the needy poor.

5. *Creating action plans to achieve objectives.* After the manager and team members agree upon objectives, action plans must be defined. Sometimes the action plan is self-evident. For example, if your objective as a call-center manager is to hire three new customer service representatives this year, you would begin by consulting with the human resources department.

6. *Reviewing performance.* Performance reviews are conducted at agreed-upon intervals. (A semiannual or annual review is typical.) Persons receive good performance reviews to the extent they attain most of the major objectives. When objectives are not attained, the manager and group member mutually analyze what went wrong. Equally important, they discuss the corrective actions. New objectives are then set for the next review period. Because establishing new objectives is part of an MBO program, the process of management by objectives can continue for the life of an organization.

Summary of Key Points

1 **Summarize a general framework for planning and apply it to enhance your planning skills.**

A generalized planning model can be used for strategic planning, tactical planning, and operational planning. The model consists of seven related and sometimes overlapping elements: defining the present situation; establishing goals and objectives; analyzing the environment in terms of forecasting aids and barriers to goals and objectives; developing action plans; developing budgets; implementing the plan; and controlling the plan. Contingency plans should also be developed.

2 **Describe the nature of business strategy.**

The explanation of business strategy chosen here emphasizes four characteristics. First, strategy involves more than operational effectiveness. Second, strategy rests on unique activities. Third, a sustainable strategic position requires trade-offs. Fourth, fit among organizational activities drives both competitive advantage and sustainability.

3 **Explain how business strategy is developed, including a SWOT analysis.**

Business strategy usually develops from planning but can also stem from a vision. Strategy is influenced by values. Gathering multiple inputs, including the technique of crowdcasting, is important in developing strategy. Strategists must also analyze the realities of the business situation to guard against false assumptions about customers, production capability, and the relevant technology. Strategy development often begins with a SWOT analysis, but first the group must prepare for the analysis. The SWOT analysis considers the strengths, weaknesses, opportunities, and threats in a given situation.

4 **Identify levels of business strategy, competitive forces, and types of business strategies.**

In a diversified business firm, strategy is formulated at the corporate level, the business level, and the functional level. Competitive forces facing the firm include customers affecting pricing, suppliers influencing pricing, substitute products, existing competition, and new market entrants. Types of strategies are as follows: Corporate-level strategies include diversification, strategic alliances, diversification of goods and services, and adherence to core competencies. Business-level strategies include product differentiation, focus, and cost leadership. Functional-level strategies include finding and retaining the best people and moving at high speed.

The right strategy or combination of strategies must be chosen with care. Current thinking suggests that strategic plans and strategy must remain flexible enough to adapt to changing circumstances.

5 **Explain the use of operating plans, policies, procedures, and rules.**

Operating plans provide the details of how strategic plans will be accomplished or implemented. They deal with a shorter time span than do strategic plans. Policies are plans set in the form of general statements that guide thinking and action in decision making. Procedures establish a customary method of handling future activities. A rule sets a specific course of action or conduct and is the simplest type of plan.

6 **Present an overview of management by objectives.**

Management by objectives (MBO) is the most widely used formal system of goal setting, planning, and review. In general, it has six elements: establishing organizational goals, establishing unit objectives, obtaining proposals from group members about their objectives, negotiating or agreeing to proposals, developing action plans, and reviewing performance. After objectives are set, the manager must give feedback to team members on their progress toward reaching the objectives.

Key Terms and Phrases

Strategic planning, 118
Operational planning, 118
Tactical planning, 118
Action plan, 121
Contingency plan, 122
Strategy, 123
Vision, 126

Mission, 126
SWOT analysis, 130
Operating plans, 140
Policies, 140
Procedures, 141
Rule, 141
Management by objectives (MBO), 142

Questions

1. In what way does planning control the future?
2. How can you use the information in this chapter to help you achieve your career and personal goals?
3. Some business owners make a statement such as, "We're too busy to bother with strategy. We have to take care of the present." What might be wrong with their reasoning?
4. Describe the purpose of (a) IBM, and (b) one of your favorite companies.

5. How realistic is Microsoft's mission (or vision)? "To enable people and businesses throughout the world to realize their full potential."
6. Using the information presented in Exhibit 4-6 as a guide, prepare an effective goal for a call center customer-service worker who is responsible for resolving call-in problems about digital cameras.
7. Give an example of how a rule could fit the corporate strategy of cost leadership.

Skill-Building Exercise 4-A: Conducting a SWOT Analysis

In this chapter you have read about the basics of conducting a SWOT analysis. Now gather in small groups to conduct one. Develop a scenario for a SWOT analysis for a group starting a chain of coffee shops, pet-care service centers, or treatment centers for online addictions. Or, conduct a SWOT analysis for reorganizing a company from one that is mostly hierarchical to one that is mostly team based. Keep in mind one of the biggest challenges in doing a SWOT analysis—differentiate between internal strengths and weaknesses and external opportunities and threats. Because most of your data are hypothetical, you will have to rely heavily on your imagination. Group leaders might share the results of the SWOT analysis with the rest of the class.

Skill-Building Exercise 4-B: Developing Business Strategy for Coca Cola

Imagine yourself as part of a strategy development team for the Coca Cola Co. You have gathered information indicating that the worldwide demand for carbonated soft drinks has been declining. More and more consumers are moving toward the purchase of specialty beverages and energy drinks such as Red Bull and flavored water. According to *Beverage Digest*, sales of non-soda drinks in the United States are rising about 14 percent per year, whereas the soda market is slipping about 2 percent. Coca Cola has diversified into a variety of bottled and canned drinks as well as water (for example, Dasani). Yet top management is concerned about Coca Cola becoming a less dominant force in the beverage world. Work as part of small team to recommended a business strategy that will help invigorate the company. Your final strategy statement should be only about 25 words long yet powerful enough to add billions of dollars in annual profit to the Coca Cola Co.

Management Now: Online Skill-Building Exercise: Business Strategy Research

The purpose of this assignment is to find three examples of business strategy by searching the Internet. Choose several companies of interest to you and search for online news articles about their strategies posted within the last sixty days. Examples would include strategies for increasing sales, introducing a new product, or combating the negative impact of a scandal or controversy. Compare the strategic plans described in the articles to the section of this chapter called "Types of Business Strategies." Attempt to match the company strategy to a type of strategy listed in the chapter.

4-A Case Problem

The Blue Ocean Strategy Team

A group of middle managers sat in a comfortable conference room overlooking Lake Superior. All five were impressed by the technology in the room, the furniture, and the refreshments. At 8:30 A.M. the meeting began, and team leader Laura spoke first.

"We all know why we are here. Baxter, our CEO, has fallen in love with Blue Ocean Strategy after reading the book and attending a conference. He thinks our conglomerate is too conventional. We go after markets in which we can compete successfully and earn a decent profit in practically all of our divisions."

Team member Ken asked, "So what's wrong with being successful? What's wrong with turning in good profits quarter after quarter and seeing our stock price rise year by year?"

Her pupils widening, Laura said, "What's wrong is that we are competing in the Red Oceans where the sharks are attacking each other and the other fish. Baxter wants us to compete in market space that does not already exist. We should be creating a new demand and then filling that demand. Baxter wants us to come up with some Blue Ocean ideas that he will then consider."

"I get it," said Carmen. "We should stay in the profitable markets our various divisions already serve. At the same time, we should get into new markets that nobody is serving. How about making battery-operated microwave ovens that will work on the moon? In a few years, we might have loads of private citizens taking trips into outer space."

"Great sense of humor, Carmen," responded Donté, "but the demand might be too small."

Laura then clicked open a PowerPoint slide listing the 58 products and services the company already provides. She told the group, "Baxter says we should forget about these markets already being served. We have to invade new markets, maybe even create a market.

"Whoever thought 40 years ago that people would walk around listening to a device that could store 1,000 tunes? Whoever thought people would pay for a package delivery service that competed with a government-backed postal service? Whoever thought people would want to read books, magazines, and newspapers on a device that looks and feels like the old Etch-A-Sketch toy?"

Bruce commented, "You are saying that as the Blue Ocean Strategy team, we have to identify a multimillion dollar market space that no other company is serving right now. The world already has millions of products and services being offered. How will our humble team identify a market of value that does not already exist?"

Laura said, "I don't know how we will find our Blue Ocean Strategy, but I do know that Baxter wants our report in 30 days. We will meet for four consecutive full-day sessions on Thursdays to get the job done. We probably will be communicating with each other between the meetings also.

"Let's get to work right now."

Discussion Questions

1. What approaches would you recommend the Blue Ocean Strategy team use to identify new market space for the conglomerate?
2. How realistic is it for Baxter to delegate the task of finding a Blue Ocean Strategy to a group of middle managers? Explain your reasoning.
3. What do you think would be the effectiveness of using the Internet to develop a Blue Ocean Strategy for the team? For example, why not go to Ask.com and enter the question, "What would be a new market space with no competition?"

4-B Case Problem

What Should Dell Do Next?

Chris Conroy works at a publisher of scientific journals in Washington, D.C. He first logged on to Dell Inc.'s Web site to browse personal computer offerings online. His laptop was dying quickly and the 31-year-old figured buying a PC on the Internet and getting it shipped home would take too long.

Conroy went to a consumer electronics store, which doesn't stock any Dell computers. There, he checked out several laptops before snapping up a Hewlett-Packard Co. model. "I could get my hands on it right then, without having to worry about it being shipped," he says.

Conroy's experience signals a fundamental problem facing Dell. For years, Dell—famous for selling products directly over the phone and Internet—was a dynamo thanks to bulk sales to corporations, mostly of desktop computers. Its direct-sales business model made the Round Rock, Texas, company a widely admired paragon of efficiency as it under-priced rivals such as H-P and Gateway, Inc. (now part of Acer Computer).

But in the past few years, buying behavior in the PC world has changed. Much of the growth has come from consumer demand rather than the business market on which Dell focused. What's more, people looking for a new home computer are increasingly turning to laptops and netbooks. There Dell is particularly weak (according to some observers): its models lack the pizzazz and features of its rivals. For laptops, especially, consumers prefer to hold and test models in a store; Dell computers are not sold in stores.

Dell still considers consumers an important market. The company has poured money into corporate products such as printers, storage systems, and computer servers. It declined some overtures from retailers to sell its wares in stores. Yet the company has one retail store to display products (but not sell them), and operates more than 170 kiosks in malls around the country, where consumers can see and order a selection of Dell products.

At the same time, rivals such as H-P and Apple Corp. have charged ahead in the consumer PC market. In particular, H-P cut costs to become competitive with Dell, began working more closely with retailers, and redoubled its marketing efforts. As Dell cut prices, H-P invested in consumer-friendly features on its notebooks.

Early in 2006, Dell expanded more slowly than the overall U.S. PC market for the first time in more than a decade. Consumers make up about 30 percent of H-P's sales, in contrast to 15 percent of Dell sales. In 2007, Dell began scrambling to contain the damage. It has overhauled its Web site and streamlined its pricing, and has introduced a new consumer advertising campaign with the tagline "Purely You." One of Dell's acquisitions was Allenware Corp., a maker of high-end videogame PCs. The company has said that deal, which boosted its offerings for consumers, was personally pushed by Michael Dell.

In 2007 Michael Dell returned to his CEO role, taking over after releasing CEO Kevin Rollins. Later that year Dell began selling $700 desktop computers at 3,400 Wal-Mart Stores.

The desktop market began cooling a few years ago as many companies slowed the pace of upgrading their computers. Meanwhile, consumers gravitated to laptops as prices fell and new wireless technology made them more useful at home and on the go. While corporate demand focused on replacing the desktops employees already had, consumers were adding second, third, and fourth computers at home as mom, dad, and the kids listened to digital music, shared digital photos, and played games. By 2010, consumers were buying more laptops than do corporations.

In late 2004, the profitability of Dell's consumer business began deteriorating. Dell told Wall Street its competitors were cutting prices to gain market share at the expense of profit, and said its focus was the high-end PC consumer. But Dell was also participating in a price war, dropping its prices as low as $299 for desktops.

Dell rolled out some new products to woo consumers. In October 2004, it released its first plasma-screen television sets, a digital music player, and a new photo printer with a built-in display to preview photos. But many consumers were wary about buying some of these products sight unseen from a company not known as a consumer electronics maker.

In May 2006, the company pledged $100 million to improve the "customer experience" and hired more than 2,000 new U.S. sales and support staff. It has since added another $50 million to the effort. Internal Dell data show that its efforts are reducing call volumes and call transfers for customers.

In 2008, Dell released a plan for several years ahead. Company representatives outlined several actions to reduce total product costs across all areas, including design, manufacturing and logistics, materials, and operating expenses. Dell was looking to accelerate growth in five areas—global consumer, enterprise, notebooks, small and medium enterprise, and emerging countries—while improving profitability and cash returns. A specific part of the growth strategy was to assist customers with their IT infrastructure. This included delivering, over the Internet, the integration of software-as-a-service applications and remote management tools.

By 2009, Dell had been restructured to intensify its focus on customers. The four customer groupings on the organization chart became consumers, corporations, mid-size and mod-size businesses, and government and educational buyers. Seven of Michael Dell's direct reports were recently appointed. The company had branched into information technology and maintenance services, software, and new hardware categories including smart phones and tablet-style computers.

Rumors had it that Dell was preparing to add social networking features as well as music and video services to Dell.com. Michael Dell wanted to create a profitable consumer business with designs as appealing as those of Apple or HP. Retail sales, including products sold at Wal-Mart stores, reached about $6 billion by 2010. By then, the consumer unit accounted for nearly 25% of Dell's revenue, but only 3% of its profits. The consumer products group therefore decided to hold back on expansion, and focus on cost control.

By 2010, Dell returned to its marketing tactic of discounting in order to win business. Among the beneficiaries of the discounting was the Indiana Office of Technology that operates more than 25,000 Dell desktop computers for state employees.

Dell said that he welcomed the challenge to prove that he could found an exceptional business and then come back in to revive a business that started to struggle. Dell also admitted that he stuck with the innovative idea of selling computers directly (Internet and phone) for too long. He added, however, "We're going to be stronger, faster, and more hyper than we've ever been. It you don't believe, then just sit back and watch."

4-B Case Problem

Discussion Questions

1. Identify several business strategies Dell has used so far, including the strategy that made the company famous.
2. Suggest a plan to Dell executives for continuing its past successes into the future.
3. What is your opinion of the quality of Dell desktops and laptops based upon what you have observed personally and what people in your network have said?

4. How has the transformation of Dell worked out as of the present?

Source: Christopher Lawton, "Consumer Demand and Growth in Laptops Leave Dell Behind," *The Wall Street Journal*, August 30, 2006, pp. A1, A9; Cliff Edwards, "Dell's Do-Over," *Business Week*, October 26, 2009, pp. 036–040; Nick Zubko, "Dell Inc.: Writing a New Program," *Industry Week* (www.industryweek. com), June 26, 2008; Justin Scheck, "Discounting Continues to Haunt Dell as Its Turnaround Struggles," *The Wall Street Journal*, February 19, 2010, p. B1; Daisuke Wakabyashi, "Dell Unit Hunts for Cost Cuts," *The Wall Street Journal*, April 28, 2010, p. B4.

CHAPTER 5

Problem Solving and Decision Making

OBJECTIVES

After studying this chapter and doing the exercises, you should be able to:

1 Differentiate between non-programmed and pro-grammed decisions.

2 Explain the steps involved in making a nonprogrammed decision.

3 Understand the major factors that influence decision making in organizations.

4 Appreciate the value and potential limitations of group decision making.

5 Understand the nature of cre-ativity and how it contributes to managerial work.

6 Describe organizational pro-grams for improving creativity and innovation.

7 Implement several sugges-tions for becoming a more creative problem solver.

When Andrew Schuman bought Hammond's Candies in 2007, the nearly 90-year-old candy company was operating in the red. Schuman, who says he knew nothing about the candy business, soon learned than an assembly-line worker, rather than an execu-tive, had dreamed up the design of the company's popular ribbon snowflake candy.

It was an "aha" moment, he says. "I thought, 'wow, we have a lot of smart people back here, and we're not tapping their knowledge.'" So Schuman then decided to offer a $50 bonus to assembly-line workers who came up with success-ful ideas to cut manufacturing costs.

"They're the ones making and packing the candy, so I thought they probably know how to do things better and more efficiently," says Schumnan, president and director of the Denver, Colorado, company that has about 90 employ-ees. The informal idea program, which is open to all Ham-mond's Candies workers, handed out more than $500 in employee bonuses in its first year of operation. One worker suggested a tweak in a machine gear that reduced workers needed on an assembly line from five to four. Another employee devised a new way to protect candy canes while en route to stores, which resulted in a 4 percent reduction in breakage.

"It's these little tiny things that someone notices that help us in the long run," says Schuman, who adds that his company has become profitable.[1]

The story about the candy company owner illustrates a couple of important points about finding imaginative ideas to move a company forward. Companies should encourage suggestions, create a mechanism for collecting ideas, and offer rewards for useful ideas. This chapter explores how managerial workers solve problems and make decisions individually and in groups. We emphasize the role of creativity and innovation in problem solving because useful new ideas are the lifeblood of most organizations.

problem
A discrepancy between ideal and actual conditions.

A **problem** is a discrepancy between ideal and actual conditions. For example, a hospital might have too many beds unoccupied when the ideal is to have an occupancy rate of 90 percent or greater. A **decision** is choosing among alternatives, such as affiliating with more doctors so as to receive more patient referrals.

decision
A choice among alternatives.

Problem solving and decision making are required to carry out all management functions. For example, when managers control, they must make a series of decisions about how to solve the problem of getting performance back to standard. Decision making can be seen as the heart of management. A distinguishing characteristic of a manager's job is the authority to make decisions.

LEARNING OBJECTIVE ①
Differentiate between nonprogrammed and programmed decisions.

NONPROGRAMMED VERSUS PROGRAMMED DECISIONS

Managerial workers make a variety of decisions. A problem that takes a new and an unfamiliar form or one that is complex or significant calls for a **nonprogrammed decision**. A complex problem contains many elements. Significant problems affect an important aspect of an organization, such as the introduction of a new service. Virtually all strategic decisions are nonprogrammed. A well-planned and highly structured organization reduces the number of nonprogrammed decisions. It does so by formulating policies to help managers know what to do when faced with a problem. Many small firms do not offer much guidance about decision making.

nonprogrammed decision
A decision that is difficult because of its complexity and the fact that the person faces it infrequently.

---

[1]Teri Evans, "Entrepreneurs Seek to Elicit Workers' Ideas," *The Wall Street Journal*, December 22, 2009, p. B7.

Within the category of nonprogrammed decisions, there are wide variations in complexity.[2] A complex nonprogrammed decision for a Harley-Davidson executive would be whether to outsource the manufacture of its heavy bikes to South Korea. It would be necessary to consider many issues, including the reputation Harley has as an American icon and the relative costs of labor and shipping. A less complex nonprogrammed decision would be whether to enlarge a manufacturing plant in Milwaukee. A complex decision is more demanding than a less complex decision, just as studying some subjects may be more difficult than studying others.

Programmed decisions are repetitive, or routine, and made according to a specific procedure. Procedures specify how to handle these routine, uncomplicated decisions. Here is an example: A person who earns $26,000 per year applies to rent a two-bedroom apartment. The manager refuses the application on the basis of an established rule that prohibits families with annual incomes of $39,000 or less from renting in the building.

Under ideal circumstances, top-level management concerns itself almost exclusively with nonroutine decisions; lower-level management handles all routine decisions. In reality, executives do make many small, programmed decisions in addition to nonprogrammed decisions. Some executives sign expense account vouchers and answer routine e-mail inquiries. Middle managers generally make both routine and nonroutine decisions. First-level managers make more routine decisions. A well-managed organization encourages all managers to delegate as many nonprogrammed decisions as possible.

The accompanying Management in Action lists some of the most important decisions ever made by managers in business, all of which were nonprogrammed.

PLAY VIDEO

Go to www.cengage. com/management/ dubrin and view the video for Chapter 5. What can you learn about this company's approach to problem solving and decision making from this video? What guiding principles do they use?

programmed decision

A decision that is repetitive, or routine, and made according to a specific procedure.

MANAGEMENT IN ACTION

Thirteen of the Greatest Management Decisions Ever Made

Many people consider good decision making to be the essence of management. A business writer for *Management Review* asked experts for their nominations of the 75 greatest decisions ever made. All these decisions were successful and all had a major impact. Here we list 11 of these decisions related directly to business (rather than to government or religion). For example, we excluded Queen Isabella's decision to sponsor Christopher Columbus's voyage to the new world in 1492. Each decision's rank among 75 is listed in brackets. At the end of the list, we add two of 20 decisions that made history, according to *Fortune*.

(continued)

---

[2]Donald C. Hambrick, Sydney Finkelstein, and Ann C. Mooney, "Executive Job Demands: New Insights for Explaining Strategic Decisions and Leader Behaviors," *Academy of Management Review*, July 2005, pp. 472–491.

MANAGEMENT IN ACTION (Continued)

1. **Walt Disney** listened to his wife and named his cartoon mouse Mickey instead of Mortimer. Entertainment was never the same after Mickey and Minnie debuted in "Steamboat Willie" in 1928. (1)
2. **Frank McNamara**, in 1950, found himself in a restaurant without money. This prompted him to come up with the idea of the Diners Club Card. This first credit card changed the nature of buying and selling throughout the world. (5)
3. **Thomas Watson Jr.**, of IBM, decided in 1962 to develop the System/360 computer, at a cost of $5 billion. Although IBM's market research suggested it would sell only two units worldwide, the result was the first mainframe computer. (7)
4. Robert **Woodruff** was president of Coca-Cola during World War II when he committed to selling Coke to members of the armed services for a nickel a bottle, starting around 1941. The decision led to enormous customer loyalty, and returning soldiers influenced family members and friends to buy Coca-Cola. (12)
5. **Jean Nidetch**, in 1961, was put on a diet in an obesity clinic in New York City. She invited six dieting friends to meet in her Queens apartment every week. The decision created Weight Watchers and the weight-loss industry. (20)
6. **Bill Gates**, in 1981, decided to license MS/DOS to IBM; IBM did not require control of the license for all non-IBM PCs. The decision laid the foundation for Microsoft's huge success and a downturn in IBM's prestige and prominence. (21)
7. A **Hewlett-Packard** engineer discovered in 1979 that heating metal in a specific way caused it to splatter. The management decision to exploit this discovery launched the ink-jet printer business and laid the groundwork for more than $6 billion in revenue for HP. (25)
8. **Sears, Roebuck and Co.**, in 1905, decided to open its Chicago mail-order plant. The Sears catalog made goods available to an entirely new customer base and provided a model for mass production (40).
9. **Ray Kroc** liked the McDonald brothers' stand that sold hamburgers, french fries, and milk shakes so much that he decided to open his own franchised restaurant in 1955 and form McDonald's Corp. Kroc soon created a giant global company and a vast market for fast food. (58)
10. **Procter & Gamble**, in 1931, introduced its brand management system, which showcased brands and provided a blueprint that management has followed ever since. (62)
11. **Michael Dell** made the decision in 1986 to sell PCs direct and build them to order. Others in the industry soon imitated Dell Computer's strategy. (73)
12. **Citibank** chairman Walter Wriston gave top-level executive John Reed the go-ahead to invest $100 million in automatic teller machines (ATMs). During a major snow storm in New York City in 1978, customers started making extensive use of these new machines that give money.
13. **King Gillette**, at his boss's urging, developed a disposable razor blade and in 1901 patented the first razor with a disposable blade. The U.S. Army gave 3.5 million Gillette razors and 32 million blades to soldiers during World War I, capturing a generation of consumers and creating the beginnings of America's throwaway culture.

Source: Stuart Crainer, "The 75 Greatest Management Decisions Ever Made," *Management Review*, November 1998, pp. 16–24; Kate Bonamici and Ellen Florian Kratz, "20 That Made History," *Fortune*, June 27, 2005, pp. 62, 80.

LEARNING
OBJECTIVE **2**
Explain the steps
involved in making
a nonprogrammed
decision.

STEPS IN PROBLEM SOLVING AND DECISION MAKING

Learning how to solve problems and make decisions properly is vitally important. Thomas H. Davenport, a professor of information technology at Babson College, observes that many managers do not pay careful enough attention to the systematic process of decision making. That may account for dramatically poor calls in recent years, such as the decision to invest in and convert into securities subprime (high-risk) mortgage loans.[3] The basic purpose of making a decision is to solve a problem, but you must analyze the problem prior to making the decision. As shown in Exhibit 5-1, and described next, problem solving and decision making can be divided into many steps.

EXHIBIT 5-1   Steps in Problem Solving and Decision Making

Managers who are thorough in their decision making will often proceed through the steps shown here.

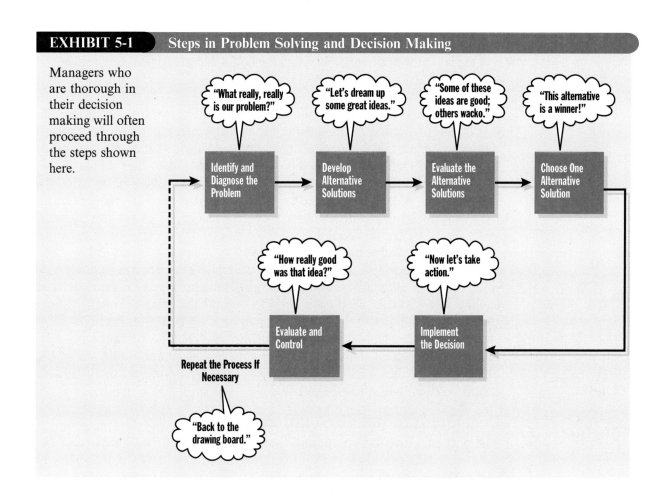

---

[3]Thomas H. Davenport, "Make Better Decisions," *Harvard Business Review*, November 2009, pp. 117–123.

Identify and Diagnose the Problem

Problem solving and decision making begin with the awareness that a problem exists. In other words, the first step in problem solving and decision making is to identify a gap between desired and actual conditions. Being attentive to the environment helps the manager identify problems, such as noticing that the department is receiving frequent criticism from outsiders and insiders. Sometimes a problem is imposed on a manager, such as when customer complaints increase. At other times, he or she must search actively for a worthwhile problem or opportunity. For example, a sales manager might actively pursue a problem by conducting an audit to find out why former customers stopped buying from the company.

A thorough diagnosis of the problem is important because the real problem may be different from the one that is suggested by a first look. The ability to think critically helps a person get at the real problem. To diagnose a problem properly, you must clarify its true nature. A frequently cited example is that a manager might attempt to reduce turnover by increasing wages. The manager assumes that workers would stay with the company longer if their wages were higher. Yet the real problem is inflexible working hours that are triggering turnover.

Develop Alternative Solutions

The second step in decision making is to generate alternative solutions. In this intellectually freewheeling aspect of decision making, all kinds of possibilities are explored, even some that seem unrealistic. Often the difference between good and mediocre decision makers is that the former do not accept the first alternative they think of. Instead, they keep digging until they find the best solution. When Jeff Bezos, the founder of Amazon.com, was searching for a way to commercialize the Internet, he made a list of the top 20 mail-order products. He then looked for where he could create the most value for customers and finally decided to sell books.[4]

Often the problem solver will find a creative alternative solution. At other times, a standard solution will work adequately. For example, one small-business owner needing money to expand the business might choose the standard alternative of borrowing from a bank or finance company. Another small-business owner might attempt the creative alternative of raising money by selling shares of the company to friends and family members. (This option creates a risk. If the company fails, the business owner will have created conflict with these people.)

Evaluate Alternative Solutions

The next step involves comparing the relative value of the alternatives. The problem solver examines the pros and cons and considers the feasibility of each. Some alternatives may appear attractive, but implementing them would be impossible or counterproductive.

---

[4]Joshua Quittner, "An Eye on the Future: Jeff Bezos Merely Wants Amazon.com to Be Earth's Biggest Seller of Everything," *Time*, December 27, 1999, p. 57.

Comparing relative value often means performing a cost and savings analysis of each alternative. Alternatives that cost much more than they save are infeasible. The possible outcome of an alternative should be part of the analysis. If an unsatisfactory outcome is almost a certainty, the alternative should be rejected. For example, if a firm is faced with low profits, one alternative would be to cut pay by 20 percent. The outcome of this alternative would be to lower morale drastically and create high turnover, so a firm should not implement that alternative. High employee turnover is so expensive that it would override the cost savings.

Choose One Alternative Solution

The process of weighing the alternatives must stop at some point. You cannot solve a problem unless you choose one of the alternatives—that is, make a decision. Several factors influence the choice. A major factor is the goal the decision should achieve. The goals sought for in making the decision are also referred to as the *decision criteria*. The alternative chosen should be the one that appears to come closest to achieving it. If two alternatives appear almost equally good after considerable deliberation, it might be helpful to seek the opinion of one more person to decide which alternative is slightly better.

Despite a careful evaluation of alternatives, ambiguity remains in most decisions. The decisions faced by managers are often complex, and the factors involved in them are often unclear. Even when quantitative evidence strongly supports a particular alternative, the decision maker may be uncertain. Human resource decisions are often the most ambiguous because making precise predictions about human behavior is so difficult. Deciding which person to hire from a list of several strong candidates is always a challenge.

Implement the Decision

Converting a decision into action is the next major step. Until a decision is implemented, it is not really a decision at all. A fruitful way of evaluating the merit of a decision is to observe its implementation. A decision is seldom good if people resist its implementation or if it is too cumbersome to implement. Suppose a firm tries to boost productivity by decreasing the time allotted for lunch or coffee breaks. If employees resist the decision by eating while working and then taking the allotted lunch break, productivity will decrease. Implementation problems indicate that the decision to boost productivity by decreasing break time would be a poor one.

Another perspective on implementation is that it represents execution, or putting plans into action. Implementation therefore involves focusing on the operations of a company or business unit. When Mark Hurd was appointed as the new CEO of Hewlett-Packard several years ago, he was praised for his decision to focus on execution rather than formulating new visions for the company. As part of execution, he focused on cost cutting and efficiency.[5]

---

[5]Adam Lashinsky, "Take a Look at HP," *Fortune*, June 13, 2005, p. 117.

His predecessor, Carly Fiorina, was often accused of focusing too much on visions and not enough on execution or business operations.

Evaluate and Control

The final step in the decision-making framework is to investigate how effectively the chosen alternative solved the problem. Controlling means ensuring that the results the decision obtained are the ones set forth during the problem-identification step. Evaluating and controlling your decisions will help you improve your decision-making skills. You can learn important lessons by comparing what actually happened with what you thought would happen. You can learn what you could have improved or done differently and use this information the next time you face a similar decision.

LEARNING
OBJECTIVE **3**
Understand the major factors that influence decision making in organizations.

bounded rationality
The observation that people's limited mental abilities, combined with external influences over which they have little or no control, prevent them from making entirely rational decisions.

BOUNDED RATIONALITY AND INFLUENCES ON DECISION MAKING

Because so many factors influence the decision maker, decision making is usually not entirely rational. Awareness of this fact stems from the research of psychologist and economist Herbert A. Simon. He proposed that bounds (or limits) to rationality are present in decision making. These bounds are the limitations of the human, particularly related to the processing and recall of information.[6] **Bounded rationality** means that people's finite (somewhat limited) mental abilities, combined with external influences over which they have little or no control, prevent them from making entirely rational decisions.

In more recent years, the irrational side of decision making became incorporated into a branch of behavioral economics called *neuroeconomics*. Behavioral economics emphasizes that people are not entirely rational decision makers. For example, many try hard to avoid losing money in the stock market instead of focusing on increasing profits. An individual might hang on to a losing stock or mutual fund too long, and a manager might hang on to a losing product for too long.[7]

Some people have superstitions about numbers. For example, a Las Vegas casino that caters to Hong Kong high-stakes gamblers skips floors 40 to 59. At the same time an affluent condominium apartment building in Hong Kong omits the 13th floor to cater to Western tastes.[8] Have you noticed that some hotels do not have a floor labeled 13? The developer who

---

[6]Herbert A. Simon, "Rational Choice and the Structure of the Environment," *Psychological Review*, 63 (1956), pp. 129–138.

[7]"Neuroeconomics," *Harvard Magazine* (http://www.harvardmagazine.com), March–April 2006, pp. 54–55; Peter Coy, "Why Logic Often Takes a Backseat: The Study of Neuroeconomics May Topple the Notion of Rational Decision-Making," *Business Week*, March 28, 2005, pp. 94–95.

[8]Carl Bialik, "Number Crushing: When Figures Get Personal," *The Wall Street Journal*, October 28, 2009, p. A19.

avoids assigning number 13 to a floor is being rational about catering to the irrationality of guests and potential guests.

Research and opinion on bounded rationality emphasize that humans use problem-solving strategies that are reasonably rapid, reasonably accurate, and in keeping with the quantity and type of information available.[9] In short, people making decisions do the best with what they have.

Often decision makers do not have the time or resources to wait for the best possible solution. Instead, they search for **satisficing decisions**, those that suffice in providing a minimum standard of satisfaction. Such decisions are adequate, acceptable, or passable. Many decision makers stop their search for alternatives when they find a satisficing one. Successful managers recognize that it is difficult to obtain every possible fact before making a decision. In the words of Lawrence Weinbach, the former top executive at Unisys and now a member of a capital management firm, "If we want to be leaders, we're going to have to make decisions with maybe 75 percent of the facts. If you wait for 95 percent, you are going to be a follower."[10]

Affected by bounded rationality, decision makers often use simplified strategies known as **heuristics**. A heuristic becomes a rule of thumb in decision making, such as the policy to reject a job applicant who does not smile during the first three minutes of the job interview. A widely used investing heuristic is as follows: The percentage of your portfolio invested in equities should equal 100 minus your age; the rest should be in fixed-income investments including cash. A 25-year-old investor would have a portfolio consisting of 25 percent interest-bearing securities, such as bonds, and 75 percent stocks. Heuristics help the decision maker cope with masses of information, but oversimplification can lead to inaccurate or irrational decision making.

A host of influences on the decision-making process contribute to bounded rationality. We describe nine such influences, as outlined in Exhibit 5-2.

Intuition

Effective decision makers do not rely on analytical and methodological techniques alone. They also use their hunches and intuition. **Intuition** is an experience-based way of knowing or reasoning in which weighing and balancing evidence are done unconsciously and automatically. Intuition is also a way of arriving at a conclusion without using the step-by-step logical process. Intuition can be based mostly on experience or mostly on feeling. The fact that experience contributes to intuition means that decision makers can become more intuitive by solving many difficult problems because accumulated facts are an asset to intuition. It also means that decision makers

satisficing decision
A decision that meets the minimum standards of satisfaction.

heuristics
A rule of thumb used in decision making.

intuition
An experience-based way of knowing or reasoning in which weighing and balancing evidence are done unconsciously and automatically.

---

[9]Gerd Gigerenzer and Reinhard Selten (eds.), *Bounded Rationality: The Adaptive Toolbox* (Cambridge, MA: MIT Press, 2001).

[10]Quoted in Jeffrey E. Garten, *The Mind of the C.E.O.* (Cambridge, MA: Perseus Publishing, 2001).

EXHIBIT 5-2   Factors Influencing Decision Making

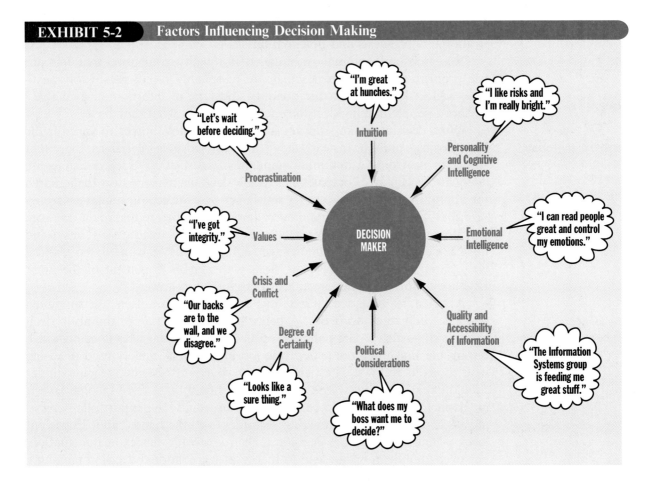

develop intuition when they perform the same work for a relatively long period of time.[11]

Intuition helps point the executive in the right direction, such as when sizing up the overall merits of the company to be acquired. Major decisions usually begin with intuition. As Henry Ford said, "If I asked consumers what they wanted, they would have told me to build a faster horse and buggy."

Personality and Cognitive Intelligence

The personality and cognitive intelligence of the decision maker influence his or her ability to find effective solutions. A particularly relevant personality dimension is a person's propensity for taking risks. A cautious, conservative person typically opts for a low-risk solution. An extremely cautious person may avoid making major decisions for fear of being wrong. Organizational pressures can influence a person's propensity for risk taking. In addition to

---

[11]Eugene Sadler-Smith and Erella Shefy, "The Intuitive Executive: Understanding and Applying 'Gut Feel' in Decision Making," *The Academy of Management Executive*, November 2004, pp. 76–91; Erik Dan and Michael G. Pratt, "Exploring Intuition and Its Role in Managerial Decision Making," *Academy of Management Review*, January 2007, pp. 33–35.

decisiveness

The extent to which a person makes up his or her mind promptly and prudently.

being related to risk taking, cautiousness and conservatism influence **decisiveness**, the extent to which a person makes up his or her mind promptly and prudently. Good decision makers, by definition, are decisive. Take the quiz presented in Exhibit 5-3 to examine your degree of decisiveness.

Perfectionism exerts a notable impact on decision making. People who seek the perfect solution to a problem are usually indecisive because they hesitate to accept the fact that a particular alternative is good enough. Optimism versus pessimism is another relevant personality dimension. Optimists are more likely to find solutions than are pessimists. Pessimists are more likely to give up searching, because they perceive situations as being hopeless.

Cognitive (or traditional) intelligence carries a profound influence on decision-making effectiveness. Today psychologists recognize other types of intelligence such as imagination, adaptability, and practical intelligence. In general, intelligent and well-educated people are more likely to identify problems and make sound decisions than are those who have less intelligence and education. A notable exception applies, however. Some intelligent, well-educated people have such a fondness for collecting facts and analyzing them that they suffer from "analysis paralysis." One plant manager put it this way: "I'll never hire a genius again. They dazzle you with facts, figures,

---

EXHIBIT 5-3   How Decisive Are You?

Answer the following questions by placing a check in the appropriate space: N = never; R = rarely; 0c = occasionally; 0f = often.

	N	R	0c	0f
1. Do you let the opinions of others influence your decisions?	—	—	—	—
2. Do you procrastinate when it's time to make a decision?	—	—	—	—
3. Do you let others make your decisions for you?	—	—	—	—
4. Have you missed out on an opportunity because you couldn't make a decision?	—	—	—	—
5. After reaching a decision do you have second thoughts?	—	—	—	—
6. Did you hesitate while answering these questions?	—	—	—	—

Scoring and interpretation: Score one point for each "often" response, two points for each "occasionally," three points for each "rarely," and four points for each "never."

19–24   You are very decisive and probably have no problem assuming responsibility for the choices you make.

13–18   Decision making is difficult for you. You need to work at being more decisive.

12 or lower   You are going to have a big problem unless you learn to overcome your timidity. When a decision has to be made, face up to it and do it!

Source: Adapted from Roger Fritz, "A Systematic Approach to Problem Solving and Decision Making," *Supervisory Management*, March 1993, p. 4. Reprinted with permission of the American Management Association.

and computer graphics. But when they get through with their analysis, they still haven't solved the problem."

It is helpful to size up the environment in terms of how much analysis is required before making a decision. It is good to avoid being both impulsive (jumping too quickly to a decision) and indecisive because of over-analysis.

A person can typically make best use of cognitive intelligence when he or she is well rested, or at least not highly fatigued. That is one reason why airlines have strict regulations about the amount of sleep pilots need before flying. An analysis of studies and theory concluded that sleep-deprived executive teams working late at night are likely to solve problems poorly and make inaccurate decisions.[12] Unfortunately, many decisions are made with limited sleep during crisis conditions.

Emotional Intelligence

emotional intelligence

The ability to connect with people and understand their emotions.

How effective you are in managing your feelings and reading other people can affect the quality of your decision making. For example, if you cannot control your anger, you are likely to make decisions motivated by retaliation, hostility, and revenge. An example would be shouting and swearing at your team leader because of a work assignment you received. **Emotional intelligence** refers to qualities such as understanding one's own feelings, empathy for others, and the regulation of emotions to enhance living. This type of intelligence generally affects the ability to connect with people and understand their emotions. If you cannot read the emotions of others, you are liable to make bad decisions such as pushing your boss too hard to grant a request. Emotional intelligence contains four key factors, all of which can influence the quality of our decisions:[13]

1. *Self-awareness.* The ability to understand your own emotions is the most essential of the four emotional intelligence competencies. Having high self-awareness allows people to know their strengths and limitations and have high self-esteem. (Effective managers seek feedback to see how well their actions are received by others. A manager with good self-awareness would recognize whether he or she was liked and exerting the right amount of pressure on people.)

2. *Self-management.* The factor is the ability to control one's emotions and act with honesty and integrity in a consistent and adaptable manner. The right degree of self-management helps prevent a person from throwing temper tantrums when activities do not go as planned. Effective workers do not let their occasional bad moods ruin their day. (A manager with high self-management skills would not suddenly decide to fire a group member because of one difference of opinion.)

---

[12]Christopher M. Barnes and John R. Hollenbeck, "Sleep Deprivation and Decision-Making Teams: Burning the Midnight Oil, or Playing with Fire?" *Academy of Management Review*, January 2009, pp. 56–66.

[13]Daniel Goleman, Richard Boyatzis, and Annie McKee, "Primal Leadership: The Hidden Driver of Great Performance," *Harvard Business Review*, December 2001, pp. 42–51.

3. *Social awareness*. This competency includes having empathy for others and having intuition about organizational problems. Socially aware workers go beyond sensing the emotions of others by showing that they care. (A team leader with social awareness, or empathy, would be able to assess whether a team member had enough enthusiasm for a project before assigning it.)

4. *Relationship management*. This competency includes the interpersonal skills of clear and convincing communication, the ability to disarm conflicts, and the ability to build strong personal bonds. Effective individuals use relationship management skills to spread their enthusiasm and solve disagreements, often with kindness and humor. (A manager with good relationship management skills would not burn bridges and would continue to enlarge his or her network of people to win support when support is needed.)

Closely related to the influence of emotional intelligence on decision making is emotional tagging, the process by which emotional information attaches to the thoughts and experiences stored in our memories.[14] For example, a manager might remember how labor-saving machinery resulted in job loss for her father when she was a teenager. As an executive in later life, this woman might resist using a voice-recognition system for routine customer service because it would mean job loss for many customer service representatives. An emotional attachment can also work in a positive direction.[15] A manager may have had a Latina nanny as a young child. Later in life he is positively predisposed toward Latinas and quick to promote a Mexican-American woman to a supervisory position. (If the woman in question has appropriate qualifications for the position, the tagging is helpful to the organization.)

Quality and Accessibility of Information

Reaching an effective decision usually requires high-quality, valid information. The ability to supply managers with high-quality information forms the major justification for information systems. Part of having quality information is being able to base decisions upon solid data. The discussion in Chapter 1 about evidence-based management emphasizes collecting information before making a decision, and we return to this topic in Chapter 6 and talk about quantitative techniques for planning and decision making.

Accessibility may be even more important than quality in determining which information is used or not used. Sometimes it takes so much time and effort to search for quality information that the manager relies on lower-quality information that is close at hand. A frequent accessibility problem is to rely on information from the Internet because it is easy to access, without stopping to investigate the date or the source of the information. Quite often the information comes from the blog of an uninformed person.

---

[14]Andrew Campbell, Jo Whitehead, and Sydney Finkelstein, "Why Good Leaders Make Bad Decisions," *Harvard Business Review*, February 2009, p. 63.

[15]Finkelstein, Whitehead, and Campbell, "How Inappropriate Attachments Can Drive Lead Leaders to Make Bad Decisions," *Organizational Dynamics*, April–June 2009, pp. 83–92.

anchoring

In the decision-making process, placing too much value on the first information received and ignoring later information.

Closely related to quality and accessibility of information is the tendency to be influenced by the first information we receive when attempting to solve a problem or make a decision. **Anchoring** occurs during decision making when the mind gives too much weight to the first information it receives. Initial impressions and estimates hold back, or anchor, later thoughts and judgments.[16] The manager who uses old or inaccurate information found on the Internet might be overly influenced by that information. Having been received first, the anchored information becomes the standard against which to judge other information. Anchoring can lead to wasting useful information received after the first information.

Political Considerations

Under ideal circumstances, managers make organizational decisions on the basis of the objective merits of competing alternatives. In reality, many decisions are based on political considerations such as favoritism, alliances, or the desire of the decision maker to stay in favor with people who wield power.

Political factors sometimes influence which data are given serious consideration in evaluating alternatives. The decision maker may select data that support the position of an influential person whom he or she is trying to please. For instance, one financial analyst, asked to investigate the cost-effectiveness of the firm owning a corporate jet, gave considerable weight to the "facts" supplied by a manufacturer of corporate jets. This information allowed her to justify the expense of purchasing the plane—the decision the CEO favored.

The *status quo trap* ties decisions to political factors. Failure to challenge the status quo often stems from worry that being critical will invite criticism from key people. Breaking away from the status quo requires action, and when we take action, we take responsibility, thus opening ourselves up to criticism.[17] A barrier many sales representatives face in selling against a dominant product in the industry results from managers' fear of being criticized if the new product were to fail. As one system administrator said, "You can never get fired for buying Cisco." (The implication is that if the manager bought Internet equipment from a smaller competitor, he would risk being reprimanded.)

Revenge is both a political and an emotional factor in decision making.[18] A person who is annoyed or irritated by another person might make a decision against that person's proposition, just to obtain revenge. Imagine that Tanya told Derek his suggestion for lowering energy costs was useless. Later, during a meeting, Tanya presents her ideas for energy conservation. Although Derek thinks the idea has merit, he points to the shortcomings in Tanya's proposal for saving energy.

A person with professional integrity arrives at what he or she thinks is the best decision and then makes a diligent attempt to convince management

---

[16]John S. Hammond, Ralph L. Keeney, and Howard Raffia, "The Hidden Traps in Decision Making," *Harvard Business Review*, September–October 1998, p. 48.

[17]Hammond, Keeney, and Raffia, "The Hidden Traps," pp. 48–49.

[18]Dan Ariely, "The End of Rational Economics," *Harvard Business Review*, July–August 2009, pp. 78–89.

of the objective merits of that solution. The person with integrity is aware of not alienating people in power, yet supports what he or she thinks is the best decision.

Degree of Certainty

The more certain a decision maker is of the outcome of a decision, the more calmly and confidently the person will make the decision. Degree of certainty is divided into three categories: certainty, risk, and uncertainty. A condition of certainty exists when the facts are well known and the outcome can be predicted accurately. A retail store manager might predict with certainty that more hours of operation will lead to more sales.

A condition of risk exists when a decision must be made based on incomplete, but accurate, factual information. Effective managers often accept a condition of risk. A calculated risk is one in which the potential return is well worth the cost that will be incurred if the effort fails. When Steve Jobs at Apple Inc. spearheaded the development of the iPod for downloading and playing music, many insiders thought the company was taking a risk with dwindling funds. However, the iPod sold well beyond even Jobs's expectations, vindicating the risky decision. Part of the factual information here was that MP3 players were an established part of the culture, along with industry sales figures for the MP3.

Crisis and Conflict

In a crisis, many decision makers panic. They become less rational and more emotional than they would be in a calm environment. Decision makers who are adversely affected by crisis perceive it to be a stressful event. They concentrate poorly, use poor judgment, and think impulsively. Under crisis, some managers do not bother dealing with differences of opinion because they are under so much pressure. A smaller number of managers perceive a crisis as an exciting challenge that energizes them toward their best level of problem solving and decision making.

A recommendation for becoming more adept at making decisions under crisis conditions is to anticipate crises. Visualize ahead of time how you will react to the situation. Visualization serves somewhat as a rehearsal for the real event. A hospital administrator might think to himself or herself, "Here is what I would do if a patient were to die during routine surgery, and the media grabed hold of the story."

Conflict relates to crisis because both can be an emotional experience. When conflict is not overwhelming and is directed at real issues, not personalities, it can be an asset to decision making. When opposing sides express different points of view, problems can be solved more thoroughly, which leads to better decisions.

Values of the Decision Maker

Ultimately, all decisions are based on values. A manager who places a high value on the personal welfare of employees tries to avoid alternatives that create hardship for workers and implements decisions in ways that lessen turmoil. Another value that significantly influences decision making is the pursuit of excellence. A manager who embraces the pursuit of excellence will search for the high-quality alternative solution.

Attempting to preserve the status quo mentioned earlier as a political factor is also a value. If you value the status quo too highly, you may fail to make a decision that could bring about major improvements. For example, a supermarket executive might not want to bother shifting part of the company's marketing efforts to social networking media. As a result, other supermarkets who have a strong presence on Facebook and comparable Web sites gain a few percentage points in market share.

Procrastination

procrastinate
To delay in taking action without a valid reason.

Many people are poor decision makers because they **procrastinate**, or delay taking action without a valid reason. Procrastination results in indecisiveness and inaction and is a major cause of self-defeating behavior. Procrastination is a deeply ingrained behavior pattern; it may be based on concerns about being judged negatively. For example, if the oil company manager delays making a decision about drilling, he or she cannot be accused of having wasted resources on an oil source of limited value.

Although too much procrastination interferes with effective decision making, rapid decision making is not always the most effective. When too much emphasis is placed on speed, financial data become less reliable, customer service might be compromised, and productivity suffers. Critical information may be withheld, alternative solutions are dismissed too readily, and risks are ignored. Good decision makers recognize the balance between procrastination and impulsiveness. We will return to the problem of procrastination in Chapter 17.

Decision-Making Styles

decision-making style
A manager's typical pattern of making decisions.

The various factors that influence the quality of decision making also contribute to a manager's typical pattern of making decisions, or **decision-making style**. For example, a manager who relies heavily on intuition will tend to make decisions quickly without agonizing over data. A manager with procrastination tendencies will ponder over as much information as possible and consult many people before reaching a decision. Kenneth R. Brousseau, the CEO of Decision Dynamics, and his colleagues have studied executive decision-making styles using a database of 120,000 people.

According to the Decision Dynamics research, decision styles differ in two fundamental ways: how information is used and how options are created. In terms of information, some managers want to pore over reams of information before making a decision. The opposite approach is to come to a decision as soon as enough information is available. (This approach is referred to as *satisficing*, as described earlier.) In terms of creating options, *single focus* decision makers are committed to taking one course of action.

In contrast, their *multifocused* counterparts generate lists of possible options and may pursue multiple courses. Combining the dimensions of using information and creating options result in four decision-making styles, as follows:[19]

1. *Decisive (one option, less information)*. Decisive decision makers value action, speed, efficiency, and consistency. Once a plan is in place they stick with it and move on to the next decision. Time is precious to this type of decision maker, and he or she fits well into a role such as brand for Procter & Gamble. For example, "Let's run a special promotion on Tide next month. Get the word out this afternoon."

2. *Flexible (many options, less information)*. The flexible style also focuses on speed, yet adaptability is emphasized. Flexible decision makers gather just enough data to choose a line of attack and quickly change course if needed. A marketing manager for Jeep with a flexible style might say, "Let's try a dealer incentive for the Dodge Nitro (sold by Jeep dealers). I've seen that work with the Cherokee. If that doesn't work, let's quickly switch to zero percent financing."

3. *Hierarchic (one option, more information)*. People using the hierarchic style analyze a great deal of information and seek input from others. They expect a decision to be final and relatively permanent. An information technology manager might say, "We have studied the problem for several months and have received inputs from hundreds of intelligent users. Our single source of new desktops and laptops will be Dell Computer."

4. *Integrative (many options, more information)*. Instead of looking for a single best solution, managers using the integrative style frame problems broadly. The integrative style uses input from many sources and makes decisions involving multiple courses of action. The decision may be modified in the future as circumstances change. An executive at Target might say, "For now, we will increase the proportion of full-time workers based on the opinions of several hundred store managers. However, we will keep our eyes on the bottom line and employee morale to see how well this shift in the proportion of full-time staff works."

Be aware that these decision-making styles exist. Reflect on your personal style and solicit feedback from others. You might recognize, for example, that you tend to collect too much data before making a decision. You might be like the potential homebuyer who collects so much information before making a purchase offer that the property is sold to someone else.

---

[19]Kenneth R. Brousseau, Michael J. Driver, Gary Hourihan, and Rikard Larsson, "The Seasoned Executive's Decision-Making Style," *Harvard Business Review*, February 2006, pp. 110–121.

Appreciate the value and potential limitations of group decision making.

group decisions
The process of several people contributing to a final decision.

GROUP PROBLEM SOLVING AND DECISION MAKING

We have described how individuals go about solving problems and making decisions. However, groups make most major decisions in organizations. **Group decisions** result when several people contribute to a final decision. Because so much emphasis has been placed on teams and participative decision making, an increasing number of decisions are made by groups rather than individuals. Group decision making is often used in complex and important situations such as developing a new product or recommending employees with the best potential for promotion. We will examine the advantages and disadvantages of group decision making, describe when it is useful, present a general problem-solving method for groups, and follow that with a specific technique.

Advantages and Disadvantages of Group Decision Making

Group decision making offers several advantages. First, the quality of the decision might be higher because of the combined wisdom of group members. A second benefit is a by-product of the first. Group members evaluate each other's thinking, so major errors are likely to be avoided. The marketing vice president of a company that sells microwave ovens, toasters, and coffee pots decided the company should sell its small appliances sell direct through e-commerce. Before asking others to begin implementing the decision, the executive brought up the matter for group discussion. A sales manager in the group pointed out that direct selling would enrage their dealers, thus damaging the vast majority of their sales. The marketing vice president decided she would back off on direct marketing until a new product was developed that would not be sold through dealers. The dealers, however, would be free to sell the products online.

Third, group decision making is helpful in gaining acceptance and commitment. People who participate in making a decision will often be more committed to the implementation than if they had not been consulted. Fourth, groups can help people overcome blocks in their thinking, leading to more creative solutions to problems.

Group decision making also has some notable disadvantages. The group approach consumes considerable time and may result in compromises that do not really solve the problem. An intelligent individual might have the best solution to the problem; relying on his or her judgment could save time.

The explosion of the space shuttle *Columbia* in 2003 presents a serious and much publicized example of the disadvantages of group decision making. Sixteen months prior to the explosion of the spaceship, the General Accounting Office concluded that the downsizing of the NASA's workforce had left it ill-equipped to manage its safety upgrade program for the shuttle. Furthermore, a Rand report released in 2002 said that "Decaying infrastructure and shuttle component obsolescence are significant contributions to a future declining safety posture." Equally significant, NASA later released a batch of e-mails revealing that dozens of NASA workers at the Johnson Space Center were aware that engineers were concerned about a potentially catastrophic re-entry for *Columbia*. A NASA official later said it would have been impossible for him to be aware of all the conversations among NASA's 18,000 employees. Furthermore, the groups of NASA officials approved the launch of *Columbia* despite all the safety warnings.[20]

groupthink

A psychological drive for consensus at any cost.

Flawed decisions of the type just described have generally been attributed to **groupthink**, a psychological drive for consensus at any cost. Groupthink makes group members lose their ability to evaluate bad ideas critically. Glen Whyte believes that many instances of groupthink are caused by decision makers who see themselves as choosing between inevitable losses. The group believes that a sure loss will occur unless action is taken. Caught up in the turmoil of trying to make the best of a bad situation, the group takes a bigger risk than any individual member would take.[21] Some of the groups of financial executives who sold securities based on subprime mortgages may have thought that without a hot new financial product on the market, their investment banks would lose out on profits. Furthermore, the executives would lose out on generous bonuses. As a consequence, high-risk investments were sold to the public.

The negative aspects of groupthink can often be avoided if the team leader encourages group members to express doubts and criticisms of proposed solutions. It is helpful to show by example that you are willing to accept criticism. It is also important for someone to play the role of the devil's advocate. This person challenges the thinking of others by asking such questions as, "Do you think employees, investors, and regulators are so stupid they will not find out that we virtually stole billions from the corporation with our wacky schemes?"

Because group decision making takes more time and people than individual decision making, it should not be used indiscriminately. Group decision making should be reserved for complex decisions of reasonable importance. Too many managers use the group method for solving such minor questions as "What should be on the menu at the company picnic?"

A General Method of Group Problem Solving

When workers at any level gather to solve a problem, they typically hold a discussion rather than rely on a formal decision-making technique. These general meetings are likely to produce the best results when they follow established decision-making steps. Exhibit 5-4 recommends steps for

---

[20]The quote is from "Inquiry Puts Early Focus on Heat Tiles," *The New York Times*, February 2, 2003; Larry Wheeler, "NASA Chief Calls on Columbia," *The New York Times*, February 28, 2003.

[21]Glen Whyte, "Decision Failures: Why They Occur and How to Prevent Them," *Academy of Management Executive*, August 1991, p. 25.

EXHIBIT 5-4 **Steps for Effective Group Decision Making**

1. **Identify the problem.** Describe specifically what the problem is and how it manifests itself.
2. **Clarify the problem.** If group members do not perceive the problem in the same way, they will offer divergent solutions. Make sure everyone shares the same definition of the problem.
3. **Analyze the cause.** To convert "what is" into "what we want," the group must understand the causes of the specific problem and find ways to overcome them.
4. **Search for alternative solutions.** Remember that multiple alternative solutions can be found to most problems.
5. **Select alternatives.** Identify the criteria that solutions must meet, and then discuss the pros and cons of the proposed alternatives. No solution should be laughed at or scorned.
6. **Plan for implementation.** Decide what actions are necessary to carry out the chosen solution.
7. **Clarify the contract.** The contract is a restatement of what group members have agreed to do, and it includes deadlines for accomplishment.
8. **Develop an action plan.** Specify who does what and when to carry out the contract.
9. **Provide evaluation and accountability.** After the plan is implemented, reconvene to discuss its progress and hold people accountable for results that have not been achieved.

Source: Adapted from Andrew E. Schwartz and Joy Levin, "Better Group Decision Making," *Supervisory Management*, June 1990, p. 4.

conducting group decision making; these are similar to the decision-making steps presented in Exhibit 5-1.

A Specific Method of Group Problem Solving: The Nominal Group Technique

nominal group technique (NGT)

A group decision-making technique that follows a highly structured format.

A manager who must make a decision about an important issue sometimes needs to know what alternatives are available and how people would react to them. Another important consideration is for the group to reach consensus. An approach called the **nominal group technique (NGT)** has been developed to fit this situation. NGT is a group decision-making technique that follows a highly structured format. The term *nominal* means that for much of the activity, the participants are a group in name only; they do not interact.

An appropriate candidate for NGT is the problem of deciding which plants of a multiplant firm should be closed because of declining demand for a product. This type of highly sensitive decision elicits many different opinions. Suppose Sherry, the division president, faces the plant-closing problem. A six-step decision process follows, using a basic version of the nominal group technique as summarized in Exhibit 5-5.[22]

[22]Andrew H. Van de Ven and Andrew L. Delbercq, "The Effectiveness of Nominal, Delphi, and Interacting Group Decision-Making Processes," *Academy of Management Journal*, December 1972, p. 606; Leigh Thompson, "Improving the Creativity of Organizational Work Groups," *Academy of Management Executive*, February 2003, p. 104; "Quality Tools: Nominal Group Technique," *American Society for Quality* (http://www.asq.org), 2004.

1. Group members (called the target group) are selected and assembled. Sherry includes her five top managers, each representing a key function of the business, and informs them in advance of the topic.
2. The group leader presents a specific question. Sherry tells the group, "Our corporate office says we must consolidate our operations. Our output isn't high enough to justify keeping five plants open. Whatever we do, we must cut operating expenses by about 20 percent. Your assignment is to develop the rationale for choosing which plant to close. However, if the group can think of another way to cut operating costs by 20 percent, I'll give it some consideration. I will want to know how you feel about the alternative you propose and how our employees might feel."
3. Individual members write down their ideas independently, without speaking to other members. Members are given a set period of time for developing their suggestions, usually about five to ten minutes. Using PowerPoint, the five managers write down their ideas about reducing operating costs by 20 percent.
4. Each participant, in turn, presents one idea to the group, projected on a large screen. The group shares the ideas in a round-robin manner. The group does not discuss the ideas. The administrative assistant summarizes each idea by writing it on a slide. Here are some of the group's ideas:

Alternative A. Close the plant with the most obsolete equipment and facilities. We all know that the Harrisburg plant is running with equipment built about 100 years ago. Close the plant in 60 days. Give

EXHIBIT 5-5	The Nominal Group Technique

Observe that when the group reaches Step 6, the job is completed except for implementation. An important purpose of the NGT is to find a high-quality solution to a problem that will result in an effective decision.

1. Small group is assembled

2. Leader presents a question or problem

3. Members write down ideas individually

4. Each participant presents one idea to group

5. Group clarifies and evaluates all suggestions

6. Alternatives are rated and best-rated one is chosen

employees six months of severance pay and assist them to find new jobs. Transfer the most outstanding staff to our other plants.

Alternative B. Close the plant with the least flexible, most unproductive workforce. A lot of employees are likely to complain about this type of closing, but the rest of the workforce will get the message that we value productive employees.

Alternative C. Forget about closing a plant. Instead, take our least productive plant and transfer its manufacturing to our other four plants. Then work diligently to get subcontracting business for the empty plant. I think our employees and stockholders will be pleased if we take such a brave stance.

Alternative D. We need a careful financial analysis of which plant is producing the lowest return on investment of capital, all factors considered. We simply close that plant. Employees will accept this decision because they all know that business is based on financial considerations.

Alternative E. Closing one plant would be too much of a hardship on one group of people. Let's share the hardship evenly. Cut everybody's pay by 25 percent, eliminate dividends to stockholders, do not replace anybody who quits or retires for the next year, and ask all our suppliers to give us a 10 percent discount. These measures would be the starting point. We could then appoint a committee to look for other savings. If everybody pulls together, morale will be saved.

5. After each group member has presented his or her idea, the group clarifies and evaluates the suggestions. At this point members are free to question the logic of the idea and express agreement and disagreement. The length of the discussion for each of the ideas varies substantially. For example, the discussion about cutting salaries 25 percent and eliminating dividends lasts only three minutes.

6. The meeting ends with a silent, independent rating of the alternatives. The final group decision is the pooled outcome of the individual votes. The target group is instructed to rate each alternative on a 1-to-10 scale, with 10 being the most favorable rating. The ratings that follow are the pooled ratings (the sum of the individual ratings) received for each alternative (50 represents the maximum score):

> Alternative A, close obsolete plant: 35
> Alternative B, close plant with unproductive workforce: 41
> Alternative C, make one plant a subcontractor: 19
> Alternative D, close plant with poorest return on investment: 26
> Alternative E, cut everybody's pay by 25 percent: 4

Sherry agrees with the group's preference for closing the plant with the least productive, most inflexible workforce. Ultimately, the board accepts Alternative B. The best employees in the factory chosen for closing are offered an opportunity to relocate to another company plant.

The NGT is effective because it follows the logic of the problem-solving and decision-making methods and allows for group participation. As a result, the group usually attains consensus. The NGT also provides a discipline and rigor that are often missing in brainstorming.

Up to this point we have explored how decisions are made and characteristics that influence the decision-making situation, and have also studied group decision making. Next, we study in depth the aspect of decision making that moves organizations forward and helps them stay competitive.

LEARNING OBJECTIVE 5
Understand the nature of creativity and how it contributes to managerial work.

creativity
The process of developing novel ideas that can be put into action.

CREATIVITY AND INNOVATION IN MANAGERIAL WORK

Creativity is an essential part of problem solving and decision making. To be creative is to see new relationships and produce imaginative solutions. **Creativity** can be defined simply as the process of developing novel ideas that can be put into action. By emphasizing the application of ideas, creativity is closely linked to innovation. To be innovative, a person must produce a new product, service, process, or procedure. Innovation can be regarded as the commercialization or implementation of creative ideas. As venture capitalist and author George Gilder notes, the true source of business growth is human creativity and entrepreneurship.[23] Managers play a key role in today's innovation-driven economy, and finding ways to generate powerful ideas has become an urgent managerial priority.[24] Leaders both generate these ideas themselves and encourage idea generation among subordinates. (Some of these methods will be described in the following pages.)

Our discussion of managerial creativity focuses on the creative personality, the necessary conditions for creativity, the creative organization, creativity programs, and suggestions for becoming more creative.

The Creative Personality

Creative people tend to be more emotionally open and flexible than their less-creative counterparts. People who rarely exhibit creative behavior may suffer from "hardening of the categories" and cannot overcome the traditional way of looking at things. In business jargon, creative people can think outside the box or get beyond the usual constraints when solving problems. Recent research suggests that an important characteristic of creative workers is *growth needs strength*. Individuals with a strong need to grow psychologically want to learn new things, stretch themselves, and strive to do better in their jobs.[25] It follows that such workers look around for useful new ideas that can be applied to the job.

---

[23]George Gilder, "The Coming Creativity Boom," *Forbes*, November 10, 2008, p. 36.

[24]Teresa M. Amabile and Mukti Khaire, "Creativity and the Role of the Leader," *Harvard Business Review*, October 2008, p. 100.

[25]Christina E. Shalley, Lucy L. Gilson, and Terry C. Blum, "Interactive Effects of Growth Need Strength, Work Contest, and Job Complexity on Self-Reported Creative Performance," *Academy of Management Journal*, June 2009, pp. 489–505.

lateral thinking
A thinking process that spreads out to find many alternative solutions to a problem.

vertical thinking
An analytical, logical process that results in few answers.

Yet another way of characterizing creative thinkers is that they sometimes break the rules. They are unconventional, as is Scott Griffith, the CEO of car-sharing service Zipcar. Not long ago, most business people would have thought it beyond reason to persuade upwardly mobile professionals to share cars. Yet what began as a counterculture movement in places such as Cambridge, Massachusetts, and Portland, Oregon has gone mainstream; Zipcar is now found in many major U.S. cities. Reservations are made online or by iPhone, thereby appealing to the techno savvy. The Zipcar user essentially rents the car for about $12 per hour. Car sharing fits an environmentally conscious urban life style. Drivers who give up their vehicles and switch to Zipcar claim to save an average of $600 per month.[26]

A key part of being creative is to think laterally. **Lateral thinking** spreads out to find alternative solutions to a problem. **Vertical thinking**, in contrast, is an analytical, logical process that results in few answers. A problem that might be addressed by lateral thinking would be to list ways in which a small-business owner could increase income. A vertical thinking problem would be to calculate how much more money the small-business owner needs each month to earn a 10 percent profit.

Conditions Necessary for Creativity

Certain individual and organizational conditions are necessary for, or at least enhance the production of, creative ideas. The most consistent of these conditions are described here and in the next section about the creative and innovative organization.

Expertise, Creative-Thinking Skills, and Internal Motivation

Creativity researcher Teresa M. Amabile summarized 22 years of research about the conditions necessary for creativity in organizations. Creativity takes place when three components join together: expertise, creative-thinking skills, and motivation.[27] *Expertise* refers to the necessary knowledge to put facts together. The more facts floating around in your head, the more likely you are to combine them in some useful way. A case in point is Deaf-Talk, a firm that offers a link between hospitals and American Sign Language interpreters. The founders, Dave Stauffer and Robert Fisher, were experts in teleconferencing equipment, and they were also knowledgeable about the needs of deaf patients, particularly when these patients face a medical emergency. With the Deaf-Talk service, a patient can be connected within minutes to a certified American Sign Language interpreter who can translate via videoconferencing equipment. Deaf-Talk also offers the services of interpreters who speak dozens of languages.[28]

---

[26]Paul Keegan, "The Best New Idea in Business," *Fortune*, September 14, 2009, pp. 42–52.

[27]Teresa M. Amabile, "How to Kill Creativity," *Harvard Business Review*, September–October 1998, pp. 78–79.

[28]"Hospitals Hook Up for Deaf," The Associated Press, February 24, 2004.

If you know how to keep digging for alternatives and avoid getting stuck in the status quo, your chances of being creative multiply. Persevering, or sticking with a problem to a conclusion, is essential for finding creative solutions. A few rest breaks to gain a fresh perspective may be helpful, but the creative person keeps coming back until a solution emerges.

The right type of motivation is the third essential ingredient for creative thought. A fascination with, or passion for, the task is more important than searching for external rewards. People will be the most creative when they are motivated primarily by the satisfaction and challenge of the work itself. The ultimate involvement in work is referred to as the **flow experience**, a condition of heightened focus, productivity, and happiness. You are experiencing flow when you are "in the zone."

flow experience
The ultimate involvement in work or a condition of heightened focus, productivity, and happiness.

The developers of the solar cooker were passionate about saving the lives of thousands of women in Chad (a country in Africa). The solar cooker uses two pieces of cardboard, tinfoil, and sunlight to cook food or boil water in bright sunlight. In the absence of a solar cooker, refugee women who fled from Darfur to Chad must go outside camp to gather firewood, running the risk of being attacked and raped. According to Rachel Andres, director of the Solar Cooker Project at Jewish World Watch, the equation is simple: "A solar cooker keeps you in camp, and that helps keep you alive."[29]

Environmental Need Plus Conflict and Tension

In addition to the internal conditions that foster creativity, two external factors over which people have little or no control. An environmental need must stimulate the setting of a goal, which is another way of saying, "Necessity is the mother of invention." For example, after Hurricane Katrina ravaged the Gulf Coast of the United States, companies attempting reconstruction projects lacked housing for workers. Among the solutions was hiring cruise ships that were stationed in the gulf as temporary hotels.

Conflict and tension that put people on edge can also foster creativity. A practical way to create this conflict is for people to challenge each other's thinking. One might say, "Offering tents as temporary housing won't attract enough construction workers to come down here. Let's try harder for a housing solution."

Encouragement from Others

Another external factor in creativity is encouragement, including a permissive atmosphere that welcomes new ideas. A manager who encourages imaginative and original thinking, and does not punish people for making honest mistakes, is likely to receive creative ideas from employees. A research study suggests that encouragement from family and friends, as well as from a supervisor, enhances creative thinking on the job.[30]

---

[29]Ranit Mishori, "The Simple Tool That Saves Women's Lives," *Parade*, March 1, 2009, p. 18.
[30]Nora Madjar, Greg R. Oldham, and Michael G. Pratt, "There's No Place Like Home? The Contributions of Work and Nonwork to Creativity Support to Employee's Creative Performance," *Academy of Management Journal*, August 2002, pp. 757–767.

Risk taking enhances creativity. Good managers find a way to encourage risk taking. Employees are sometimes hesitant to make creative suggestions for fear of being zapped if new ideas fail when implemented. If employees know that it is okay to fail, more will take chances. For people to sustain creative effort, they must feel that their work matters to the employer. The manager might say, "I love your idea for reducing shipping costs. Keep up the good work." In this way, the employee might be encouraged to take a risk.

The Creative and Innovative Organization

It's important to recognize that certain managerial and organizational practices foster creativity. When thinking about organizational creativity and innovation, recognize that the two concepts apply to services and processes as well as to products. Service innovations include online bill payments and a smart phone application for ordering take-out food. Novel processes, such as the extraordinary computer network used by Google and the inventory management system deployed by Amazon, are a key part of profitability.

Seven categories of activities summarize much of what is known about what managers can do to establish a creative atmosphere, as described next.[31] The combination of all or several of these activities contributes to a culture of innovation. Convincing evidence for the importance of the organizational culture comes from a study of 750 publicly held companies across 17 nations. The major finding was that a corporate culture that fosters innovation is the single most important factor in determining whether a company will produce radical innovations.[32]

1. *Challenge.* Giving employees the right type and amount of challenge helps provide a creative atmosphere. Employees should be neither bored with the simplicity of the task nor overwhelmed by its difficulty. A good creativity inducer for a new sales representative might be for the manager to say, "How would you like to go through our ex-customer file and attempt to bring back 5 percent of them? It would have a great impact on profits."

2. *Freedom.* To be creative, employees should have the freedom to choose how to accomplish a goal, but not which goal to accomplish. For example, creativity would be encouraged if a manager said to a group member, "I would like to improve our Facebook presence; you figure out how." A creative result would be less likely if the manager said, "I would like to improve our service, and this is what I want you to do."

---

[31]Amabile, "How to Kill Creativity," pp. 81–84; Pamela Tierney, Steven M. Farmer, and George B. Graen, "An Examination of Leadership and Employee Creativity: The Relationship of Traits and Behaviors," *Personnel Psychology*, Autumn 1999, pp. 591–620; Amabile and Khaire, "Creativity and the Role of the Leader," pp. 100–109.

[32]Gerard Tellis, Jaideep Prabhu, and Rajesh Chandy, "Radical Innovation Across Nations: The Preeminence of Corporate Culture," *Journal of Marketing*, January 2009, pp. 3–23.

3. *Resources.* Managers must allot time and money carefully to enhance creativity. Tight deadlines can get the creative juices flowing, but people still need enough time to let creative ideas swirl around in their heads. Employees also need large enough budgets to purchase the equipment and information necessary to get the job done. It is important that the budget approval process for funding worthwhile ideas not be overly restrictive. Robert Iger, the CEO of Walt Disney Company, suggests that to manage creativity well, the approval process should not be unduly rigorous.[33]

4. *Rewards and recognition for innovative ideas.* Even though internal motivation is essential for innovation, external rewards and recognition are also helpful. The introductory case about the candy company rewarding process innovation illustrates this point. Borrego Solar Systems in San Diego holds quarterly employee contests promoting original thinking, each with a $500 prize. One contest seeks the best business innovation, which must be carefully documented in terms of the problem the idea solves and its costs, risks, and benefits. The other competition rewards the best "knowledge brief," which encourages employees to share information that can benefit the entire company.[34]

5. *Allocating time for innovative thinking.* Workers need time to think in order to be creative. 3M has long been recognized as a business firm that supports creativity. One of the leading companywide programs lets workers invest 15 percent of their time on their own projects. In the past, it was not necessary that such projects fit into the strategic business plan. One of the most successful projects to come from the program is Post-it® notes, a top-selling product in the United States. In recent years, the new 3M CEO has demanded data about the marketing feasibility of a product before giving financial support. Other companies offer employees time to pursue pet-project programs as a way of enhancing creativity and innovation. At Google, for example, engineers have "20 percent time" in which they are free to pursue projects about which they are passionate.[35]

6. *Building on the ideas of others.* As described earlier, encouragement facilitates creativity. A specific form of encouragement that contributes to innovation is looking for the kernel of value in the imaginative suggestions of others and then adding value to those ideas. At Pixar Animation Studios, the producer of animated movies, the process for developing technologies and movies entails collaboration and idea sharing from the start. Pixar's 1,000 employees are taught the technique of *plussing* during orientation and training. When an idea is offered in a meeting, it is restated and added to. Co-workers do not say "no but." Instead, they

---

[33]Merissa Marr, "Redirecting Disney," *The Wall Street Journal*, December 5, 2005, p. B1.

[34]Evans, "Entrepreneurs Seek to Elicit Workers' Ideas," p. B7.

[35]Ed Frauenheim, "On the Clock But Off on Their Own: Pet Project Programs Set to Gain Wider Acceptance," *Workforce Management*, April 24, 2006, p. 40.

say "yes and." Another idea-building statement is "Yes, that would work, and if we also...." Adding a plus to the ideas of co-workers appears to produce better results in terms of innovation.[36]

7. *Greater diversity in groups.* Managers can also cultivate creativity by establishing a group of people with diverse backgrounds. Intellectual diversity, in particular, fans the fire of creativity. A variety of perspectives lead to thinking outside the box and challenging existing paradigms. Tom Preston, the former head of MTV, then Viacom, says that one of the tips for managing a creative organization is to hire passionate, diverse employees.[37]

Here are three companies that have been successful in fostering creativity and innovation, as designated by *Bloomberg Business Week.* The three make use of many of the practices mentioned in the last several pages.[38]

- Apple has rocked the smart-phone world with the iPhone, prompting rivals to imitate the touch-screen design.
- The Tata Group, a Mumbai-based conglomerate, developed a $2,500-automobile for the masses. This automobile is inexpensive, in part, because of a distribution model that sells the auto in kits. (The final price may exceed $2,500, and not many countries will authorize its use because of safety concerns).
- In recent years Coca-Cola brought the excitement of race cars and high-tech creativity to the redesign of its Freestyle fountain-drink dispensers, with one machine dispensing more than 100 different drinks. The machines are based on Microsoft technology and style points from the designers of Italian sports cars.

LEARNING OBJECTIVE 6
Describe organizational programs for improving creativity and innovation.

Organizational Programs for Improving Creativity and Innovation

Another aspect of the creative organization is formal programs or mechanisms for creativity improvement. Four such mechanisms include creativity training, brainstorming, systematically gathering ideas, and appropriate physical surroundings.

Creativity Training

A standard approach to enhancing individual and organizational creativity is to offer creativity training to many workers throughout the organization. Much of creativity training encompasses the ideas already covered in this chapter, such as learning to overcome traditional thinking and engaging in

---

[36]Kathy Gurchiek, "Motivating Innovation," *HR Magazine*, September 2009, p. 33.

[37]Matthew Karnitschnig, "Mr. MTV Moves Up," *The Wall Street Journal*, January 9, 2006, p. B1.

[38]Michael Arndt and Bruce Einhorn, "The 50 Most Innovative Companies," *Bloomberg Business Week*, April 25, 2010, pp. 38–40.

some type of group problem-solving activity. A variety of techniques are used to encourage more flexible thinking, such as engaging in child play, squirting each other with water guns, and scavenger hunts. An extreme technique is to deprive participants of food and rest for 24 hours; some believe that when their defenses are weakened, they are mentally equipped to "think differently." Other creativity-training techniques are more cerebral, such as having participants solve puzzles and ask "what if" questions.

Brainstorming

brainstorming
A group method of solving problems, gathering information, and stimulating creative thinking. The basic technique is to generate numerous ideas through unrestrained and spontaneous participation by group members.

The best-known method of improving creativity, as well as working on real problems, is **brainstorming**. This technique is a method of problem solving carried out by a group. Brainstorming is standard practice for solving real problems facing a company; it is also a creativity-training technique. Group members spontaneously generate numerous solutions to a problem without being discouraged or controlled. Alex Osborn, the founder of modern brainstorming, believed that one of the main blocks to organizational creativity was the premature evaluation of ideas. The presence of a trained facilitator greatly enhances the productivity of brainstorming meetings.[39]

Brainstorming produces ideas; it is not a technique for working out details during the first meeting. Some types of business problems are well suited to brainstorming, such as coming up with a name for a new sports car, identifying ways to attract new customers, and making cost-cutting suggestions. People typically use brainstorming when looking for tentative solutions to nontechnical problems, yet the technique is also used to improve software and systems.

An example of an appropriate application of brainstorming in business took place at Microsoft Corp. in choosing a new name for its search engine, Live. Microsoft hired a firm named Interbrand, which established a group of eight employees to brainstorm around themes such as "speed" and "relevance." Within six weeks, the group came up with 2,000 names, and then reduced the list to 600. Interbrand finally submitted around 55 names to Microsoft, which in turn submitted eight to focus groups. "Bing" was the final choice for the search engine name, over such alternatives as "Kumo" and "Hook." Lawyers and linguists also got involved in the final selection to avoid any trademark infringements or offensive meaning of the term *bing* in another language.[40] (Yes, Bing is a type of cherry and a family name but that did not deter Microsoft.)

By brainstorming, people improve their ability to think creatively. To achieve the potential advantages of brainstorming, the session must be conducted properly. Exhibit 5-6 presents rules for conducting a brainstorming session. The technique continues to evolve. One new suggestion is to assign

---

[39]Thompson, "Improving the Creativity of Organizational Work Groups," p. 97; Michael Myser, "When Brainstorming Goes Bad," *Business 2.0*, October 2006, p. 76.

[40]Michael Mechanic, "How Bing Gots Its Name," *Mother Jones* (http://motherjones.com), July 13, 2009.

EXHIBIT 5-6	Rules for Conducting a Brainstorming Session

RULE 1 Enroll five to eight participants. If you have too few people, you lose the flood of ideas; if you have too many, members feel that their ideas are not important, or too much chatter may result. Set a meeting limit of about 60 minutes because creativity tends to come in intense bursts, and these bursts are mentally draining.

RULE 2 Give everybody the opportunity to generate alternative solutions to the problem. Have them call out these alternatives spontaneously. Encouraging members to prepare for the meeting will often help participation. One useful modification of this procedure is for people to express their ideas one after another, to decrease possible confusion.

RULE 3 Do not allow criticism or value judgments during the brainstorming session. Make all suggestions welcome. Above all, members should not laugh derisively or make sarcastic comments about other people's ideas.

RULE 4 Encourage freewheeling. Welcome bizarre ideas. It is easier to tone down an idea than it is to think one up.

RULE 5 Strive for quantity rather than quality. The probability of discovering really good ideas increases in proportion to the number of ideas generated.

RULE 6 Encourage members to piggyback, or build, on the ideas of others.

RULE 7 The facilitator should record each idea or audio-record the session. Disallow participants from taking notes on a notebook computer or BlackBerry rather than actively participating. Written notes should not identify the author of an idea because participants may worry about saying something foolish.

RULE 8 After the brainstorming session, edit and refine the list of ideas and choose one or two for implementation.

Source: Parts of rules 1 and 8 are from "Finding Inspiration in a Group," *Business 2.0*, April 2005, p. 110.

fieldwork to participants prior to the meeting. Staffers from the design firm Ideo wanted to devise new high-tech gadgets for children. The team split into three groups: The first group did no preparation; the second group did some background reading; and the third group visited toy stores. The toy-store group produced the highest-quality ideas along with the highest quantity, said Ideo general manager Tom Kelley.[41] Another suggestion is to allow natural light into the brainstorming workspace. A sterile, windowless room may not be conducive to idea generation.

---

[41]"Finding Inspiration in a Group," *Business 2.0*, April 2005, p. 110.

The rules of brainstorming can also be regarded as goals, as proposed by Robert C. Lichfield, a professor of organizational behavior at Washington & Jefferson College.[42] For example, the brainstorming team leader might think, "My goal in today's session will be to give everybody the opportunity to generate alternative solutions to the problem."

Brainstorming can be conducted through e-mail and other online collaboration tools—it's generally referred to as *electronic brainstorming*. The online collaboration tool might include video, audio, file sharing, and sketch pads.[43] In brainstorming by e-mail, group members simultaneously enter their suggestions into a computer. The ideas are distributed to the screens of other group members. Or ideas can be sent back at different times to a facilitator who passes the contributions along to other members. In either approach, although group members do not talk to each other, they are still able to build on each other's ideas and combine ideas.

Systematically Gathering Ideas

A powerful approach to developing an innovative organization is to systematically gather ideas from people inside and outside the firm. A within-company technique is to set quotas for employee suggestions, including the demand that employees bring a useful idea to a meeting. Being creative becomes a concrete work goal. The oldest approach to systematically gathering ideas is the humble suggestion box. Employees write ideas on paper and put them into a box, and they are often given cash awards for useful ideas. In recent years, the wooden box is often replaced by an online system for offering suggestions. Quite often the suggestions gathered have to do with human resources management, but many product and process ideas and energy-saving suggestions often show up.

Another approach to systematically gathering ideas is for workers to visit with workers of a partner company in order to better understand each other's perspectives and perhaps arrive at some shared ideas. The accompanying Management in Action illustrates this approach.

Appropriate Physical Surroundings

Creativity is facilitated when the physical environment allows for the flow of ideas. This might be a room with natural light, as previously mentioned. Physical spaces for innovation should be designed to encourage informal conversations. Break rooms are useful, and so are atriums. The presence of whiteboards throughout the corridors encourages the sudden exchange of complicated ideas that benefit from a diagram. Open work areas that allow for desks turned toward each other also facilitate the exchange of idea through conversation.

---

[42]Robert C. Litchfield, "Brainstorming Reconsidered: A Goal-Based View," *Academy of Management Review*, July 2008, pp. 649–668.

[43]Chris Penttila, "Fantastic Forum," *Entrepreneur*, September 2005, p. 92.

Despite the merits of physical spaces for idea sharing, many workers need private space to do their best creative thinking. After developing a creative idea, the person might want to refine the idea by interacting with others. Yet time for independent thinking, away from the buzz of the office, is also important. Microsoft makes sure that employees required to do creative work have access to private space, as well as the opportunity for group interaction.

As has been described, creativity and innovation are considered highly important in most organizations. Yet caution is in order. A company must focus on the most important creative ideas and not attempt every good idea. Too many new products and services developed at the same time can lead to more complexity than the company can manage. The company must optimize revenues and profits by focusing on the most promising new offerings.[44] Yet if creativity and innovation are ignored, a company will not have promising new offerings (such as the typewriter, electric coffee pot, personal computer, and smart phone) upon which to concentrate.

LEARNING
OBJECTIVE 7
Implement several suggestions for becoming a more creative problem solver.

Self-Help Techniques for Improving Creativity

In addition to participating in organizational programs for creativity improvement, you can help yourself become more creative in other ways. Becoming a more creative problem solver and decision maker requires that you increase the flexibility of your thinking. Reading about creativity improvement or attending one or two brainstorming sessions is insufficient. You must also practice the methods described in the following sections. As with any serious effort at self-improvement, you must exercise the self-discipline to implement these suggestions regularly. Creative people must also be self-disciplined to carefully concentrate on going beyond the obvious in solving problems.

Six Specific Creativity-Building Suggestions

To develop habits of creative thinking, you must regularly practice the suggestions described in the list that follows.[45]

1. Keep track of your original ideas by maintaining an idea notebook or a computer file. Few people have such uncluttered minds that they can recall all their past flashes of insight when they need these insights.
2. Stay current in your field and be curious about your environment. Having current facts at hand gives you the raw material to link information creatively. (In practice, creativity usually takes the form of associating

---

[44]Mark Gottfredson and Keith Aspinall, "Innovation Versus Complexity," *Harvard Business Review*, November 2005, pp. 62–71; Robin Hanson, "The Myth of Creativity," *Business Week*, July 3, 2006, p. 134.

[45]Eugene Raudsepp, "Exercises for Creative Growth," *Success*, February 1981, pp. 46–47; Mike Vance and Diane Deacon, *Think Out of the Box* (Franklin Lakes, NJ: Career Press, 1995); Interview with John Cleese, "Test: Can You Laugh at His Advice?" *Fortune*, July 6, 1998, pp. 203–204.

MANAGEMENT IN ACTION

Procter & Gamble and Google Swap Workers to Spur Innovation

At Procter & Gamble Co. (P&G), the corporate culture is so rigid that employees jokingly call themselves "Proctoids." In contrast, Google Inc. staffers are urged to wander the halls on company-provided scooters and brainstorm on public whiteboards. Now this odd couple thinks they have something to gain from one another—so they've started swapping employees. So far, about two dozen staffers from the two companies have spent weeks participating in each other's staff training programs and sitting in on meetings where business plans get hammered out. Previously, neither company had granted this kind of access to outsiders.

Closer ties are crucial to both sides. P&G, which spends more money each year on advertising than any other company, is waking up to the reality that the next generation of laundry-detergent, paper towels and skin-cream buyers now spends more time online than watching TV.

According to marketing research data, consumers age 18 to 27 say they use the Internet nearly 13 hours per week, compared to 10 hours of TV. Currently P&G—so famously thorough at understanding consumers, it even tracks people's tooth-brushing strokes—spends only a sliver of its ad budget online.

"We're trying to open the eyes of our brand managers," says P&G's Stan Joosten, whose title is "digital innovation manager," a job that didn't exist until spring 2007.

The idea of the employee swap between the two companies gained momentum a few years ago when P&G's then global marketing officer, Jim Stengel, expressed concern that one of the biggest initiatives in the company's laundry-soap history—a switch to small bottles with a more concentrated formula—didn't include enough of an online search-term marketing campaign. The issue: Without an online campaign, Tide buyers searching the Internet to figure out why the detergent bottle shrank might not be directed to Tide's own Web site.

As part of a month-long job swap at P&G's headquarters, a mixed group of Google and P&G staffers crowded into P&G's archives to study the 62-year history of Tide. Sessions like these are a key part of P&G's training of up-and-coming brand managers.

Questions
1. In what way might swapping employees between P&G and Goggle spur innovation?
2. Why would a Google employee be interested in learning about the history of Tide?
3. What kind of skills and knowledge do you think would be good for a "digital innovation manager"?

Source: Ellen Byron, "A New Odd Couple: Google, P&G Swap Workers to Spur Innovation," *The Wall Street Journal*, November 19, 2008, pp. A 1, A 18.

ideas that are non-associated, such as the idea of selling movie tickets with the idea of selling through vending machines.) The person who routinely questions how things work (or why they do not work) is most likely to have an idea for improvement.

3. Improve your sense of humor, including your ability to laugh at your own mistakes. Humor helps reduce stress and tensions, and you will be more creative when you are relaxed.

4. Adopt a risk-taking attitude when you try to find creative solutions. You will inevitably fail a few times. The best-known tale about creativity is that Thomas Edison got the light bulb right after 99 false starts.

5. Identify the times when you are most creative and attempt to accomplish most of your creative work during that period. Most people are at their peak of creative productivity after ample rest, so try to work on your most vexing problems at the start of the workday. Schedule routine decision making and paperwork for times when your energy level is lower than average.

6. When faced with a creativity block, step back from the problem and engage in a less mentally demanding task for a brief pause, or even a day. Sometimes, while doing something quite different, your perspective becomes clearer; creative alternatives will flash into your head when you return to your problem. Although creative problem solvers are persistent, they will sometimes put a problem away for awhile so they can come back stronger. The solution will eventually emerge. Patent whiz Steve Harrington says, "When you have a problem, it doesn't leave you alone until you have a solution."[46]

Play the Roles of Explorer, Artist, Judge, and Lawyer

One method for improving creativity incorporates many of the suggestions discussed so far. It requires you to adopt four roles in your thinking. First, you must be an *explorer*. Speak to people in different fields to get ideas you can use. Second, be an *artist* by stretching your imagination. Strive to spend about 5 percent of your day asking "what if?" questions. For example, an executive in a swimsuit company might ask, "Sunbathing causes skin cancer. What if the surgeon general decides that we must put warning labels on bathing suits?" Third, know when to be a *judge*. After developing some wild ideas, evaluate them. Fourth, achieve results with your creative thinking by playing the role of *lawyer*. Negotiate and find ways to implement your ideas within your field or place of work. You may spend months or years getting your best ideas implemented.[47] One of the biggest hurdles in bringing about innovation in an organization is to obtain funding for your brainchild.

Engage in Appropriate Physical Exercise

A well-accepted method of stimulating creativity is to engage in physical exercise. Stephen Ramocki, a marketing professor at Rhode Island College, found that a single aerobic workout is sufficient to trigger the brains of students into high gear—and that the benefit lasted for a minimum of two

---

[46]David Tyler, "Patent Whiz Runs Out of Room on His Wall," Rochester, New York *Democrat and Chronicle*, September 13, 2006, p. 9D.

[47]"Be a Creative Problem Solver," *Executive Strategies*, June 6, 1989, pp. 1–22.

hours. Gary Kasparov, the chess champion, is a gym fanatic and an extraordinary intellect. He believes that his physical fitness has improved his skill in chess.

One explanation of why exercise facilitates creativity is that exercising pumps more blood and oxygen into the brain. Exercise also enhances activity in the frontal lobe, the region of the brain involved in abstract reasoning and attention.[48] The fact that physical exercise can boost creative thinking should not be interpreted in isolation. Without other factors going for the manager, such as a storehouse of knowledge and passion for the task, physical exercise will not lead to creative breakthroughs.

---

[48]Richard A. Lovett, "Jog Your Brain: Looking for a Creative Spark? Hop to the Gym," *Psychology Today*, May/June 2006, p. 55.

Summary of Key Points

1 **Differentiate between nonprogrammed and programmed decisions.**

Unique and complex decisions are nonprogrammed decisions; programmed decisions are repetitive or routine and made according to a specific procedure.

2 **Explain the steps involved in making a nonprogrammed decision.**

The recommended steps for solving problems and making nonprogrammed decisions call for a problem solver to identify and diagnose the problem, develop alternative solutions, evaluate the alternatives, choose an alternative, implement the decision, evaluate and control, and repeat the process if necessary.

3 **Understand the major factors that influence decision making in organizations.**

Bounds (or limits) to rationality are present in decision making, leading many people to make decisions that suffice. Neuroeconomics helps explain the irrational side of decision making. People vary in their decision-making ability, and the situation can influence the quality of decisions. Factors that influence the quality of decisions are intuition, personality and cognitive intelligence, emotional intelligence, quality and accessibility of information, political considerations, degree of certainty, crisis and conflict, values of the decision maker, and procrastination. Decision-making style focuses on a combination of how information is used and how options are created (for example, decisive—one option, less information).

4 **Appreciate the value and potential limitations of group decision making.**

Because many people contribute, group decision making often results in high-quality solutions. It also helps people feel more committed to the decision. However, the group approach consumes considerable time, may result in compromise solutions that do not really solve the problem, and may encourage groupthink. Groupthink occurs when consensus becomes so important that group members lose their ability to evaluate ideas. It is likely to occur when decision makers must choose between inevitable losses. Group decision making should be reserved for complex decisions of reasonable importance.

General problem-solving groups are likely to produce the best results when the decision-making steps are followed closely. The nominal group technique (NGT) is recommended for a situation in which a manager wants to know what alternatives are available and how people will react to them and wants consensus. Using the technique, a small group of people contribute written thoughts about the problem. Other members respond to their ideas later. Members rate each other's ideas numerically, and the final group decision is the value of the pooled individual votes.

5 **Understand the nature of creativity and how it contributes to managerial work.**

Creativity is the process of developing novel ideas that can be put into action. Creative people are generally more open and flexible than their less creative counterparts, and they are willing to break the rules. They are also better able to think laterally.

Creativity takes place when three components join together: expertise, creative-thinking skills, and internal motivation. Perseverance in digging for a solution is important, and so is an environmental need that stimulates the setting of a goal. Conflict and tension can prompt people toward creativity. Encouragement contributes to creativity. Certain managerial and organizational practices foster creativity and innovation. To establish a creative atmosphere, managers can (a) provide the right amount of job challenge, (b) give freedom regarding how to reach goals, (c) provide the right resources, (d) give rewards and recognition for creative ideas, (e) allocate time for innovative thinking, and (f) promote greater diversity in groups.

6 **Describe organizational programs for improving creativity and innovation.**

One organizational program for improving creativity is to conduct creativity training. Brainstorming is the best-known method of improving creativity. The method can be conducted by e-mail and by means of online collaboration tools. Systematically gathering ideas inside and outside the company often enhances creativity, as does appropriate physical surroundings.

 Implement several suggestions for becoming a more creative problem solver.

Self-discipline improves creative thinking ability. Creativity-building techniques include staying current in your field and being curious about your environment, improving your sense of humor, and having a risk-taking attitude. A broad approach for improving creativity is to assume the roles of explorer, artist, judge, and lawyer. Each role relates to a different aspect of creative thinking. Engaging in appropriate physical exercise can stimulate the brain to think creatively

Key Terms and Phrases

Problem 152
Decision, 152
Nonprogrammed decision, 152
Programmed decisions, 153
Bounded rationality, 158
Satisficing decisions, 159
Heuristics, 159
Intuition, 159
Decisiveness, 161
Emotional intelligence, 162
Anchoring, 164

Procrastinate, 166
Decision-making style, 166
Group decisions, 168
Groupthink, 169
Nominal group technique (NGT), 170
Creativity, 173
Lateral thinking, 174
Vertical thinking, 174
Flow experience, 175
Brainstorming, 179

Questions

1. Describe a problem the manager of a new restaurant might face and point to the actual and ideal conditions in relation to this problem.
2. How might emotional factors in decision making influence whether top-level management at one company decides to purchase a competitor?
3. How might the use of Internet search engines help you make better decisions on the job?
4. Which one of the factors that influence decision making would likely give you the most trouble? What can you do to position this factor more in your favor?
5. Assume that the director of a social agency was exploring different alternatives for decreasing the number of homeless people in the area. Describe how a political factor might influence his or her decision making.
6. It is widely accepted that the generation of creative and innovative ideas is important for the survival of an organization. What should management do with a bunch of apparently useless ideas it receives?
7. Describe the general approach a firm of five real-estate developers might take to use the nominal group technique for deciding which property to purchase next.

Skill-Building Exercise 5-A: Stretching Your Imagination

A global contest was organized by Stanford University through its Technology Ventures Program. Anyone in the world was permitted to enter. The assignment was to take ordinary rubber bands and "add value" to them (make them more useful). Entries were submitted by video posted on YouTube. Entrants were people from many different occupations, including computer scientists. The winner received The Genius Award.

Here is where you fit in. Working alone or brainstorming with others, come up with at least six ways of adding value to a rubber band or a bunch of rubber bands. You must stretch your imagination to be successful. After the brainstorming sessions have been completed, perhaps taking 10 minutes of class time, a representative of each group might share results with the class. Students might then assign a Genius Award to the entry that seems the most useful. Or, the instructor might be the judge.

Source: The facts about the contest stem from Lee Gomes, "Our Columnist Judges a Brainstorming Bee, And Meets a Genius," *The Wall Street Journal*, March 5, 2008, p. B1.

Skill-Building Exercise 5-B: Choose an Effective Domain Name

Huddle in small groups and use brainstorming techniques. Your task is to develop original domain names for several products or services. An effective domain name is typically one that is easy to remember and one that will capture potential customers in an uncomplicated Web search. This exercise is difficult because "cybersquatters" grab unclaimed names they think business owners might want and then sell these names later. For example, a cybersquatter (or domain name exploiter) might develop or buy the domain name www.dogfood.com, hoping that an e-tailer of dog food will want this name in the future. The owner of dogfood.com would charge a company like Pet Smart every time a surfer who wanted to purchase dog food over the Internet entered dogfood.com and was then linked to Pet Smart.

After your team has brainstormed possible domain names, search the Internet to see whether your domain name is already in use. Simply enter the name you have chosen followed by .com into your browser. Or visit the site of a company such as http://www.DomainCollection.com/Inc. After you have developed your list of domain names not already in use, present your findings to the rest of the class.

- Hair salons
- Replacement parts for antique or classic autos
- A used-car chain
- Massage therapy salons
- Personal loans for people with poor credit ratings
- Recycled steel for manufacturers
- Choose one of your own

Management Now: Online Skill-Building Exercise: Learning About Creativity Training

Use the Internet to learn more about what companies are doing to enhance employee creativity. Be specific when you make an entry in your search engine to avoid being deluged with a choice of Web sites far removed from your topic. In your search engine, enter a sample phrase such as "creativity training programs for business." When you have located one or two sites and/or online newspaper articles posted within the last 12 months that give some details about a training program, compare the information you've found to the information in this chapter about creativity training. Note similarities and differences and be prepared to discuss your findings in class.

5-A Case Problem

What to Do with All These False Emergency Patients?

During her twenty-minute rest break at 3 A.M., Sue Abrams, M.D., rolled her eyes when Ken Raskins, a hospital administrator, asked her how she was doing. "It's real nice of you Ken, to drop by the emergency room to get a feel for what life is like in the trenches," said Sue.

"You know it. The emergency room doctors and nurses know it. And the rest of the ER medical and support staff know it. We've got the same enormous problem in our ER that is sweeping the country. The ER has lost most of its original purpose, and the change is choking the staff."

"I think I know what you're getting at," said Ken. "But please give me an update on the problem so I can take it up with the senior administrators."

"Stated simply," said Sue, "I estimate that only about one-third of the patients who come to the ER are facing a real emergency. They are using the ER for such reasons as avoiding having to visit a doctor during the day, or simply to get treatment for a minor illness or injury."

"I'm listening, and I'll take a few written notes," responded Ken. "Can you give me a few specifics?"

"Okay," said Sue with a sigh of exasperation. "I'll give you a handful of examples before I have to get back to the next hypochondriac in the ER.

- A mother brought in her two children with ordinary colds. She told me she thought her children were dying from the swine flu.
- An older man said he wanted to be treated for a stroke because he felt a twitching over his left eye.
- A pregnant teenager came in with her boyfriend. She said she had a six-pack of beer

that evening and she wanted to know whether her binge drinking had harmed the fetus.

- A young guy came in with a swollen hand. He said he got so mad that he hit the door in his apartment; he wanted to know what he should do for his hand."

Ken said sympathetically, "I understand that from a medical standpoint these types of visits to the ER seem unwarranted. Yet a lot of people do not understand what constitutes a true medical emergency."

Sue retorted, "Yet we still have a critical problem. We are clogging our ER beyond limits. It's gotten to the point where it is difficult to find nurses, nurse's aides, and physician assistants who will work in our ER."

Ken finished the conversation by saying, "You are right Sue. We've got to do something with all these false emergency patients. I'll get this problem on the hospital administrator's agenda. Most likely, we'll ask you and other ER staff to provide some input. That's providing you have enough energy left to attend a meeting."

Discussion Questions

1. What is the problem facing the ER staff in terms of the discrepancy between the ideal and actual conditions?
2. How might the hospital staff go about resolving the problem or problems described by Sue Abrams?
3. For what reasons should the ER staff and the hospital administrators care if some of the visitors to the emergency room are really not experiencing an emergency?

5-B Case Problem

Staples' Invention Quest

Henry Ford. Thomas Alva Edison. Adrian Chernoff. Adrian Chernoff? Maybe Chernoff isn't a household name like the first two inventors, but the 33-year-old Royal Oak, Michigan, man certainly shows potential. Chernoff's claim to fame—a handy little office product called Rubber Bandits—started gracing the shelves of every Staples store in North America a few years ago. The labelling bands, which retail at $2.99, also have their own Web site and can be purchased online through Staples.

The General Motors Corp. employee was one of the finalists in an annual Staples' Invention Quest. The contest is part of a broad effort by Staples to develop an exclusive product line to distinguish its private brand from those of competitors. Inaugurated several years ago, the contest is aimed at budding inventors looking to create the next Post-it note or better. About 10,000 entries are received annually. In recent years, school children have been involved in the contest. Besides giving inventors the gratification of seeing their ideas hit the shelves in 1,600 office superstores, Staples promises to share the profits. Winners of the contest receive $25,000 and as much as an 8 percent royalty have. One year's winner was a California man who created WordLock, a combination lock that allows users to select their combinations using letters rather than the traditional set of numbers.

Chernoff walked away with $5,000, a licensing agreement with the office-supply store, and the official title of inventor. "The best part for me right now is seeing it actually make its way

in the market place," Chernoff said. "The product is going into practice in the real world."

Maybe an extra-large rubber band with a wear-and-tear-resistance label won't solve the world's problems. But Rubber Bandits do make it easier to bundle and label piles of paperwork. And it definitely makes a nice workplace projectile, although Chernoff says that was not its original purpose.

Chernoff centered his career on creativity. In addition to a bachelor's degree and two master's degrees from the University of New Mexico (in business and engineering), his résumé includes jobs working on robots for the National Aeronautics and Space Administration and designing new rides for The Walt Disney Co.

Rubber Bandits popped into his mind on a shuttle bus ride between Denver and Boulder, Colorado, where he was visiting a brother. He started pondering office efficiency and the problems people have of losing things in the shuffle.

Discussion Questions
1. Why should Rubber Bandits be classified as a creative idea?
2. What does this story illustrate about how creative ideas surface?
3. In what way might having studied both business and engineering helped Adrian Chernoff become an inventor?

Source: Karen Dyris, "Staples Hunting for Next Wave of Ideas, Inventors," *Detroit News* syndicated story, May 10, 2005; William M. Bulkeley, "Got a Better Letter Opener? Staples Solicits Inventive Ideas from the Public for Products It Can Sell Exclusively," *The Wall Street Journal*, July 13, 2006, pp. B1, B6.

CHAPTER 6

Quantitative Techniques for Planning and Decision Making

C aterpillar Inc. recently told its steel suppliers that it would more than double its purchases of the metal in the present year, even if the company's sales did not rise one iota. In fact, the heavy-equipment maker had been boosting orders to suppliers for everything from big tires and hydraulic tubes to shatterproof glass.

Caterpillar's inventory buildup is attributed to the "bullwhip effect." Economists call it a bullwhip because even small increases in demand can cause a big snap in the need for parts and materials further down the supply chain. A big question in the mind of Caterpillar is how well suppliers are positioned to ramp up production. Bottlenecks and other headaches may occur as spot shortages cause unexpected price hikes and hamper companies' ability to meet demand.

That's why Caterpillar took the unusual step of visiting with key suppliers to ensure they had the resources to quickly boost output. In extreme cases, the equipment maker is helping suppliers get financing. Caterpillar said that even if demand for its equipment was flat in 2010—an unlikely projection it calls its "Great Recession scenario"—it would still need to boost production in its factories 15 percent just to restock dealer inventories and meet ongoing customer demand.

Meanwhile, output at Caterpillar's suppliers would have to rise by 30 percent to 40 percent in this scenario because Caterpillar would also be refilling its shelves. Executives at Caterpillar, though, are betting on growth. In that case, demand for parts would jump even more. If Caterpillar increases its production by 15 percent, says company CEO Jim Owens, a Ph.D. economist, "many of our suppliers would more than double their shipments to us."[1]

The Caterpillar analysis of its inventory needs illustrates several aspects of modern management. First, decisions are based on facts and data. Second, scenarios of the future are imagined in order to be prepared. Third, managing inventory well is part of being a successful business. To make planning and decision making more accurate, a variety of techniques based on the scientific method, mathematics, and statistics have been developed. This chapter will provide sufficient information for you to acquire basic skills in several widely used techniques for planning and decision making. You can find more details about these techniques in courses and books about production and operations management and accounting.

All these quantitative tools are useful, but they do not supplant human judgment and intuition. For example, a decision-making technique might tell a manager that it will take four months to complete a project. He or she might say, "Could be, but if I put my very best people on the project, we can beat that estimate."

As you read and work through the various techniques, recognize that software is available to carry them out. A sampling of appropriate software is presented in Exhibit 6-1. Before using a computer to run a technique, however, it is best to understand the technique and try it out manually or with a calculator. Such firsthand knowledge can prevent accepting computer-generated information that is way off track. Similarly, many people use spell checkers without a good grasp of word usage. The results can be misleading and humorous, such as "Each of our employees is assigned to a *manger*" or "The company picnic will proceed as scheduled *weather* or not we have good *whether.*"

---

[1]Excerpted from Timothy Aeppel, "' Bullwhip' Hits Firms as Growth Snaps Back," *The Wall Street Journal*, January 27, 2010, pp. A1, A6.

EXHIBIT 6-1	Software for Quantitative Planning and Decision-Making Techniques

Managers and professionals generally rely on computers to make use of quantitative planning and decision-making techniques. Examples of applicable software are presented at the right, and should be referred to for on-the-job-application of these techniques.

Forecasting Techniques	Excel-Based ForecastX™ (John Galt Solutions Inc.); Forecast Pro (Business Forecast Systems Inc.); PROPHIX; spreadsheet programs can also be used to make forecasts based on trend data.
Gantt Charts and Milestone Charts	SmartDraw; E Project Management Software
PERT Diagrams	MinuteMan Plus (MinuteMan Systems); Envision Software; PERT Chart EXPERT (Critical Tools Inc.)
Break-Even Analysis	Orion Business Center; Business Plan Software
Decision Trees	TreeAge; SmartDraw
Economic Order Quantity (EOQ)	Software would be superfluous, use pocket calculator. However, the EOQs that you calculate can be entered into a spreadsheet and updated as needed.
Just-in-Time (JIT) Inventory Management	Blue Claw Database Design; Just-in-Time Software Solutions
Pareto Diagrams	Envision Software; SPC for Excel
All Techniques Combined	Enterprise software controls an entire company's operations, linking them together. The software automates finance, manufacturing, and human resources, incorporating stand-alone software such as that designed for PERT and break-even analysis. Enterprise software also helps make decisions based on market research. Specific types of enterprise software have several different names. (Four key suppliers are SAP, Oracle, Siebel, and NEC Enterprise Software Solutions.)

LEARNING
OBJECTIVE **1**

Explain how managers use data-based decision making.

data-driven management

An attitude and approach to management rather than a specific technique that stems from data-based decision making.

DATA-BASED DECISION MAKING

Numbers and facts often influence managerial decision making. **Data-driven management** refers to the idea that decisions are based on facts rather than impressions or guesses.[2] The idea is straightforward: Before making a decision of consequence, the managerial worker should gather facts that could influence the outcome of the decision. The quantitative techniques described in this chapter assist the process of data-driven management, yet simply gathering relevant facts can make data-driven management possible.

The discussion about using high-quality information in making decisions (Chapter 5) is part of data-driven management. People who are scientifically oriented use data-driven management quite naturally. Executive dashboards, described in Chapter 14, give managers access to a wide variety of real-time information such as items sold, profit, and spending versus budget.

---

[2]http://www.pheatt.emporia.edu/courses/2002/, accessed November 17, 2006.

Many managers want to see the data before accepting a suggestion from a subordinate. Marissa Mayer, the vice president for search products and user experiences at Google Inc., is one such manager. One of her "9 notions of innovation" is "Don't politic, use data." She discourages the use of "I like" in meetings, pushing staffers instead to use "metrics."[3] How might this use of data work in practice?

During a meeting with Mayer, a staff member might make the comment, "I don't think we have much to worry about from A9.com, the Amazon.com search engine. Almost nobody has heard about it or is using it." Mayer might reply, "Get back to me when you can cite some hard data about how many people are using A9.com instead of Google when they conduct a search. At that point we can decide on the competitive threat posed by A9."

Data-driven management is more of an attitude and approach than a specific technique, and it is hardly new. You attempt to gather relevant facts before making a decision of consequence. Suppose a small-business owner wants to repaint the walls inside the office. The office manager suggests buying a premium brand of paint because such paint stays fresher looking longer and does not chip as readily. The data-driven manager would say, "Where is the evidence that if we have the painter use premium paint the walls will look better longer and resist chipping? Show me the evidence."

Although data-driven management is preferable in most situations, intuition and judgment still contribute to making major decisions. At times relevant data may not be available, so acting on hunches can be essential. A major new source of recruiting for truckers is early retiree couples who enjoy heavy travel.[4] Before actively recruiting older people as potential truckers to help with the acute trucker shortage, several trucking association executives guessed that this demographic group might be attracted to trucking. Now trucking managers have some data to work with in terms of recruiting retiree couples. During the Great Recession, trucking companies were swamped with applications for trucker positions. As the economy drifted back toward normal, recruiting reliable people to become truckers resurfaced as a concern.

The accompanying Management in Action presents more details of how a successful manager relies heavily on data before making major decisions.

<table>
<tr><td>LEARNING
OBJECTIVE ②
Explain the use of
forecasting
techniques in
planning.</td></tr>
</table>

FORECASTING METHODS

All planning involves making forecasts, or predicting future events. Forecasting is important because if a manager fails to spot trends and react to them before the competition does, the competition can gain an invaluable edge. As noted in an executive newsletter: "The handwriting is on the wall. The way your business reacts to newly emerging trends is perhaps the best barometer of your future success."[5] In recognition of the importance of understanding

---

[3]Michelle Conlin, "Champions of Innovation," *Business Week*, June 2006, p. IN 20.

[4]Stephanie Chen, "How Baby Boomers Turn Wanderlust into Trucking Careers," *The Wall Street Journal*, August 24, 2006, pp. A1, A8.

[5]Daniel Levinas, "How to Stop the Competition from Eating Your Lunch," *Executive Focus*, May 1998, pp. 55–58.

MANAGEMENT IN ACTION

Data-Driven Decision Making at Hewlett-Packard

When Mark Hurd was named chief executive of Hewlett-Packard Co. in March 2005, the board gave him a clear mission: fix the giant computer and printer make, which was suffering from slow growth and inconsistent results. Hurd took a big step forward attempting to fulfil that mandate when he embarked on a sweeping plan in July 2005 to cut costs and restructure the company. He planned to lay off 14,500 employees, or about 10 percent of the company's global workforce, modify its pension benefits, and revamp its sales force in an effort to make the company more efficient and better able to service customers. (All of these plans were implemented by 2007.)

But before Hurd could attempt to fix HP, he had to figure out HP. Shortly after arriving at the Palo Alto, California, company, the 48-year-old former chief executive of NCR Corp. set about to collect information methodically. He spent time with senior executives, conducted extensive business reviews and even travelled with sales people to meet HP customers firsthand. He visited HP offices and factories from Boise to Beijing. At each site he spoke to employees and sought feedback. In all, he has collected more than 5,000 e-mails from HP staffers. With his findings, Hurd built two computer models—one financial and the other an operating model—designed to help plot the company's course.

"I have a pretty standard process," Hurd said. Getting out into the field "is some of the best market research I can get."

After reviewing the businesses at each site, Hurd typically held an employee "coffee talk" in the afternoon. For him, the aim is to trigger feedback from employees so that they can unearth facts not covered by managers. Many visits are dominated "by the biggest personalities," he says. "But it's some of the people who don't speak up who send the crispest two-page e-mails."

About 320 new e-mails arrive every day, the company says. Hurd has also encouraged staffers to call him directly: Hearing someone's voice helps him understand what they are emphasizing and their emotion, he says.

Then came the rigorous analysis. Back at his Palo Alto office, Hurd reviewed the findings from a site visit or business review with executives. Based on a series of spreadsheets, these models change daily as Hurd adds new facts and thoughts from his travels, such as the number of salespeople in an office versus the size of a sales territory, and ruminations on what kinds of capabilities must be added to or subtracted from a facility.

The goal of the models is to winnow down all the information being collected onto a single page that lays out a vision of HP's future and how to get there. "I want to get everything between us and the goal line on a piece of paper," says Hurd.

Hurd points out that although he is heavily involved in decision making, he relies on the collective intelligence of his executive team. Upon being recognized as "The Chronicle 200's CEO of the year," Hurd said, "Running a company like HP, which is so global and so diversified, is absolutely a team sport. I'm very honored to receive the recognition."

Hurd left HP in 2010 because of his involvement in an expense account irregularity, but is still regarded as a data-driven manager.

Case Questions
1. Why might employees and customers be a valuable source of input for Hurd in making decisions about the future of HP?
2. In what way is employee input shaping the future of HP?
3. What, if any, ethical issues might there be in collecting input from employees about fixing the company, then laying off 14,500 of them?

Sources: Excerpted from Pui-Wing Tam, "Rewiring Hewlett-Packard," *The Wall Street Journal*, July 20, 2005, p. B1; Final paragraph based on information from Ryan Kim, "Mark Hurd Has Earned a Name at Hewlett-Packard, *SFGate.com, (San Francisco Chronicle)*, April 20, 2008.

the future, almost every large business or government agency performs some type of formalized forecasting.[6] The forecasts used in strategic planning are especially difficult to make because they involve long-range trends. Unknown factors might crop up between the time the forecast is made and the time about which predictions are made. This section will describe approaches to and types of forecasting.

Qualitative and Quantitative Approaches

Forecasts can be based on both qualitative and quantitative information. Most of the forecasting done for strategic planning relies on a combination of the two. *Qualitative* methods of forecasting consist mainly of subjective hunches. For example, an experienced executive might predict that the high cost of housing will create a demand for small, less-expensive homes, even though this trend cannot be quantified. One qualitative method is a **judgmental forecast**, a prediction based on a collection of subjective opinions. It relies on analysis of subjective inputs from a variety of sources, including consumer surveys, sales representatives, managers, and panels of experts. For instance, a group of potential homebuyers might be asked how they would react to the possibility of purchasing a compact, less-expensive home.

Quantitative forecasting methods involve either the extension of historical data or the development of models to identify the cause of a particular outcome. A widely used historical approach is **time-series analysis**. This technique is simply an analysis of a sequence of observations that have taken place at regular intervals over a period of time (hourly, weekly, monthly, and so forth). The underlying assumption of this approach is that the future will be much like the past. When the changes in the external environment are slow and consistent, time-series analyses are the most accurate. An example of slow and consistent change would be the aging of the population, whereas a rapid and consistent change would be the consumer use of media technology.

Exhibit 6-2 shows a basic example of a time-series analysis chart. This information might be used to make forecasts about when people would be willing to take vacations. Such forecasts would be important for the resort and travel industry. A time-series forecast works best in a relatively stable situation. For example, an unusually strong or weak hurricane season makes it difficult to predict the demand for home improvement materials. If you use a spreadsheet program such as Excel to make forecasts, you will find that the input data are part of a time-series analysis. The future trends projected are based on historical data.

Many firms use quantitative and qualitative approaches to forecasting. Forecasting begins with a quantitative prediction, which provides basic data about a future trend. An example of a quantitative prediction is the forecast of a surge in demand for flat-screen television receivers, 50 inches or greater.

---

[6]"Forecasting in Business," *Encyclopedia of Business and Finance* (www.endnotes.com), February 11, 2011.

PLAY VIDEO

Go to www.cengage.com/management/dubrin and view the video for Chapter 6. What can you observe about how Recycline uses data from watching this video?

judgmental forecast
A qualitative forecasting method based on a collection of subjective opinions.

time-series analysis
An analysis of a sequence of observations that have taken place at regular intervals over a period of time (hourly, weekly, monthly, and so forth).

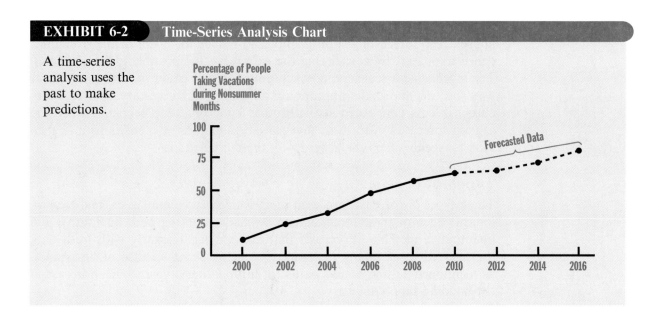

EXHIBIT 6-2   **Time-Series Analysis Chart**

A time-series analysis uses the past to make predictions.

Next, the qualitative forecast is added to the quantitative forecast, somewhat as a reality check. For example, a quantitative forecast might predict that if the current growth trend continues, every household in North America will contain three 50-inch TV sets by 2015.

The quantitative forecast is then adjusted according to the subjective data supplied by the qualitative forecast. In this case, it could be reasoned that the growth trend was extrapolated too aggressively. In many instances, a quantitative forecast will serve as a reality check on the qualitative forecasts because numerical data are more accurate than intuition.

Three errors or traps are particularly prevalent when making forecasts or estimates.[7] One is the *overconfidence trap*, whereby people overestimate the accuracy of their forecasts. A CEO might be so confident of the growth of her business that she moves the company into expensive new headquarters. Based on her confidence, she does not prepare contingency plans in case the estimated growth does not take place. A second problem is the *prudence trap*, in which people make cautious forecasts "just to be on the safe side." Being safe can mean taking extra measures not to be caught short. A restaurant owner might buy ten extra boxes of strawberries "just to be safe." If the strawberry desserts go unsold, the owner is stuck unless he can make strawberry pudding for tomorrow's menu.

A third problem is the *recallability trap*, whereby forecasts are influenced by extremely positive or negative incidents we recall. If a manager vividly recalls success stories from global expansion to Singapore, he might overestimate the chances of succeeding in that country this time.

---

[7]John S. Hammond, Ralph L. Keeney, and Howard Raiffa, "The Hidden Traps in Decision Making," *Harvard Business Review*, September–October 1998, pp. 55–58.

Being aware of these traps can help you take a more disciplined approach to forecasting. For example, to reduce the effect of the overconfidence trap, start by considering the extremes—the possible highs and lows. Try to imagine a scenario in which your forecast could be way too high or way too low and make appropriate adjustments if necessary. For a reality check, discuss your forecasts with other knowledgeable people. To become a good forecaster, you must make a large number of predictions and then look for feedback on the accuracy of these predictions.

Types of Forecasts

Three types of forecasts are used most widely: economic, sales, and technological. Each of these forecasts can be made by using both qualitative and quantitative methods. Forecasts that are updated regularly with fresh data are referred to as *rolling forecasts*. The presence or absence of hurricanes, as mentioned earlier, would be useful in updating a yearly sales forecast in the building-supply industry.

Economic Forecasting

No single factor is more important in managerial planning than predicting the level of future business activity. Strategic planners in large organizations rely often on economic forecasts made by specialists they hire. Planners in smaller firms are more likely to rely on government forecasts or speak to other business people. However, forecasts about the general economy do not necessarily correspond to business activity related to a particular product or service. Assume that you are a manager at an office-supply company such as Office Max or Staples. The following forecast prepared by the World Future Society might prompt you to stock up on home-office systems:

> *More than 100 million people will telecommute to work by the year 2015. This increase will distribute worldwide wealth more rapidly, save energy, reduce global pollution, and transfer real estate values.*[8]

A major factor in the accuracy of forecasts is time span: Short-range predictions are more accurate than long-range predictions. Strategic planning is long-range planning, and many strategic plans must be revised frequently to accommodate changes in business activity. For example, a sudden recession may abort plans for diversification into new products and services.

Sales Forecasting

The sales forecast is usually the primary planning document for a business. Even when the general economy is robust, an organization needs a promising sales forecast before it can be aggressive about capitalizing on new opportunities. Strategic planners themselves may not be involved in making sales

---

[8]*Special Report: Forecasts for the Next 25 Years*, p. 3 (Published by the World Future Society, 2004).

forecasts, but to develop master plans they rely on forecasts from the marketing unit. For instance, the major tobacco companies have embarked on strategic plans to diversify into a number of nontobacco businesses, such as soft drinks and food products. An important factor in their decision to implement this strategic plan was a forecast of decreased demand for tobacco products in the domestic market. The cause for decreased demand was health concerns of the public, and numerous antismoking campaigns.

According to marketing consultant Terry Elliott, sales forecasts are likely to be more accurate if they are based on several types of data. A manager of a home-electronics store might include the following data sources in preparing a sales forecast for the present year: (1) average sales volume per square foot for similar stores in similar locations and size, (2) the number of households within five miles who intend to purchase home electronic devices, and (3) sales revenues for each type of item or service offered. A service might be in-home installation of electronic products. Elliott also recommends that the owner generate three figures: pessimistic, optimistic, and realistic. The pessimistic forecast might alert the owner to the importance of lining up credit or conserving cash.[9]

Feedback from the field sales force often provides useful input for forecasts. The people in the field know the realities of consumer demand, and might have an inkling of what customers will want in the future.[10] One of the reasons some television sets now have an Internet capability is because customers often said to store associates, "I wish I didn't have to get up from watching television just to check my e-mail and favorite Web sites."

Technological Forecasting

A technological forecast predicts what types of technological changes will take place. Technological forecasts allow a firm to adapt to new technologies and thus stay competitive. For example, forecasts made in the late 1990s about the explosive growth of e-commerce enabled many firms to ready themselves technologically for the future. At first a lot of the activity was unprofitable, but the majority of industrial and consumer companies that prepared to buy and sell over the Internet soon found it to be profitable. By mid-2000, technological forecasts were made of the abundant availability of Wi-Fi at places of work, airports, hotels, and restaurants. This forecast encouraged the manufacture and marketing of portable computers and personal digital assistants suited for the wireless environment. (*Wi-Fi* refers to Wireless Fidelity, a high-speed, high-capacity network built on radio signals.)

Scenario Planning to Make Good Use of Forecasts

Forecasting is a way of predicting what will happen in the future. To make effective use of such knowledge, it is helpful to plan how to respond

---

[9]Terry Elliott, "Sales Forecasting by Multiple Methods Is Most Accurate," *About Small Business: Canada* (http://www.sbinfocanada.about.com), Accessed November 17, 2006.

[10]Gopinathan Thachappilly, "Revenue Forecasts Initiate Business Planning," http://businessmanagement.suite101, November 15, 2009.

Scenario planning
The process of preparing responses to predicted changes in conditions.

to the forecasted events. **Scenario planning** is the process of preparing responses to predicted changes in conditions.[11] With scenario planning, you prepare for what the future might look like. The practice of scenario planning was pioneered in the U.S. military in the 1950s and gained popularity in a few major business corporations in the 1970s. With the turbulence in recent times, including the airplane attacks on the World Trade Center on September 11, 2001, scenario planning has made a comeback.

A good use of scenario planning would be to figure out in advance how to deal with a serious disruption in business such as that caused by a hurricane. At the same time, it would be helpful to plan for a substantial increase in business such as that caused by a hurricane. A building-supply company might face the latter problem.

One of many companies now making serious use of scenario planning is JDS Uniphase Corp, a manufacturer of fiber-optic telecommunications equipment. A few years ago, as input from sales representatives showed early signs of a decrease in demand, company management started planning for the worst-case scenario. Sales orders began to decrease. The company decided to kill some products, combine two of its divisions, outsource more manufacturing to contractors, and close three factories with seven research-and-development sites, eliminating 400 jobs.[12] It is possible for scenario planning to lead to optimistic outcomes, such as a baby-products company preparing for a forecasted surge in births.

The Delphi Technique for Increasing the Accuracy of Forecasts

Delphi Technique
A form of group decision making designed to provide group members with one another's ideas and feedback while avoiding some of the problems associated with interacting groups.

The approaches to forecasting can be made more systematic, and a little more quantitative, if the several people who make forecasts on the same trend are pooled. Each forecaster commenting on the forecast made by the other forecasts can also increase accuracy. Using the **Delphi Technique**, a facilitator gathers the forecasts, as well as the reasons for them, from the specialists in the panel. (The Delphi Technique is a form of group decision making designed to provide group members with one another's ideas and feedback while avoiding some of the problems associated with interacting groups.) All the panelists then receive each other's forecasts and reasons for the forecasts, and comment about this information. After several rounds of reviews, the forecasts are refined and the facilitator submits the final forecast. Ideally, the forecasters attain consensus on the final forecast. An example of a final forecast might be, "By 2020, one-half of car buyers in the United States and Canada will want to purchase a hybrid vehicle."

---

[11]Cari Tuna, "Pendulum Is Swinging Back on 'Scenario Planning,'" *The Wall Street Journal*, July 6, 2009, p. B6.
[12]Ibid.

LEARNING
OBJECTIVE **3**
Describe how to
use Gantt charts,
milestone charts,
and PERT planning
techniques.

GANTT CHARTS AND MILESTONE CHARTS

Two basic tools for monitoring the progress of scheduled projects are Gantt charts and milestone charts. Closely related to each other, they both help a manager keep track of whether activities are completed on time. Both techniques include the use of numbers, so they can be classified as quantitative.

Gantt Charts

Gantt chart
A chart that depicts
the planned and actual
progress of work
during the life of the
project.

During the era of scientific management, Henry Gantt developed a chart for displaying progress on a project. An early application was tracking the progress of building a ship.[13] A **Gantt chart** graphically depicts the planned and actual progress of work over the period of time encompassed by a project. Gantt charts are especially useful for scheduling one-time projects such as constructing buildings, making films, or building an airplane. Charts of this type are also called time-and-activity charts, because time and activity are the two key variables they consider. Time is plotted on the horizontal axis; activities are listed on the vertical axis.

Despite its simplicity, the Gantt chart is a valuable and widely used control technique. It also provides the foundation of more sophisticated types of time-related charts such as the PERT diagram described later.

Exhibit 6-3 shows a Gantt chart used to schedule the opening of a small office building. Gantt charts used for most other purposes would have a similar format. At the planning phase of the project, the manager lays out the schedule by using rectangular boxes. As each activity is completed, the appropriate box is shaded. At any given time, the manager can see which activities have been completed on time. For example, if the building owner has not hired a contractor for the grounds by August 31, the activity would be declared behind schedule.

The Gantt also depicts dependent activities such as, in Exhibit 6-3, hiring contractors being dependent on first securing the building permit. The dependent activities must be completed in sequence. Other activities are nondependent or "parallel." For example, some developers obtain leases before a building is completed.

The Gantt chart presented here is quite basic. On most Gantt charts, the bars are movable strips of plastic. Different colors indicate scheduled and actual progress. Mechanical boards with pegs to indicate scheduled dates and actual progress can also be used. Some managers and specialists now use computer graphics to prepare their own high-tech Gantt charts. You can also use a spreadsheet to construct a Gantt chart, and many different software packages are available for preparing these charts.

Because Gantt charts are used to monitor progress, they also act as control devices. When the chart shows that the building-permit activity has fallen behind schedule, the manager can investigate the problem and solve it. The Gantt chart gives a convenient overall view of the progress made against the

---

[13]"Gantt Chart," *NetMBA* (http://www.netmba.com/operations/project/gantt), accessed November 17, 2006, p. 1.

EXHIBIT 6-3   **A Gantt Chart Used for Opening a Small Office Building**

A Gantt chart helps keep track of progress on a project.

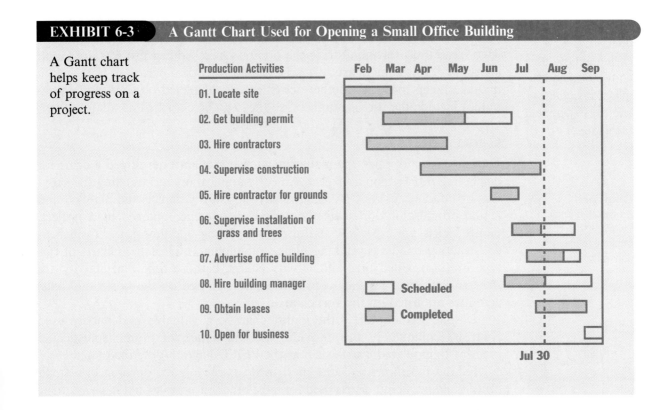

schedule. Its disadvantage is that it does not furnish enough details about the subactivities that must be performed to accomplish each general item.

Milestone Charts

milestone chart
An extension of the Gantt chart that provides a listing of the subactivities that must be completed to accomplish the major activities listed on the vertical axis.

A **milestone chart** is an extension of the Gantt chart, and some more advanced Gantt charts make provision for the milestones. The milestone chart provides a listing of the subactivities that must be completed to accomplish the major activities listed on the vertical axis. The inclusion of milestones, which are the completion of individual phases of an activity, adds to the value of a Gantt chart as a scheduling and control technique. Each milestone serves as a checkpoint on progress. In Exhibit 6-4, the Gantt chart for constructing a small office building has been expanded into a milestone chart. The numbers in each rectangle represent milestones. A complete chart would list each of the 33 milestones. In Exhibit 6-4 only the milestones for obtaining leases (including screening tenants) and the opening date are listed.

PROGRAM EVALUATION AND REVIEW TECHNIQUE

Gantt and milestone charts are basic scheduling tools, exceeded in their basic versions only in simplicity by a to-do list. A more complicated method of scheduling activities and events uses a network model. The model depicts

EXHIBIT 6-4	A Milestone Chart Used for Opening a Small Office Building

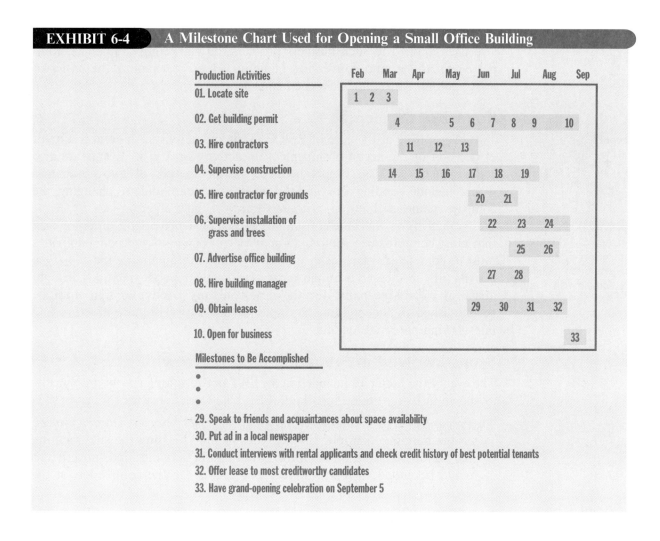

Production Activities

	Feb	Mar	Apr	May	Jun	Jul	Aug	Sep
01. Locate site	1 2 3							
02. Get building permit		4		5	6	7 8 9		10
03. Hire contractors		11	12	13				
04. Supervise construction		14	15	16	17 18	19		
05. Hire contractor for grounds					20 21			
06. Supervise installation of grass and trees						22 23	24	
07. Advertise office building						25 26		
08. Hire building manager						27 28		
09. Obtain leases						29 30	31 32	
10. Open for business								33

Milestones to Be Accomplished

-
-
-

29. Speak to friends and acquaintances about space availability
30. Put ad in a local newspaper
31. Conduct interviews with rental applicants and check credit history of best potential tenants
32. Offer lease to most creditworthy candidates
33. Have grand-opening celebration on September 5

program evaluation and review technique (PERT)

A network model used to track the planning activities required to complete a large-scale, nonrepetitive project. It depicts all of the interrelated events that must take place.

all the interrelated events that must take place for a project to be completed. The most widely used network-modeling tool is the **program evaluation and review technique (PERT)**. It is used to track the planning activities required to complete a large-scale, nonrepetitive project. PERT was originally developed in 1958 by the U.S. Department of Defense to assist with the Polaris mobile submarine launch project.

Quite often Gantt charts and PERT are used together, with the Gantt chart being laid out first because it provides a useful list of all the activities that must be performed in a project. PERT has the potential to reduce the time and cost required to complete a project because activities can be sequenced efficiently. A scheduling technique such as PERT is useful when certain tasks must be completed before others if the total project is to be completed on time. In the small office building example, the site of the building must be specified before the owner can apply for a building permit. (The building commission will grant a permit only after approving a specific location.) The PERT diagram indicates such a necessary sequence of events.

PERT is used most often in engineering and construction projects. It has also been applied to such business problems as marketing campaigns, company relocations, and convention planning. Here we examine the basics of PERT, along with a few advanced considerations.

Key PERT Concepts

event

In the PERT method, a point of decision or the accomplishment of a task.

Two concepts lie at the core of PERT: event and activity. An **event** is a point of decision or the accomplishment of an activity or a task. Events are also called *milestones*. The events involved in the merger of two companies would include sending out announcements to shareholders, changing the company name, and letting customers know of the merger.

activity

In the PERT method, the physical and mental effort required to complete an event.

An **activity** is the time-consuming aspect of a project or simply a task that must be performed. Before an activity can begin, its preceding activities must be completed—such as installing dry wall before painting the wall. One activity in the merger example is to work with a public relations firm to arrive at a suitable name for the new company. Activities that must be accomplished in the building example include supervising contractors and interviewing potential tenants.

Steps Involved in Preparing a PERT Network

The events and activities included in a PERT network are laid out graphically, as shown in Exhibit 6-5. Preparing a PERT network consists of four steps:

1. *Prepare a list of all activities and events necessary to complete the project.* In the building example, the activities include locating the site, securing the building permit, and so forth. Many more activities and subactivities could be added to this example. The events are the completion of the activities such as (C) hiring the contractors.

EXHIBIT 6-5   A PERT Network for Opening a Building

Each numeral in the diagram equals the expected time for an activity, such as 5 weeks to locate site (between circles A and B) and 13 weeks to supervise installation of grass and trees (between circles E and F). The critical path is the estimated time for all the activities shown above the thick arrows (13 + 30 + 6 + 13 + 8 + 14 + 8 + 1 = 93).

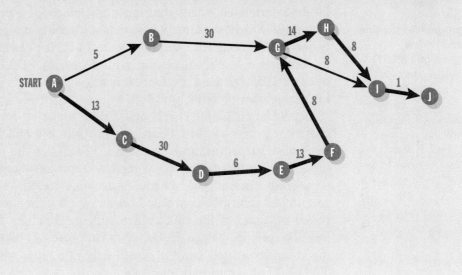

2. *Design the actual PERT network, relating all the activities to each other in the proper sequence.* Anticipating all the activities in a major project requires considerable skill and judgment. In addition, activities must be sequenced—the planner must decide which activity must precede another. In the building example, the owner would want to hire a grounds contractor before hiring a building manager.

3. *Estimate the time required to complete each activity.* This step must be done carefully because the major output of the PERT method is a statement of the total time required by the project. Because the time estimate is critical, several people should be asked to make three different estimates: optimistic time, pessimistic time, and probable time.

Optimistic time (O) is the shortest time an activity will take if everything goes well. In the construction industry, the optimistic time is rarely achieved because so many different trades are involved in completing a project.

Pessimistic time (P) is the amount of time an activity will take if everything goes wrong (as it sometimes does with complicated projects such as installing a new subway system).

Most probable time (M) is the most realistic estimate of how much time an activity will take. The probable time for an activity can be an estimate of the time taken for similar activities on other projects. For instance, the time needed to build a cockpit for one aircraft might be based on the average time it took to build cockpits for comparable aircraft in the past.

After the planner has collected all the estimates, he or she uses a formula to calculate the **expected time**. The expected time is the time that will be used on the PERT diagram as the needed period for the completion of an activity. As the following formula shows, expected time is an "average" in which most probable time is given more weight than optimistic time and pessimistic time.

expected time
The time that will be used on the PERT diagram as the needed period for the completion of an activity.

$$\text{Expected time} = \frac{O + 4M + P}{6}$$

(The denominator is six because O counts for one, M for four, and P for one.)

Suppose the time estimates for choosing a site location for the building are as follows: optimistic time (O) is two weeks; most probable time (M) is five weeks; and pessimistic time (P) is eight weeks. Therefore,

$$\text{Expected time} = \frac{2 + (4 \times 5) + 8}{6} = \frac{30}{6} = 5 \text{ weeks}$$

As each event or milestone is completed, the project manager can insert the actual time required for its completion. The updates are helpful because if the completion time turns out to be the pessimistic one, more resources can be added to shorten the activity required to attain the next event.

critical path
The path through the PERT network that includes the most time-consuming sequence of events and activities.

1. Calculate the **critical path**, *the path through the PERT network that includes the most time-consuming sequence of events and activities.* The path with the longest elapsed time determines the length of the entire project. To calculate the critical path, you must first add the times needed to complete the activities in each sequence. The logic behind the

critical path is this: A given project cannot be considered completed until its lengthiest component is completed. For example, if it takes six months to get the building construction permit, (and six months for the other components) the office-building project cannot be completed in less than one year, even if all other events are completed earlier than scheduled. Sudden changes in the time required for an activity can change the critical path, such as unanticipated delays in obtaining enough plywood for the building project.

Exhibit 6-5 shows a critical path that requires a total elapsed time of 93 weeks. This total is calculated by adding the numerals that appear beside each thick line segment. Each numeral represents the number of weeks scheduled to complete the activities between lettered labels. Notice that activity completion must occur in the sequence of steps indicated by the direction of the arrows. In this case, if 93 weeks appeared to be an excessive length of time, the building owner would have to search for ways to shorten the process. For example, the owner might be spending too much time supervising the construction.

When it comes to implementing the activities listed on the PERT diagram, control measures play a crucial role. The project manager must ensure that all critical events are completed on time. If activities in the critical path take too long to complete, the overall project will not be completed on time. If necessary, the manager must take corrective action to move the activity along. Such action might include hiring additional workers, dismissing substandard workers, or purchasing more productive equipment.

Advanced Considerations in PERT

Considering that PERT is used for projects as complicated as building a new type of airliner, the process can become quite complex. In practice, PERT networks often specify hundreds of events and activities. Each small event can have its own PERT diagram. Software is available to help perform the mechanics of computing paths. The PERT Chart EXPERT shown in Exhibit 6-6 is one such program. Here we look at two concepts that are used in complex applications of PERT.

Refined Calculation of Expected Times

The optimistic, pessimistic, and most probable times should be based on a frequency distribution of estimates. Instead of using one intuitive guess as to these durations, a specialist collects all available data about how long comparable activities took. For example, wiring a cockpit took seven weeks in ten different cases; six weeks in five cases; five weeks in three cases; and so forth. The optimistic and pessimistic times are then selected as the lower and upper ten percentiles of the distribution of times. In other words, it is optimistic to think that an event will be completed as rapidly as suggested by the briefest 10 percent of estimates. Also, it is pessimistic to think that the event will be completed in the longest 10 percent of estimated times. (Remember, the expected time is calculated based on a weighted average of the optimistic, most probable, and pessimistic times.)

EXHIBIT 6-6	The PERT Chart EXPERT Software

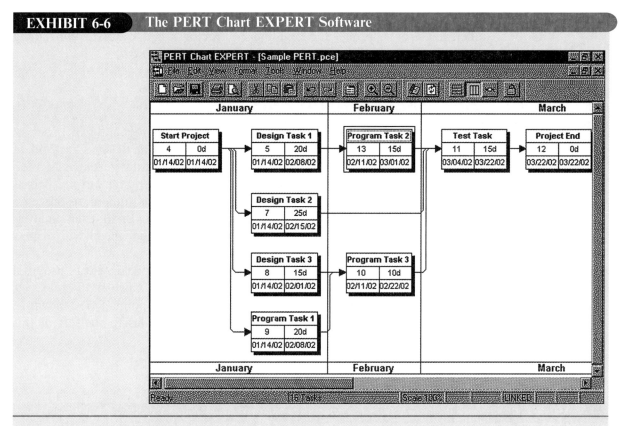

Source: Reprinted with permission from http://www.criticaltools.com.

It is often difficult to obtain data for comparable activities, so quantified guesswork will be required. To illustrate, a project manager might guess, "If we attempted to drill a hole for oil through that ice cap 100 times, I think it would take us 60 days, 15 times, 90 days, 20 times, 110 days, 25 times, and 130 days, 40 times." The guesses provided by this project manager might be combined with those of another specialist, before calculating the pessimistic, optimistic, and most probable times.

Resource and Cost Estimates

In addition to estimating the time required for activities, advanced applications of PERT estimate the amount of resources required. Before a building contractor would establish a price for erecting a building, it would be prudent to estimate how much and what types of equipment would be needed. It would also be essential to estimate how many workers of different skills would be required. Considering that payroll runs about two-thirds of the cost for manufacturing, miscalculating costs can eliminate profits.

The resource and cost estimates can be calculated in the same manner as time estimates. Resource and cost estimates can then be attached to events, thereby suggesting at which point in the project they will most likely be incurred. For example, the building contractor might estimate that siding specialists will not be needed until 90 days into the project.

BREAK-EVEN ANALYSIS

"What do we have to do to break even?" is asked frequently in business. Managers often find the answer through **break-even analysis**, a method of determining the relationship between total costs and total revenues at various levels of production or sales activity. Managers use break-even analysis because—before adding new products, equipment, or human resources—they want to be sure that the changes will pay off. Break-even analysis tells managers the point at which it is profitable to go ahead with a new venture.

Exhibit 6-7 illustrates a typical break-even chart. It deals with a proposal to add a new product to an existing line. The point at which the Total Costs line and the Revenue line intersect is the break-even point. Sales shown to the right of the break-even point represent profit. Sales to the left of this point represent a loss.

EXHIBIT 6-7	Break-Even Chart for Adding a New Product to an Existing Line

A break-even chart indicates at what point a venture becomes profitable.

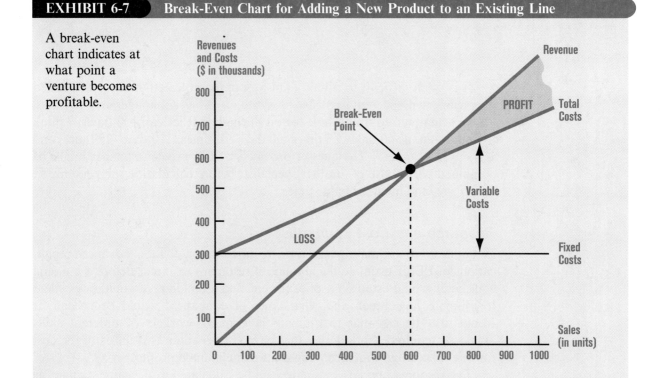

Break-Even Formula

The break-even point (BE) is the situation in which total revenues equal fixed costs plus variable costs. It can be calculated with the following standard formula:

$$BE = \frac{FC}{P - VC}$$

where

P = selling price per unit

VC = variable cost per unit, the cost that varies with the amount produced

FC = fixed cost, the cost that remains constant no matter how many units are produced

The chart in Exhibit 6-7 is based on the plans of a small company to sell furniture over the Internet. For simplicity, we provide data only for the dining room sets. The average selling price (P) is $1,000 per unit; the variable cost (VC) is $500 per unit, including Internet commission fees for sales made through major Web sites. The fixed costs are $300,000.

$$BE = \frac{\$300,000}{\$1,000 - \$500} = \frac{\$300,000}{\$500} = 600 \text{ units}$$

Under the conditions assumed and for the period of time in which these costs and revenue figures are valid, a sales volume of 600 dining room sets would be required for the furniture company to break even. Any volume above that level would produce a profit and anything below it would result in a loss. (We are referring to online sales only. Sales through their customary channels would be figured separately.) If the sales forecast for dining room sets sold through e-commerce is more than 600 units, it would be a good decision to sell online. If the sales forecast is for fewer than 600 units, the furniture company should not attempt e-commerce for now. However, if the husband-and-wife team is willing to absorb losses now to build for the long range, they might start e-commerce anyway. Break-even analysis would tell the owners how much money they are likely to lose. An encouraging note is that small operations such as the furniture company in question have typically profited from e-tailing.

Break-even analyses must be calculated frequently because fixed and variable costs may change quite suddenly. Imagine that you were the manager of a package-delivery service. One of your variable costs, gasoline, might fluctuate weekly. A fixed cost such as truck insurance might change every six months. As an enterprise grows, new fixed costs arise; for example, a growing company might hire a human resources outsourcing firm to take care of payroll and benefits administration.

Advantages and Limitations of Break-Even Analysis

Break-even analysis helps managers keep their thinking focused on the volume of activity that will be necessary to justify a new expense. The technique is useful because it applies to a number of operations problems. Break-even analysis can help a manager decide whether to drop an existing product from the line, to replace equipment, or to buy rather than make a part.

Break-even analysis has some drawbacks. First, it is only as valid as the estimates of costs and revenues that managers use to create it. Second, the relationship between variable costs and sales may be complicated. Exhibit 6-7 indicates that variable costs and sales increase together in a direct relationship. In reality, unit costs may decrease with increased volume. It is also possible that costs may increase with volume. Suppose that increased production leads to higher turnover because employees prefer not to work overtime. A caution about break-even analysis: the break-even point is a calculation, not a forecast. Just because the business owner above must sell 600 dining room sets to break even, it does not mean there is a demand for this many units.

Break-even analysis relates to decisions about whether or not to proceed. The next section will examine a more complicated decision-making technique that relates to the desirability of several alternative solutions.

DECISION TREES

decision tree

A graphic illustration of the alternative solutions available to solve a problem.

Another useful planning tool is called a **decision tree**, a graphic illustration of the alternative solutions available to solve a problem. Analyzing the outcomes of a few alternative actions before making a decision is useful because it helps predict whether you have made a decision that produces the most favorable, or least painful, consequences.[14] Decision trees are designed to estimate the outcome of a series of decisions. As the sequences of the major decision are drawn, the resulting diagram resembles a tree with branches.

A decision tree extends from a starting point through a series of branches until two or more final results are reached at the opposite end. The diagram may continue to branch, as more options are chosen. Using this information, the manager computes the expected values and adds them for the two alternatives. An **expected value** is the average value incurred if a particular decision is made a large number of times. Sometimes the alternative would earn more, and sometimes less, with the expected value being the alternative's average return.

expected value

The average return on a particular decision being made a large number of times.

To illustrate the essentials of using a decision tree for making financial decisions, consider a manager from a mining company in Alaska who is deciding on the feasibility of digging for gold. Discussions with staff accountants and mining engineers suggest the following expected outcomes (conditional values) for a first gold dig: 10 percent chance of having a very successful dig; 20 percent chance of having moderately successful dig; 10 percent chance of breaking even; and 60 percent chance of losing a moderate amount of money. These figures are conditional; they depend on such factors as the amount of gold in the ore under the ground and the reliability of the equipment. Liking the conditional values, the manager decides to take a chance with mining for gold and lays out the decision tree shown in Exhibit 6-8.[15]

---

[14]Carole Matthews, "Decision Making with Decision Trees," *Inc.com*, April 2003, p. 1.

[15]The idea for this particular layout of a basic decision tree is based on "Decision Tree," www.referenceforbusiness.com.

EXHIBIT 6-8	First-Dig Decision Tree for Gold Mining Manager

A decision tree helps predict if you have made a decision that produces the most favorable outcome.

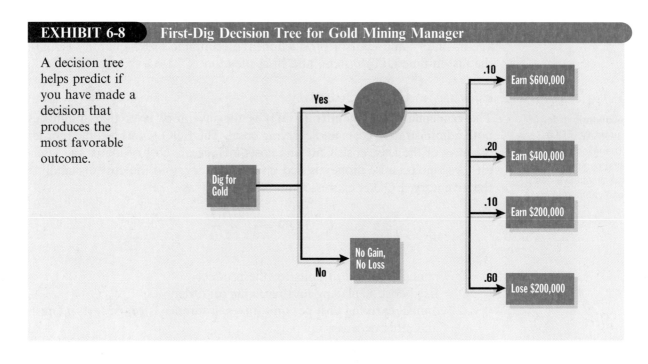

The expected financial outcome from the first dig is a profit of $40,000, calculated as follows: .10 × $600,000 + .20 × $400,000 + .10 × $200,000 − .60 × $200,000 = $40,000. Or, $60,000 + $80,000 + $20,000 − $120,000 = $40,000. Our manager, says, "Sounds good. I will go for the gold for the first dig."

The advantage of a decision tree is that it can be used to help make sequences of decisions. After one dig for gold, the manager may think of expanding. One of the many ways in which the decision tree could continue would be for the manager to use more advanced equipment or to conduct two digs at the same time. New conditional values would have to be calculated for these branches.

LEARNING OBJECTIVE ⑤
Describe how to manage inventory by using the economic order quantity (EOQ), the just-in-time (JIT) system, and LIFO versus FIFO.

INVENTORY CONTROL TECHNIQUES

Managers of manufacturing and sales organizations face the problem of how much inventory to keep on hand. If a firm maintains a large inventory, goods can be made quickly, customers can make immediate purchases, and orders can be shipped rapidly. However, stocking goods is expensive. The goods themselves are costly, and the money tied up in inventory cannot be invested elsewhere. Dell Computers and Target are examples of companies that owe some of their competitive advantage to their efficient management of inventory. Dell minimizes the need for large inventory by building a computer only after an order is received. Of course, Dell still keeps lots of computer components on hand, but they do not have warehouses filled with yet-to-be sold computers. Target collaborates with its suppliers to keep shelves stocked with the right amount and quantity of merchandise to minimize inventory accumulation.

This section will describe three decision-making techniques used to manage inventory and control production: the economic order quantity (EOQ), the just-in-time (JIT) system, and brief mention of LIFO versus FIFO.

Economic Order Quantity

economic order quantity (EOQ)

The inventory level that minimizes both administrative costs and carrying costs.

The **economic order quantity (EOQ)** is the inventory level that minimizes both administrative costs and carrying costs. The EOQ represents the reorder quantity of the least cost. Carrying costs include the cost of loans, the interest foregone because money is tied up in inventory, and the cost of handling the inventory. EOQ is expressed mathematically as

$$\text{EOQ} = \sqrt{\frac{2\,DO}{C}}$$

where
D = annual demand in units for the product
O = fixed cost of placing and receiving an order
C = annual carrying cost per unit (taxes, insurance, storage cost, interest, and other expenses)

The economic order quantity is found to be the most useful when a company has repetitive purchasing and demand for an item, such as truck tires or hospital supplies. Let us return to our furniture example. Assume that the annual demand for coffee tables is 100 units and that it costs $1,000 to order each unit. Furthermore, suppose the carrying cost per unit is $200. The equation to calculate the most economic number of coffee tables to keep in inventory is

$$
\begin{aligned}
\text{EOQ} &= \sqrt{\frac{2 \times 100 \times \$1,000}{\$200}} \\
&= \sqrt{\frac{\$200,000}{\$200}} \\
&= \sqrt{1,000} \\
&= 32 \text{ coffee tables (rounded figure)}
\end{aligned}
$$

Therefore, the owners of the online furniture store conclude that the most economical number of coffee tables to keep in inventory during the selling season is 32. (The assumption is that the company has a large storage area.) If the figures entered into the EOQ formula are accurate, EOQ calculations can vastly improve inventory management.

Just-in-Time System

just-in-time (JIT) system

A system to minimize inventory and move it into the plant exactly when needed.

An important thrust in manufacturing is to keep just enough parts and components on hand to fill current orders. The **just-in-time (JIT)** system is an inventory control method designed to minimize inventory and move it into the plant exactly when needed. Note also that JIT is part of a manufacturing system that focuses on making manufacturing more efficient by eliminating waste wherever possible.

The key principle of the system is to eliminate excess inventory by producing or purchasing parts, subassemblies, and final products only when—and in the exact amounts—needed. JIT helps a manufacturing division stay *lean* by minimizing waste. JIT is often referred to as lean manufacturing because waste of "fat" is minimized. A lean manufacturing organization adopts a culture of continuously looking for ways to be more efficient. A specific example would be redesigning a work area from a linear operation to a U-shaped station to improve efficiency.[16]

The JIT is quantitative in the sense that it relies heavily on numbers, such as the number of parts and components accumulated as inventory. Under JIT, the company would track data such as the number of hours or days of accumulated inventory. Imagine the small furniture company having raw wood delivered to its door within an hour or so after an order is received over the Internet. JIT is generally used in a repetitive, single-product manufacturing environment. The system is now also used to improve operations in sales and service organizations.

Reducing waste is the core JIT philosophy. Three such wastes are overproduction, waiting, and stock. *Overproduction waste* can be reduced by producing only what is needed when an order is received. *Waiting waste* can be reduced by synchronizing the work flow, such as technicians preparing a housing for a computer monitor when the internal mechanisms are coming down the line. *Stock waste* can be reduced by keeping inventory at a minimum.

Procedures and Techniques

Just-in-time inventory control is part of a system of manufacturing control. It involves many different techniques and procedures. Seven of the major techniques and procedures are described in the list that follows.[17] Knowing them provides insight into the system of manufacturing used by many successful Japanese companies and others.

1. *Kanbans.* The JIT system of inventory control relies on *kanbans*, or cards, to communicate production requirements from the final point of assembly to the manufacturing operations that precede it. (A computerized equivalent of the physical card can be used.) When an order is received for a product, a kanban is issued that directs employees. The finishing department selects components and assembles the product. The kanban is then passed back to earlier stations. This kanban tells workers to resupply the components. New stock is ordered when stock reaches the reorder level. Kanban communication continues all the way back to the material suppliers. In many JIT systems, suppliers locate their companies so they can be close to major customers. Proximity

---

[16]Neal Haldene, "Novi Center Teaches Lean Way of Working," *Detroit News* (http://www .detnews.com), September 21, 2006.

[17]Ramon L. Aldag and Timothy M. Stearns, *Management*, 2nd ed. (Cincinnati: South-Western College Publishing, 1991), pp. 645–646.

allows suppliers to make shipments promptly. At each stage, parts and other materials are delivered just in time for use.

2. *Demand-driven pull system.* The JIT technique requires producing exactly what is needed to match the demand created by customer orders. Demand drives final assembly schedules, and assembly drives subassembly timetables. The result is a pull system—that is, customer demand pulls along activities to meet that demand.

3. *Short production lead times.* A JIT system minimizes the time between the arrival of raw material or components in the plant and the shipment of a finished product to a customer.

4. *High inventory turnover (with the goal of zero inventory and stockless production).* Levels of finished goods, work in process, and raw materials are purposely reduced. Raw material in a warehouse is regarded as waste, and so is idle work in process. (A person who applied JIT to the household would regard backup supplies of ketchup or motor oil as shameful!)

5. *Designated areas for receiving materials.* Certain areas on the shop floor or in receiving and shipping departments are designated for receiving specific items from suppliers. At a Toyota plant in Japan, the receiving area is about half the size of a football field. The designated spaces for specific items are marked with yellow paint.

6. *Designated containers.* Specifying where to store items allows for easy access to parts and it eliminates counting. For example, at Toyota the bed of a truck has metal frame mounts for exactly eight engines. A truckload of engines means eight engines—no more, no less. No one has to count them.

7. *Neatness.* A JIT plant that follows Japanese tradition is immaculate. All unnecessary materials, tools, rags, and files are discarded. The factory floor is as neat and clean as the showroom.

Advantages and Disadvantages of the JIT Inventory System

Manufacturing companies have realized several benefits from adopting JIT. The expenses associated with maintaining a large inventory can be dramatically reduced, providing suppliers do not raise their prices for making deliveries as needed. JIT controls can lead to organizational commitment to quality in design, materials, parts, employee–management and supplier–user relations, and finished goods. With minimum levels of inventory on hand, finished products are more visible and defects are more readily detected. Quality problems can be attacked before they escalate to an insurmountable degree. Low levels of inventory shorten cycle times.

Despite the advantages JIT management can offer large manufacturers, it has some potential disadvantages. Above all, a JIT system must be placed in a supportive or compatible environment. JIT is applicable only to highly repetitive manufacturing operations such as car or residential furnace manufacturing. Also, product demand must be predictable with a minimum of surges in demand. Reliable suppliers are needed.

Small companies with short runs of a variety of products often suffer financial losses from JIT practices. One problem they have is that suppliers are often unwilling to promptly ship small batches to meet the weekly needs of a small customer.

The savings from JIT management can be deceptive. Suppliers might simply build up inventories in their own plants and add that cost to their prices. JIT inventory practices leave a company vulnerable to work stoppages, such as a strike. With a large inventory of finished products or parts, the company can continue to meet customer demand while the work stoppage is being settled.

Finally, JIT may lead to manufacturing efficiencies, but efficiency alone does not make for a great organization. For example, Dell ultimately ran into problems with competitors taking away some of its market share by introducing products more in demand. Dell management, as described in Case 4-B, then swung into action with the introduction of new products to regain some of its prominence.

LIFO versus FIFO

Another method of inventory control is more a method of accounting than it is a method of managing physical inventory, yet it does relate to stocking inventory. Imagine that you were running a tire warehouse and had hundreds of tires of many sizes in stock. When an automotive service center ordered four tires, would you ship the oldest tires in your warehouse? Or would you ship the tires you most recently acquired? Which tires you ship could have important implications.

Last In, First Out (LIFO)
Selling an item first that was received last in inventory.

First In, First Out (FIFO)
Selling an item first that has been in inventory the longest.

Last In, First Out (LIFO) means that when there is more than one item in stock, you sell the most recently received items first, before you sell older inventory. In the example at hand, you sell the latest four tires you received from the manufacturer. The rationale here is that the newest is probably the most expensive. **First In, First Out (FIFO)** means that when there is more than one item in stock, you sell the one you have had in inventory the longest.

In choosing between LIFO and FIFO, you have both physical and financial considerations. Getting rid of older inventory first can be a good idea because the longer something sits around, the higher the probability the item will be damaged or the packing will begin to look old and torn. If the company has borrowed money to purchase inventory, you want to move the inventory you have been paying for the longest. This is particularly true for business firms such as automobile and boat dealers.

One of several financial and tax considerations is that if you value inventory at the cost of the time you purchased it, your profits will look better when you sell at today's prices. In returning to the tire example, suppose you sell your four tires to the service center for $400. If you ship four tires for which you paid $50 each three years ago, your gross profit would be $200 (four tires times $50). You have to pay income tax on $200. However, if you ship four tires for which you paid $75 each last month, your profit is now $100. You have earned less profit, but you will pay less tax. (Consult your accounting professor or tax accountant for the latest rulings! For example, it might be possible to value the older tires at today's prices, thus reducing your reported revenue.)

LEARNING
OBJECTIVE 6
Describe how to identify problems using a Pareto diagram.

PARETO DIAGRAMS FOR PROBLEM IDENTIFICATION

Pareto diagram
A bar graph that ranks types of output variations by frequency of occurrence.

Managers and professionals frequently must identify the major causes of their problem. For example, "What features of our product are receiving the most complaints from consumers?" or "Our agency is offering more services to the public than we can afford. Which services might we drop without hurting too many people?" One problem-identification technique uses a **Pareto diagram**, a bar graph (or histogram) that ranks types of output variations by frequency of occurrence. Managers and other workers often use Pareto diagrams to identify the most important problems or causes of problems that affect output quality. Identification of the "vital few" allows management or product improvement teams to focus on the major cause of a production or service problem. Based on quantitative data, effort is then directed where it will do the most good.

An example of Pareto analysis is an investigation of the delay associated with processing credit card applications. The data are grouped in the following categories:[18]

- No signature
- Residential address not valid
- Non-legible handwriting
- Already a customer
- Other

As Exhibit 6-9 shows, the cause of a problem is plotted on the x-axis (horizontal). The cumulative effects both in frequency and percent are plotted on the y-axis (vertical). In a Pareto diagram, the bars are arranged in descending order of height (or frequency of occurrence) from left to right across the x-axis. As a consequence, the most important causes are at the left of the chart. Priorities are then established for taking action on the few causes that account for most of the effect. According to the Pareto principle, generally 20 percent or fewer of the causes contribute to 80 percent or more of the effects. It is widely recognized, for example, that about 20 percent of the customers of an industrial company account for 80 percent of sales. About 20 percent of customers account for about 80 percent of complaints.

At one point a crisis-management team of Ford managers and professionals did a Pareto analysis of problems with Bridgestone/Firestone tires

---

[18]Kerri Simon, "Pareto Chart," *Six Sigma* (http://www.isixsigma.com), accessed November 18, 2006.

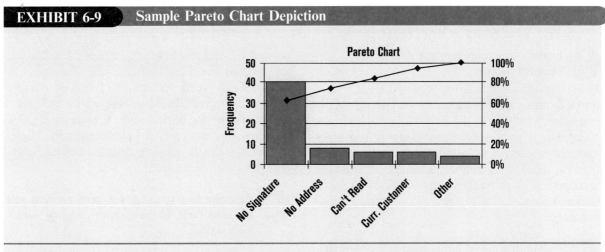

EXHIBIT 6-9   **Sample Pareto Chart Depiction**

Source: Kerri Simon, "Pareto Chart," *Six Sigma* (http://www.isixsigma.com), accessed November 18, 2006.

used on the Ford Explorer. The Ford team analyzed the data based on tire sizes that had more than 30 reported warranty claims. The key results of their analysis, reported as follows, strongly support the Pareto principle:

> *Of 2,498 complaints involving eight separate size categories, 2,030, or 81 percent, involved the 15-inch P235/75R15 models, which included the Firestone ATX and Wilderness tires. Of the 1,699 reported complaints of tread separations on 13 different size tires, 1,424, or 84 percent, were for the P234/75R15 series of tires used on Ford's Explorer and Bronco SUVs and its F-150 and Ranger pickup trucks.*[19]

As you probably observed, one model created 81 percent of the problems and another series 84 percent. Although the 80/20 (Pareto) principle is a general guide, it is a close approximation of reality in many situations.

The Pareto Diagram fits data-driven management and decision making. In the example in Exhibit 6-9, the manager can say, "About 80 percent of our credit card applications are being rejected because the signature is missing. I think we can coach our customers to do a better job signing their applications."

---

[19]Bill Vlasic, "Tire Recall Rife with Blame, Tragedy," *The Detroit News*, March 9, 2000.

Summary of Key Points

1 **Explain how managers use data-based decision making.**

Using data-driven management, decisions are based on facts rather than impressions or guesses. Many managers want to see the data before accepting a suggestion from a subordinate. Data-driven management is more of an attitude and approach than it is a specific technique. Although data-driven management is preferable in most situations, intuition and judgment still contribute to making major decisions.

2 **Explain the use of forecasting techniques in planning.**

All planning includes making forecasts, both qualitative and quantitative. A judgmental forecast makes predictions on subjective opinions. Time-series analysis is a widely used method of making quantitative forecasts. Three widely used forecasts are economic, sales, and technological. Scenario planning helps managers prepare for the outcomes of forecasts, both negative and positive. The Delphi Techniques can improve the accuracy of forecasts because specialists working alone prepare forecasts and comment on the forecasts prepared by others in the group.

3 **Describe how to use Gantt charts, milestone charts, and PERT planning techniques.**

Gantt and milestone charts are simple methods of monitoring schedules that are particularly useful for one-time projects. Gantt charts graphically depict the planned and actual progress of work over the period of time encompassed by a project. A milestone chart lists the subactivities that must be completed to accomplish the major activities.

Managers use PERT networks to track complicated projects when sequences of events must be planned carefully. In a PERT network, an event is a point of decision or accomplishment. An activity is the task that must be performed to complete an event. To complete a PERT diagram, a manager must sequence all the events and estimate the time required for each activity. The expected time for each activity takes into account optimistic,

pessimistic, and probable estimates of time. The critical path is the most time-consuming sequence of activities and events that must be followed to implement the project. The duration of the project is determined by the critical path. Frequency distributions are sometimes used to calculate expected times, and PERT can be used to estimate resources and costs that will be needed.

4 **Describe how to use break-even analysis and decision trees for problem solving and decision making.**

Managers use break-even analysis to estimate the point at which it is profitable to go ahead with a new venture. It is a method of determining the relationship between total costs and total revenues at various levels of sales activity or operation. Break-even analysis determines the ratio of total fixed costs to the difference between the selling price and the variable cost for each unit. The results of break-even analysis are often depicted on a graph. Break-even analysis must be done frequently because fixed and variable costs change.

A decision tree provides a quantitative estimate of the best alternative. It is a tool for estimating the outcome of a series of decisions. When sequences of major decisions are drawn, they resemble a tree with branches.

5 **Describe how to manage inventory using the economic order quantity (EOQ), the just-in-time (JIT) system, and LIFO versus FIFO.**

The economic order quantity (EOQ) is a decision-support technique widely used to manage inventory. The EOQ is the inventory level that minimizes both ordering and carrying costs. The EOQ technique helps managers in a manufacturing or sales organization decide how much inventory to keep on hand.

Just-in-time (JIT) inventory management minimizes stock on hand. Instead, stock is moved into the plant exactly when needed. Although not specifically a decision-making technique, JIT helps shape decisions about inventory. The key principle underlying JIT systems is the elimination of excess inventory by producing or purchasing items only when and in the exact amounts needed. JIT is part of lean manufacturing.

JIT processes involve (1) kanbans, or cards for communicating production requirements to the previous operation; (2) a customer demand-driven system; (3) short production lead times; (4) high inventory turnover; (5) designated areas for receiving materials; (6) designated containers and (7) neatness throughout the factory.

JIT inventory management is best suited for repetitive manufacturing processes. One drawback of JIT is that it places heavy pressures on suppliers to build up their inventories to satisfy sudden demands of their customers who use the system.

LIFO versus FIFO helps manage inventory, but is mostly an accounting technique. With LIFO, you sell the last item received first. With FIFO, you sell first the item you have had in inventory the longest.

 Describe how to identify problems using a Pareto diagram.

Problems or causes of problems can often be identified by a problem-identification technique called the Pareto diagram. The Pareto principle stems from the diagram, and suggests that about 20 percent or fewer of the causes contribute to 80 percent or more of the effects.

Key Terms and Phrases

Data-driven management, 193
Judgmental forecast, 196
Time-series analysis, 196
Scenario planning, 200
Delphi Technique, 200
Gantt chart, 201
Milestone chart, 202
Program evaluation and review
   technique (PERT), 203
Event, 204
Activity, 204

Expected time, 205
Critical path, 205
Break-even analysis, 208
Decision tree, 210
Expected value, 210
Economic order quantity (EOQ), 212
Just-in-time (JIT) system, 212
Last In, First Out (LIFO), 215
First In, First Out (FIFO), 215
Pareto diagram, 216

Questions

1. Why would a heavy equipment company like Caterpillar hire a Ph.D. in economics as the CEO?
2. Visualize yourself as the manager of an athletic club. Give three examples of data you might be able to use in making decisions about how to improve the profitability of the club.
3. Gantt charts have been around for almost 100 years, and they are now implemented with software. Why do Gantt charts have such staying power?
4. Describe two possible job applications for a PERT network.
5. How might the Pareto principle apply to the profits an automobile company earns on the sales of its vehicles?
6. At least one-half of new restaurants fail within the first couple of years, even when these restaurants appear to be busy much of the time. How might two of the techniques described in this chapter help prevent someone opening a restaurant that is doomed to fail?
7. An important part of management is dealing with people. Where is the human touch in any of the techniques described in this chapter?

Skill-Building Exercise 6-A: Developing a PERT Network

Use the following information about a safety improvement project to construct a PERT diagram.

Be sure to indicate the critical path with a dark arrow. Work individually or in small groups.

EVENT	DESCRIPTION	TIME REQUIRED (UNITS)	PRECEDING EVENT
A	Complete safety audit	6	none
B	Benchmark	15	A
C	Collect internal information	6	A
D	Identify safety problems	3	B, C
E	Identify improvement practices	7	D
F	Elicit employee participation	20	A
G	Implement safety program	6	E, F
H	Measure results	8	G

Source: Adapted and reprinted with permission from Raymond L. Hilgert and Edwin C. Leonard Jr., *Supervision: Concepts and Practices of Management,* 6th ed. (Cincinnati: South-Western College Publishing, 1995), p. 191.

Skill-Building Exercise 6-B: Break-Even Analysis

On recent vacation trips to Juarez, Mexico, you noticed retail stores and street vendors selling inexpensive digital cameras. (The photo stores also sold brand-name digital cameras at close to U.S. prices.) The prices for the inexpensive cameras ranged from $25 to $40 U.S. A flash of inspiration hit you. Why not sell Mexican-assembled digital cameras back home to Americans, using a van as your store? Every three months you would drive the 350 miles to Mexico and load up on these novelty digital cameras. You are thinking of negotiating to receive large-quantity discounts.

You would park your van on busy streets and nearby parks, wherever you could obtain a permit. Typically you would display the cameras outside the van, but on a rainy day people could step inside. Your intention is to operate your traveling camera sale about 12 hours per week. If you could make enough money from your business, you could attend classes full-time during the day. You intend to sell the cameras at an average price of $65 a unit.

Based on preliminary analysis, you have discovered that your primary fixed costs per month would be $550 for payments on a van, $175 for gas and maintenance, $75 for insurance, and $60 for a street vendor's permit. You will be driving to Mexico every three months at $600 per trip, resulting in a $200 per month travel cost. Your variable costs would be an average of $30 per camera and 45¢ for placing each camera in an attractive box.

1. How many cameras must you sell each month before you start to make a profit?
2. If the average cost of your cameras rises to $35, how many cameras must you sell each month if you hold your price to $65 per unit?

Management Now: Online Skill-Building Exercise: The Reality of the Pareto Principle

The Pareto principle has become entrenched in management thinking: 80 percent of effects are created by 20 percent of causes. We regularly hear such glib statements as "20 percent of our customers account for 80 percent of our sales." The text furnished other examples of the Pareto principle. Conduct research on the Internet to find at least one example of the 80/20 rule that has taken place in the last six months. Perhaps a recent product recall will prove fruitful, such as one model of a product creating the vast majority of the problems. At the same time, see whether you can find evidence that refutes the reliability of this principle or rule. In other words, can you find a current example of a situation in which 20 percent of the causes did not produce 80 percent of the effects?

6-A Case Problem

Retro Is Our Future

The management team at Bally Hoo Fashions was gathered in Puerto Rico for their annual February executive meeting. The sales for the previous year totaled $85 million, and net profits hit $11.2 million. Both figures were the highest in company history even after adjusting for inflation, putting CEO Julia and the rest of the team in a jubilant mood.

During the first evening of the meeting, just before dinner, Julia addressed the team in these words: "You folks may have heard the rumor, but I want to confirm it and expand a little. I have spotted a great opportunity for Bally Hoo, and I have had to look in the rear view mirror to get a clear picture of the future.

"A dominant trend in the fashion world, especially for people under age 30, is the retro look. I'm talking about designs that go back to the disco look of the 1960s, and the Elvis Presley craze. I am proposing that we invest about $10 million in setting up Bally Hoo Retro boutiques across the country and in Canada. We will also sell our retro fashions to our major retailers."

"I have some concerns, Julia," said Kelly, the director of marketing. "What makes you so confident that there is a future in retro fashions?"

Julia replied, "I'm getting all sorts of vibes in that direction. The Elvis impersonator festivals are stronger than ever. I am seeing more photos on the Internet of restored 1957 Chevys recently. My teenage daughter told me that tunes from Nat King Cole, Barbara Streisand, and Frank Sinatra are hot in her school. Her boyfriend has started to grow sideburns and

productions of "Grease" are running across the country."

Trent, the chief financial officer said, "You are our leader Julia, and you have shown great fashion intuition in the past. But despite our recent prosperity, $10 million is a big gamble on a long shot like bringing back styles from over 50 years ago."

Julia replied, "The great companies became great by making big bets on long shots. Look at how well Apple did in betting on iPods and iPhones."

With a concerned expression, Trent said, "Julia, Apple didn't invest in rotary dial phones or phonographs. Steve Jobs and company bet on leading-edge products."

With an exasperated expression, Julia said, "Okay, I can feel the cold water splashing on my face. Tomorrow morning, we will spend a few hours trying to determine whether our future is in retro."

Discussion Questions

1. How should the management team at Bally Hoo make an informed judgment about the future demand for retro clothing styles?
2. What is your evaluation of the creative thinking of Julia?
3. Should Kelly and Trent be reprimanded for insubordination?
4. If you were a consultant to Bally Hoo Fashions, what would you advise them on the feasibility of establishing a chain of retro boutiques and selling retro clothing to retailers? What is the source of information for your recommendations?

6-B Case Problem

Just-In-Time Worries at the University of Utah Hospital

Like many big hospitals, the University of Utah Hospital carries a 30-day supply of drugs, in part because it would be too costly or wasteful to stockpile more. Some of its hepatitis vaccine supply has been diverted to the hurricane-ravaged Gulf, leaving it vulnerable should an outbreak occur closer to home. About 77 other drugs are in short supply because of manufacturing and other glitches, such as a drug maker shutting down a factory.

"The supply chain is horribly thin," says Erin Fox, a drug-information specialist at the Salt Lake City Hospital. In the event of a pandemic flu outbreak, that chain is almost certain to break. Thousands of drug-company workers in the United States and elsewhere could be sickened, prompting factories to close. Truck routes could be blocked and borders may be closed, particularly perilous at a time when 80 percent of raw materials for U.S. drugs come from abroad. The likely result: shortages of important medicines—such as insulin, blood products, or the anesthetics used in surgery—quite apart from any shortages of medicine to treat the flu itself.

A problem facing Utah Hospital, as well as other hospitals, is that production of drugs takes place offshore because that's cheaper. The federal government doesn't intervene as a guaranteed buyer of flu drugs, as it does with weapons. Investors and tax rules conspire to eliminate redundancy and reserves. Antitrust rules prevent private companies from collaborating to speed development of new drugs.

A report issued by the Trust for America's Health, a public-health advocacy group in Washington, concluded that 40 percent of the states lack enough backup medical supplies to cope with a pandemic flu or other major disease outbreak.

"Most, if not all, of the medical products or protective-device companies in this country are operating almost at full capacity," says Michael Osterholm, director of the Center for Infectious Disease Research and Policy at the University of Minnesota. "That's the reality of today's economy: just-in-time delivery with no surge capacity."

One significant concern is what Michael Leavitt, the secretary of health and human services, described in an interview as the "Albertson's syndrome," referring to the grocery-store chain. At the first sign of panic, all supplies disappear from shelves, something that routinely happens when there is the threat of even a modest storm.

Discussion Questions

1. How suitable is the just-in-time inventory management system for the University of Utah Hospital (as well as for other large hospitals)?
2. What recommendations would you make to the hospital in question to have drugs available to deal with a pandemic or other emergency?

Source: Bernard Wysocki Jr. and Sarah Lueck, "Just-in-Time Inventories Make U.S. Vulnerable in a Pandemic," *The Wall Street Journal*, January 12, 2006, pp. A1, A7.

CHAPTER 7

Job Design and Work Schedules

A few years ago, it took 20 to 30 craftsmen to put together each Louis Vuitton Reade tote bag. Over the course of about eight days, individual workers would sew together leather panels, glue in linings, and attach handles. Later on, inspired by car maker Toyota Corporation and egged on by management consultants from McKinsey & Company, the venerable French luxury-goods house discovered efficiency. Today, teams of 6 to 12 workers, each performing several tasks, can assemble the $680 shiny, LV-logo bags in a single day.

The factory floor changes are part of a sweeping effort by Louis Vuitton to serve customers better by keeping its boutiques fully stocked with popular merchandise—to operate, in other words, more like a successful modern retailer. Its supply-chain overhaul includes changes to its distribution system and to the way salespeople serve customers in its tony stores.

For years, high-end fashion houses like Louis Vuitton—best known for its expensive brown-and-gold logo bags—paid far more attention to product design, craftsmanship, and image than to the mechanics of keeping the stores stocked. When new designs caught on, they often sold

OBJECTIVES

After studying this chapter and doing the exercises, you should be able to:

1. Explain the four major dimensions of job design plus job specialization and job descriptions.

2. Describe job enrichment, including the job characteristics model.

3. Describe job involvement, enlargement, and rotation.

4. Explain how workers use job crafting to modify their jobs.

5. Illustrate how ergonomic factors can be part of job design.

6. Summarize the various modified work schedules.

7. Explain how job design can contribute to a high-performance work system.

out, and the companies were often ill prepared to speed up production and distribution.

Chic but less-expensive fashion labels such as Zara and H&M have thrived by spotting trends quickly and filling shelves with new products every fortnight. Their success has forced higher-end rivals to rethink how they do business. Part of the overhaul by Louis Vuitton to stay competitive was to make its manufacturing process more flexible, borrowing techniques pioneered by car makers and consumer-electronics companies.

Tampering with Vuitton's production poses a risk to the brand's image. Customers pay hundreds of dollars for its logo canvas bags, for example, partly because they have bought into the notion that skilled craftsmen make them the old-fashioned way. Although the company has been modernizing gradually for some time, its reputation for high-quality hand-crafted products is still vital to its success.

The new factory format is called Pégase (Pegasus in English), after the mythological winged horse and a Vuitton rolling suitcase. Under the new system, it takes less time to assemble bags, in part because they no longer sit around on carts waiting to be moved from one workstation to another. That enables the company to ship fresh collections to its boutiques every six weeks—more than twice as frequently as in the past. "It's about finding the best ratio between quality and speed," says Patrick-Louis Vuitton, a fifth-generation member of the company's founding family, who is in charge of special orders.[1]

The Louis Vuitton story illustrates how modifying job design is a major part of helping a company stay competitive. By adding tasks to the production workers' jobs, the workers became more productive to the point that the tote bag could be produced in one day. (Yet the company does not want to lose the benefits of workers having expertise.) Improving job design can contribute to the success of a workplace in many manufacturing and service settings. Employers use a variety of job designs and work schedules to increase productivity and job satisfaction. Modifying job design and giving workers more control over schedules are the two major topics of this chapter.

To accomplish complex tasks, such as building ships or operating a hotel, you must divide work among individuals and groups. Subdividing

---

[1]Adapted from Christina Passariello, "Louis Vuitton Tries Modern Methods on Factory Lines," *The Wall Street Journal*, October 9, 2006, pp. A1, A15.

the overall tasks of an enterprise can be achieved in two primary ways. One way is to design specific jobs to be accomplished by individuals and groups. A shipbuilding company must design jobs for welders, metal workers, engineers, purchasing agents, and contract administrators. In addition, workers may be assigned to teams that assume responsibility for productivity and quality. The other primary way of subdividing work assigns tasks to units within the organization—units such as departments and divisions.

This chapter will explain basic concepts relating to job design, such as making jobs more challenging and giving employees more control over their working hours and place of work. We also look at how workers often shape their own jobs, the importance of ergonomics, and job designs for high-performance work systems. The next chapter will describe how work is divided throughout an organization.

LEARNING OBJECTIVE ❶

Explain the four major dimensions of job design plus job specialization and job descriptions.

 PLAY VIDEO

Go to www.cengage.com/management/dubrin to view the video for Chapter 7. What type of workforce does this company have, and why does that create challenges in scheduling?

job design

The process of laying out job responsibilities and duties and describing how they are to be performed.

FOUR MAJOR DIMENSIONS OF JOB DESIGN PLUS JOB SPECIALIZATION AND JOB DESCRIPTION

A useful starting point in understanding job design is to examine the major dimensions or components of jobs. **Job design** is the process of laying out job responsibilities and duties and describing how they are to be performed. The different ways in which work can be designed has been studied for a long time. Frederick P. Morgeson and Stephen E. Humphrey have integrated this information, added a study of their own with 540 job holders, and arrived at a new understanding of job dimensions and the nature of work.[2] Each of the four dimensions has several components. Almost any job, from door person to CEO, can be described according to how much of each dimension and sub-dimension is contained in the job. Because the dimensions refer to what an incumbent actually does on the job, understanding these dimensions leads to an understanding of the nature of work.

These dimensions and sub-dimensions are described next, and outlined in Exhibit 7-1. In this section we explain job specialization and job descriptions because they are a logical follow-up to knowing job dimensions. The various approaches to job design described in this chapter contain similar dimensions, and this new framework includes many previous findings about job design.

[2]The entire discussion in this section is based on Frederick P. Morgeson and Stephen E. Humphrey, "The Work Design Questionnaire (WDQ): Developing and Validating a Comprehensive Measure for Assessing the Job Design and the Nature of Work," *Journal of Applied Psychology*, November 2006, pp. 1321–1329. The Morgeson and Humphrey article is based partly on much of the research on job enrichment and the job characteristics model presented later in this chapter.

EXHIBIT 7-1	The Four Job Dimensions and Their Sub-Dimensions

Task Characteristics	Social Characteristics
Work-scheduling autonomy	Social support
Decision-making autonomy	Initiated interdependence
Work-methods autonomy	Received interdependence
Task variety	Interaction outside organization
Task significance	Feedback from others
Task identity	
Feedback from the job	Contextual Characteristics
	Ergonomics
Knowledge Characteristics	Physical demands
Job complexity	Work conditions
Information processing	Equipment use
Problem solving	
Skill variety	
Specialization	

Source: Abridged from Frederick P. Morgeson and Stephen E. Humphrey, "The Work Design Questionnaire (WDQ): Developing and Validating a Comprehensive Measure for Assessing the Job Design and the Nature of Work," *Journal of Applied Psychology*, November 2006, p. 1327.

Task Characteristics

Task characteristics focus on how the work itself is accomplished and the range and nature of the tasks associated with a particular job. A task characteristic for a manager at a steel mill might be using a spreadsheet to make a time-series analysis of the demand for recycled steel by manufacturers of washing machines.

Autonomy in general refers to how much freedom and independence the incumbent has to carry out his or her work assignment. The freedom aspect includes (a) work scheduling, (b) decision making, and (c) work methods. A steel manager with high autonomy might decide when to do the forecast, make decisions based on the forecast, and choose the method for making the forecast (maybe not using a spreadsheet).

Task variety refers to the degree to which the job requires the worker to use a wide range of tasks, such as the steel-mill manager making forecasts, selecting employees, and motivating workers. *Task significance* indicates the extent to which a job influences the lives or work of others, whether inside or outside the organization. Because the steel our manager helps produce is contained in the vehicles and home appliances of many people, the manager's job has high task significance.

Task identity reflects the extent to which a job involves a whole piece of work that can readily be identified. An audiologist who administers hearing tests to customers in a shopping mall has high task identity. A business analyst who performs financial analysis that only contributes to a larger report has low task identity.

Feedback from job refers to the extent to which the job provides direct and clear information about task performance. The focus is on feedback directly from the job itself, as opposed to feedback from others. An installer of satellite TV has considerable feedback because before leaving the customer's home, he or she knows if the rig is working. One of the potential frustrations in a manager's job is that the manager does not know right away if he or she has done any good, such as in attempting to motivate workers.

Knowledge Characteristics

An obvious job dimension is the demand for knowledge, skill, and ability placed on a job holder because of the activities built into the job. The security person at the door of a bar must know the difference between a valid I.D. card and a fake I.D. card. A chief financial officer must understand the various ways in which *profits* might be stated.

Job complexity refers to the degree to which the job tasks are complex and difficult to perform. Work that involves complex tasks requires high-level skills and is mentally demanding and challenging. Even some basic jobs, such as a production technician's, have become more complex because of the math and computer skills required to carry out these jobs. Most managerial positions involve high complexity, including the many skills described in Chapter 1 and throughout this book.

Information processing refers to the degree to which a job requires attending to and processing data and information. (Information is the result of making data useful, such as making sense of a survey about customer satisfaction.) Some jobs require higher levels of monitoring and processing information than others. As managers dash about consulting their BlackBerry, a high level of information processing is required. A student's life is filled with processing information, as is the life of a professional-level worker in any field.

Problem solving refers to the degree to which a job requires unique ideas or solutions, and it also involves diagnosing and solving nonroutine problems and preventing or fixing errors. Creativity is often required to perform effective problem solving. Without problem-solving skills, a worker could be replaced by software or a handbook. Managers and professional-level workers are essentially problem solvers, yet some managerial jobs require heavier problem solving than others. For example, the CEO of Ford Motor Company at one time had to solve the problem of how to make the automotive division profitable.

Skill variety refers to the extent to which a job requires the incumbent to use a variety of skills to perform the work. Skill variety and task variety are not the same thing because the use of multiple skills is different from the performance of multiple tasks. Your task might be to assemble a PowerPoint presentation, and you would need a variety of skills to perform this one task. Among the skills would be keyboarding, operating software, data analysis, and being artistic.

Specialization refers to the extent to which a job involves performing specialized tasks or possessing specialized knowledge and skills. Depth of knowledge and skill is required to be an effective municipal-bond analyst or brain surgeon. A manager's job is typically that of a generalist rather than a specialist, yet the manager is most likely a specialist on the way to becoming a manager. A basic example would be a purchasing specialist later becoming a purchasing manager. Later, we add a few more comments about job specialization to highlight its importance in defining jobs and careers.

Social Characteristics

Social characteristics relate to the interpersonal aspects of a job or the extent to which the job requires interaction with others. *Social support* refers to the degree to which a job involves the opportunity for advice and assistance from others in the workplace. Social support often contributes to the job holder's well-being, as in being able to turn to coworkers for technical assistance.

Interdependence reflects the degree to which the job depends on others—and others depend on the job—to accomplish the task. Visualize a team putting together a proposal for a large government contract to build an airplane. The various team members must provide input about manufacturing time and cost figures, such as the quality of a particular component being somewhat dependent on how much money is available for its manufacture.

Interaction outside the organization refers to how much the job requires the employee to interact and communicate with people outside the organization. Customer-contact workers obviously interact with outsiders, and so do C-level managers such as a CFO speaking with Wall Street financial analysts. *Feedback from others* refers to the extent to which other workers in the organization provide information about performance. Supervisors and coworkers are typical sources of feedback, yet feedback can also be received from those outside the immediate work area. For example, a senior manager might encounter a specialist in the hallway and say, "Jackie, I heard you're doing a great job for us. Keep up the good work."

Contextual Characteristics

Contextual characteristics refer to the setting or environment of the job, such as working in extreme temperatures. *Ergonomics* indicates the degree to which a job allows correct posture or movement. A chicken cutter in a poultry factory might suffer from tendonitis as a result of the repetitive movements, whereas most managerial jobs do not risk ergonomics problems except for too much keyboarding and mouse utilization.

Physical demands refer to the level of physical activity or effort required for the job, particularly with respect to physical strength, endurance, effort, and activity. The job of a furniture mover obviously has high physical demands; however, many managerial positions have heavier physical demands than outsiders imagine. Among these demands can be travelling a lot, which requires endurance, lugging a heavy laptop computer and accessories, standing for long hours at a trade show, and working long hours.

Work conditions relate directly to the environment in which the work is performed, including the presence of health hazards, noise, temperature, and cleanliness of the workplace. A project manager on a building site faces more environmental challenges than does his or her counterpart working in a climate-controlled office. *Equipment use* is a sub-dimension of contextual characteristics that reflects the variety and complexity of the technology and equipment incorporated into the job. Although managers are not ordinarily considered equipment operators, they often make use of computers, printers, personal digital assistants, telephones, pocket calculators, and even coffee pots.

Job Dimension Differences between Professional and Nonprofessional Jobs

As we described the dimensions, we made several references to occupational differences with regard to the dimensions. Morgeson and Humphrey collected data on differences between the dimensions of the occupational categories of professionals (such as managers, accountants, and engineers) and nonprofessionals (such as food preparation specialists and personal-service providers). Nonprofessional jobs required more physical demands. Professionals scored significantly higher on several work characteristics:

- Job complexity
- Information processing
- Problem solving
- Skill variety
- Work-scheduling autonomy
- Decision-making autonomy
- Work-methods autonomy
- Work conditions (more favorable)

Another analysis within the study compared the job demands of occupations that were human-life focused (such as a supervisor) against those that were nonhuman-life focused (such as a lab technician). The human-life–focused jobs scored higher on the dimension of significance, or impact on others.

A career suggestion here: If you think the dimensions in the bulleted list and the dimension of significance are important, you would be more satisfied occupying a professional job rather than a nonprofessional job.

Job Specialization and Job Design

A major consideration in job design is how specialized the job holder must be (as discussed in the specialization sub-dimension of knowledge characteristics). **Job specialization** is the degree to which a jobholder performs only a limited number of tasks. Specialists handle a narrow range of tasks especially well. High occupational-level specialists include the investment consultant who specializes in municipal bonds and the surgeon who concentrates on liver

job specialization
The degree to which a job holder performs only a limited number of tasks.

transplants. Specialists at the first occupational level are often referred to as entry-level workers, production specialists, support workers, or operatives.

A generalized job requires the handling of many different tasks. An extreme example of a top-level generalist is the owner of a small business, who performs such varied tasks as making the product, selling it, negotiating with banks for loans, and hiring new employees. An extreme example of a generalist at the first (or entry) occupational level is the maintenance worker who packs boxes, sweeps floors, shovels snow in winter, mows the lawn, and cleans the lavatories.

Advantages and Disadvantages of Job Specialization

Job specialization allows for the development of expertise at all occupational levels. When employees perform the same task repeatedly, they become highly knowledgeable and highly skilled. Many employees derive status and self-esteem from being experts at some task. Specialized jobs at lower occupational levels require less training time and less learning ability, which can be a key advantage when the available labor force lacks special skills. For example, McDonald's could never have grown so large if each restaurant had needed expert chefs. Newcomers to the workforce can quickly learn such specialized skills as preparing hamburgers and french fries. These newcomers can be paid entry-level wages—an advantage from a management perspective only!

Job specialization has disadvantages. Coordinating the workforce can be difficult when several employees do small parts of one job. Somebody must take responsibility for pulling together the small pieces of the total task. Although some employees prefer narrow specialized jobs, many more prefer broad tasks that give them a feeling of control over what they are doing. Although many technical and professional workers join the workforce as specialists, they often become bored by performing a narrow range of tasks.

Automation and Job Specialization

Automation has been used to replace some aspects of human endeavor in the office and the factory ever since the Industrial Revolution. Automation typically involves a machine that performs a specialized task previously performed by people. Automation is widely used in factories, offices, and stores. A major purpose of automation is to increase productivity by reducing the labor content required to deliver a product or service. A representative example is robotic equipment that can polish parts. Kason Industries in Atlanta, Georgia, found that the robotic polisher costing $500,000 paid for itself in two years.[3]

Two automation devices in the retail store are optical scanners and the automatic recording of remaining inventory when a customer checks out. The computerization of the workplace represents automation in hundreds of ways, such as personal computers decreasing the need for clerical support

---

[3]Michael E. Kanell, "Productivity Lull Raises Concerns," *The Atlanta Journal Constitution* (http://www.ajc.com), November 24, 2006.

in organizations. Today, only high-level managers have personal secretaries. Others rely on their computers to perform many chores. E-mail and text messaging have automated the delivery of many types of messages, including sending photos and graphics, once sent by postal mail or messenger service around the world. Automation enhances job satisfaction when annoying or dangerous tasks are removed, and automation does not result in job elimination. When automation helps a business organization become more productive, the net result is often the creation of more jobs. A curious case in point is the self-service kiosks at many McDonald's restaurants. Sales have increased so much where kiosks are installed that owners found it necessary to add two more employees at each store.[4]

Job Description and Job Design

job description

A written statement of the key features of a job along with the activities required to perform it effectively.

Before choosing a job design, managers and human resource professionals develop a job description. The **job description** is a written statement of the key features of a job and the activities required to perform it effectively. Sometimes a description must be modified to fit basic principles of job design. For example, the job description of a customer-service representative might call for an excessive amount of listening to complaints, thus creating too much stress. Exhibit 7-2 presents a job description of a middle-level manager.

The various job dimensions described earlier are found in job design, even when these dimensions are not made explicit in the design. For example, in the job description for branch manager, the knowledge characteristics are heavy. The manager also has demands on social characteristics, as in hiring new insurance agents and developing new businesses.

LEARNING
OBJECTIVE **2**

Describe job enrichment, including the job characteristics model.

JOB ENRICHMENT AND THE JOB CHARACTERISTICS MODEL

Job enrichment is an approach to including more challenge and responsibility in jobs to make them more appealing to most employees. At its best, job enrichment gives workers a sense of ownership, responsibility, and

---

EXHIBIT 7-2	*Job Description for Branch Manager, Insurance*

Manages the branch office, including such functions as underwriting, claims processing, loss prevention, marketing, and auditing, and resolves related technical questions and issues. Hires new insurance agents, develops new business, and updates the regional manager regarding the profit-and-loss operating results of the branch office, insurance trends, matters having impact on the branch-office function, and competitor methods. The manager makes extensive use of information technology to carry out all of these activities, including spreadsheet analyses and giving direction to establishing customer databases.

---

[4]Charles Fishman, "The Toll of a New Machine," *Fast Company*, May 2004, p. 95.

job enrichment
An approach to including more challenge and responsibility in jobs to make them more appealing to employees.

accountability for their work. Because job enrichment leads to a more exciting job, it often increases employee job satisfaction and motivation. People usually work harder at tasks they find enjoyable and rewarding, just as they put effort into a favorite hobby. The general approach to enriching a job is to build into it more planning and decision making, controlling, and responsibility. Most managers have enriched jobs; most data entry specialists do not.

Characteristics of an Enriched Job

The design of an enriched job includes as many of the characteristics in the following list as possible, based on the pioneering work of Frederick Herzberg and on updated research.[5] (Exhibit 7-3 summarizes the characteristics and consequences of enriched jobs.) The person holding the job must perceive these characteristics to be part of the job. You will notice that characteristics 1, 4, and 5 are also found as sub-dimensions of the four major dimensions that were described earlier in this chapter. Supervisors and group members frequently have different perceptions of job characteristics. For example, supervisors are more likely to think that a job has a big impact on the organization.[6] A worker who is responsible for placing used soft-drink cans in a recycling bin might not think his job is significant. The supervisor

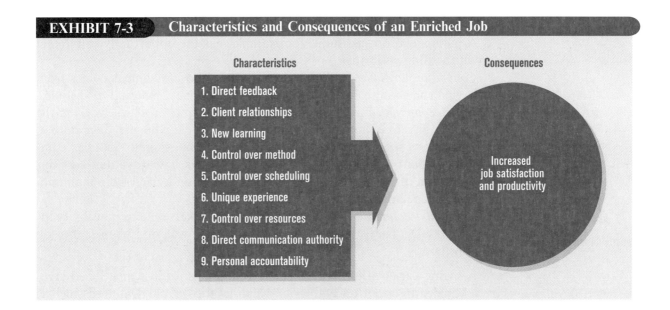

EXHIBIT 7-3 **Characteristics and Consequences of an Enriched Job**

Characteristics

1. Direct feedback
2. Client relationships
3. New learning
4. Control over method
5. Control over scheduling
6. Unique experience
7. Control over resources
8. Direct communication authority
9. Personal accountability

Consequences

Increased job satisfaction and productivity

[5]Frederick Herzberg, "The Wise Old Turk," *Harvard Business Review*, September–October 1974, pp. 70–80; Nico W. Van Yperen and Mariët Hagedoorn, "Do High Job Demands Increase Intrinsic Motivation or Fatigue or Both? The Role of Job Control and Job Social Support," *Academy of Management Journal*, June 2003, pp. 339–348.

[6]Marc C. Marchese and Robert P. Delprino, "Do Supervisors and Subordinates See Eye-to-Eye on Job Enrichment?" *Journal of Business and Psychology*, Winter 1998, pp. 179–192.

might perceive the individual to be contributing to the social-responsibility goal of creating a cleaner, less-congested environment—a green job.

The following are the characteristics of an enriched job:

1. *Direct feedback.* Employees should receive immediate evaluation of their work. This feedback can be built into the job (such as the feedback that closing a sale gives a sales representative) or provided by the supervisor.

2. *Client relationships.* A job is automatically enriched when an employee has a client or customer to serve, whether that client is inside or outside the firm. Serving a client is more satisfying to most people than performing work solely for a manager.

3. *New learning.* An enriched job allows its holder to acquire new knowledge. The learning can stem from job experiences or from training programs associated with the job.

4. *Control over method.* When a worker has some control over which method to choose to accomplish a task, his or her task motivation generally increases. An office manager, for example, might be told to decrease building energy costs by 10 percent. She would be deemed to have control over method if empowered to decide *how* to decrease costs, for example, by adjusting the thermostat or finding a lower-cost energy supplier.

5. *Control over scheduling.* The ability to schedule one's work contributes to job enrichment. Scheduling includes the authority to decide when to tackle which assignment and having some say in setting working hours.

6. *Unique experience.* An enriched job exhibits unique qualities or features. A public-relations assistant, for example, has the opportunity to interact with visiting celebrities.

7. *Control over resources.* Another contribution to enrichment comes from having some control over resources such as money, material, or people.

8. *Direct communication authority.* An enriched job provides workers the opportunity to communicate directly with people who use their output. A software specialist with an enriched job, for example, handles complaints about the software he or she developed. The advantages of this dimension of an enriched job are similar to those derived from maintaining client relationships.

9. *Personal accountability.* In an enriched job, workers take responsibility for their results. They accept credit for a job done well and blame for a job done poorly.

A highly enriched job with all nine characteristics just mentioned gives the jobholder an opportunity to satisfy high-level psychological needs such as self-fulfillment. Sometimes, the jobs of managers are too enriched, with too much responsibility and too many risks. A job with some of these characteristics would be moderately enriched. An impoverished job has none. Information technology workers are another occupational group that may suffer from over-enriched jobs. Working with computers and software at an advanced level may represent healthy job enrichment for many workers—working directly with information technology gives a person direct feedback, new learning, and personal accountability. However, many other computer workers feel stressed by the complexity of information technology, the amount of continuous learning involved, and frequent hardware and software breakdowns beyond the control of the worker.

The Job Characteristics Model of Job Enrichment

job characteristics model

A method of job enrichment that focuses on the task and interpersonal dimensions of a job.

Expanding the concept of job enrichment creates the **job characteristics model**, a method of job enrichment that focuses on the task and interpersonal dimensions of a job.[7] As Exhibit 7-4 shows, five measurable characteristics improve employee motivation, satisfaction, and performance. All five characteristics have been incorporated into the four major dimensions of job design and were defined previously.

As Exhibit 7-4 reports, these core job characteristics relate to critical psychological states or key mental attitudes. Skill variety, task identity, and task significance lead to a feeling that the work is meaningful. The task dimension of autonomy leads quite logically to a feeling of responsibility for work outcomes. The feedback dimension leads to knowledge of results. According to the model, a redesigned job must lead to these three psychological states in

| EXHIBIT 7-4 | The Job Characteristics Model of Job Enrichment |

Job enrichment can be made more precise and scientific by following the model presented here.

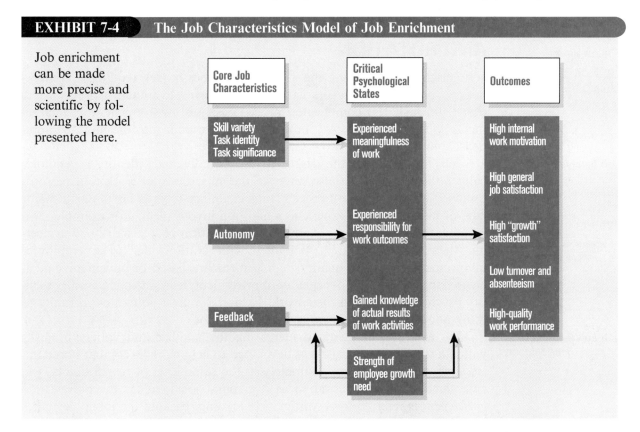

---

[7]John Richard Hackman and Greg R. Oldham, *Work Redesign* (Reading, MA: Addison-Wesley, 1980), p. 77.

workers so that they can achieve the outcomes of internal motivation, job satisfaction, low turnover and absenteeism, and high-quality performance.

Guidelines for Implementing a Job Enrichment Program

The notation in Exhibit 7-4, strength of employee growth need, provides guidelines for managers. The link between the job characteristics and outcomes strengthens as workers want to grow and develop. Before implementing a program of job enrichment, a manager must first ask whether the workers need or want more responsibility, variety, and growth. Some employees already have jobs that are adequately enriched. Many employees do not want an enriched job because they prefer to avoid the challenge and stress of responsibility. Brainstorming is useful for pinpointing changes that will enrich jobs for those who want enrichment.[8] The brainstorming group would be composed of job incumbents, supervisors, and perhaps an industrial engineer. The workers' participation in planning changes can be useful. Workers may suggest, for example, how to increase client contact or how they could self-schedule some tasks.

LEARNING OBJECTIVE **3**

Describe job involvement, enlargement, and rotation.

JOB INVOLVEMENT, ENLARGEMENT, AND ROTATION

Job enrichment, including the job characteristics model, requires a comprehensive program. Managers can improve the motivational aspects of job design through less complicated procedures: job involvement, job enlargement, and job rotation. All three processes are built into the more comprehensive job enrichment program.

job involvement
The degree to which individuals identify psychologically with their work.

Job involvement is the degree to which individuals identify psychologically with their work. It also refers to the importance of work to a person's total self-image. If an insurance claims examiner regards his job as a major part of his identity, he experiences high job involvement. For example, at a social gathering the claims examiner would inform people shortly after meeting them, "I'm a claims examiner with Nationwide." The employee-involvement groups in quality management are based on job involvement. By making decisions about quality improvement, team members ideally identify psychologically with their work. Exhibit 7-5 gives you an opportunity to think about job involvement as it applies to you.

job enlargement
Increasing the number and variety of tasks within a job.

Job enlargement refers to increasing the number and variety of tasks within a job. The technique was developed to help workers combat boredom. Because the tasks are approximately at the same level of responsibility, job enlargement is also referred to as horizontal job loading. In contrast, *job enrichment* is referred to as vertical job loading, because the jobholder takes on higher-level job responsibility. The claims examiner would experience job

---

[8]J. Barton Cunningham and Ted Eberle, "A Guide to Job Enrichment and Redesign," *Personnel*, February 1990, p. 59.

EXHIBIT 7-5   How Involved Are You?

Indicate how strongly you agree with the following statements by circling the number that appears below the appropriate heading: DS = disagree strongly; D = disagree; N = neutral; A = agree; AS = agree strongly. Respond in relation to a present job, the job you hope to have, or schoolwork.

	DS	D	N	A	AS
1. My work is the biggest contributor to my self-image.	1	2	3	4	5
2. Work is only a way of getting other things in life that I want.	5	4	3	2	1
3. The most meaningful things that happen to me involve my work.	1	2	3	4	5
4. I often concentrate so hard on my work that I'm unaware of what is going on around me.	1	2	3	4	5
5. If I inherited enough money, I would spend the rest of my life in leisure activities.	5	4	3	2	1
6. I attempt to minimize interruptions in my work, such as shifting my attention to a Web site unrelated to the task at hand.	1	2	3	4	5
7. I am very much emotionally involved personally in my work.	1	2	3	4	5
8. Most things in life are more important than work.	5	4	3	2	1
9. Working full time blocks me from doing a lot of things in life I would prefer to do.	5	4	3	2	1
10. My work is usually the most exciting part of my day.	1	2	3	4	5

Score_____

Scoring and interpretation: Total the numbers circled, and then use the following guide to interpretation.

45–50   Your attitudes suggest intense job involvement. Such attitudes should contribute highly to productivity and satisfaction.

28–44   Your attitudes suggest a moderate degree of job involvement. To sustain a high level of productivity, you would need to work toward becoming more involved in your work.

10–27   Your attitudes suggest a low degree of job involvement. It would be difficult to sustain a successful, professional career with such low involvement.

Source: The idea for the job involvement scale stems from Myron Gable and Frank Dangello, "Job Involvement, Machiavellianism, and Job Performance," *Journal of Business and Psychology*, Winter 1994, p. 163.

enlargement if he were given additional responsibilities such as examining claims for boats and motorcycles as well as automobiles.

As responsibilities expand in job enlargement, jobholders usually find themselves juggling multiple priorities. Two, three, four, or even more demands might be facing the worker. In one approach to handling multiple priorities, a jobholder ranks them in order of importance and then tackles the most important one first. With this approach, the lowest-priority tasks may be neglected. In a more recommended approach, the jobholder finishes the top-priority task and then moves immediately to all other tasks. Top-priority items can be tackled again after the lesser tasks have been completed. If the manager or team leader insists that a specific task must be done immediately, it is good office politics to work on that task first. Some catch-up time at night or on weekends might then be invested to avoid falling behind on other projects.

A new approach to job enlargement has surfaced as a way for companies to reduce compensation costs when new positions are filled. In one variation of this approach, a mid-level position is combined with a junior position. The position is then advertised and offered at a lower salary. In another variation of job enlargement, senior people who are hired later find that they are responsible for performing their own work as well as tasks that were formerly the responsibility of subordinates. A specific example of adding responsibilities to a position to save compensation costs relates to hiring. For example, a new chief marketing officer might be expected to also handle ordinary media tasks such as negotiating rates for advertising.[9]

job rotation
A temporary switching of job assignments.

Job rotation is a temporary switching of job assignments. Formal programs of job rotation usually last about one year.[10] In this way, employees develop new skills and learn about how other aspects of the unit or organization work. However, the potential advantages of job rotation are lost if a person is rotated from one dull job to another. A motivational form of job rotation would be for the claims examiner to investigate auto and small-truck claims one month and large-truck claims the next. When a worker is rotated from one job to another, the position he or she left behind should be adequately staffed. When two competent workers switch jobs, the potential problem takes care of itself.

Job rotation helps prevent workers from falling into a rut and feeling bored. In addition to learning new skills, job rotation gives workers an opportunity to learn more about how the organization operates. A marketing specialist who was rotated into a finance position for six months commented, "Now I really understand firsthand how every penny counts when the company is attempting to obtain a good return on investment."

Job enlargement and job rotation offer similar advantages and disadvantages to the individual and the organization. Through job enlargement and job rotation, workers develop a broader set of skills, making them more valuable and flexible. Pushed to extremes, however, job enlargement and rotation lead to feelings of overwork.

---

[9]Dana Mattioli, "Help Wanted: Senior-Level Job, Junior Title Pay," *The Wall Street Journal*, August 12, 2008, p. D1.

[10]Margaret Fiester, "Job Rotation, Total Rewards, Measuring Value," *HR Magazine*, August 2008, p. 33.

LEARNING
OBJECTIVE **4**
Explain how
workers use job
crafting to modify
their jobs.

JOB CRAFTING AND JOB DESIGN

In the traditional view of a job, a competent worker carefully follows a job description; good performance means that the person accomplishes what is specified in the job description. A contemporary view sees a job description as only a guideline; the competent worker exceeds the constraints of a job description. He or she takes on constructive activities not mentioned in the job description.

The flexible work roles carried out by many workers contribute to the move away from tightly following job descriptions that are too rigid. An emerging trend finds companies hiring people "to work" rather than to fill a specific job slot. For example, as the pharmaceutical industry has become increasingly competitive and unpredictable, Pfizer has shifted its hiring strategy to find workers who are versatile. The giant drug maker now hires and develops employees who can shift from one position to another. In the past, the company hired mostly on the basis of job descriptions. Now, Pfizer evaluates what competencies (such as problem solving and communications skills) the candidate demonstrates.[11]

Workers sometimes deviate from their job descriptions by modifying their job to fit their personal preferences and capabilities. According to the research of Amy Wrzesniewski and Jane E. Dutton, employees craft their jobs by changing the tasks they perform and their contacts with others to make their jobs more meaningful.[12] To add variety to her job, for example, a team leader might make nutritional recommendations to team members. The team leader alters her task of coaching about strictly work-related issues to also coaching about personal health. In this way, she broadens her role in terms of her impact on the lives of work associates.

job crafting
The physical and
mental changes
individuals make in the
task or relationship
aspects of their job.

Job crafting refers to the physical and mental changes individuals make in the task or relationship aspects of their job. Three common types of job crafting include (1) the number and types of job tasks, (2) the interactions with others on the job, and (3) one's view of the job. The most frequent purpose of crafting is to make the job more meaningful or enriched. A cook, for example, might add flair to a meal; this is not required, but it injects a little personal creativity. Job crafting is modeled after the pride that craftsmen and craftswomen take in their work, such as a person who makes boots or furniture by hand.

Job crafting can also take place at the group level, whereby the group collaboratively decides how to improve and enlarge the position. A study with teachers and aides in 62 childcare centers found that crafting by the group resulted in better job satisfaction and performance.[13] An example of

---

[11]Jessica Marquez, "A Talent Strategy Overhaul at Pfizer," *Workforce Management*, February 12, 2007, pp. 1, 3.

[12]Amy Wrzesniewski and Jane E. Dutton, "Crafting a Job: Revisioning Employees as Active Crafters of Their Work," *The Academy of Management Review*, April 2001, pp. 179–201.

[13]Carrie Leana, Eileen Appelbaum, and Iryna Shevchuk, "Work Process and Quality of Care in Early Childhood Education: The Role of Job Crafting," *Academy of Management Journal*, December 2009, pp. 1169–1192.

job crafting by childcare teachers and aides would be offering guidance to parents on how to involve children in activities at home other than watching television and playing video games.

Exhibit 7-6 illustrates these three forms of job crafting and shows how crafting affects the meaning of work. After studying the exhibit, consider whether you have ever engaged in job crafting.

The discussion of the various approaches to job design can provide useful information about how jobs can be made more satisfying and lead to higher productivity. However, another explanation of why workers are attracted to and perform well in particular jobs is missing. **Job embeddedness** refers to the array of forces attaching people to their jobs. Three dimensions are included in job embeddedness.[14] First are links—the formal or informal connections to people in the organization or community. (You might stick with a job because you love your city.) Second is sacrifice, the perceived cost of material or psychological benefits you would forfeit if you left the job. (You might decide that relocation to another geographic area to find new employment would not be worth the many associated costs.) Third is fit, compatibility, or comfort with the organizational environment and the external environment. (You might not find you job to be fascinating, but you think highly of the company and enjoy your community.)

job embeddedness
The array of forces attaching people to their jobs.

EXHIBIT 7-6	Forms of Job Crafting	
Form	Example	Effect on Meaning of Work
Changing number, scope, and type of job tasks	Design engineers engage in changing the quality or amount of interactions with people, thereby moving a project to completion.	Work is completed in a more timely fashion; engineers change the meaning of their jobs to be guardians or movers of projects.
Changing quality and/or amount of interaction with others encountered in the job	Hospital cleaners actively care for patients and families, integrating themselves into the workflow of their floor units.	Cleaners change the meaning of their jobs to be helpers of the sick; they see the work of the floor unit as an integrated whole of which they are a vital part.
Changing the view of the job	Nurses take responsibility for all information and "insignificant" tasks that may help them to care more appropriately for a patient.	Nurses change the way they see the work to be more about patient advocacy, as well as high-quality technical care.

Source: Adapted from Amy Wrzesniewski and Jane E. Dutton, "Crafting a Job: Revisioning Employees as Active Crafters of Their Work," *The Academy of Management Review*, April 2001, p. 185.

---

[14]Peter W. Hom et al. "Explaining Employment Relationships with Social Exchange and Job Embeddeness," *Journal of Applied Psychology*, March 2009, p. 281.

LEARNING
OBJECTIVE **5**
Illustrate how
ergonomic factors
can be part of job
design.

ergonomics
The practice of
matching machines to
worker requirements.

ERGONOMICS AND JOB DESIGN

A key principle of job design is that the job should be laid out to decrease the chances that it will physically harm the incumbent. According to the U.S. Occupational and Health Agency (OSHA), **ergonomics** is the science of fitting the worker to the job. Ergonomics seeks to minimize the physical demands on workers and optimize system performance, and therefore has considerable relevance to job design. Three principles of ergonomics are recommended when designing jobs:

- Workers should be able to adopt several different postures that are safe and comfortable.
- Workers who exert muscular force should be encouraged to use the largest muscle groups (such as using the legs and body to help lift a box rather than only the arms).
- Whenever possible, workers should be able to perform regular work activities in the middle range of joint movement.[15]

It is important that managers help prevent ergonomic problems for ethical and humanitarian reasons. In addition, injuries and illnesses stemming from ergonomic problems drive up health costs, including insurance premiums.

Musculoskeletal Disorders Including Carpal Tunnel Syndrome

A frequent problem in factories, mills, supermarkets, and offices is work-related musculoskeletal disorders (MSDs), problems involving muscles and bones. There are more than 100 musculoskeletal disorders that can occur when there is a mismatch between the physical requirements of the job and the physical capacity of the human body. Overuse is a common problem. A supermarket cashier might stay in good shape working a few hours a day, but lifting several hundred bags of groceries in eight hours can create severe back injury. OSHA believes that designing check-out counters to reduce ergonomic risk factors, such as twisting or extended reaching, can improve cashier effectiveness and productivity.

Solutions to some potential ergonomic problems can be quite simple. For example, working the back of a deep display case to face or stock merchandise can be awkward and uncomfortable, especially when heavy items are involved. One solution to this problem OSHA recommends is to use display cases that are stocked from the back. The product, such as cartons of milk, slides down an inclined shelf so that it is always in front of the customer. The employee stocking the shelf experiences less physical strain.[16]

---

[15]"Ergonomics," http://www.referencesforbusiness.com/management/Em-Exp/Ergnomics. html, accessed November 26, 2006, p. 1.

[16]"Ergonomics for the Prevention of Musculoskeletal Disorders—Guidelines for Retail Grocers," http://www.osha.gov/ergonomics/guidelines/retailgrocery/retailgrocery.html, accessed November 26, 2006, p. 4.

cumulative trauma disorders

Injuries caused by repetitive motions over prolonged periods of time.

Musculoskeletal disorders also include **cumulative trauma disorders**—injuries caused by repetitive motions over prolonged periods of time. These disorders now account for almost half of occupational injuries and illnesses in the United States. Any occupation involving excessive repetitive motions, as with a bricklayer, meat cutter, or fishery worker, can lead to cumulative trauma disorder. Vibrating tools such as jackhammers also cause such disorder. The use of computers and other high-tech equipment, such as price scanners, contributes to the surge in the occurrence of cumulative trauma disorders.

carpal tunnel syndrome

The most frequent cumulative trauma disorder; it occurs when frequent wrist bending results in swelling, leading to a pinched nerve.

Extensive keyboarding places severe strain on hand and wrist muscles and often leads to **carpal tunnel syndrome**. This syndrome occurs when frequent bending of the wrist causes swelling in a tunnel of bones and ligaments in the wrist. The nerve that gives feeling to the hand is pinched, resulting in tingling and numbness in the fingers. Overuse of the computer mouse is a major contributor to wrist and tendon injury. The symptoms of carpal tunnel syndrome are severe. Many workers suffering from the syndrome are unable to differentiate hot and cold by touch; some lose finger strength. They often appear clumsy because they have difficulty with everyday tasks such as tying their shoes or picking up small objects. Treatment of carpal tunnel syndrome may involve surgery to release pressure on the median nerve. Another approach is anti-inflammatory drugs to reduce tendon swelling. You have probably seen students and coworkers wearing braces on their wrists; others have had operations to ease the problem of carpal tunnel syndrome.

To help prevent and decrease the incidence of cumulative trauma disorders, many companies select equipment designed for that purpose. Exhibit 7-7 depicts a workstation based on ergonomic principles developed to engineer a good fit between person and machine. In addition, the following steps can help prevent cumulative trauma disorders:[17]

- Analyze each job with an eye toward possible hazards, including equipment that is difficult to operate.
- Install equipment that minimizes awkward hand and body movements. Try ergonomically designed keyboards to see whether they make a difference.
- Encourage workers to take frequent breaks; rotate jobs so that repetitive hand and body movements are reduced.
- Encourage workers to maintain good posture when seated at the keyboard. Poor posture can lead to carpal tunnel syndrome from extending the wrists too far and to neck ache and backache.
- Make less use of the mouse by using more key commands. Overuse of the mouse can cause repetitive motion injury. Find ways to use the opposite hand more, such as for tapping function keys.

Workers who spend nonworking hours using a keyboard increase the probability of developing carpal tunnel syndrome. Other factors that

---

[17]Albert R. Karr, "An Ergo-Unfriendly Home Office Can Hurt You," *The Wall Street Journal,* September 30, 2003, p. D6; "Preventing Carpal Tunnel Syndrome," *HRfocus.* August 1995, p. 4.

EXHIBIT 7-7   An Ergonomically Designed Workstation

- Screen is below eye level.

- Elbows are on same level with the home key row, keeping wrists and lower arms parallel to the floor.

- Back and thighs are supported.

- Upper legs are parallel to the floor.

- Feet are placed flat on the floor.

- Task lamp supplements adequate room lighting.

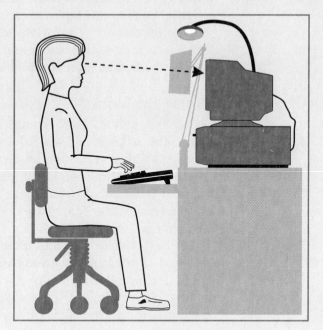

predispose workers to carpal tunnel syndrome are obesity, particularly when the obese person is diabetic, and shortages of vitamins B6 and C.[18]

Back Problems[19]

Back pain remains one of the most common complaints in the workplace; approximately 270,000 cases of workplace-related back injuries and illnesses are reported in the United States each year. Many cases of back pain stem from ergonomics problems, including long periods of time hunched over a computer monitor. The best way to prevent back pain is to first examine workplace practices and then take administrative action. Lisa Brooks, manager of ergonomics and safety programs at General Electric in Fairfield, Connecticut, says that employers who make a good-faith effort to provide ergonomic support and try to engineer hazards out of the workplace are likely to get employee cooperation.

The good posture shown in Exhibit 7-7 will help prevent back problems and so will knowing how to lift properly (bend at the knee, not from the waist). The initiatives taken by FedEx to prevent back injuries represent a useful illustration of how such injuries can be prevented. Because delivery

[18]William Atkinson, "The Carpal Tunnel Conundrum," *Workforce*, September 2002, p. 17.

[19]This section is mostly based on Nancy Hatch Woodward, "Easing Back Pain: Prevent Back Injuries from Crippling Your Business," *HR Magazine*, April 2008, pp. 56–60.

workers must be able to lift 75 pounds and because new employees have the most back problems, FedEx take steps to help employees achieve better physical condition. Employees are taught how to stretch prior to their shifts, how to lift and put down packages properly, and how to find alternatives to lifting (such as sliding and pushing or pulling). Employees also use back-support belts, which are useful in conjunction with other safety initiatives.

Noise Problems

Repetitive motion disorders and other musculoskeletal disorders, including tendonitis, sciatica, and lower-back pain, are well-publicized ergonomic problems. Another recurring problem relates to uncomfortable noise levels. Although industrial noise problems are usually associated with manufacturing and mills, the constant buzz in offices also can create discomfort and physical problems. Many workers complain about the ringing of personal cell phones during the work day.

An experiment was conducted in which 40 female clerical workers were assigned to either a low-noise control group or three hours of low-intensity noise designed to simulate open-office noise levels. Workers exposed to the noise experienced negative consequences not experienced by the control (comparison) group. One effect was an increase in epinephrine, a hormone that enters the urine in response to stress. The group exposed to noise performed less well on a puzzle given to participants. The group exposed to noise also made less use of office furniture features designed to provide opportunities for postural adjustment during the work day.[20] In this way one ergonomics problem (noise) could lead to other ergonomic problems (repetitive motion disorder and back problems).

LEARNING OBJECTIVE 6
Summarize the various modified work schedules.

modified work schedule

Any formal departure from the traditional hours of work, excluding shift work and staggered work hours.

MODIFIED WORK SCHEDULES AND JOB DESIGN

A key characteristic of job enrichment is giving workers authority in scheduling their own work. Closely related is the widespread practice of giving workers some choice in deviating from the traditional five-day, 40-hour workweek. A **modified work schedule** is any formal departure from the traditional hours of work, excluding shift work and staggered work hours. Shift work presents enough unique managerial challenges to warrant discussion here. Modified work schedules include flexible working hours, a compressed workweek, job sharing, telecommuting, and part-time and temporary work.

Modified work schedules serve several important organizational purposes in addition to being part of job design. They potentially increase job satisfaction and motivation and attract workers who prefer to avoid a traditional schedule. Modified work schedules are popular with the physically disabled because the rigors of commuting may decrease. Many single parents need

---

[20]Gary W. Evans and Dana Johnson, "Stress and Open-Office Noise," *Journal of Applied Psychology*, October 2000, pp. 779–783.

flexible hours to cope with childcare. Flexible working hours are popular with many employees, and working at home continues to gain popularity with a subset of the workforce. However, many workers are reluctant to ask employers for more flexibility during a period of widespread downsizing.

Flexible Working Hours

Many employees exert some control over their work schedules through a formal arrangement of flexible working hours. Such employees work core hours, such as from 10:00 a.m. to 3:30 p.m., and then choose which hours they work between 7:00 a.m. and 10:00 a.m. and between 3:30 p.m. and 6:30 p.m. Exhibit 7-8 presents a basic model of flexible working hours. Time-recording devices frequently monitor employees' required hours for the week.

Flexible working hours are far more likely to be an option for employees on the nonexempt payroll. Such workers receive additional pay for work beyond 40 hours per week and premium pay for Saturdays and Sundays. Managers, professional-level workers, and salespeople generally have some flexibility in choosing their work hours. Managers and professionals in corporations work an average of 55 hours per week, making concerns about a 40-hour-per-week flextime schedule irrelevant.

Many employers believe that flexible working hours decrease employee absenteeism and stress and enhance productivity. Flexible working hours tend to increase efficiency during core times and decrease the need for overtime because more gets accomplished during the core.[21]

Despite the popularity of flexible working hours, many of these programs were placed on hold during the Great Recession.[22] Many employees

EXHIBIT 7-8	A Typical Flexible-Working-Hours Schedule

Flexible working hours have a fixed core time in the middle.

Flexible Arrival Time	Fixed Core Time (designated lunch break)	Flexible Departure Time
7:00 a.m. 10:00 a.m.		3:30 p.m. 6:30 p.m.

Sample schedules: Early Schedule, 7:00–3:30
Standard Schedule, 9:00–5:30
Late Schedule, 10:00–6:30

---

[21]"Introducing Flexible Working Hours Into Your Organization," in *Business: The Ultimate Resource* (Cambridge, MA: Perseus Publishing, 2002), p. 358.

[22]Jennifer Schramm, "Work/Life On Hold?" *HR Magazine*, October 2008, p. 120.

hesitate to take advantage of flexible working hours (as well as other work/life programs) for fear of being perceived as not strongly committed to the organization. In a survey of 505 employees, 59 percent indicated they were reluctant to ask their employer about flexible working options. The most common reason given was fear of the perception that they were not serious about their careers.[23]

A major problem for the career-oriented employee who chooses flextime is that meetings might be held at times outside the employee's scheduled time. Suppose you have agreed to work from 7 a.m. until 4 p.m. on Thursday. The team leader schedules an important meeting at 4:30. You now face a conflict between taking care of personal obligations and appearing to be a dedicated worker.

Flextime programs are often the result of employee requests. Answering the following questions can help the manager evaluate a flextime request.[24] (The same questions also apply generally to other types of modified work schedules.)

1. *Does the nature of the job allow for a flexible schedule?* Employees who must turn around work quickly or respond to crises might not be good candidates for flexible working hours. Negative indicators for flextime include other employees being inconvenienced by the altered schedule and a job that requires frequent interaction with others.

2. *Will this individual work well independently?* Some employees thrive on working solo and may be in the office at 6 a.m. or 7 p.m. Others lose momentum when working alone. Does the employee have a high level of initiative and self-motivation?

3. *Are you comfortable managing a flex-worker?* A manager who feels the need to frequently monitor the work of employees will become anxious when the employees are working by themselves during noncore hours.

4. *Can you arrange tasks so the employee will have enough to do when you or other workers are not present?* Some employees find ways to make a contribution on their own, while others must be fed work in small doses.

5. *Are you comfortable with not seeing employees in the office and with empowering them to work on their own?* For flexible work arrangements to be effective, the manager must feel comfortable when the flex-workers are empowered to work without much supervision.

Sometimes flexible work schedules are informal, with managers granting flexibility as needed. Smith-Winchester, a Michigan company that provides advertising and other business communication services, has a year-round

---

[23]*BNA Daily Labor Report* article cited in "Workers May Want Flexibility, but Don't Always Ask for It," *Leading for Results*, sample issue 2006. Published by Ragan's Management Resources.

[24]"A Time for Change? Maybe Not—Flextime Isn't for Everyone," *WorkingSMART*, September 1996, pp. 1–2; Jessica Marquez, "Citigroup to Train Managers on Flex-Work Arrangements," November 17, 2008, pp. 8, 10.

policy that permits workers to leave early as needed, as long as they make up the time. The company also grants workers five personal days a year.[25]

Compressed Workweek

compressed workweek

A full-time work schedule that allows 40 hours of work in less than five days.

A **compressed workweek** is a full-time work schedule that allows 40 hours of work in less than five days. The usual arrangement is 4–40 (working four 10-hour days). Many employees enjoy the 4–40 schedule because it enables them to have three consecutive days off. Employees often invest this time in leisure activities or part-time jobs. A 4–40 schedule usually allows most employees to be off Saturdays and Sundays. Important exceptions include police workers, hospital employees, and computer operators. As mentioned in Chapter 3 in relation to sustainability, the four-day workweek is gaining popularity in state and municipal government offices.

Compressed workweeks are popular with employees whose lifestyle fits such a schedule, and morale increases for employees who want more days off. However, the 4–40 week has built-in problems. Some employees do not want so much time away from work each month. Many workers are fatigued during the last two hours of the day and suffer from losses in concentration. From a personal standpoint, working for ten consecutive hours can be inconvenient, and the 4–40 workweek can create conflict with childcare arrangements.

Telecommuting and the Remote Workforce

telecommuting

An arrangement with one's employer to use a computer to perform work at home or in a satellite office.

An estimated 8 percent of the U.S. workforce conducts most of its work away from the company office, with this estimate showing wide variation.[26] **Telecommuting** is an arrangement in which employees use computers to perform their regular work responsibilities at home, in a satellite office, or from a remote worksite. Because they are located away from the traditional workplace, such workers are often referred to as part of the *remote* or *distributed workforce*. Self-employed people who work at home are not classified as remote workers.

Telecommuting also takes place at coffee shops, Wi-Fi (or Internet) cafés, boats, and RVs (recreational vehicles). Sun Microsystems and Microsoft are among the employers that provide remote touchdown spaces in suburban locations that allow workers to access secure networks and collaborate with other workers without having to drive long distances. Another possibility for working remotely is to work from a community center alongside other telecommuters.

Employees who telecommute usually use computers linked to the company's main office. Others simply use e-mail or text messaging to communicate with people in the traditional office. Sending input to company

---

[25]Joyce M. Rosenberg, "Bosses Can Help Relieve Holiday Pressure," Associated Press, November 27, 2006.

[26]Tali Arbel, "Census: Home Workers Grew In First Part of Decade," *www.philly.com*, January 26, 2010.

Web sites is another possibility. Telecommuters often attend meetings on company premises and stay in contact by telephone and teleconferences.

Advantages of Telecommuting

Telecommuting can work well with self-reliant and self-starting employees who have relevant work experience. Work-at-home employees usually volunteer for such an arrangement. As a result, they are likely to find telecommuting satisfying. Employees derive many benefits from working at home: easier management of personal life; lowered costs for commuting, work clothing, and lunch; much less time spent commuting; and fewer distractions such as office noise. During a recession, telecommuting offers several unique advantages. As the housing market slows, it becomes more difficult for some workers to relocate to accept a new job. When the job market is weak, it becomes more difficult for both marriage partners to find a job in the same city. If one of the partners can telecommute, a *commuter marriage* (partners living in separate cities) is avoided.[27]

Telecommuting offers the following advantages to the employer:[28]

1. *Increased productivity*. Surveys consistently show that telecommuting programs increase productivity, usually by at least 25 percent. AT&T managers consistently report that they gain about one extra productive hour per day when working at home. The gain comes from saving time by not physically commuting, the ability to concentrate better by not being distracted, and better time management. Cisco Systems also reports a 25 percent increase in productivity among telecommuters. American Express Company telecommuters processed 26 percent more calls and produced 43 percent more business than their traditional-office counterparts. Turnover tends to be lower among telecommuters. Work design consultant Jim Ware notes that distributed workers are more productive because they spend less time commuting, gabbing in hallways, and sitting in unproductive meetings.[29] (A contributing factor to the productivity advantage of telecommuters is that they tend to be well educated and self-motivated.)

2. *Low overhead*. Because there are fewer people on the premises, the company can operate with less office space. A vice president of marketing research operations noted that, because of its work-at-home program, the company was able to greatly expand its client load without acquiring additional space. At Sun Microsystems, Inc., nearly one-half of employees are part of the distributed workforce, saving the company $300

---

[27]Jennifer Schramm, "Work Turns Flexible," *HR Magazine*, March 2009, p. 88.

[28]John A. Pearse II, "Successful Corporate Telecommuting with Technology Considerations for Late Adopters," *Organizational Dynamics*, January–March 2009, pp. 16–25; John Sullivan, "Time to Telecommute," *Workforce Management*, June 23, 2008, p. 66; Michelle Conlin, "The Easiest Commute of All," *Business Week*, December 12, 2005, p. 79.

[29]Ware is cited in "Workplace 1.5: Managing Teleworkers—at Home, at Work, at Starbucks," *Fast Company*, November 2005, p. 105.

million annually in real-estate costs. (Sun would probably have to sell $3 billion in equipment to earn the same profit.)

3. *Access to a wider range of employee talent.* Companies with regular work-at-home programs are usually deluged with résumés from eager job applicants. The talent bank includes parents (mostly mothers) with young children, employees who find commuting unpleasant, and others who live far away from their firms. The Department of Labor regards telecommuting as an option for disabled workers who traditionally have few opportunities in the workplace. Many disabled workers have talents that otherwise might be overlooked.

4. *Direct contribution to green initiatives.* Telecommuting makes a major contribution to sustaining the environment because people who work at home drive their vehicles less. As a result, air quality improves and atmospheric ozone levels decrease. Less congested highways and streets make for a more attractive environment.

Disadvantages of Telecommuting

Work-at-home programs must be used selectively because they pose disadvantages for both employee and employer. The careers of telecommuters may suffer because they are not visible to management. Many telecommuters complain of the isolation from coworkers. There are also societal implications. Telecommuting may translate into less highway traffic and fewer meals eaten in restaurants. As a result, the service-station owners and fast-service restaurant proprietors have less income.

Telecommuters can feel exploited if they must work on company problems late into the night and on weekends. The many potential distractions at home make it difficult for some, but not all, telecommuters to concentrate on work. Telecommuters are sometimes part-time employees who receive limited benefits and are paid only for what they produce. As one data entry specialist said, "If I let up for an afternoon, I earn hardly anything." Working at home can reinforce negative tendencies: It will facilitate a workaholic to work harder and longer, and it will give a procrastinator ample opportunity to delay work.[30]

Telecommuting programs can be disadvantageous to the employer because building loyalty and teamwork is difficult when so many workers are away from the office. Several years ago, a group of Hewlett-Packard employees who managed the company's internal software and computers were no longer allowed to telecommute. The HP chief information officer made the change as part of a plan to increase face-to-face interaction and team effectiveness in the information technology unit.[31]

It's difficult to supervise telecommuters who are not performing measured work—working at home gives an employee much more latitude in

---

[30]Jenny C. McCune, "Telecommuting Revisited," *Management Review*, February 1998, p. 13.

[31]Ed Frauenheim, "Telecommuting Cutbacks at HP Represent Shift," *Workforce Management*, June 26, 2006, p. 4.

attending to personal matters during work time. Many teleworkers conduct work at coffee shops, and some may lose focus on company goals during the working day.

A major concern is that the organization misses out on some of the creativity that stems from the exchange of ideas in the traditional office. Another problem is that telecommuting can make workers feel self-employed, rather than part of the organization.[32] A worker who spends very little time on company premises is less likely to express a sentiment such as "I am a Yahoo! woman."

To maximize the advantages and minimize the disadvantages of telecommuting, managers should follow a few key suggestions presented in Exhibit 7-9. If you are in the process of building your career and want to develop valuable contacts on the job, minimize telecommuting. Establishing face-to-face relationships remains highly important for career advancement.

Job Sharing

job sharing

A work arrangement in which two people who work part-time share one job.

Another way to accommodate workers is to give them half a job. **Job sharing** is a work arrangement in which two people who work part-time share one job. Salary and benefits are prorated for the half-time workers. The sharers divide the job according to their needs. They may work selected days of the workweek, or one person might work mornings and the other afternoons. The job sharers might be two friends, a husband and wife, or two employees who did not know each other before sharing a job. For complex jobs, the sharers may spend work time discussing it.[33]

Employees wanting to share a job often feel that personal responsibilities preclude their ability to work full time. Job sharing allows for a sense of balance in one's life and allows employees to hold on to a career. A typical job-sharing situation involves two friends who want a responsible position but can only work part-time. Job sharing offers the employer an advantage in that two people working half time usually produce more than one person working full time; this is particularly noticeable in creative work. If one employee is sick, the other is available to handle the job half the time.

Part-Time and Temporary Work

Part-time work is a modified work schedule offered by about two-thirds of employers. The category of part-time workers includes employees who work reduced weekly, annual, or seasonal hours and those who have project-based occasional work. For example, a marketing brand manager might work full days on Mondays, Wednesdays, and Fridays. Many people, such as students

---

[32]Sherry M. B. Thatcher and Xiumei Zhu, "Changing Identities in a Changing Workplace: Identification, Identity, Enactment, Self-Verification, and Telecommuting," *Academy of Management Review*, October 2006, p. 1079.

[33]Dawn Rosenberg McKay, "Job Sharing: An Interview, Part I," http://www.careerplanning.about.com, accessed November 27, 2006.

EXHIBIT 7-9   How to Manage Teleworkers

1. *Develop a formal telecommuting policy.* The expectations of teleworkers should be made explicit in writing. The type of electronic equipment required to telecommute should be specified, including software. Employees must know how much the company will pay for or subsidize home-office equipment. The policy should cover many of the points in this list. Having a formal policy is an effective way of knowing if workers are abusing the system.

2. *Choose the right type of work for working at home.* If a job requires frequent monitoring, such as reviewing progress on a complex report, it is not well suited for telecommuting. Jobs requiring the use of complicated, large-scale equipment, such as medical laboratory work or manufacturing, cannot be done off premises. Work that requires clients or customers to visit the employee is best done on company premises. In general, positions with measurable work output are best suited for working at home.

3. *Teleworkers should be chosen with care.* Working at home is best suited for self-disciplined, well-motivated, and deadline-conscious workers. Make sure the telecommuter has a suitable home environment for telecommuting. The designated work area should be as separate from the household as possible and relatively free from distractions, including interaction with family members, friends, and domestic animals.

4. *Agree early on the number of days or months for telecommuting.* The optimum number of days depends somewhat on the position and the worker. For corporate telecommuters, about two days per week of working at home is typical.

5. *Clearly define productivity goals and deadlines.* The more measurable the work output, such as lines of computer code or insurance claims forms processed, the better suited it is for telecommuting. Collect weekly data that relate to the results being achieved, such as orders filled or cases settled.

6. *Keep in contact through a variety of means, including e-mail and instant messaging, telephone, phone meetings, and conference calls.* Agree on working hours during which the teleworker can be reached. Remember, the manager is not disturbing the worker at home by telephoning that person during regularly scheduled working hours. Also, agree on how frequently the worker will be checking e-mail.

7. *Use telecommuting as a reward for good performance in the traditional office.* Poor performers should not be offered the opportunity to telecommute. Employees who volunteer to become telecommuters should be accepted only if they can demonstrate average or above-average performance records.

8. *Make periodic visits to the workers at home, but give them appropriate lead time.* During the visit, look to see if equipment is being used in a way that is ergonomically sound. Field visits, as long as they are not perceived as spying, communicate the fact that teleworkers are an important part of the team.

9. *Arrange for telecommuters to sometimes communicate with each other at a predetermined time.* The value of physical interaction is reinforced by the many face-to-face business meetings that take place at even the most technologically advanced companies with telecommuting programs. The availability of instant messaging, video conferencing, and webinars facilitates teleworkers communicating with each other simultaneously.

Sources: "Don't Give Up On Telecommuters," *Manager's Edge*, July 2006, p. 8; "Managing Telecommuters: Taking the Mystery Out of Tracking Work from Afar," *Executive Strategies*, March 1998, p. 6; "What Is the Future of Telework?" p. 6; Stephen L. Schilling, "The Basics of a Successful Telework Network," *HRfocus*, June 1999, p. 10; John A. Pearse II, "Successful Corporate Telecommuting with Technology Considerations for Late Adopters," *Organizational Dynamics*, January–March 2009, p. 22.

and semi-retired people, choose part-time work because it fits their lifestyle. Others work part time because they cannot find full-time employment.

Temporary employment is at an all-time high, with some employers even hiring part-time managers, engineers, lawyers, and other high-level workers. Part-time and temporary employees collectively constitute one-fourth to one-third of the workforce. Given that they are hired according to, or contingent upon, an employer's need, they are referred to as **contingent workers**. Some contingent workers receive modest benefits. Other contingent workers function as independent contractors who are paid for services rendered but who do not receive benefits. A familiar example would be a plumber hired by a business owner to make a repair. The plumber sets the wage and receives no benefits.

contingent workers
Part-time or temporary employees who are not members of the employer's permanent workforce.

Contingent employment now affects even executive positions, particularly managers who can execute strategy and bring about operational efficiencies.[34] Another approach to contingent employment for executives is interim appointment. Interim executives are sometimes hired from outside to help a company through a restructuring or a scandal (such as a top-level manager indicted for insider trading). Empty posts are sometimes filled with interim managers. If the manager performs well in the position, he or she might be offered a permanent slot.[35]

Many employees enjoy part-time work, which allows them to willingly trade the low pay for personal convenience. Employers, particularly in the retailing and restaurant industries, are eager to hire contingent workers to avoid the expense of hiring full-time workers. Paying limited or no benefits to part-time workers can save employers as much as 35 percent of the cost of full-time compensation, and contingent workers can be laid off if business conditions warrant such action. Some seasonal businesses, such as gift-catalog sales firms, hire mostly part-time workers.

The accompanying Management in Action illustrates the hiring of an executive as a contingent worker.

Shift Work

To accommodate the needs of employers rather than employees, many workers are assigned to shift work. The purpose of shift work is to provide coverage during nonstandard hours. The most common shift schedules are days (7 a.m. to 3 p.m.), evenings (3 p.m. to 11 p.m.), and nights (11 p.m. to 7 a.m.). Manufacturing uses shift work to meet high demand for products without having to expand facilities. It is more economical to run a factory 16 or 24 hours per day than to run two or three factories 8 hours per day. Service industries make even more extensive use of shift work to meet the demands

---

[34]Sarah E. Needleman, "Employers Tap Executives for Temporary Jobs," *The Wall Street Journal*, May 13, 2008, p. D6.

[35]Melissa Korn, "Making a Temporary Stint Stick," *The Wall Street Journal*, February 8, 2010, p. D6; Michele Conlin, "Test-Drives in the C-Suite," *Business Week*, October 19, 2009, p. 054.

MANAGEMENT IN ACTION

Be Our Guest Hires Part-Time CFO

During a downturn in the economy several years ago, Al Lovata, chief executive of Be Our Guest Inc., cut expenses for his party equipment rental business by laying off staff and reducing workers' salaries. He credits an "outsourced" chief financial officer with helping him prepare for the worst of the economic downturn.

The Boston-based company had sales growth in the double digits for several years, but revenues fell flat during the Great Recession. Then, thanks to the part-time CEO's guidance, the company became stable; revenue was down 24 percent to 30 percent, but profitability was higher than in the previous months, says the chief executive. "If we hadn't had this service, we would still be struggling," Lovata says.

Be Our Guest is not alone. Some other small-business owners in need of accounting help to balance their books and guide them out of a financial black hole are renting CFOs rather than hiring them. The strategy emerged at a time when the deep recession had forced small companies to look for money-saving alternatives that can yield good returns yet avoid substantial overhead costs.

"They're looking for ways to streamline and be as efficient as they can," says Glenn Dunlap, a cofounder of Milestone Advisors LLC, a small-business consulting firm in Indianapolis that provides CEO services.

Questions

1. In what way might being a part-time CFO represent a good career opportunity for the accountant involved?
2. How well motivated to do a good job might a part-time CFO be in comparison to one who works full time?
3. Part-time professional workers sometimes make the same contribution as a full-time counterpart, yet they receive half the pay. How fair is that?

Source: Raymund Flandez, "For Rent: Chief Financial Officer," *The Wall Street Journal*, September 28, 2009, p. B7.

of customers around the clock. Shift work is necessary in public service operations such as police work, fire fighting, and healthcare.

Catering to clients in faraway time zones may require some modification of a typical shift. For example, a stockbroker in Seattle, Washington, must be on call to converse with clients in Tokyo, Japan. According to the Sleep Channel, nearly 20 percent of employees in industrialized countries are assigned to shift work that requires them to drastically change their sleep habits weekly or even daily. Changes in the work shift affect circadian rhythm; similar to jet lag, this desynchronizes the body's sleep-wake schedule.[36]

Shift work involves more than a deviation from a traditional work schedule. It creates a lifestyle that affects productivity, health, family, and social life. Approximately 20 percent of shift workers report falling asleep during work, leading to more accidents and lower productivity. The average

---

[36]"Shift Work Sleep Disorder," http://www.sleepdisorderchannel.com/shiftwork, accessed November 27, 2006.

incidence of drug and alcohol triples, fostering an increase risk of errors and accidents. Many industrial catastrophes (such as shipwrecks, oil spills, and chemical leaks) have taken place during the night (graveyard) shift. People who work in nontraditional hours that interfere with their biological clock are also at risk for automobile crashes.[37]

Many shift workers experience difficulty in integrating their schedules with the social needs of friends and families. With proper training, employees can adjust better to shift work. A major consideration is to sleep well and comfortably; this often involves using draperies to create darkness in the room and sleeping at regular times.

LEARNING OBJECTIVE **7**
Explain how job design can contribute to a high-performance work system.

JOB DESIGN AND HIGH-PERFORMANCE WORK SYSTEMS

As implied throughout this chapter, a major purpose of job design is to enhance job performance and productivity. Job design contributes to work systems that perform exceptionally well. High-performing work systems have been proposed in terms of both manufacturing settings and the total work environment. Because essentially every topic in the formal study of management is geared toward producing a high-performing work system, we look at both approaches briefly.

High-Performance Work Systems in a Manufacturing Environment

High-performing work systems based on the contribution of individual workers overlap with several components of job enrichment and the job characteristics model. A **high-performance work system** is a way of organizing work so that frontline workers participate in decisions that have an impact on their jobs and the wider organization.

high-performance work system

A way of organizing work so that frontline workers participate in decisions that have an impact on their jobs and the wider organization.

The United Auto Workers and other labor unions favor high-performance work systems as a way of saving jobs by boosting the productivity of U.S. manufacturing plants. However, for a plant to boost productivity, four workplace practices must be incorporated into the operation of the plant. First, the workers must have a reasonable degree of autonomy in their jobs, such as making decisions about job tasks and work methods. Second, workers must have access to coworkers, managers, and supporting professionals such as manufacturing engineers and product designers. Third, the teams on the production floor must be self-managing to a large extent. Fourth, problem-solving and quality-improvement teams must function away from assembly line responsibilities. Most of these ideas will be touched upon again in the study of effective work groups, in Chapter 13.

Another consideration is that these four practices must be supported by the company's overall approach to human resource management. Among

---

[37]"Shift Work," http://www.sleepeducation.com, updated July 10, 2007.

these supportive human resource practices are extensive screening of new employees to establish a high-quality workforce, increased training for production workers, a commitment to employment security, and financial incentives linked to group performance.[38]

A team of seven researchers investigated the impact of high-performing work systems on organizational productivity. The human resource practices of empowerment, extensive training, and teamwork were compared to operational initiatives such as quality management, just-in-time inventory systems, advanced manufacturing technology, and supply-chain partnering. The relative merits of these practices were investigated by a study of 308 companies in the United Kingdom over 22 years, during a time when they implemented some or all of the seven practices just mentioned. Organizational performance tended to increase with empowerment and extensive training. The impact was strongest when teamwork was adopted. The researchers were not able to demonstrate that the operational initiatives boosted productivity.[39]

Another large study found support for the idea that high-performance work practices enhance productivity and satisfaction. The setting for the study was 21 retailers in the United States, with over 1,700 employees surveyed about the impact of empowerment on their work. It was found that empowered employees were more likely to experience job satisfaction, feel greater commitment to the company, and attain high job performance. All these positive outcomes were more likely to occur when the workers felt that their employers cared about them and valued their work.[40]

High-Performance Jobs through Adjusting Worker Resources

Another twist on high-performance work systems and job design is to adjust resources available to all workers. According to Harvard Business School professor Robert Simons, for a company to attain its potential, each employee's supply of organizational resources should equal his or her demand, or need, for these resources. The same supply–demand balance must apply to every function, every business unit, and the entire organization. To carry out his or her job, each employee must find answers to four questions:

1. What resources do I control for accomplishing my tasks?
2. What measures will be used to evaluate my performance?

---

[38]"High Performance Work Systems: What's the Payoff?" http://www.uaw.org/publications/jobs_pay, accessed November 22, 2006; Eileen Appelbaum, Thomas Bailey, Peter Berg, and Arne Kallbgberg, *Manufacturing Advantage* (Ithaca, NY: Cornell University Press, 2000).

[39]Kamal Birdi et al, "The Impact of Human Resource and Operational Management Practices On Company Productivity: A Longitudinal Study," *Personnel Psychology*, Autumn 2008, pp. 467–501.

[40]Marcus Butt et al, "Individual Reaction to High Involvement Work Practices: Investigating the Role of Empowerment and Perceived Organizational Support," *Journal of Occupational Health Psychology*, April 2009, pp. 122–136.

3. With whom must I interact and whom must I influence to achieve my goals?

4. How much support can I expect when I ask for assistance?

Each question refers to the four basic *spans* of a job. Question 1 refers to the control span; Question 2, accountability; Question 3, influence; and Question 4, support. Each span can be adjusted so that it is narrow or wide or somewhere between the extremes. When the manager adjusts resources to the right settings, the job can be designed to allow a talented individual to execute the company's strategy with success. If the resources are adjusted incorrectly, the worker will be less effective.

The heart of this proposed system is an executive manipulating resources as if they were a high-to-low sliding volume control. According to this system of achieving high performance, the supply of resources for each job and each unit must be equivalent to demand. This means that the span of control plus span of support must equal the span of accountability plus span of influence. An example of this type of fine-tuning would be in making adjustment in spans for a marketing and sales manager at a software company. The manager might be given a narrow span of control and a relatively wide span of accountability. The discrepancy would be geared toward forcing the manager to be entrepreneurial. Workers who lack resources yet who are still accountable for outcomes such as market share and customer satisfaction must take an entrepreneurial, innovative approach.[41]

The approach to job design just presented is usually implemented by a top-level manager. The several other approaches to job design described in this chapter are much more realistic for most managers.

---

[41]Robert Simons, "Designing High-Performance Jobs," *Harvard Business Review*, July–August 2005, pp. 54–72.

Summary of Key Points

 Explain the four major dimensions of job design plus job specialization and job descriptions.

The four major dimensions of job design are task characteristics, knowledge characteristics, social characteristics, and contextual characteristics. Each dimension has sub-dimensions. Professional and nonprofessional jobs differ on sub-dimensions; professional jobs have more complexity, information processing, and problem solving. Human-life–focused jobs score higher on the dimensions of significance.

Job specialization is the degree to which a jobholder performs only a limited number of tasks. Specialists are found at different occupational levels. Job specialization enhances workforce expertise at all levels and can reduce training time at the operative level. Specialization, however, can lead to problems. Coordinating the work of specialists can be difficult, and some employees may become bored. Automation contributes to job specialization. A major purpose of automation is to increase productivity by reducing the labor content required to deliver a product or service.

 Describe job enrichment, including the job characteristics model.

Job enrichment calls for increasing challenges and responsibility, which makes jobs more appealing to most employees. The person holding the job must perceive these enriched characteristics of a job. An enriched job provides direct feedback, client relationships, new learning, control over methods, scheduling by the employee, unique experience, control over resources, direct communication authority, and personal accountability.

Expanding on the idea of job enrichment creates the job characteristics model, which focuses on the task and interpersonal dimensions of a job. Five characteristics of jobs improve employee motivation, satisfaction, and performance: skill variety, task identity, task significance, autonomy, and feedback. These characteristics relate to critical psychological states, which in turn lead to outcomes such as internal motivation, satisfaction, low absenteeism, and high quality.

Implementing job enrichment begins by finding out which employees want an enriched job. The employees most likely to want and enjoy enriched jobs are those with a strong need for personal growth.

 Describe job involvement, enlargement, and rotation.

Job involvement reflects psychological involvement with one's work and how much work is part of the self-image. Job enlargement increases the number and variety of job tasks. Job rotation switches assignments and can contribute heavily to career development.

4 **Explain how workers use job crafting to modify their jobs.**

The rigidity of some job descriptions does not fit the flexible work roles carried out by many workers. Following an emerging trend, many companies hire people "to work" rather than to fill a specific job slot. Another way of deviating from job descriptions is for workers to modify the job to fit their personal preferences and capabilities. Employees often craft their jobs by changing the tasks they perform and their contacts with others to make their jobs more meaningful.

The idea of job embeddedness helps explain the many forces that attach people to their job beyond job design.

5 **Illustrate how ergonomic factors can be part of job design.**

A key principle of job design is that the job should be laid out to decrease the chances that it will physically harm the incumbent. Ergonomics seeks to minimize the physical demands on workers and optimize system performance. Musculoskeletal (muscle and bone) injuries include cumulative trauma disorders—injuries caused by repetitive motions over prolonged periods of time, which occur in many different types of work. Workstations can be designed to minimize these problems by such measures as supporting the back and thighs and permitting workers to place the feet flat on the floor. Back problems are widespread in the workplace, and many of these problems can be prevented through ergonomics. Uncomfortable noise levels present another ergonomic problem to be addressed.

6 **Summarize the various modified work schedules.**

Work scheduling is another part of job design. A modified work schedule departs from the traditional hours of work. Modified work-scheduling options include flexible working hours, a compressed work-week, an alternative workplace and telecommuting, job sharing, and part-time and temporary work. Shift work involves more than a deviation from a traditional work schedule; it creates a lifestyle that affects productivity, health, family, and social life.

 Explain how job design can contribute to a high-performance work system.

A high-performing work system organizes work so that frontline workers participate in decisions that have an impact on their jobs and the wider organization. Such a work system includes job autonomy, access to support from work associates, self-managing work teams, and problem-solving and quality-improvement teams. The company human resource management approach should support the high-performing work system.

A proposed approach to high-performing work systems is to adjust resources available to workers. For a company to attain its potential, each employee's supply of resources should equal demand for these resources.

Key Terms and Phrases

Job design, 226
Job specialization, 230
Job description, 232
Job enrichment, 233
Job characteristics model, 235
Job involvement, 236
Job enlargement, 236
Job rotation, 238
Job crafting, 239
Job embeddedness, 240

Ergonomics, 241
Cumulative trauma disorders, 242
Carpal tunnel syndrome, 242
Modified work schedule, 244
Compressed workweek, 247
Telecommuting, 247
Job sharing, 250
Contingent workers, 252
High-performance work system, 254

Questions

1. At one time, some companies hired talented people at a good salary with the assignment to simply "do something useful, and profitable." Were these hiring managers irresponsible? What kind of worker could perform well in such a position?
2. In about 35 words, write the job description for (a) a restaurant manager, (b) the top executive at Macy's, and (c) the head coach of one of your favorite athletic teams.
3. Why is job rotation often more exciting to workers than job enlargement?

4. What are the benefits of frequent job rotation for a person who would like to become a high-level manager?
5. How might a customer-service representative who works at the call center for a consumer electronics company craft his or her job?
6. Would you be satisfied as a telecommuter or remote worker? Why or why not?
7. How would a manager know if the jobs he or she supervised fit well into a high-performance work system?

Skill-Building Exercise 7-A: The Ideal Home-Based Office

Gather into teams of about five people to design an ideal office at home for a professional worker. Take about 20 minutes to develop suggestions for the following aspects of a home office: (1) hardware and software, (2) equipment other than computers, (3) furniture, (4) ergonomics design, (5) office layout, and (6) location within home. Consider both productivity and job satisfaction when designing your office. After the designs are completed, the team leaders might present the design to the rest of the class.

Skill-Building Exercise 7-B: The Job-Improvement Interview

Interview two people performing essentially the same job (two accountants, two truck drivers, or two clerical support workers). Probe for information about what these workers like and dislike about their jobs, and what improvements they would like to see. Based on your interview findings and the information in this chapter, prepare a 150-word report on how to improve the job in question. Make recommendations for improving both job satisfaction and productivity.

Management Now: Online Skill-Building Exercise: Best Jobs

The assignment here is to gain insight into how intensely some people like their jobs, and to speculate what managers can do to create more such jobs. Conduct an Internet search to find three jobs that could qualify for a "best job" trophy. Focus your search on an article written or a blog posted within the last 90 days. After finding these jobs, identify the factors that make these jobs so rewarding and satisfying to people. What interest might you have in holding one of these jobs?

7-A Case Problem

The Sub Shop Blues

Serge runs a profitable chain of five rapid-service restaurants that sell submarine sandwiches, non-alcoholic beverages, and related snacks such as potato chips and pretzels. Customers either take out the sandwiches or eat them on the restaurant premises. "Serge's Subs" also caters to local businesses for luncheon parties and to homes for sports gathering.

Asked to identify his biggest management challenge, Serge replied, "Keeping good employees. Most of our workers are part-timers. Some are students, some are older people. Most of them want part-time employment. Making a submarine sandwich may look easy, but there is skill involved. For example, you have to remember what the customer asked for. A beginner might ask the same question a few times about what the customer wants on the sub.

"It takes a few weeks for a sub maker to get sharp, and to move quickly enough to take care of a surge in orders, like Friday lunch.

"The problem is that too many of the good sub makers leave after a couple of months. My store managers have to keep finding and training new employees."

Asked what he and his managers have attempted so far to increase retention, Serge replied, "We tried increasing pay 15 cents per hour. We are also being more generous about allowing employees to make their own subs to eat on premises or take home.

"So far these two initiatives haven't had much of an effect on reducing turnover."

Asked what reason workers give for leaving, Serge answered. "Sometimes a worker will say that he or she needs more money. Sometimes the answer is that school has become too demanding. Sometimes a senior person will say that he or she finds the work too physically demanding, especially standing up all the time.

"But the biggest complaint I get is that the work is boring. Instead of thinking of preparing a sub as a work of art, a lot of the guys and gals say that the work is boring. Once you've prepared a hundred sandwiches, they're all the same."

"So far, I haven't figured out how to make the job of our basic worker more interesting."

Discussion Questions
1. How does this case relate to job design?
2. What recommendations might you offer Serge for making the position of sub shop preparer more satisfying?
3. What else can Serge do to find out what is lacking in the job of sub shop preparer?

7-B Case Problem

The Telecommuting Challenge at Broadbent Distributors

Margot is the vice president of administration at Broadbent Beverages, a bottler and distributor for approximately 25 beverage companies. Much like the bottling companies for the best-known soft drink manufacturers, Broadbent does much of the behind-the-scenes work, such as bottling, packaging, and shipping beverages.

As more beverage companies are doing their own bottling and distribution, and profit margins are getting thinner, Margot and other Broadbent executives have been looking for ways to trim costs. One cost-cutting measure Margot proposed about one year ago was to expand its telecommuting program. She calculated that the company could reduce office space by 25 percent if just 10 percent more workers did not require permanent office space. The telecommuters could work from home about four days per week and share much more limited space on their day in the office. Margot also explained to other Broadbent executives that the company would most likely enjoy productivity gains from the telecommuting program.

In collaboration with other executives and middle managers, Margot developed a list of positions eligible for telecommuting: accounts receivable specialist, business development representatives, benefits specialist, purchasing manager, and truck dispatcher. Workers who volunteered to telecommute would be given the opportunity, yet no workers would be forced to telecommute.

Thirty-one employees volunteered for telecommuting at first, and within six months, 42 employees were telecommuting at least two days per week. The telecommuters themselves had good reports about their experience. Several talked about their work lives being less stressful; many agreed that cutting back a little on commuting improved the quality of their lives; and at least one dozen employees said they enjoyed contributing to a green environment by spending less time on the road.

Despite the praiseworthy comments from the telecommuters, several middle managers and supervisors began to complain about the work-at-home program. Dan, the director of accounting, complained, "I may be old fashioned, but I don't consider my accounts receivable specialist really working when she spends Friday morning at Starbucks poking at her laptop. If she were in the office, she would be processing a lot more invoices."

Midge, the marketing manager, said, "I want to get together a group of reps so we can brainstorm a complex customer problem. But there's only one rep on the premises, so I have to schedule the brainstorming session for a later date. This same problem has happened to me a few times."

Cal, the dispatching supervisor, expressed his concerns about telecommuting in these words: "With half the dispatchers away from the office at a given time, it is tough to solve simple problems. Instead of just walking down the hall to iron out a small problem, we have to exchange dozens of e-mails, or make dozens of phone calls. It doesn't feel like our department is part of a real company any longer."

Margot made note of all the positives and negatives said about the telecommuting program and decided to dig into the problem later in the week.

Discussion Questions

1. Explain the extent to which you agree with the complaints about telecommuting.
2. How fair is the assessment of Midge and Cal that group problem solving is made more difficult when workers are telecommuting?
3. What advice can you offer Margot to have a telecommuting program better accepted by the managers?

CHAPTER 8

Organization Structure, Culture, and Change

The appointment of a new chief executive at Procter & Gamble could spark broader management changes at the consumer products giant as it tries to better control its sprawling empire and keep certain executives from quitting, people familiar with the matter said a few years ago. P&G said that operations chief Robert McDonald would become chief executive officer, succeeding A. G. Lafley who had held the post for nine years. The appointment put a 29-year veteran of the consumer-goods maker in charge just as it grappled with the global recession and new competitive threats to its brands, which include Crest, Tide, and Pantene.

McDonald gave the employees a hint of what was coming next: He planned to reduce the levels of management between entry-level positions and the chief executive to seven levels, he said at a town-hall style meeting at a P&G's Cincinnati headquarters. At the time there were about nine levels of managers between new hires and the CEO office.

McDonald also said he wouldn't replace himself as chief operating officer and would assume the title of president, eliminating another high-profile job opening. As CEO, McDonald planned to "create a simpler, flatter and more

OBJECTIVES

After studying this chapter and doing the exercises, you should be able to:

1. Describe the bureaucratic organization structure and discuss its advantages and disadvantages.

2. Explain the major ways in which organizations are divided into departments.

3. Describe four modifications of the bureaucratic structure.

4. Identify key factors that influence the selection of organization structure.

5. Specify how delegation, empowerment, and decentralization spread authority in an organization.

6. Identify major aspects of organizational culture.

7. Describe key aspects of managing change, including gaining support for change.

agile organization," he said. "This is a priority because simplification reduces cost, improves productivity, and enhances employee satisfaction."

These changes were perceived by some as a nod to one of P&G's critical challenges: its sometimes cumbersome bureaucracy and slow decision-making processes. During a recent decade, P&G grew into a behemoth, doubling its annual sales to $83.5 billion. The company has 138,000 employees spanning more than 60 countries. That scale made it sometimes difficult to respond to competitive threats such as competitors' lower-priced products.[1]

The story about the new CEO of a giant consumer-products company illustrates how organization structure can be related to productivity, satisfaction, and even culture (such as an emphasis on deliberate decision making). The story also hints at the importance of organizational change. The major topics in this chapter are organization structure, culture, and change. All three topics are fundamental aspects of how organizations function.

BUREAUCRACY AS AN ORGANIZATION STRUCTURE

In Chapter 7, we described how the tasks of an organization are divided into jobs for individuals and groups. Companies also subdivide work through an **organization structure**—the arrangement of people and tasks to accomplish organizational goals. The structure specifies who reports to whom and who does what, and it is also a method for implementing a strategy or for accomplishing the purpose of the organization. For example, top management at Subway wants to sell millions and millions of sandwiches and beverages, so it places thousands of stores and counters in convenient locations, even at some service stations.

A **bureaucracy** is a rational, systematic, and precise form of organization in which rules, regulations, and techniques of control are specifically defined. Think of bureaucracy as the traditional form of organization; other structures are variations of, or supplements to, bureaucracy. Do not confuse the word *bureaucracy* with bigness. Although most big organizations are bureaucratic, small firms can also follow the bureaucratic model. An example might be a small, carefully organized bank.

---

[1]Excerpted from Ellen Byron and Joann S. Lublin, "Appointment of New P&G Chief Sends Ripples Through Ranks," *The Wall Street Journal*, June 11, 2009, p. B3.

Principles of Organization in a Bureaucracy

The entire classical school of management contributes to our understanding of bureaucracy. Yet the essence of bureaucracy can be identified by its major characteristics and principles as listed next:

1. *Hierarchy of authority.* The dominant characteristic of a bureaucracy is that each lower organizational unit is controlled and supervised by a higher one. The person granted the most formal authority (the right to act) occupies the top place of the hierarchy. Exhibit 8-1 presents a bureaucracy as pyramid shaped. The number of employees increases substantially as one moves down each successive level. Most of the formal authority concentrates at the top and decreases with each lower level.

2. *Unity of command.* A classic management principle, **unity of command** states that each subordinate receives assigned duties from one superior only and is accountable to that superior. In the modern organization, many people serve on projects and teams in addition to reporting to their regular boss, thus violating the unity of command principle.

3. *Task specialization.* In a bureaucracy, division of labor is based on task specialization. To achieve task specialization, organizations designate separate divisions or departments such as new product development, customer service, and information technology. Workers assigned to these organizational units employ specialized knowledge and skills that contribute to the overall effectiveness of the firm.

unity of command
The classical management principle stating that each subordinate receives assigned duties from one superior only and is accountable to that superior.

EXHIBIT 8-1   **The Bureaucratic Form of Organization**

In a bureaucracy, power is concentrated at the top, yet many more employees occupy lower levels in the organization. Note that team leaders are typically found at the first level or middle level of management.

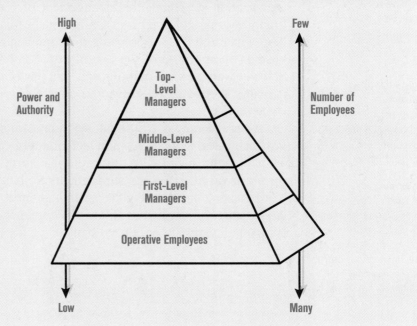

4. *Responsibilities and job descriptions*. Bureaucracies are characterized by rules that define the responsibilities of employees. In a highly bureaucratic organization, each employee follows a precise job description and therefore knows his or her job expectations. The responsibility and authority of each manager is defined clearly in writing. Responsibility defined in writing lets managers know what is expected of them and what limits are set to their authority.

5. *Line and staff functions*. A bureaucracy identifies the various organizational units as line or staff. Line functions involve the primary purpose of an organization or its primary outputs. In a bank, line managers supervise work related to borrowing and lending money. Staff functions assist the line functions. Staff managers take responsibility for important functions such as human resources and purchasing. Although staff functions do not deal with the primary purposes of the firm, they play an essential role in achieving the organization's mission.

Go to www.cengage.
com/management/
dubrin and view the
video for Chapter 8. As
you watch the video,
think about how you
would describe
EvoGear's corporate
culture and structure.

Advantages and Disadvantages of Bureaucracy

Bureaucracy made modern civilization possible. Without large, complex organizations to coordinate the efforts of thousands of people, we would not have airplanes, automobiles, skyscrapers, universities, vaccines, or space satellites. Many large bureaucratic organizations such as Microsoft and McDonald's continue to grow at an impressive pace. A major reason that hierarchies continue to thrive is that they fill the basic need for order and security. People want order, predictability, and structures they can understand. For example, they want to be able to be in touch with the tech center when a desktop computer breaks down. Hierarchies help us satisfy other psychological needs through such mechanisms as career ladders; belonging to a stable organization gives us a feeling of identity.[2] Organizations such as banks, pharmaceutical firms, and hospitals must follow tight regulations for the good of the public.

Advantages A major advantage of a bureaucracy is that organizational members know who is responsible for what—everyone knows who has the authority to make a particular decision. One of the first major initiatives Carol Bartz took when she became CEO of Yahoo! in 2009 was to clarify who was responsible for what type of decisions so innovation could move forward.[3] People who develop new ideas for products or services find it reassuring to present their ideas to a manager with the authority to implement them.

Traditional bureaucracies facilitate vertical integration whereby a company controls materials, product development, manufacturing, and distribution. In

---

[2]Harold J. Leavitt, "Why Hierarchies Thrive," *Harvard Business Review*, March 2003, p. 99; Leavitt, *Top Down: Why Hierarchies Are Here to Stay and How to Manage Them More Effectively* (Boston: HBS Press, 2004).

[3]"A Question of Management," *The Wall Street Journal*, June 2, 2009, p. R4.

an era of outsourcing and subcontracting, the 100-year-old strategy of vertical integration still has a place in building a strong, unified organization. For example, a few years ago Larry Ellison, the CEO of Oracle, purchased Sun Microsystems. At once, Oracle was transformed into a more powerful company that developed and produced software, computers, and computer components. Ellison said, "It's back to the future." PepsiCo, Boeing, and General Motors have also moved further into vertical integration in recent years.[4]

In an attempt to make their companies less bureaucratic, many executives eliminate policies, rules, and regulations. These procedures often embody an invaluable source of effective organizational practices. Paul S. Adler says, "Having tossed out the manuals, many organizations discover that their employees are frustrated because now they have to improvise without even a common melody line let alone a complete score."[5]

Disadvantages Despite the contributions of bureaucracy, several key disadvantages exist. A bureaucracy can be rigid in handling people and problems. Its well-intended rules and regulations sometimes create inconvenience and inefficiency. For example, requiring several layers of approval to make a decision causes the process to take a long time. Another substantial problem in a pronounced bureaucracy is that many workers pass responsibility to another department for dealing with a problem. A typical comment is, "You will have to be in touch with (another department) to solve that problem."

Any structure in which strong divisions or departments exist lends itself to a silo mentality in which members of one group feel competitive with other groups to the extent that cooperation suffers. For example, the pharmaceutical group might compete for resources with the over-the-counter medicine group in a medical products company. A situation at Sony portrays an example of the silo problem. A few years ago one of management's biggest challenges was to break down silos and get rival factions to cooperate. Specifically, the e-book device was bogged down by infighting among rival camps.[6]

Other frequent problems in a bureaucracy are frustration caused by red tape, slow decision making based on the layers of approval required, and frequent meetings. During the Haitian earthquake crisis in 2010, vital medical supplies were sometimes blocked from getting through to people in need because of a lengthy customs procedure required by the Haitian government.

---

[4]Ben Worthen, Cari Tuna, and Justin Scheck, "Companies More Prone to Go 'Vertical,'" *The Wall Street Journal*, November 30, 2009, p. A1.

[5]Paul S. Adler, "Building Better Bureaucracies," *Academy of Management Executive*, November 1999, pp. 26–37.

[6]Cliff Edwards, Kenji Hall, and Ronald Grover, "Sony Chases Apple's Magic," *Business Week*, November 10, 2008, pp. 48–51.

To examine your own orientation to the bureaucratic form of organization, take the self-quiz presented in Exhibit 8-2.

EXHIBIT 8-2	**Understanding Your Bureaucratic Orientation**

Respond to each statement, "mostly agree" (MA) or "mostly disagree" (MD). Assume the mindset of attempting to learn something about you rather than impressing a prospective employer.

		MA	MD
1.	I value stability in my job.		
2.	I like a predictable organization.		
3.	I enjoy working without the benefit of a carefully specified job description.		
4.	I would enjoy working for an organization in which promotions were generally determined by seniority.		
5.	Rules, policies, and procedures generally frustrate me.		
6.	I would enjoy working for a company that employed 95,000 people worldwide.		
7.	Being self-employed would involve more risk than I'm willing to take.		
8.	Before accepting a position, I would like to see an exact job description.		
9.	I would prefer a job as a freelance landscape artist to one as a supervisor for the Department of Motor Vehicles.		
10.	Seniority should be as important as performance in determining pay increases and promotion.		
11.	It would give me a feeling of pride to work for the largest and most successful company in its field.		
12.	Given a choice, I would prefer to make $100,000 per year as a vice-president in a small company than $120,000 per year as a middle manager in a large company.		
13.	I would feel uncomfortable if I were required to wear an employee badge with a number on it.		
14.	Parking spaces in a company lot should be assigned according to job level.		
15.	I would generally prefer working as a specialist to performing many different tasks.		
16.	Before accepting a job, I would want to make sure that the company had a good program of employee benefits.		
17.	A company will not be successful unless it establishes a clear set of rules and regulations.		
18.	I would prefer to work in a department with a manager in charge than to work on a team where managerial responsibility is shared.		
19.	You should respect people according to their rank.		
20.	Rules are meant to be broken.		
	Score:		

(continued)

| EXHIBIT 8-2 | Understanding Your Bureaucratic Orientation *(continued)* |

Scoring and interpretation: Give yourself one point for each statement you responded to in the bureaucratic direction, then total your score.

1. Mostly agree	8. Mostly agree	15. Mostly disagree
2. Mostly agree	9. Mostly disagree	16. Mostly agree
3. Mostly disagree	10. Mostly agree	17. Mostly agree
4. Mostly agree	11. Mostly agree	18. Mostly agree
5. Mostly disagree	12. Mostly disagree	19. Mostly agree
6. Mostly agree	13. Mostly disagree	20. Mostly disagree
7. Mostly agree	14. Mostly agree	

15–20   You would enjoy working in a bureaucracy.

8–14   You would experience a mixture of satisfactions and dissatisfactions if working in a bureaucracy.

0–7   You would most likely be frustrated by working in a bureaucracy, especially a large one.

Source: Adapted and updated from Andrew J. DuBrin, *Human Relations: A Job Oriented Approach*, 5th ed. (Upper Saddle River, NJ: Prentice Hall, 1991), pp. 434–435.

LEARNING OBJECTIVE

Explain the major ways in which organizations are divided into departments.

departmentalization
The process of subdividing work into departments.

functional departmentalization
An arrangement that defines departments by the function each one performs, such as accounting or purchasing.

DEPARTMENTALIZATION

Bureaucratic and other forms of organization subdivide the work into departments or other units to prevent total confusion. Can you imagine an organization of 300,000 people, or even 300, in which all employees worked in one large department? The process of subdividing work into departments is called **departmentalization**. This chapter uses charts to illustrate four frequently used forms of departmentalization: functional, geographic, product–service, and customer. In practice, most organization charts show a combination of the various types; they are said to have hybrid organization structures.

Functional Departmentalization

Functional departmentalization defines departments by the function each one performs, such as accounting or purchasing. Dividing work according to activity is the traditional way of organizing the efforts of people. In a functional organization, each department carries out a specialized activity such as information processing, purchasing, sales, accounting, or maintenance. Exhibit 8-3 illustrates an organization arranged on purely functional lines. The major subdivisions further divide along their own functional lines as shown in Exhibit 8-4. The exhibit shows the functional organization within the materials management department.

EXHIBIT 8-3 — Functional Departmentalization Within the Davenport Machine Company

Observe that each box below the level of CEO indicates an executive in charge of a specific function or activity, such as sales and marketing.

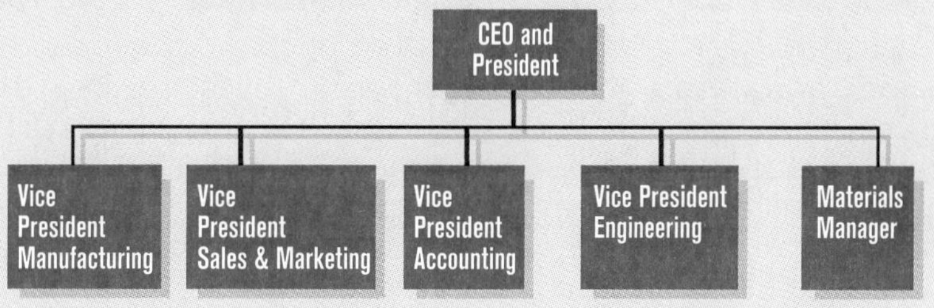

```
                        CEO and President
   Vice President   Vice President      Vice President   Vice President   Materials
   Manufacturing    Sales & Marketing   Accounting       Engineering      Manager
```

The list of advantages and disadvantages of the functional organization, the traditional form of organization, reads the same as for bureaucracy. Functional departmentalization works particularly well when large batches of work must be processed on a recurring basis and when the expertise of specialists is required. As with any form of departmentalization, a major problem is that the people within a unit may not communicate sufficiently with workers in other units.

The accompanying Management in Action illustrates how a functional structure can sometimes be used to improve organizational effectiveness.

Geographic Departmentalization

geographic departmentalization

An arrangement of departments according to the geographic area or territory served.

Geographic departmentalization is an arrangement of departments according to the geographic area or territory served. In this organization structure, people performing all the activities for a firm in a given geographic area report to one manager who often has a title such as *Regional Vice President*. Marketing divisions often use territorial departmentalization; the sales force may be divided into northeastern, southeastern, midwestern, northwestern, and southwestern regions.

Geographic departmentalization that divides an organization into geographic regions generally works well for international business. Yet in a

EXHIBIT 8-4 — Functional Departmentalization Within a Department of the Davenport Machine Company

Observe that the materials management department, as with other departments, has its own functional structure.

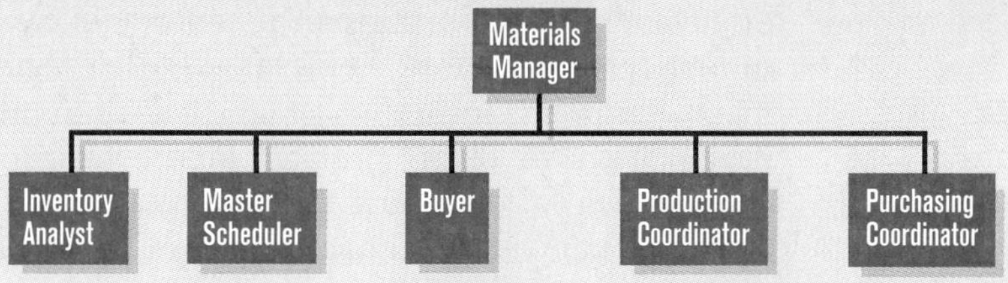

```
                    Materials Manager
   Inventory   Master      Buyer   Production    Purchasing
   Analyst     Scheduler           Coordinator   Coordinator
```

MANAGEMENT IN ACTION

In January, a few years ago, cellphone giant Nokia Corp. threw itself off balance. The Finnish company had previously divided its cellphone business into three groups based on market segments: consumer phones, feature-heavy smart phones, and business phones. Instead, Nokia executives carved the cellphone unit into two functional groups: those developing the phones and those creating the company's growing software-and-services offerings.

The reorganization allowed Nokia to focus more attention on software and services, an increasingly important part of its business. It also created an organization that is "unstable by design." The two units are encouraged to challenge each other, says Mikko Kosonen, a former Nokia strategy chief who advised the executive team on the new corporate structure.

One potential friction point: whether Nokia's software should be reserved for the company's cellphones or marketed to other hardware makers, a question with the potential to affect the profits each unit can make. But units no longer set their own financial targets, one of many tactics that force executives to resolve their differences rather than fight. That mix of tension and collaboration is designed to "keep the organization awake," says Kosonen, who recently authored a book on strategic agility with Yves Diz, a professor at the Instead business school in Fontainbleau, France. "The very things that make you great will kill you—unless you take the medicine to stay agile," says Kosonen.

Questions

1. Why is dividing the cellphone unit into groups (developing phones and developing software and services) classified as a functional structure?
2. How might this new organization structure take away a little from Nokia's ability to satisfy customer needs?

Source: Excerpted from Phred Dvorak, "Experts Have a Message for Managers: Shake It Up," *The Wall Street Journal*, June 16, 2008, p. B8.

new global business trend, organizations develop a central structure that serves operations in various geographic locations. A case in point is Ford Motor Company. To economize, Ford merged its manufacturing, sales, and product development operations in North America, Europe, Latin America, and Asia.

A key advantage of geographic departmentalization is that it allows for decision making at a local level, where the personnel are most familiar with the problems and the local culture, including tastes in fashion, product styling, and food. Geographic departmentalization also presents some potential disadvantages. The arrangement can be quite expensive because of duplication of costs and effort. For instance, each region may build service departments (such as for purchasing) that duplicate activities carried out at headquarters. A bigger problem arises when top-level management experiences difficulty controlling the performance of field units. To deal with this problem, many multinational corporations supplement the geographic structure by coordinating functional activities across regions. For example, a food processor might want to make sure that the same health standards are followed in all parts of the world.

Product–Service Departmentalization

product-service departmentalization

The arrangement of departments according to the products or services they provide.

Product–service departmentalization is the arrangement of departments according to the products or services they provide. When specific products or services are so important that the units that create and support them almost become independent companies, product–service departmentalization makes sense. The departments of this size are usually labeled divisions. With very successful products, the organizational unit making the product becomes a division. One example is the wireless product division of Verizon.

Exhibit 8-5 presents a version of product–service departmentalization at General Electric. Notice that the four divisions offer products or services with unique demands. For example, the sale of technology infrastructure is a different business than lending money to business firms. Notice also that the same customer might purchase services from one or more divisions. For example, a large business purchasing a wind turbine from one major division might also borrow money to finance a new machine and to pay for advertising on NBC. As a consequence, the structure is not strictly customer departmentalization.

Organizing by product line offers numerous benefits; employees focus on a product or service, which allows each division or department the maximum opportunity to grow and prosper. An important marketing and sales advantage is that sales representatives are assigned to one product or service group in which they become experts, rather than being sales generalists. Several years ago Hewlett-Packard shifted back to product-specific reps; they would no longer be sending generalist account reps up against the "razor-focused sales people from the likes of Dell, printer specialist Lexmark International Inc., and storage giant EMC Corp."[7]

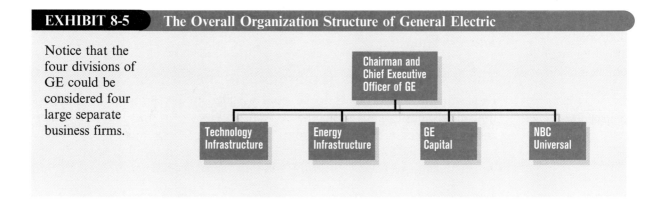

EXHIBIT 8-5   The Overall Organization Structure of General Electric

Notice that the four divisions of GE could be considered four large separate business firms.

---

[7]Peter Burrows, "The Un-Carly Unveils His Game Plan," *Business Week*, June 27, 2005, p. 36.

In a smooth-running organization with open communication, the various product or service units cooperate with each other for mutual benefit. A case in point is the healthcare giant Johnson & Johnson. A division that develops an improved method of delivering drugs (such as a skin patch) would typically share that development with another division. Human care could improve pet care and vice versa! Similar to geographic departmentalization, grouping by product or service fosters high morale and allows decisions to be made at the local level. Departmentalization by product poses the same potential problems as geographic departmentalization. It can be expensive because of duplication of effort, and top-level management may find it difficult to control the separate units.

Product–service departmentalization also takes the form of organizational groups created to better service customer needs. This type of structure is referred to as customer departmentalization. In 2009, Dell Inc. reorganized its commercial businesses into three worldwide units to serve customers better and to reduce geographic barriers. The new units were (a) large enterprise, (b) public sector, and (c) small and mid-size businesses. Customer needs as well as the sales process could be quite different among the units.[8] For example, it might take seven months of negotiation to sell 500 laptop computers to a government agency but only an hour to sell a two-person advertising agency one notebook computer.

LEARNING OBJECTIVE **3**

Describe four modifications of the bureaucratic structure: the matrix structure; flat structures, downsizing, and outsourcing; the horizontal structure; and power sharing at the top.

MODIFICATIONS OF THE BUREAUCRATIC ORGANIZATION

To overcome some of the problems of the bureaucratic (including the functional) structure, several other organization structures have been developed. Virtually all large organizations combine bureaucratic and less bureaucratic forms. This section describes three popular modifications of bureaucracy: the matrix organization; flat structures, downsizing, and outsourcing; and the horizontal structure. We also describe power sharing at the very top of the organization; it represents a slight variation from a bureaucratic organization structure.

The Project and Matrix Organizations

project organization
A temporary group of specialists working under one manager to accomplish a fixed objective.

Departmentalization tends to be poorly suited to performing special tasks that differ substantially from the normal activities of a firm. **Project organization**, in which a temporary group of specialists works under one manager to accomplish a fixed objective, offers one widely used solution to this problem. Used most extensively in the military, aerospace, construction, motion

---

[8]Christopher Helman, "Dell's Reboot," *Forbes,* February 2, 2009, p. 29; Ben Charny and Justin Scheck, "Dell Elevates Insiders in Strategy Change," *The Wall Street Journal*, January 2, 2009, p. A11.

picture, and computer industries, project management is so widespread that software has been developed to help managers plot out details and make all tasks visible. The project manager has long been a central figure in getting major tasks accomplished, such as seeing a new product to completion. Project managers serve as a linking pin between an organization providing service and the client.[9] An example would be a project manager at the General Electric division that services airplane engines spending time on the premises of United Airlines to help with the service project.

matrix organization
A project structure superimposed on a functional structure.

The best-known application of project management is the **matrix organization**, a project structure superimposed on a functional structure. Matrix organizations evolved to capitalize on the advantages of project and functional structures while minimizing their disadvantages. Jay R. Galbraith, professor emeritus at the International Institute for Management Development, says that matrix organizations are a natural consequence of working in today's complex business environment.[10] The project groups act as mini-companies within the firm in which they operate. The group usually disbands after completing its mission. In some instances, the project proves so successful that it becomes a new and separate division of the company.

Exhibit 8-6 shows a popular version of the matrix structure. Notice that functional managers exert some functional authority over specialists assigned to the projects. For example, the quality manager occasionally meets with the quality specialists assigned to the projects to discuss their professional activities. The project managers hold line authority over the people assigned to their projects. For the matrix organization to work well there should be an assumed balance of power between the two bosses.

The project managers borrow resources from the functional departments; this is a feature that distinguishes the matrix from other organizational structures. Each person working on the project reports to two superiors: the project manager and the functional manager. For example, observe the quality analyst in the lower right corner of Exhibit 8-6. The analyst reports to the manager of quality three boxes above him or her and to the project manager for the thermo pumps project located five boxes to the left.

Users of the matrix structure include banks, insurance companies, aerospace companies, and educational institutions. Colleges often use matrix structures for setting up special interest programs. Among them are African American studies, industrial training, and an executive MBA program. A director who uses resources from traditional departments heads each of these programs. IBM has used the matrix structure with considerable success, partially because the complexity of the company demands complex structures.

---

[9]Jay R. Galbraith, *Designing Matrix Organizations That Actually Work: How IBM, Procter & Gamble, and Others Design for Success* (San Francisco: Jossey-Bass, 2009), p. 247.

[10]Shelia Simsarian Webber and Maria T. Torti, "Project Managers Doubling as Client Account Executives," *Academy of Management Executive*, February 2004, p. 70.

EXHIBIT 8-6	Matrix Organization in an Energy-Equipment Company

Personnel assigned to a project all report to two managers: a project head and a functional manager.

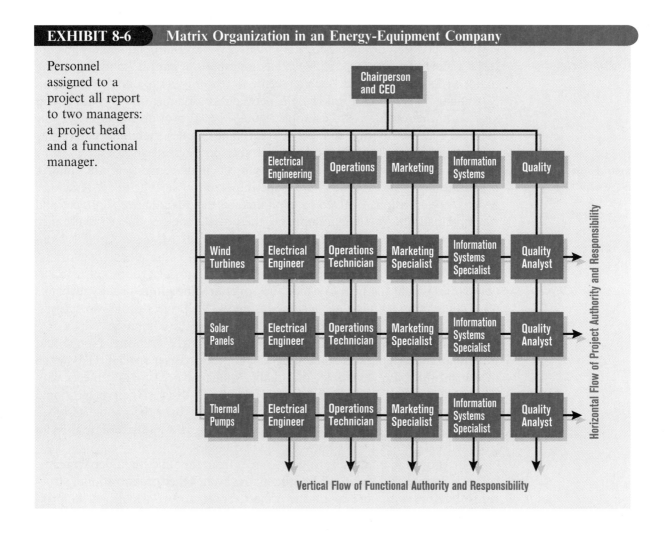

Flat Structures, Downsizing, and Outsourcing

Three closely related approaches to simplifying an organization structure include creating flat structures, downsizing, and outsourcing. Reducing the number of layers typically makes an organization less bureaucratic.

Flat Structures

Organizations with a bureaucratic structure tend to accumulate many layers of managers and often too many employees in general. You may recall that Procter & Gamble had eleven levels of management when the new CEO was appointed. Top management may decide to create a **flat organization structure,** a form of organization with relatively few layers. A flat organization structure acts less bureaucratically for two reasons. First, fewer available managers review the decisions of other workers. Second, a shorter chain of command means that managers and workers at lower levels can make decisions more independently.

flat organization structure

A form of organization with relatively few layers of management, making it less bureaucratic.

span of control
The number of workers reporting directly to a manager.

An important consequence of creating flat structures leaves the remaining managers with a larger **span of control**—the number of workers reporting directly to a manager. A large span of control works best with competent and efficient managers and group members. When group members do relatively similar work, the manager can supervise more people.

Computer-based approaches to sending information to workers have been a major force toward flattening organization structures. Workers have a lot of the information they need to accomplish their work without consulting a manager.[11] However, management writer Mark Henricks observes that an organization can be too flat. The key is to make sure your organization doesn't have too many managers—nor too few. When you have too little hierarchy, decisions don't get made or are made wrongly by employees who lack experience, accountability, or motivation to do the work of the missing managers.[12]

Downsizing

In Chapter 3 we analyzed downsizing as it related to social responsibility. Downsizing can also be viewed as a way of simplifying an organization to make it less bureaucratic. Under ideal circumstances, downsizing also leads to better profits and higher stock prices. The motivation behind most downsizings of both assets (such as company divisions or buildings) and workers comes from the drive to reduce costs and increase profits. Yet, downsizing can be expensive. Among the costs associated with downsizing that must be considered are severance pay, supplements to early retirement plans, disability claims, and lowered productivity resulting from possible decline in staff morale.

An analysis of companies over an 18-year period conducted by business professor Wayne F. Cascio of Colorado State University paints a grim picture of extensive layoffs. He concluded that companies that cut the deepest relative to the competition delivered smaller profits and weaker stock returns for as long as nine years following a recession.[13] As management consultant Bob Legge observes, "Laying off people means losing the investment a company has made in hiring and training. It will cost more to replace lost people when growth resumes—if you even can find similar talent."[14]

---

[11]Adam Bryant, "Structure? The Flatter the Better," *The New York Times* (www.nytimes.com), January 22, 2010.

[12]Mark Henricks, "Falling Flat?" *Entrepreneur*, January 2005, p. 70.

[13]Study reported in Scott Thurm, "Recalculating the Cost of Big Layoffs," *The Wall Street Journal*, May 5, 2010, p. B1.

[14]Quoted in Deb Koen, "Many Alternatives Companies Can Use to Avoid Laying Off," *Democrat and Chronicle*, Rochester, New York, February 1, 2009, p. 2E.

For downsizing to help the company in the long run, *it should be part of a business strategy to improve the company, not just a stopgap measure to save money.* Examples would be using downsizing to eliminate duplication of jobs after a merger or to exit a business that does not fit a new strategy. *Eliminating low-volume and no-value activities* provides an early step in effective restructuring. This *activity-based reduction* systematically compares the costs of a firm's activities to their value to the customer. In searching for low-value activity, workers monitor the output of others. *Keeping the future work requirements in mind* also contributes to effective restructuring. Letting go of people who will be an important part of the firm's future rarely provides an effective answer to overstaffing. *Sensible criteria should be used to decide which workers to let go.* In general, the poorest performers should be released first. Offering early retirement and asking for voluntary resignations also leads to less disruption. Laid-off workers should be *offered assistance in finding new employment or reorienting their career.*

A comprehensive principle of downsizing or resizing a company is to *involve employees in the resizing process.* Top-level management may have to decide which employees will be terminated, yet workers can be involved in making suggestions about how the work should be reassigned. At a successful resizing in a publishing company, middle-level managers helped design the resized organization. They identified opportunities to eliminate unnecessary work and redeploy workers to support more profitable divisions of the publisher.[15]

Outsourcing

Outsourcing is part of globalization; it is also part of the organization structure when other companies perform part of your work. Domestic outsourcing is a major part of hiring other companies to perform work. By outsourcing, a company can reduce its need for employees and physical assets and their associated costs. Outsourcing to low-wage regions saves money if the work is performed properly. Productivity can increase because work is performed more economically. A major justification for outsourcing is that a company is likely to profit when it focuses its effort on activities it performs best, while noncore activities such as human resources, payroll processing, and information systems are performed by outside experts.

As outsourcing evolves, considerable core work, including research and development and marketing, is being outsourced. Companies such as Dell, Motorola, and Philips purchase complete designs for some digital devices from Asian developers. Later the designs are modified to the well-known company's specifications and labeled with the company's brand.[16] Outsourcing also takes the form of subcontracting in which another company

---

[15]Mitchell Lee Marks and Kenneth P. De Meuse, "Resizing the Organization: Maximizing the Gain While Minimizing the Pain of Layoffs, Divestitures, and Closings," *Organizational Dynamics*, No. 1, 2005, p. 28.

[16]Peter Engardio and Bruce Einhorn, "Outsourcing," *Business Week*, March 21, 2005, p. 86.

functions like a complete manufacturing plant—sometimes for high quality, expensive products. An example is that Porsche, the German sports car manufacturer, has contracted manufacturing since 1997 to Valmet Automotive of Finland. Valmet produces about one-third of the total output of Porsche, including the Cayman and the Boxster.[17]

United Parcel Service (UPS) exemplifies how far outsourcing has advanced. The world's largest delivery company provides a wide variety of services for other companies through its subsidiary, UPS Supply Chain Solutions. The services other companies outsource to UPS include emergency electronic repairs, fixing laptops, installing giant X-ray machines, operating customer-service hotlines, packaging consumer electronics, and issuing corporate credit cards. The type of work Supply Chain provides lends itself to domestic outsourcing because much of the work is needed urgently. UPS stores every conceivable part in its giant warehouse in Louisville, Kentucky, so it can perform repairs quickly.[18] (For this type of operation, the just-in-time inventory system would be counterproductive because speed of repair is a success factor.) Outsourcing partners such as UPS work so closely with their customers that they become virtually part of their client's business.

homeshoring

Moving customer service into workers' homes as a form of telecommuting.

A rapidly growing development in outsourcing is **homeshoring,** or moving customer service into workers' homes as a form of telecommuting. Instead of customer service work being performed at domestic and foreign call centers, it is performed by telecommuters. At JetBlue Airways, reservation agents work from home as company employees. The majority of the new homeshoring jobs are for independent contractors given assignments by outsourcing companies. Home-based agents are typically stay-at-home moms with a higher level of education than call center workers. Two key advantages of homeshoring are that the workers know the culture of the country and are a flexible, just-in-time workforce with shifts lasting as little as 15 minutes. During the Great Recession the talent level of home-based workers increased because so many competent workers had been downsized and were eager to work from home.[19]

Outsourcing is a form of organization structure that management must carefully evaluate. Outsourcing may save money and provide expertise not available in-house, yet there is much to be said for building a company with a loyal workforce that has company pride. Great companies such as Colgate Palmolive and Google did not achieve their greatness through outsourcing every conceivable business process.

---

[17]Carter Dougherty, "Porsche Finds Fortune from Unlikely Outsourcing," *The New York Times* (www.nytimes.com), April 3, 2009.

[18]Chuck Salter, "Surprise Package," *Fast Company*, February 2004, pp. 62–66.

[19]Michele Conlin, "Call Centers in the Rec Room," *Business Week*, January 23, 2006, pp. 76–77; Jeremy Smerd, "Outsourcing on the Home Front," *Workforce Management*, May 18, 2009, p. 33.

The Horizontal Structure (Organization by Team and Process)

In the traditional, or functional, organization, people in various organization units are assigned specialized tasks such as assembly, purchasing, marketing, and shipping. In another approach to organization structure, a group of people concern themselves with a process, such as filling an order or developing a new product. Instead of focusing on a specialized task, all team members focus on achieving the purpose of all the activity, such as getting a product in the hands of a customer.

horizontal structure
The arrangement of work by teams that are responsible for accomplishing a process.

A **horizontal structure** is the arrangement of work by multidisciplinary teams that are responsible for accomplishing a process. Exhibit 8-7 illustrates a horizontal structure, as do the projects shown in Exhibit 8-6. The employees take collective responsibility for customers, and they work together to accomplish the task. Instead of one department handing off work to another department, the team members work together on the task of meeting customer requirements. A horizontal structure can therefore be considered a team structure, and teams will be reintroduced in Chapter 13. It would be difficult today to find a business, governmental, not-for-profit, or educational organization that made no use of the team structure.

As with other modifications of the bureaucratic structure, the horizontal structure coexists with vertical structures. The process teams offer a balanced focus so that employees direct their effort and attention toward adding value for the customer.[20] The UPS groups that provide packaging services for clients use a horizontal structure; a project manager is responsible for assuring

EXHIBIT 8-7   A Horizontal Organization Structure

In a horizontal organization, even though specialists are assigned to the team, they are expected to understand one another's tasks and perform some of those tasks as needed.

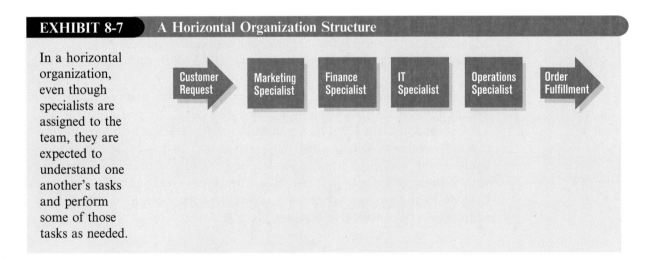

Customer Request → Marketing Specialist → Finance Specialist → IT Specialist → Operations Specialist → Order Fulfillment

[20]Frank Ostroff, *The Horizontal Organization: What the Organization of the Future Actually Looks Like and How It Delivers Value to Customers* (New York: Oxford University Press, 1999); Ann Majchrzak and Qianwei Wang, "Breaking the Functional Mind-Set in Process Organizations," *Harvard Business Review*, January 1998, p. 21.

that client needs are met. The team members focus on a single purpose such as "We must get these Nikon cameras packed and ready for shipment."

reengineering
The radical redesign of work to achieve substantial improvements in performance.

Switching from a vertical (task) emphasis to a horizontal (process) emphasis can be done through **reengineering,** the radical redesign of work to achieve substantial improvements in performance. Reengineering searches for the most efficient way to perform a large task. At the same time, reengineering is process innovation because it searches for new ways to perform the same process, such as revamping the way merchandise is ordered and shipped to a department store. Reengineering emphasizes uncovering wasted steps, such as people handing off documents to others to obtain approvals. E-commerce considerably reengineers the work of sales representatives. If goods are exchanged over the Internet, the need for industrial sales representatives shrinks.

As a result of reengineering, work is organized horizontally rather than vertically. The people in charge of the process function as team leaders who guide the team toward the completion of a core process such as new product development or filling a complicated order. Key performance objectives for the team would include "reduce cycle time," "reduce costs," and "reduce throughput time." Team members must usually develop a process mentality instead of the task mentality of focusing on their specialty.

The push toward the horizontal structures and a process mentality should not be embraced without qualification. Having a task-mentality remains important because expertise is still crucial in many endeavors. A building construction team, for example, still relies on highly proficient specialists such as mechanical and electrical engineers. Wouldn't you prefer to ride in an elevator that was designed by a highly proficient specialist?

Informal Structures and Communication Networks

informal organization structure
A set of unofficial relationships that emerge to take care of events and transactions not covered by the formal structure.

The formal structures described in this chapter are an essential part of planning how work is performed. Nevertheless, an organization chart does not tell the whole story of how work gets accomplished. The **informal organization structure** is a set of unofficial relationships that emerge to take care of events and transactions not covered by the formal structure. The informal structure supplements the formal structure by adding a degree of flexibility and speed. A widespread application of the informal structure is the presence of "tech fixers" who supplement the technical support center. For example, marketing assistant Jason might be skilled at resolving software problems created by computer viruses. As a consequence, many people call on Jason for some quick assistance even though the formal organization indicates that they should use the tech center for help with virus problems.

Informal structures are also referred to as informal networks because of the focus on how people use personal contacts to obtain information in a hurry and get work done.[21] The informal networks reveal how well

---

[21]Rob Cross and Laurence Prusak, "The People Who Make Organizations Go—Or Stop," *Harvard Business Review*, June 2002, p. 104.

connected people are, as well as how work really gets done. Spotting talent is an application of mapping the informal network. Some of the most respected workers might not be found on the organization chart but could be indicated by a network map because of the number of times these individuals are consulted by other workers. The highly respected workers might be tapped for key projects.[22]

social network analysis

The mapping and measuring of relationships and links between and among people, groups, and organizations.

The informal organization can be revealed by **social network analysis**, the mapping and measuring of relationships and links between and among people, groups, and organizations.[23] The nodes in the network are the people; the links show relationships or flow between and among the nodes, as shown in Exhibit 8-8. Notice that Rathin is an important node in the network because he is linked with Lisa, Anna, and Brett. Social network analysis helps explain how work gets accomplished in a given unit, such as shown in the interactions among Susan, Tim, and Tara on the right side of Exhibit 8-8. Perhaps the three of them mutually discuss credit risks. The interrelations can become quite complicated because of the many number of people and interactions between and among them.

EXHIBIT 8-8   **A Basic Unit of a Social Network Analysis**

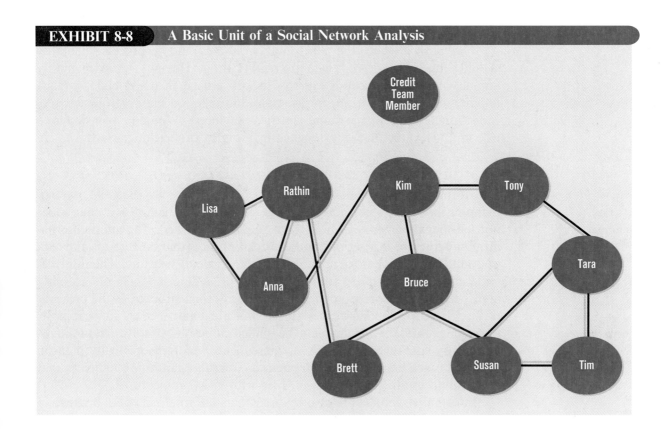

---

[22]Jena McGregor, "The Office Chart That Really Counts: Mapping Informal Relationships at a Company Is Revealing and Useful," *Business Week*, February 27, 2006, pp. 48–49.

[23]Valdis Krebs, "Social Network Analysis: A Brief Introduction," 2009.

Social network analysis helps management survey the informal interactions among employees that can lead to innovative ideas. At the same time, the maps can point to areas where workers should be collaborating but are not. In this way the maps help facilitate knowledge sharing. The maps can also be used to pinpoint the interactions one manager has, so he or she can give the information to a successor.

Also as part of informal networks, all organization structures described so far in this chapter are influenced by information technology. Workers from various units throughout an organization can solve problems together through information networks without being concerned with "who reports to whom," as indicated by organization charts. Entry-level workers can leap-frog layers of management and communicate directly with senior executives through e-mail. Now, as in the past, entry-level workers almost never telephone a member of upper management.

Enough different organization structures have been described to create some confusion and blurring. Exhibit 8-9 indicates the unique aspect of each structure. We have added the conglomerate structure, referring to a collection of independent companies under one corporate roof. Although the term is fading from frequent use, conglomerates still exist; General Electric is one of the best known.

Power Sharing at the Highest Level of Management

In a pure bureaucracy the person at the top of the pyramid would have considerable power. At the same time, all members of the organization would know who is ultimately responsible for the success and failure of the organization—where "the buck stops." Concerns about the complexity of the top position have led to two modifications in the organization structure of the executive suite: splitting the roles of the chairman and CEO, and the use of co-CEOs. We describe these two divisions of labor separately.

You may have noticed that many executives at the very top of a business firm hold the title of chairman and CEO. Less frequently, you find that the positions of chairman, or chairwoman, and CEO are held by two different people. Many management specialists who seek improved corporate governance recommend that one person should not hold these two posts. One person holding the post of chairman and CEO concentrates too much power in the hands of a single executive and permits too much unchecked power. Having a separate CEO and chairperson allows the CEO to concentrate on managing the company and spend less time interacting with other members of the board.[24] With the CEO focusing on operations, the chairperson is free to focus on long-term strategy. The counterargument is that when one person is chairman and another CEO, it leads to confusion in leadership. Managers and other workers in the company wonder who is really in charge.

---

[24]"Splitting Up the Roles of CEO and Chairman: Reform or Red Herring? *Knowledge@ Wharton*, June 2, 2004.

EXHIBIT 8-9   Unique Feature of Various Organization Structures

Type of Structure or Modification	Unique Feature or Emphasis
Bureaucracy	Hierarchical, with clear rules and regulations
Functional	Departments are defined by the function, or activity, they perform
Geographic	Departments are defined by their geographic location
Product–Service	Departments or divisions are defined by the major product or service they offer
Matrix	A project, or program, structure is superimposed on a functional structure
Flat and Downsized	One or more layers is removed from the structure, and the staff is reduced
Outsourcing and Homesourcing	Work activities are deployed outside the organization, including having it performed at peoples' homes
Horizontal or Team	Work is performed by multidisciplinary teams, and communication among workers is enhanced
Informal	People work cooperatively to fill in the gaps not taken care of by the formal organization
Hybrid	A structure that combines several of the above structures, such as a traditional bureaucracy also having several product or service divisions
Conglomerate	A large company that is really a collection of loosely related independent companies, with a minimum of direction and control from headquarters

In general, it appears that whether one person holds both titles has little influence on the financial performance of the firm.[25] Someone who is an outstanding manager and leader and highly ethical can probably hold both posts of chairperson and CEO.

When the job is perceived as too big for one person to handle, it is possible to divide the responsibilities of the CEO position. In the co-CEO arrangement, the two executives work together as a team and make joint decisions. Few public companies have co-CEOs, but the number of family businesses using co-CEOs has doubled in recent years.[26] Two prominent companies that use the co-CEO form of power sharing are SAP, the German software maker, and Martha Stewart Living Ominmedia Inc., the media and merchandising company.

---

[25]Ed Frauenheim, "Co-CEOs: Two at the Top," *Workforce Management*, May 18, 2009, p. 41.

[26]Cited and quoted in Shira Ovide, "Martha Stewart Living CEO Steps Down," *The Wall Street Journal*, June 12, 2008, p. B3.

Power sharing might work well in many marriages, but it is an awkward arrangement in the executive suite. Paul Bernard, an executive coach and management consultant, says that although they are not unusual, the track record of co-CEO arrangement is dismal. "Inevitably what will happen is that someone will be pushed out."[27]

LEARNING
OBJECTIVE **4**

Identify key factors
that influence the
selection of
organization
structure.

Key Factors That Influence the Selection of an Organization Structure

With so many organization structures, how do managers choose the best one? The answer lies in contingency management, the idea that the most effective structure depends on certain factors. Among these factors are strategy, technology, size, financial condition, and environmental stability.

1. *Strategy and goals.* As described in the history of management presented in Chapter 1, structure is supposed to follow strategy. Assume that the strategy of a business machine company is to be the friend of small businesses and individuals who want to operate business equipment in their homes. The company would choose a geographically dispersed marketing organization that gives them maximum access to small customers such as OfficeMax and Radio Shack.

2. *Technology.* High-technology firms such as aerospace companies make extensive use of flexible structures such as project and matrix structures. Relatively low-technology firms such as lumber mills and refuse-collection firms rely more on bureaucratic structures. Organizations based on digital technology, such as Cisco Systems and Amazon.com, typically use horizontal and network structures for two key reasons.[28] The primary reason is that the technology allows for linking workers, customers, and suppliers. A more subtle reason is that information technology–oriented workers are naturally inclined toward horizontal, free-flowing communication.

3. *Size.* As an organization grows and matures, it inevitably needs centralized controls and some degree of bureaucracy or formalization. Yet when the firm becomes very large, it is necessary to develop smaller, more flexible units such as projects and task forces. These units help the firm remain adaptive, and they are found in every large organization. Large size and bureaucracy, however, are not synonymous. Some small firms, such as a local bank, might be bureaucratic because they are tightly regulated by banking laws.

4. *Financial condition of the firm.* Size influences structure, and the financial condition of the firm influences both size and structure. Many large business organizations have moved toward a flatter structure to trim costs. Trimming the number of corporate positions influences structure; with

---

[27]Rob Cox and Antony Currie, "Separate Lives, Always: Regardless of the Economy, CEO and Chairman Jobs Should Be Independent," *The Wall Street Journal*, May 10–11, 2008, p. B14.

[28]Richard L. Daft, *Management*, 7th ed. (Mason, Ohio: Thomson/South-Western, 2005), p. 380.

fewer headquarters executives left to supervise divisions, decision-making authority becomes more decentralized.

5. *Environmental stability.* When a business firm faces an uncertain and unstable environment, such as the market for high-fashion clothing or domestic electronics, it needs a highly flexible structure. Task forces and projects are often called into action to deal with a rapidly changing marketplace. Conversely, a more bureaucratic structure is better suited to dealing with more certain (stable) environments. An example is the market for Crayola Crayons and related products, which has proved to be both recession-proof and resistant to competitors.

LEARNING
OBJECTIVE **5**
Specify how delegation, empowerment, and decentralization spread authority in an organization.

DELEGATION, EMPOWERMENT, AND DECENTRALIZATION

Collective effort would not be possible, and organizations could not grow and prosper, if a handful of managers did all the work themselves. In recognition of this fact, managers divide up their work. Subdividing work through the process of departmentalization has already been described. The section that follows will discuss subdivision of work using the chain of command through delegation, empowerment, and decentralization.

Delegation of Responsibility and Empowerment

delegation
Assigning formal authority and responsibility for accomplishing a specific task to another person.

empowerment
The process by which managers share power with group members, thereby enhancing employees' feelings of personal effectiveness.

Delegation refers to assigning formal authority and responsibility for accomplishing a specific task to another person. If managers do not delegate any of their work, they are acting as individual contributors—not true managers. Some managers are hesitant to delegate because they dislike giving up control, which explains why *control* freaks are poor at delegation. Delegation relates closely to **empowerment**, the process by which managers share power with group members, thereby enhancing employees' feelings of personal effectiveness. Delegation is a specific way of empowering employees and increasing motivation.

A major goal of delegation is the transfer of responsibility as a means of increasing one's own productivity. At the same time, delegation allows team members to develop by learning how to handle responsibility and become more productive. Even though a manager may hold a group member responsible for a task, final accountability belongs to the manager. (To be accountable is to accept credit or blame for results.) If the group member fails miserably, the manager must accept the final blame; the manager chose the person who failed.

Delegation and empowerment lie at the heart of effective management. For example, a study was conducted with management teams in 102 hotel properties in the United States. A major finding was that empowering leadership increased the sharing of job knowledge among employees and increased effective teamwork. In turn, the improved knowledge sharing and teamwork were related to good performance.[29]

---

[29]Abhishek Srivastava, Kathryn M. Bartol, and Edwin A. Locke, "Empowering Leadership in Management Teams: Effects on Knowledge Sharing, Efficacy, and Performance," *Academy of Management Journal*, December 2006, pp. 1239–1251.

Following the five suggestions presented next improves the manager's chance of increasing productivity by delegating to and empowering individuals and teams.[30] (Note that teams as well as individuals can be the unit of delegation and power sharing.)

1. *Assign duties to the right people.* The chances for effective delegation and empowerment improve when capable, responsible, well-motivated group members receive the delegated tasks. The manager must be aware of the strengths and weaknesses of staff members to delegate effectively. However, if the purpose of delegation is to develop a group member, the present capabilities of the person receiving the delegated tasks are less important. The manager is willing to accept some mistakes as the cost of development.

2. *Delegate the whole task and step back from the details.* In the spirit of job enrichment, a manager should delegate an entire task to one subordinate rather than dividing it among several. So doing gives the group member complete responsibility, enhances motivation, and gives the manager more control over results. After the whole task is delegated, step back from the details. If a manager cannot let go of details, he or she will never be effective at delegation or empowerment.

3. *Give as much instruction as needed.* Some group members will require highly detailed instructions, while others can operate effectively with general instructions. Many delegation and empowerment failures occur because instruction was insufficient. *Dumping* is the negative term given to the process of dropping a task on a group member without instructions. Under ideal circumstances, delegating should be an opportunity for coaching employees and sharing skills with them.

4. *Retain some important tasks for yourself.* Managers should retain some high-output or sensitive tasks for themselves. In general, the manager should handle any task that involves the survival of the unit or employee discipline. However, which tasks the manager should retain always depends on the circumstances. Strategic planning is ordinarily not delegated except to obtain input from group members. Sales managers often keep one or two key accounts for themselves.

5. *Obtain feedback on the delegated task.* A responsible manager does not delegate a complex assignment to a subordinate and then wait until the assignment is complete before discussing it again. Managers must establish checkpoints and milestones to obtain feedback on progress.

Decentralization

decentralization
The extent to which authority is passed down to lower levels in an organization.

Decentralization is the extent to which authority is passed down to lower levels in an organization. It comes about as a consequence of managers

---

[30]Sharon Gazda, "The Art of Delegating," *HR Magazine*, January 2002, pp. 75–77; "Boost Delegation with This Master List," *Manager's Edge*, June 2002, p. 7; "The Power of Power Sharing," *HR/OD*, July–August 1998, p. 2.

delegating work to lower levels. The term also refers to decentralization by geography. Geographic decentralization often results in passing down authority; managers in the decentralized units are granted decision-making authority. Unless so noted, this text uses the term *decentralization* in reference to authority. **Centralization** is the extent to which authority is retained at the top of the organization. Decentralization and centralization lie on two ends of a continuum. No firm operates as completely centralized or decentralized.

How much control top management wants to retain determines how much an organization is decentralized. Organizations favor decentralization when a large number of decisions must be made at lower organizational levels, often in response to customer needs. Johnson & Johnson, the medical and personal care products giant, favors decentralization, in part, because the company consists of a collection of different businesses, many with vastly different customer requirements. Division management is much more aware of these needs than are people at company headquarters. In general, a centralized firm exercises more control over organization units than a decentralized firm.

Many firms centralize and decentralize operations simultaneously. Certain aspects of their operations are centralized, whereas others are decentralized. Rapid-service franchise restaurants such as Subway, Long John Silver's, and Wendy's illustrate this trend. Central headquarters exercises tight control over such matters as menu selection, food quality, and advertising. Individual franchise operators, however, make human resource decisions such as hiring.

An advanced technique of juggling the forces of centralization and decentralization simultaneously is for decentralized units to remain somewhat autonomous, yet cooperate with each other for the common good. For example, the basic structure of Johnson & Johnson is a decentralized firm with 204 nearly autonomous units organized into three divisions: drugs, medical and diagnostic devices, and consumer products (such as Band-Aids and Johnson's Baby Powder). J&J is considered by many to be the reference company for decentralization. The current emphasis at J&J is for the autonomous divisions to cooperate with each other to achieve better products. For example, sutures from one division are coated with drugs from another to help prevent infections.[31]

Microsoft Corp. is another company in which top-level management has searched for ways to get better cooperation across divisions in order to enhance innovation. According to CEO Steve Ballmer, Microsoft tries to find the right balance between being a conglomerate and a monolithic operating company (highly centralized).[32]

centralization

The extent to which authority is retained at the top of the organization.

---

[31]Amy Barrett, "Staying on Top," *Business Week*, May 5, 2003, p. 62; "Johnson & Johnson CEO William Weldon: Leadership in a Decentralized Company," *Knowledge@Wharton*, June 25, 2008.

[32]Robert A. Guth, "Ballmer Aims to Find Microsoft's Balance," *The Wall Street Journal*, June 27, 2008, p. B6.

LEARNING
OBJECTIVE **6**

Identify major
aspects of
organizational
culture, including
its determinants
and how it is
learned, managed,
and sustained.

**organizational
culture (or corporate
culture)**
The system of shared
values and beliefs that
actively influence the
behavior of
organization
members.

ORGANIZATIONAL CULTURE

Organization structure has sometimes been referred to as the *hard side* of how a firm operates; understanding the *soft side* of an organization is also essential. **Organizational culture (or corporate culture)** is the system of shared values and beliefs that actively influence the behavior of organization members. The term *shared* implies that many people are guided by the same values and that they interpret these values in the same way. Values develop over time and reflect a firm's history and traditions. It's important to understand organizational culture because it is a major factor in the success of any company. In the words of Douglas R. Conant, the dynamic CEO of Campbell Soup Co., "If you want to be a sustainably good company, you have to have a sustainably good culture."[33]

This section describes significant aspects of organizational culture: how it is learned and its determinants, dimensions, consequences, and management and maintenance.

Determinants of Organizational Culture

Many forces shape a firm's culture. Often its origin lies in the values, administrative practices, and personality of the founder or founders. The leader's vision can have a heavy impact on culture; John Chambers' dreamed of Cisco Systems becoming one of the world's greatest companies in history. Steve Jobs, the co-founder of Apple Inc., exemplifies how a leader's personality can help influence the culture. Jobs is recognized as a high-tech visionary who has attracted many talented people to his companies. (Jobs has also served as CEO of Pixar, but his influence is greater at Apple.) Jobs' pronounced personal traits and behaviors (arrogance and smugness) spill over to the culture of Apple; most workers believe that they are part of a superior group of people and that whatever they produce is "outrageously good." Part of the culture is to denounce the competition.

The culture in which a society operates helps determine the culture of the firm. Sooner or later, society's norms, beliefs, and values find their way into the firm. Societal values are communicated through such means as the media, conversations, and education. The emphasis on sexual and racial equality in U.S. society has become incorporated into the value culture of many employers. The emphasis on collegiality translates into harmony and cooperation in the workplace at many Scandinavian companies, including Nokia. Another perspective on national culture is that the introduction of values from another society into a retail business can be a competitive advantage. For example, the Korean values of high quality, reliability, and spotless factories have helped fuel the success of the Hyundai and Kia car brands in the United States.

---

[33]Quoted in Harold Brubaker, "Souper Saver," *Philadelphia Inquirer* (http://www.philly.com), July 25, 2006, p. 1.

The industry to which a firm belongs helps shape its culture. For example, a public utility will have a culture different from a food manufacturer of comparable size. Heavy competition and low profit margins may force the food manufacturer to operate at a faster pace than the utility, which usually competes with only several other utilities.

Dimensions of Organizational Culture

subculture

A pocket in which the organizational culture differs from the dominant culture and from other pockets of the subculture.

The dimensions of organizational culture help explain the subtle forces that influence employee actions. In addition to the dominant culture of a firm, the subculture also influences behavior. A **subculture** is a pocket in which the organizational culture differs from the dominant culture and from other pockets of subculture. A frequently observed difference in subcultures can be found between the marketing and production groups, even in such matters as dress and behavior. The marketing people are likely to be more style conscious and people oriented. Six dimensions significantly influence organizational culture.[34]

1. *Values.* Values provide the foundation of any organizational culture. The organization's philosophy expressed through values guides behavior on a day-to-day basis. Representative values of a firm might include ethical behavior, concern for employee welfare, a belief that the customer is always right, a commitment to quality, and a belief in the importance of equality and independence. An emphasis on teamwork is another key value.

   A pervasive value is the importance of formality. For example, a heavily bureaucratic culture believes strongly in formality, including following procedures and protocol. Another value of significance is an emphasis on truthfulness and candor. In a culture characterized by candor, workers resist telling others what they want to hear.[35]

2. *Relative diversity.* The existence of an organizational culture assumes some degree of homogeneity. Nevertheless, organizations differ in terms of how much deviation can be tolerated. Many firms are highly homogeneous; executives talk in a similar manner and even look alike. Those executives promote people from similar educational backgrounds and fields of specialty into key jobs. The diversity of a culture reflects itself in the dress code. Some organizations insist on uniformity of dress, requiring men to wear a jacket and tie when interacting with customers or clients. Strongly encouraging all workers to conform to dress-down Fridays discourages diversity.

3. *Resource allocations and rewards.* The allocation of money and other resources exerts a critical influence on culture. The investment of

---

[34]J. Steven Ott, *The Organizational Culture Perspective* (Chicago: Dorsey Press, 1989), pp. 20–48; Personal communication from Lynn H. Suksdorf, Salt Lake City Community College, October 1998.

[35]James O'Toole and Warren Bennis, "What's Needed Next: A Culture of Candor," *Harvard Business Review*, June 2009, pp. 54–61.

resources sends a message to people about what is valued in the firm. If a customer-service department is fully staffed and nicely furnished, employees and customers can assume that the company values customer service.

4. *Degree of change*. The culture in a fast-paced, dynamic organization differs from that of a slow paced, stable one. A highly competitive environment might encourage a fast-paced climate. Top-level managers, by the energy or lethargy of their stance, send signals about how much they welcome innovation. The degree of change influences whether a culture can take root and how strong that culture can be.

5. *A sense of ownership*. The movement toward employee stock ownership creates an ownership culture and inspires workers to think and act like owners. An ownership culture increases loyalty, improves work effort, and aligns worker interests with those of the company. An ownership culture can be reflected in such everyday actions as conserving electricity, making gradual improvements, and not tolerating sloppiness by coworkers. An ownership culture can backfire, however, if employee wealth stays flat or decreases as a result of stock ownership.

6. *Strength of the culture*. The strength of the culture, or how much influence it exerts, emerges partially as a by-product of the other dimensions. A strong culture guides employees in everyday actions. It determines, for example, whether an employee will inconvenience himself or herself to satisfy a customer. Without a strong culture, employees are more likely to follow their own whims; they may decide to please customers only when convenient. A research study with 123 organizations found that the climate (or culture) tended to be strongest when it was unambiguous, either clearly bureaucratic or clearly flexible.[36]

These dimensions represent a formal and systematic way of understanding organizational culture. In practice, people use more glib expressions in describing culture, as illustrated in Exhibit 8-10.

How Workers Learn the Culture

socialization

The process of coming to understand the values, norms, and customs essential for adapting to the organization.

Employees learn the organizational culture primarily through **socialization**, the process of coming to understand the values, norms, and customs essential for adapting to the organization. Socialization is a method of indoctrinating employees into the organization in such a way that they perpetuate the culture. The socialization process takes place mostly by imitation and observation.

Another important way in which workers learn the culture is through the teachings of leaders, as implied in the cultural dimension of resource allocations and rewards. Organizational members learn the culture to some extent

---

[36]Marcus W. Dickson, Christian J. Resick, and Paul J. Hanges, "When Organizational Climate Is Unambiguous, It Is Also Strong," *Journal of Applied Psychology*, March 2006, pp. 351–364.

EXHIBIT 8-10   A Sampling of Organizational Cultures of Well-Known Companies

IKEA. Very informal, with roots in Swedish culture. Emphasis on informality, cost consciousness, and a humble, down-to-earth approach. Workers are allowed considerable responsibility.

Nike. Go-it alone, insular culture characterized by a desire for growth within, rather than taking on the hassles of integrating a merger with another company. Very difficult for outside executives to be accepted by the inner circle.

Apple Inc. Attitude of smugness and superiority, with a tendency to perceive other technology companies as mere imitators of the real thing (Apple). These attitudes are strengthened with the success of the iPod, iPhone, and iTab. Intense fondness for innovation and free thinking, combined with a strong dislike for bureaucracy.

Honda Motors. Very strong culture that emphasizes quick thinking, conservative investments,

a willingness to candidly examine its own weaknesses and accept painful realities. Company executives prefer to stick with what they do best. Company de-emphasizes hierarchy and is more interested in technology than finance.

Zappos (subsidiary of Amazon.com). The core company value calls for workers to have fun yet stay focused. The ultimate business goal of founder Tony Hsieh is to cultivate happiness. Company managers practice the belief that treating employees well leads to good treatment of customers. A playful attitude permeates the company. To enhance happiness and group solidarity, more than one-half of company employees are on the company-wide Twitter feed. The event planner for employee activities holds the title "Cruise Ship Captain." Job applicants are asked, "How weird are you?" to asses their fit with the Zappos culture.

Sources: Katarina Kling and Ingela Goteman, "IKEA CEO Anders Dahlvig on International Growth and IKEA's Unique Corporate Culture and Brand Identity," *Academy of Management Executive,* February 2003, pp. 26–29; 31–37; Carleen Hawn, "If He's So Smart …" *Fast Company,* January 2004, pp. 68–74; Ian Rowldey, "What Put Honda in the Passing Lane," *Business Week,* October 19, 2009, pp. 057–058; Carlin Flora, "Paid to Smile," *Psychology Today,* September/October 2009, pp. 58–59; Ed Frauenheim, "Jungle Survival," *Workforce Management,* September 14, 2009, pp. 18–22.

by observing what leaders pay attention to, measure, and control. Suppose a coworker of yours is praised publicly for doing community service. You are likely to conclude that an important part of the culture is to help people outside the company. Senior executives will sometimes publicly express expectations that help shape the culture of the firm, such as demanding data-driven decision making.

Workers also learn the culture by hearing repeated stories that illustrate company values. For example, at FedEx workers hear stories about how someone went beyond the call of duty to deliver a package during a storm, or how a driver rescued a person caught in a flood. The value illustrated is outstanding service to customers and the community.

Consequences and Implications of Organizational Culture

The attention to organizational culture stems from its pervasive impact on organizational effectiveness. Exhibit 8-11 outlines several key consequences of organizational culture. The right organizational culture *contributes to gaining competitive advantage and therefore achieving financial success.* The consistently strong performance of Google can be partially attributed to its culture that values intelligence, imagination, and hard work.

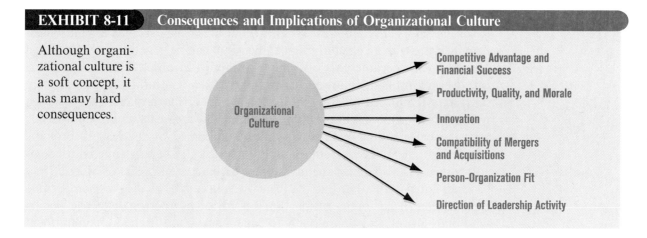

EXHIBIT 8-11 **Consequences and Implications of Organizational Culture**

Although organizational culture is a soft concept, it has many hard consequences.

Organizational Culture →
- Competitive Advantage and Financial Success
- Productivity, Quality, and Morale
- Innovation
- Compatibility of Mergers and Acquisitions
- Person-Organization Fit
- Direction of Leadership Activity

The right organizational culture can enhance *productivity, quality,* and *morale.* A culture that emphasizes productivity and quality encourages workers to be more productive and quality conscious. A synthesis of many studies found that organizational culture is related to quality practices related to attitudes (such as top management support for quality). These practices, in turn, were related to manufacturing performance.[37] A culture that values the dignity of human beings fosters high morale and job satisfaction. A corporate culture that *encourages creative behavior contributes to innovation,* as described in Chapter 5 about problem solving and decision making. Amazon chief executive Jeff Bezos notes that a culture of experimentation is crucial in a fast-changing world. He says, "Invention always leads you down paths that people think are weird."[38]

At times a culture that facilitates high quality and business success can become smug and complacent, believing that it cannot fail. A recent example is Toyota, a company envied for its manufacturing techniques. Toyota was subject to the largest automobile recall in history in 2010. The problems related to both uncontrolled acceleration and brake problems. Analysts describe a Toyota management team culture characterized by self-love and arrogance that had become too insular to handle the flawed vehicle problem. The company had received some warnings about accelerator problems stemming back to 2002. Another cultural problem might have been that managers and workers in Japanese corporations have a difficult time delivering bad news to executives. Also, there is shame and embarrassment associated with admitting to problems in a company noted for exceptional product quality.[39]

---

[37]Micahel Naor, Susan Goldstein, Kevin Linderman, and Roger Schroeder, "The Role of Culture as Driver of Quality Management and Performance: Infrastructure versus Core Quality Practices," *Decision Sciences,* vol. 39, 2008, pp. 671–702.

[38]Quoted in Robert D. Hof, "How to Hit a Moving Target," *Business Week,* August 21/28, 2006, p. 81.

[39]Bill Saporito, "Toyota Tangled," *Time,* February 22, 2019, pp. 26–30.

A reliable predictor of success in merging two or more firms is *compatibility of their respective cultures.* When the cultures clash, such as a hierarchical firm merging with an egalitarian one, the result can be negative synergy. When Merrill Lynch became part of Bank of America in order to survive, a large turnover of brokers followed shortly thereafter. Cultural differences were cited as a major reason for the dissatisfaction of the brokers. One concern was that the cost-conscious culture of Bank of America was not compatible with the big-spending Wall Street culture embodied by the Merrill brokers. Another problem was that the Bank of America CEO at the time had repeatedly voiced his disdain for the investment banking gunslingers of Merrill.[40]

Individuals can contribute to their own success by *finding a good person–organization fit,* an organization that fits his or her personality. The person who finds a good fit is more likely to experience job satisfaction, commitment to the organization, and a lesser interest in quitting.[41] Similarly, an organization will be more successful when the personalities of most members fit its culture.

Organizational culture powerfully influences the *direction of leadership activity.* Top-level managers spend much of their time working with the forces that shape the attitudes and values of employees at all levels. Leaders in key roles establish what type of culture is needed for the firm and then shape the existing culture to match that ideal. This is why outsiders are sometimes brought in to head a company.

Managing and Sustaining the Culture

After a new CEO is appointed, the person typically makes a public statement such as this: "My number-one job is to change the culture." A manager might do the following to bring about change and assure that a healthy corporate culture is maintained.

- Serve as a role model for the desired attitudes and behaviors. Leaders must behave in ways consistent with the values and practices they wish to see imitated throughout the organization. For example, if the CEO wants to move the culture toward higher risk taking, he or she must take risks such as investing in new products and services and experimenting with new organization structures.
- Establish a reward system that reinforces the culture, such as suggestion awards to promote innovation. At Boeing Co., CEO W. James McNerney Jr. wanted to create a common culture and work toward a shared goal. To discourage negative internal competition and the hoarding of information, part of executive compensation is based on how well managers share information with other units across the company.[42]

---

[40]Randall Smith, "Merrill's Broker Chief Quits BofA," *The Wall Street Journal,* January 6, 2009, p. C2; Heidi N. Moore, "BofA, Merrill Still Merging," *The Wall Street Journal,* April 21, 2009, p. C5.

[41]Amy L. Kristof-Brown, Ryan D. Zimmerman, and Erin C. Johnson, "Consequences of Individuals' Fit at Work: A Meta-Analysis of Person-Job, Person-Organization, Person-Group, and Person-Supervisor Fit," *Personnel Psychology,* Summer 2005, p. 310.

[42]Stanley Holmes, "Cleaning Up Boeing," *Business Week,* March 13, 2006, p. 64.

- Select candidates for positions at all levels whose values mesh with the values of the desired culture. Many firms hire only those candidates whose work and school suggest that they might be good team players—a cultural value.

- Sponsor new training and development programs that support the desired cultural values. Top management might sponsor diversity training to support the importance of cultural diversity, or training in quality to support the value of quality.

- Disseminate widely the type of cultural change required. General Motors had long been known for having a highly bureaucratic, slow-moving, low risk-taking organizational culture that some thought interfered with its competitiveness. When Ed Whitacre was appointed as chairman (and later CEO), he held a conference at which he told 800 GM workers, "We want you to step up. We don't want any bureaucracy. We're not going to make if you don't take a risk." The address was broadcast over the Internet to GM employees worldwide. As a follow-up to the conference, Whitacre urged his top-level managers to make decisions more on their own rather than asking for approval.[43]

A suggestion in relation to organizational culture is to find employment where you fit the culture or quickly adapt your values and behavior to create a fit. For example, if the culture emphasizes data-driven decision making and a highly disciplined approach to management, act in this manner to survive and prosper.

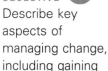

LEARNING
OBJECTIVE

Describe key aspects of managing change, including gaining support for change, and the DICE framework for successful change management.

MANAGING CHANGE

To meet their objectives, managers must manage change effectively almost daily. Change in the workplace relates to any factor with an impact on people. This includes changes in technology, organization structure, competition, human resources, and budgets. The concept of change management contains five components: (1) change at the individual versus organizational level, (2) a model of the change process, (3) resistance to change, (4) gaining support for change, and (5) bringing about planned change through Six Sigma. Knowledge of these components helps in managing change that affects oneself and others.

Creating Change at the Individual versus the Organizational Level

Much useful change in organizations takes place at individual and small group levels rather than at the organizational level. Quite often individual contributors, middle-level managers, and team leaders identify a small

[43]Quoted in "GM CEO Shuffles Managers, Seek Culture Changes," Associated Press, December 2, 2009; Sharon Terlep, "GM's Plodding Culture Vexes Its Impatient CEO," *The Wall Street Journal*, April 7, 2010, p. B1.

need for change and make it happen. For example, a supermarket manager observed that several meat department workers did not understand fractions. He suggested that each supermarket should have a designated "fraction trainer" who would assist meat workers who could not work with fractions.

One study researched the effective change brought about by individuals in a variety of organizations. Each of the more than 100 participants was identified as a "mover and shaker," someone who brought about constructive change. Constructive change included, for example, modifying a software product so as to open new markets. A common characteristic of these people who brought about change was a greater focus on results rather than on trying not to offend anyone. At the same time, they concentrated more on exerting individual initiative than on blending into the group.[44]

Change at the organizational level receives much more attention than the small, incremental changes brought about by individuals. One of these major changes has already been described: changing the organizational culture. Later we describe how Six Sigma changes an organization. Change at the organizational level can be regarded as change in the fundamental way in which the company operates, such as moving from a government-regulated utility to a competitive organization.

The Unfreezing-Changing-Refreezing Model of Change

Psychologist Kurt Lewin developed a three-step analysis of the change process widely used by managers to help bring about constructive change.[45] Many other approaches to initiating change stem from this simple model illustrated in Exhibit 8-12. *Unfreezing* involves reducing or eliminating resistance to change. As long as employees oppose a change, it will not be implemented effectively. To accept change, employees must first deal with and resolve their feelings about letting go of the old. Only after people have dealt effectively with endings can they readily make transitions.

EXHIBIT 8-12	The Change Process

To bring about change, you have to break old habits, create new ones, and solidify the new habits.

Unfreezing → Changing → Refreezing

---

[44]Alan H. Frohman, "Igniting Organizational Change from Below: The Power of Individual Initiative," *Organizational Dynamics*, Winter 1997, pp. 39–53.

[45]Kurt Lewin, *Field Theory and Social Science* (New York: Harper & Brothers, 1951). The Lewin quote in the following page is from the same source.

Changing, or moving on to a new level, usually involves considerable two-way communication, including group discussion. According to Lewin, "Rather than a one-way flow of commands or recommendations, the person implementing the change should make suggestions. The people who are changing should be encouraged to contribute and participate." *Refreezing* includes pointing out the success of the change and looking for ways to reward people involved in implementing the change.

Resistance to Change

Before a company's managers can gain support for change, they must understand why people resist change. People resist changes for reasons they think are important. The most common is the fear of an unfavorable outcome, such as less money or personal inconvenience. People resist change for many reasons. Some simply don't want to break well-established habits. Change may be unwelcome because it upsets the balance of an activity, even something as simple as the old system of in-person meetings versus video conferencing. Underlying all forms of resistance to change are emotions and feelings; the manager wanting to bring about change must make good use of his or her emotional intelligence.

Personality factors also contribute to resistance to change. For example, a rigid person might be more naturally disposed to maintaining the status quo. Workers who feel they lack the skills to deal effectively with the change, such as working in a team rather than individually, will sometimes resist change. Even when people do not view a change as potentially damaging, they may sometimes cling to a system they dislike rather than change. According to folk wisdom, "People would rather deal with the devil they know than the devil they do not know."

Workers may resist change because of weaknesses in the proposed changes that have been overlooked or disregarded by management. Two researchers about change, Jeffery D. Ford and Laurie W. Ford, suggest along these lines that resistance is really a form of feedback, frequently provided by workers who know more about day-to-day operations than a high-level manager. For example, managers might not be aware of how upset many customers would be when a voice recognition system replaces live customer-service agents. Because workers have more contact with customers, they might predict the customer dissatisfaction. The resistance, or feedback, can be turned into lively conversation that gives the change effort a higher profile.[46]

Gaining Support for Change

Gaining support for change, and therefore overcoming resistance, is an important managerial responsibility. A study investigated how organizational

---

[46]Jeffrey D. Ford and Laurie W. Ford, "Decoding Resistance to Change," *Harvard Business Review*, April 2009, p. 100.

change in 32 different public and private organizations affected employees' commitment to the change and their broader commitment to the organization. One of the conclusions reached was that long-term benefits of change occur only when employees actively work to support the change and are aligned with the organization's goals and values.[47] Here we look at eight techniques for gaining support for change.

1. *Allow for discussion and negotiation.* Support for change can be increased by discussing and negotiating the more sensitive aspects of the change. It is important to acknowledge the potential hardships associated with the change, such as longer working hours or higher output to earn the same compensation. The two-way communication incorporated into the discussion helps reduce some employee concerns. Discussion often leads to negotiation, which further involves employees in the change process.

2. *Allow for participation.* To overcome resistance to change, allow people to participate in the changes that will affect them. In applying this concept, a manager can allow employees to set their own rules to increase compliance. A powerful participation technique is to encourage people who already favor the change to help in planning and implementation. These active supporters of the change will be even more strongly motivated to enlist the support of others. Participation is also useful because it gives the manager additional input into developing a careful plan for the change, including implementation.

3. *Point out the compelling reasons for change, including the financial benefits.* A good way to prepare employees for change is to point out the most compelling reasons why the status quo will no longer be effective; for example, the competition may be gaining ground. The compelling reason will often create a sense of urgency. Given that so many employees express concern about the financial effects of work changes, it is helpful to discuss these effects openly. If employees will earn more money as a result of the change, this fact can be used as a selling point. For example, a company owner told his employees, "I know you are inconvenienced and upset because we have cut way back on clerical support. But some of the savings will be invested in bigger bonuses for you." Much of the grumbling subsided.

4. *Establish a sense of urgency.* The presentation of compelling reasons for change will often create a sense of urgency, but the change agent may have to go even further. According to John Kotter of the Harvard Business School, a sense of urgency is more likely to be created when both the hearts and heads of employees are enlisted. In other words, an appeal must be made to both emotion and reason. Telling a human-interest

---

[47]Donald B. Fedor, Steven Caldwell, and David M. Herold, "The Effect of Organizational Changes on Employee Commitment: A Multilevel Investigation," *Personnel Psychology,* Spring 2006, p. 26.

story about the need for change can help enlist emotions and the intellect.[48] For example, one division president explained how her uncle who owned a film-developing store slowly went out of business because he did not shift fast enough to services that fit the digital age.

5. *Use a visual people can relate to.* The Target Company was at one time lagging behind current trends in clothing. Target was selling the previous year's fashions by purchasing imitations and selling them in the current year. Color was frowned upon because khaki and gray sold well enough. Soon some Target managers began coaxing the company's very cautious buyers, bringing in large glass jars containing M&M candies to demonstrate how enticing bright colors could be. The intention of the visual was also to demonstrate the importance of putting trendier offerings on display. Target's transition from cheap dowdiness to affordable and trendy fashion was underway.[49]

6. *Avoid change overload.* Too much change too soon leads to negative stress. Too many sweeping changes in a brief period of time, or too many simultaneous changes, causes confusion; it leads to foot dragging about workplace innovation. When change is perceived as excessive, employees often focus too much on the change and not enough on primary tasks related to product, service, or customers. Explaining how the large-scale changes fit the company strategy can sometimes lessen the sting of change.

7. *Allow for first-hand observation of successful change.* Support for change can sometimes be overcome by giving workers an opportunity to see first-hand an example of a model of the change in question.[50] Suppose, for example, top management decides that the company should shift to virtually paperless operation without administrative support. Many managers and staff professionals would be quite skeptical. If feasible, it would be helpful for a small team of company skeptics to visit a company that has become a paperless office. Seeing is believing, and it helps overcome resistance to change.

8. *Get the best people behind the program.* A powerful tactic for bringing about change is to enlist the cooperation of people whom others in the organization respect, people who are flexible. Workers who enjoy change and who are influential among their peers might be encouraged to communicate their attitudes about change, perhaps by posting them on a social networking Web site (without revealing company secrets.)

The above techniques for overcoming resistance to change are more likely to be successful when the manager has a good working relationship

---

[48]John Kotter, *A Sense of Urgency* (Boston: Harvard Business School Press, 2008).

[49]Christopher F. Chabris, "Old Habits Die Hard," *The Wall Street Journal*, February 19, 2010, p. A13; Book review of Chip Heath and Dan Heath, *Switch: How to Change Things When Change Is Hard* (New York: Broadway, 2009).

[50]Jeffrey Pfeffer, *The Human Equation: Building Profits by Putting People First* (Boston, MA: Harvard Business School Press, 1998), pp. 126–128.

with staff members. Allowing for discussion and participation is less likely to be perceived as manipulation when the manager is trusted.

Six Sigma and Planned Change

Implementing efforts to become a more quality-conscious firm can be classified as a total systems approach to organization change. Having high-quality goods and services is considered a necessary minimum to compete effectively. Most customers today require highquality standards from vendors. One such standard is Six Sigma, named for the mathematical concept that identifies 3.4 errors in 1 million opportunities. (The figure is derived from the area under the normal curve from -6 to $+6$ standard deviations from the mean.) A number of organizations formalized this quality standard as part of companywide programs for attaining high quality. With initial capital letters, **Six Sigma** refers to a philosophy of driving out waste and improving quality, and the cost and time performance of a company.

Six Sigma
Refers to a philosophy of driving out waste and improving quality, and the cost and time performance of a company.

Four companies that have used Six Sigma programs in some or all their divisions are GE, the Vanguard Group (investment management), Hyundai, and Xerox. A few years ago when revenue growth was slowing, Google hired a chief financial officer, Patrick Pichette, who was trained in Six Sigma. Two of his major goals were to reduce inefficiencies and delay spending where feasible.[51]

Six Sigma is a data-driven method for achieving near-perfect quality, with an emphasis on preventing problems. The focus is on identifying, quantifying, and eliminating errors in business processes. Six Sigma emphasizes statistical analysis and measurement in design, manufacturing, and the entire area of customer-oriented activities. Decision making becomes heavily based on numbers. Six Sigma also contains a strong behavioral aspect, with a focus on motivating people to work together to achieve higher levels of productivity.

Six Sigma implementation calls for creating specialized positions in the company instead of placing additional responsibility on already overburdened managers and specialists. Employees chosen to be "black belts" (or Six Sigma specialists) work full time as project leaders. Six Sigma teams carry out most of an organization's quality improvement efforts. Everyone else in the company should be involved to some extent in the change effort.[52] As with all programs of organizational improvement, top management commitment is vital.

An example of the application of Six Sigma to fix a quality problem took place in a manufacturing unit of Xerox. Software for translating technical manuals into foreign languages could not deal with some of the engineering

---

[51]Jessica E. Sacellaro and Scott Morrison, "Google Gears Down for Tougher Times," *The Wall Street Journal*, December 3, 2008, p. A13.

[52]Sara Fister Gale, "Building Frameworks for Six Sigma Success," *Workforce*, May 2003, pp. 64–69.

jargon. Identifying and eradicating the problematic phrases led to more rapid translations, fewer errors, and savings of up to $1 million.[53]

Six Sigma, as with other quality programs, can help an organization achieve reliable products and services. However, the program must fit into the company culture. Companies more attuned to Six Sigma are those where the culture emphasizes discipline and measurement, such as Xerox and Pitney-Bowes. Six Sigma is less likely to be accepted in a more free-wheeling and less disciplined culture such as a large advertising agency. A concern about pushing too far with Six Sigma is that it sometimes takes away from the innovation and customer relationships partially because of its heavy emphasis on measurement and paperwork (or electronic work).[54]

---

[53]Faith Arner and Adam Aston, "How Xerox Got Up to Speed," *Business Week*, May 3, 2004, p. 104.

[54]Brian Hindo and Brian Grow, "Six Sigma: So Yesterday?" *Business Week*, June 2007, p. 11.

Summary of Key Points

1 **Describe the bureaucratic form of organization and discuss its advantages and disadvantages.**

The most widely used form of organization is the bureaucracy, a multilevel organization in which authority flows downward and rules and regulations are carefully specified. Bureaucracies can be highly efficient organizations that are well suited to handling repetitive, recurring tasks. People know who is responsible for what, and vertical integration of the company is possible. A bureaucracy fits the human need for order and security, among other needs. Bureaucracies may be rigid in terms of handling people and problems, and decision-making delays are frequent.

2 **Explain the major ways in which organizations are divided into departments.**

The usual way of subdividing effort in organizations, particularly in bureaucracies, is to create departments. Three common types of departmentalization are functional, geographic, and product–service. Product–service departmentalization also takes the form of groups that better service customer needs.

3 **Describe four modifications of the bureaucratic structure.**

Projects are temporary groups of specialists. The matrix organization consists of a project structure superimposed on a functional structure. Personnel assigned to the projects within the matrix report to a project manager and also to a functional manager. Flat organizations have fewer layers than traditional hierarchies; these are often the result of downsizing. They are created for such purposes as reducing human resource costs and speeding up decision making. Downsizing can be looked upon as a way of simplifying an organization to make it less bureaucratic. Downsizing must be done carefully or it can backfire in terms of increasing efficiency. By outsourcing, a company can reduce its need for employees, physical assets, and associated payroll costs. Outsourcing is part of globalization. It becomes part of your organization structure when other companies perform part of your work. Homeshoring, or having

customer-service work performed in workers' homes, is a trend that is growing rapidly.

Another approach to organization structure is to organize horizontally. In this way a group of people concern themselves with a process, such as filling an order or developing a new product. Team members focus on their purpose rather than their specialty and take collective responsibility for customers. Switching from a task emphasis to a process emphasis can often be done through reengineering.

In addition to the formal structures, organizations also make use of informal structures such as personal relationships and networks to accomplish work. Information technology facilitates communication in all types of organization structures. A slight deviation from the bureaucratic structure is to share power in the executive suite by having the chairperson position separate from the CEO; another option is to have co-CEOs.

4 **Identify key factors that influence the selection of organization structure.**

The most effective structure depends on four key factors. The organization's strategy and goals are the most influential factor. High technology favors a flexible structure, whereas low technology favors bureaucracy. Large size often moves a company toward bureaucracy. Finances influence structure because flatter structures lower costs. An unstable environment favors a flexible structure.

5 **Specify how delegation, empowerment, and decentralization spread authority in an organization.**

Delegation is assigning formal authority and responsibility to another person for accomplishing a task. Delegation fosters empowerment. The manager remains accountable for the result of subordinates' efforts. Effective delegation includes assigning duties to the right people and obtaining feedback on the delegated task. Decentralization stems from delegation. It is the extent to which authority is passed down to lower levels in an organization. Decentralization sometimes refers to geographic dispersion. Although units may be decentralized and autonomous, in some organizations these units cooperate with one another for the common good.

 Identify major aspects of organizational culture.

The organizational culture is shaped by such forces as the values and personality of the founder, the attitudes of top-level managers, society, and the industry. Six key dimensions of organizational culture are values, relative diversity, resource allocation and rewards, degree of change, a sense of ownership, and the strength of culture. Employees learn the culture primarily through socialization, including story telling.

Culture has important consequences and implications for factors such as competitive advantage, productivity, quality, and morale. Top management is responsible for shaping, managing, and controlling culture. Although culture is slow to change, the manager can take positive steps to bring about change. The manager can act as a role model, impose a new approach through edict, reward behaviors that fit the desired cultural values, select the right people, and conduct training programs and conference calls to bring about the desired culture.

 Describe key aspects of managing change, including gaining support for change.

Change can take place at the individual and small group levels as well as at the organizational level. A model of change suggests that the process has three stages: unfreezing attitudes, attitude change, and refreezing to point out the success of the change. People resist change for reasons they think are important, the most common of which is the fear of an unfavorable outcome.

Ten techniques for gaining support for change are as follows: allow for discussion and negotiation; allow for participation; point out the financial benefits; avoid change overload; point out the compelling reasons for change, including the financial benefits; establish a sense of urgency; use a visual people can relate to; allow for first-hand observation of successful change; and get the best people behind the program.

Six Sigma is an important organizational change strategy. It is a data-driven method for achieving near-perfect quality, administered by Six Sigma teams with the cooperation of most managers and executives.

Key Terms and Phrases

Organization structure, 263
Bureaucracy, 263
Unity of command, 264
Departmentalization, 268
Functional departmentalization, 268
Geographic departmentalization, 269
Product–service departmentalization, 271
Project organization, 272
Matrix organization, 273
Flat organization structure, 274
Span of control, 275
Homeshoring, 277

Horizontal structure, 278
Reengineering, 279
Informal organization structure, 279
Social network analysis, 280
Delegation, 284
Empowerment, 284
Decentralization, 285
Centralization, 286
Organizational culture (or corporate culture), 287
Subculture, 288
Socialization, 289
Six Sigma, 298

Questions

1. Over the years, large business organizations have steadily reduced the number of layers in the organization structure. What purposes has this profound change in structure served?

2. Small and medium-sized companies are often eager to hire people with experience in a large, successful bureaucratic firm such as IBM or General Foods. What might be the reason behind the demand for these workers with experience in a bureaucracy?

3. If you were the CEO of a large organization, would you want to share responsibility with a co-CEO? Why or why not?

4. What can first-level and middle-level managers and team leaders do about shaping the culture of a firm?

5. What can you tell about the organizational culture of a large retailer just by visiting a couple of their stores?

6. Many career counselors believe that you are more likely to succeed in an organization in which you fit the culture. How could you determine before joining an organization whether you fit its culture?

7. How can a manager tell whether an employee is resisting change?

Skill-Building Exercise 8-A: Comparing Organization Structures

Work individually or in groups to identify the organization structure at a local company or any type of organization. It may be possible to accomplish the task by e-mail and telephone. Whatever structure you find, provide some kind of explanation for why the particular structure is useful for the organization. For example, a hospital would have a departmental structure such as "emergency room" and "ob-gyn." The reason would be that the departments serve clienteles with radically different needs. Compare your organization structures in class, and see how many different types were found.

Skill-Building Exercise 8-B: The Art of Delegation

Delegation is one of the most important managerial skills, yet delegation does not come easily to most people. Three major problems in delegating are (a) neglecting to check progress, (b) telling someone exactly how to perform the task, and (c) checking up on someone too frequently. Consult the chapter section about delegation, empowerment, and decentralization for suggestions about effective delegation as you perform this exercise. Your task is to delegate a work or personal-life task to somebody within the next ten days. Then reflect on what happened in terms of such factors as these:

- How much difficulty did you have in getting the person to accept the delegation?
- How much checking up on the person was needed?
- Did the task get accomplished?
- What did you learn about delegation?

Management Now: Online Skill-Building Exercise: Analyzing an Organizational Culture

Even though some have no written description, every organization has a culture. Search the Internet for several articles posted within the last 12 months about one of your favorite companies, and search that company's Web site. Find at least three statements that describe its culture (for example, "this is a highly disciplined organization where every worker keeps focused on the goal," or "this place is a bunch of cowboys and cowgirls running wild"). Arrive at a tentative conclusion about the company's culture, based on your findings.

8-A Case Problem

Redesigning PepsiCo

Assume that you are asked to assist in the re-design of the organization structure at PepsiCo. Assume also that PepsiCo has the structure drawn below for its major products. PepsiCo Chairwoman and CEO Indra Nooyi presents one reason she would like to see a new organization structure: "We have some of the world's strongest brands and some of the world's greatest marketers, but never have we integrated our marketing efforts in a holistic, global and disciplined fashion across the PepsiCo enterprise. We want to integrate our brand marketing efforts and stay ahead of macro consumer trends with a deeper level of sophistication."

In creating your revised organization structure you will be working closely with Jill Beraud, the Global Chief Marketing Officer at PepsiCo. Her goal is to build PepsiCo's food

and beverage brands on an international scale and integrate the company's entire marketing efforts.

Discussion Questions

1. Draw a revised organization structure that will help PepsiCo attain the marketing integration it seeks.
2. In addition to implementing the new structure you have drawn, what steps can Beraud take to facilitate an integration of marketing efforts across the major brands at PepsiCo?

Sources: The quote from Nooyi is from Joe Guy Collier, "Pepsi Picks Its First Chief Marketing Officer," *The Atlanta Journal Constitution* (www.ajc.com), December 3, 2008. The information about Beraud is from Natalie Zmuda, "Jill Beraud: Global Chief Marketing Office, PepsiCo," *Advertising Age* (www.adage.com), June 1, 2009. The organization structure presented for PepsiCo is hypothetical.

8-B Case Problem

The Corporate Culture Picnic

Matt Larson is the CEO of Exterior Light Inc. a company that manufactures and installs external lighting for municipalities, malls, and athletic stadiums. Working closely with Helen Ono, the vice president of administration and human resources, he organizes a company picnic every summer. The tradition has endured for 25 years.

Four hundred of the company's 440 people attended the picnic this year, held at Larson's summer home on lakefront property. The picnic facilities featured a volleyball area, a 22-foot inflatable slide, pony rides, face painters, temporary tattoos, miniature golf, an open beer-and-wine bar for adults, and a fully stocked Good Humor truck. Larson, Ono, and the other corporate officials worked the grill, which included meat products and vegetarian choices. According to the accounting department, the picnic cost $49,000 including reimbursed travel costs for employees working in field locations.

Perry Sanders, an accounts payable specialist attending the picnic, commented to Larson, "Geez Matt, I hope you and the other four hundred people stuffing themselves today are getting a bang for the buck. Today's fun will probably run a tab of $49,000. Those bucks would look pretty good if they were used to fatten our bottom line."

Larson retorted, "Perry, take off your accountant's hat for a few moments. Our annual picnic sends a clear signal that it's part of our culture to treat people well, and for our employees to work together in a friendly, cooperative environment."

After the last guest had left, Larson and Sanders chatted about the value of the picnic some more; they were joined by Ono. When she heard about the challenge to the picnic, she chimed in. "I'm a human resources professional, not a drumbeater for the company picnic, and I like Matt's point about the picnic communicating the culture. Setting up lighting systems requires a lot of cooperation across department and geographic lines. Seeing so many of your colleagues in person creates a culture of cooperation and teamwork."

Barbara Lyons, the director of marketing, said, "I saw a little of this friendliness go too far. The open bar led to too much random hugging, kissing, and patting. If you get sexually harassed at a company picnic, it is as serious as harassment in the office."

Ono replied, "Good point Barbara. I think I know who you are talking about. Some of our field technicians get a little too macho at the picnic. We'll have to send out a polite reminder before next year's picnic."

Larson rested his chin on the thumb of a clenched fist and said, "So you folks think there might be less expensive and time-consuming ways of communicating our culture of caring and teamwork? Let's leave the door open on this topic and return to it at a staff meeting."

Sanders said, "I don't want to be the Abominable No Man, but we need to calculate the return on investment from these picnics. Are we getting a cultural bang for the buck?"

Discussion Questions

1. Do Sanders, Ono, and Lyons have the right to challenge the annual picnic's value in communicating the corporate culture values?
2. How would company management at Exterior Lighting know whether the picnic was an effective way of communicating the cultural values of caring for people and teamwork?
3. What, if anything, should management do about possible sexual harassment at the company picnic?
4. Aside from a picnic, how might top management communicate the company's culture?

CHAPTER 9

Human Resource and Talent Management

OBJECTIVES

After studying this chapter and doing the exercises, you should be able to:

1. Explain how human resource and talent management is part of business strategy.

2. Describe the components of talent management.

3. Present an overview of recruitment and selection.

4. Present an overview of employee orientation, training, and development.

5. Explain the basics of a performance evaluation system.

6. Summarize the basics of employee compensation.

7. Understand the role of labor unions in human resource management.

Concerned a brain drain could hurt its long-term ability to compete, Google Inc. is tackling the problem with its typical tool: an algorithm. A few years ago, the Internet search giant began crunching data from employee reviews and promotion and pay histories in a mathematical formula Google says can identify which of its 20,000 employees are most likely to quit.

The input to the formula includes information from surveys and peer reviews—Google says the algorithm has already identified employees who felt underused, a key complaint among those who think about leaving. Applying a complex equation to a basic human resource problem is pure Google, a company that made using heavy data to drive decisions one of its "Ten Golden Rules."

The move is one of a series Google has made to prevent its most promising engineers, designers, and sales executives from leaving at a time when its once powerful draws— a start-up atmosphere and soaring stock price—have been diluted as the company got bigger. Laszlo Bock, who runs Google's human resources programs, said he pushed to expand the company's talent planning process. Google's algorithm is part of that effort.

Several years ago current and former Googlers said the company was losing talented employees who felt they had less opportunity to make an impact as the company matured. Several said Google provided little formal career planning, and some found the company's human resource programs too impersonal.

Google says it can do little to keep executives who want to run their own company, but it is determined to retain top product managers and engineers who create new services and technologies. And it claims to be succeeding. "We haven't seen the most critical people leave," said Bock.[1]

The story about Google illustrates, among other ideas, that even a famous and prosperous business organization must carefully examine its human resources practices and how it manages talent in order retain the right people. Many of the activities traditionally included in staffing and human resource management are now referred to as **talent management** because employees represent the talent the organization needs to function. An instructive definition of talent management is "a deliberate approach to attract, develop, and retain people with the aptitude and abilities to meet current and future organizational needs."[2]

talent management
A deliberate approach to attract, develop, and retain people with the aptitude and abilities to meet current and future organizational needs.

This chapter deals with key aspects of human resource and talent management, including how to fit into business strategy the subactivities of recruitment and selection, training, development, evaluation, and compensation. All managers engage in human resource management to some extent when they engage in activities such as recruiting, selecting, training, and evaluating employees. The human resource department assists in these activities and provides leadership.

LEARNING OBJECTIVE **1**

Explain how human resource management is part of business strategy.

HUMAN RESOURCE MANAGEMENT AND BUSINESS STRATEGY

The modern role for human resource professionals is that of a partner in helping the organization implement its business strategy. In the words of many HR professionals, "We finally have a seat at the executive table." The implication is that human resource management is an integral part of business strategy. (Human resource management is often referred to as *strategic human resource* management.) Without effective human resource

---

[1]Scott Morrison, "Google Searches for Staffing Answers," *The Wall Street Journal*, May 19, 2009, p. B1.

[2]Derek Stockley, "Talent Management Concept—Definition and Explanation," www.deredstockely.com, accessed February 25, 2010.

management, the company cannot accomplish high-level goals such as competing globally, grabbing market share, and being innovative. For example, unless talented and imaginative employees are recruited (even through outsourcing) innovation cannot be sustained. (This helps explain the emergence of the term *talent management*.) A major purpose of HRM is to maximize human capital so workers achieve the goals of the organization.

An indicator of the importance of human resource management to business strategy is that many present and former human resource management executives serve as outside directors on boards. A recent survey by executive search firm Spencer Stuart found that 7 percent of its U.S. board placements were present or prior heads of human resources, up sharply from previous years. U.S. companies seeking these human resource executives value their insight on key issues such as executive pay, management succession, and successful acquisition.[3]

In many organizations, however, human resource managers and professionals are still seen as occupying a minor operational role, carrying out activities such as processing payroll, filing government forms about equal employment opportunity, and recruiting and selecting entry-level workers. In small enterprises, the HR function might be part of the office manager's or owner's responsibility.

A specific way in which HRM contributes to business strategy is by helping to build high-performance work practices. Several of these approaches were mentioned in Chapter 7 in the discussion about designing jobs for high performance and establishing flexible working hours. Aspects of high-performance work practices described in the present chapter include selection, incentive compensation, and training. The self-managing teams described in Chapter 13 also contribute to high performance. A recent integration of 92 studies found that organizations can increase their performance by 20 percent by implementing high-performance work practices—the relationship is more evident in manufacturing than service settings. The results demonstrate that human resource methods contribute substantially to an organization's performance goals.[4]

PLAY VIDEO

Go to www.cengage.com/management/dubrin and view the video for Chapter 9. As you watch this video, what can you learn about this company's approach to managing their employees?

LEARNING OBJECTIVE ❷
Describe the components of organizational staffing.

THE TALENT MANAGEMENT MODEL AND STRATEGIC HUMAN RESOURCE PLANNING

In the model in Exhibit 9-1, the talent management (the same as staffing) process flows in a logical sequence. Although not every organization follows the same steps in the same sequence, talent management ordinarily proceeds in the way this section will discuss. Software is available to support every

---

[3]Study cited in Joann S. Lublin, "HR Executives Suddenly Get Hot," *The Wall Street Journal*, December 14, 2009, p. B5.

[4]James Combs, Yongmei Liu, Angela Hall, and David Ketchen, "How Much Do High-Performance Work Practices Matter? A Meta-Analysis of Their Effects on Organizational Performance," *Personnel Psychology*, Autumn 2006, pp. 501–528.

| EXHIBIT 9-1 | The Organization Talent Management Model |

Under ideal circumstances, organization staffing would proceed through the stages as shown, and would improve employee retention. Terminating employees might also be considered part of staffing.

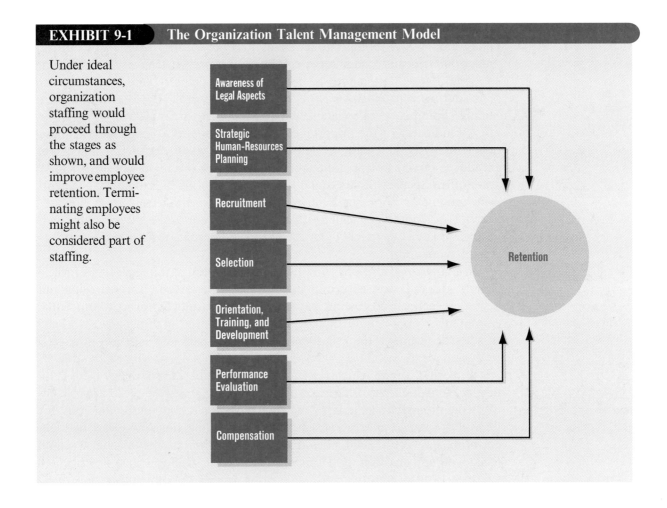

aspect of talent management. Although this software may be impressive from a technical standpoint, it does not necessarily mean that (a) human judgment is not required in making judgments about people, and (b) the content in the software was prepared by a human resources professional.

The arrows pointing to "Retention" in the model suggest that a major strategy of staffing is to retain valuable employees and that any aspect of talent management can contribute to retention. For example, selecting the right person for the job increases the probability that he or she will enjoy the job and stay with the firm. The chapter opener about Google illustrates the importance business firms attach to retention of the right talent.

Turnover (employees not being retained) occurs mainly due to individual, environmental, and workplace factors; these three main factors often work in combination.[5] An example of an *individual factor* might be that a

---

[5]Joseph Rosse and Robert Levin, *Talent Flow: A Strategic Approach to Keeping Good Employees, Helping Then Grow, and Letting Them Go* (San Francisco: Jossey-Bass, 2001).

person is not smart enough to cope with all the new learning in a job so he or she quits. If the job had been modified, the person might have stayed. *Environmental factors* include the economy. Employees are more likely to explore job possibilities outside the firm during good economic conditions and times of low unemployment. Workers who believe they are working for an outstanding company are less likely to poke around for a new job even during boom times.

Workplace factors include job enrichment and emotional support given to workers, both of which are likely to reduce turnover. However, an employee who wants to live in another climate might quit even an enriched job. Managers have more control over workplace than individual or environmental factors in reducing turnover.

A study found that approximately 70 percent of HR managers thought that employee retention is a primary business concern, and 40 percent reported that turnover is increasing. The study also concluded that long-term demographic changes, including the retiring baby boomer population, might aggravate the problem. Among the retention strategies suggested by the study are enhancing compensation (including benefits), providing opportunities for professional growth and development, creating opportunities for work–life balance, and improving communication with employees.[6] All these topics are discussed in this chapter and other places in the text.

Because many studies suggest that turnover occurs at a higher rate during the early stages of employment, talent management processes must start working early.[7] Employees who feel they cannot meet new job demands become discouraged. Managers must pay careful attention to the new hire who is adapting to the new position and the organization.

job embeddedness
A theory of turnover suggesting that a combination of many factors influences whether employees stay with a firm.

Job embeddedness theory (described in Chapter 7) suggests that a combination of many factors influences whether employees stay with a firm. Among these influences are factors about the job itself, such as bonds with coworkers, the fit between one's skills and job demands, and organization-sponsored community service that the employee perceives as valuable. Off-the-job factors influencing retention include personal, family, and community commitments. For example, a person is less likely to relocate for job purposes when he or she has good contacts on the job and the family is committed to staying in the community.[8]

Another useful finding is that when coworkers feel embedded, they create an atmosphere that encourages staying with the job rather than quitting. Job embeddedness is somewhat contagious.[9]

---

[6]Study cited in Susan Meisinger, "Workforce Retention: A Growing Concern," *HR Magazine*, April 2006, p. 12.

[7]Peter W. Hom, Loriann Roberson, and Aimee D. Ellis, "Challenging Conventional Wisdom About Who Quits: Revelations from Corporate America," *Journal of Applied Psychology*, January 2008, pp. 1–34.

[8]Brooks C. Holtom, Terence R. Mitchell, and Thomas W. Lee, "Increasing Human and Social Capital by Applying Job Embeddedness Theory," No. 4, 2006, p. 319.

[9]Will Felps et al, "Turnover Contagion: How Coworkers' Job Embeddedness and Job Search Behaviors Influence Quitting," *Academy of Management Journal*, June 2009, pp. 545–561.

EXHIBIT 9-2	Federal Laws Prohibiting Job Discrimination

- Title VII of the Civil Rights Act of 1964 (Title VII) prohibits employment discrimination based on race, color, religion, sex, or national origin.
- The Equal Pay Act of 1963 (EPA) protects men and women who perform substantially equal work in the same establishment from sex-based wage discrimination.
- The Age Discrimination in Employment Act of 1967 (ADEA) protects individuals who are 40 years of age or older.
- Title I and Title V of the Americans with Disabilities Act of 1990 (ADA) prohibits employment discrimination against qualified individuals with disabilities in the private sector, and in state and local governments.

- Sections 501 and 505 of the Rehabilitation Act of 1973 prohibits discrimination against qualified individuals with disabilities who work in the federal government.
- The Civil Rights Act of 1991, which, among other things, provides monetary damages in cases of intentional employment discrimination.

The U.S. Equal Employment Opportunity Commission (EEOC) enforces all of these laws. EEOC also provides oversight and coordination of all federal equal employment opportunity regulations, practices, and policies.

Source: http://www.eeoc.gov/abouteeo/overview_laws.html.

Legal Aspects of Staffing

Federal, state, provincial, and local laws influence every aspect of talent management. Managers and human resource specialists must keep the major provisions of these laws in mind whenever they make decisions about any phase of employment. Exhibit 9-2 summarizes major pieces of U.S. federal legislation that influence various aspects of staffing—not just employee selection. Canada has comparable legislation in both the federal and provincial levels. Managers must be aware that such legislation exists and be familiar with the general provisions of each law or executive order. When a possible legal issue arises, the manager should review the relevant legislation in depth and confer with a company specialist in employment law.

A key aspect of implementing the spirit and letter of employment discrimination law in the United States has been affirmative action programs. To comply with the Civil Rights Act of 1964, employers with federal contracts or subcontracts must develop programs to end discrimination. **Affirmative action** consists of complying with antidiscrimination law and correcting past discriminatory practices. Under an affirmative action program, employers actively recruit, employ, train, and promote minorities and women who may have been discriminated against by the employer in the past, which resulted in their underrepresentation in certain positions.

Complying with affirmative action requires extensive documentation such as an analysis of compensation paid to minority group members and

affirmative action
An employment practice that complies with antidiscrimination law correcting past discriminatory practices.

recruitment and hiring goals for affected groups. Part of an affirmative action plan might include a career development program for Native American workers to help them qualify for management positions.

A national debate continues over whether any person in a competitive situation deserves a preference because of race, ethnicity, or sex. The opposing point of view to affirmative action programs is that race, ethnicity, or sex should not be a factor in making employment or business decisions. For example, a job candidate should not be given an edge over other applicants because she is a Hispanic female. What is your opinion on this issue?

One way to understand how these laws might affect the individual is to specify the discriminatory practices prohibited by these laws. Under Title VII, the ADA, and the ADEA, it is illegal to discriminate in any aspect of employment, including hiring and firing; compensation, assignment, or classification of employees; transfer, promotion, layoff, or recall; job advertisements; recruitment; testing; use of company facilities; training and apprenticeship programs; fringe benefits; pay, retirement plans, and disability leave; or other terms and conditions of employment. Discriminatory practices under these laws also include the following:

- Harassment on the basis of race, color, religion, sex, national origin, disability, or age.
- Retaliation against an individual for filing a charge of discrimination, participating in an investigation, or opposing discriminatory practices.
- Employment decisions based on stereotypes or assumptions about the abilities, traits, or performance of individuals of a certain sex, race, age, religion, or ethnic group, or individuals with disabilities.
- Denying employment opportunities to a person because of marriage to, or association with, an individual of a particular race, religion, national origin, or an individual with a disability. Title VII also prohibits discrimination because of participation in schools or places of worship associated with a particular racial, ethnic, or religious group.

Although these forms of discrimination may appear clear-cut, a good deal of interpretation is required to decide whether a given employee is the subject of discrimination. For example, assume that a woman files a charge of sex discrimination. Later on she is bypassed for promotion. She claims the company is now seeking revenge. Yet the company claims that she did not have the appropriate interpersonal skills to be promoted to a supervisory position.

In an effort to comply with anti-discrimination legislation, employers continue to adjust their practices based on recent court rulings, sometimes to the disadvantage of a particular demographic group. During the Great Recession, employees in their 20s and 30s found themselves at a risk of a layoff, according to labor lawyers. The reason was that employers wanted to avoid age discrimination lawsuits by using a "last one in, first one out" policy for layoffs. As a result, more senior, and often older, employees were less likely to be laid off.[10] (A young and talented worker might say that he or she was the victim of reverse age discrimination.)

Among the remedies awarded to individuals judged to have been discriminated against are back pay, promotion and reinstatement. In many cases, the employer pays attorney's fees and court costs. Compensatory and punitive damages are also possible.

Strategic Human Resource and Talent Management Planning

Staffing begins with a prediction about how many and what types of people will be needed to conduct the work of the firm. Such activity is referred to as **strategic human resource planning** (also referred to as strategic talent management planning). It is the process of anticipating and providing for the movement of people into, within, and out of an organization to support the firm's business strategy. Management attempts, through planning, to have the right number and right kinds of people at the right time.

Business strategy addresses the financial priorities of the organization with respect to identifying type of business, product direction, profit targets, and so forth. Matthew Schuyler, chief human resources officer for Capital One, says, "The key to workforce planning is to start with the long-term vision of the organization and its future business goals and work back from there." The full engagement of business unit leaders and line managers is required for workforce (human resource) planning to be effective.[11]

Human resource planning addresses the question "What skills are needed for the success of this business?" Planning helps identify the gaps between current employee competencies and behavior and the competencies and behavior needed in the organization's future.

Strategic human resource planning consists of four basic steps:[12]

1. *Planning for future needs.* A human resource planner estimates how many people, and with what abilities, the firm will need to operate in the foreseeable future.
2. *Planning for future turnover.* A planner predicts how many current employees are likely to remain with the organization. The difference between this number and the number of employees needed leads to the next step.
3. *Planning for recruitment, selection, and layoffs.* The organization must engage in recruitment, employee selection, or layoffs to attain the required number of employees. A major choice between the commitment strategy in which the firm seeks to develop its own human capital and the secondary strategy of acquiring human capital in the market must be made.

strategic human resource planning

The process of anticipating and providing for the movement of people into, within, and out of an organization to support the firm's business strategy.

---

[10]Dana Mattioli, "With Jobs Scarce, Age Becomes an Issue," *The Wall Street Journal*, May 19, 2009, p. D4.

[11]Quoted in Fay Hansen, "The Long View," *Workforce Management*, April 21, 2008, p. 1.

[12]James A. F. Stoner and R. Edwards Freeman, *Management*, 4th ed. (Prentice Hall, 1989), p. 331; Peter Bamberger and Ilan Meshoulam, *Human Resource Strategy: Formulation, Implementation, and Impact* (Thousand Oaks, CA: Sage, 2000).

Most firms find a balance between training and promoting current employees and hiring needed talent from the outside.

4. *Planning for training and development.* An organization always needs experienced and competent workers. This step involves planning and providing for training and development programs that ensure the continued supply of people with the right skills.

Strategic business plans usually involve shifting around or training people. Human resource planning is an important element in the success of strategies. Human resource planning can also be a strategic objective in itself. For example, one strategic objective of PepsiCo is the development of talented people. Human resource planning contributes to attaining this objective by suggesting on- and off-the-job experiences to develop talent.

LEARNING OBJECTIVE **3**
Present an overview of recruitment and selection.

recruitment
The process of attracting job candidates with the right characteristics and skills to fill job openings.

RECRUITMENT

Recruitment is the process of attracting job candidates with the right characteristics and skills to fit job openings. The preferred recruiting method is to begin with a large number of possible job candidates and then give serious consideration to a much smaller number. However, if few candidates are available, the recruiter must be less selective or not fill the position.

Purposes of Recruitment

A major purpose of recruitment and selection is to find qualified employees who fit well into the culture of the organization. Most job failures are attributed to workers being a "poor fit" rather than to poor technical skills or lack of experience. The poor fit often implies poor relationships with coworkers. A positive person-organization fit is usually based on a mesh between the person's values and those of the organization. For example, a person who values technology and diversity among people—and is qualified—would be a good candidate to work for Xerox. A synthesis of many studies indicates that person-organization fit is positively related to job satisfaction, commitment to the firm, and intention to quit.[13] An important implication is that a good person-organization fit helps increase retention.

Another key purpose of recruiting is to sell the organization to high-quality prospective candidates. Recruiters must select candidates who can function in one job today and be retrained and promoted later, as company needs dictate. Flexible candidates of this type are in demand—a recruiter may need to sell the advantages of his or her company to entice a candidate to work there. An important principle of successful recruiting is to present an honest picture of the firm about such factors as growth opportunities, the amount of travel, and the type of culture.[14]

---

[13]Amy L. Kristof-Brown, Ryan D. Zimmerman, and Eric C. Johnson, "Consequences of Individuals' Fit at Work: A Meta-Analysis of Person-Job, Person-Organization, Person-Group, and Person-Supervisor Fit," *Personnel Psychology*, Summer 2005, p. 310.

[14]Carolyn Brandon, "Truth in Recruitment Branding," *HR Magazine*, November 2005, pp. 89–96.

Job Descriptions and Job Specifications

A starting point in recruiting is to understand the nature of the job to be filled and the qualifications sought. Toward this end, the recruiter should be supplied with job descriptions and job specifications. The job description explains in detail what the jobholder is supposed to do: it is a vital document in human resource planning and performance evaluation. An exception is that in some high-level positions, such as CEO, the person creates part of his or her own job description. A **job specification** (or person specification) stems directly from the job description. It is a statement of the personal characteristics needed to perform the job. A job specification usually includes the education, experience, knowledge, and skills required to perform the job successfully.

Many firms see job descriptions and job specifications decreasing in relevance, as explained in the study of job design in Chapter 7. Organizations often expect workers to occupy flexible roles rather than specific positions in order to meet the need for rapid change. An example of flexibility might be expecting a worker to learn new job-related software: a job description might mention specific software that must be mastered.

Recruiting Sources

The term *recruitment* covers a wide variety of methods for attracting employees to the firm, even through such methods as handing out personal business cards to people met while skiing. Recruiting sources are classified into four major categories, as described below. Exhibit 9-3 presents a more detailed breakdown of recruiting sources used by a variety of companies. It's easy to see that being referred by another employee or using the Internet are the two most productive paths to finding a job.

job specification
A statement of the personal characteristics needed to perform the job.

| **EXHIBIT 9-3** | **Sources of External Hires** |

Employee referrals continue to be the leading source of quality hires, followed by company Web sites.

Employee referrals 27.3
Company Web sites 20.1
Job boards 12.3
All other 10.1
Direct sourcing 7.8 (Candidates applying directly to the company, including inviting these candidates to apply.)
College 3.6
Print/media 3.4

Search engine marketing 3.3
Career fairs 3.2
Temp-to-hire 3.1
Third-party agencies 2.7
Rehires 2.4

Walk-ins 0.8

Source: Based on data from CareerXroads Eighth Annual Source of Hire Study, reported in Ed Frauenheim and Gonzalo Hernández, "Logging Off of Job Boards," *Workforce Management*, June 22, 2009, p. 25.

1. *Present employees.* As a standard recruiting method, companies post job openings and encourage current employees to apply. Managers often recommend current employees for transfer or promotion. A human resources information system can identify current employees with the right skills and competencies, which minimizes the need to reject unqualified internal applicants. Temporary workers are another source of potential full-time workers, providing the company has a temp-to-hire agreement with the employment agency.

2. *Referrals by present and former employees.* For established firms, present employees can be the primary recruiters. Satisfied employees may be willing to nominate relatives, friends, acquaintances, and neighbors for job openings. The effectiveness of current employees in the recruiting process comes from their ability to explain the culture of the firm to prospects. For example, they can point out that the company expects its employees to work hard and long.[15] Former employees who left the company on good terms can be effective recruiting sources. An angry former employee might be prompted to refer poorly qualified candidates.

3. *Online recruiting including company Web sites.* The Internet is a standard tool for recruiting job candidates. It offers hundreds of Web sites free to job candidates, and sometimes to employers. Online recruiting includes listing open positions on company Web sites and on job boards, and surfing sites for possible candidates. A key part of the service is the job board for posting openings, to which candidates submit their credentials. Many companies focus their online recruiting on the career section of the company Web site. Many job seekers go directly to company Web sites instead of using job boards.

   Online recruiting also occurs by means of company pages developed to attract possible candidates on social networking Web sites such as Facebook, LinkedIn, and Twitter. These pages often contain information and discussion boards aimed at students. The social Web site offers the advantage of allowing for continuing dialogue with potential job candidates. Some recruiters scan social networking sites looking for potential talent. A person's Facebook page might reveal considerable job-related information about him or her. A potential employer might find an interesting person on a social networking site and proceed to track down blogs that individual posted to learn more about the prospect.[16]

4. *External sources other than online approaches.* Potential employees outside an organization can be reached in many ways. The best known of these methods is a recruiting advertisement—print, radio, and sometimes television. Other external sources include (a) placement offices, (b) private and public employment agencies, (c) labor union hiring halls, (d) walk-ins (people who show up at the firm without invitation), and

---

[15]Kerri Koss Morehart, "How to Create an Employee Referral Program That Really Works," *HRfocus*, January 2001, pp. 3–4.

[16]Mark Henricks, "Recruiting 2.0," *Entrepreneur*, February 2009, p. 56.

(d) write-ins (people who write unsolicited job-seeking letters). Labor union officials believe that unions simplify the hiring process for employers because only qualified workers are admitted to the unions.

Finding employees or finding a job is best done through a variety of methods mentioned here. A major consideration regarding which recruiting source will be the most effective is whether the company is seeking active job seekers or passive candidates—those who are not looking for a job but could be enticed. In many cases, people with the appropriate skills and talent to fill a given position are employed elsewhere. They may not be fully content with their present position, but have not yet begun a job search.[17] Referrals and the scanning of social networking sites are likely to be effective in tracking down passive candidates. Web sites that advertise job and other external sources tend to be more effective in recruiting active job seekers.

Global Recruiting

Global recruiting presents unique challenges. Multinational businesses must have the capability to connect with other parts of the globe to locate talent. Company recruiters must meet job specifications calling for multiculturalism (being able to conduct business in other cultures) in addition to more traditional skills. To fill international positions, the recruiter may have to develop overseas recruiting sources. The recruiter may also require the assistance of a bilingual interviewer to help assess the candidate's ability to conduct business in more than one language.

Global recruiting for managers can be difficult because candidates must be found who can blend the work practices of two cultures. A Dell representative noted in relation to finding a manager for a facility in China that veteran executives in China often have a Confucian mind-set that views hands-on management as suited to lower-level workers. Dell needs leaders and higher-level workers familiar with the Chinese business culture but also willing to use a hands-on approach to daily operations.[18]

SELECTION

Qualified candidates are the lifeblood of the firm. An important goal of selection is to fill as many positions as possible with "A" players, or top-level performers.[19] Even in the most basic jobs, some people outperform others; for example, some custodial technicians exceed standards for creating a clean workplace.

---

[17]Julie Bos, "Rebuilding Recruitment: Top Strategies in a Recovering Economy," *Workforce Management*, January 2010, p. 30.

[18]Ed Frauenheim, "Dell Reboots Recruitment for International Approach," *Workforce Management*, April 10, 2006, p. 24.

[19]Michelle V. Rafter, "Get Your 'A' Players Here!" *Workforce Management*, March 3, 2008, pp. 1, 20–28.

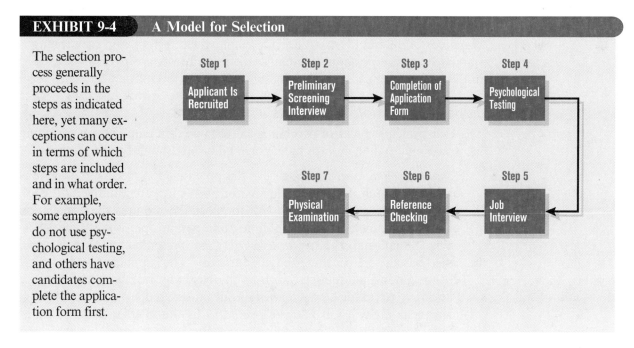

EXHIBIT 9-4   A Model for Selection

The selection process generally proceeds in the steps as indicated here, yet many exceptions can occur in terms of which steps are included and in what order. For example, some employers do not use psychological testing, and others have candidates complete the application form first.

Step 1 — Applicant Is Recruited
Step 2 — Preliminary Screening Interview
Step 3 — Completion of Application Form
Step 4 — Psychological Testing
Step 5 — Job Interview
Step 6 — Reference Checking
Step 7 — Physical Examination

Selecting the right candidate for a job is part of a process that includes recruitment, as shown in Exhibit 9-4. Recruiting sources such as Web sites and print ads typically generate hundreds of unqualified applicants and a few valuable candidates. A hiring decision is based on information gathered in two or more of these steps. For instance, a person might receive a job offer if he or she was impressive in the interview, scored well on the tests, and had good references. Another important feature of this selection model allows for an applicant to be rejected at any point. An applicant who is abusive to the employment specialist might not be asked to fill out an application form.

Preliminary Screening Interview

Selection begins when candidates come to the attention of the recruiter, often by cover letter and job résumé. If candidates come close to fitting the job specifications, a brief screening interview follows, frequently by telephone. The purpose of the screening interview is to determine whether the candidate should be given further consideration. One area of disqualification would be for the candidate to demonstrate such poor oral communication skills, especially for a job requiring considerable customer contact. "Knockout" questions are sometimes used to quickly disqualify candidates. Assume a person applying for a supervisory position in a nursing home is asked, "How well do you get along with senior citizens?" A candidate who responds, "Very poorly" is immediately disqualified.

An important suggestion here is to be at your best for the telephone interview, including total concentration on the tasks at hand. Rehearse your presentation in advance.

Psychological Testing

Hundreds of different tests are used in employment testing, and such testing is standard practice in about one-half of firms. All tests are psychological tests in the sense that measuring human ability is an important part of psychology.

Types of Psychological Tests

The four principle types of psychological tests used in employment screening are situational judgment, aptitude, personality, and honesty and integrity.

1. *Situational judgment tests* measure the potential for success in situations or scenarios that describe a dilemma or problem representative of the job under consideration. Dealing with the problem requires the application of relevant knowledge, skills, abilities, and perhaps personality characteristics. Situational judgment tasks may be presented in written, oral, video-based, or computer-based formats. The applicant often must choose among alternatives, such as the best way to deal with an angry customer. Areas of competence typically measured by situational judgment tests include job knowledge and skills, interpersonal skills, teamwork, leadership, and personality tendencies such as agreeableness.[20] An advantage of situational judgment tests is that they tend to be perceived as fair by job applicants because the simulations appear to be relevant.

2. *Aptitude tests* measure the potential for performing satisfactorily on the job, given sufficient training. Mental ability tests, the best-known variety of aptitude tests, measure the ability to solve problems and learn new material. Mental ability tests measure such specific aptitudes as verbal reasoning, numerical reasoning, and spatial relations (the ability to visualize in three dimensions). Tests of *emotional intelligence* are gaining in popularity; in these, the candidate is measured on the ability to deal with people's feelings and emotions. Emotional intelligence can also be classified as an aspect of personality.

3. *Personality tests* measure personal traits and characteristics that could be related to job performance. The use of personality tests still sparks controversy, but research during the past decade shows a positive connection between certain personality tests and subsequent job performance. Critics express concern that these tests invade privacy and are too imprecise to be useful. Nevertheless, personality factors can profoundly influence job performance. Personality tests are increasingly used to screen applicants for entry-level jobs at call centers, retail stores, and other customer-contact positions.[21] Exhibit 9-5 lists the major personality factors related to job performance.

---

[20]Michael S. Christian, Bryan D. Edwards, and Jill C. Bradley, "Situational Judgment Tests: Constructs Assessed and a Meta-Analysis of their Criterion-Related Validities," *Personnel Psychology*, Spring 2010, p. 84.

[21]Erin White, "Personality Tests Aim to Stop 'Fakers'," *The Wall Street Journal*, November 6, 2006, p. B3.

EXHIBIT 9-5   **The Big Five Personality Factors**

Many psychologists believe that the basic structure of human personality is represented by what they call the Big Five factors. These factors influence job performance. Conscientiousness, for example, is related to the tendency to produce quality work. Furthermore, these factors can be measured by psychological tests.

I. **Neuroticism**. This factor relates to whether a person is anxious, depressed, angry, embarrassed, emotional, or worried. A person of low neuroticism—or high emotional stability—is calm and confident, and usually in control.

II. **Extraversion**. Extraversion (which is the same as extroversion) relates to whether a person is social, gregarious, assertive, talkative, or active. A shy person scores high on introversion.

III. **Openness to experience**. This factor relates to whether a person is imaginative, cultured, curious, original, broad-minded, intelligent, or artistically sensitive.

IV. **Agreeableness**. This factor relates to whether a person is courteous, flexible, trusting, good-natured, cooperative, forgiving, soft hearted, or tolerant.

V. **Conscientiousness**. This factor relates to whether a person is careful, thorough, responsible, organized, or prepared. Conscientiousness also relates to whether a person is hard-working, achievement-oriented, and persevering.

A recent study with middle managers in an energy company suggests that personality tests are good predictors of management performance with respect to both the task and interpersonal aspects of the job. The personality factors measured were those presented in Exhibit 9-5. Management performance was measured in terms of judgments by both superiors and subordinates, providing more insight into performance than judgments of performance made by superiors only. Subordinate judgments were made using 360 degree feedback ratings (described later in this chapter).[22]

4. *Honesty and integrity tests* are designed to measure a person's honesty or integrity as it relates to job behavior. (Honesty relates most specifically to lying, whereas integrity refers to sticking with your principles.) These tests are frequently used in workplaces such as retail stores, banks, and warehouses where employees have access to cash or merchandise. Other work, in which employees could damage computers or access secret documents, for example, also requires a prediction of employee honesty. A major factor measured by integrity tests is social conscientiousness. People who score high on this personality factor show a much greater likelihood of following organizational rules. Despite controversy, honesty and integrity tests are widely used. Years of experience with integrity and honesty tests indicates that these tests can help identify job

---

[22]In-Sue Oh and Christopher M. Berry, "The Five-Factor Model of Personality and Managerial Performance: Validity Gains Through the Use of 360 Degree Performance Ratings," *Journal of Applied Psychology*, November 2009, pp. 1498–1513.

candidates with a propensity to steal and engage in other counterproductive behavior (such as computer hacking).[23]

Validity and Equal Employment Opportunity

The EEOC insists that psychological tests (integrity tests included) be scientifically accurate, job-related, and not discriminatory against any group. These rules also apply to other selection instruments, including application forms and interviews. A specific provision requires a validity study when a selection procedure shows an adverse impact on any race, sex, or ethnic group. A *validity study* is a statistical and scientific method of seeing whether a selection device does predict job performance. Do high scorers perform well on the job? Do low scorers tend to be poor performers? An adverse impact as defined by the EEOC occurs when the selection ratio (acceptance rate) for protected groups is less than four-fifths of the selection ratio for the unprotected group. For example, if 80 out of 100 white males are accepted through a company-wide selection procedure, then 64 out of 100 Latino males should be accepted ($4/5 \times 80 = 64$).

A 2009 Supreme Court ruling favored white firefighters in New Haven, Connecticut, who challenged the city's decision to reject the results of a promotion exam because none of the specific group of black applicants scored high enough to advance. The court also stated that employers must ensure that employment tests do not discriminate, yet they cannot modify the results to favor one ethnic group over others. Many human resource professionals interpreted the new ruling to mean that the use of valid psychological tests continues to be acceptable employment practice.[24]

The most consistent finding about the effectiveness of psychological tests in predicting job performance stems from a long series of studies concerning general intelligence and conscientiousness. In general, employees who have good problem-solving ability and are conscientious are likely to perform well in most jobs.[25] (These findings assume that the employee also has the necessary education and job skills. Yet for basic jobs, dependability and the ability to learn are more important than experience and existing skills.) General problem-solving ability is measured by mental ability tests and conscientiousness by a Big Five personality test. A straightforward explanation of these findings is that a bright person will learn quickly, and a conscientious person will try hard to get the job done.

[23]Leonard D. Goodstein and Richard I. Lanyon, "Applications of Personality Assessment to the Workplace: A Review," *Journal of Business and Psychology*, Spring 1999, p. 317; James E. Wanek, Paul R. Sackett, and Deniz S. Ones, "Towards an Understanding of Integrity Test Similarities and Differences: An Item-Level Analysis of Seven Tests," *Personnel Psychology*, Winter 2003, pp. 873–894.

[24]Carl Tuna, Nathan Koppel, and Michael Sanserino, "Job-Test Ruling Cheers Employers," *The Wall Street Journal*, July 1, 2009, p. B1.

[25]Orlando Behling, "Employee Selection: Will Intelligence and Conscientiousness Do the Job?" *Academy of Management Executive*, February 1998, pp. 77–86; Goodstein and Lanyon, "Applications of Personality Assessment," p. 295.

The Job Interview

The job interview is more comprehensive than the screening interview, covering topics such as education, work experience, special skills and abilities, hobbies, and interests. Interviewers frequently use the candidate's résumé as a source of topics. For example, "I notice you have worked for four employers in three years. Why is that?" Testing results may also provide clues for additional questioning. If a candidate scored low on a scale measuring conscientiousness, the interviewer might ask about the candidate's punctuality and error rate.

Employment interviews are more valid when the interviewer is trained and experienced. Evidence also suggests that when the interviewer carefully follows a format, predictions about job performance tend to be more accurate.[26] Validity may increase when several candidates are interviewed for each position, because comparisons can be made among the applicants.

Job interviews serve a dual purpose. The interviewer tries to decide whether the interviewee is appropriate for the organization. At the same time, the interviewee tries to decide whether the job and organization fit him or her. An important approach to helping both the organization and the individual to make the right decision is to offer a **realistic job preview,** a complete disclosure of the potential negative features of a job to a job candidate.[27] For example, an applicant for a tech support-center position might be told, "At times customers will scream and swear at you because a computer file has crashed. Around holiday time many frustrated customers go ballistic." Telling job applicants about potential problems leads to fewer negative surprises and less turnover.

Exhibit 9-6 presents guidelines for conducting a job interview. Several of the suggestions reflect a screening approach referred to as **behavioral interviewing**; the answers to many of the questions reveal actual job behaviors relevant to a given position. The airline marketing manager might be instructed, "Give me an example of what you have done in the past to compete with a lower-price competitor." Susan Docherty, the head of the United States sales, service, and marketing team at General Motors, uses behavioral interview questions frequently. She notes as follows:

One of the first questions I ask is "Can you describe a decision that you made, or a situation that you were involved in, that was a failure?"And I don't need to know how they got to the failure. But I need to know what they did about it. How they handled that is the best illustration of whether or not they're an innovative thinker and are comfortable taking some risk.[28]

realistic job preview
A complete disclosure of the potential negative features of a job to a job candidate.

behavioral interviewing
A style of interviewing in which the interviewer asks questions whose answers reveal behaviors that would be either strengths or weaknesses in a given position.

[26]Richard A. Posthuma, Frederick Pl. Morgeson, and Michael A. Campion, "Beyond Employment Interview Validity: A Comprehensive Narrative Review of Recent Research and Trends Over Time," *Personnel Psychology*, Spring 2002, p. 42.

[27]Robert D. Bretz Jr. and Timothy A. Judge, "Realistic Job Previews: A Test of the Adverse Self-Selection Hypothesis," *Journal of Applied Psychology*, April 1998, pp. 330–337.

[28]Quoted in Adam Bryant, "Now, Put Yourself in My Shoes," *The New York Times* (nytimes.com), February 7, 2010.

EXHIBIT 9-6   Guidelines for Conducting an Effective Selection Interview

1. **Prepare in advance**. Prior to the interview, carefully review the applicant's job application form and résumé. Keep in mind several questions worthy of exploration, such as "I notice you have done no previous selling. Why do you want a sales job now?" Job candidates who submit a video résumé will often provide some additional areas for questioning, such as asking about the quality of the candidate's oral communication skills and ability to smile at customers.

2. **Find a quiet place free from interruptions**. Effective interviewing requires careful concentration. Also, the candidate deserves the courtesy of an uninterrupted interview. Do not access e-mail, look at the computer screen, use a BlackBerry, or engage in telephone conversations during the interview.

3. **Take notes during the interview**. Take notes on the content of what is said during the interview. Also, record your observations about the person's statements and behavior. For example, "Candidate gets very nervous when we talk about previous work history."

4. **Use a brief warm-up period**. A standard way of relaxing a job candidate is to spend about five minutes talking about neutral topics, such as the weather. This brief period can be extended by asking about basic facts, such as the person's address and education.

5. **Ask open-ended questions**. To encourage the employee to talk, ask questions that call for more than a one- or two-word answer. Sometimes a request for information—a statement like "Tell me about your days at business school"—works like an open-ended question.

6. **Follow an interview format**. Effective interviewers carefully follow a predetermined interview format. They ask additional questions that are based on responses to the structured questions.

7. **Encourage the job candidate**. The easiest way to keep an interviewee talking is to give that person encouragement. Standard encouragements include "That's very good," "How interesting," "I like your answer," and "Excellent."

8. **Dig for additional details**. When the interviewee brings up a topic worthy of exploration, dig for additional facts. Assume the interviewee says, "I used to work as a private chauffeur, but then I lost my driver's license." Noticing a red flag, the interviewer might respond, "Why did you lose your license?"

9. **Spend most of the interview time listening**. An experienced job interviewer spends little time talking. It is the interviewee who should be doing the talking.

10. **Provide the candidate ample information about the organization**. Answer any relevant questions.

If the candidate lacks much job experience, a behavioral question can be asked about a characteristic important to the job, such as resiliency.[29] The candidate might be asked, "Tell me about how you acted the last time you were rejected for something you really wanted?"

To personalize the job interview process, go through the checklist presented in Exhibit 9-7 just to assure that you are on the top of your game for your next interview.

---

[29]Andrea C. Poe, "Graduate Work: Behavioral Interviewing Can Tell You If an Applicant Just Out of College Has Traits Needed for the Job," *HR Magazine*, October 2003, pp. 95–100.

EXHIBIT 9-7 The Job Interviewee Checklist

Most readers are already familiar with most of the behaviors and attitudes associated with having a successful job interview. Nevertheless, going through the checklist of behaviors presented below in the form of questions can serve as a quick reminder of how to be at your best during a job interview.

1. Have I visited the organization's Web site to learn more about the company, and done an Internet search to read a few articles about the company?
2. Have I investigated which style of clothing (such as business formal versus business casual) would be preferred by HR and the interviewing manager?
3. Do I plan to look relaxed and fresh during the interview by resting, exercising, and showering as close to interview time as feasible?
4. Have I rehearsed a discussion of my strengths and areas for needed development?
5. Have I rehearsed a scenario of how I solved a difficult job problem or took care of an emergency?
6. Can I describe my job and educational history without hesitation?
7. Am I prepared to put away my cell phone (and keep it turned off) or personal digital assistant during the entire interview?
8. Will I be able to resist the temptation of frequently glancing at the interviewer's computer monitor?
9. Do I have a few intelligent questions in mind to ask the interviewer?
10. Am I prepared to listen to the interviewer as well as ask questions?
11. Will I ask questions about the nature of the work and challenges instead of asking about factors such as vacation time and personal leave time?
12. Will I be able to refrain from making negative statements about people I worked with in the past?
13. Will I be able to give examples of how I have been a team player?
14. Will I be able to give examples of having taken on some leadership responsibility (even for a project)?
15. Am I prepared to look relaxed and smile frequently?
16. Am I prepared to make a few comments about current events if the topic is relevant to the interview?
17. Am I prepared to explain how I would like to make a contribution?
18. Will I be able to refrain from talking about how this job will give me the experience I need to achieve my career goals?
19. Will I make only statements of facts about me that can be verified?
20. If the job interests me, will I have enough courage to indicate that I would accept an offer?
21. After the interview is completed will I remember to thank the interviewer for his or her time?

Interpretation: I can hear you saying "Duh" in response to a few of the above checklist items. Yet, you would be surprised how many candidates—even for top-level executive positions—blow job interviews by violating these suggestions. The more yes answers you gave, and assuming you are qualified for the position, the better your chances are for receiving a job offer.

Reference Checking and Background Investigation

A **reference check** is an inquiry to a second party about a job candidate's suitability for employment. The two main topics explored in reference checks are past job performance and the ability to get along with coworkers. Asking about any evidence of violent behavior has become more common. Former and prospective employers have a qualified privilege to discuss an employee's past performance. As long as the information is given to a person with a legitimate interest in receiving it, discussion of an employee's past misconduct or poor performance is permissible under law. Many state laws hold employers blameless if the information they share with a reference checker is truthful and without malice.[30] In spite of such rulings, many past employers are hesitant to provide complete references because job applicants have legal access to written references unless they specifically waive this right in writing (Privacy Act of 1974).

reference check
An inquiry to a second party about a job candidate's suitability for employment.

Background investigations are closely related to **reference checks**—they focus on information from sources other than former employers. The growth of databases accessible through the Internet has facilitated reference checking. Areas investigated include driving record, possible criminal charges or convictions, creditworthiness, disputes with the IRS, and coworkers' and neighbors' comments about a candidate's reputation. Many employers believe that a good credit record reflects dependability. A concern for both employers and job candidates is that many credit reports are inaccurate.

Standard practice today is for prospective employers to search the Web, including social networking Web sites, for negative and positive information about a candidate. Candidates with popular names such as Susan Johnson or Robert Anderson often advise potential employers in advance as to their full identifying information.

One justification for background investigations is that so many job candidates present untrue information in résumés and job interviews. The Society of Human Resource Managers reports that approximately 53 percent of job candidates lie to some extent on their résumés.[31] The many financial scandals in the executive suite in recent years have prompted more thorough background investigations of candidates for top-level management positions. Executives have been found to misrepresent facts on their résumé, such as a college degree that was never earned.

Physical Examination and Drug Testing

The physical examination remains a key part of preemployment screening. The exam gives some indication as to the person's physical ability to handle the requirements of particular jobs. For example, a person with a history of four heart attacks would be a poor candidate for a high-stress managerial position. The physical exam also provides a basis for later comparisons. This step lessens the potential for an employee to claim that the job caused a particular injury or disease. For example, after one year on the job, an employee might claim that the job created a fusion of two vertebrae. If the preemployment physical showed evidence of two fused vertebrae, the employer would have little to fear from the claim.

---

[30]Joe Mullich, "Cracking the ex-Files," *Workforce Management*, September 2003, pp. 51–54.

[31]Data presented in "Fake It and You're Busted," *TimesJobs.com*, January 23, 2009, p. 1.

Many companies test all job applicants for use of illegal drugs. (Executives and entry-level workers can be drug abusers.) Abuse of prescription drugs is a widespread problem. Testing for substance abuse includes blood analysis, urinalysis, analysis of hair samples, observations of eyes, and examination of skin for punctures.

Some people raise the concern that inaccurate drug testing may unfairly deny employment to worthy candidates. A strong argument in favor of drug testing, however, is that employees who are drug abusers may create such problems as lowered productivity, lost time from work, and misappropriation of funds. Accident and absenteeism rates for drug (as well as alcohol) abusers are substantial; those employees also experience more health problems.

Cross-Cultural Selection

As with cross-cultural recruitment, most of the selection guidelines and techniques already mentioned can be applied cross-culturally. Many selection devices, such as widely used psychological tests, are published in languages besides English, especially Spanish. Managers and employment interviewers gathering information about job candidates from other countries should familiarize themselves with key facts about the other culture. For example, in some countries a baccalaureate (or "bac") is equivalent to an American high school diploma, not a bachelor's degree.

A key aspect of cross-cultural selection is choosing workers who will fit well as *expatriates*, those individuals sent to work in affiliates in other countries. One predictor of success is the desire for an out-of-the-country assignment. Key personality traits of relevance for overseas assignments are flexibility, openness to experience, sense of humor, and interest in others. Matching the person's style to the culture is another key success factor. A human resources professional says, "You could have a top sales person in the United States who is aggressive and a high achiever, but who will fail in Japan for the very reason he's a success in the United States."[32]

After being recruited, job candidates pass through all the selection screens, such as the physical exam, before being hired. After making the hiring decision and applicant acceptance, human resource specialists and new employees complete all the necessary forms, such as those relating to taxes and benefits. Next is orientation.

LEARNING OBJECTIVE ④
Present an overview of employee orientation, training, and development.

ORIENTATION, TRAINING, AND DEVELOPMENT

Most firms no longer operate under a "sink or swim" philosophy when it comes to employee learning. Instead, employees are oriented to the firm, and later trained and developed.

---

[32]The quote and information in the same paragraph are from Andrea C. Poe, "Selection Savvy," *HR Magazine*, April 2002, p. 78.

Employee Orientation (Onboarding)

employee orientation program
A formal activity designed to acquaint new employees with the organization.

An **employee orientation program** (also referred to as onboarding) formally acquaints new employees with the company and imparts information about the corporate culture. The onboarding experience is significant because it helps the new employee feel committed to the firm and less likely to leave shortly. Part of the orientation may deal with small but important matters such as the availability of parking stickers. Large firms offer elaborate orientation programs conducted by human resource specialists. The program may include tours of the buildings, talks by department heads, video presentations, printed and online information, and visits to the company Web site.

Employee orientation also conveys to new employees the specific nature of their jobs and expectations about performance. In some firms, a buddy system is part of the orientation. A buddy, a peer from the new employee's department, shows the new employee around and fills in information gaps. A growing orientation practice is to assign a new employee a mentor who will help him or her better understand the organization and also serve as a resource person for resolving problems. The mentor is supposed to check in regularly to discuss progress, even by instant messaging.

Another aspect of orientation is informal socialization. In this process, coworkers introduce new employees to aspects of the organizational culture. Coworkers might convey, for example, how well motivated a new employee should be or the competence level of key people in the organization. The new employee might also be advised of informal practices such as taking turns at bringing donuts and bagels for coworkers. The disadvantage of informal orientation is that it may furnish the new employee with misinformation.

The most successful onboarding programs work with groups of employees. Some aspects of some programs last up to one to two years. In addition to presenting factual information, the program should help newcomers build relationships with peers and managers. Caela Farren, CEO of a career development and talent management firm, states, "Companies that have a well thought-out formal period including training, tours, and opportunities to speak with executives have the best retention rates."[33]

Training and Development

training
Any procedure intended to foster and enhance learning among employees, particularly directed at acquiring job skills.

Training and development deal with systematic approaches to improve employee skills and performance. **Training** is any procedure intended to foster and enhance learning among employees and particularly directed at acquiring job skills. Rapid changes in technology and the globalization of business have spurred the growth of training programs. Training programs exist to teach hundreds of different skills such as equipment repair, performance evaluation, software utilization, and budget preparation. Training can develop both hard skills (technical, scientific, and numerical) and soft

---

[33]Quoted in Bridget Mintz Testa, "Onboarding Success," *Workforce Management*, September 22, 2008, p. 29.

skills (interpersonal skills and attitudes). Employee training and development are based on the belief that developing talent internally is a good investment.

Training and development are so important to many big companies that the organizational unit responsible for such activity is labeled a *university*. Examples include McDonald's Hamburger University, Apple University, and Pixar University. The purpose of Burger King University is to train franchisees. None of these corporate universities is authorized to grant degrees by the state in which it operates.

A substantial amount of skills training in industry is delivered through computers, including the Internet. **E-learning** is a Web-based form of computer-based training. Some learning programs are computer-based without being delivered over the Internet. For example, a CD might be used for product training. An e-learning course is usually carefully structured, with specific lesson plans for the student. E-learning helps deal with the challenge of training workers who are geographically dispersed. Placing learning modules on social networking Web sites is a form of e-learning gaining some momentum.

Another feature of e-learning is that it is often interactive. The computer provides a stimulus or prompt, to which the trainee responds. The computer then analyzes the response and provides feedback to the student. A question in a customer service course might ask trainees to evaluate the following response to a customer complaint: "If you don't like my answer, go speak to my boss." A message would appear, suggesting that the trainee take more ownership of the problem.

Related to e-learning is delivering training content via MP3 players or iPods, enabling workers to receive training at any spare moment or just-in-time (for example, when trying to understand how to use a new machine or fix a customer problem). The system works by transforming training content into podcasts: employees can train anywhere, even on an airplane or while bike riding. Steve Arneson, senior vice president of learning and development at Capital One (financial services), emphasizes that audio learning is part of the company's focus on blended learning—classroom, multimedia, and written materials.[34]

Despite the substantial contribution and growth of e-learning, many students learn better when they can interact with fellow students and instructors. Nonverbal cues, so important for many types of learning, are minimal when interacting with software.

Many companies are now taking a balanced approach of classroom training combined with e-learning. Computer-based learning is effective in helping workers learn conceptual information and hard skills such as product information and principles of customer service. Developing interpersonal skills requires face-to-face practice. For example, Home Depot relies heavily on computers for training cashiers how to make change and process credit cards. Personal mentoring is used more often to coach store associates

e-learning

A Web-based form of computer-based training.

---

[34]Elizabeth Agnvall, "Just-in-Time Training," *HR Magazine*, May 2006, pp. 66–71.

about product knowledge and dealing with customers.[35] As with telecommuting, many workers lack self-discipline and self-motivation to follow through with e-learning.

Employee training is often conducted by company leaders. Jennifer Gratton, director of learning and development for 1-800-Got-Junk?, takes a novel approach to training. She creates simulated radio shows with a conference call phone line. Gratton says, "I, or one of the other leaders, will be the host of the call, so there's no cost for that. We schedule these calls at a few different times during the day to reach different time zones, from Boston to Sydney, Australia. Then we record the 20-minute training session and it becomes an MP3 file."[36]

development
A form of personal improvement that usually consists of enhancing knowledge and skills of a complex and unstructured nature.

Development is a form of personal improvement that usually consists of enhancing knowledge and skills of a complex and unstructured nature. For example, a development program might help managers become better leaders or develop multicultural skills. Management development now deals with two broad types of learner expectations. One extreme is a demand for bite-sized, job-related, on-demand learning, such as consulting a smart phone to learn how to calculate return on investment. At the other extreme is enrollment in a university program to escape a time-pressured, and often unreflective (no time to think about learning), learning environment.[37]

Managers play an important role in most types of training and development, particularly with respect to on-the-job training and development. We return to the topic of manager as teacher in discussions about mentoring in Chapter 10 and coaching in Chapter 16.

Most of this text and its accompanying course could be considered an experience in management training and development. The next paragraphs describe two vital aspects of training and development for employees and managers: needs assessment and the selection of an appropriate training program.

Needs Assessment and Selecting an Appropriate Training Program

Before embarking on a training program, an organization must determine what type of training is needed. When training programs fail, both traditional training and e-learning, it is often because there is no connection between learning and defined business needs.[38] Such an assessment generally benefits from including a job analysis and asking the managers themselves, their managers, and group members about the managers' need for training.

---

[35]Joe Mullich, "A Second Act for E-Learning," *Workforce Management,* February 2004, p. 51; George Anders, "Companies Find Online Training Has Its Limits," *The Wall Street Journal,* March, 2007, p. 83.

[36]Reported in Kathryn Tyler, "15 Ways to Train on the Job," *HR Magazine,* September 2008, p. 106.

[37]Steven J. Armstrong and Eugene Sadler-Smith, "Learning on Demand, at Your Own Pace, in Rapid Bite-Sized Chunks: The Future of Management Development?" *Academy of Management Learning & Education,* December 2008, p. 573.

[38]Sister Fister Gale, "Making E-Learning More Than Pixie Dust," *Workforce,* March 2003, p. 58.

| EXHIBIT 9-8 | A Sample Listing of Training Programs versus Development Programs |

Training programs listed in the left column are often included in a program of management development.

The programs on the right, however, are rarely considered to be specific skill-based training programs.

Training Programs	Management Development
World-class customer service	Effective team leadership
Applying ergonomics to the office	Gourmet cooking for teamwork
Introduction to human resources law	Strategic leadership
Salary administration	Maintaining a healthy workforce
Preventing and controlling sexual harassment	Strategic diversity
Telemarketing skills	Developing cultural sensitivity
Understanding financial statements	Open book management
Getting started in e-commerce	Principle-centered leadership
Fundamentals of e-learning	Retaining valued employees
Six Sigma basics	Becoming a charismatic leader
Dealing with difficult employees	Strategic human resources planning
Accident prevention	Building a social networking presence

Training and development needs can be identified for the entire organization, or portions of it. For example, an entire organization might be trained in how to use social networking to enhance the company's image.

Despite the importance of matching training and development programs to specific individual and organizational needs, universal training needs also require attention. The training would include elements such as communication, motivation, decision making, coaching, and time management.

After needs are assessed, a program must often be tailored to fit company requirements. The person assigning employees to training and development programs must be familiar with their needs for training and development, know the content of various programs, and enroll employees in programs that will meet their needs. Exhibit 9-8 presents a sample listing of training and development programs.

In addition to training and development programs, substantial learning takes place outside of the classroom and away from the computer. Many employees learn job skills and information by asking questions, sharing ideas, and observing each other. Such learning is spontaneous, immediate, and task specific. Much **informal learning** takes place in meetings, on breaks, and in customer interactions. The digitalization of information facilitates informal learning because workers can exchange information so readily.[39] Some companies have installed high round tables and white boards in

informal learning
Any learning in which the learning process is not determined or designed by the organization.

---

[39]Nancy Day, "Informal Learning Gets Results," *Workforce*, June 1998, p. 31; Marcia L. Conner, "Informal Learning," *Ageless Learner*, 1997–2005, http://agelesslearner.com/intros/informal.html, p. 2.

corridors and common areas around the company so workers can informally exchange ideas in addition to small talk.

LEARNING
OBJECTIVE

Explain the basics of a performance evaluation system.

PERFORMANCE EVALUATION (OR APPRAISAL)

Up to this point in the staffing model, employees have been recruited, selected, oriented, and trained. The next step is to evaluate performance. A **performance evaluation (or appraisal)** is a formal system for measuring, evaluating, and reviewing performance. The term *performance* appears self-explanatory. An analysis of dozens of studies indicates that performance has three major components:[40]

performance evaluation

A formal system for measuring, evaluating, and reviewing performance.

- *Task performance* is the accomplishment of duties and responsibilities associated with a given job (such as maintaining inventory at a profitable level).
- *Citizenship performance* is behavior that contributes to the goals of the organization by contributing to its social and psychological environment (such as voluntarily help a coworker with a technical problem).
- *Counterproductive performance* is voluntary behavior that harms the well-being of the organization (such as consistently insulting customers).

When managers evaluate performance, they are thinking of these components even when they are not explicitly aware of the components. For example, when a manager rates marketing assistant Maria "outstanding," the manager is most likely reacting to the fact that Maria (a) accomplished her marketing tasks, (b) was a cooperative company citizen, and (c) did not engage in counterproductive behavior such as disrupting meetings or regularly arriving late to work.

forced rankings

An offshoot of evaluating employees against a performance standard in which employees are measured against one another.

An offshoot of evaluating employees against a performance standard is to use **forced rankings** in which employees are measured against each other. Using this system, employees are ranked into three, four, or five "baskets." The baskets represent the best workers, the worst workers, and intermediate categories. One ranking approach is to force employees into the categories of "Top 20 percent, Vital 70 percent, and Bottom 10 percent." In some companies including GE, the rankings are considered guidelines over time; every grading period need not force workers forced into the bottom 10 percent. Forced rankings are also referred to as "rank and yank"; the employees ranked in the bottom basket are dismissed—often during a downsizing. Sometimes the bottom 10 percent is coached and trained toward higher performance.[41]

Forced rankings are highly controversial. A major criticism is that a manager might be responsible for a group of outstanding performers, yet be forced to declare a few as "bottom performers." Teamwork and cooperation

---

[40]Maria Rotundo and Paul R. Sackett, "The Relative Importance of Task, Citizenship, and Counterproductive Performance to Global Ratings of Job Performance: A Policy-Capturing Approach," *Journal of Applied Psychology*, February 2002, pp. 66–80.

[41]Steve Bates, "Forced Rankings," *HR Magazine*, June 2003, pp. 63–68; Jack and Suzy Welch, "The Case for 20-70-10," *Business Week*, October 2, 2006, p. 108.

are likely to suffer under such a zero-sum game. The emphasis on team structures changes performance appraisals in two major ways. One, groups as well as individuals are now subject to regular evaluation. Another change comes in the widespread use of multirating systems whereby several workers evaluate an individual. The most frequently used multirater system is **360-degree feedback**, in which a person is evaluated by most of the people with whom he or she interacts. An evaluation form for a manager might incorporate input from the manager's manager, all group members, other managers at his or her level, and even a sampling of customers when feasible. The manager's manager would then synthesize all the information and discuss it with him or her. Dimensions for rating a manager might include "gives direction," "listens to group members," "coaches effectively," and "helps the group achieve key results."

360-degree feedback
A performance appraisal in which a person is evaluated by a sampling of all the people with whom he or she interacts.

The rationale for using 360-degree feedback for performance evaluation is based on its ability to present a complete picture of performance. This technique is used as much for management and leadership development as for performance appraisal. As with most human resources programs, 360-degree evaluation for both evaluation and development works best when it begins with top-level managers and then cascades down through the organization.[42] The system is dependent on the raters giving honest, legitimate evaluations to friends and people they dislike.

Purposes of Performance Evaluation

Performance evaluations serve a number of administrative purposes and they can help the manager carry out the leadership function. A major purpose is to decide whether an employee should receive a merit increase and how large that increase should be. The evaluation process also identifies employees with potential for promotion. High-performing teams can be identified as well. Employee reviews are widely used to provide documentation for discharging, demoting, and downsizing employees who are not meeting performance standards.

Performance appraisals help managers carry out the leadership function in several ways. Suggesting areas for needed improvement can increase productivity. Also, the manager can help employees identify their needs for self-improvement and self-development. Appraisal results can be used to motivate employees by providing feedback on performance. Finally, a performance appraisal gives employees a chance to express their ambitions, hopes, and concerns, thereby enhancing career development.

Design of the Performance Evaluation System

traits
Stable aspects of people; closely related to personality.

Performance evaluation methods are usually designed to measure traits, behavior, or results. **Traits** are stable aspects of people, which are closely related to personality. Job-related traits include enthusiasm, dependability,

---

[42]John W. Fleenor, Sylvester Taylor, and Craig Chappelow, *Leveraging the Impact of 360-Degree Feedback* (San Francisco: Pfeiffer, 2008).

behavior
In performance evaluation, what people actually do on the job.

results
In performance evaluation, what people accomplish, the objectives they attain.

and honesty. **Behavior**, or activity, is what people do on the job. Job-related behavior includes working hard, keeping the work area clean, maintaining a good appearance, and showing concern for customer service. A worker's level of activity in company social networking sites might provide some clues to how frequently his or her opinion is sought by other workers. The content of the worker's blogs might provide hints about how well he or she represents the company to the community. **Results** are what people accomplish, the objectives they attain. Following is an example of a performance factor on an employee evaluation form that focuses on results:

	5	4	3	2	1
	☐	☐	☐	☐	☐
Quality of work is the accuracy and thoroughness of work.	Consistently unsatisfactory	Occasionally unsatisfactory	Consistently satisfactory	Sometimes superior	Consistently superior

Many performance evaluation systems consider results as well as traits and behaviors. For example, a worker might have achieved work goals (results), and also be described as having initiative (a behavior linked to a trait). The performance evaluation system should encourage some risk-taking behavior even if it could mean not reaching agreed-upon goals. Without prudent risk taking, innovation would be stifled.[43]

Employees are most satisfied with performance evaluation when they participate in the process. Participation can take a number of forms: jointly setting goals with the manager, submitting a self-appraisal as part of the evaluation, and having the opportunity to fully discuss the results.[44]

Many workers dislike having their performance evaluated; many managers dislike evaluating workers, particularly when negative feedback is involved. Some researchers propose eliminating performance appraisals. Such a move would be tantamount to abolishing grades in school. One alternative to performance appraisals is regular face-to-face conversations between managers and workers about performance, at least three or four times annually. Frequent reviews are particularly important during rapidly changing business conditions because priorities may change; for example, there may be a sudden need to cut costs or increase sales. Managers make written note of any problems workers experience; this creates the necessary documentation to support discipline or termination.[45] Regular conversations

---

[43]Jena McGregor, "The Struggle to Measure Performance," *Business Week*, January 9, 2006, p. 28.

[44]Brian D. Cawley, Lisa M. Keeping, and Paul E. Levy, "Participation in the Performance Appraisal Process and Employee Reactions: A Meta-Analytic Review of Field Investigations," *Journal of Applied Psychology*, August 1998, pp. 615–633.

[45]Jena McGregor, "The Struggle to Measure Performance," *Business Week*, January 9, 2006, p. 28; McGregor, "The Midyear Review's Sudden Impact," *Business Week*, July 6, 2009, pp. 50–52.

that accommodate documentation of poor performance simply translate into an informal system of performance appraisal, not its replacement.

Human resources writer Samuel A. Culbert suggests the use of performance *previews* instead of *reviews*. The manager and direct reports discuss how they, as teammates, will work together even more effectively and efficiently than they have done in the past (thereby overcoming problems). Of course, the organization still needs an evaluation of each worker's performance for administrative purposes.[46]

LEARNING OBJECTIVE 6
Summarize the basics of employee compensation.

COMPENSATION

Compensation, including pay and benefits, plays a major role in talent management (which also includes attracting and retaining valued employees in general, particularly during a labor shortage). Even when a firm is downsizing, key employees will be recruited and retained by juggling benefits. Compensation attracts considerable management attention because it constitutes about two-thirds of the cost of running most enterprises. Here we look at several types of pay and employee benefits. Chapter 11 will describe how compensation is used as a motivational device.

Types of Pay

Wages and salary are the most common forms of pay. Wages are payments to employees for their services, computed on an hourly basis or on the basis of the amount of work produced. Salary is an annual amount of money paid to a worker; it does not depend directly on output or hours worked. Nevertheless, future salary is dependent to some extent on how well the worker produced in the previous year. Many workers are eligible for bonuses or incentives to supplement their salary.

job evaluation
The process of rank-ordering jobs, based on job content, to demonstrate the worth of one job in comparison to another.

To determine how much a given job should receive in wages or pay, many companies perform a **job evaluation**, the rank-ordering of jobs based on job content, to demonstrate the worth of one job in comparison to another. Among the factors contributing to the content of a job are education, skill, mental demands, and physical demands. Each factor receives a weight, and the weights are added to determine how many points a job is worth. The greater the total points, the higher the pay.[47]

variable pay
When the amount of money a worker receives is partially dependent on his or her performance.

The major thrust in compensation for workers at all levels is **variable pay**, in which the amount of money a worker receives is partially dependent on performance. A worker might receive a bonus for having surpassed a performance standard, or a salary increase for the same reason. Performance-based compensation is increasing rapidly as employers struggle to remain competitive in price yet attract and retain capable workers. The assumption

---

[46]Samuel A. Culbert, "Get Rid of the Performance Review," *The Wall Street Journal*, October 20, 2008, p. R4.

[47]Deborah Keary, Saundra Jackson, and Vicki Neal, "Job Evaluations, Health Coverage, Discipline," *HR Magazine*, January 2004, p. 39.

MANAGEMENT IN ACTION

Goodyear Tire Stretches Compensation Dollars

Jobs at Goodyear Tire & Rubber Co., the largest tire maker in the United States, were coveted mainly because everyone from janitors to skilled machine operators could expect to eventually earn more than $20 an hour and generous benefits. That rich compensation is now slipping away. New workers hired under Goodyear's latest labor agreement earn just $13 an hour with fewer benefits for the first three years; many will likely never achieve the lofty pay packages of the past.

"Nobody is sticking their paycheck in my face and saying, 'Look what I made,' but you can't help thinking about it," says Ronald Guffey, a 43-year-old former corrections officer who signed on for a $13 job at Goodyear's sprawling plant in Gadsen, Alabama. Scott Bruton, a fellow tire builder who does the same job as Guffey, has been at the plant since 1984 and earns $23 an hour. "If I was doing the same job, working just as hard, and earning what they make, I'd be resentful," he says. Few people, he says, talk openly about the pay issue on the factory floor. "I feel sorry for these guys," continues Guffey.

Goodyear is like a growing number of old-line companies that have decided two-tier systems are the only way to keep domestic factories viable. Detroit's traditional Big Three automakers reached deals several years ago with the United Autoworkers union that will let them hire a group of workers that receive lower pay and benefits. The new workers will be paid roughly the same amount as Toyota Motor Corp.'s U.S. workers.

Case Questions
1. How does the two-tier system of wages for production workers compare to downsizing as a useful way of reducing operating costs for the company?
2. What impact might global outsourcing have on the wages paid to tire builders at this Goodyear factory in Gadsen, Alabama?
3. Suppose a new Goodyear tire maker does not want to work for a starting wage of $13. What can he or she do about it?

Source: Excerpted from Timothy Aeppel, "Pay Scales Divide Factory Floors," *The Wall Street Journal*, April 9, 2008, p. B4.

stack-ranking

A ranking system that requires managers to rank each employee within each unit and distribute raises and bonuses accordingly.

is that a talented worker will accept lower guaranteed pay if higher incentive pay is possible.[48]

Another approach to variable pay, **stack-ranking**, requires managers to rank each employee within each unit and distribute raises and bonuses accordingly. Yahoo! uses stack ranking to help retain top performers. According to the method, each member of a group of 25 people would be ranked 1 through 25, with person number 1 receiving the biggest share of the raise and bonus money allotted to the group. If the person ranked 25 was meeting job standards, he or she could still receive a raise or bonus. During performance evaluation, the Yahoo! workers are not told their specific ranking.[49]

---

[48]Jessica Marquez, "Premium on Productivity," *Workforce Management*, November 7, 2005, p. 22.

[49]Jena McGregor, "The Struggle to Measure Performance," *Business Week*, January 9, 2006, p. 28.

Employee Benefits

An **employee benefit** is any noncash payment given to workers as part of compensation for their employment. Employee benefits cost employers about 35 percent of salaries. An employee earning $40,000 per year in salary probably receives a combined salary and benefit package of $54,000. Under ideal circumstances, employee benefits should be linked to business strategy, meaning that these benefits should reward employees for achieving key business goals. Some companies only offer tuition assistance for courses that directly improve job performance. Honda of America reimburses an engineer for studying fuel cell technology, but would not reimburse an engineer for a course in acupuncture.

Exhibit 9-9 presents a representative list of employee benefits organized by type and frequency. Organizations vary considerably in the benefits and services they offer employees. No one firm is likely to have the same portfolio of benefits, particularly nonstandard benefits such as back massage services or on-company-premises dry-cleaning. One of the most humanitarian benefits is cash given to financially strapped families who face emergencies. For example, top-level management at 1-800 Contacts, a contact-lens vendor, has established an "associate outreach fund." One worked was assisted in making mortgage payments after a spouse was laid off.[50]

Benefits, especially healthcare insurance and pensions, have been looked upon carefully by management in recent years as a detriment to competing successfully against foreign competitors who do not bear such a heavy cost. In many countries, for example, health care is paid for directly or administered by the federal government. Many business firms in recent years have either decreased benefits to current employees or required them to pay a larger share, particularly with respect to healthcare. Many companies have eliminated healthcare and pension benefits, claiming they can no longer afford them.

One way to reduce the cost of healthcare insurance is to shift workers to a *consumer driven health plan* in which the worker assumes a much larger deductible before receiving reimbursement from the insurance company. For example, the worker might pay the first $1,000 in healthcare fees before reimbursement. Eleven percent of large employers now make a high-deductible plan their only healthcare benefit. "Consumer driven" refers to the idea that the worker (as a consumer) is likely to be sensitive to price and consume healthcare services only when really needed. Unhealthy employees tend to quickly burn through the deductible and are no longer sensitive to price, so the employer's cost savings may not be substantial.[51]

---

[50]"Best of the Juggle," *The Wall Street Journal*, September 8, 2009, p. B13.

[51]Jeremy Smerd, "Aetna Official Says CDHP Alone Won't Cut Costs," *Workforce Management*, August 14, 2006, p. 6; Smerd, "Bedside Manner in Switching to a Consumer Plan," *Workforce Management*, May 22, 2006, p. 33.

EXHIBIT 9-9   A Variety of Employee Benefits

Employers find that the right package of benefits will increase the chances an individual will stay with the firm for a relatively long time.

Common Health-Care Benefits

Health and dental insurance
Life insurance
Drug prescription program
Mental health insurance
Employee assistance program
Weight-loss program as part of
wellness program

Common Financial Benefits

ATM
Direct deposit
Credit union
Educational assistance
Defined-contribution retirement plan
Automobile allowance/expenses
Incentive bonus plan
Employee stock ownership
Financial counseling as part of
employee assistance program

Common Family-Friendly Benefits

Dependent care flexible spending
account
Flexible working hours
Compressed workweeks
Telecommuting
Job sharing
Bring child to work in emergency
Child-care referral service

Common Personal Services

Professional development opportunities
(seminars, conferences, courses, and so on)
Professional memberships
Casual dress everyday
Casual dress one day per week
Organization-sponsored sports teams
Food services/subsidized cafeteria
Club memberships

Less Common Benefits of All Types

On-site health-care clinics
Free lunches served on premises
Financial planning and counseling outside of
employee assistance program
Oil change/auto care
Massage therapy at work area
Lactation rooms for mothers of infants
Car-pooling subsidy
Company-supported childcare center
Company-supported eldercare center
Subsidizde cost of elder care
On-site laundry
Drop off packages for shipping service
Naptime during the workday
Animal pet health insurance
Bringing babies to work permitted
Animal pet allowed on company premises

Source: Stephanie Armour, "Voluntary Benefits Retain Their Luster," *USA Today* syndicated story, December 29, 2003; "What Benefits Are Companies Offering Now?" *HRfocus*, June 2000, p. 6; Jennifer Saranow, "Anybody Want to Take a Nap?" *The Wall Street Journal*, January 24, 2005, p. R5.

Few companies any longer offer the traditional benefit plan in which retirees are given a fixed pension for life, adjusted upward annually for inflation. Instead most employers offer a defined contribution plan, often referred to as a 401(k) plan. The employee contributes to the plan, and the employer often matches the employee contribution in part or in full. The money paid into the plan is tax deferred and earnings accrue on a tax-deferred basis. Employees usually have a broad choice of investments. Employees who quit take the 401(k) with them, as they would with any personal investment. For the employer, a 401(k) plan avoids such costs as $65,000 a year in pension paid to a worker who leaves at 55 and lives to be 100. If employees are diligent enough to invest seriously during their career, their portable 401(k) nest egg will be sufficient for retirement.

A strategic perspective about employee benefits combined with other humane management practices, such as empowerment and recognition, is that they contribute to worker sustainability. Simply, put workers stay healthier physically and mentally, and live longer, when they are treated well. Stanford University professor or organizational behavior, Jeffrey Pfeffer notes that when a company stresses its workers, costs are passed on to the health care system, such as public clinics and emergency rooms.[52] Humane treatment of employees is therefore socially responsible.

THE ROLE OF LABOR UNIONS IN HUMAN RESOURCE MANAGEMENT

LEARNING OBJECTIVE **7**
Understand the role of labor unions in human resource management.

When a public or private organization is unionized, the labor union influences almost all human resource programs and practices. A major purpose of a labor union is to attain fair treatment for workers in such areas as compensation; this includes health and retirement benefits, safe working conditions, working hours, job security, and work-life programs.

According to the United States Bureau of Labor Statistics, about 12.3 percent of wage and salary workers are union members; this number has been essentially stable for several years. The union membership rate has declined from a high of 20.1 percent in 1983, partially because of the manufacturing decline in North America. The unionization rate for government workers is 37.4 percent; the rate for private industry workers is 7.2 percent. The most heavily unionized public sector workers are teachers, police officers, and firefighters. Among private industries, transportation and utilities have the highest union membership rate at 22.2 percent. Twelve percent of manufacturing workers are organized.[53]

Because the manufacturing sector has been the hardest hit by foreign competition, union leaders are often unable to push for improved compensation including wages and health retirement benefits. Company executives threaten to send work offshore when union demands are too high. Another anti-union tactic, as in the case of automotive parts supplier Delphi Corporation, is to declare bankruptcy and have a judge nullify the union–management contract. Delphi then hired temporary workers at a lower wage rate to replace the union workers.

A concern management has had about unions over many years, particularly in manufacturing, is that union leaders attempt to avoid flexible work

---

[52]Jeffrey Pfeffer, "Building Sustainable Organizations: The Human Factor," *Academy of Management Perspectives,* February 2010, p. 43.

[53]This section follows closely "Union Members Summary," *Bureau of Labor Statistics News,* January 22, 2010.

rules that allow workers to rotate jobs as demanded by shifts in work assign-ments. For example, a welder would not be allowed to pitch in as a parts assembler. Another concern is that in some industries, union demands for compensation have made it difficult for companies to remain competitive. General Motors was able to operate profitably in Asia for a long time, but not in the United States, because the GM workers in Asia were not repre-sented by the United Auto Workers Union. Foreign car makers have estab-lished manufacturing facilities in several Southern states in recent years because of generous tax benefits and laws that make it easier to build a largely non-union workforce.[54] Union counterarguments are that workers should (a) receive a fair share of profits, and (b) not be expected to receive low wages to compensate for management bungling.

A reasonably balanced point of view is that when employers offer work-ers what they want and need, employee desire to unionize diminishes. Human resource strategies and policies like these discourage union activity; they are the type of demands labor unions typically seek.

- Fair and consistent policies and practices
- Open-door management policies (workers are free to discuss problems with management)
- Competitive pay and benefits
- Employee trust and recognition[55]

Many instances exist of healthy partnerships between management and labor unions in which both sides gain advantage. According to the American Rights to Work Group, Costco and Harley-Davidson are companies that partner well with unions.

1. *Costco Wholesale Corporation (International Brotherhood of Teamsters).* By providing wages and benefits above industry standards, this retail membership warehouse chain demonstrates that treating employees well is good for business.
2. *Harley-Davidson Motor Company (International Association of Machi-nists, United Steel Workers).* This leading motorcycle manufacturer part-ners with its employees' unions at every level; this boosts productivity and quality and keeps jobs in America.[56]

Perhaps not every business firm is in a position to have such progressive labor relations, yet the message is clear; working well with all stakeholders is associated with business success.

[54]Paulo Prada and Dan Fitzpatrick, "South Could Gain as Detroit Struggles," *The Wall Street Journal*, November 20, 2008, p. B1.

[55]Erin Patton, "How Can We Prevent a Union from Organizing in Our Company?" *HR Magazine*, September 2009, p. 28.

[56]Quoted from "The Labor Day List: Partnerships that Work," *American Rights to Work*, September 2005, pp. 1–2.

Summary of Key Points

1 **Explain how human resource and talent management is part of business strategy.**

Human resource and talent management is an integral part of business strategy. Without effective human resource management, the company cannot accomplish high-level goals such as competing globally, grabbing market share, and being innovative.

2 **Describe the components of talent management.**

The talent management (or staffing) model consists of seven phases: awareness of the legal aspects of staffing; strategic human resources planning; recruitment; selection; orientation, training and development; performance appraisal; and compensation. All phases can influence employee retention.

3 **Present an overview of recruitment and selection.**

Recruitment is the process of attracting job candidates with the right characteristics and skills to fit job openings and the organizational culture. Job descriptions and job specifications are necessary for recruiting. External and internal sources are used in recruiting, including online job boards, company Web sites, and social networking sites.

Candidates who perform well are the lifeblood of the firm. Selecting the right candidate from among those recruited may involve a preliminary screening interview, psychological and personnel testing, a job interview, reference checking, and a physical examination. The four types of psychological and personnel tests used most frequently in employee selection are situational judgment, aptitude, personality, and honesty and integrity. Tests should be scientifically accurate and nondiscriminatory toward any group.

Interviews are more valid when the interviewer is trained and experienced. Job interviews help both the interviewer and the interviewee acquire important information. Behavioral interviewing helps make the interview job-related. Job simulations are essentially a job tryout. Reference checks and background investigations are useful in making sound selection decisions, as is the physical examination.

4 **Present an overview of employee orientation (onboarding), training, and development.**

An employee onboarding program helps acquaint the newly hired employee with the firm. Training includes any procedure intended to foster and enhance employee skills. Development is a form of personal improvement that generally enhances knowledge and skills of a complex and unstructured nature. A needs assessment should be conducted prior to selecting training and development programs.

5 **Explain the basics of a performance evaluation system.**

A performance evaluation (or appraisal) is a standard method of measuring, evaluating, and reviewing performance of individuals and teams. The 360-degree appraisal involves feedback from many people. The forced-ranking method compares employees to each other. Performance evaluations serve important administrative purposes, such as helping managers make decisions about pay increases and promotions and carry out the leadership function. Appraisal systems measure traits, behavior, and results; some systems take into account more than one factor.

6 **Summarize the basics of employee compensation.**

Workers are typically paid wages or salaries, bonuses, and sometimes additional payment for job skills. The purpose of job evaluations is to determine how much a job is worth. Variable pay is used to motivate employees and reduce company expenses. Employee benefits are a major part of compensation. Compensation is a major factor in recruiting and retaining employees, yet expensive benefits such as health insurance and pensions have been reduced in recent years to help companies face global competition.

7 **Understand the role of labor unions in human resource management.**

The labor union influences almost all human resource programs and practices. A major purpose of a labor union is to attain fair treatment for workers in such areas as compensation, health and retirement benefits, safe working conditions, flexible working hours, job security, and work-life programs. Companies can counterinfluence unions by offering the type of compensation, policies, and work practices that workers would like to have. Many instances exist of healthy partnerships between management and labor unions, as described by the American Rights to Work Group.

Key Terms and Phrases

Talent management, 306
Job embeddedness, 309
Affirmative action, 310
Strategic human resource planning, 312
Recruitment, 313
Job specification, 314
Realistic job preview, 321
Behavioral interviewing, 321
Reference check, 323
Employee orientation program, 326
Training, 326
E-learning, 327

Development, 328
Informal learning, 329
Performance evaluation (or appraisal), 330
Forced rankings, 330
360-degree feedback, 331
Traits, 331
Behavior, 332
Results, 332
Job evaluation, 333
Variable pay, 333
Stack-ranking, 334
Employee benefit, 335

Questions

1. What is your opinion about paying human resource managers as much as managers in other functions such as marketing, operations, and finance?
2. What would you see as the advantages and disadvantages of keeping your résumé on a popular social networking site if you are currently employed?
3. Why should a manager who does not work in the human resources department be familiar with the various aspects of talent management?
4. Noted psychologist David McLelland once said, "They say you can teach a squirrel to fly. But it's easier to hire the eagle." Assuming that's true, what implications does the statement have for staffing and human resource management?
5. What have you learned about talent management that you might apply to your own job search?
6. Why do so many people dislike performance evaluations?
7. Several Web sites have emerged that claim they can tell you how to cheat on personality tests so you will appear desirable to employers who use these tests as part of their candidate screening. What is your opinion of the ethics of such Web sites?

Skill-Building Exercise 9-A: Presenting Yourself in 30 Seconds

A well-accepted belief about recruiters, hiring managers, and employment interviewers is that they form a quick impression of a candidate, often within the first ten seconds. With this fact in mind, develop a 30-second opening presentation about yourself with the goal of creating a favorable impression on people making judgments about your job qualifications. Facts to pack into your 30-second statement might include your name, type of work sought, education, experience, and key accomplishments. Be creative. Many job seekers have found the 30-second self-promotion speech invaluable when meeting with recruiters or attending job fairs. Give your 30-second presentation to a few fellow students to obtain their feedback, and return the favor to them.

Skill-Building Exercise 9-B: The Selection Interview

Assume the role of manager or employment interviewer of tech support for Apple Inc. The support center provides support to customers who already own Apple computers and consumer electronic devices including the iPod, iPhone, and iPad. After thinking through the job demands of a tech support center representative, conduct a 15-minute interview of a classmate who pretends to apply for the tech support center rep position. Before conducting the interview, review the guidelines in Exhibit 9-6. Other students on your team might observe the interview and then provide constructive feedback.

Management Now: Online Skill-Building Exercise: Recruiting on the Net

Place yourself in the role of a manager who is recruiting qualified job applicants to fill one or more of the following positions: (a) sales representative of machine tools, (b) customer service supervisor who speaks English and Spanish, and (c) social networking marketing specialist. Use the Internet to conduct your search for a pool of candidates. A good starting point might be the job boards (Web sites for job hunters). Limit your search to candidates who appear to have posted their credentials within the last 60 days. Remember, in this exercise you are looking for job candidates, not a position for yourself. Try to determine whether you can locate job applicants without paying an employer fee.

9-A Case Problem

The Scrutinized Job Candidates

Kelly is a partner at a recruiting firm in Chicago, Illinois. She explains that a job candidate's behavior comes under careful watch the moment he or she arrives at the placement firm. "We use whatever data we can to build a portrait of you."

The receptionist notices whether you are using your cell phone to make calls and send and receive text messages. We also look to see if you are scrolling through apps on your smart phone rather than reading the employer's annual report. She may also keep tabs on your hygiene habits, such as whether you sneeze into the air instead of a handkerchief or facial tissue.

Suppose a candidate is escorted to an interviewer's office door, and the candidate marches right in even though the interviewer is involved in a call. Kelly thinks that's a faux pas, with it being better to wait outside the office until the call is completed. After you get started with the interview, and you peek at your smart phone from time to time, you can appear socially inept. Kelly says that several times in recent months, aspiring vice presidents have pulled out smart phones during interviews with one of the partners at the placement firm. The candidates were told sternly that it was time to shut down their device. It is better to check on a work crisis before and after the interview.

Kelly will often suggest that candidates take their car to a restaurant for lunch because the car is parked nearby. First Kelly observes the cleanliness of the vehicle both inside and out. When a vehicle looks like a Dumpster on the inside or is excessively dirty on the outside, she assumes that the candidate is sloppy and disorganized. Kelly, as well as the other partners in the firm, also makes a few inferences about the way the candidate drives. A candidate who drives beyond the speed limit or races through yellow lights is regarded as possibly irresponsible. On the other hand a candidate who drives too slowly might be perceived as too cautious for a job requiring high imagination.

Kelly has observed that a few candidates will swear at other drivers who cut them off or wait too long to start driving when the light turns green. She regards such behavior as reflectting poor emotional control.

Similar with many other recruiters, Kelly asks the receptionist how she was treated by the candidate. She notes, "One time we immediately disqualified a candidate because he started ordering the receptionist around. Offered a soft drink, he insisted on a fresh fruit drink. Later, he asked the receptionist to bring up the MSBN Website on her desktop so he could check the stock market results."

Discussion Questions

1. How fair is it for the recruiters described here to reject candidates because they display poor manners, such as receiving e-mail messages during the job interviews?
2. Of what significance is it if the candidate who is waiting scrolls through applications on a smart phone instead of reading the company annual report?
3. How valid is Kelly's belief that the way a person drives is related to job performance in aspects of a job that does not involve driving?
4. What lessons do these recruiters have for graduates seeking entry-level technical and professional jobs?

9-B Case Problem

Performance Rankings at Portland Events Planners

Rob is the founder and owner of Portland Events Planners, a company that plans events for a wide variety of companies in and around the Portland area. The events include trade shows, product demonstrations, business conferences at hotels, and videoconferences. A staff of five professionals performs the activities necessary for selling the company's services to businesses and for doing the event planning. Rob is involved in the same activities of obtaining new business and event planning. The six professionals are assisted by an administrative staff of four people.

After five years of operation without one, Rob decides that it is time to implement a formal performance evaluation system. After studying the idea of performance evaluation and speaking to a talent management professional in his network, Rob decides that most performance-evaluation systems are too top-down. He thinks that he would like a more democratic system of performance evaluation, particularly because the staff work closely together as a team. Rob decided on a performance evaluation method that focused on each team member rating the contribution of all other team members, supplemented by his own rating.

Next, Rob sent an e-mail to all staff members explaining his evaluation system. The e-mail was followed up by a staff meeting to discuss the new system before its implementation. Rob began the meeting with a brief explanation:

"As described in my e-mail, the new evaluation system is quite simple. Each of you will anonymously rate the contribution of each staff member to our company's success on a 1-to-10 scale, with 10 indicating a super contribution. I will also give a rating, so the maximum rating anyone could have would be 60, a score of 10 from each of the six raters. The minimum score you could receive would be a six. I will allocate salary increases based somewhat on the results of the evaluation. What do you think, gang? I want you to react one by one."

The five staff members of Portland Event Planners reacted as follows:

Linda: "I like the system because it is objective. Of course, the ratings tell us nothing about what each of us is doing right or wrong."

Tom: "Rob, I like the idea of peer input. But I'm afraid that your ratings will simply reflect how much we like each other. So, I'm expecting to receive 59 points." [Laughter from the team.]

Kitty: "I see some good things about this new system. The system seems objective because we wind up with numerical ratings. But the system is really subjective; you will not be making salary decisions based on tangible, measured accomplishments."

José: "I disagree with Kitty. Most of our sales and our planning is really a joint effort. It is difficult to pin down who among us really accomplished what on his or her own. I'd say, let's give the new system a chance."

Laura: "Rob, I see some merit in this system. But before endorsing it, I want your assurance that you will sit down with us one by one and discuss the ratings. I think you should also give each of us your personal feedback."

With a reflective look, Rob replied, "I've really learned a lot this morning about your high level of professionalism and your interest in performance evaluation. Let me think about what you have told me, and I will get back to you."

Discussion Questions

1. What is your evaluation of the system of performance evaluation Rob is proposing?
2. Explain which two suggestions from the team members you think are the most valid.
3. Considering the nature and size of Portland Events Planners, what type of performance evaluation system do you recommend Rob implement?

Leadership

The crash had hit Silicon Valley as hard as anywhere else. The only consolation was that this time, at least, it didn't start here. But while other firms were hunkering down and trying to survive, networking giant Cisco Systems continued to strive forward. "Even in this downturn," said chairman and CEO John Chambers, sitting at the table in his modest memento-crammed office, "We intend to be the most aggressive we've ever been."

A decade ago Cisco was known for building the switching systems (routers) that find the most efficient path for information on the Internet. These days it has a presence in just about every corner of the Web's infrastructure—from networking hardware (switches, gateways, and the like) to network management software to the router that runs the wireless network in your home.

Cisco had no major layoffs during the economic downturn and made no salary cuts. Furthermore, the company announced its intention to pursue 30 disparate new market areas—from sports to the smart grid (delivering electricity efficiently through digital technology) to cloud computing (using thousands of computers to share work)—simultaneously.

"You never want to waste a good crisis," Chambers says with a smile, as he publicly predicted an average 12% to 17% annual growth over the course of the next five years whatever happens to the economy in the short term. "We basically wrote the press release for five years from now," he said, "and now we plan to live up to it."

Chambers credits his parents (an obstetrician/gynecologist father and a psychologist mother who also ran a restaurant) with giving him a doctor's approach to business problems. "They taught me to focus on the long-term health of the patient, and not to treat symptoms but the underlying problem."

As is mentioned in every biography of the man, John Chambers is a severe dyslexic, although that didn't keep him from earning a law degree from West Virginia University and an MBA from Indiana University. "He had this optimistic attitude about everything," his childhood reading therapist would say. "He was just not going to fail. One thing I notice as I hear him now on TV is that he still has that attitude."[1]

The story about the successful executive in the Internet equipment field illustrates how the right type of leader can direct others through good times and bad times. The story also explains that successful leaders can overcome personal adversity. **Leadership** is the ability to inspire confidence and support among the people who are needed to achieve organizational goals.[2] This chapter focuses on leadership in business firms, which is important at every organizational level. For example, an office manager who is an effective leader helps keep the company running smoothly by motivating and encouraging the office workers to perform at their best. Successful professionals, regardless of their job titles, generally possess leadership capabilities. In order to cope with frequent change and to solve problems, people exercise initiative and leadership in taking new approaches to their job. In the modern organization, people slip in and out of leadership roles such as a temporary assignment as a task force leader.

In this chapter we describe the characteristics and behaviors of leaders in organizations, useful leadership theories, leadership during times of adversity, and key leadership skills.

leadership
The ability to inspire confidence and support among the people who are needed to achieve organizational goals.

---

[1]Michael S. Malone, "The Weekend Interview with John Chambers: Silicon Valley Survivor," *The Wall Street Journal*, July 25–26, 2009, p. A11.

[2]W. Chan Kim and Renee A. Maubourgne, "Parables of Leadership," *Harvard Business Review*, July–August 1992, p. 123.

LEARNING OBJECTIVE **1**

Differentiate between leadership and management.

THE LINK BETWEEN LEADERSHIP AND MANAGEMENT

Today's managers must know how to lead as well as manage in order to have an effective organization. (You will recall that leadership—along with planning, organizing, and controlling—is one of the basic functions of management.) Three representative distinctions between leadership and management follow:[3]

* Management is more formal and scientific than leadership. It relies on universal skills such as planning, budgeting, and controlling. Management is a set of explicit tools and techniques based on reasoning and testing that can be used in a variety of situations.
* Leadership involves having a vision of what the organization can become. Leadership requires eliciting cooperation and teamwork from a large network of people and keeping the key people in that network motivated, using every manner of persuasion.
* Managing focuses on continuous improvement of the status quo, whereas leadership is a force for change that compels a group to innovate and depart from routine. Leadership requires having a vision.

 PLAY VIDEO

Go to www.cengage.com/management/dubrin and view the video for Chapter 10. You'll see that even a town must have leadership. How would you describe this town's leaders? What challenges are they facing?

Effective leadership and management are both required in the modern workplace; to be an effective leader, one must also be an effective manager.[4] Managers must be leaders, but leaders must also be good managers. Workers must be inspired and persuaded, but they also need assistance in developing a smoothly functioning workplace. Henry Mintzberg asks, "How would you like to be managed by someone who doesn't lead? …Well then why would you want to be led by someone who doesn't manage?" A leader who doesn't manage will most likely not know what is going on in his or her operation.[5]

One such effective manager and leader is Kevin Johnson, the president of the Windows platform and services division at Microsoft. He has been described as a hard-headed operator with the shrewdness of Bill Gates and the personal skills of Oprah Winfrey. "I love business, I love technology, I love customers, and I love people," he says.[6]

Exhibit 10-1 presents an overview of the link between leadership and management. It also highlights several of the major topics presented in this chapter. The figure illustrates that to bring about improved productivity and morale, managers do two things. First, they use power, authority, influence,

---

[3]John P. Kotter, *A Force for Change: How Leadership Differs from Management* (New York: Free Press, 1990); David Fagiano, "Managers versus Leaders," *Management Review*, November 1997, p. 5; Herminia Ibarra and Otilia Obodaru, "Women and the Vision Thing," *Harvard Business Review*, January 2009, p. 65.

[4]Gary Yukl and Richard Lepsinger, "Why Integrating the Leading and Managing Roles is Essential for Organizational Effectiveness," *Organizational Dynamics*, No. 4, 2005, pp. 361–373.

[5]Henry Mintzberg, *Managing* (San Francisco: Berrett-Koehler), 2009, p. 8.

[6]"Star Power," *Fortune*, February 6, 2006, p. 58.

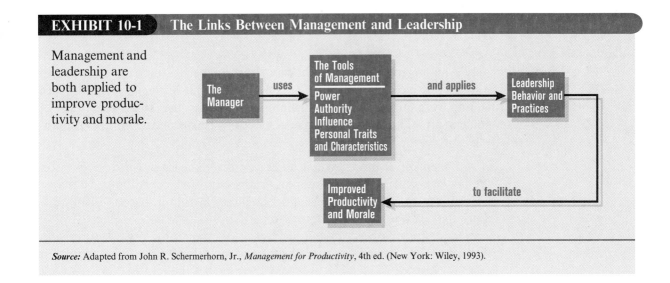

EXHIBIT 10-1   The Links Between Management and Leadership

Management and leadership are both applied to improve productivity and morale.

The Manager → uses → The Tools of Management: Power, Authority, Influence, Personal Traits and Characteristics → and applies → Leadership Behavior and Practices → to facilitate → Improved Productivity and Morale

Source: Adapted from John R. Schermerhorn, Jr., *Management for Productivity*, 4th ed. (New York: Wiley, 1993).

and personal traits and characteristics. Second, they apply leadership behaviors and practices.

THE LEADERSHIP USE OF POWER AND AUTHORITY

LEARNING OBJECTIVE **2**
Describe how leaders are able to influence and empower team members.

power
The ability or potential to influence decisions and control resources.

authority
The formal right to get people to do things or the formal right to control resources.

Leaders influence people to do things through the use of power and authority. **Power** is the ability or potential to influence decisions and control resources. Powerful people have the potential to exercise influence, and they exercise it frequently. For example, a powerful executive might influence an executive from another company to do business with his or her company. **Authority** is the formal right to get people to do things or the formal right to control resources. Factors within a person, such as talent or charm, help them achieve power. Only the organization, however, can grant authority. To understand how leaders use power and authority, we examine the various types of power, influence tactics, and how leaders share power with team members. Understanding these different approaches to exerting influence can help a manager become a more effective leader.

Types of Power

Leaders use various types of power to influence others. However, the power exercised by group members, or subordinates, acts as a constraint on how much power leaders can exercise. The list that follows describes the types of power exercised by leaders and sometimes by group members.[7]

---

[7]John R. P. French Jr. and Bertram Raven, "The Bases of Social Power," in Dorwin Cartwright and Alvin Zander (eds.), *Group Dynamics: Research and Theory* (New York: Harper & Row, 1960), pp. 607–623.

1. *Legitimate power* is the authentic right of a leader to make certain types of requests. These requests are based on internalized social and cultural values in an organization. It is the easiest type of influence for most subordinates to accept. For example, virtually all employees accept the manager's authority to conduct a performance evaluation.

2. *Reward power* is a leader's control over rewards of value to the group members. Exercising this power includes giving salary increases and recommending employees for promotion. Wealth leads to considerable reward power; being an extremely wealthy leader has become almost synonymous with power.

3. *Coercive power* is a leader's control over punishments. Organizational punishments include assignment to undesirable working hours, demotion, and firing. Effective leaders generally avoid heavy reliance on coercive power because it creates resentment and sometimes retaliation.

4. *Expert power* derives from a leader's job-related knowledge as perceived by group members. This type of power stems from having specialized skills, knowledge, or talent. Expert power can be exercised even when a person does not occupy a formal leadership position. An advertising copywriter with a proven record of writing winning ad slogans has expert power, and so does a marketing manager who knows how to create demand for a product.

5. *Referent power* refers to the ability to control based on loyalty to the leader and the group members' desire to please that person. Having referent power contributes to being perceived as charismatic, but expert power also enhances charisma.[8] Part of the loyalty to the leader is based on identification with the leader's personal characteristics. Referent power and charisma are both based on the subjective perception of the leader's traits and characteristics.

6. *Subordinate power* is any type of power that employees can exert upward in an organization, based on justice and legal considerations. This type of power restricts the extent to which power can be used to control them. For example, certain categories of workers cannot be asked to work overtime without compensation, and a worker need not put up with being sexually harassed by the boss.

The preservation of power can be important to executives, even for an exemplary leader such as John Chambers at Cisco. To help implement the many acquisitions he plans, he established 48 councils so managers can make decisions without waiting for his approval. Two former Cisco executives say that the arrangement of councils is an effective way for Chambers to consolidate power. Diluting authority by spreading it among a number of councils (or committees) may prevent any one manager from gaining too

---

[8]Jeffrey D. Kudisch et al., "Expert Power, Referent Power, and Charisma: Toward the Resolution of a Theoretical Debate," *Journal of Business and Psychology*, Winter 1995, p. 189.

much control. The same skeptics said that heirs apparent at Cisco rarely lasted at the company for very long.[9]

Despite some constraints on leadership power, a small number of executives abuse power; for example, they use the corporate jet for personal vacations and pay for personal services such as home renovation with company funds.

Influence Tactics

In addition to various types of power, leaders use many other influence tactics to get things done. Influence tactics are especially important in the modern organization, where you often have to influence people over whom you lack formal authority. Various groups team up informally to accomplish work without the benefit of a command-and-control hierarchy. Eight frequently used influence tactics follow. Exhibit 10-2 presents statements used for research purposes to measure three of these influence tactics.

1. *Leading by example* means that the leader influences group members by serving as a positive model of desirable behavior. A manager who leads by example shows consistency between actions and words. For example, suppose a firm has a strict policy on punctuality. The manager explains the policy and is always punctual. The manager's words and actions provide a consistent model. A popular connotation of leading by example is for the manager to demonstrate a strong work ethic by working long and hard, and expecting others to do the same.

2. *Leading by values* means the leader influences people by articulating and demonstrating values that guide the behaviors of others. Using values to influence others is similar to the organizational culture guiding behavior. Ideal values for a leader to pursue include mutual respect, trust, honesty, fairness, kindness, and doing good.[10] According to Medtronic executive Bill George, an important part of leading by values is to be authentic by staying true to your values, such as being more concerned about employee welfare than trying to appease outside financial analysts.[11]

3. *Assertiveness* refers to being forthright in your demands. It involves expressing what you want done and how you feel about it. Assertiveness also refers to making orders clear. A supervisor might say, for example, "This break room is a mess. It nauseates me, and I want it cleaned up by tomorrow morning at 8:30."

---

[9]Peter Burrows, "Cisco's Extreme Ambitions," *Business Week*, November 30, 2009, pp. 026–029.

[10]Manuel London, *Principled Leadership and Business Diplomacy: Value-Based Strategies for Management Development* (Westport, CT: Quorum Books, 1999).

[11]Bill George, *Authentic Leadership: Rediscovering the Secrets to Creating Lasting Value* (San Francisco: Jossey-Bass, 2003).

| **EXHIBIT 10-2** | **The Measurement of Three Organizational Influence Tactics** |

Person to be described: (Quite often a person's immediate manager.)

Instructions: The purpose of this questionnaire is to learn more about the different ways people try to influence each other in work organizations. Please describe how much the person indicated above uses each type of behavior in an effort to influence you. For each behavior item, select one of the following response choices, and write the number for your choice on the line provided.

1. I can't remember him/her ever using this tactic with me
2. He/she very seldom uses this tactic with me
3. He/she occasionally uses this tactic with me
4. He/she uses this tactic moderately often with me
5. He/she uses this tactic very often with me

Ingratiation

___ 1. Says you have the special skills or knowledge needed to carry out a request.
___ 2. Praises your past performance or achievements when asking you to do a task.
___ 3. Praises your skill or knowledge when asking you to do something.
___ 4. Says you are the most qualified person when asking you to perform a task.

Exchange

___ 5. Offers something you want in return for your help on a task or project.
___ 6. Offers to do something for you in exchange for you carrying out a request.
___ 7. Offers to do a specific task or favor for you in the future in return for your help and support now.
___ 8. Offers to do something for you in the future in return for your help now.

Coalition

___ 9. Mentions the names of other people who endorse a proposal when asking you to support it.
___10. Gets others to explain to you why they support a proposed activity or change that you are being asked to support or help implement.
___11. Brings someone along for support when meeting with you to make a request or proposal.
___12. Asks someone you respect to help influence you to carry out a request or support a proposal.

Source: Gary Yukl, Charles F. Seifert, and Carolyn Chavez, "Validation of the Extended Influence Behavior Questionnaire," *The Leadership Quarterly*, October 2008, pp. 618–620. © Gary Yukl

4. *Rationality* means appealing to reason and logic. Strong leaders use this tactic frequently. Pointing out the facts of a situation to group members in order to get them to do something is an example of rationality. For example, a middle-level manager might tell a supervisor, "If our department goes over budget this year, we are likely to be cut further next

year." Knowing this information, the supervisor will probably become more cost conscious. Appealing to reason and logic works best when the leader is perceived as knowledgeable.

5. *Ingratiation* refers to getting somebody else to like you, often through the use of political skill. A typical ingratiating tactic would be to act in a friendly manner just before making a demand. Effective managers treat people well consistently to get cooperation when it is needed. A representative example is Timothy D. Cook, the second-in-command executive at Apple Inc. Part of his ability to influence others is based on his being so well liked. Cook is said to have "the courtly demeanor of a Southern Gentleman."[12]

6. *Exchange* is a method of influencing others by offering to reciprocate if they meet your demands. Leaders with limited expert, referent, and legitimate power are likely to use exchange and make bargains with subordinates. A manager might say to a group member, "If you can help me out this time, I'll go out of my way to return the favor." Using exchange is like using reward power. The emphasis in exchange, however, is that the manager goes out of his or her way to strike a bargain that pleases the team members.

7. *Coalition formation* is a way of gaining both power and influence. A **coalition** is a specific arrangement of parties working together to combine their power, thus exerting influence on another individual or group. Coalitions in business are a numbers game—the more people you can get on your side, the better. For example, a manager might band with several other managers to gain support for a major initiative such as merging with another company.

8. *Joking and kidding* are widely used to influence others on the job. Good-natured ribbing is especially effective when a straightforward statement might be interpreted as harsh criticism. In an effort to get an employee to stop Internet surfing so much during the work day, the supervisor said, "I know that you have 7,000 friends on Facebook, but please stay in touch with only your business contacts during the day."

So which influence tactic should a leader choose? Leaders are unlikely to use all the influence tactics in a given situation. Instead, they tend to choose an influence tactic that fits the demands of the circumstances. For example, leading by values works best when a manager is highly placed in the organization and the influencing need not be done in a hurry. Rationality might work best in a fast-paced team setting such as a meeting to discuss a product introduction.

Although influence tactics are presented here from the standpoint of the leader using them, recognize that in today's organization influence runs in many directions. Leaders influence subordinates, subordinates influence leaders, and people at various organization levels influence each other. Many

coalition
A specific arrangement of parties working together to combine their power, thus exerting influence on another individual or group.

---

[12]Nick Wingfield, "Apple's No. 2 Has Low Profile, High Impact," *The Wall Street Journal*, October 16, 2006, p. B9.

workers are considered to be active agents who influence and are influenced by others.[13] Relevant examples here include a group member influencing the manager to try a new system of minimizing inventory, and one division manager influencing another to give telecommuting a try in her division.

Employee Empowerment and the Exercise of Power

Chapter 8 emphasized empowerment as a way of distributing authority in the organization. Empowerment is a way for leaders to share power, also referred to as shared leadership. When leaders share power, employees experience a greater sense of personal effectiveness and job ownership. Sharing power with group members enables them to feel better about themselves and become better motivated. The extra motivation stems from a feeling of being in charge. An important use of empowerment is to enhance customer service. As employees acquire more authority to take care of customer problems, these problems can be handled promptly, sometimes right on the spot.

A cornerstone belief underlying empowerment is that leadership in a team can and should be shared. Shared leadership also means that leadership should flow between individuals on teams, depending on the nature of the task and the skills of the team members. Not only do leaders share power with team members, they also share power with each other. According to management professors Craig L. Pearce, Charles C. Manz, and Henry P. Sims, Jr., teams that share leadership consistently outperform those whose leadership is centralized in the hands of a top-down designated leader.[14] In this respect, empowerment enhances performance.

A key component of empowerment is the leader's acceptance of the employee as a partner in decision making. Because the team member's experience and information are regarded as equal to those of the leader, he or she shares control. Both the leader and team member must agree on what is to be accomplished. The partnering approach to empowerment builds trust between the employee and the leader.[15] Mark Pincus, the founder and chief executive of Zynga, a provider of online social games, practices empowerment regularly. He provides this example:

> *We had this really motivated, smart receptionist. She was young. We kept outgrowing our phone systems, and she kept coming back and saying, "Mark, we've got to buy a whole new phone system." And I said:*

---

[13]Analysis by Richard Osburn in book review of May Uhl-Bien and Russ Marion, *Complexity Leadership: Conceptual Foundations* (Charlotte, NC: Information Age Publishing, 2008). The review appears in *Academy of Management Review*, October 2008, p. 1015.

[14]Craig L. Pearce, Charles C. Manz, and Henry P. Sims Jr., "Where Do We Go from Here? Is Shared Leadership the Key to Team Success?" *Organizational Dynamics*, July–September 2009, pp. 234–239.

[15]Frank J. Navran, "Empowering Employees to Excel," *Supervisory Management*, August 1992, p. 5.

"I don't want to hear about it. Just buy it. Go figure it out." She spent a week or two meeting every vendor and figuring it out. She ended up running our whole office."[16]

Self-Leadership and Empowerment

self-leadership
The process of influencing oneself.

For empowerment to work well, people must exercise **self-leadership**, the process of influencing oneself.[17] Self-leadership is possible because most people have the capacity to lead themselves, particularly when faced with difficult yet important tasks. At the same time, people are intrinsically (internally) motivated to perform well when they engage in challenging tasks, as in job enrichment. A manager could give the group an opportunity to practice self-leadership with an assignment such as this: "We need to find a way to boost productivity 10 percent in our division starting next month. I am going to Ireland on a business trip for ten days. You can stay in touch with me by e-mail if you like, but the assignment is yours. When I return, I will accept your three best suggestions for boosting productivity."

According to Charles C. Manz, Henry Sims, and Christopher P. Neck, managers can help group members to practice effective self-leadership through three core steps.[18] First, the leader must set an example of self-leadership through such means as setting his or her own goals, making work enjoyable, and accepting rather than avoiding challenges. Second, the leader should give encouragement and instruction in self-leadership skills. Asking appropriate questions can be helpful: What goals have you established? What aspects of your work give you the biggest kick? What obstacles have you overcome lately? Third, the leader should reward accomplishment in self-leadership, such as giving feedback on progress and praising initiative. The manager returning from a trip might say (if true), "These two productivity boosting suggestions you made look like winners. I really appreciate the way you followed through on this project."

Cross-cultural Factors and Empowerment

Empowerment as a leadership technique works better in some cultures than in others. To the extent that cultural values support the manager sharing power with group members, the more likely it is that empowerment will lead to higher productivity and morale. A team of researchers investigated how well the management practice of empowerment fit different cultures. Data were collected from employees from a U.S.-based multinational

---

[16]"Corner Office—Mark Pincus—Every Worker Should be C.E.O. of Something," *The New York Times* (www.nytimes.com), February 3, 2010, p. 2.

[17]Charles C. Manz and Christopher P. Neck, *Mastering Self-Leadership: Empowering Yourself for Personal Excellence*, 3rd ed. (Upper Saddle River, NJ: Pearson Prentice Hall, 2004), p. 5; Neck and Manz, *Mastering Self-Leadership*, 4th ed., 2007.

[18]Manz and Neck, *Mastering Self-Leadership*, pp. 138–139; Charles Manz and Henry P. Sims Jr., "Self-Management as a Substitute for Leadership: A Social Learning Theory Perspective," *Academy of Management Review*, No. 5, 1980, pp. 361–367.

corporation with operations in the United States, Mexico, Poland, and India. The results associated with empowerment varied with the country and culture. Workers in the United States, Mexico, and Poland had favorable views of their supervisors when they used a high degree of empowerment. Indian employees, however, rated their supervisor low when empowerment was high. (Indians value unequal power between superiors and subordinates, and expect the supervisor to retain most of the power.)[19]

LEARNING OBJECTIVE ❸
Identify important leadership characteristics and behaviors.

CHARACTERISTICS, TRAITS, AND BEHAVIORS OF EFFECTIVE LEADERS

Understanding leadership requires an understanding of leaders as individuals. This section will highlight findings about the personal characteristics and behaviors of effective managerial leaders. An assessment of the characteristics and behaviors of leaders translates into the idea that these same positive attributes of a leader will facilitate his or her effectiveness in comparable settings, such as customer service departments in different companies.

The term *effective* is essential for understanding the relevance of leadership. An effective leader makes a positive impact on the organization or group in terms of productivity and morale. Having the right traits and characteristics facilitates effectiveness, but these traits, characteristics, and behaviors alone do not constitute leadership effectiveness. Fortunately for students of leadership, an analysis of 20 years of studies shows that the right type of leader does improve organizational performance.[20]

A key point to recognize in your development as a leader is that leadership encompasses a wide variety of personal qualities and behaviors that could be relevant in a given situation. David Corderman, chief of the Leadership Development Institute at the FBI, notes: "Effective leadership entails such a wide variety of behaviors and skills across an extensive array of circumstances that no one person could possibly be born with all of the qualities necessary to serve in that capacity for all situations. Effective leadership therefore involves in most cases a substantial degree of acquired learning."[21]

Characteristics and Traits of Effective Leaders

Possessing certain characteristics and traits does not in itself guarantee success. Yet effective leaders differ from others in certain respects. Studying leadership traits is also important because a person who is perceived to embody certain traits is more likely to be accepted as a leader. For example,

---

[19]Christopher Robert et al., "Empowerment and Continuous Improvement in the United States, Mexico, Poland, and India: Predicting Fit on the Dimensions of Power Distance and Individualism," *Journal of Applied Psychology*, October 2000, pp. 643–658.

[20]Robert B. Kaiser, Robert Hogan, and S. Bartholomew Craig, "Leadership and the Fate of Organizations," *American Psychologist*, February–March 2008, pp. 96–110.

[21]Quoted in "What Is Leadership? The FBI Takes It On," *Executive Leadership*, October 2006, p. 4, Adapted from *The FBI Law Enforcement Bulletin*.

people see managers whom they believe to be good problem solvers as able to help overcome obstacles and create a better workplace. Hundreds of human qualities can enhance leadership effectiveness in some situations. Recent scholarly writing emphasizes that leadership effectiveness arises from the combined influence of several characteristics.[22] For example, to develop strategy leaders need high intelligence and self-confidence and also effective interpersonal skills to implement the strategy. Here we present a sampling of factors relevant to many work settings. [23]

power motivation
A strong desire to control others and resources or get them to do things on your behalf.

1. *Drive and passion.* Leaders are noted for the effort they invest in their work and the passion they have for work and work associates. Carol Bartz, the CEO of Yahoo, observes, "If you're not excited, how can you get others excited? People will know. It's like how kids and dogs can sense when people don't like them."[24]

2. *Power motive.* Successful leaders exhibit **power motivation**, a strong desire to control others and resources and get them to do things on your behalf. A leader with a strong power need enjoys exercising power and using influence tactics. A manager who uses power constructively would more likely be promoted rapidly in an ethical corporation. Bill Gates, formerly of Microsoft, exemplifies a power-obsessed leader who aggressively pursued a market domination strategy. He now uses his power through his foundation to help combat malnutrition and AIDS throughout the world.

3. *Self-confidence combined with humility.* Self-confidence contributes to effective leadership in several ways, in addition to being part of leadership efficacy. Above all, self-confident leaders project an image that encourages subordinates to have faith in them. Self-confidence also helps leaders make some of the tough business decisions they face regularly. When a dose of humility is combined with self-confidence, the leader is likely to be even more influential. A key aspect of humility is being able to put other people in the limelight, thereby enhancing their self-esteem.[25]

4. *Trustworthiness and honesty.* Trust is regarded as one of the major leadership attributes. Continuing waves of downsizings, financial scandals, and gigantic compensation to executives have eroded employee trust

---

[22]Stephen J. Zaccaro, "Trait-Based Perspectives on Leadership," *American Psychologist*, January 2007, p. 12.

[23]Sean T. Hannah, Bruce J. Avolio, Fred Luthans, and P.D. Harms, "Leadership Efficacy: Review and Future Directions," *Leadership Quarterly*, December 2008, pp. 669–692; Timothy A. Judge, Ronald F. Piccolo, and Tomek Kosalka, "The Bright and Dark Sides of Leader Traits: A Review and Theoretical Extension of the Leader Trait Paradigm," *The Leadership Quarterly*, December 2009, pp. 855–875; Orlando Behling, "Employee Selection: Will Intelligence and Conscientiousness Do the Job?" *Academy of Management Executive*, February 1998, pp. 77–86.

[24]"Top Leaders Tell their Secrets," *Fortune*, December 12, 2005, p. 128.

[25]Martha Finney, *In the Face of Uncertainty: 25 Top Leaders Speak Out on Challenge, Change, and the Future of American Business* (New York: AMACOM, 2002).

and commitment in many organizations. Effective leaders know they must build strong employee trust to obtain high productivity and commitment. A major strategy for being perceived as trustworthy is to make your behavior consistent with your intentions. Such behavior is referred to as leadership authenticity. Practice what you preach and set the example. Allowing group members to participate in decisions is another trust builder.[26]

A recent study in a medical healthcare system looked at the effects of trusting supervisors and management in relation to both job tasks and interpersonal relations. Trusting the supervisor with respect to interpersonal relationships had the biggest impact on positive job behaviors. Both types of trust in supervisors and management tended to have a positive impact on job satisfaction and commitment to the organization.[27] The relevance of this study is that it demonstrates that having trust in leaders and managers helps the organization.

Closely related to trustworthiness and honesty is being open with employees about the financial operations and other sensitive information about the company. In an **open-book company** every employee is trained, empowered, and motivated to understand and pursue the company's business goals. In this way employees become business partners. A company in Texas that repairs airplane parts reduced the bill for shop supplies by 91 percent through open-book management. One saving was to substitute heavy-duty tape that cost $25 a roll with tape that cost $2.50 per roll.[28]

To help you link the abstract concept of trust to day-by-day behavior, take the self-quiz in Exhibit 10-3. You might use the same quiz in relation to any manager you have worked for.

5. *Good intellectual ability, knowledge, and technical competence.* Effective leaders are good problem solvers and knowledgeable about the business or technology for which they are responsible. They are likely to combine academic intelligence with practical intelligence (the ability to solve everyday problems based on experience). An analysis of 151 studies found a positive relationship between intelligence and the job performance of leaders. The relationship is likely to be higher when the leader plays an active role in decision making and he or she is not overly stressed.[29] The intellectual

open-book company

A firm in which every employee is trained, empowered, and motivated to understand and pursue the company's business goals.

---

[26]Kurt T. Dirks and Donald L. Ferrin, "Trust in Leadership: Meta-Analytic Findings and Implications for Research and Practice," *Journal of Applied Psychology*, August 2002, p. 622; Rob Goffee and Gareth Jones, "Managing Authenticity: The Paradox of Great Leadership," *Harvard Business Review*, December 2005, pp. 86–94.

[27]Jixia Yang and Kevin W. Mossholder, "Examining the Effects of Trust in Leaders: A Bases and Foci Approach," *Leadership Quarterly*, February 2010, pp. 50–63.

[28]John Case, "HR Learns How to Open the Books," *HR Magazine*, May 1998, p. 72; Stan Luxenberg, "Open Those Books: Boost Your Biz by Sharing Info," *Business Week Small Biz*, Summer 2006, p. 32.

[29]Timothy A. Judge, Amy E. Colbert, and Remus Ilies, "Intelligence and Leadership: A Quantitative Review and Test of Theoretical Propositions," *Journal of Applied Psychology*, June 2004, pp. 542–552.

ability required for leadership also involves thinking on a grand scale about the organization, as in formulating business strategy.

Technical competence, or knowledge of the business, often translates into close attention to details about products and services. Steve Jobs of Apple Inc. represents one of the most outstanding examples of how a leader's knowledge of the business, combined with creative thinking, contributes to organizational success. During his medical leave of absence from the company in 2009, Jobs continued to work on Apple's major strategies and products. His involvement included working on the user interface of the iPhone operating system.[30]

6. *Sense of humor.* An effective sense of humor is an important part of a leader's job. In the workplace, humor relieves tension and boredom, defuses hostility, and helps build relationships with group members. The manager who makes the occasional witty comment is likely to be perceived as approachable and friendly.

7. *Emotional intelligence.* Effective leaders demonstrate good emotional intelligence, the ability to manage themselves and their relationships effectively. Emotional intelligence broadly encompasses many traits and behaviors related to leadership effectiveness, including self-confidence, empathy, passion for the task, and visionary leadership. Being sensitive to the needs of others (and not insulting or verbally abusing them) is another part of emotional intelligence. Richard Anderson, the chief executive of Delta Airlines, provides us an everyday example of the relevance of emotional intelligence. He says that the most important leadership lesson he has learned is to be patient and not lose his temper. Anderson notes that when a leader loses his or her temper, it squelches debate and sends the wrong signal about how you want your organization to run.[31]

Another important aspect of emotional intelligence is to create good feelings in those being led. The good moods and positive emotions help group members perform at their best; they become excited about the task and might even be more creative. One way in which leaders bring about good moods is to encourage the positive expression of feelings in others and avoid being cranky, hostile, and miserable themselves.[32]

8. *Leadership efficacy.* A good way of concluding how personal characteristics contribute to leadership effectiveness is the comprehensive trait of **leadership efficacy.** This refers to a specific form of efficacy (or feeling effective) associated with the level of confidence in the knowledge, skills,

---

[30]Yukari Iwatani Kane, "Job Maintains Grip at Apple," *The Wall Street Journal,* April 11–12, 2009, p. A1.

[31]Cited in Adam Bryant, "He Wants Subjects, Verbs and Objects," *The New York Times* (nytimes.com), April 26, 2009, p. 1.

[32]Daniel Goleman, "Leadership That Gets Results," *Harvard Business Review,* March–April 2000, p. 80; Goleman, Richard Boyatzis, and Annie McKee, *Primal Leadership: Realizing the Power of Emotional Intelligence* (Boston: Harvard Business School Press, 2002).

EXHIBIT 10-3	Behaviors and Attitudes of a Trustworthy Leader

The following behaviors and attitudes characterize leaders who are generally trusted by their group members and other constituents. After you read each characteristic, indicate whether this behavior or attitude is one you have developed already, or does not fit you at present.

	Fits Me	Does Not Fit Me
1. Tells people he or she is going to do something, and then always follows through and gets it done	☐	☐
2. Is described by others as being reliable	☐	☐
3. Keeps secrets and confidences well	☐	☐
4. Tells the truth consistently	☐	☐
5. Minimizes telling people what they want to hear	☐	☐
6. Is described by others as "walking the talk"	☐	☐
7. Delivers consistent messages to others in terms of matching words and deeds	☐	☐
8. Does what he or she expects others to do	☐	☐
9. Minimizes hypocrisy by not engaging in activities he or she tells others are wrong	☐	☐
10. Readily accepts feedback on behavior from others	☐	☐
11. Maintains eye contact with people when talking to them	☐	☐
12. Appears relaxed and confident when explaining his or her side of a story	☐	☐
13. Individualizes compliments to others rather than saying something like "You look great" to a large number of people	☐	☐
14. Does not expect lavish perks for himself or herself while expecting others to go on an austerity diet	☐	☐
15. Does not tell others a crisis is pending (when it isn't) just to gain their cooperation	☐	☐
16. Collaborates with others to make creative decisions	☐	☐
17. Communicates information to people at all organizational levels	☐	☐
18. Readily shares financial information with others	☐	☐
19. Listens to people and then acts on many of their suggestions	☐	☐
20. Generally engages in predictable behavior	☐	☐

Scoring: These statements are mostly for self-reflection, so no specific scoring key exists. However, the more statements that fit you, the more trustworthy you are—assuming you are answering truthfully. The usefulness of this self-quiz increases if somebody who knows you well answers it for you to supplement your self-perceptions.

and abilities associated with leading others. It helps to believe that you can accomplish the job when you take on a leadership role. The feeling of efficacy can be based on some of the traits already described, including self-confidence and intellectual ability suited to the leadership task.

Behaviors and Skills of Effective Leaders

Traits alone are not sufficient to lead effectively. A leader must also behave in certain ways and possess key skills. The actions or behaviors described in the following list are linked to leadership effectiveness. Recognize, however, that behaviors are related to skills. For example, in giving emotional support to team members, a leader uses interpersonal skills. A valuable part of understanding leadership behaviors is to know that they can be learned and can be translated into doable tasks.[33] In reality, leaders are neither born nor made; they are a combination of genetic predisposition and learning. For example, you might have good native cognitive intelligence but you must cultivate thinking big to become an effective executive. Leadership behaviors and skills include the following:

1. *Is adaptable to the situation.* Adaptability reflects the contingency viewpoint: A tactic is chosen based on the unique circumstances at hand. Research with trauma resuscitation teams (as in an emergency room) at a medical center documents this tried and true observation about leadership behavior. Empowering leadership was found to be more effective when severity of the trauma was low (for example, a broken leg) and team experience was high. In contrast, directive leadership was more effective when trauma severity was high (for example, a gunshot wound to the head) or when the team was inexperienced.[34] Another important aspect of adaptability is a leader's ability to function effectively in different situations, such as leading equally well in a manufacturing or office setting or even with a different cultural group. A former Coke director said of Muhtar Kent, the CEO of Coca Cola Company, "He can meet with the janitor in a bottling plant and minutes later go meet with a prime minister and be equally effective."[35] The ability to size up people and situations and adapt tactics accordingly is a vital leadership behavior.

2. *Establishes a direction for and demands high standards of performance from group members.* A major contribution of the leader at any level is to point the group in the right direction or work with them to figure out what the group should be doing. The direction becomes a clear vision of the future. Maigread Eichten, president and chief executive of FRS, a maker of energy drinks, points out that her job is not to make everybody happy. Instead, she says, "My job is to chart the right course

[33]Sharon Daloz Parks, *Leadership Can Be Taught: A Bold Approach for a Complex World* (Harvard Business School Press, 2005).

[34]Seokhwa Yun, Samer Faraj, and Henry P. Sims Jr., "Contingent Leadership Effectiveness of Trauma Resuscitation Teams," *Journal of Applied Psychology*, November 2005, pp. 1288–1296.

[35]Duane D. Stanford, "Coke's New President is Polished, Worldly," *The Atlanta Journal-Constitution*, December 8, 2006.

and, at the end of the day, I leave this building and if I feel like I've done the right thing and people respect me, I'm happy."[36]

After setting a direction, effective leaders consistently hold group members to high standards of performance, which raises productivity. (The leader might also set high standards for directions already in place.) Setting high expectations for subordinates becomes a self-fulfilling prophecy. People tend to live up to the expectations set for them by their superiors. Setting high expectations might take the form of encouraging team members to establish difficult objectives.

3. *Is visible and maintains a social presence.* An effective way of making an impact as a leader is to be visible to group members and maintain a presence. Leaders are often tempted to stay in their own work area performing analytical work or dealing with e-mail. Being visible allows for spontaneous communication with group members and creates a relaxed atmosphere in which to hear about problems. Being visible also creates the opportunity for coaching group members. Jeff Immelt, the chairman and CEO of General Electric, believes that being visible is essential for carrying out his leadership role. He spends more than one-half his time on the road visiting customers, employees, and shareholders.[37]

4. *Provides emotional support to group members.* Supportive behavior toward subordinates usually increases leadership effectiveness. A supportive leader frequently gives encouragement and praise: "Jack, if it were not for your super effort over the weekend, we couldn't have opened the store today." The emotional support generally improves morale and sometimes improves productivity. Being emotionally supportive comes naturally to the leader who has empathy for people and who is a warm person.

5. *Gives frequent feedback and accepts feedback.* Giving group members frequent feedback on their performance is another vital leadership behavior. The manager rarely can influence the behavior of group members without appropriate performance feedback. Feedback helps in two ways. First, it informs employees of how well they are doing, so they can take corrective action if needed. Second, positive feedback encourages subordinates to keep up the good work. The late John Wooden was one of the greatest basketball coaches in history, and became a leadership advisor. He emphasized how listening for feedback contributes to learning. He said that you must listen to those under your supervision and to your superiors. "We'd all be a lot wiser if we listened more—not just hearing the words, but listening and not thinking about what we're going to say."[38]

---

[36]Quoted in "Corner Office: The CEO Must Decide Who Swims," *The New York Times*, (www.nytimes.com), August 24, 2009, p. 1.

[37]Carol Hymowitz, "GE Chief is Charting His Own Strategy, Focusing on Technology," *The Wall Street Journal*, September 23, 2003, p. B1.

[38]Quoted in Casey Feldman, "Game Changers," *Fortune*, July 21, 2008, p. 54.

6. *Plays the role of servant leader.* Some effective leaders believe that their primary mission is to serve the needs of their constituents, including employees, customers, and communities. They measure their effectiveness in terms of their ability to help others. Because servant leaders are more concerned about the needs of their constituents, they usually show qualities such as patience, honesty, good listening skills, and appreciation of others. Instead of seeking individual recognition, servant leaders see themselves as working for the group members. Another defining characteristic of servant leaders is their high level of integrity. The servant leader uses his or her talents to help group members. For example, if the leader happens to be a good planner, he engages in planning because it will help the group attain its goals.[39]

Many academic administrators see themselves as servant leaders; they take care of administrative work so instructors can devote more time to teaching and scholarship. To be an effective servant leader, a person needs the many leadership traits and behaviors described in this chapter.

LEADERSHIP STYLES

LEARNING
OBJECTIVE **4**
Describe
participative
leadership,
authoritarian
leadership, the
Leadership Grid,
situational
leadership, and
entrepreneurial
leadership.

leadership style
The typical pattern of behavior that a leader uses to influence his or her employees to achieve organizational goals.

participative leader
A leader who shares decision making with group leaders.

Another important part of the leadership function is **leadership style**. It is the typical pattern of behavior that a leader uses to influence his or her employees to achieve organizational goals. Several different approaches to describing leadership styles have developed over the years. Most of these involve how much authority and control the leader turns over to the group. The historically important Theory X and Theory Y presented in Chapter 1 can be interpreted as two contrasting leadership styles. First, this section will describe two basic leadership styles, the participative and the autocratic. We then describe the Leadership Grid, the situational model of leadership, and the entrepreneurial leadership style. A skill-building exercise at the end of the chapter gives you a chance to measure certain aspects of your leadership style.

Participative Leadership Style

A **participative leader** is one who shares decision making with group members. The modern organization generally favors this model. In this complex world, the leader does not have all the answers. Shared leadership mentioned in relation to empowerment might be considered an approach to carrying out the participative style. Team leaders use the participative style so frequently that participative leadership is also referred to as the *team leadership style*. Participative leadership takes many forms. The group decision-making

---

[39]Robert K. Greenleaf, *The Power of Servant Leadership* (San Francisco: Berrett-Koehler Publishers Inc., 1998); Robert C. Liden, Sandy J. Wayne, Haoi Zhao, and David Henderson, "Servant Leadership: Development of a Multidimensional Measure and Multi-Level Assessment," *Leadership Quarterly*, April 2008, pp. 161–171.

techniques described in Chapter 5 are participative because group input is relied on heavily.

Three closely related subtypes of participative leaders include consultative, consensus, and democratic. *Consultative leaders* confer with subordinates before making a decision. However, they retain the final authority to make decisions. *Consensus leaders* encourage group discussion about an issue and then make a decision that reflects the general opinion (consensus) of group members. All workers who will be involved in the consequences of a decision have an opportunity to provide input. A decision is not considered final until all parties involved agree with the decision. *Democratic leaders* confer final authority on the group. They function as collectors of opinion and take a vote before making a decision.

Although a pure democratic style of leadership may seem unsuited to business, it has been a cornerstone philosophy at the highly successful Brazilian equipment supplier, Semco. Of the employees' 3,000 votes on a variety of work issues, CEO Ricardo Semler gets only one. Employees even played a major role in setting their own compensation.[40]

Participative leadership works well with people who want to share decision making and whose cultural values accept group members sharing leadership. Using consensus and democratic leadership is time consuming and results in much time spent in physical and electronic meetings. Executive Chairman Bill Ford Jr. said, in analyzing the problems at Ford Motor Company, "Maybe one of the drawbacks of our culture is that we've been too democratic, and that may have slowed us down."[41] Ford Motor later rebounded from these problems in part due to faster decision making.

Autocratic Leadership Style

autocratic leader
A task-oriented leader who retains most of the authority for himself or herself and is not generally concerned with group members' attitudes toward decisions.

Autocratic leaders retain most of the authority for themselves. They make decisions in a confident manner and assume that group members will comply. An autocratic leader is not usually concerned with group members' attitudes toward the decision. Typical autocratic leaders tell people what to do; they assert themselves and serve as models for group members. During a crisis, autocratic leadership is often welcome because group members want someone to point them in the right direction in a hurry. In a crisis, the situation may be so dire that the leader does not have sufficient time to attain consensus on a recovery plan.

Many autocratic leaders practice hands-on-management, meaning that they get involved in the details of the operation. When the leader has good expertise, the hands-on approach can be helpful in teaching others and in getting key tasks accomplished. Pushed to extreme, the hands-on style can create morale problems. A case in point is Massimo F. d'Amore, the CEO

---

[40]"Ricardo Semler's Huge Leap of Faith," *Executive Leadership*, April 2006, Adapted from Lawrence M. Fisher, "Ricardo Semler Won't Take Control," *strategy + business*.

[41]Bryce G. Hoffman, "Mulally Already Shaking up Ford," *The Detroit News* (http://www.detnews.com), September 22, 2006.

of PepsiCo Americas Beverages. He placed himself in the center of brand management, hiring and firing ad agencies and helping to develop and edit commercials. His hands-on style annoyed marketing executives and a few left voluntarily. D'Amore recognizes that he bruised a few egos, yet explained that changes needed to be implemented rapidly.[42]

Donald Trump is a power-oriented business leader and celebrity with a brusque and autocratic leadership style. He contributes heavily to decisions such as which type of marble to choose for a hotel lobby. Trump is well liked by construction workers and by many staff members. "The Donald" may be autocratic, but he is not vicious. In Trump's words, "One of the most important lessons my parents taught me was to treat people with respect, even if I'm angry with them."[43]

Leadership Grid Leadership Styles

Several approaches to understanding leadership styles focus on two major dimensions of leadership: tasks and relationships. Research extending over 50 years has shown that the dimensions of tasks and relationships contribute to both performance and satisfaction. Task behavior is more related to performance; relationship behaviors are more closely related to satisfaction.[44] The best known approach to basing style on tasks and relationships is the **Leadership Grid.**® It is based on different integrations of the leader's concern for production (results) and people (relationships). The Grid (a.k.a., The Managerial Grid) is part of a comprehensive program of management and leadership training that addresses the fundamental values and attitudes that influence behavior. The Grid has evolved over the years; its most recent version is presented in Exhibit 10-4.

Concern for results is rated on the Grid's horizontal axis. Concern for production includes results, bottom line, performance, profits, and mission. Concern for people is rated on the vertical axis; it includes concern for group members and coworkers. Both concerns are leadership attitudes or ways of thinking about leadership. Each of these concerns (or dimensions) exists in varying degrees along a continuum from 1 to 9. A manager's standing on one concern is not supposed to influence his or her standing on the other. As shown in Exhibit 10-4, the Grid encompasses seven leadership styles.

The developers of the grid argue strongly for the value of sound management (9, 9). According to their research, the sound management approach pays off. It results in improved performance, low absenteeism and turnover,

Leadership Grid®
A visual representation of different combinations of a leader's degree of concern for task-related issues.

---

[42]Burt Helm, "Blowing Up Pepsi," *Business Week*, April 27, 2009, p. 032.

[43]Quoted in Robert Kiyosaki, "Why the Rich Get Richer," *Yahoo! Finance* (http://www.finance.yahoo.com), November 29, 2006.

[44]Timothy A. Judge, Ronald F. Piccolo, and Remus Ilies, "The Forgotten Ones? The Validity of Consideration and Initiating Structure in Leadership Research," *Journal of Applied Psychology*, February 2004, pp. 36–51.

EXHIBIT 10-4 **The Leadership Grid™**

The Managerial Grid graphic below is a very simple framework that elegantly defines seven basic styles that characterize workplace behavior and the resulting relationships. The seven managerial Grid styles are based on how two fundamental concerns (concern for people and concern for results) are manifested at varying levels whenever people interact.

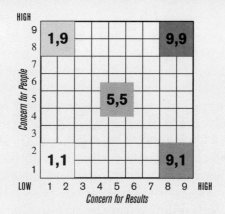

The Seven Managerial Grid Styles:

9,1 Controlling (Direct & Dominate)

I expect results and take control by clearly stating a course of action. I enforce rules that sustain high results and do not permit deviation.

1,9 Accommodating (Yield & Comply)

I support results that establish and reinforce harmony. I generate enthusiasm by focusing on positive and pleasing aspects of work.

5,5 Status Quo (Balance & Compromise)

I endorse results that are popular but caution against taking unnecessary risk. I test my opinions with others involved to assure ongoing acceptability.

1,1 Indifferent (Evade & Elude)

I distance myself from taking active responsibility for results to avoid getting entangled in problems. If forced, I take a passive or supportive position.

PAT Paternalistic (prescribe & Guide)

I provide leadership by defining initiatives for myself and others. I offer praise and appreciation for support, and discourage challenges to my thinking.

OPP Opportunistic (Exploit & Manipulate)

I persuade others to support results that offer me private benefit. If they also benefit, that's even better in gaining support. I rely on whatever approach is needed to secure an advantage.

9,9 Sound (Contribute & Commit)

I initiate team action in a way that invites involvement and commitment. I explore all facts and alternative views to reach a shared understanding of the best solution.

and high morale. Team management relies on trust and respect, which help bring about good results.[45]

Applied to the executive suite, the team management approach can result in a high-commitment, high-performance organization. CEOs of these exceptional companies earn the trust of people through their willingness to accept candid feedback. They are heavily engaged with their people and build strong relationships with them. At the same time, they mobilize their employees around a focused agenda (or business purpose) and concentrate on one or two initiatives. Two examples of high-commitment, high-performance CEOs are Russ Fradin of Hewitt Associates (human resource services) and James W. Griffith of Timkin (anti-friction products, transmissions, and specialty steel).[46] Keep in mind, however, that if you visited one of these companies you would not find that every employee is highly committed and highly productive despite the overall success of the company.

Situational Leadership®II (SLII)

Situational leadership II (SLII)

A concept that explains how to match leadership style to capabilities of group members on a given task.

In another major perspective on leadership, effective leaders adapt their leadership style to the requirements of the situation (such as whether the group is facing a crisis and swift, decisive action is called for by the leader).[47] Many other variables are also important, such as the organizational culture and the characteristics of group members. **Situational leadership II (SLII)**, a concept identified by Kenneth H. Blanchard and his colleagues, explains how to match leadership style to capabilities of group members on a given task.[48] For example, you might need less guidance from the supervisor when you are skilled in a task than when you are performing a new task.

Situational Leadership II is designed to increase the frequency and quality of conversations about performance and professional development between managers and group members so that competence is developed, commitment takes place, and turnover among talented workers is reduced. Leaders are taught to use the leadership style that matches or responds to the needs of the situation.

Situational Leadership II stems from the original situational model that has been widely studied in leadership and used in training programs. The major premise of SLII is that the basis for effective leadership is managing the relationship between a leader and a subordinate on a given task. The major concepts of the SLII model are presented in Exhibit 10-5. According to SLII, effective leaders adapt their behavior to the level of *commitment* and

[45]Robert R. Blake and Anne Adams McCanse, *Leadership Dilemmas—Grid Solutions* (Houston: Gulf Publishing, 1991).

[46]Russel A. Eisenstat et al, "The Uncompromising Leader," *Harvard Business Review*, July–August 2008, pp. 50–57.

[47]Victor H. Vroom and Arthur G. Jago, "The Role of the Situation in Leadership," *The American Psychologist*, January 2007, pp. 17–24.

[48]Kenneth H. Blanchard, David Zigarmi, and Robert Nelson, "Situational Leadership after 25 Years: A Retrospective," *Journal of Leadership Studies 1*, 1993, pp. 22–26: "Building Materials Leader Builds Better Leaders," http://www.kenblanchard.com.

EXHIBIT 10-5	Situational Leadership II (SLII)

For best results on a given task, the leader is required to match style to the developmental level of the group member.

Each quadrant indicates the desired match between leader style and subordinate developmental level.

Supporting (relationship behaviors) ↕

Style 3	Style 2
Supporting: Low on directing and high on supporting behaviors	**Coaching:** High on directing and high on supporting behaviors
Developmental level 3	**Developmental level 2**
Capable but cautious performer: Growing competence and variable commitment	**Disillusioned learner:** Some competence but low commitment
Style 4	Style 1
Delegating: Low on directing and low on supporting behaviors	**Directing:** High on directing and low on supporting behaviors
Developmental level 4	**Developmental level 1**
Self-reliant achiever: Highest level of commitment and competence	**Enthusiastic Beginner:** Low competence but high commitment

◄———————— **Directing (task-related behaviors)** ————————►

competence of a particular subordinate to complete a given task. For example, team member Russ might be committed to renting some empty office space by year-end and also highly skilled at such activity. Or he might feel that the task is drudgery and he might not have much skill in selling office space. The combination of the subordinate's commitment and competence determines his or her *developmental level*, as follows:

- **D1**—Enthusiastic Beginner. The learner has low competence but high commitment.
- **D2**—Disillusioned Learner. The individual has gained some competence but has experienced several setbacks. Commitment at this stage is low.
- **D3**—Capable but Cautious Performer. The learner has growing competence, yet commitment is variable.
- **D4**—Self-reliant Achiever. The learner has high competence and commitment.

Situational Leadership II explains that effective leadership depends on two independent behaviors: *supporting* and *directing*. Supporting refers to relationship behaviors such as listening, giving recognition, communicating, and encouraging. Directing refers to task-related behaviors such as giving careful directions and controlling. As shown in Exhibit 10-4, the four basic styles are as follows:

- **S1**—Directing. High directive behavior/low supportive behavior.
- **S2**—Coaching. High directive behavior/high supportive behavior.

- **S3**—Supporting. Low directive behavior/high supportive behavior.
- **S4**—Delegating. Low directive behavior/low supportive behavior.

A key point of SLII is that no one style is best: an effective leader uses all four styles depending on the subordinate's developmental level on a given task. The most appropriate leadership style among S1 to S4 corresponds to the subordinate developmental levels of D1 to D4 respectively. Specifically, enthusiastic beginners (D1) require a directing (S1) leader; disillusioned learners (D2) need a coaching (S2) leader; capable but cautious workers (D3) need a supporting-style (S3) leader; and self-reliant achievers (D4) need a delegating (S4) style of leader.

Situational leadership represents a consensus of thinking about leadership behavior in relation to group members: competent people require less specific direction than do less competent people. The model has gone through several versions. There is evidence to support the advice to give new employees more direction and to use more supportive behavior and less direct behavior as the employee becomes more experienced in the task.[49]

The model is also useful because it builds on other explanations of leadership that emphasize the role of task and relationship behaviors. As a result, it has proved to be useful as the basis for leadership training. Because the situational model also corroborates common sense, it is intuitively appealing. You can benefit from this model by attempting to diagnose the commitment and competence of group members before choosing the right leadership style.

A challenge in applying SLII is that the leader must stay tuned into which task a group member is performing at a given time and then implement the correct management style. Given that assignments change rapidly and group members often work on more than one task in a day, the leader would have to keep shifting styles. SLII presents categories and guidelines so precisely that it gives the impression of infallibility. In reality, leadership situations are less clear cut than the four quadrants suggest. Also, the prescriptions for leadership will work only some of the time. For example, many supervisors use a coaching style (S2) with a disillusioned learner (D2) and still achieve poor results.

The Entrepreneurial Leadership Style

Interest in entrepreneurial leadership is intense because start-up companies and other small enterprises are an important source of new employment. Many new small businesses arise to meet the demand of larger firms that outsource work. Managers who initiate one or more innovative business enterprises show several similarities in leadership style. Entrepreneurs often possess the following personal characteristics and behaviors:

1. *A strong achievement need.* Entrepreneurs have stronger achievement needs than most managers. Building a business is an excellent vehicle

---

[49]Geir Thompson and Robert P. Vecchio, "Situational Leadership Theory: A Test of Three Versions," *Leadership Quarterly*, October 2009, p. 846.

for accomplishment. The high achiever shows three consistent behaviors and attitudes. He or she (a) takes personal responsibility to solve problems, (b) attempts to achieve moderate goals at moderate risks, and (c) prefers situations that provide frequent feedback on results (readily found in starting a new enterprise).[50] As part of their achievement need, entrepreneurs are often in a hurry to get projects accomplished and move on to the next project.

2. *High enthusiasm, creativity, and visionary perspective.* Related to the achievement need, entrepreneurs are typically enthusiastic, creative, and visionary. Their enthusiasm makes them persuasive. As a result, entrepreneurs are often perceived as charismatic by their employees and customers. The enthusiasm of entrepreneurs propels them into a hurrying mode much of the time. Creativity is needed to find new business ideas. Successful entrepreneurs carefully observe the world around them, in constant search for their next big marketable idea, leading to a vision. They see opportunities others fail to observe. One example is Andy Taylor, who founded Enterprise Rent-a-Car. The opportunity he saw was to build a car rental agency that specialized in renting cars to airline travelers and people whose cars were being repaired. Enterprise is now a major player in the car rental business.

3. *Uncomfortable with hierarchy and bureaucracy.* Entrepreneurs, by temperament, are not ideally suited to working within the mainstream of a bureaucracy. Many successful entrepreneurs are people who were frustrated by the constraints of a bureaucratic system. Once the typical entrepreneur launches a successful business, he or she often hires a professional manager to take over the internal workings of the firm. The entrepreneur is then free to concentrate on making sales, raising capital, and pursuing other external contacts. One of the reasons entrepreneurs have difficulty with bureaucracy is that they focus their energies on products, services, and customers. Some entrepreneurs are gracious to customers and moneylenders but brusque with company insiders.

The leadership styles described here relate directly to the leadership behavior of adaptability to the situation. Leaders who achieve the best results do not stick with one leadership style. The effective executive selects the best style to fit a given situation, much as a golfer selects the appropriate club for a particular shot. Imagine that Louisa starts her business career as a manager of a fast-service restaurant. Most of the workers are inexperienced and poorly motivated, so Louisa focuses on giving them emotional support and showing them how to perform basic tasks such as preparing sandwiches to specification. Later in her career Louisa becomes a home-office executive in the same company. Louisa can now focus on her creative and strategic side, and provide subordinates more latitude.

---

[50]David C. McClelland, *The Achieving Society* (New York: Van Nostrand Reinhold, 1961).

LEARNING OBJECTIVE 5
Describe transformational and charismatic leadership.

TRANSFORMATIONAL AND CHARISMATIC LEADERSHIP

The study of leadership often emphasizes the **transformational leader**—the one who helps organizations and people make positive changes in the way they do things. Transformational leadership combines charisma, inspirational leadership, and intellectual stimulation. It plays an especially critical role in the revitalization of existing business organizations. The transformational leader develops new visions for the organization and mobilizes employees to accept and work toward attaining these visions.

An example of a transformational leader is William Bratton, the Los Angeles Chief of Police and former police commissioner of New York City. In two years Bratton turned New York into one of the safest large cities in the United States; he has made substantial progress in combating crime in Los Angeles. He had previously turned around four other law enforcement agencies. During a time of austerity, Bratton convinced the city that adding 1,000 police officers was a good investment because it reduced costs associated with crime. Among these costs of high crime are the loss of business and lower property values resulting in small tax revenues. Based on his success in transforming big-city police departments, Bratton later founded Altegrity Risk International, a security consulting firm in New York City. Bratton's plan is to bring the best of American policing to the most dangerous places in the world including Kabul, Afghanistan.[51]

This section will describe how transformations take place, the role of charisma, how to become charismatic, and the downside of charismatic leadership.

How Transformations Take Place

The transformational leader attempts to overhaul the organizational culture or subculture and to make a difference in people's lives. To bring about the overhaul, transformations take place in one or more of three ways.[52] First, the transformational leader raises awareness of the importance and value of certain rewards and how to achieve them. He or she points out the pride workers would experience if the firm were to become number one in its field. Second, the transformational leader gets people to look beyond their self-interests for the sake of the work group and the firm. Such a leader might say, "I know you would like more healthcare benefits, but if we don't cut expenses, we'll all be out of a job." Third, the transformational leader helps people go beyond a focus on minor

transformational leader
A leader who helps organizations and people make positive changes in the way they do things.

---

[51]W. Chan Kaim and Renée Mauborgne, "Tipping Point Leadership," *Harvard Business Review*, April 2003, pp. 60–69; "Chief William J. Bratton's Welcome Message," http://www.lapdblo.typepad.com, May 11, 2006; Gabriel Kahn, "Top Cop In Los Angeles Says Cutting Crime Pays," *The Wall Street Journal*, November 29–30, p. A9.; Susan Berfield, "Bill Bratton, Globocop," *Bloomberg Business Week*, April 12, 2010. pp. 49, 50.

[52]John J. Hater and Bernard M. Bass, "Superiors' Evaluations and Subordinates' Perceptions of Transformational and Transactional Leadership," *Journal of Applied Psychology*, November 1988, p. 69; Nick Turner et al., "Transformational Leadership and Moral Reasoning," *Journal of Applied Psychology*, April 2002, pp. 304–311.

satisfactions to a quest for self-fulfillment. He or she might explain, "I know that a long lunch break is nice. But just think, if we get this project done on time, we'll be the envy of the company."

One of many studies indicating that transformational leadership makes a difference in performance was conducted by Robert T. Keller with 118 research and development project teams from five firms. Subordinate perceptions of transformational leadership (including charisma) were measured by a standard measure of such leadership. The results demonstrated that transformational leadership was positively related to technical quality of the projects produced; they were performing on schedule one year later. Even more impressive, perceptions of transformational leadership were related to the five-year profitability of the products developed by the project teams as well as product speed to market.[53]

The impact of transformational leadership can also be indirect. A study of 94 top management teams in credit unions found that leaders perceived to be transformational were better able to get other members of the team to agree on the importance of certain goals, such as improving customer service. Agreement on goal importance, in turn, was associated with better organizational importance.[54]

Charismatic Leadership

charisma

The ability to lead or influence others based on personal charm, magnetism, inspiration, and emotion.

A leader's personality can be a big part of his or her effectiveness. **Charisma** is the ability to lead or influence others based on personal charm, magnetism, inspiration, and emotion. To label a leader as charismatic does not mean that everybody shares that opinion. Even the most popular and inspiring leaders are perceived negatively by some members of their organization or constituency. Quite often these negative perceptions are communicated on blogs and social networking sites. Charismatic leadership is important because it often leads to enhanced motivation and satisfaction among subordinates. A study with firefighters demonstrated that the firefighters under the command of an officer they perceived to be charismatic were happier than their counterparts working for an officer perceived to be non-charismatic.[55] The list that follows presents leaders' qualities that relate specifically to charisma.[56]

---

[53]Robert T. Keller, "Transformational Leadership, Initiating Structure, and Substitutes for Leadership: A Longitudinal Study of Research and Development Project Team Performance," *Journal of Applied Psychology*, January 2006, pp. 202–210.

[54]Amy E. Colbert, Amy L. Kristof-Brown, Bret H. Bradley, and Murray R. Barrick, "CEO Transformational Leadership: The Role of Goal Importance Congruence in Top Management Teams," *Academy of Management Journal*, February 2008, pp. 81–96.

[55]Amir Erez et al, "Stirring the Hearts of Followers: Charismatic Leaders and the Transferal of Affect," *Journal of Applied Psychology*, May 2008, pp. 602–613.

[56]Alan J. Dubinsky, Francis J. Yammarino, and Marvin A. Jolson, "An Examination of Linkages Between Personal Characteristics and Dimensions of Transformational Leadership," *Journal of Business and Psychology*, Spring 1995, p. 315; Timothy A. Judge and Joyce E. Bono, "Five-Factor Model of Personality and Transformational Leadership," *Journal of Applied Psychology*, October 2000, pp. 751–765; Stephen Denning, "Stories in the Workplace," *HR Magazine*, September 2008, pp. 129–132.

1. *Vision.* Charismatic leaders offer an exciting image of where the organization is headed and how to get there. A vision is more than a forecast; it describes an ideal version of the future for an organization or organizational unit. Being visionary is almost synonymous with charisma. Helmut Panke, the former chairman of German automaker BMW, was regarded as visionary. He was fond of saying such things as, "Every model we make has to earn the right to wear the BMW badge."[57]

2. *Masterful communication style.* To inspire people, charismatic and transformational leaders use colorful language and exciting metaphors and analogies. A former CEO of Coca-Cola told people, "We give people around the world a moment of pleasure in their daily lives." Another key aspect of the communication style of transformational leaders is that they tell captivating stories that relate to the goals of the firm. For example, some leaders use the fairy tale "The Three Little Pigs" to illustrate how business firms must make products and services stronger to withstand competitive force. Telling interesting stories with a message is also part of the masterful communication style. For instance, a division head might tell a true story of how workers at the division once saved the company by working 60 hours a week to win a vital government contract.

3. *Elicits trust.* People believe so strongly in the integrity of charismatic leaders that they will risk their careers to pursue the leader's vision. When a charismatic leader leaves an organization, several subordinates often follow the leader to his or her next firm.

4. *Energy and action orientation.* Similar to entrepreneurs, most charismatic leaders are energetic and serve as a model for getting things done on time.

5. *Inspiring leadership.* Partly as a result of the four preceding characteristics, transformational and charismatic leaders emotionally arouse people to the point that they want to achieve higher goals than they thought of previously. In short, the charismatic leader stands as an inspiration to many others.

Charisma may indeed be related to personality factors, but often a leader is perceived as charismatic because he or she attained outstanding performance. For example, a study found that CEOs tended to be perceived as charismatic following good organizational performance. Yet CEOs being perceived as charismatic was not related to future good business results.[58] It is possible that good organizational performance leads to charisma rather than the opposite.

---

[57]Quoted in Rich Karlgaard, "Four Styles of Leadership," *Forbes*, November 2, 2009, p. 23.

[58]Bradely R. Agle, Nandu J. Nagarajan, Jeffrey A. Sonnenfeld, and Dhinu Srinivasan, "Does CEO Charisma Matter? An Empirical Analysis of the Relationships among Organizational Performance, Environmental Uncertainty, and top Management Perceptions of CEO Charisma," *Academy of Management Journal*, February 2006, pp. 161–174.

Developing Charisma

Managers can improve their image as charismatic by engaging in favorable interactions with group members through a variety of techniques.[59] A starting point is to *use visioning*. Develop a dream about the future of your unit and discuss it with others. *Make frequent use of metaphors.* Develop metaphors to inspire the people around you. After a group has experienced a substantial setback, it's common to say, "Like the phoenix, we will rise from the ashes of defeat." *It is important to inspire trust and confidence.* Get people to believe in your competence by making your accomplishments known in a polite, tactful way.

Be highly energetic and goal oriented so your energy and resourcefulness become contagious. To increase your energy supply, exercise frequently, eat well, and get ample rest. It is important to express your emotions. Freely express warmth, joy, happiness, and enthusiasm. *Smile frequently*, even when you are not in a happy mood. A warm smile indicates a confident, caring person, which contributes to perceptions of charisma. *Make everybody you meet feel important.* For example, at a company meeting shake the hand of every person you meet. Another way of making people feel important is giving them assignments in which they have a high chance of succeeding; then give positive feedback.

A relatively easy characteristic to develop is to *multiply the effectiveness of your handshake*. Shake firmly without creating pain, and make enough eye contact to notice the color of the other person's eyes. When you take that much trouble, you project care and concern. Finally, *stand up straight and use nonverbal signs of self-confidence*. Practice good posture and minimize fidgeting and speaking in a monotone.

David Brandon, now the athletic director at the University of Michigan and former CEO of Domino's Pizza, provides a good illustration of a transformational and charismatic leader. During his first eight years at Domino's he unleashed the company's once patriarchal culture and created an energized and fast-growing company. Brandon is highly people focused and uses such techniques as creating new labels for business functions. Human resources became "People First" and marketing became "Build the Brand." Brandon frequently praises people, offers financial incentives for reaching goals, and tells stories with messages about company values. His human relations skills are outstanding. A colleague at the University of Michigan commented, "He comes off very kind and engaging and interested. A nice person. He cares."[60]

---

[59]Andrew J. DuBrin, *Personal Magnetism: Discover Your Own Charisma and Learn How to Charm, Inspire, and Influence Others* (New York: AMACOM, 1997), pp. 93–111; Monica Larner, "The Man Who Saved Ferrari," *Business Week*, March 8, 1999, pp. 74–75.

[60]Dorothy Bourdet, "Domino Effect," *Detroit News Online*, December 9, 2006; Mark Snyder, "A Lifetime of Leadership leads David Brandon to Michigan Job," *freep.com*, March 8, 2010.

The Downside of Charismatic Leadership

Charismatic business leaders are seen as corporate heroes when they can turn around a failing business or launch a new enterprise. Charismatic leaders whose efforts benefit others are sometimes referred to as socialized charismatics. Nevertheless, this type of leadership has a dark side. Some charismatic leaders manipulate and take advantage of people, such as by getting them to invest retirement savings in risky company stock. Some charismatic leaders are unethical and lead their organizations toward illegal and immoral ends. People are willing to follow the charismatic leader down a quasi-legal path because of his or her charisma. Bernard Madoff, the former CEO and chairman of his own investment company and the ex-president of NASDAQ, was perceived as charming and persuasive. He encouraged individual consumers and stock brokers to invest money in his firm and swindled people out of an estimated $50 billion. After he was sent to prison, it was reported that Madoff was well liked by his fellow prisoners. However, he was eventually assaulted by another prisoner over a dispute about money the assailant thought Madoff owed him. Madoff was hospitalized because of his injuries including a broken nose (according to another inmate).[61]

Another concern about some charismatic business leaders is that they begin to perceive themselves as superstars who accomplish most of the company leadership personally. Some of these charismatic executives become caught up in receiving publicity and mingling with politicians and investors, neglecting the operations of the business. Because of this, low-key executive leaders—especially those who focus on internal operations—are more in style than previously. One such example is Mark Hurd, the former chairman and CEO of Hewlett-Packard; he is moderately charismatic, yet considered to be a whiz at making a company more efficient (despite his expense account irregularities at HP).

THE LEADER AS A MENTOR AND COACH

mentor
A more experienced person who develops a protégé's abilities through tutoring, coaching, guidance, and emotional support.

Another vital part of leadership is directly assisting less experienced workers to improve their job performance and advance their careers. A **mentor** is a more experienced person who develops a protégé's abilities through tutoring, coaching, guidance, and emotional support. The mentor helps the person being mentored grow by challenging him or her to deal with difficult situations (such as joining a task force) or with a difficult work problem. The idea of mentoring traces back to ancient Greece, when warriors entrusted their sons to the tutor Mentor. Although never out of style, mentoring is more important than ever as workers face complex and rapidly changing job demands. Coaching deals with helping others improve performance; it will be described more fully in Chapter 16. Quite often the mentor is also a coach, but a manager who coaches another person may not be a mentor. The manager mentioned in the chapter opener functioned as both a mentor and coach.

---

[61]Dionne Searcey and Amir Efrati, "Madoff Beaten in Prison," *The Wall Street Journal*, March 18, 2010, p. A3.

The mentor, a trusted counselor and guide, is typically a person's manager or team leader. Mentors are typically within the field of expertise of the protégé, but can also come from another specialty. For example, a manufacturing manager might mentor an accountant. A leader can be a mentor to several people at the same time, and successful individuals often have several mentors during their career.

Helping the protégé solve problems is an important part of mentoring. Mentors help their protégés solve problems by themselves and make their own discoveries. A comment frequently made to mentors is, "I'm glad you made me think through the problem. You put me on the right track." A mentor can also give specific assistance in technical problem solving. If the mentor knows more about the new technology than the protégé, he or she can shorten the person's learning time. Many developments in communication technology are likely to be taught by a coworker serving as a mentor, because a manager often has less current technology knowledge than a group member.

Mentoring has traditionally been an informal relationship based on compatibility between two personalities. As with other trusted friends, good chemistry should exist between the mentor and the protégé. Many mentoring programs assign mentors to selected new employees. Formal mentors often supplement the work of managers by assisting a newcomer to acquire job skills and understand the organization culture.

shadowing

Directly observing the work activities of the mentor by following the manager around for a period of time, such as one day per month.

A recently popular approach to mentoring is **shadowing**, or directly observing the work activities of the mentor by following the manager around for a period of time, a day or a month. The protégé might be invited to strategy meetings, visits with key customers, discussions with union leaders, and the like. The protégé observes how the mentor handles situations, and a debriefing session might be held to discuss how and why certain tactics were used.

To capitalize on the potential advantages of mentoring, develop or build on good relationships with superiors and request feedback on performance at least once a year. Find and identify an informal mentor who is willing to be an advocate for your upward mobility within the organization, help you learn the informal rules of the workplace, and help you make valuable contacts. Your mentor will help you identify the informal rules of the company that are helpful in navigating through the organization. (An example would be "Never turn down a request from upper management.")

A mentor usually becomes a better manager because of mentoring. Keith R. Wyche, the president, U.S. Operations of Pitney Bowe's Management Services, observes that mentoring enhances the leadership capacity of the mentor. "The first law of leadership," he says, "is a true leader helps create future leaders. It also helps the mentor move from being just successful to being significant. Individual success is admirable, but taking time to help others achieve success is much more satisfying and significant."[62]

---

[62]Quoted in Laura Egodigwe, "His Brother's Keeper: A Mentor Learns the True Meaning of Leadership of Leadership," *Black Enterprise*, December 2006, p. 69.

LEARNING
OBJECTIVE **7**

Pinpoint leadership
approaches to
dealing with
adversity and
crises.

LEADERSHIP DURING ADVERSITY AND CRISIS

As suggested at many places in this book, an important role of both managers and leaders is to help the group deal with adversity and crisis. Adversity and crises may take such forms as a downturn in business, a sudden surge in workload that workers perceive as overwhelming, hurricanes, fire damage, a massive product recall, and workplace violence. The accompanying Management in Action gives an example of leading during a crisis created by a natural disaster. Almost all the principles and techniques of leadership would be helpful during difficult times, but here we pinpoint ten behaviors and actions that are particularly relevant for a leader dealing with adversity and crisis.[63]

MANAGEMENT IN ACTION

Safety Coordinator Sherry Black Copes with a Tornado at a Caterpillar Plant

Nearly every bulldozer, dump truck, and excavator made by Caterpillar Inc. depends on high-pressure couplings that for years were made only in a small factory in Oxford, Mississippi. By concentrating production in one place, Caterpillar lowered costs and controlled its supply chain. But the strategy was a high-stakes gamble: Any problem that shut down this 300-person plant could halt equipment production around the world, cause thousands of temporary layoffs, and result in tens of millions of dollars in lost sales.

On February 5, 2008, catastrophe struck. At 5:37 p.m., Sherry Black, the plant's health and safety coordinator, received a text message from a weather-alert service: A tornado 18 miles away was swirling toward the factory. In seconds, Black hustled about 80 second-shift workers into two cinder-block-walled locker rooms that serve as one of the factory's emergency shelters.

Minutes later, Black was patrolling the plant when she heard what she thought was hail battering the roof. She dove beneath a desk. While the tornado roared overhead, Black, a petite 46-year-old, worried she wouldn't survive to see the birth of a grandchild. When silence fell over the plant, she scrambled out, grabbed a flashlight, and rushed to the shelters.

No one was seriously hurt. Workers shuffled out of the darkened plant. A rotten-egg stench from a natural-gas leak fouled the air. After lightning flashed, Black noticed that part of the roof was missing. The storm had disabled the plant and its key metal-stamping presses.

Case Questions

1. In what way did Sherry Black exercise leadership in the circumstances surrounding the tornado?
2. If you were a Caterpillar executive, would you recognize Sherry Black for her efforts? Or was she simply following her job description as the plant safety coordinator?

Source: Ilan Brat, "Rebuilding After a Catastrophe," *The Wall Street Journal*, May 19, 2009, p. B1.

---

[63]James O'Toole and Warren Bennis, "What's Needed Next: A Culture of Candor," *Harvard Business Review*, June 2009, pp. 54–61; Ronald Heifetz, Alexander Grashow, and Marty Linsky, "Leadership in a Permanent Crisis," *Harvard Business Review*, July–August 2009, pp. 62–69; Emily Thorton, "Managing through a Crisis: The New Rules," *Business*

1. *Make tough decisions quickly.* The best accepted principle of crisis leadership is that the leaders should take decisive action to remedy the situation. Ron Sargent became CEO of office supplies retailer Staples one week before the September 11, 2001, terrorist attacks and in the midst of a recession. After the attacks, Sargent had to choose between cutting payroll or reducing product lines to save money. He worked quickly to eliminate consumer-oriented products such as Britney Spears backpacks, hurting profit margins in the short term but saving jobs and keeping customer service strong.[64]

2. *Serve as a model by being resilient.* Effective managerial leaders are resilient: They bounce back quickly from setbacks such as budget cuts, demotions, and terminations. Leadership resiliency serves as a positive model for employees at all levels when the organization confronts difficult times. During such times, effective leaders sprinkle their speech with clichés such as "Tough times don't last, but tough people do," or "When times get tough, the tough get going." Delivered with sincerity, such messages are inspirational to many employees and may help stabilize morale.

3. *Present a plan for dealing with the adversity or crisis.* A key part of managing a crisis well is to present a plan for dealing with the crisis while at the same time behaving in a calm and reassuring manner. When Meg Whitman, the former CEO of eBay, was at a company meeting in Germany, the managers present were concerned about a weakness in their business. She suggested that additional marketing spending would help boost activity; no one should panic because there were many solutions at their disposal.[65] To implement a plan for coping with adversity, the management team must be disciplined, paying attention to operational details, listening to customer complaints, and communicating new developments with each other.

4. *Appear confident and trustworthy.* Group members must trust that the leader or leaders can deal with the crisis. Trust can be attained by communicating openly, honestly, and often about the crisis. In dealing with a crisis, it is helpful for the leader to project confident body language, such as appearing relaxed while delivering the crisis plan.

5. *Focus on the future.* Part of being visionary is focusing on the future when the present is filled with difficulty. The leader of a software company might tell the group that technology investment has dipped for the present but that companies will soon recognize that they cannot compete well in the long run if they don't upgrade their information technology soon. A bold move to focus on the future is to get into the scavenger mode. For example, a CEO might buy out a struggling competitor and hire talented people who have been laid off by competitors. Top-management might purchase real estate at distressed prices to later earn a big increase in market value.

Week, January 19, 2009, pp. 030–034; Geoff Covin, "The Upside of the Downturn," *Fortune*, June 8, 2009, pp. 58–62.

[64]Douglas MacMillan, "Survivor: CEO Edition," *Bloomberg Business Week*, March 1, 2010, p. 34.

[65]Adam Lashinsky, "Meg and the Machine," *Fortune*, September 1, 2003, p. 70.

6. *Communicate widely about the problem.* When tough times hit, it pays to increase communication about the problems facing the company or unit and discuss what might be done to improve the situation. Communicating with workers throughout the organization gives them an opportunity to provide leadership. In one company, a technician suggested focusing more on servicing existing equipment than on attempting to sell new equipment during the recession. Communicating with customers and their customers can bring forth useful information about how long the tough times will remain. The business can be reconfigured to meet the new reality, such as finding the least painful ways to cut costs.

7. *Change to meet changing circumstances.* A bold leadership move is to change the thrust of a company's activities to adapt to changing circumstances. When the condominium market in Florida started softening several years ago, real estate magnate Jorge Perez expanded in Latin America and found particular success in Mexico. He says, "I tell my people all the time that the minute we stop changing as a company, we die."[66]

8. *Stick with constructive core values.* Leaders who keep their company or division focused on core values are likely to endure difficult times. Neglecting core values to help overcome adversity can create permanent damage. Take this humble example: A well-known underwear company decided to cope with lower sales volume by cutting costs on the manufacture of men's briefs. The lower-cost briefs looked fine but they tore apart at the waistband after several washings. Word spread quickly about the defective briefs, and the company lost accounts with several major retail chains. The core value compromised here was offering only high-quality goods to the public.

9. *Divide major problems into smaller chunks.* Give workers bits of the major problem to work on so they feel less overwhelmed by the adversity facing them and the company. For example, if the company is hurting for cash, one group of employees might search for items in the office or factory that could be sold on an auction Web site. Another group of workers might search for ways to reduce shipping costs by 10 percent. Other groups would be assigned different adversity-fighting tasks. When an obstacle is framed as too large, too complex, or too challenging, workers might feel overwhelmed and freeze in their tracks.

10. *Lead with compassion.* Crises can take a heavy emotional toll on workers. Compassionate leadership encompasses two related sets of actions. The first is to create an environment in which affected workers can freely discuss how they feel, such as a group meeting to talk about the adversity, crisis, or disaster. The second is to create an environment in which the workers who experience or witness pain can find a method to alleviate their own suffering or that of others. The leader might establish a

---

[66]Quoted in Neil H Simon, "Five Top CEOs Share Hot Tips for Thriving in the Cold Economy," *Hispanic Business*, June 2008, p. 76

special fund to help the families who were victims of a disaster such as a hurricane or earthquake or give workers access to grief counseling.

LEADERSHIP SKILLS

LEARNING OBJECTIVE **8**
Identify the skills that contribute to leadership.

As already explained, leadership involves personal qualities, behaviors, and skills. A skill refers to a present capability, such as the ability to resolve conflict or create a vision statement. Many of these leadership skills have been mentioned or implied throughout the book. A prime example would be the five general skills for managers described in Chapter 1: technical, interpersonal, conceptual, diagnostic, and political. For example, to exercise strategic leadership, a manager would need to have strong conceptual skills. To inspire people, a leader would need interpersonal skills, and to negotiate well, he or she would need good political skills. To be an effective face-to-face leader, the manager would need coaching skills as described in Chapter 16.

The leadership roles presented in Chapter 1 directly associated with leadership skills are as follows: negotiator, coach, team builder, technical problem solver, and entrepreneur. The following checklist provides some additional skills that can contribute to leadership effectiveness, depending on the people and the task.

- Sizing up situations in order to apply the best leadership approach
- Exerting influence through various approaches such as rational persuasion, inspirational appeal, and assertiveness
- Motivating team members through such specific techniques as goal setting and positive reinforcement
- Motivating people from diverse cultures and nations
- Resolving conflict with superiors and group members
- Solving problems creatively in ways that point group members in new directions
- Developing a mission statement that inspires others to perform well
- Leading a group through adversity

As implied by this discussion, leadership involves dozens of different skills. An effective manager's toolkit combines various skills according to the leader's needs and the situation. Holding a leadership position offers a wonderful opportunity for personal growth through skill development.

Summary of Key Points

Differentiate between leadership and management.

Management is a set of explicit tools and techniques based on reasoning and testing that can be used in a variety of situations. Leadership is concerned with vision, change, motivation, persuasion, creativity, and influence.

2 Describe how leaders are able to influence and empower team members.

Power is the ability to get other people to do things or the ability to control resources. Authority is the formal right to wield power. Six types of power include legitimate, reward, coercive, expert, referent (stemming from charisma), and subordinate. Through subordinate power, team members limit the authority of leaders. To get others to act, leaders also use tactics such as leading by example, leading by values, assertiveness, rationality, ingratiation, exchange, coalition formation, and joking and kidding.

Empowerment is the process of sharing power with team members to enhance their feelings of personal effectiveness. A key belief of empowerment is that leadership in a team can and should be shared. Empowerment increases employee motivation, because the employee is accepted as a partner in decision making. For empowerment to work well, people must exercise self-leadership; cross-cultural factors in the acceptance of empowerment must be considered.

3 Identify important leadership characteristics and behaviors.

Certain personal characteristics are associated with successful managerial leadership in many situations, including the following: drive and passion; power motive; self-confidence combined with humility; trustworthiness and honesty; good intellectual ability, knowledge, and technical competence; sense of humor; emotional intelligence; and leadership efficacy.

Effective leaders must demonstrate adaptability, establish a direction and set high standards of performance, be visible and maintain a social presence, and provide emotional support to group members.

They should give and accept feedback, and perhaps be a servant leader.

4 Describe participative leadership, authoritarian leadership, the Leadership Grid, situational leadership, and entrepreneurial styles of leadership.

Leadership style is the typical pattern of behavior that a leader uses to influence employees to achieve organizational goals. Participative leaders share decision making with the group. One subtype of participative leader is the consultative leader, who involves subordinates in decision making but retains final authority. A consensus leader also involves subordinates in decision making and bases the final decision on group consensus. A democratic leader confers final authority on the group. Autocratic leaders attempt to retain most of the authority.

The Leadership Grid classifies leaders according to how much concern they have for both results and people. Sound management, with its high emphasis on results and people, is considered the ideal.

The Situational Leadership II model explains how to match the leadership style to the capabilities of group members on a given task. The basic premise of SLII is that the basis for effective leadership is managing the relationship between a leader and a subordinate on a given task. Effective leaders adapt to the level of commitment and competence of a subordinate. The leader adjusts the amount of supporting and directing, which results in the four leadership styles shown in Exhibit 10-5.

Entrepreneurial leaders often have a strong achievement need, high enthusiasm and creativity, and a visionary perspective. They are uncomfortable with hierarchy and bureaucracy, often because they focus their energies on products, services, and customers.

Describe transformational and charismatic leadership.

The transformational leader helps organizations and people make positive changes. He or she combines charisma, inspirational leadership, and intellectual stimulation. Transformations take place through such means as pointing to relevant rewards, getting people to look beyond self-interest, and encouraging people to work toward self-fulfillment. Charismatic leaders provide vision and masterful communication. They can inspire trust and help people feel capable, and they are action-oriented. Performing well may lead to being perceived as charismatic. Some charismatic leaders are unethical and use their power to accomplish illegal and immoral ends. Managers can improve their image as charismatic by engaging in favorable interactions with group members through a variety of techniques including visioning and an effective handshake.

 Explain the leadership role of mentoring and coaching.

Mentoring is more important than ever as workers face complex and rapidly changing job demands. Coaching is part of mentoring. Mentors help protégés solve problems by themselves and make their own discoveries. Mentoring can be an informal or formal relationship. Shadowing is a useful part of mentoring.

 Pinpoint leadership approaches to dealing with adversity and crises.

An important role of leaders and managers is to help the group deal with adversity and crisis. Included here are: make tough decisions quickly; be a model of resilience; present a plan for the adversity or crisis; appear confident and trustworthy; focus on the future; communicate widely about the problem; change to meet changing circumstances; stick with core values; divide problems into chunks; and lead with compassion.

8 **Identify the skills that contribute to leadership.**

To be an effective leader, a manager must possess a wide variety of skills, many of which are described throughout this chapter and this book. Among these diverse skills are exerting influence, motivating others, and solving problems creatively.

Key Terms and Phrases

Leadership, 346
Power, 348
Authority, 348
Coalition, 352
Self-leadership, 354
Power motivation, 356
Open-book company, 357
Leadership style, 362

Participative leader, 362
Autocratic leader, 363
Leadership Grid®, 364
Situational leadership II (SLII), 366
Transformational leader, 370
Charisma, 371
Mentor, 374
Shadowing, 375

Questions

1. In what way does a first-level supervisor play an important leadership role in the organization?
2. Describe how a businessperson could be an effective leader yet an ineffective manager. Also describe how a businessperson could be an effective manager yet an ineffective leader.
3. Which of the influence tactics described in this chapter do you think is the least ethical? Explain your reasoning.

4. How would a leader know whether a given subordinate, or group of subordinates, is trustworthy enough to be empowered?
5. The entrepreneurial spirit has become increasingly welcome in corporations of all sizes. What do you think you could do to develop your entrepreneurial spirit?
6. Suppose you believed that you would be more effective as a leader or potential leader if you

were more charismatic. What would be a realistic action plan for you to begin this month to become more charismatic?

7. What experiences have you already had in life that would prepare you for leading subordinates through adversity?

Skill-Building Exercise 10-A: My Leadership Journal

A potentially important technique to aid in your development as a leader is to maintain a journal or diary of your experiences. Make a journal entry within 24 hours after you carried out a significant leadership action or failed to do so when the opportunity arose. Record entries dealing with leadership opportunities both capitalized upon and missed. An example: "A few of my neighbors were complaining about all the vandalism in the neighborhood. Cars were getting dented and scratched and headlights were being smashed. A few bricks were thrown into home windows. I volunteered to organize a neighborhood patrol. The patrol actually helped cut back on the vandalism." Or, in contrast: "A few of my neighbors.... into home windows. I thought to myself that someone else should take care of the problem. My time is too valuable."

Also include in your journal entries about feedback you receive on your leadership ability, leadership traits you appear to be developing, and key leadership ideas you read about. Review your journal monthly and note progress you think you have made in developing your leadership skills. Also consider preparing a graph of your leadership skill development. The vertical axis can represent skill level on a 1-to-100 scale, and the horizontal axis might be divided into time intervals such as calendar quarters.

Skill-Building Exercise 10-B: What Style of Leader Are You?

Directions: Answer the following questions, keeping in mind what you have done or think you would do in the scenarios and attitudes described.

	Mostly True	Mostly False
1. I am more likely to take care of a high-impact assignment myself than turn it over to a group member.	——	——
2. I would prefer the analytical aspects of a manager's job rather than working directly with group members.	——	——
3. An important part of my approach to managing a group is to keep the members informed almost daily of any information that could affect their work.	——	——
4. It is a good idea to give two people in the group the same problem and then choose what appears to be the best solution.	——	——
5. It makes good sense for the leader or manager to stay somewhat aloof from the group in order to facilitate making a tough decision when necessary.	——	——
6. I look for opportunities to obtain group input before making a decision, even on straightforward issues.	——	——
7. I would reverse a decision if several group members presented evidence that I was wrong.	——	——
8. Differences of opinion in the work group are healthy.	——	——

9. I think that activities to build team spirit, such as the team fixing up a poor family's house on a Saturday, are an excellent investment of time. —— ——

10. If my group were hiring a new member, I would like the person to be interviewed by the entire group. —— ——

11. An effective team leader today uses e-mail for about 98 percent of communication with team members. —— ——

12. Some of the best ideas are likely to come from group members rather than from the manager. —— ——

13. If our group were planning a banquet, I would seek input from each member on what type of food should be served. —— ——

14. I have never seen a statue of a committee in a museum or park, so why bother making decisions by committee if you want to be recognized? —— ——

15. I dislike it intensely when a group member challenges my position on an issue. —— ——

16. I typically explain to group members how they should accomplish an assigned task. —— ——

17. If I were out of the office for a week, most of the important work in the department would be accomplished anyway. —— ——

18. Delegation of important tasks is something that would be (or is) very difficult for me. —— ——

19. When a group member comes to me with a problem, I tend to jump right in with a proposed solution. —— ——

20. When a group member comes to me with a problem, I typically ask that person something like, "What alternative solutions have you thought of so far?" —— ——

Scoring and Interpretation: The answers in the participative/team-style leader direction are as follows:

Mostly True: 3, 6, 7, 8, 9, 10, 12, 13, 17, 20
Mostly False: 1, 2, 4, 5, 11, 14, 15, 16, 18, 19

Skill development: The quiz you just completed is also an opportunity for skill development. Review the 20 questions and look for implied suggestions for engaging in participative leadership. For example, question 20 suggests that you encourage group members to work through their own solutions to problems. If your goal is to become an authoritarian leader, the questions can also serve as useful guidelines. For example, question 19 suggests that an authoritarian leader looks first to solve problems for group members.

Skill-Building Exercise 10-C: Learning from Failed Leadership

Find a written story about a business or sports leader who was fired from a leadership position for either performance or moral issues. Find at least two accounts of the failure. Identify several traits or behaviors that contributed to the leader being ousted from his or her position. What did you learn from the situation that could help you avoid experiencing the same problem?

Management Now: Online Skill-Building Exercise: Developing
Charisma Tips from the Net

A section in this chapter offered suggestions for becoming more charismatic. Search the Internet for additional suggestions and compare them to the suggestions in the text. Restrict your search to suggestions posted within the last twelve months. Be alert to contradictions and offer a possible explanation for them. You might want to classify the suggestions into two categories: those dealing with the inner person, and those dealing with more superficial aspects of behavior. A suggestion of more depth would be to become a visionary; a suggestion of less depth would be to wear eye-catching clothing.

You might consult a search engine. Use a search phrase such as "How to become more charismatic." An all-encompassing phrase such as "developing leadership effectiveness" is unlikely to direct you to the information you need. You might consult a search engine and look for information about developing charisma.

10-A Case Problem

Michelle Rhee Makes Waves in D.C.

Michelle Rhee took over responsibility for the 144 schools in Washington D.C. in June 2007, when Mayor Adrian Fenty appointed her Chancellor, District of Columbia Public Schools. Her appointment stunned people connected with the D.C. school system. Age 37 at the time, Rhee had no experience running a school. The challenge seemed overwhelming with 45,000 students who collectively ranked last in math among 11 urban school systems. Within two years of becoming chancellor, Rhee was hated by teachers and feared by principals.

When invited to interview for the position, Rhee was running a nonprofit organization called the New Teacher Project, which helps schools recruit good teachers. Rhee, who is Korean-American, was from Ohio, rather than Washington D.C., and she was interviewing for a position in a majority African-American city. She now says, "I was the worst pick on the face of the earth." However, Rhee was once an elementary teacher in Baltimore; that experience taught her that good teachers could alter the lives of children.

Two years after Rhee's appointment, test scores released by the U.S. Department of Education showed that Washington's fourth-graders made the largest gains in math among big city school systems during a two-year period. Rhee has replaced ineffective principals, laid off teachers based on "quality, not by seniority," and shuttered failing schools.

Some of Rhee's thinking about her role as chancellor is revealed in her comments in relation to several aspects of her work, as described next.

How to Lead: I often get in trouble for saying this, but I actually think it's true—that collaboration and consensus building and all those things are quite frankly overrated. No CEOs run their company by committees. Why should we run a school district by committee? The bottom line is that in order to run an effective organization, you need one leader who has clear vision for what needs to happen and the authority to make that happen.

Firing Employees: We had to conduct a reduction in force of about 500 employees in the district. And that included about 250 or so teachers. We made the decision that we were going to conduct the layoffs by quality, not by seniority. It caused this firestorm. From a managerial standpoint, it would make no sense to do a layoff by seniority only. In a school district that is struggling as hard as ours is, we have to be able to look at the quality and value that different employees are adding.

Rhee recognizes that she has been often criticized, but she suggests that some ruthlessness is required. "Have I rubbed people the wrong way? Definitely. If I changed my style, I might make people a little more comfortable" she says. "But I think there's real danger in acting in a way that makes adults feel better. Because where does that stop?"

Money for Nothing: We spend more money per child in this city than almost any other urban jurisdiction in the country, and our results are at the absolute bottom. So it goes against the idea that you have to put more money into education, and that's how you are going to fix it.

It comes down to two basic things about why we spend so much money and the results aren't as good. First is a complete and utter lack of accountability in this system. And the second is a lack of political courage on the part of most of the people who are running cities and school districts.

We have a system in which you could have been teaching for 25, 30 years. Every year, you could actually take your children backward—not just not improve their learning as much as you should, but your kids can move backward in your classroom every year—and you will continue to have a job. You will continue to get your step raise. You will continue to get your negotiated union increases. Where else can that happen, except in public education? So that lack of public accountability is a significant problem.

And then on the courage part, I think that when you're talking about making the difficult decisions that are necessary in this climate—closing schools, firing teachers, removing principals, et cetera—those are the things that make most politicians run for the hills because it makes your phone ring off the hook and people are saying oh, don't close this school, don't fire this person.

Discussion Questions

1. Identify three leadership traits in which Michelle Rhee scores high or low and cite your evidence.
2. What recommendations can you offer Rhee to help her become an even more effective leader?
3. How would you classify Rhee's leadership style, using one or more of the styles presented in this chapter?
4. Assume that Rhee held a leadership position in your field of interest. Explain whether you would enjoy working for her.

Source: The opening facts in the story are from Amanda Ripley, "Can She Save Our Schools?" *Time*, December 8, 2008, p. 36. The quote about ruthlessness is from p. 40 of the same article. "Who's Got Michelle Rhee's Back? *The Wall Street Journal* (editorial), December 14, 2009. p. A24. The interview comments are from Michelle Rhee, "An Educated Work Force," *The Wall Street Journal*, November 23, 2009, p. R3.

10-B Case Problem

Is Julia Too Empowering?

Julia is the director of the municipal bond group of a financial services firm. Julia has four managers reporting to her, each of whom supervises a unit of the group: retail sales, institutional sales, customer service, and internal administration.

Laura, the branch director and company vice president, heard rumblings that the group was not receiving enough supervision, so she decided to investigate. During a dinner meeting requested by Laura, she asked Julia about her approach to leading the group. Julia replied:

> *"I am leading my four managers as if they are all responsible professionals. I believe in management by exception. Unless I am aware of a problem, I am hesitant to get involved in how my managers conduct their work. Don't forget that as the head of the municipal bond group, I have some responsibility for spending time with major customers as well as meeting with you and other senior executives. I do hold a weekly meeting, and conduct my annual performance reviews as required."*

Laura thanked Julia for having attended the dinner, and said that the meeting was informative. With Julia's permission, Laura said that she would be visiting the municipal bond group to have a few casual conversations with the four managers.

When asked about Julia's leadership, the first manager said his nickname for Julia was Macro Julia; instead of being a micromanager, she went to the other extreme and was a *macromanager* who had minimal contact with the group. He added that at times Julia didn't seem to even care what was happening. The manager said, "I recently asked Julia's advice about finding a good contact who could introduce me to the pension fund manager of a hospital. Julia told me that a big part of my job was to develop contacts on my own."

The second manager Laura spoke to said that she enjoyed working with Julia because she was a nice person who didn't get in her hair. "I don't need a boss to remind me to attain my goals or get my work done on time. A little smile of encouragement here and there is all I need," the manager said.

The third manager said to Laura, "I think Julia would be a great manager for me a few years down the road. But right now, I do not want to feel so much on my own. Julia is a talented person who I could learn from. Yet she is more involved with customers and higher-level management than she is with her managers. I'm new in the field, so I could use more of a coaching style of manager."

The fourth manager said, "I remember meeting Julia a few times, but I don't remember much about her. You said she is my manager? I don't care if my comments get back to her, because I'm joining a competitor next month."

Discussion Questions

1. To what extent has Julia chosen the right approach to leading the managers in her unit of the financial services firm?
2. What advice can you offer Julia to be a more effective leader?
3. What advice can you offer Laura to help Julia be a more effective leader?
4. Explain whether you think Laura was justified in asking Julia's direct reports about Julia's approach to leadership.

CHAPTER 11

Motivation

O ne recent May, employees of Student Media Group in Newark, Delaware, started noticing things popping up in the office: a 50-inch plasma television screen, a ping-pong table, a Wii videogame player, and a fridge stocked with free soda and snacks. They wondered what was going on.

After three salespeople were laid off during the spring and revenue fell 40 percent year-to-year in the first four months of the year, the owner of the college advertising company sensed a bad vibe among the 19 remaining employees that he didn't want to continue. He invested $3,000 on perks to motivate his staff.

"Let's show our employees that we're not scared," says Paul Alford, chief executive of Springboard Inc., which owns Student Media Group. "Let's see if this inspires them. It did." By the end of May, sales were at $1.5 million for the year, up 10% from the same period last year. Alford says the action had a big impact on the staff. "It was really the catalyst that got people believing," he says.[1]

OBJECTIVES

After studying this chapter and doing the exercises, you should be able to:

1. Explain the relationship between motivation and performance.
2. Present an overview of major theories of need satisfaction in explaining motivation.
3. Explain how goal setting is used to motivate people.
4. Describe the application of positive reinforcement including recognition and praise to worker motivation.
5. Explain the conditions under which a person will be motivated according to expectancy theory.
6. Describe the role of financial incentives, including profit sharing, and gainsharing in worker motivation.

---

[1]Raymund Flandez, "Rewards Help Soothe Hard Times," *The Wall Street Journal*, July 7, 2009, p. B4.

The story about the college advertising company illustrates how deliberate steps to motivate workers can pay off in terms of increased productivity. For many managers, the purpose of motivation is to get people to work hard toward achieving company objectives. Understanding motivation is also important because low motivation contributes to low-quality work, superficial effort, indifference toward customers, and high absenteeism and tardiness.

The term motivation refers to two different but related ideas. From the standpoint of the individual, motivation is an internal state that leads to the pursuit of objectives. Personal motivation affects the initiation, direction, intensity, and persistence of effort. (A motivated worker gets going, focuses effort in the right direction, works with intensity, and sustains the effort.) From the standpoint of the manager, motivation is the process of getting people to pursue objectives. Both concepts have an important meaning in common. **Motivation** is the expenditure of effort to accomplish results. The effort results from a force that stems from within the person. The manager, team leader, or group can be helpful in igniting the force.

This chapter will present several theories or explanations of motivation in the workplace. In addition, it will provide descriptions of specific approaches to motivating employees. All the ideas presented in this chapter can be applied to motivating oneself as well as others. For instance, when you read about the expectancy theory of motivation, ask yourself: "What rewards do I value strongly enough that I will work extra hard?"

motivation

The expenditure of effort to accomplish results.

LEARNING OBJECTIVE **1**

Explain the relationship between motivation and performance.

THE RELATIONSHIP BETWEEN MOTIVATION, PERFORMANCE, AND ENGAGEMENT

Many people believe the statements "You can accomplish anything you want" and "Think positively and you will achieve all your goals." In truth, motivation is but one important contributor to productivity and performance. Abilities, skills, and the right equipment are also indispensable. An office assistant might be strongly motivated to become a brand manager for Cheerios at General Mills, but she must first acquire knowledge about marketing and project management, develop her leadership skills, and make the right connections—among other factors.

Exhibit 11-1 shows the relationship between motivation and performance. It can also be expressed by the equation $P = M \times A$, where P refers to performance, M to motivation, and A to ability. Note that skill and technology contribute to ability. For instance, if you are skilled at using information technology and you have the right hardware and software, you can accomplish the task of producing a company Web site. Engagement in the diagram is essentially an extension of motivation, referring to the level of commitment workers make to their employer. Engagement is reflected in employee willingness to stay with the firm and go beyond the call of duty.[2]

P = M × A

An expression of the relationship between motivation and performance, where P refers to performance, M to motivation, and A to ability.

[2]Ed Frauenheim, "Downturn Puts New Emphasis on Engagement," *Workforce Management*, July 20, 2009, p. 8

EXHIBIT 11-1 | **Motivation and Ability as Factors in Performance**

Motivation does contribute substantially to performance, but not as directly as many people think.

▶ **PLAY VIDEO**

Go to www.cengage.
com/management/
dubrin and view the
video for Chapter 11.
What is this
company's approach
to motivation? What
did you learn about the
relationship between
motivation and
performance?

The engaged employee works joyfully toward achieving organizational objectives.

Gaining employee commitment is especially important in the current era because several studies have found that most American workers are not fully engaged in their work.[3] They do what is expected of them but do not contribute extra mental and physical effort to be outstanding. Many of these workers want to be good organizational citizens, yet many of them feel they have a poor relationship with the supervisor or believe that the organization does not care about them. According to a Gallup study, about 70 percent of employees are "disengaged," meaning that they are no longer committed to the company. Furthermore, the longer employees stay, the more disengaged they become.[4]

Employee engagement is widely thought to have a payoff to the organization. An analysis by Best Buy provides some quantitative evidence of its importance. Company officials contend that a two percent increase in employee engagement at one of its electronic stores translates, on overage, to a $100,000 annual rise in sales at that location.[5] Engagement is measured by a questionnaire.

Decreased job security caused by downsizing and outsourcing and global outsourcing, along with reduced benefits, are probable contributors to less than full engagement by many employees. An exception is that some employees work harder during a recession, hoping to preserve their jobs. Another indirect way in which difficult times increases engagement and commitment is that employees who have survived layoffs sometimes have more energy and commitment to the organization than they had before. The struggle to accomplish more with fewer resources tends to build a spirit of teamwork.

---

[3]Quoted in Steve Bates, "Getting Engaged," *HR Magazine*, February 2004, p. 46; Updated by the Gallup Organization 2009 in Frauenheim, "Downturn Puts New Emphasis on Engagement."

[4]Ibid.

[5]Michelle Conlin, "Is Optimism a Competitive Advantage?" *Business Week*, August 24 and 31, 2009, p. 052.

This curious phenomenon appears to take place when managers have acted in a helpful and responsible way during the downturn.[6]

The techniques described in this chapter, as well as other places in this text, are designed to help employees commit to the organization. High-performance work design as described in Chapter 7 leads to commitment. High motivation for a given task is different from emotional commitment that translates into intense motivation for a long period of time. The process works as follows:

Day-by-day motivation and good treatment of workers	→	Long-term motivation of workers	→	Emotional commitment to the firm	→	Competitive advantage	→	Elevated profits and stock price

Group norms also contribute to both motivation and performance. If group norms and organizational culture encourage high motivation and performance, the individual worker will feel compelled to work hard. To do otherwise isolates the worker from the group and the culture. Group norms and an organizational culture favoring low motivation will often lower individual output.

A manager contributes to performance by motivating group members, improving their ability, and helping to create a positive work culture. Before studying specific explanations of motivation, do the accompanying self-assessment quiz (Exhibit 11-2). Taking the quiz will give you a preliminary idea of your current level of knowledge about motivation.

LEARNING OBJECTIVE **2**

Present an overview of major theories of need satisfaction in explaining motivation.

need

A deficit within an individual, such as a craving for water or affection.

MOTIVATION THROUGH NEED SATISFACTION

The simplest explanation of motivation is one of the most powerful: People are willing to expend effort toward achieving a goal because it satisfies one of their important needs. A **need** is a deficit within an individual, such as a craving for water or affection. Self-interest is thus a driving force. The principle is referred to as "What's in it for me?" or WIIFM (pronounced wiff'em). Reflect on your own experiences. Before working hard to accomplish a task, you probably want to know how you will benefit. If your manager asks you to work extra hours to take care of an emergency, you will most likely oblige. Underneath you might be thinking, "If I work these extra hours, my boss will think highly of me. As a result, I will probably receive a good performance evaluation and maybe a better-than-average salary increase."

Our behaviors are ruled partly by our need intensity; for example, an intense desire for recognition might propel a person to win an employee-of-the month award.[7] Similarly, people are motivated to fulfill needs that

---

[6]"Workplace Challenges: Managing Layoffs and Motivating Those Left Behind," *Knowledge@Wharton*, November 24, 2009, p. 4.

[7]Piers Steel and Cornelius J. König, "Integrating Theories of Motivation," *Academy of Management Review*, October 2006, pp. 895–897.

EXHIBIT 11-2   Self-Assessment Exercise: My Approach to Motivating Others

Describe how often you act or think in the way indicated by the following statements when attempting to motivate another person. Use the following scale: very infrequently (VI); infrequently (I); sometimes (S); frequently (F); very frequently (VF).

	VI	I	S	F	VF
1. I ask the other person what he or she is hoping to achieve in the situation.	1	2	3	4	5
2. I attempt to figure out whether the person has the ability to do what I need done.	1	2	3	4	5
3. When another person is heel-dragging, it usually means he or she is lazy.	5	4	3	2	1
4. I tell the person I'm trying to motivate exactly what I want.	1	2	3	4	5
5. I like to give the other person a reward up front so he or she will be motivated.	5	4	3	2	1
6. I give lots of feedback when another person is performing a task for me.	1	2	3	4	5
7. I like to belittle another person enough so that he or she will be intimidated into doing what I need done.	5	4	3	2	1
8. I make sure that the other person feels treated fairly.	1	2	3	4	5
9. I figure that if I smile nicely enough I can get the other person to work as hard as I need.	5	4	3	2	1
10. I attempt to get what I need done by instilling fear in the other person.	5	4	3	2	1
11. I specify exactly what needs to be accomplished.	1	2	3	4	5
12. I generously praise people who help me get my work accomplished.	1	2	3	4	5
13. A job well done is its own reward. I therefore keep praise to a minimum.	5	4	3	2	1
14. I make sure to let people know how well they have done in meeting my expectations on a task.	1	2	3	4	5
15. To be fair, I attempt to reward people about the same no matter how well they have performed.	5	4	3	2	1
16. When somebody doing work for me performs well, I recognize his or her accomplishments promptly.	1	2	3	4	5
17. Before giving somebody a reward, I attempt to find out what would appeal to that person.	1	2	3	4	5
18. I make it a policy not to thank somebody for doing a job he or she is paid to do.	5	4	3	2	1
19. If people do not know how to perform a task, their motivation will suffer.	1	2	3	4	5
20. If properly designed, many jobs can be self-rewarding.	1	2	3	4	5

Total score _____

Scoring and interpretation: Add the numbers circled to obtain your total score.

90–100   You have advanced knowledge and skill with respect to motivating others in a work environment. Continue to build on the solid base you have established.

50–89   You have average knowledge and skill with respect to motivating others. With additional study and experience, you will probably develop advanced motivational skills.

20–49   To effectively motivate others in a work environment, you will need to greatly expand your knowledge of motivation theory and techniques.

Source: The idea for this quiz and a couple of statements stem from David A. Whetton and Kim S. Cameron, *Developing Management Skills*, 3rd ed. (New York: HarperCollins, 1995), pp. 358–359.

are not currently satisfied. The need-satisfaction approach requires two key steps in motivating workers. First, you must know what people want—what needs they are trying to satisfy. To learn what the needs are, you can ask directly or observe the person. You can obtain knowledge indirectly by getting to know employees better. To gain insight into employee needs, find out something about the employee's personal life, education, work history, outside interests, and career goals.

Second, you must give each person a chance to satisfy needs on the job. To illustrate, one way to motivate a person with a strong need for autonomy is to allow that person to work independently.

This section examines needs and motivation from three related perspectives. First, we describe the best-known theory of motivation, Maslow's need hierarchy. Then we discuss several specific needs related to job motivation, including four basic human drives. Finally, we move on to an updated version of another cornerstone idea, Herzberg's two-factor theory.

Maslow's Need Hierarchy

Maslow's need hierarchy

The motivation theory that arranges human needs into a pyramid-shaped model with basic physiological needs at the bottom and self-actualizing needs at the top.

deficiency needs

Lower-order needs that must be satisfied to ensure a person's existence, security, and requirements for human contact.

growth needs

Higher-order needs that are concerned with personal development and reaching one's potential.

Based on his work as a clinical psychologist, Abraham M. Maslow developed a comprehensive view of individual motivation.[8] **Maslow's need hierarchy** arranges human needs into a pyramid-shaped model with basic physiological needs at the bottom and self-actualization needs at the top. (See Exhibit 11-3.) Lower-order needs, called **deficiency needs**, must be satisfied to ensure a person's existence, security, and requirements for human contact. Higher-order needs, or **growth needs**, are concerned with personal development and reaching one's potential. Before higher-level needs are activated, the lower-order needs must be satisfied. The five levels of needs are described next.

1. *Physiological needs* refer to basic bodily requirements such as nutrition, water, shelter, moderate temperatures, rest, and sleep. Most office jobs allow us to satisfy physiological needs. Naps to reduce stress and boost productivity help workers satisfy an important physiological need. Fire fighting is an occupation with potential to frustrate some physiological needs. Smoke inhalation can block the satisfaction of physiological needs.

2. *Safety needs* include the desire to be safe from both physical and emotional injury. Many workers who hold dangerous jobs would be motivated by the prospects of obtaining safety. For example, computer operators who are suffering from cumulative trauma disorder would prefer a job that requires less intense pressure on their wrists. Any highly stressful job can frustrate the need for emotional safety.

---

[8]Abraham M. Maslow, "A Theory of Human Motivation," *Psychological Review*, July 1943, pp. 370–396; Abraham M. Maslow, *Motivation and Personality* (New York: Harper & Row, 1954), Chapter 5.

EXHIBIT 11-3   **Maslow's Need Hierarchy**

As you move up the hierarchy, the needs become more difficult to achieve. Some physiological needs could be satisfied with pizza and a soft drink, whereas it might take becoming rich and famous to satisfy the selfactualization need.

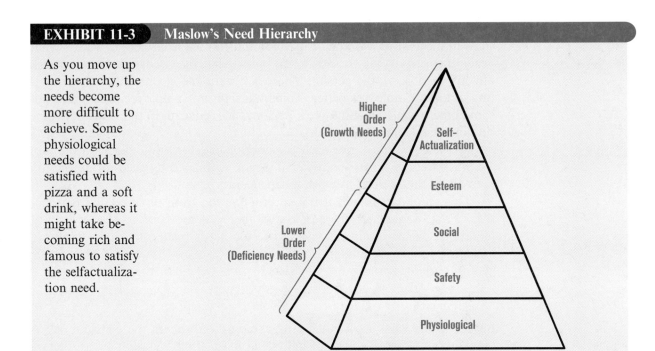

3. *Social needs* are the needs for love, belonging, and affiliation with people. Managers can contribute to the satisfaction of these needs by promoting teamwork and allowing people to discuss work problems with each other. Many employees see their jobs as a major source for satisfying social needs.

4. *Esteem needs* reflect people's desire to be seen by themselves and others as a person of worth. Occupations with high status are a primary source for the satisfaction of esteem needs. Managers can help employees satisfy their esteem needs by praising the quality of their work.

5. *Self-actualization needs* relate to the desire to reach one's potential. They include needs for self-fulfillment and personal development. True self-actualization is an ideal to strive for, rather than something that automatically stems from occupying a challenging position. Self-actualized people are those who are becoming all they are capable of becoming. Managers can help group members move toward self-actualization by giving them challenging assignments and the chance for advancement and new learning.

Maslow's need hierarchy is a convenient way of classifying needs; it has spurred thousands of managers to take the subject of human motivation more seriously. Its primary value lies in recognition of the importance of satisfying needs in order to motivate employees. Furthermore, Maslow shows why people are difficult to satisfy. As one need is satisfied, people want to satisfy other needs or different forms of the same need. The need hierarchy has helped three generations of students understand that it is normal to be constantly searching for new satisfactions.

The need hierarchy is relevant in the current era because so many workers have to worry about satisfying lower-level needs. Job security and having limited or no healthcare benefits are still concerns for many workers. Even when finding new employment is relatively easy, many workers feel their security is jeopardized when they must worry about conducting a job search to pay for necessities.

Specific Needs People Attempt to Satisfy

Maslow's need hierarchy refers to classes of needs; it represents but one way of understanding human needs. The work setting offers the opportunity to satisfy dozens of psychological needs. This section will describe six of the most important of these needs.

Achievement, Power, and Affiliation

achievement need
The need that refers to finding joy in accomplishment for its own sake.

affiliation need
A desire to have close relationships with others and to be a loyal employee or friend.

According to David McClelland and his associates, much job behavior can be explained by the strength of people's needs for achievement, power, and affiliation.[9] The power need (or motive) has already been described in relation to leadership. The **achievement need** refers to finding joy in accomplishment for its own sake. High achievers find satisfaction in completing challenging tasks, attaining high standards, and developing better ways of doing things. Entrepreneurs typically have strong achievement needs. The **affiliation need** is a desire to have close relationships with others and to be a loyal employee or friend. Affiliation is a social need, while achievement and power are self-actualizing needs.

A person with a strong need for affiliation finds compatible working relationships more important than high-level accomplishment and the exercise of power. Successful executives, therefore, usually have stronger needs for achievement and power than for affiliation. Workers with strong affiliation needs typically enjoy contributing to a team effort. Befriending others and working cooperatively with them satisfies the need for affiliation.

Recognition

recognition need
The desire to be acknowledged for one's contributions and efforts and to feel important.

The workplace provides a natural opportunity to satisfy the **recognition need**, the desire to be acknowledged for one's contributions and efforts and to feel important. A manager can thus motivate many employees by making them feel important. Exhibit 11-4 gives you an opportunity to think through your own need for recognition. Employee needs for recognition can be satisfied both through informal recognition and by formal recognition programs, as will be described later in the chapter.

---

[9]Michael J. Stahl, "Achievement, Power, and Managerial Motivation: Selecting Managerial Talent with Job Choice Exercise," *Personnel Psychology*, Winter 1983; David C. McClelland, *Power: The Inner Experience* (New York: Irvington, 1975).

EXHIBIT 11-4   How Much Do I Crave Recognition?

Respond to the following statements on the following scale: disagree strongly (DS); disagree (D); neutral (N); agree (A); agree strongly (AS).

	DS	D	N	A	AS
1. I keep (or would keep) almost every plaque, medal, or trophy I have ever received on display in my living quarters.	1	2	3	4	5
2. I feel a nice warm glow each time somebody praises my efforts.	1	2	3	4	5
3. When somebody tells me "nice job," it makes my day.	1	2	3	4	5
4. When I compliment someone, I am looking for a compliment in return.	1	2	3	4	5
5. I would rather win an "employee-of-the-month" award than receive a $100 bonus for my good work.	1	2	3	4	5
6. If I had the resources to make a large donation to charity, I would never make the donation anonymously.	1	2	3	4	5
7. Thinking back to my childhood, I adored receiving a gold star or similar acknowledgment from my teacher for my good work.	1	2	3	4	5
8. I would rather be designated as *Time* magazine's Person of the Year than be one of the world's richest people.	1	2	3	4	5
9. I love to see my name in print.	1	2	3	4	5
10. I do not receive all the respect I deserve.	1	2	3	4	5

Total score _____

Scoring and interpretation: Add the circled numbers to obtain your total score.
- 45–50: You have an above-average recognition need. Recognition is a strong motivator for you. You will be happiest in a job where you can be recognized for your good deeds.
- 25–44: You have an average need for recognition and do not require constant reminders that you have done a good job.
- 10–24: You have a below-average need for recognition and like to have your good deeds speak for themselves. When you do receive recognition, you would prefer that it be quite specific to what you have done, and not too lavish. You would feel comfortable in a work setting with mostly technical people.

The Need to Feel Proud

Wanting to feel proud motivates many workers even though *pride* is not exactly a psychological need. Striving to experience the emotion of pride most likely stems from the desire to satisfy the needs for self-esteem and self-fulfillment. Being proud of what you accomplish is more of an internal (intrinsic) motivator than an external (extrinsic) motivator such as receiving a gift. Giving workers an opportunity to experience pride can be a strong internal motivator.

Imagine that you are the assistant service manager at a company that customizes corporate jets to meet the requirements of individual clients. Your manager asks you to prepare a PowerPoint presentation of trends in equipment problems. You make your presentation to top management, the group applauds, executives shake your hand, and later you receive several congratulatory e-mail messages. One of the many emotions you experience is likely to be pride in having performed well. You are motivated to keep up the good work.

Workers can also experience pride in relation to external motivators. For example, a worker might receive a crystal vase for having saved the company thousands of dollars in shipping costs. The vase might be more valuable to the worker as a symbol of accomplishment than as a household decoration. The feeling of pride stems from having accomplished a worthwhile activity (saving the company money) rather than from being awarded a vase.

According to consultant Jon R. Katzenbach, managers can take steps to motivate through pride. A key tactic is for the manager to set his or her compass on pride, not money. It is more important for workers to be proud of what they are doing day by day than for them to be proud of reaching a major goal. The manager should celebrate "steps" (small goals) as much as the "landings" (the major goal). The most effective pride builders are masters at identifying and recognizing the small achievements that will instill pride in their people.[10]

Risk Taking and Thrill Seeking

The willingness to take risks and pursue thrills is a need that has grown in importance in the high-technology era. Many people work for employers, start businesses, and purchase stock with uncertain futures. Both the search for giant payoffs and daily thrills motivate these individuals, and they are attracted to high-stress careers such as computer security specialists or investment banking.[11] A strong craving for thrills may have some positive consequences for the organization, including willingness to perform such dangerous feats as setting explosives, capping an oil well, controlling a radiation leak, and introducing a product in a highly competitive environment. However, extreme risk takers and thrill seekers can create problems such as a disproportionate number of vehicular accidents and imprudent investments. Risk takers in the financial field sometimes get involved in developing and selling high risk investments that can bankrupt a firm and lead to criminal investigation.

A manager can appeal to the need for risk taking and thrill seeking and enhance the motivation of a person so inclined by rewarding good behavior with adventuresome assignments such as the following:

- Dealing with an irate, hostile customer
- Working on a product development team under time constraints
- Repairing equipment under heavy time pressures and customer demands
- Attending dangerous team-building activities such as cliff hanging and race-car driving

---

[10]Cited in John A. Byrne, "How to Lead Now," *Fast Company*, August 2003, p. 66.

[11]Christopher Munsey, "Frisky, but Risky," *Monitor on Psychology*, July/August 2006, p. 40.

If you are too strong a thrill seeker, you must be on guard for your own safety and that of others while on the job. Or, you could seek thrills off the job, such as mountain climbing and betting on changes in foreign currencies.

Four Drives or Needs Hardwired Into Our Brains

Research in the fields of neuroscience, biology, and evolutionary psychology supports the long-held belief that need satisfaction is a major part of human motivation. Certain drives or needs are hardwired into our brains; how well they are satisfied influences our emotions and our behavior. First is the *drive to acquire scarce goods* to bolster our sense of well being. This helps explain why a promotion might be motivational. Second is the *drive to bond* with people and organizations. This helps explain why working for an organization, or belonging to a work group, brings us pride and is motivational. Third is the *drive to comprehend* or make sense of our corner of the world. Employees are motivated by positions that enable them to learn and grow. Fourth is the *drive to defend* ourselves, our accomplishments, people we care about, and our ideas against external threats. A worker's resistance to change or a quest for job security could be a manifestation of the drive to defend.[12]

The various approaches to motivation described in this chapter as well as in Chapter 7 about job design and work schedules help workers satisfy directly or indirectly the four drives or needs just described.

Herzberg's Two-Factor Theory

two-factor theory of work motivation

The theory contending that there are two different sets of job factors. One set can satisfy and motivate people, and the other set can only prevent dissatisfaction.

The study of the need hierarchy led to the **two-factor theory of work motivation**, which focuses on the idea of two different sets of job factors. One set of factors can satisfy and motivate people. The other can only prevent dissatisfaction. The late industrial psychologist Frederick Herzberg and his associates interviewed hundreds of professionals about their work.[13] They discovered that some factors of a job give people a chance to satisfy higher-level needs. Such elements are satisfiers or motivators. A *satisfier* is a job factor that, if present, leads to job satisfaction. Similarly, a *motivator* is a job factor that, if present, leads to motivation. When a motivator is not present, the effect on motivation is neutral rather than negative.

Satisfiers and motivators generally refer to the content (the heart or guts) of a job. These factors are achievement, recognition, challenging work, responsibility, and the opportunity for advancement. All the factors are self-rewarding. The important implication for managers is that most people can be motivated by providing an opportunity to do interesting work or to be promoted. The two-factor theory thus underlies the philosophy of job design through job enrichment and the job characteristics model, as described in Chapter 7.

---

[12]Nitin Nohria, Boris Groysberg, and Linda-Elong Lee, "Employee Motivation: A Powerful New Model," *Harvard Business Review*, July–August 2008, pp. 78–84.

[13]Frederick Herzberg, *Work and the Nature of Man* (Cleveland: World, 1966).

Herzberg also discovered that some job elements are more relevant to lower-level needs than upper-level needs. Referred to as dissatisfiers, or hygiene factors, these elements are noticed primarily by their absence. A *dissatisfier* is a job element that, when present, prevents dissatisfaction; it does not, however, create satisfaction. People will not be satisfied with their jobs just because hygiene factors are present. For example, not having a handy place to park your car would create dissatisfaction; having a place to park would not make you happier about your job.

Dissatisfiers relate mostly to the context of a job (the job setting or external elements). These include relationships with coworkers, company policy and administration, job security, and money. All these factors deal with external rewards. Money, however, does work as a satisfier for many people. A key point of the two-factor theory is that the opposite of satisfaction is no satisfaction—not dissatisfaction. Similarly, the opposite of dissatisfaction is no dissatisfaction—not satisfaction.

The two-factor theory has prompted managers to ask, "What really motivates our employees?" Herzberg's assumption—that all workers seek more responsibility and challenge on the job—may be incorrect. It is more likely that people in higher-level occupations strive for more responsibility and challenge. A key take-away from Herzberg's theory is that intrinsic motivation is a major form of motivation; it is the basis for job enrichment as well as job crafting. But even in a given occupational group, such as managers or production workers, not everybody has the same motivational pattern. Many workers are motivated by a secure job when they have heavy financial obligations.

The two-factor theory becomes more current when we look at job factors that are considered important today for attracting, motivating, and retaining professional workers of the millennial generation (born in 1980 or later). In terms of suggestions to managers, these motivator and hygiene factors are as follows:

- *Let them have a life.* Millennials are wary of their parents' 80-hour workweeks; liberal vacation policies are a must.
- *No time clocks, please.* Recent grads are willing to work long hours if they set the schedule. Lockheed Martin allows employees to work nine-hour days and take alternate Fridays off.
- *Give them responsibility.* An opportunity to work on fulfilling projects and develop projects of their own is important to millennials. PepsiCo allows young employees with potential to manage a small team within six months of joining.
- *Feedback and more feedback.* Career-planning advice and frequent performance appraisals are helpful in retaining new hires.
- *Giving back matters.* Today's young workers expect to have the opportunity to engage in community service. Wells Fargo encourages its employees to teach financial literacy classes in the community.[14]

---

[14]Lindsey Gerdes, "The Best Places to Launch a Career," *Business Week*, September 18, 2006, p. 70.

LEARNING
OBJECTIVE **3**
Explain how goal
setting is used to
motivate people.

MOTIVATION THROUGH GOAL SETTING

Goal setting plays an important role in most formal motivational programs and managerial methods of motivating employees. The premise underlying goal theory is that behavior is regulated by values and goals. A value is a strongly held personal standard or conviction. It is a belief about something important to the individual, such as dignity of work or honesty. Our values create within us a desire to behave consistently with them. If an executive values honesty, the executive will establish a goal of trying to hire only honest employees. He or she would therefore make extensive use of reference checks and honesty testing. A **goal** is an overall condition one is trying to achieve, or a conscious intention to act. Exhibit 11-5 summarizes some of the more consistent findings and the following list describes them.[15]

goal
An overall condition
one is trying to
achieve, or a
conscious intention
to act.

1. *Specific goals lead to higher performance than do generalized goals.* Telling someone to "do your best" is a generalized goal. A specific goal would be "Decrease the turnaround time on customer inquiries to an average of two working days."
2. *Performance generally increases in direct proportion to goal difficulty.* The harder one's goal, the more one accomplishes. An important exception occurs, however, when goals are too difficult. Difficulty in reaching the goal leads to frustration, which in turn leads to lowered performance. On the other hand, lofty goals can be inspirational. A **superordinate goal** is

superordinate goals
An overarching goal
that captures the
imagination.

EXHIBIT 11-5   **The Basics of Goal Theory**

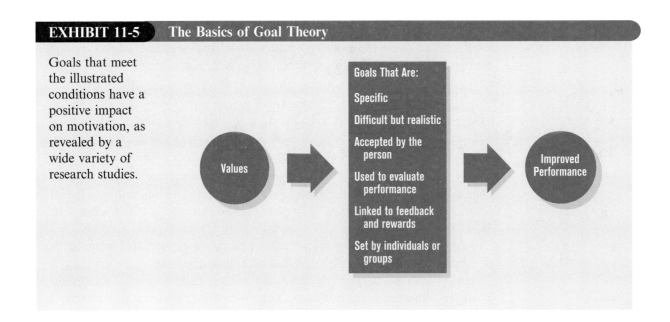

Goals that meet the illustrated conditions have a positive impact on motivation, as revealed by a wide variety of research studies.

Values → Goals That Are: Specific; Difficult but realistic; Accepted by the person; Used to evaluate performance; Linked to feedback and rewards; Set by individuals or groups → Improved Performance

---

[15]Edwin A. Locke and Gary P. Latham, *A Theory of Goal Setting and Task Performance* (Upper Saddle River, NJ: Prentice Hall, 1990); Gary P. Latham, "Goal Setting: A Five-Step Approach to Behavior Change," *Organizational Dynamics*, Vol. 32, No. 3, 2003, pp. 309–317.

an overarching goal that captures the imagination of people.[16] The superordinate goal is similar to a vision; it relates to an ideal and is often inspirational. The construction manager of a sewer-pipe company might explain to all workers that "We are working together to improve sanitation and help rid the world of deadly diseases stemming from poor sewage systems."

3. *Before goals can improve performance, the employee must accept them.* If you reject a goal, you will not incorporate it into your planning. For this reason, it is often helpful to discuss goals with employees rather than imposing the goals on them. Participating in setting goals has no major effect on the level of job performance except when it improves goal acceptance. Yet participation is valuable because it can lead to higher satisfaction with the goal-setting process.

4. *Goals are more effective when they are used to evaluate performance.* When workers know that their performance will be evaluated in terms of how well they attained their goals, the impact of goals increases. Management by objectives is built around this important idea.

5. *Goals should be linked to feedback and rewards.* Workers should receive feedback on their progress toward goals and be rewarded for reaching them. Rewarding people for reaching goals is perhaps the best-accepted principle of management. Feedback is also important because it is a motivational principle within itself. The process of receiving positive feedback encourages us to repeat the behavior; receiving negative feedback encourages us to discontinue the behavior. A practical way of building more feedback into goal setting is to set achievable short-term goals. In this way, goal accomplishment gets measured more frequently, giving the goal setter regular feedback. Because many people do not have the patience and self-discipline to work long and hard without seeing results, short-term goals also increase motivation.

6. *Group goal setting is as important as individual goal setting.* Having employees work as teams with a specific team goal, rather than as individuals with only individual goals, increases productivity. The combination of the compatible group and individual goals is more effective than either individual or group goals.

Pygmalion effect

The idea that people live up to the expectations set for them.

Closely related to goal theory is the **Pygmalion effect**—the idea that people live up to the expectations set for them. If the manager establishes high goals and projects confidence that these goals will be achieved, the workers will rise to the occasion. The confidence might be projected through such means as a firm handshake or an accepting smile. Holding high expectations for employees can help overcome some of the motivational problems of a low work ethic. Many employees with a low work ethic will change their attitudes and behaviors if management expects them to perform well.[17]

[16]Latham, "Goal Setting: A Five-Step Approach," p. 309.

[17]Dov Eden, *Pygmalion in Management: Productivity as a Self-fulfilling Prophecy* (Lexington, MA: Lexington Books, 1990).

A potential problem with relying on goals to motivate workers is that they might use unethical means to attain goals. In the words of a team of researchers, "Goal setting is a prescription-strength medication that has both powerful positive effects and formidable negative side effects."[18] Examples of negative effects of clinging to goals include booking sales for a quarter in which the money is yet to be received and using low-quality components in order to attain a cost goal for a part. To meet profit goals, some CEOs will cut back on research and development, fire capable workers, and sell off valuable company assets.

A risk specialist wrote this about financial goal setting: "In over 30 years as a banker, I have seen the toll that the relentless pressure to turn in ever better quarterly and annual numbers has on business and personal ethics."[19] Another problem with goals is that the continual pursuit of goals that stretch your capability can be stressful, causing workers to extend their workweek to "make their numbers."

To overcome this potential problem with goals, it is important for the worker pursuing the goal and the goal setter to agree on the method of attaining the goal. Unethical and dysfunctional methods might be declared out of bounds.

<table>
<tr><td>

LEARNING OBJECTIVE ④

Describe the application of positive reinforcement including recognition and praise to worker motivation.

behavior modification

A way of changing behavior by rewarding the right responses and punishing or ignoring the wrong responses.

</td></tr>
</table>

POSITIVE REINFORCEMENT AND RECOGNITION PROGRAMS

Rewarding workers for doing the right thing is a widely accepted principle. Positive reinforcement is part of **behavior modification,** a way of changing behavior by rewarding the right responses and punishing or ignoring the wrong responses. A *reward* is something of value received as a consequence of having attained a goal.

Positive reinforcement increases the probability that behavior will be repeated by rewarding people for making the right response. The phrase "increases the probability" is noteworthy. No behavior modification strategy guarantees that people will always make the right response in the future. However, it increases the chance that they will repeat the desired behavior. The term *reinforcement* means that the behavior (or response) is strengthened or entrenched. For example, pressing F7 in Word to reach the spelling and grammar function has been reinforced so many times that it is now probably automatic. Pressing F5 to refresh a Web site is probably done so infrequently that people must pause and think before making the response.

Positive reinforcement is the most effective behavior modification strategy. Most people respond better to being rewarded for the right response

---

[18]Lisa D. Ordóñez, Maurice E. Schweitzer, Adam D. Galinksy, and Max H. Bazerman, "On Good Scholarship, Goal Settings, and Scholars Gone Wild," *Academy of Management Perspectives,* August 2009, pp. 82–87.

[19]Quoted in Carol Hymowitz, "Readers Share Tales of Jobs Where Strategy Became Meeting Target," *The Wall Street Journal,* March 22, 2005, p. B1.

than to being punished for the wrong response; receiving a bonus for good customer service is more motivating than being fined for poor customer service. Here we describe the successful application of positive reinforcement, and using recognition and praise to motivate workers. Both recognition and praise are part of reinforcement. We will also describe cross-cultural differences in the effectiveness of specific rewards.

Rules for Application of Positive Reinforcement

Positive reinforcement may take the form of an overall company program, such as within a highly structured behavior modification program, or a rewards and recognition program. Managers use positive reinforcement more frequently, on an informal, daily basis. The following list presents suggestions for making effective use of positive reinforcement, whether as part of a company program or more informally.

1. *State clearly what behavior will lead to a reward, and supply ample feedback.* The nature of good performance, or the goals, must be agreed to by both manager and group member. Clarification could take this form: "What I need are inventory reports without missing data. When you achieve this, you'll be credited with good performance." As workers attain performance goals, they should receive frequent feedback. Telling people they have done something correctly, or notifying them by e-mail, are efficient forms of feedback.

2. *Use appropriate rewards.* An appropriate reward proves effective when it is valued by the person being motivated. Examine the list of rewards in Exhibit 11-6. Note that some have more appeal to you than do others. The best way to motivate people is to offer them their preferred rewards for good performance. Managers should ask employees what they are interested in attaining. A seven-year-long case history analysis of call center workers found that promotional opportunities—not pay increases— were the most effective rewards. Part of the reason for the appropriateness of promotion as a reward is it brought along formal recognition as well as changes in status and responsibilities.[20]

3. *Make rewards contingent on good performance.* Contingent reinforcement means that getting the reward depends on giving a certain performance. Unless a reward is linked to the desired behavior or performance, it will have little effect on whether the behavior or performance is repeated. For example, saying "You're doing great" in response to anything an employee does will not lead to good performance. If the manager reserves the "doing great" response for truly outstanding performance, he or she may reinforce the good performance.

4. *Administer rewards intermittently.* Positive reinforcement can be administered under different types of schedules. The most effective and sensible

---

[20]Philip Moss, Harold Salzman, and Chris Tilly, "Under Construction: The Continuing Evolution of Job Structures in Call Centers," *Industrial Relations*, Vol. 47, pp. 173–208.

A large number of potential rewards can be used to motivate individuals and teams, and many of them are low-cost or no-cost. An important condition for a reward is the perception of its value by the individual being motivated. The viewpoint of the reward giver alone about the value of a reward is not sufficient.

Monetary

Salary increases or bonuses

Instant cash awards

Company stock

Bonus or profit sharing

Stock options

Paid personal holiday (such as birthday)

Extra paid-vacation days

Movie, concert, or athletic event tickets

Free or discount airline tickets

Discounts on company products or services

Gift selection from online catalog

Race-car driving camp

Job and Career Related

Challenging work assignment

Empowerment of employee

Change of job status from temporary to permanent

Promise of job security

Assignment to high-prestige team or project

Favorable performance evaluation

Freedom to choose own work activity
Promotion

Flexible working hours

Creating own schedule for peak work loads

Do more of preferred task

Role as boss's stand-in when he or she is away

Job rotation

Seminars and continuous education

Opportunity to set own goals

Food and Dining

Business luncheon paid by company

Company picnics

Department parties or banquet

Lunch catered into office

Recognition and Pride Related

Compliments

Encouragement

Access to confidential information

Pat on back or handshake

Public expression of appreciation

Meeting of appreciation with executive

Open note of thanks distributed by e-mail

Flattering letter from customer distributed by e-mail

Employee-of-the-month award

Wall plaque indicating accomplishment

Visit to manager's office just to receive praise

Team uniforms, hats, or T-shirts

Designated parking space for outstanding performance

Status Symbols

Bigger office or cubicle

Office or cubicle with window

Freedom to personalize work area

Private office

Time Off

Three-day weekend

Company time bank with deposits made for unusual success

Time off gift certificates

Personal leave days for events chosen by employee

Sources: Melinda Ligos, "Those Year-End Bonuses Aren't Always Green," *The New York Times* (http://nytimes.com) December 28, 2003; "Do Incentive Rewards Work?" *HRfocus,* October 2000, pp. 1, 14–15; "Retain Top Workers with Time Off," *Manager's Edge,* October 2006; Cindy Krischer Goodman, "Managers Use Perks for Young Workers," *McClatchy Newspapers,* September 24, 2006. Julie Bos, "Building Engagement in an Economic Crisis," *Workforce Management,* April 20, 2009, p. 30.

type is an intermittent schedule in which rewards are administered often, but not always, when the appropriate behavior occurs. A reward loses its effect if given every time the employee makes the right response. Thus intermittent rewards sustain desired behavior for a longer time by helping to prevent the behavior from fading away when it is not rewarded. In addition to being more effective, intermittent rewards are generally more practical than continuous rewards. Few managers have enough time to dispense rewards every time team members attain performance goals.

5. *Administer rewards promptly.* The proper timing of rewards may be difficult because the manager is not present at the time of good performance. In this case, an e-mail message, text message, or phone call of appreciation within several days of the good performance is appropriate. Some managers are posting Tweets these days to post public notes of appreciation.

6. *Change rewards periodically.* Rewards grow stale quickly; they must be changed periodically. A repetitive reward can even become an annoyance. How many times can one be motivated by the phrase "nice job"? Suppose the reward for making a sales quota is an iPad. How many iPads can one person use (assuming the award is not re-gifted)?

7. *Make the rewards visible.* When other workers notice the reward, its impact multiplies because the other people observe what kind of behavior is rewarded. Assume that you were informed about a coworker's exciting assignment, given because of high performance. You might strive to accomplish the same level of performance.

8. *Reward groups and teams as well as individuals.* To improve organizational productivity, both groups and individuals should receive rewards for good performance. A combination of group and individual rewards encourages teamwork yet does not discourage outstanding individual performance. As Jack and Suzy Welch recommend, "When an individual or team does something notable, make a big deal of it. Announce it publicly, talk about it at every opportunity. Hand out awards."[21]

Positive Reinforcement Effectiveness

Positive reinforcement has a long history of improving productivity on the job, including the control of absenteeism.[22] Discount-store chain Dollar General turned to the behavior modification company Aubrey Daniels International to tackle absenteeism when it reached 16 percent at the company's distribution center. Dollar General introduced a point system, put workers into teams, and drew a racetrack on the wall with each team represented by a race car. Using positive reinforcement principles, team members could earn

---

[21]Jack and Suzy Welch, "Keeping Your People Pumped," *Business Week*, March 27, 2006, p. 122.

[22]Alexander D. Stajkovic and Fred Luthans, "Differential Effects of Incentive Motivators on Work Performance," *Academy of Management Journal*, June 2001, pp. 580–590.

points by arriving on time. If they arrived late, they could earn points for their teams in other ways such as by returning from breaks on time. Each day, the race cars advanced by the number of points earned.

Jeff Sims, the Dollar General senior vice president, says, "And we talked to all of our supervisors and got rid of the punishing behavior of yelling at them if they were late. We started thanking them for coming to work and then saying, 'We really need your help to get those points tomorrow morning.' " After a certain number of laps were completed, the team with the most points was authorized to choose the food served at the distribution center. Within two weeks of the program's introduction, attendance had moved up to 95 percent (from 84 percent).[23]

You may think the Dollar General motivational approach is hokey, but there is a message. With even modest rewards, positive reinforcement can help a company attain key goals.

The power of positive reinforcement to change behavior is being successfully applied to develop a healthier workforce in many companies. Data indicate that incentives from $51 to $100 can increase participation in smoking cessation and weight management programs and encourage workers to get biometric screenings. Incentives of greater than $100 are associated with higher participation in health risk appraisals.[24] The payoff to the company includes lower health-insurance costs and higher productivity; healthy workers concentrate better, have more energy, and are absent less frequently.

Employee Recognition and Reward Programs and Informal Recognition

As indicated in Exhibit 11-6, positive reinforcement for workers often takes the form of tangible rewards as well as recognition and praise. A combination of recognition and rewards, along with informal praise, is likely to be the most motivational. Here we describe these two related approaches separately.

Recognition and Reward Programs

About one half of companies of all sizes have formal *recognition and reward* programs as managers attempt to retain the right employees, and keep workers productive who worry about losing their jobs or having no private work area. These recognition programs usually include the term *reward* because good performers are recognized with rewards. Among the rewards are dinner certificates, watches and jewelry, candles, plaques, and on-the-spot cash awards (around $25 to $50) for good performance. Employee recognition programs are so widespread that several companies, including Maritz Inc.,

---

[23]Todd Henneman, "Daniels' Scientific Method," *Workforce Management*, October 10, 2005, p. 46.

[24]Susan J. Wells, "Getting Paid for Staying Well," *HR Magazine*, February 2010, p. 59.

specialize in developing reward incentive and recognition programs for other companies.[25]

Yum Brands, the world's largest restaurant company whose divisions include Taco Bell, KFC, and Pizza Hut, is widely recognized for its programs of rewards and recognition. When Chairman and CEO David C. Novak became president of KFC, he wanted to break through the clutter of recognition so he gave away rubber chickens. He would give an outstanding KFC chef a rubber chicken along with a $100 check, and the event was photographed. Novak now gives way big sets of smiling teeth with legs on them for people walking the talk on behalf of the customer. Part of his reasoning is that many people quit because they do not feel appreciated.[26]

More sophisticated recognition programs recognize behavior that supports organizational values, so the awards are a reminder of what is important to the company. TEOCO, an information technology company near Washington DC, links rewards to the company name and values. Managers give on-the-spot "TEO-Star" awards when they observe workers displaying one of the company's core values: alignment with interests of employees, clients, and community; integrity, honesty, and respect; courageous action; and striving for progress through ownership.[27] An IT technician might receive such an award for salvaging a client's data during a blackout.

Recognition rewards became increasingly popular as a way of motivating workers and boosting productivity during the Great Recession as less money was available for salary increases and bonuses. Many companies, including Rockwell Collins and Ford Motor Company, unleashed a slew of inexpensive rewards such as praise, thank-you notes, and $25 gift cards.[28]

Teams, as well as individuals, should receive recognition to enhance motivation. Motivation consultant Bob Nelson recommends that to build a high-performing team, the manager should acknowledge the success of all team members. As with individual recognition, a personal touch works best. Examples include a manager thanking group members for their involvement, suggestions, and initiatives. Holding a group luncheon for outstanding team performance is also a potential motivator.[29] *Potential* is emphasized because team recognition does not take into account individual differences in preferences for rewards. For example, some employees object to group luncheons because it diverts time they might want to use for personal purposes.

---

[25]Sheree R. Curry, "Family Turmoil Aside, the Incentives Business Has Proved Rewarding for Maritz," *Workforce Management*, July 2005, p. 74.

[26]Adam Bryant, "At Yum Brands, Rewards for Good Work," *The New York Times* (nytimes.com), July 12, 2009, p. 3

[27]"Branded Recognition," *Manager's Edge*, December 2006, p. 4.

[28]Dana Mattioli, "Rewards for Extra Work Come Cheap In Lean Times," *The Wall Street Journal*, January 4, 2010, p. B7.

[29]Bob Nelson, "Does One Reward Fit All?" *Workforce*, February 1997, pp. 67–70.

As with most motivation and retention programs, recognition and rewards must be carefully planned, otherwise they may backfire and lose money for the company. One example is giving out turkeys or gift baskets at holiday time that many employees perceive to be insulting and patronizing. An advanced procedure is to ask employees what types of recognition they prefer.

Informal Recognition Including Praise

Praising workers for good performance is a major type of informal recognition. As Jim Weddle, CEO of retail broker Edward Jones, said a couple of years ago, "The retail brokerage business isn't great right now, so I've been asking managers to simply tell folks that they're appreciated."[30] An effective form of praise describes the worker's performance rather than merely making an evaluation. Describing good performance might take this form: "You turned an angry customer into an ally who has referred new business to us." A straightforward evaluation would be "You did a great job with that angry customer." Even more effective would be to combine the two statements.

Generic praise, such as telling all workers on the team that they are doing a great job, can be discouraging, because the team members will not feel they are being recognized as individuals. A useful principle of effective praise is that it should be true, sincere, deserved, and meaningful. Here is an example of praising good performance:

> *Karla, you made a terrific presentation this morning. I especially liked the charts you used to illustrate the budget choices we are facing. That really helped me make sense of a complicated issue, and I appreciate the work you put into it.*[31]

Although praise costs no money and only requires a few moments of time, many workers feel they do not receive enough praise. Managers therefore have a good opportunity to increase motivation by the simple act of praising good deeds. Other informal approaches to recognizing good performance include a manager or team leader taking an employee to lunch, offering a sincere handshake, and putting flowers on an employee's desk. E-mail and text messages are other handy tools for giving praise and recognition. Exhibit 11-7 provides a list of statements of praise that might be used with team members.

Cross-Cultural Differences in Needs and Suitable Recognition Awards

A person's culture can influence which needs are strongest for him or her, and therefore which approach to recognizing and motivating that person is the most effective. A manager can study different cultures in general to get some ideas, but it is also important to make some observations within the

---

[30]Quoted in "The Three-Minute Manager," *Fortune*, November 24, 2008, p. 28.

[31]"Raise Workplace Morale Without Spending a Dime," *Communication Briefings*, April 2010, p. 1.

| **EXHIBIT 11-7** | **21 Ways to Say "Well Done"** |

Sometimes, offering praise is harder than it should be. In a busy office, it's easy to forget to compliment and voice your appreciation. But praise can really make a team member's day. Here are some reminders of how easy it really is to say, "Thanks, well done."

1. I'm proud you're on my team.
2. Congratulations on a terrific job.
3. You're so helpful. Thank you.
4. You really made a difference by...
5. Thanks so much for your considerate effort.
6. I really admire your perseverance.
7. You've made my day because of...
8. You're a champion.
9. Wow, what an incredible accomplishment.
10. Great effort. You make us all look good.
11. I have great confidence in you.
12. You've grasped the concept well.
13. Your customer service skills are sensational.
14. Your sales results are outstanding.
15. You're a valuable part of the team.
16. Your efforts are really making a difference.
17. You are hitting high productivity.
18. Our customers are crazy about you.
19. You have helped us attain our goals.
20. Your work ethic motivates the team.

work group. According to popular stereotype, a worker raised in Japan would more likely be motivated by recognition in private than by public recognition. In contrast, an American-raised worker would be more likely to experience need satisfaction when given public recognition such as during a staff meeting.

On a more superficial level than psychological needs, cultural differences exist about suitability of recognition gifts. Globoforce CEO Eric Mosley notes that companies should be sensitive to differences in desirability of gift certificates. The United States has a department-store culture, so awarding American workers gift certificates to big retail chains and restaurants is desirable. Italians may prefer gift certificates to a small fashion boutique, and Germans, a sports store. In most parts of Asia, gift certificates are not prevalent, and employees would prefer a tangible gift as a reward.[32]

Cross-cultural differences in standards of living also influence the effectiveness of recognition awards. In the United States, an outstanding performer might be rewarded with a luxury item such as a Mont Blanc pen or watch worth $1,000 retail. In India or China, where standards of living are still rising and where bicycles remain an important mode of transportation, $1,000 might be better invested to buy a motor bike for a top employee. Incentives consultant Eugene Less says, "You might not give a moped away in the U.S., but giving one in China or India is a huge thing."[33]

---

[32]Sheree R. Curry, "A Reward in the U.S. May Not Be a Reward Overseas," http://www.workforce.com, July 2005.

[33]Irwin Speizer, "Incentives Catch On Overseas, but Value of Awards Can Too Easily Get Lost in Translation," *Workforce Management*, November 21, 2005, p. 46.

Despite cultural and geographic differences, the manager must still investigate. In general, a moped is a better gift than an expensive fountain pen for a high-performing Chinese worker. Nevertheless, beauty products giant Mary Kay has found that pink cell phones, pink Buicks, and pink Cadillacs are cherished gifts for outstanding sales representatives in China.[34]

LEARNING
OBJECTIVE **5**
Explain the
conditions under
which a person will
be motivated
according to
expectancy theory.

EXPECTANCY THEORY OF MOTIVATION

According to the **expectancy theory of motivation**, people will put forth the greatest effort if they expect the effort to lead to performance that in turn leads to a reward. The various versions of expectancy theory suggest that a process similar to rational gambling determines choices among courses of action. Employees are motivated by what they expect will be the consequences of their efforts. At the same time, they must be confident they can perform the task.[35]

**expectancy theory of
motivation**

The belief that people
will expend effort if
they expect the effort
to lead to performance
and the performance
to lead to a reward.

A Basic Model of Expectancy Theory

Expectancy theory integrates important ideas found in other generally accepted motivation theories, including those presented in this chapter. Exhibit 11-8 presents a basic version of expectancy theory. According to the version of expectancy theory developed by Victor H. Vroom, four conditions must exist for motivated behavior to occur.[36]

Condition A refers to *expectancy*, which means that people will expend effort because they believe it will lead to performance. In this $E{\rightarrow}P$ expectancy, subjective probabilities range between 0.0 and 1.0. Rational people ask themselves, "If I work hard, will I really get the job done?" If they evaluate the probability as being high, they probably will invest the effort to achieve the goal. People have higher $E{\rightarrow}P$ expectancies when they have the appropriate skills, training, and self-confidence.

EXHIBIT 11-8   Basic Version of Expectancy Theory of Motivation

An individual will be motivated when:

A. The individual believes effort (E) will lead to favorable performance (P)—that is, when $E{\rightarrow}P$ (also referred to as expectancy).
B. The individual believes performance will lead to favorable outcome (O)—that is,

when $P{\rightarrow}O$ (also referred to as instrumentality).
C. Outcome or reward satisfies an important need (in other words, valence is strong).
D. Need satisfaction is intense enough to make effort seem worthwhile.

---

[34]Martin Booe, "Sales Force at Mary Kay China Embraces the American Way," *Workforce Management*, April 2005, pp. 24–25.

[35]Steel and König, "Integrating Theories of Motivation," p. 893.

[36]Victor H. Vroom, *Work and Motivation* (New York: Wiley, 1964).

Condition B is based on the fact that people are more willing to expend effort if they think that good performance will lead to a reward. This is referred to as $P{\to}O$ instrumentality. It, too, ranges between 0.0 and 1.0. (*Instrumentality* refers to the idea that the behavior is instrumental in achieving an important end.) The rational person says, "I'm much more willing to perform well if I'm assured that I'll receive the reward I deserve." A cautious employee might even ask other employees whether they received their promised rewards for exceptional performance. To strengthen a subordinate's $P{\to}O$ instrumentality, the manager should give reassurance that the reward will be forthcoming.

Condition C refers to *valence*, the value a person attaches to certain outcomes. The greater the valence, the greater the effort. Valences can be either positive or negative. If a student believes that receiving an A is important, he or she will work hard. If a student believes that avoiding a C or a lower grade is important, he or she will work hard. Valences range from -1 to $+1$ in most versions of expectancy theory. A positive valence indicates a preference for a particular reward. A clearer picture of individual differences in human motivation spreads valences out over a range of -100 to $+100$.

Most work situations present the possibility of several outcomes, with a different valence attached to each. Assume that a project manager is pondering whether becoming a project manager professional (**PMP**) would be worth the effort. The list that follows cites possible outcomes or rewards from achieving certification, along with their valences (on a scale of -100 to $+100$).

* Status from being a PMP, 75
* Promotion to senior project manager, 95
* Plaque to hang on office wall, 25
* Bigger salary increase next year, 90
* Letters of congratulations from friends and relatives, 50
* Expressions of envy from one or two coworkers, -25

Valences are useful in explaining why some people will put forth the effort to do things with low expectancies. For example, most people know the chance of winning a lottery, inventing something as successful as the Internet, or writing a best-selling novel is only one in a million. Nevertheless, a number of people vigorously pursue these goals. They do so because they attach an extraordinarily positive valence to these outcomes (perhaps 100!).

Condition D indicates that the need satisfaction stemming from each outcome must be intense enough to make the effort worthwhile. Would you walk two miles on a hot day for one glass of ice water? The water would undoubtedly satisfy your thirst need, but the magnitude of the satisfaction would probably not be worth the effort. A production technician turned down a promotion to the position of inspector because the raise offered was only 50 cents per hour. The worker told his supervisor, "I need more money. But I'm not willing to take on that much added responsibility for $30 a week."

Implications for Management

Expectancy theory has several important implications for the effective management of people. The theory helps pinpoint what a manager must do to motivate group members and diagnose motivational problems.[37]

1. *Individual differences among employees must be taken into account.* Different people attach different valences to different rewards, so a manager should try to match rewards with individual preferences. Behavior modification also makes use of this principle.

2. *Help workers feel that they are making progress toward their goals.* One of the components of expectancy theory deals with feeling that your effort will lead to good performance, so workers have a desire to believe they are making headway in their jobs. A multiyear study tracking hundreds of knowledge workers found that the top motivator of performance is the feeling of making progress. The study found that when workers feel they are making headway in their jobs, or when they receive support that helps them overcome obstacles, their drive to succeed is at its highest.[38]

3. *Rewards should be closely tied to those actions the organization sees as worthwhile.* For example, if the organization values customer service, people should be rewarded for providing good customer service. Home Depot has a program called Orange Juiced that offers store employees bonuses as much as $2,000 for exceptional customer service.[39]

4. *Employees should be given the appropriate training and encouragement.* An investment in training will strengthen their subjective hunches that effort will lead to good performance.

5. *Employees should be presented with credible evidence that good performance does lead to anticipated rewards.* A manager should reassure employees that good work will be both noticed and rewarded. As part of this implication, managers must listen carefully to understand the perceived link employees make between hard work and rewards. If instrumentality is unjustifiably low, the manager must reassure the employee that hard work will be rewarded.

6. *The meaning and implications of outcomes should be explained.* It can be motivational for employees to know the values of certain outcomes. If an employee knows that a high rating on a performance evaluation increases the chances of receiving favorable assignments and promotions, plus a bigger salary increase, he or she will strive harder to perform well.

[37]Walter B. Newsom, "Motivate Now!" *Personnel Journal*, February 1999, pp. 51–52.

[38]Teresa M. Amabile and Steven J. Kramer, "What Really Motivates Workers," *Harvard Business Review*, January–February 2010, pp. 44–45.

[39]Bruce Upbin, "Hammered," *Forbes*, January 8, 2007, p. 37.

LEARNING
OBJECTIVE **6**
Describe the role
of financial
incentives,
including profit
sharing and
gainsharing, in
worker motivation.

MOTIVATION THROUGH FINANCIAL INCENTIVES

A natural way to motivate workers at any level is to offer them financial incentives for good performance. Linking pay to performance improves the motivation value of money. Using financial incentives to motivate people fits principles of positive reinforcement and punishment. Financial incentives, however, predate behavior modification. The paragraphs that follow discuss linking pay to performance, profit sharing and gainsharing, employee stock ownership and stock options, and problems associated with financial incentives. Exhibit 11-9 outlines this information.

A useful principle for using financial incentives to motivate workers at all levels is to investigate which incentives are most appealing to groups and individuals. Many workers are motivated to work hard for salary increases, yet some others would work harder for the opportunity to obtain a bonus or stock options. Another group of workers might value increased health benefits more than a salary increase.[40] Another key principle is for managers to explain clearly to employees how performance is linked to pay, including the fact that unethical behavior will not be tolerated as a way of attaining a performance goal. The accompanying Management in Action illustrates how individual preferences might be built into an incentive plan.

Linking Pay to Performance Including Bonuses

Financial incentives are more effective when they are linked to (or contingent upon) good performance. Production workers and sales workers have long received contingent financial incentives. Many production workers receive, after meeting a quota, bonuses per unit of production. Most industrial sales representatives receive salary plus commissions.

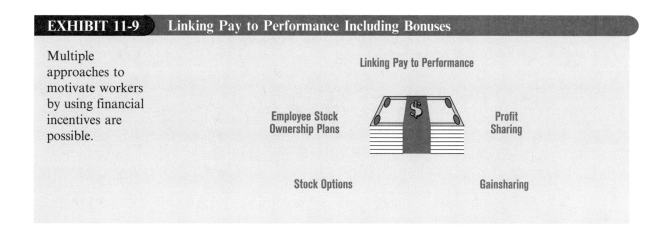

EXHIBIT 11-9	**Linking Pay to Performance Including Bonuses**

Multiple approaches to motivate workers by using financial incentives are possible.

Linking Pay to Performance

Employee Stock Ownership Plans

Profit Sharing

Stock Options

Gainsharing

---

[40]Pamela Babcock, "Find What Workers Want," *HR Magazine*, April 2005, p. 51.

Managers increasingly use bonuses to retain and motivate employees. Bonuses help control fixed costs, and also tend to keep employees focused on business objectives.[41] Human resources specialists also see equitable salaries and merit pay as a way of keeping employees engaged. Conversely, the lack of merit pay can readily disengage workers.[42] When times are tight, pay for performance can be used to focus on the most valuable contributors so they can be recognized, motivated, and retained.[43]

Exhibit 11-10 presents a typical approach to linking employee pay to performance, a plan that is often referred to as merit pay. Such a plan has become an almost universal method of distributing wage and salary increase in the United States and in many other countries.[44] The U.S. Federal government, however, makes quite limited use of merit pay, with only about 0.1 percent of salaries awarded in bonuses. Note carefully in Exhibit 11-10 the information about assigning lump sum payments, rather than percentages, to each performance category. This approach helps more junior workers receive large merit increases. A cost-of-living adjustment is not considered

---

EXHIBIT 11-10 **Guidelines for Performance-Based Merit Increases at a Hospital**

Merit pay is additional income earned for meeting performance standards.

Performance Level of Staff Members	Merit Increase (Percentage of Pay)
Demonstrate exceptional performance and make outstanding contributions during the year	4.75–5.50
Give consistently productive performance that meets all standards and exceeds some	3.75–4.74
Give consistently productive performance that meets expectations	2.00–3.74
Demonstrate performance that is not wholly satisfactory, even though some expectations may be met or even exceeded	1.00–1.99
Generally fail to meet key expectations and standards; substantial improvement is necessary and essential	0.00

Note: To help equalize wages more, some organizations assign an absolute amount of salary increase to each performance category. For example, all workers in the top category would receive a $2,500 increase; those in the second category $1,500; those in the third category, $1,000; and those in the fourth category, zero dollars. Assigning absolute dollar amounts to each category prevents junior workers receiving relatively small increases because their base pay is so much lower. Under the new system a more junior top-performing worker making $30,000 per year would receive a new salary of $32,500 ($30,000 + $2,500). Under the old percentage system, his or her maximum new salary might be $31,650 ($30,000 + 0.055 × $30,000).

---

[41]Study cited in Erin White, "Employers Increasingly Favor Bonuses to Raises," *The Wall Street Journal*, August 28, 2006, p. B3.

[42]Fay Hansen, "Money Talks," *Workforce Management*, November 16, 2009, pp. 27–31.

[43]Mark Henricks, "Pay for Performance," *Entrepreneur*, November 2008, p. 77.

[44]Fay Hansen, "Merit-Pay Payoff?" *Workforce Management*, November 3, 2008, p. 33.

MANAGEMENT IN ACTION

Workers at Skyline Construction Choose Own Mix of Salary and Bonus

Mark Trento and Adam Chelini had a rare opportunity last year. They got to pick their own salaries, in a range between $125,000 and $150,000. The catch: Choosing a lower salary meant a shot at a larger bonus. Trento, a vice-president for San Francisco-based Skyline Construction Inc., chose the safety of $150,000. Chelini, a Skyline senior project manager, opted for $125,000 and wound up with a larger bonus than he would have received otherwise. While neither would say what his bonus was, both say they were happy with their choices.

Trento and Chelini are among 15 participants in Skyline's unusual management compensation system, which lets employees put a portion of their pay at risk. Compensation experts say the approach is rare and potentially risky, but Skyline employees say it offers flexibility and motivates them to succeed.

Executives at Skyline, which specializes in building and renovating commercial interiors, introduced the plan in 2005 when employees bought the company from its former owners. During a brainstorming session on cutting costs, a project manager proposed the idea to encourage Skyline's biggest earners to take lower upfront salaries, says Chief Executive David Hayes. The idea proved popular. Twelve of the 15 eligible managers in one year chose lower salaries and higher potential bonuses. "It's their way of throwing a little skin in the game," Hayes says.

Skyline's plan works by adjusting managers' commission targets, allowing them to accrue bigger bonuses for exceeding their targets. Other bonus factors include nonfinancial measures such as customer satisfaction and timely project completion. Only top managers were included in the plan because they have the biggest influence on profits. An employee-owned company, Skyline shares profits with its 82 employees through a separate long-term equity plan.

Hayes says that the pick-your-salary plan has been a success, noting that Skyline's revenues grew from $42 million to $76 million during a three-year period. All four senior executives at Skyline regularly opt for lower salaries and higher potential bonuses. Hayes says the plan fits well with Skyline's culture, which focuses on open-book management and employee ownership. "Owners get more reward for taking risk," he says. "That's business, and that's the entrepreneurial spirit that we are seeking to capture."

Case Questions

1. Why might being given some choice in the mix of guaranteed salary and bonus be motivational?
2. What kind of motivational problem might Skyline senior managers have in a year when the company did not generate a profit?
3. What does the analogy "skin in the game" imply from a motivational standpoint?
4. Given the opportunity, what mix of salary and bonus would you choose? Why?

Source: Cari Tuna, "Pay, Your Own Way: Firm Lets Workers Pick Salary," *The Wall Street Journal*, July 7, 2008, p. B6.

merit pay because it is not related to performance. Merit pay for both individual contributors and managers is based on actual results.

An increasing effort of managers and compensation specialists to link pay to performance supports many business strategies—workers receive financial incentives for performing in ways consistent with the business strategy. The Home Depot bonuses for good customer service mentioned above came about because the company was not rated as highly on customer service as management wanted, so improved customer service was incorporated into strategy.

For a pay-for-performance plan to be successful, performance must be measured carefully and regularly. Most pay-for-performance plans are based somewhat on qualitative measures such as supervisory ratings. Whenever possible, quantitative measures of performance such as sales completed, productivity, turnover, patents, return on investment, and customer satisfaction results should also included.

Profit Sharing and Gainsharing

The pay plans mentioned so far link rewards to individual effort. Numerous organizations attempt to increase motivation and productivity through a company-wide plan linking incentive pay to increases in performance. Here we describe profit sharing in general, and a specific form of sharing profits called gainsharing.

Profit Sharing

profit-sharing plan
A method of giving workers supplemental income based on the profitability of the entire firm or a selected unit.

Profit-sharing plans give workers supplemental income based on the profitability of the entire firm or a selected unit. The motivational principle is that employees will work harder to contribute to profitability when they will eventually share some of the profits. The larger the company, the more difficult it is for the individual employee to visualize how his or her work efforts translate into corporate profits. Ideally, all employees must be committed to working for a common good. Employee contributions to profits may take a variety of forms such as product quantity, product quality, reduced costs, or improved business processes.

A major challenge in administering profit-sharing plans and any of the other financial incentives described here is making precise judgments about who should receive how much, and whether the variable pay contributes to organizational performance.

Gainsharing

gainsharing
A formal program allowing employees to participate financially in the productivity gains they have achieved.

Another approach to profit sharing focuses on productivity increases more directly attributable to worker ideas and effort. **Gainsharing** is a formal program that allows employees to participate financially in the productivity gains they have achieved. It is accomplished through establishing a payout formula and involving employees. Productivity gains are typically manufacturing related, but can also be in service, such as customer service.

Rewards are distributed after performance improves. As in other forms of profit sharing, the participants can be the entire organization or a unit within the firm. Gainsharing is based on factors in the work environment that employees can control directly. Rewards are shared with all members of the gainsharing unit, regardless of individual contribution toward productivity improvement.[45]

The formulas used in gainsharing vary widely, but share common elements. Managers begin by comparing what employees are paid to what they sell or produce. Assume that labor costs make up 50 percent of production costs. Any reductions below 50 percent are placed in a bonus pool. Part of the money in the bonus pool is shared among workers. The company's share of the productivity savings in the pool can be distributed to shareholders as increased profits. The savings may allow managers to lower prices, a move that could make the company more competitive.

The second element of gainsharing is employee involvement. Managers establish a mechanism that actively solicits, reviews, and implements employee suggestions about productivity improvement. A committee of managers and employees reviews the ideas and then implements the most promising suggestions. The third key element is employee cooperation. To achieve the bonuses for productivity improvement, group members must work harmoniously with each other. Departments must also cooperate with each other, because some suggestions involve the work of more than one organizational unit.[46]

Employee Stock Ownership and Stock Option Plans

Another way of motivating workers with financial incentives is to make them part owners of the business through stock purchases. Two variations of the idea of giving workers equity in the business are stock ownership and stock option plans. Stock ownership can be motivational because employees participate in the financial success of the firm as measured by its stock price. If employees work hard, the company may become more successful and the value of the stock increases. Executives are motivated by plans that award them company shares. If the stock increases in value, the executive can sell it and generate a profit.

Under an *employee stock ownership plan* (ESOP), employees at all levels in the organization are given stock. The employer contributes either shares of its stock or the money to purchase the stock on the open market. Stock shares are usually deposited in employee retirement accounts. Upon retirement, employees can choose to receive company stock instead of cash. ESOPs are also significant because they offer tax incentives to the employer.

---

[45]Luis R. Gomez-Meija, Theresa M. Welbourn, and Robert M. Wiseman, "The Role of Risk Sharing and Risk Taking Under Gainsharing," *Academy of Management Review*, July 2000, p. 493; http://www.gainsharing.com.

[46]Susan C. Hanlon, David C. Meyer, and Robert K. Taylor, "Consequences of Gainsharing: A Field Experiment Revisited," *Group and Organization Management*, Vol. 19, No. 1 (1994), pp. 87–11; http://www.gainsharing.com, accessed March 12, 2010.

For example, some of the earnings paid to the retirement fund are tax deductible.

Employee stock ownership plans are popular because they are easy to understand and because they contribute to an ownership culture. The only notable downside is that employees might rely too heavily on company stock, forgoing the advantages of a diversified investment portfolio. If the company stock plunges dramatically, the value of the employee's investments shrinks to almost nothing. Ten years after stocks in general began their decline in 2001 they had still not returned to their all-time high.

Employee stock options are more complicated than straightforward stock ownership. Stock options give employees the right to purchase company stock at a specified price at some point in the future. If the stock rises in value, the employee can purchase it at a predetermined discount. Thousands of workers in the information technology field, particularly in Silicon Valley, have become millionaires and multimillionaires with their stock options— particularly those who cashed in their options at the right time.

Stock options can be risky. When it comes time for employees to cash in their options, the stock price could be much less than the option (strike) price. If the stock sinks below the designated purchase price, the option is worthless. Many workers who chose relatively small base pay and big options will be especially disappointed should the stock market plunge. Stock options then become a source of discouragement and anger rather than motivation. To help remedy the situation, many technology companies enable employees to exchange *underwater* options for new options that are more likely to be profitable. (An *underwater option* is one whose strike price is more than the stock's current value, or the water level.) The new lower-price options are more likely to be exercised.[47]

Stock options have encouraged practices of questionable ethics. For example, a high-ranking official backdates the option price to a time when it was much lower than the time at which the holder of the options wants to sell the stock.[48] A few instances have been found in which backdates were forged to make the grants seem legitimate. The person is assigned a "favorable date." The ethical issue is that the option holder is almost guaranteed a big profit even if the stock did not increase in value from the time the original option was issued.

Problems Associated with Financial Incentives

Although financial incentives are widely used as motivators, they can create problems. A major problem is that workers may not agree with managers about the value of their contributions. Financial incentives can also pit individuals and groups against each other. The result may be unhealthy

[47]Gregory Zuckerman, "Tech Companies Find Options Hard to Kick," *The Wall Street Journal,* August 11, 2003, p. C1.

[48]Craig Matsuda, "I Did the Work, Now Pay Me," *Entrepreneur,* November 2009, pp. 78–79.

competition rather than cooperation and teamwork. Some managers believe that giving equal increases to all members of the team promotes teamwork.

Another concern is that merit pay decisions are based on performance evaluations, and the evaluations might be too subjective. As implied in the criticisms of goals, huge financial incentives can prompt financial managers to make high-risk investments that can result in major losses for investors, such as selling securities based on mortgages held by people with poor credit.

Many critics of financial incentives are concerned that American business executives siphon off too much money from corporations that could go to shareholders, employees, and to customers in the form of lower prices. Top-level managers may deserve large financial rewards for good performance, but how much is too much? A representative example is that Wells Fargo (a major investment and commercial bank) chief executive John G. Stumpf received $18.7 million in cash and stock for 2009.[49]

People who justify such high executive compensation say the large payments are necessary to attract and retain top talent and to keep the executives motivated. And besides, executive pay is a small percentage of total revenues. You have probably heard the same argument for paying some professional athletes $20 million per year. Another argument in favor of giant compensation for executives is that managerial skills are highly valued in society, and top business managers and leaders are worth at least as much as entertainment stars.

The most researched argument against financial rewards is that it focuses the attention of workers too much on the external reward such as money or stocks. In the process, the workers lose out on intrinsic rewards such as joy in accomplishment. Instead of being passionate about the work they are doing, people become overly concerned with the size of their reward. This distinction is important because intrinsic motivation is more intense and longer lasting than the external motivation of financial incentives.[50] One argument is that external rewards do not create a lasting commitment. Instead, they create temporary compliance, such as working hard in the short run to earn a bonus. A frequent problem with merit pay systems is that a person who does not receive a merit increase for one pay period then feels that he or she has been punished.

In reality, workers at all levels want a combination of internal (intrinsic) rewards and financial rewards along with other external rewards such as praise. Workers also want a work environment that enables them to manage their lives well off the job, such as ample vacation and some flexibility in working hours. Workers search for meaning and satisfaction as well as

---

[49]Eric Dash, "Wall St.'s Biggest Bonuses Go to Not-So-Big Names," *The New York Times* (nytimes.com) February 11, 2010, p. 1.

[50]One such argument is presented in Daniel H. Pink, *Drive: The Surprising Truth about What Motivates Us* (New York: Riverhead, 2010).

financial rewards.[51] The ideal combination is to offer exciting (intrinsically motivating) work to people, and simultaneously pay them enough money so they are not preoccupied with matters such as salary and bonuses.

A useful perspective for managers is that for financial rewards to be effective motivators, they must be combined with meaningful responsibility, respect for the worker, constructive relationships on the job, and recognition. All these factors combined make for an effective motivation strategy.[52]

[51]Gardiner Morse, "Why We Misread Motives," *Harvard Business Review*, January 2003, p. 18.
[52]R. Brayton Bowen, "Today's Workforce Requires New Age Currency," *HR Magazine*, March 2004, p. 101.

Summary of Key Points

Explain the relationship between motivation and performance.

From the standpoint of the individual, motivation is an internal state that leads to the pursuit of objectives. From the standpoint of the manager, motivation is an activity that gets subordinates to pursue objectives. The purpose of motivating employees is to get them to achieve results and commitment. A problem today is that so many workers are not engaged in their work. Motivation is but one important contributor to productivity and performance. Other important contributors are abilities, skills, technology, and group norms.

Present an overview of major theories of need satisfaction in explaining motivation.

Workers can be motivated through need satisfaction, particularly because most people want to know "What's in it for me?" First, needs must be identified. Second, the person must be given an opportunity to satisfy those needs.

Maslow's need hierarchy states that people strive to become self-actualized. However, before higher-level needs are activated, certain lower-level needs must be satisfied. When a person's needs are satisfied at one level, he or she looks toward satisfaction at a higher level. Specific needs playing an important role in work motivation include achievement, power, affiliation, recognition, pride, risk taking and thrill seeking. Recent research suggests that four needs or drives are hardwired into the brain related to acquiring things, bonding with others, comprehending our part of the world, and defending ourselves.

The two-factor theory of work motivation includes two different sets of job motivation factors: Satisfiers and motivators, when present, increase satisfaction and motivation. Satisfiers and motivators generally relate to the content of a job. They include achievement, recognition, and opportunity for advancement. Dissatisfiers prevent dissatisfaction, but they do not create satisfaction or motivation. Dissatisfiers relate mostly to the context of a job. They include company policy and administration, job security, and money. Current satisfiers for young workers include flexible work schedules and engaging in community service.

Explain how goal setting is used to motivate people.

Goal setting is an important part of most motivational programs, and it is a managerial method of motivating group members. It is based on these ideas: (a) specific goals are better than generalized goals; (b) the more difficult the goal, the better the performance, yet superordinate goals are important; (c) only goals that are accepted improve performance; (d) goals are more effective when used to evaluate performance; (e) goals should be linked to feedback and rewards; and (f) group goal setting is important. The Pygmalion effect contributes to goal setting. Too strong a focus on goals can lead to unethical behavior to attain them.

Describe the application of positive reinforcement including recognition and praise to worker motivation.

Positive reinforcement is a behavior modification strategy that focuses on rewarding workers for making the right response. Suggestions for the informal use of positive reinforcement in a work setting include (a) state clearly what behavior leads to a reward and supply feedback, (b) use appropriate rewards, (c) make rewards contingent on good performance, (d) administer intermittent rewards, (e) administer rewards promptly, (f) change rewards periodically, (g) make rewards visible, and (h) reward the team as well as the individual.

Motivating employees through recognition takes the form of both formal reward and recognition programs and informal recognition and praise given by managers. Cross-cultural differences in needs and suitable recognition awards should be taken into account.

Explain the conditions under which a person will be motivated according to expectancy theory.

Expectancy theory contends that people will expend effort if they expect the effort to lead to performance and performance to reward. According to the expectancy model presented here, a person will be motivated if the person believes effort will lead to performance, performance will lead to a reward, the reward satisfies an important need, and need satisfaction is intense enough to make the effort seem worthwhile.

6 **Describe the role of financial incentives, including profit sharing and gainsharing, in worker motivation.**

A natural way to motivate workers at any level is to offer financial incentives for good performance. Linking pay to performance improves the motivational value of financial incentives.

Profit-sharing plans give out money related to company or large-unit performance. Gainsharing is a formal program that allows employees to participate financially in productivity gains they have achieved. Bonuses are distributed to employees based on how much they decrease the labor cost involved in producing or selling goods. Employee involvement in increasing productivity is an important part of gainsharing.

Employee stock ownership plans set aside a block of company stock for employee purchase, often redeemable at retirement. Stock option plans give employees the right to purchase company stock at a specified price at some future time. Both plans attempt to motivate workers by making them part owners of the business. Stock option plans have been subject to the abuse of backdating the strike price.

Financial motivators can create problems, such as executives siphoning off too much money from shareholders, employees, and even customers. Financial incentives also encourage workers to focus on the reward instead of the work. For best results, financial incentives should be combined with internal motivators such as meaningful responsibility and recognition.

Key Terms and Phrases

Motivation, 389
$P = M \times A$, 389
Need, 391
Maslow's need hierarchy, 393
Deficiency needs, 393
Growth needs, 393
Achievement need, 395
Affiliation need, 395
Recognition need, 395

Two-factor theory of work motivation, 398
Goal, 400
Superordinate goal, 400
Pygmalion effect, 401
Behavior modification, 402
Expectancy theory of motivation, 410
Profit-sharing plans, 416
Gainsharing, 416

Questions

1. Complaints are often heard about employees who spend most of their time at work using smart phones to send and receive text messages and access the Internet. What program might be effective in motivating these time-wasting workers to spend more time working?

2. Suppose that you as a manager figure out that Jennifer, one of your team members, has strong intrinsic motivation. What would you do with this information to motivate Jennifer to higher levels of performance?

3. How could you use expectancy theory to increase your own motivation level?

4. What similarities do you see between motivating professional athletes and workers in business?

5. What information does this chapter have to offer the manager who is already working with a well-motivated team?

6. Some managers object to systematic approaches to motivating employees by expressing the thought, "Why should we go out of our way to motivate workers to do what they are paid to do?" What is your reaction to this objection?

7. How would a company know if recognition awards, such as an expensive watch containing the company logo, actually contributed to employee motivation or retention?

Skill-Building Exercise 11-A: Recognizing the Good Work of Others

The evidence about the effectiveness of recognition and other forms of positive reinforcement is impressive. However, we want you to study the results of recognition first hand. Think of someone who performs a service for you whom you might have an opportunity to see more than once or twice. Examples here include cashiers at a supermarket, servers at a restaurant, or bank tellers. When you receive good service from that person, give him or her appropriate recognition (or a super tip, if tipping is expected). When you encounter that person again, see whether he or she behaves differently or performs at an even higher level. If no change occurs, analyze the reason for the lack of change. For example, is there a possibility that you did not deliver the recognition effectively?

Skill-Building Exercise 11-B: Identifying the Most Powerful Motivators

The class divides itself into small groups. Working alone, group members first attach a valence to all the rewards in Exhibit 11-8. Use the expectancy theory scale of −100 to +100. Next, do an analysis of the top ten motivators identified by the group, perhaps by calculating the average valence attached to the rewards that at first glance were assigned high valences by most group members. After each group has identified its top ten motivators, the group leaders can post the results for the other class members to see. After comparing results, answer these questions:

1. What appear to be the top three motivators for the entire class?
2. Do the class members tend to favor internal or external rewards?
3. Did career experience or gender influence the results within the groups?
4. Of what value to managers would this exercise be in estimating valences?

Management Now: Online Skill-Building Exercise: Analyzing a Motivational Program

Hundreds of programs for motivating employees are described on the Internet. Find one motivational program of interest to you posted within the last six months, perhaps one that includes a video presentation. After reading about the program and/or watching the video, answer these questions:

1. Which theory of motivation appears to underlie the work of the program?

2. How acceptable do you think the program would be to the employees who are meant to be motivated by the program?
3. What edge might this motivational program have over managers simply thanking workers for a job well done?

11-A Case Problem

We Need More Engagement Around Here

Peggy Bates is the CEO of a regional HMO (health maintenance organization) with 25 local offices serving business and nonprofit organizations. The competition for business has become more intense in recent years as organizations continue to look for ways to reduce costs for medical and dental insurance. A particular concern is that a given company might shift to another HMO if that healthcare provider can offer lower costs.

Peggy expressed her concern at a meeting with the management staff in these words: "I think our HMO could provide better service and lower costs if our employees put in more effort. A lot of the employees I have seen are so laid back, and almost indifferent. They don't seem to have a sense of urgency.

"I don't think that by simply downsizing the company we will reduce costs. Having fewer workers to accomplish our important work would just make things worse. We would get less work accomplished, and the quality would suffer."

After listening to Peggy, Jerry Falcone, the vice president of marketing, commented: "Peggy, you might be right about some of our employees not being totally engaged in our efforts. Yet, I cannot understand why. Taking care of people's health is one of the most important responsibilities in the world. I mean, we are often increasing life span as well as saving lives."

Melissa Mitchell, director of human resources, said: "Jerry, from your point of view, you are correct. Healthcare is a noble undertaking. Yet when a person is seated at a keyboard and terminal for eight hours processing claims, he or she might not feel like an angel of mercy.

"We can speculate all we want about how well our employees are engaged and motivated, and what we should do about the situation. I propose that we get some data so we can learn more about the nature of the problem we are working with. I propose we hire a human resources consulting firm to conduct a survey about employee engagement. It could prove to be a good investment."

Peggy said with a smile, "Here I am concerned about our costs being too high, and Melissa makes a suggestion for spending money."

Case Exhibit: Data from Employee Attitude Survey

Question	Percent Yes	Percent No
1. Do you know what is expected of you at work?	72	28
2. Do you have the opportunity to do what you do best every day?	55	45
3. Do you put your full effort into the job most days?	44	56
4. Do you think your immediate boss is doing a good job?	85	15
5. Do you expect to be working for this company for at least another three years?	34	66
6. Do you ever take work home with you (assuming you have the type of work that can be done off company premises)?	41	59
7. In the past year, have you had opportunities at work to learn and grow?	38	62
8. How satisfied are you with your compensation (salary and benefits combined)?	69	31

Melissa retorted, "Peggy, I am talking about *investing*, not spending money. If we could boost our employee level of motivation 10 percent, we would get a tremendous return on investment."

Peggy, Melissa, and the rest of the executive team agreed on hiring a firm to conduct the survey. Four months later, the survey was completed and the results presented to management. The consultant, Ken Hui, focused on the data presented in the accompanying Exhibit as the key findings of the survey. He said, "Folks, here is the meat of the study. Let's discuss calls for action that are revealed by the data."

Discussion Questions

1. How bad is employee motivation and engagement as revealed by the Exhibit?
2. What actions can management take to increase motivation?
3. Should management focus on intrinsic, or extrinsic, motivators in attempting to enhance the motivation and engagement level of these HMO workers?

11-B Case Problem

Justin Tries a Little Recognition

Justin is a super-franchiser for a large chain of soup-and-sandwich shops. He owns twelve shops in the same region, having invested $2 million to own these stores. Half of the investment in the stores came from inheritance and investments Justin had made prior to becoming a franchisor. The other half of the money was borrowed, so Justin feels considerable pressure to earn enough gross profit from the stores in order to make his debt payments and earn a living.

Justin concluded that he needed to increase revenues from his stores about 15 percent in order to net enough profit for a comfortable living. He believed that his business processes were good enough to make a profit, and that the company was giving his franchise operations enough marketing and advertising support. Justin also thought that his managers were running efficient operations. He was concerned, however, that they weren't trying hard enough to achieve good customer service by encouraging the order takers at the stores to pay more attention to customers. For example, when Justin visited the stores (or sent a family member in his place), it seemed that the order takers didn't smile enough or ask frequently enough, "What else would you like with your order?"

Justin decided that he shouldn't micromanage by telling the store managers how to motivate their staffs. Yet he decided to discuss with his managers what he wanted—more profit by doing a better job of motivating the order takers and cashiers. He also pointed out to his twelve store managers that he would be rewarding and recognizing their accomplishments in boosting store revenues. After consulting with the managers, Justin established the goal of a 15 percent increases in revenues within 12 months.

Two weeks after the goal-setting discussions with the 12 store managers, Justin announced that he would be recognizing and rewarding a 15 percent or better increase in revenue with two of the following forms of recognition:

- A wall plaque designating the manager as a "Store Manager of the Year"
- A year's membership in an athletic club for the manager and a spouse or partner
- A bonus equivalent to two percent of annual salary
- An iPad
- An expense paid trip for the manager and his family for one day at an amusement park or a theme park

Justin waited for responses from his managers to the proposed recognition plan. He received several e-mail messages acknowledging an appreciation of his program, yet no burst of enthusiasm. Justin thought to himself, "I guess the managers don't understand how great it feels to be recognized for making a tough financial target. When they earn their recognition awards, I'm sure I will see a lot more enthusiasm."

Discussion Questions

1. What advice can you give Justin Salisbury about the most likely motivational consequences of his recognition program?
2. What other form of recognition should Justin offer the store managers?
3. Would it be better for Justin to have a recognition program aimed directly at the order-takers and cashiers than at their managers? Explain your reasoning.

CHAPTER 12

Communication

OBJECTIVES

After studying this chapter and doing the exercises, you should be able to:

1. Describe the steps in the communication process.
2. Recognize the major types of nonverbal communication in the workplace.
3. Explain and illustrate the difference between formal and informal communication channels.
4. Identify major communication barriers in organizations.
5. Develop tactics for overcoming communication barriers.
6. Describe how to conduct more effective meetings.
7. Describe how organizational (or office) politics affects interpersonal communication.

Loveday Madzika says his boss at accounting giant KPMG gripes that he isn't assertive enough when it comes to getting financial information from some of his auditing clients. That is why Madzika, 33, has been sent to Richard Newman, a body language coach hired by KPMG in London to teach its accountants the art of using and decoding body language.

Newman tells Madzika to recite the nursery rhyme, "Mary Had a Little Lamb." The point? To show the accountant that body language can change how people react to something as innocent as a child's nursery rhyme. The first time Madzika sings the ditty in front of six colleagues he flashes a brilliant smile. He tries again, but he can't seem to mix the nursery rhyme with a more serious stance. Only after Newman shoved Madzika about 15 feet across the floor did he belt out the song with more of an edge. Madzika lifted his sternum, as Newman had suggested, and sang the song more forcefully—and without smiling. "I pushed back," says Madzika.

Also at KPMG, it was the job of Jason Allan, an investment consultant and senior manager, to give advice to trustees of pension funds and other institutions. Many of his clients were much older than Allan, 30. In a session,

Newman immediately spotted flaws in his body language. When Allan sat, his legs tended to saw from side to side, detracting from his gravitas. A short time later Allan advised trustees at a big company to move money into corporate bonds. One resisted the move, griping that advisers dispense advice but don't take responsibility. Rather than rising to the bait, Allan challenged the trustee. He sat calmly, keeping his legs still. Speaking in a slow and measured voice, he got into the details of his presentation. The meeting, Allan says, was a success.[1]

Many readers are probably wondering why a conservative accounting firm would want staff professionals to recite a nursery rhyme or keep their legs from swaying back and forth. The reason is that the accounting giant in question wants to have every possible edge in dealing with clients. Without effective communication, relationships with clients and employees can be damaged.

Communication has been described as the glue that holds the organization together. According to one study, companies with highly effective internal communication posted shareholder returns over a five-year period that were 57 percent higher than those of companies that communicated less well with employees.[2] Sales are won when the sales staff has the skills to develop rapport with customers, to listen, to inform, and to solve problems—either in person, by telephone, or by e-mail.[3] Looking at the negative side, poor communication is the number one problem in virtually all organizations and the cause of most problems.

Communication is an integral part of all managerial functions. Unless managers communicate with others, they cannot plan, organize, control, or lead. Effective communication is a leader's most potent tool for inspiring workers to take responsibility for creating a better future (implementing the vision).[4] Person-to-person communication is as much a part of managerial, professional, technical, and sales work as running is a part of basketball and soccer. Furthermore, the ability to communicate effectively relates closely to career advancement. Employees who are poor communicators are often bypassed for promotion, particularly if the job includes people contact. Well-known investor and executive Warren Buffet told a group of business students that good communication skills are the most important skills needed to succeed.[5]

The information in this chapter is designed to improve communication among people in the workplace. Two approaches are used to achieve this

---

[1] Anita Raghavan, "Watch Your Body Language," *Forbes*, March 16, 2009, pp. 92–93.

[2] Study reported in Eric Krell, "The Unintended Word," *HR Magazine*, August 2006, pp. 51–52.

[3] David Saxby, "Sales Unfold Naturally When You Train Employees to Be Skilled Communicators with Customers," (http://www.measure-x.com/tips/salesunfold.html), accessed June 25, 2004.

[4] John Hamm, "The Five Messages Leaders Must Manage," *Harvard Business Review*, May 2006, p. 114.

[5] Josh Funk, "Buffet Devotes Time to College Students," Associated Press, April 14, 2006.

end. First, the chapter describes key aspects of organizational communication, including communication channels and barriers and the use of social networking sites for internal communication. Second, the chapter presents many suggestions about how managers and others can overcome communication barriers and conduct effective meetings. We also study a subtle aspect of communications called organizational politics.

THE COMMUNICATION PROCESS

Anytime people send information back and forth to each other, they are communicating. **Communication** is the process of exchanging information by the use of words, letters, symbols, or nonverbal behavior. Sending messages to other people, and having the messages interpreted as intended, generally proves to be complex and difficult. The difficulty arises because communication depends on perception. People may perceive words, symbols, actions, and even colors differently, depending on their background and interests.

A typical communication snafu took place at a product-improvement meeting. The supervisor said to a technician, "Product desirability is in the eye of the beholder." The technician responded, "Oh, how interesting." Later the technician told the rest of the team, "It's no use striving for product improvement. The boss thinks product desirability is too subjective to achieve." The supervisor's message—that the consumer is the final judge of product desirability—got lost in the process; communication failed.

Steps in the Communication Process

Exhibit 12-1 illustrates the complexity of the communication process. This diagram simplifies the baffling process of sending and receiving messages. The model of two-way communication involves four major steps, each subject to interference, or noise. The four steps are encoding, transmission, decoding, and feedback.

LEARNING OBJECTIVE 1

Describe the steps in the communication process.

communication
The process of exchanging information by the use of words, letters, symbols, or nonverbal behavior.

 PLAY VIDEO

Go to www.cengage.com/management/dubrin and view the video for Chapter 12. What communication techniques have been used in Greensburg, Kansas? How did these methods affect the town?

EXHIBIT 12-1   **The Communication Process**

Exchanging message as intended is complex because noise, or interference, so often gets in the way.

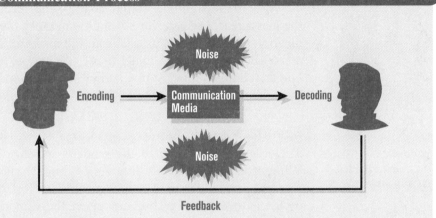

Encoding the Message

encoding

The process of organizing ideas into a series of symbols designed to communicate with the receiver.

Encoding is the process of organizing ideas into a series of symbols, such as words and gestures, designed to communicate with the receiver. Word choice strongly influences communication effectiveness. The better a person's grasp of language, the easier it is for him or her to encode. Appropriate choices of words or any other symbol increase the chance that communication will flow smoothly. The supervisor mentioned at the beginning of this section chose to use the somewhat vague phrase: "Product desirability is in the eye of the beholder." A more effective message might be: "Product desirability is measured by customer acceptance."

Communication Media

The message is sent via a communication medium such as voice, e-mail, instant message, blog, or telephone. Selecting a medium that fits the message contributes to its effectiveness. In general, more emotional, sensitive, and negative topics, such as disciplining a worker or offering a promotion, are better communicated face-to-face. It would be appropriate to use the spoken word to inform a coworker that his shirt was torn. It would be inappropriate to send the same message through e-mail or voice mail because the message might appear too harsh and ridiculing. Many messages in organizations are communicated nonverbally, through the use of gestures and facial expressions. For example, a smile from a superior in a meeting effectively communicates the message "I agree with your comment."

Decoding the Message

decoding

The communication stage in which the receiver interprets the message and translates it into meaningful information.

In **decoding**, the receiver interprets the message and translates it into meaningful information. Barriers to communication often surface at the decoding step. People may interpret messages according to their psychological needs and motives. The technician mentioned earlier may have been looking for an out—a reason not to be so concerned about achieving high standards. He may have interpreted the message in a way that minimized the need to strive for product desirability.

After understanding comes action—the receiver does something about the message. If the receiver acts in the manner the sender wants, the communication process is successful. From the manager's perspective, the success of a message is measured in terms of the action taken by a group member. Understanding alone is not sufficient. Many people understand messages but take no constructive action.

Feedback

feedback

The communication stage in which the receiver responds to the sender's message.

The receiver's response to the sender's message is referred to as **feedback**. Without feedback, it is difficult to know whether a message has been received and understood. Many people are offended when they are forced to listen to a message but not given the opportunity for feedback. Seven months before Robert Nardelli was fired as CEO of Home Depot, he held an annual meeting in which he knew he would be criticized for his gigantic compensation and the company's low stock price. Nardelli convinced other board members to stay away from the meeting and limited shareholder questions to one minute. His attempt to limit dialogue reinforced his public image as a callous and entrenched corporate leader,[6] an autocratic leader who does not want to listen to criticism.

The feedback step also includes the reactions of the receiver. If the receiver takes actions as intended by the sender, the message has been received satisfactorily. Because it results in a message sent from the receiver to the original sender, action represents a form of feedback. Suppose a small-business owner receives this message from a supplier: "Please send us $450 within 10 days to cover your overdue account. If we do not receive payment within 10 days, your account will be turned over to a collection agent." The owner understands the message but decides not to comply because the parts for which the $450 is owed were defective. The owner's noncompliance is not due to a lack of understanding.

The feedback from the receiver to the sender is likely to be better accepted when it contains an analysis, rather than merely an opinion.[7] An opinion would be, "Your idea about sending payroll notices exclusively online is bad." An analysis on the same subject would be, "Many of our employees do not have computers, so it would be difficult for them to access the information that previously came in the mail to their homes."

Many missteps can occur between encoding and decoding a message. **Noise**, or unwanted interference, can distort or block the message. Later in the chapter, the discussion of communication barriers will examine the problem of noise and how it prevents the smooth flow of ideas between sender and receiver.

noise
In communication, unwanted interference that can distort or block a message.

LEARNING OBJECTIVE **2**

Recognize the major types of nonverbal communication in the workplace.

nonverbal communication

The transmission of messages by means other than words.

NONVERBAL COMMUNICATION IN ORGANIZATIONS

The most obvious modes of communication are speaking, writing, and sign language. A substantial amount of interpersonal communication also occurs through **nonverbal communication**, the transmission of messages by means other than words. Nonverbal communication usually supplements rather than substitutes for writing, speaking, and sign language. The general purpose of nonverbal communication is to express the feeling behind a message, such as nodding one's head vigorously to indicate an emphatic "yes." Six frequently used aspects of nonverbal communication are presented next.

1. *Hand and body gestures.* Your hand and body movements convey specific information to others. Frequent gesturing shows a positive attitude

---

[6]Joann S. Lublin, Ann Zimmerman, and Chad Terhune, "Behind Nardelli's Abrupt Exit: Executive's Fatal Flaw: Failing to Understand New Demands on CEOs," *The Wall Street Journal*, January 4, 2007, p. A12.

[7]Seth Godin, "How to Give Feedback," *Fast Company*, March 2004, p. 103.

toward another person. In contrast, dislike or disinterest usually produces few gestures. An important exception here occurs when some people wave their hands while in an argument, sometimes to the point of making threatening gestures. The type of gesture displayed also communicates a specific message. For example, moving your hand toward your body in a waving motion communicates the message "Come here, I like you" or "Tell me more." Palms spread outward indicate perplexity. According to the body language expert mentioned at the outset of the chapter, putting hands palms down indicates that someone means business. For instance, when negotiating over price, "palms down" indicates that a potential buyer intends to walk away.[8]

Somewhat related to hand gestures is the handshake that we all know is part of how people judge your self-confidence. A study involving college students enrolled in a career course found that the rated quality of handshake was related to interviewer hiring recommendations. The relationship between a firm handshake and being recommended for hire was stronger for women than men. Interviewers apparently were particularly impressed by a woman with a firm handshake.[9]

2. *Facial expressions and movement.* The particular look on a person's face and movements of the person's head provide reliable cues as to approval, disapproval, or disbelief. A smile from the receiver often indicates support for what you are saying.

3. *Posture.* Another widely used clue to a person's attitude is his or her posture. Leaning toward another person suggests a favorable attitude toward the message a person is trying to communicate. Tilting your head and leaning in indicates your concern and attentiveness. Leaning backward communicates the opposite. Standing up straight generally conveys self-confidence, while slouching can be interpreted as a sign of low self-confidence.

4. *Body placement.* The placement of one's body in relation to someone else is widely used to transmit messages. Facing a person in a casual, relaxed style indicates acceptance. Moving close to another person also generally indicates acceptance. Moving too close may be perceived as a violation of personal space, and the message sender will be rejected. Speechwriter and speaking coach Nick Morgan says that to effectively relate to an audience, you need a kinesthetic connection (effective movement of the body). This would include the other forms of nonverbal communication as well as moving around effectively. For example, vary the distance between yourself and your audience, and do not turn away from the audience to cue your next slide.[10]

---

[8]Raghavan, "Watch Your Body Language," p. 93.

[9]Greg L. Stewart et al, "Exploring the Handshake in Employment Interviews," *Journal of Applied Psychology*, September 2008, pp. 1139–1146.

[10]Nick Morgan, "The Kinesthetic Speaker: Putting Action Into Words," *Harvard Business Review*, April 2001, p. 115.

5. *Voice quality.* Aspects of the voice such as pitch, volume, tone, and speech rate may communicate confidence, nervousness, and enthusiasm. People often judge intelligence by how a person sounds. The most annoying voice quality is a whining, complaining, or nagging tone.[11] Another aspect of voice quality is a person's accent. A study conducted in Texas found that job candidates with strong regional accents were less likely to be offered a high-prestige job or one with high public contact. The recommendation offered is to soften but not necessarily completely change a regional accent because a complete change could make a person feel unnatural.[12] Many professionals hire speech pathologists to serve as voice coaches and thereby improve their chances for career advancement. The emphasis is not on speech therapy but on voice beautification, which allows a person to come across as more intelligent and persuasive.[13]

6. *Clothing, dress, and appearance.* The image a person conveys communicates such messages as "I feel powerful" and "I think this meeting is important." For example, wearing one's best business attire to a performance evaluation interview would communicate that the person thinks the meeting is important. Manner of dress also communicates how willing the employee is to comply with organizational standards. By deviating too radically from standard, such as wearing a suit on casual dress day, the person communicates indifference.

In addition to helping people communicate effectively, nonverbal communication has other applications. One example is to assist in screening airline passengers who might be a security threat. Unusual body language such as trembling, lack of eye contact with security officials, and a swollen carotid artery (in the neck) could suggest a passenger with evil intent. Wearing a big coat on a summer day would be an example of unusual and suspicious behavior. Odd gestures and split-second expressions could indicate an attempt to conceal emotions. Passengers displaying any of the preceding behaviors would then be interviewed for further screening. Screening possible security threats by nonverbal communication rather than by cultural stereotypes is much more acceptable to defenders of civil liberties.[14]

Keep in mind that many nonverbal signals are ambiguous. For example, a smile usually indicates agreement and warmth, but at times it can indicate nervousness. Even if nonverbal signals are not highly reliable, they are used to judge your behavior, particularly in meetings.

[11]Jeffrey Jacobi, *The Vocal Advantage* (Upper Saddle River, NJ: Prentice-Hall, 1996).

[12]Carla D'Nan Bass, "Strong Accent Can Hurt Chances for Employment," *Knight Ridder*, October 1, 2000.

[13]Jennifer Saranow, "A Personal Trainer for Your Voice," *The Wall Street Journal*, February 3, 2004, pp. D1, D4.

[14]Daniel Michaels, "Queues Caused by Airport Searches Spur Calls for Passenger Profiling," *The Wall Street Journal*, August 17, 2006, p. A5.

ORGANIZATIONAL CHANNELS AND DIRECTIONS OF COMMUNICATION

Messages in organizations travel over many different channels, or paths. Communication channels can be formal or informal, and can be categorized as downward, upward, horizontal, or diagonal. The widespread use of communication technology including e-mail, instant messaging, text messaging, intranets, and Web conferencing has greatly facilitated sending messages in all directions.

Formal Communication Channels

**formal
communication
channels**

The official pathways
for sending
information inside and
outside an
organization.

Formal communication channels are the official pathways for sending information inside and outside an organization. The organization chart formally indicates the channels messages are supposed to follow. By carefully following the organization chart, a maintenance technician would know how to transmit a message to the chief operating officer. In many large organizations, the worker may have to go through as many as eight management or organizational levels. Modern organizations, however, make it easier for lower-ranking workers to communicate with high-level managers.

Specific Channels for Exchanging Information Including Social Media

Formal channels include publications such as intranets, e-mail, videoconferences, Web conferences, and physical meetings. The company *blog* is a formal communication channel rapidly growing in use. A point of potential confusion here is that the blog, a formal channel, is written in a casual, informal way. Blogs were first used by businesses to communicate with customers in a personal, direct manner. The blog communicates professional information, but with a soft, human touch. For example, a product manager for single-use cameras might say, "Just the other day, I heard from an off-the-road bike rider, Lily. She carries a few single-use cameras with her to every rally. Lily says she would rather smash one of our cameras than her $600 digital rig."

Many companies now use social media Web sites, particularly Twitter and Facebook, to supplement or substitute for a blog. Even when a company does not have its own Facebook page, Facebook contains a link to the company's Web site. One of thousands of possible examples is the department store chain Macy's. On Facebook, you will be directed to their Web site. You will also find hundreds of mentions of Macy's, but these are not formal company communications.

Social networking sites are sometimes used as a vehicle for employees to communicate with each other. To supplement e-mail, employees would send each other tweets or posts on Twitter or Facebook. (A potential problem, of course, is that workers who send and receive company messages on social networking sites can readily become distracted by outside messages.) As a variation of this technique, some companies establish an internal Web site that resembles a social networking site used by the public. At the company SunGard, the purpose of a Twitter-like system called Yammer is to allow workers to see what others are doing, share information, collaborate, and brag about their successes.[15]

The company blog or social media site can be used to communicate with employees in a relaxed, casual tone. Employees and customers can interact with the blog by providing comments that can be a source of valuable feedback to management. These comments are communicated directly to other visitors to the site.

If an employee publishes a blog with company information but the blog is not authorized by the company, this does not constitute a formal communication channel. Many employees have been fired for making nasty statements about their employers on their blogs. Revealing trade secrets on your blog can also get you fired.

Formal channels such as Web conferencing are particularly important for companies with large numbers of employees who are geographically dispersed. In a Web conference, a number of people visit a designated Web site at the same time in an interactive fashion, often with voice capability. A prime example of Web conferencing use is the consulting firm Accenture, which has 178,000 employees and offices in 160 cities throughout the world. Professional staff members spend most of their time at client sites, so staying in touch electronically is particularly useful. Accenture employees also communicate by e-mail, text messages, and phone.[16]

The use of information technology to enhance formal communication continues to evolve, with RSS (really simple syndication) being one example. It is the technology that enables Web sites and blogs to send out automatic updates about new content that workers might need to know, including price changes and inventory shortages. The updates can be sent via e-mail, mobile phones, or through a browser.

Management by Walking Around

One important communication channel can be classified as both formal and informal. With management by walking around, managers intermingle freely with workers on the shop floor, in the office, with customers, and at company social events. By spending time in personal contact with employees, the manager enhances open communication. Because management by walking around is systematic, it could be considered formal. However, a manager who circulates throughout the company violates the chain of command and invites more informal communication. Visualize yourself as a manager doing a walk-around. Exhibit 12-2 offers you a few suggestions.

[15]Adam Bryant, "Structure? The Flatter, the Better," *The New York Times* (nytimes.com), January 17, 2010, p. 2.

[16]Jessica Marquez, "Connecting a Virtual Workforce," *Workforce Management,* September 22, 1998, pp. 1, 18–25.

EXHIBIT 12-2 | **How to Succeed in Management by Walking Around**

Here's a checklist of walk-around tips a manager can start using today, as provided by communications consultant Linda Duyle:

- *Get out of the office.* Dedicate some time each week to get out and talk with your workforce.
- *Leave behind your cell phone and BlackBerry.* Minimize distractions that can tug on your attention. You want to demonstrate courtesy and respect during your time on the floor.
- *Start slowly.* Don't feel the need to dive right into your discussion even if you have prepared an agenda. Effective listening requires you to focus on the person with whom you are speaking. Clear your mind of distractions.
- *Make eye contact.* Look directly at the people with whom you are speaking.
- *Make it two-way communication.* When you're asked a question that you can't answer, tell the employee that you don't have the answer but will get back to him or her.

- *Be honest.* If times are tough, don't sugar-coat reality. For example, if the company lost a big contract, bring it up in your casual conversation.
- *Process information.* You may want to bring a small notepad with you to write down questions or comments that you'd like to remember or that require follow-up. You will learn some great new things about your people and operations.
- *Show appreciation.* Thank the person for his or her time and comments.
- *Never quit.* People may not be comfortable during the early months of the walk-around process. But as they see you more frequently and your willingness to be visible, comfort in the process will improve.

Source: Adapted and abridged from Linda Dulye, "Get Out of Your Office," *HR Magazine*, July 2006, pp. 100–101.

Informal Communication Channels

informal communication channel

An unofficial network that supplements the formal channels in an organization.

Organizations could not function by formal communication channels alone. Another system of communication, called an **informal communication channel**, is also needed. The informal organization structure is created from informal communication networks. Informal communication channels form the unofficial network that supplements the formal channels. Most of these informal channels arise out of necessity. For example, people sometimes depart from the official communication channels to consult with a person with specialized knowledge. For example, a marketing manager might consult with a worker from another department who is up to date on hip-hop culture. Anytime two or more employees consult each other outside formal communication channels, an informal communication channel has been used. Here we look at four aspects of informal communication channels: networks created by leaders, capitalizing on informal networks, chance encounters, and the grapevine (including rumors).

Networks Created by Leaders

Leaders make extensive use of informal networks to accomplish goals. Successful leaders have a knack for knowing whom to tap to get things done. For example, Melissa in finance might be highly creative when cost-cutting ideas are needed, and Tim in human resources might be outstanding at nego-tiating with union leaders.

Based on a study of 30 emerging leaders, Herminia Ibarra and Mark Hunter identified three distinct forms of networking.[17] *Operational network-ing* is aimed at doing one's assigned task more effectively. It involves culti-vating stronger relationships with coworkers whose membership in the network is clear. Some of these relationships may be part of the formal struc-ture, such as getting cost data from a member of the finance department. *Personal networking* engages cooperative people from outside the organiza-tion in a person's effort to develop personally and advance. This type of net-working might involve being mentored on how to deal with a challenge, such as dealing with the problem of sexual harassment by a senior manager. *Stra-tegic networking* focuses networking on attaining business goals directly. At this level, the manager creates a network that will help identify and capitalize on new opportunities for the company, such as breaking into the Indian market.

Capitalizing on Informal Networks

In Chapter 8, social network analysis was described in relation to the infor-mal organization structure. Here we present a few additional ways in which managers can capitalize on the potential contribution of informal networks. A somewhat confusing fact to keep in mind, however, is that in-house net-works of experts, or communities of practice, are becoming integrated into formal management structures in some companies. Richard McDermott and Douglas Archibald, consultants and adjunct professors at the Warwick Business School, offer several suggestions for making best use of these infor-mal networks (that are sometimes formal).

1. *Focus on issues important to the organization.* Sustainable communities of practice tackle real problems that have been defined by upper manage-ment, rather than working completely on their own. At the pharmaceuti-cal firm Pfizer, communities of practice work on the vital issue of drug safety. The communities of practice are divided into safety councils and networks, with membership in the networks being voluntary.
2. *Establish community goals and deliverables.* As the informal networks have become more formal, they should be assigned goals and deliver-ables (or end-products). At ConocoPhillips a functional group might be responsible for the major goal, while the network group contributes to its attainment. For example, when the company planned to improve the performance of its well operations, the functional team formed a well-optimization network. The network then figured out how to reduce unplanned losses in relation to impaired equipment by 10 per-cent annually.

---

[17]Herminia Ibarra and Mark Hunter, "How Leaders Create and Use Networks," *Harvard Business Review*, January 2007, pp. 40–47.

MANAGEMENT IN ACTION

Victor Gulas Draws a Map of Connections

To boost productivity at engineering firm MWH, executive Victor Gulas asks employees which colleagues they talk to, and whom they turn to for help. Then he draws a "map" of the connections. The map reveals dark patches around employees who work closely with others and lighter areas where there's little interaction. Gulas says that the map shows communication gaps, information bottlenecks, and underutilized employees. "It's making the invisible visible," he says.

MWH, a $1 billion closely held Broomfield, Colorado, firm specializing in water projects, started using social network analysis in 2003, when executives sought to reduce costs and improve cooperation among their seven technology centers. There was so little communication that the Denver and Pasadena, California, centers each created programs to track employee-address changes without knowing the other had done similar work.

Gulas, who runs information technology and human resources, employed network analysis after hearing a lecture by Rob Cross, a University of Virginia management professor. His first analysis showed that information flowed well inside each location, but not among them. Workers in Denver had little contact with those in Walnut Creek, California, and even less with colleagues in Christchurch, New Zealand. Most communication was funneled through bosses. One group in Pasadena rarely spoke to other teams. "There were silos and there were gatekeepers," says Gulas.

Gulas worked to remove those bottlenecks, repeating the analysis to check progress. He sent U.S. workers to fill vacation openings in the U.K. because the analysis showed that those groups didn't talk much. He hired executive coaches for his top managers to help them become less authoritarian and more collaborative.

Micki Nelson, who oversees technology under Gulas, says she reviews the network analysis when setting goals for her teams: She sends less-well-known workers on trips to other offices. One analysis asked employees to rate how interactions with colleagues affected their energy levels: she hired an acting coach for a manager pinpointed as "low energy."

Gulas says the social networking analysis helps MWH's bottom line. The firm's technology costs declined to 3.6 percent of revenue from 5.2 percent during a seven-year period. Network analysis is spreading to other parts of the company.

Case Questions
1. Why might social network analysis have reduced technology costs at this engineering firm?
2. Why might employees working closely with each other benefit this large engineering firm?

Source: Phred Dvorak, "Engineering Firm Charts Ties: Social Mapping Helps MWH Uncover Gaps," *The Wall Street Journal,* January 26, 2009, p. B7.

3. *Provide real governance.* The networks, or communities of practice, should not be allowed to float on their own. Instead, the networks should report to one or more senior managers. Pfizer's communities are sponsored by two top-level managers, the heads of Drug Safety Research and Development and Safety and Risk Management.
4. *Set high management expectations.* Members of top management should take the communities of practice seriously whether they are classified as

formal or informal structures. Frequent meetings and updates should be scheduled with community leaders, and ample recognition should be given for goal attainment.[18]

The accompanying Management in Action describes how a company uses informal networks to enhance organizational effectiveness. The description supports directly the information presented about informal structures in Chapter 8.

Chance Encounters

Unscheduled informal contact between managers and employees can be an efficient and effective informal communication channel.[19] Spontaneous communication events may occur in the cafeteria, near the water fountain, in the halls, and on the elevator. For example, during an elevator ride, a manager might spot a purchasing agent and ask, "Whatever happened to the just-in-time inventory purchasing proposal?" In two minutes the manager might obtain the information that would typically be solicited in a meeting or e-mail exchange. Also, the chance meeting might trigger the manager's thinking of the topic. A chance encounter differs from management by walking around in that the latter is a planned event; the former occurs unintentionally.

The Grapevine and Rumor Control

Two key aspects of informal communication channels are the gossip and rumor carried on the grapevine and how to control those rumors.

The Grapevine, Gossip, and Rumors

grapevine
The informal means by which information is transmitted in organizations.

The **grapevine** is the informal means by which information is transmitted in organizations. As such, it is the major informal communication channel. The term grapevine refers to tangled pathways that can distort information. Rumors and gossip are the two major components of the grapevine. Conditions of anxiety and uncertainty breed rumors. Rumors are typically about something people wish to happen (such as double bonuses this year) or something people dread (such as jobs being outsourced).

Gossip is fueled by the need for affiliation and helps people bond. By sharing information, we develop a sense of trust and intimacy.[20] Gossip is usually spread by word of mouth, but electronic transmission is also a vehicle. Positive gossip travels over the grapevine. (Did you hear that our accounts payable supervisor is getting married for the first time at age 57?)

---

[18]Richard McDermott and Douglas Archibald, "Harnessing Your Staff's Informal Networks," *Harvard Business Review*, March 2010, pp. 82–89.

[19]John P. Kotter, *The General Manager* (New York: The Free Press, 1991).

[20]Zak Stambor, "Bonding Over Others' Business," *Monitor on Psychology*, April 2006, pp. 58–59.

The negative type travels even faster. (Did you hear that our chief ethics officer was convicted of DWI?)

According to psychology professor and rumor expert Nicholas DiFonzo, gossip can help workers by alerting them to problems. Informing a coworker, for example, about the boss' negative idiosyncrasies can help her avoid later unpleasantness (such as being reprimanded for having used clipart in a PowerPoint presentation).[21]

The grapevine often creates a bigger impact on employees than do messages sent over formal channels. Messages received through formal communication channels often carry the perception of stale news. Information usually travels along the grapevine with considerable speed.

Approximately three-fourths of messages transmitted along the grapevine are true. Because so many grapevine messages are essentially correct, employees believe most of them. Nevertheless, messages frequently become distorted and misunderstood. By the time a rumor reaches the majority of employees, it is likely to contain false elements. An example would be the case of a company CEO who gave a personal donation to a gay-rights group. The funds were to be used to promote local legislation in favor of equal employment opportunities for gay people. The last version of the story that traveled over the grapevine took this form: "The CEO has finally come out of the closet. He's hiring three gay managers and is giving some year-end bonus money to the Gay Alliance."

Rumor Control

False rumors can be disruptive to morale and productivity and can create employee stress. Some employees take actions that hurt the company and themselves in response to a rumor. Employees might leave a firm in response to rumors about an impending layoff. The valuable workers often leave first because they have skills and contacts in demand at other firms. Severe negative rumors dealing with products or services, especially about product defects or poisonings, must be neutralized to prevent permanent damage to an organization. A couple of years ago rumors spread quickly that part of a human finger was found in a bowl of chili eaten at a fast-food restaurant. (It would not be fair to mention the restaurant.) The company had to work hard to explain the truth—a woman planted the finger so she could sue the company. She had pulled such a stunt in the past with another restaurant chain.

Rumors can be combated by enhancing formal communication. Employees naturally seek more information during times of intense rumors. Move quickly on reaching a decision, such as changing from a traditional company pension to a 401(k) plan where employees make a larger contribution, rather than waiting for so many departments to sign off on it.[22] Explain why you cannot comment or give full information. For example, during the

---

[21]Nicholas DiFonzo, "When Gossip Is Good," *The Wall Street Journal*, December 12–13, 2009, p. W3.

[22]Francine Russo, "Meet the Nicheperts," *Time*, October 9, 2006, p. A29.

preliminary stages of a merger, management is legally obligated to make no comment.

Confirm the rumor. For example, "Yes, it is true. We are going to outsource the manufacture of all paper clips and staples." Encourage employees to discuss rumors they hear with you. Be readily accessible, and practice management by walking around. Make it clear that you are willing to clear up rumors and that you will investigate whatever facts you do not have at hand.[23]

Communication Directions

communication network

A pattern or flow of messages that traces the communication from start to finish.

Messages in organizations travel in four directions: downward, upward, horizontally, and diagonally. Over time, an organization develops communication networks corresponding to these directions. A **communication network** is a pattern or flow of messages that traces the communication from start to finish.

In *downward communication*, messages flow from one level to a lower level. For example, a supervisor gives orders to a team member, or top-level managers send an announcement to employees. A guiding principle of downward communication is that the company must be *transparent* (rather than opaque or hidden) in terms of revealing information to company insiders and outsiders. A representative example is El Dorado Furniture, located in South Florida. Several years ago, top-level managers gathered its workers over three days for motivational seminars to reassure employees that their jobs were secure. Jesus Capo, the chief information officer, said, "We wanted to make sure employees on the floor, in our decorating department, and on our cleaning crew are working toward the same goal and treating our customers with respect."[24]

Upward communication transmits messages from lower to higher levels in an organization. Although it may not be as frequent as downward communication, it is equally important. Upward communication tells management how well messages have been received. The upward communication path also provides an essential network for keeping management informed about problems. Management by walking around and simply speaking to employees facilitate upward communication. Many companies develop their own programs and policies to facilitate bottom-up communication. Four such approaches follow:

1. *Open-door policy.* An open-door policy allows any employee to bring a gripe to top management's attention—without first checking with his or her immediate manager. The open-door policy can be considered a grievance procedure that helps employees resolve problems. The policy enhances upward communication because it informs top management about problems employees are experiencing.

---

[23]"Make the Rumor Mill Work for You," *Executive Leadership*, May 2003, p. 7.

[24]Quoted in Cindy Krischer Goodman, "Firms with Happy Employees More Likely to Weather Economic Storm," *The Miami Herald* (www.miamiherald.com), April 29, 2009.

2. *Town hall meetings.* Top-level executives at many companies meet with employees in a town hall format to gather employee concerns and opinions. For example, General Electric conducts three-day town hall meetings across the company, attended by a cross section of about 50 company personnel— senior and junior managers and salaried and hourly workers. Facilitators encourage the audience to express their concerns freely. Participants evaluate various aspects of their business, such as reports and meetings. They discuss whether each one makes sense and attempt to resolve problems. By using upward communication, GE attempts to achieve more speed and simplicity in its operations.

3. *Complaint program and hotlines.* Many organizations institute formal complaint programs. Complaints sent up through channels include those about supervisors, working conditions, personality conflicts, sexual harassment, and inefficient work methods.

4. *Blogs.* Blogs are useful vehicles for upward communication, while at the same time being a vehicle for downward communication. The employee has the opportunity to interact with the message sent by management, such as "We plan to base more of your compensation on variable pay next year." The employee might reply, "Sounds good to me so long as I have the opportunity to earn more money."

Through *horizontal communication,* managers and other workers send messages to others at the same organizational level. Horizontal communication frequently takes the form of coworkers from the same department talking to or sending e-mail and intranet messages to each other. Coworkers who fail to share information with and respond to each other are likely to fall behind schedules and miss deadlines. Horizontal communication provides the basis for cooperation. People need to communicate with each other to work effectively in joint efforts. For example, they advise each other of work problems and ask each other for help when needed. Moreover, extensive lateral communication enhances creativity. Exchanging and "batting around" ideas with peers sharpens imagination.

Diagonal communication is the transmission of messages to higher or lower organizational levels in different departments. A typical diagonal communication event occurs when the head of the marketing department needs some pricing information. She sends an e-mail to a supervisor in the finance department to get his input. The supervisor, in turn, sends an e-mail to a specialist in the data processing department to get the necessary piece of information. The marketing person has thus started a chain of communication that goes down and across the organization.

Organizational Learning as Part of Communication in Organizations

An important output of both formal and informal communication channels is the transmission of information to other workers so as to advance knowledge and learning throughout the organization. An effective organization

learning organization

An organization that is skilled at creating, acquiring, and transferring knowledge.

engages in continuous learning by proactively adapting to the external environment. In the process, the organization profits from its experiences. Instead of repeating the same old mistakes, the organization learns. A **learning organization** is skilled at creating, acquiring, and transferring knowledge. It also modifies its behavior to reflect new knowledge and new insights.[25] All of these activities are facilitated by effective communication.

Learning organizations find ways to manage knowledge more productively and encourage organization members to share information by communicating relevant topics to each other. IBM defines **knowledge management** as the ways and means by which a company leverages its knowledge resources to generate business value. More simply, knowledge management involves "getting the right knowledge to the right people at the right time."[26]

knowledge management

The ways and means by which a company leverages its knowledge resources to generate business value.

Most organizations employ many people with useful knowledge, such as how to solve a particular problem. Because this information may be stored solely in one person's brain, other workers who need the information do not know who possesses it. Systematizing such knowledge develops a sort of corporate yellow pages.

In addition to the specialized work of the *chief information (or knowledge) officer* in a learning organization, managers also manage knowledge. They should actively contribute to knowledge management. Firms that fail to codify and share knowledge lose the knowledge of workers who leave. Shared knowledge, such as knowing who the real decision makers are within a particular customer's business, can be retained. In a learning organization, considerable learning takes place in teams as members share expertise. A major block to knowledge sharing is that many workers jealously guard their best ideas, believing that their creative ideas are their ticket to success. The chief information officer and the manager must work hard to overcome people's natural resistance to sharing their best ideas.

LEARNING OBJECTIVE 4

Identify major communication barriers in organizations.

BARRIERS TO COMMUNICATION

Barriers to communication influence the receipt of messages, as shown in Exhibit 12-3. The input is the message sent by the sender. Barriers to communication, or noise, affect throughput, the processing of input. Noise poses a potential threat to effective communication because it can interfere with the accuracy of a message. The output in this model is the message as received.

Interference occurs most frequently when a message is complex, arouses emotion, or clashes with a receiver's mind-set. An emotionally arousing message deals with such topics as money or personal inconvenience, such as change in working hours. A message that clashes with a receiver's usual way of viewing things requires the person to change his or her typical pattern

---

[25]David A. Garvin, "Building a Learning Organization," *Harvard Business Review*, July–August 1993, p. 80.
[26]"Are You Up to Speed on Knowledge Management?" *HR Focus*, August 2005, pp. 5–6.

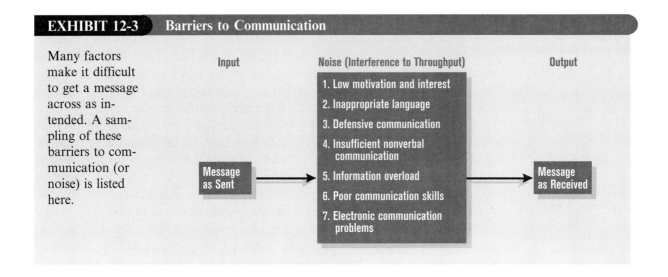

EXHIBIT 12-3   **Barriers to Communication**

Many factors make it difficult to get a message across as intended. A sampling of these barriers to communication (or noise) is listed here.

Input

Message as Sent

Noise (Interference to Throughput)

1. Low motivation and interest
2. Inappropriate language
3. Defensive communication
4. Insufficient nonverbal communication
5. Information overload
6. Poor communication skills
7. Electronic communication problems

Output

Message as Received

of receiving messages. To illustrate this problem, try this experiment. The next time you order food at a restaurant, order the dessert first and the entrée second. The server will probably not hear your dessert order.

Low Motivation and Interest

Many messages never get through because the intended receiver is not motivated to hear the message or is not interested. The challenge to the sender is to frame the message in such a way that it appeals to the needs and interests of the receiver. This principle can be applied to conducting a job campaign. When sending a message, the job seeker should emphasize the needs of the prospective employer. An example would be: "If I were hired, what problem would you like me to tackle first?" Many job seekers send low-interest messages of this type: "What advancement opportunities would there be for me?" Sending a message at the right time contributes to motivation and interest. Messages should be sent at a time when they are most likely to meet with a good reception, such as asking for new equipment when the company is doing quite well.

Inappropriate Language

The language used to frame a message must be suited to the intended receivers. Language can be inappropriate for a host of reasons. Two factors of language that are of particular significance in a work setting—semantics and difficulty level—may affect appropriateness.

Semantics is the study of meaning in language forms. The message sender should give careful thought to what certain terms will mean to receivers. Take, for example, the term *productive*. To prevent communication barriers, you may have to clarify this term. Assume a manager says to the group members, "Our department must become more productive." Most employees will correctly interpret the term to mean "more efficient," but some employees will interpret it as "work harder and longer at the same rate of pay." Consequently, these latter employees may resist the message.

The difficulty level of language affects receiver comprehension. Communicators are typically urged to speak and write at a low difficulty level. At times, however, a low difficulty level is inappropriate. For instance, when a manager communicates with technically sophisticated employees, using a low difficulty level can create barriers. The employees may perceive the manager as patronizing and may tune him or her out. The use of jargon, or insider language, is closely related to difficulty level. When dealing with outsiders, jargon may be inappropriate; with insiders (people who share a common technical language), it may be appropriate.

Defensive Communication

defensive communication
The tendency to receive messages in a way that protects self-esteem.

An important general communication barrier is **defensive communication**—the tendency to receive messages in a way that protects self-esteem. Defensive communication also allows people to send messages to make themselves look good. People communicate defensively through the process of *denial*, the suppression of information one finds uncomfortable. It serves as a major barrier to communication because many messages sent in organizations are potentially uncomfortable. Top management might decide, for example, to require employees to enroll in a physical fitness program so the company might be able to reduce healthcare costs. Many physically unfit employees might dismiss the requirement as simply a joke.

Insufficient Nonverbal Communication

Effective communicators rely on both verbal and nonverbal communication. If verbal communication is not supplemented by nonverbal communication, messages may not be convincing, as the following situation illustrates. For example, if the manager expresses approval for an idea with a blank facial expression, the approval message might not get through. As one worker said, "My manager is a zombie, so I never know what she is really thinking."

Information Overload

information overload
A condition in which an individual receives so much information that he or she becomes overwhelmed.

Information overload occurs when an individual receives so much information that he or she becomes overwhelmed. As a result, the person does a poor job of processing information and receiving new messages. A contributing factor to errors made on the job, such as not following through on sending a needed document, is that so many workers are suffering from information overload. Many managers suffer from information overload because of extensive e-mail and instant messages, in addition to the phone messages, text messages, the intranet, blogs, and trade magazines. Some managers receive as many as 150 e-mail messages daily. The problem of being overloaded by e-mail is intensified by including too many people on the distribution list. Many workers are learning how to manage e-mail better, such as dealing with e-mail during certain blocks of time, yet information overload is still a widespread problem.

Poor Communication Skills

A message may fail to register because the sender lacks effective communication skills. The sender might garble a written or spoken message so severely that the receiver cannot understand it, or the sender may deliver the message so poorly that the receiver does not take it seriously. Documents prepared by humanresource departments and lawyers can be difficult to understand because the terminology must be precise to meet legal requirements. For most purposes, the average reader should be able to understand the intent of the written message. Unclear voice-mail messages, including difficult-to-follow return numbers or e-mail addresses, are a widespread problem. Another form of poor communication skills stems from not focusing on the receiver while sending a message. When speaking on the phone, it is helpful to focus on the other person rather than reading e-mails or doing other work at the same time.

Communication barriers can also result from deficiencies within the receiver. A common barrier is a receiver who is a poor listener. Have you ever encountered a person who repeats "okay" several times but then does nothing in response to your request?

Electronic Communication Problems

Information technology plays a major role in workplace communication, yet it creates several problems, including information overload. The problems associated with e-mail are representative of these barriers, particularly the problem of impersonality. Many people conduct business with each other exclusively by e-mail and instant messaging, thus missing out on the nuances of human interaction. Some managers and staff professionals discourage face-to-face meetings with workers who ask for help and instead demand communication by e-mail.

Face-to-face communication offers the advantage of a smile and an expression of sympathy through a nod of the head. When somebody asks or answers a question in person rather than through e-mail, it is easier to probe for more information. Many people supplement their e-mail messages with emoticons to add warmth and humor. Yet many times, an electronic message can seem much harsher than a spoken message.

E-mail, in general, is better suited to communicating routine rather than complex or sensitive messages. When dealing with sensitive information, it is better to deliver the message face to face or at least in a phone conversation. In this way both parties can have questions answered and minimize misunderstandings. Electronic communication is poorly suited for expressing disagreement because you cannot react immediately to the receiver's response. Don G. Lents, the chairman of an international law firm, says, "You should never engage in disagreement electronically. If you are going to disagree with somebody, you certainly don't want to do it by e-mail, and if possible you don't even want to do it by phone. You want to do it face to face."[27] Laying off workers through e-mail or text messaging is particularly insensitive, and creates a poor company reputation.

A subtle communication barrier erected by electronic communication, especially e-mail, is that messages sent and received on company equipment are not fully confidential.[28] Knowing that company officials have the ability to read any e-mail sent on the system, many workers are hesitant to fully state their opinions in an electronic message. For example, a manager might want to inform a team member that her proposal for updating the purchasing system will never be approved because "Our vice president won't spend a dime to fix anything this year." Instead the manager writes, "All proposals involving the expenditure of money are subject to careful review this year." So the team member does not get the full meaning of the communication.

Videoconferencing is another example of an electronic device that has built-in communication problems despite its many productivity advantages. Exchanging information back and forth through webcams is perceived as too impersonal by some businesspeople. Videoconferencing saw a big boost after the terrorist attacks of September 11, 2001, but cooled down shortly thereafter. The motivation to save money during the Great Recession gave videoconferencing another surge.

Computer graphic presentations, such as PowerPoint, present problems of their own. In most organizations, PowerPoint presentations are expected. Some major suggestions for communicating effectively with slide presentations are to maintain eye contact with your audience and avoid looking too much at your slides, thereby giving the impression that you are reading the slides to your audience. Another suggestion is to present enough slides to keep the audience interested and focused, but do not overwhelm them with slides containing considerable detail.

LEARNING OBJECTIVE **5**
Develop tactics for overcoming communication barriers.

OVERCOMING BARRIERS TO COMMUNICATION

Most barriers to communication are surmountable. First, however, you must be aware that these potential barriers exist. Then as part of a strategy to overcome the barriers, you develop a tactic to deal with each one. For example, when you have an important message to deliver, make sure you answer the following question from the standpoint of the receiver: "What's in it for me?" This section will describe eight strategies and tactics for overcoming communication barriers. Exhibit 12-4 lists the strategies.

---

[27]Quoted in Joe Sharkey, "E-Mails Saves Time, but Being There Says More," *The New York Times* (www.nytimes.com), January 26, 2010.

[28]William P. Smith and Filiz Tabak, "Monitoring Employee E-mails: Is There Any Room for Privacy?" *Academy of Management Perspectives*, November 2009, pp. 33–48.

EXHIBIT 12-4	Overcoming Communication Barriers

The chances of getting around the noise in the communication process increase when the sender uses specific strategies and tactics.

1. Understand the receiver
2. Communicate assertively and directly
3. Use two-way communication and ask for clarification
4. Elicit verbal and nonverbal feedback
5. Enhance listening skills
6. Unite with a common vocabulary
7. Be sensitive to cultural differences
8. Engage in metacommunication

Effective Communication

Understand the Receiver

A common communication error is to think about communication as tool for getting others to agree with you. It is more effective to strive for under-standing rather than agreement.[29] Understanding the receiver provides a strategy that can assist in overcoming every communication barrier. For example, part of understanding the receiver comes from an awareness that he or she may be overloaded with information or poorly motivated.

Achieving understanding takes empathy, the ability to see things as another person does. Empathy leads to improved communication because people more willingly engage in dialog when they feel understood. Communication improves because empathy builds rapport with the other person. Rapport, in turn, further improves communication. You may notice that conversation flows smoothly when you achieve rapport with a work associate or friend.

Communicate Assertively and Directly

Many people create their own communication barriers by expressing their ideas in a passive or indirect mode. If, instead, they explain their ideas explic-itly and directly—and with feeling—the message is more likely to be received. Being assertive also contributes to effective communication because assertiveness enhances persuasiveness. When both sides are persuasive, they are more likely to find a shared solution.[30] Notice the difference between a passive (indirect) phrasing of a request and an assertive (direct) approach:

Passive
Team member: By any chance would there happen to be some money left over in the budget? If there is, I would like to know.

---

[29]Timothy G. Habbershon, "Can't We All Just Get Along?" *Business Week Small Biz*, Summer 2005, p. 16.

[30]Jay A. Conger, "The Necessary Art of Persuasion," *Harvard Business Review*, May–June 1998, p. 86.

Manager: I'll have to investigate. Try me again soon.
Assertive
Team member: We have an urgent need for a high-speed color copier in our department. Running to the document center to use their copier is draining our productivity. I am therefore submitting a requisition for a high-speed color copier.
Manager: Your request makes sense. I'll see what's left in the budget right now.

Informative Confrontation

Another use of assertiveness in overcoming communication barriers in the workplace is **informative confrontation**, a technique for inquiring about discrepancies, conflicts, and mixed messages.[31] Confronting people about the discrepancies in their message provides more accurate information. As a manager, here is how you might handle a discrepancy between verbal and nonverbal messages:

You're talking with a team member you suspect is experiencing problems. The person says, "Everything is going great" (verbal message). At the same time the team member is fidgeting and clenching his fist (nonverbal message). Your informative confrontation might be to say: "You say things are great, yet you're fidgeting and clenching your fist."

informative confrontation
A technique of inquiring about discrepancies, conflicts, and mixed messages.

Repeating Messages, and Using Multiple Channels

As another way of being assertive, you repeat your message and use multiple channels. If you are persistent, your message is more likely to be received. An important message should be repeated when it is first delivered and repeated again one or two days later. Repetition of the message becomes even more effective when more than one communication channel is used. Effective communicators follow up spoken agreements with written documentation. The use of multiple channels helps accommodate the fact that some people respond better to one communication mode than another. For example, a supervisor asked an employee why she did not follow through with the supervisor's request that she wear safety shoes. The employee replied, "I didn't think you were serious. You didn't send me an e-mail."

Being Direct

Another way of being assertive is to be direct, rather than indirect and evasive, when delivering bad news. A manager might say, "Today is a good day for a change," when he has to deliver some bad news about staff members

---

[31]William Cormier and Sherilyn Cormier, *Interviewing Strategies for Helpers* (Monterey, CA: Brooks/Cole, 1990).

being demoted or the loss of a major customer. Indirect communication of this type is often referred to as *spin,* putting a bright face on a bad situation.

Powerful Words

Closely related to communicating assertively is the technique of sprinkling speaking and writing with words and expressions that connote power. Frank Luntz, a business communications specialist, has discovered five words that resonate in today's world of business. These five power-packed words are (1) consequences, (2) impact, (3) reliability, (4) mission, and (5) commitment.[32] To impress a subordinate you might say, "The consequences of your work will have an impact on the reliability of our service, thereby fulfilling our mission and enhancing your commitment." Other powerful words these days include sustainability, recession-resistant, transparent, and user-friendly.

Use Two-Way Communication and Ask for Clarification

A dialog helps reduce misunderstanding by communicating feelings as well as facts. At times a brief amount of small talk, such as commenting on a popular movie or sporting event, can set the stage for comfortable two-way communication. Both receiver and sender can ask questions of each other in two-way communication. Here is an example:

> *Manager: I want you here early tomorrow. We have a big meeting planned with our regional manager.*
> *Employee: I'll certainly be here early. But are you implying that I'm usually late?*
> *Manager: Not at all. I know you come to work on time. It's just that we need you here tomorrow about 30 minutes earlier than usual.*
> *Employee: I'm glad I asked. I'm proud of my punctuality.*

A manager who takes the initiative to communicate face to face with employees encourages two-way communication. Two-way interaction also overcomes communication barriers because it helps build connections among people. Interaction is also useful in obtaining clarification on what the other person means by a phrase such as "you need to provide better customer service." One of the reasons that instant messaging is used frequently in business is that it allows for more immediate two-way communication and clarification than does e-mail. The telephone is making a comeback as a communications device because it allows for more authentic two-way communication than does e-mail.[33] Some small enterprises have even moved to a "no e-mail Friday" to encourage more personal and two-way communication among employees.

---

[32]Frank Luntz, "Words that Pack Power," *Business Week,* November 3, 2008, p. 106.

[33]Jared Sandberg, "Employees Forsake Dreaded Email For the Beloved Phone," *The Wall Street Journal,* September 26, 2006, p. B1.

Elicit Verbal and Nonverbal Feedback

To be sure that the message has been understood, ask for verbal feedback. A recommended managerial practice is to conclude a meeting with a question such as, "To what have we agreed this morning?" The receiver of a message should also take the responsibility to offer feedback to the sender. The expression "This is what I heard you say" is an effective feedback device. Feedback can also be used to facilitate communication in a group meeting. After the meeting, provide everyone in attendance with written follow-up to make sure they all left with the same understanding.

It is also important to observe and send nonverbal feedback. Nonverbal indicators of comprehension or acceptance can be more important than verbal indicators. For example, the manner in which somebody says "Sure, sure" can indicate whether that person is truly in agreement. If the "Sure, sure" is a brush-off, the message may need more selling. The expression on the receiver's face can also be a clue to acceptance or rejection.

Enhance Listening Skills

Many communication problems stem from the intended receiver not listening carefully. Managers need to be good listeners because so much of their work involves eliciting information from others in order to solve problems. Based on his 65 years of consulting and writing, Peter Drucker said that a rule for managers is to listen first, speak last.[34] Reducing communication barriers takes active listening. **Active listening** means listening for full meaning, without making premature judgments or interpretations. Five suggestions should be followed.[35]

active listening
Listening for full meaning without making premature judgments or interpretations.

1. *The receiver listens for total meaning of the sender's message.* By carefully analyzing what is said, what is not said, and nonverbal signals, you will uncover a fuller meaning in the message.
2. *The receiver reflects the message back to the sender.* Show the sender that you understand by providing summary reflections such as "You tell me you are behind schedule because our customers keep modifying their orders."
3. *The sender and receiver both understand the message and engage in a concluding discussion.* In the preceding situation, the manager and the employee would converse about the challenges of making on-time deliveries despite changes in customer requirements.
4. *The receiver asks questions instead of making statements.* For example, do not say, "Maurice, don't forget that the Zytex report must be completed

[34]Peter F. Drucker, "What Makes an Effective Executive," *Harvard Business Review*, June 2004, p. 63.

[35]Andrew E. Schwartz, "The Importance of Listening: It Can't Be Stressed Enough," *Supervisory Management*, July 1991, p. 7; "Train Yourself in the Art of Listening," *Positive Leadership*, p. 10, sample issue, 2001; "Five Keys to Effective Listening," *Black Enterprise*, March 2005, p. 113.

on Friday morning." Rather, ask, "Maurice, how is the Zytex report coming along? Any problems with making the deadline?" By asking questions you will start the type of dialog that facilitates active listening.

5. *The receiver does not blurt out questions as soon as the sender is finished speaking.* Being too quick to ask questions gives the impression that you were formulating your reply rather than listening. Before you ask a question, paraphrase the speaker's words. An example is, "So what you're saying is...." Then, ask your question. Paraphrasing followed by asking a question will often decrease miscommunication.

Note that active listening incorporates the two previous suggestions about two-way communication and eliciting verbal and nonverbal feedback.

Unite with a Common Vocabulary

People from the various units within an organization may speak in terms so different that communication barriers are erected. For example, the information technology group and the marketing group may use some words and phrases not used by the other. Steve Patterson recommends that managers first identify the core work of a business, and then describe it in a shared business vocabulary.[36] All key terms should be clearly defined, and people should agree on the meaning. Assume that a company aims to provide "high-quality broadband service." Workers should agree on the meaning of high quality in reference to broadband. The various departments might retain some jargon and their unique perspectives but a common language would unite them.

Be Sensitive to Cultural Differences

Effective communication in a global environment requires sensitivity to cultural differences. Awareness of these potential barriers alerts you to the importance of modifying your communication approach. The list that follows presents several specific ideas to help overcome cross-cultural communication barriers.

- *Show respect for all workers.* An effective strategy for overcoming cross-cultural communication barriers is to simply respect all others in the workplace. A key component of respect is to perceive other cultures as different from but not inferior to your own. Respecting other people's customs can translate into specific attitudes, such as respecting one coworker for wearing a yarmulke on Friday and another for wearing native African dress to celebrate Kwanzaa.

- *Use straightforward language and speak clearly.* When working with people who do not speak your language fluently, speak in an easy-to-understand manner. Look for signs of poor comprehension, such as

---

[36]Steve Patterson, "Returning to Babel," *Management Review*, June 1994, pp. 44–48.

not asking any questions or nodding in agreement with everything you say. Minimize the use of idioms and analogies specific to your language. Particularly difficult for foreigners to interpret are sports analogies such as "This should be a slam dunk" or "We pulled the hat trick."

- *Be alert to cultural differences in customs and behavior.* To minimize cross-cultural communication barriers, recognize that many subtle job-related differences in customs and behavior may exist. You must search for these differences if you have regular contact with workers from another culture. For example, Asians may feel uncomfortable when asked to brag about themselves in the presence of others, even during a job interview. From their perspective, calling attention to oneself at the expense of another person is rude and unprofessional.

- *Be sensitive to differences in nonverbal communication.* Be alert to the possibility that a person from another culture may misinterpret your nonverbal signal. Hand gestures are especially troublesome. When communicating with people from another country, take caution in using the popular thumbs-up signal accompanied by a smile to indicate acceptance and contentment. The signal connotes acceptance and agreement in many cultures, but could be interpreted as a vulgarity in others. (It could be argued that the agreement signal is really verbal communication because it is a symbol.)

- *Do not be diverted by style, accent, grammar, or personal appearance.* Although these superficial factors all relate to business success, they are difficult to interpret when judging a person from another culture. It is therefore better to judge the merits of the statement or behavior.[37] A brilliant individual from another culture may still be learning your language and may make basic mistakes in speaking your language.

- *Be attentive to individual differences in appearance.* A major cross-cultural insult is to confuse the identity of people because they are members of the same race or ethnic group. Research experiments suggest that people have difficulty seeing individual differences among people of another race because they code race first. They may think, "She has the lips of an African American." However, people can learn to search for more distinguishing features, such as a dimple or eye color.[38]

- *Pronounce correctly the names of people you interact with from other countries.* Communication is much smoother when you correctly pronounce the name of another person. This is a challenge for many Americans who are accustomed to names with one or two syllables that are easy to pronounce, such as Bob or Anna. A trouble spot for many people whose only language is English is that "H" and "J" are silent in

---

[37]David P. Tulin, "Enhance Your Multi-Cultural Communication Skills," *Managing Diversity*, Vol. 1, 1992, p. 5.

[38]Siri Carpenter, "Why Do 'They All Look Alike'?" *Monitor on Psychology*, December 2000, p. 44.

some languages.[39] Suppose one of your work or personal associates has the first name "Hyuntak." After listening to his name for the first time, develop a phonetic spelling that will help you pronounce the name in the future. (How about "High-oon-tack"?)

Engage in Metacommunication

metacommunicate
To communicate about a communication to help overcome barriers or resolve a problem.

A frequent response to a communication problem is to ignore the barrier by making no special effort to deal with the problem—a "take it or leave it" approach to communicating. Another possibility is to **metacommunicate**, or communicate about your communication to help overcome barriers or resolve a problem. If you are a manager faced with heavy deadline pressures, you might say to a group member, "I might appear brusque today and tomorrow. Please don't take it personally. It's just that I have to make heavy demands on you because the group is facing a gruesome deadline." Metacommunicating also helps when you have reached a communication impasse with another person. You might say, for example, "I'm trying to get through to you, but you either don't react to me or you get angry. What can I do to improve our communication?"

LEARNING OBJECTIVE 6

Describe how to conduct more effective meetings.

HOW TO CONDUCT AN EFFECTIVE MEETING

Much of workplace communication, including group decision making, takes place in meetings. When conducted poorly, meetings represent a substantial productivity drain, including wasted money. Team specialist Kimberly Douglas points out that few companies have enough spare time to waste in unproductive meetings.[40] Most of the information presented in this chapter and in Chapter 5, which discussed decision making, applies to meetings. The following suggestions apply to those who conduct physical and electronic meetings, and some are also relevant for participants. By following these suggestions, you increase the meeting's effectiveness as a vehicle for collaborative effort and communication.

1. *Meet only for valid reasons.* Many meetings lead to no decisions because they lacked a valid purpose in the first place. Meetings are necessary only in situations that require coordinated effort and group decision making. The purpose of the meeting is usually included in the agenda. E-mail messages can be substituted for meetings when factual information must be disseminated and discussion is unimportant. Having clear objectives contributes to the validity of a meeting.[41]

2. *Start and stop on time, and offer refreshments.* Meetings appear more professional and action-oriented when the leader starts and stops on time. If

---

[39]Kathleen Begley, "Managing Across Cultures at Home," *HR Magazine*, September 2009, p. 115.

[40]Cited in "5 Tips for Better Meetings," The Associated Press, November 9, 2009.

[41]Stuart R. Levine, "Make Meetings Less Dreaded," *HR Magazine*, January 2007, p. 107.

the leader waits for the last member to show up, much time is lost and late behavior is rewarded. Stopping the meeting on time shows respect for the members' time. Offering refreshments is a tactic that emphasizes the importance of the meeting and enhances satisfaction with it.

3. *Keep comments brief and to the point.* A major challenge facing the meeting leader is to keep conversation on track. Verbal rambling by participants creates communication barriers because other people lose interest. An effective way for the leader to keep comments on target is to ask the contributor of a non sequitur, "In what way does your comment relate to the agenda?"

4. *Avoid electronic distractions.* Many people attending meetings pretend to be focused on the meeting but instead are doing other work on their laptops, or responding to information outside the meeting by using wireless e-mail devices. Get the group to agree not to be performing other work, as is mandated during executive meetings at Ford Motor Company. As a reward, offer briefer meetings with more accomplished.

5. *Capitalize on technology when appropriate.* Although electronic devices can be distracting at meetings, they can also make a major contribution. One example is group decision-making software. Web sites are now being used by boards of governors at several large companies to replace masses of information formerly hauled to meetings in oversized briefing binders. For example, directors at the AIM Management Group Inc. have switched to running paperless meetings. All the information they need is stored on a Web site; using a laptop computer, members click on a specific page as needed.[42] (We assume that board members can be trusted not to go surfing during the meetings.) Or, if participants have keen vision, the meeting leader can flash the Web pages on a giant screen.

6. *Encourage critical feedback and commentary.* Meetings are more likely to be fully productive when participants are encouraged to be candid with criticism and negative feedback. Openness helps prevent groupthink and also brings important problems to the attention of management.

7. *Strive for wide participation.* One justification for conducting a meeting is to obtain a variety of input. Although not everybody is equally qualified to voice a sound opinion, everyone should be heard. A key role for the meeting leader is to facilitate the meeting so that participation is widespread. Asking participants for their point of view is a good facilitation technique. A skillful leader may have to limit the contribution of domineering members and coax reticent members to voice their ideas. Asking participants to bring several questions to the meeting will often spur participation. If the meeting leader spends the entire time reading a Power-Point presentation, participation will be discouraged. The slides should supplement the meeting and be starting points for discussion.

---

[42]Jaclyne Badal, "Goodbye Briefing Books: A Paperless Board Meeting? It's Starting to Happen," *The Wall Street Journal*, October 23, 2006, p. R11.

8. *Solve small issues ahead of time with e-mail.* Meetings can be briefer and less mundane when small issues are resolved ahead of time. E-mail is particularly effective for resolving minor administrative issues, and also for collecting agenda items in advance.

9. *Consider "huddling" when quick action is needed.* A huddle is a fast-paced, action-oriented way to bring workers together into brief meetings to discuss critical performance issues. A department store manager might bring together five floor managers ten minutes before opening to say, "We have a line-up of about 500 customers waiting to get in because of our specials today. Is everybody ready for the rush of excitement? What problems do you anticipate?" The huddle is particularly important when it would be difficult for the workers to attend a long meeting.[43]

10. *Ensure that all follow-up action is assigned and recorded.* All too often, even after a decision has been reached, a meeting lacks tangible output. Distribute a memo summarizing who is responsible for taking what action and by what date.

LEARNING OBJECTIVE 7

Describe how organizational (or office) politics affects interpersonal communication.

organizational politics

Informal approaches to gaining power or other advantage through means other than merit or luck.

ORGANIZATIONAL POLITICS AND INTERPERSONAL COMMUNICATION

At various places in our study of management we mention political factors. For example, Chapter 1 describes political skill as essential to success as a manager, and Chapter 5 describes the role of political factors in decision making. Politics affects communication because so much interpersonal communication in organizations is politically motivated. Our communication is often shaped by a desire to gain personal advantage. As used here, **organizational politics** refers to informal approaches to gaining power or other advantage through means other than merit or luck.

As managers rely more on personal influence and less on hierarchy, people tend to recognize the more positive aspects of organizational politics. For example, a team of management researchers defines political skill as "an interpersonal style that combines social awareness with the ability to communicate well. People who practice this skill behave in a disarmingly charming and engaging manner that inspires confidence, trust, and sincerity."[44] A series of studies showed that if political skills are wielded effectively, it can enhance one's reputation. (This is true because working smoothly with others is a valuable skill.) Having a positive reputation was shown to improve job performance ratings.[45]

---

[43]Pamela Babcock, "Sending the Message," *HR Magazine*, November 2003, p. 70.

[44]Gerald R. Ferris, Pamela L. Perrewé, William P. Anthony, and David C. Gilmore, "Political Skill at Work," *Organizational Dynamics*, Spring 2000, p. 25.

[45]Yongmei Liu et al, "Dispositional Antecedents and Outcomes of Political Skill in Organizations: A Four-Study Investigation with Convergence," *Journal of Vocational Behavior*, 2007, pp. 146–165.

In this section we describe a sampling of political tactics, classified as relatively ethical versus relatively unethical. We also mention what managers can do to control politics. Exhibit 12-5 gives you an opportunity to think through your own political tendencies.

Relatively Ethical Political Tactics

A political tactic might be considered relatively ethical if used to gain advantage or power that serves a constructive organizational purpose. For example, you might want to get an influential executive on your side so you can implement a company wellness program. Five useful and relatively ethical tactics are described next.

1. *Develop power contacts.* After you have identified powerful people in your network, establish alliances with them. To use this tactic you may need to bring influential people into your network. Cultivating friendly, cooperative relationships with organization members and outsiders can advance the cause of the manager or professional. These people can support your ideas or directly assist you with problem solving. Power contacts are also essential because they can recommend you for promotion or high-visibility assignments. Social media Websites such as LinkedIn and Facebook are only a starting point in developing useful contacts. In-person meetings are still the medium of choice for building truly useful contacts. For example, Sheryl Sandberg, the chief operating officer of Facebook, holds networking events with other powerful women in her living room.[46]

2. *Be courteous, pleasant, and positive.* Having good human relations skills creates many more friends than enemies. It can help you be chosen for good team assignments and keep you off the downsizing list. It is widely acknowledged by human resource specialists that courteous, pleasant, and positive people are the first to be hired and the last to be fired (assuming they are also technically qualified).

3. *Create a positive image.* A positive image can be created through such means as keeping your voice calm and well modulated, dressing fashionably, and matching your humor to others around you. Speaking well is critical, and being courteous, pleasant, and positive also contributes to a positive image.

4. *Ask satisfied customers to contact your boss.* A favorable comment by a customer receives considerable weight because customer satisfaction is a top corporate priority. If a customer says something nice, the comment will carry more weight than one from a coworker or subordinate; coworkers and subordinates might praise a person for political reasons. Customers' motivation, on the other hand, is assumed to be pure because they have little concern about pleasing suppliers.

---

[46]Patricia Sellers, "The New Valley Girls," *Fortune*, October 13, 2008, p. 154.

EXHIBIT 12-5 **The Positive Organizational Politics Questionnaire**

Answer each question "mostly agree" or "mostly disagree," even if it is difficult for you to decide which alternative best describes your opinion.

	Mostly Agree	Mostly Disagree
1. Pleasing my boss is a major goal of mine.	____	____
2. I go out of my way to flatter important people.	____	____
3. I am most likely to do favors for people who can help me in return.	____	____
4. Given the opportunity, I would cultivate friendships with powerful people.	____	____
5. I will compliment a coworker even if I have to think hard about what might be praiseworthy.	____	____
6. If I thought my boss needed the help, and I had the expertise, I would show him or her how to use an electronic gadget for personal life.	____	____
7. I laugh heartily at my boss's humor, so long as I think he or she is at least a little funny.	____	____
8. I would not be too concerned about following a company dress code, so long as I looked neat.	____	____
9. If a customer sent me a compliment through e-mail, I would forward a copy to my boss and another influential person.	____	____
10. I smile only at people in the workplace whom I genuinely like.	____	____
11. An effective way to impress people is to tell them what they want to hear.	____	____
12. I would never publicly correct mistakes made by the boss.	____	____
13. I would be willing to use my personal contacts to gain a promotion or desirable transfer.	____	____
14. I think it is a good idea to send a congratulatory note to someone in the company who receives a promotion to an executive position.	____	____
15. I think office politics is only for losers.	____	____

Scoring and interpretation: Give yourself a plus 1 for each answer that agrees with the keyed answer. Each question that receives a score of plus 1 shows a tendency toward playing positive organizational politics. The scoring key is as follows:

1. Mostly agree	9. Mostly agree
2. Mostly agree	10. Mostly disagree
3. Mostly agree	11. Mostly agree
4. Mostly agree	12. Mostly agree
5. Mostly agree	13. Mostly agree
6. Mostly agree	14. Mostly agree
7. Mostly agree	15. Mostly disagree
8. Mostly disagree	

1–6	Below-average tendency to play office politics
7–11	Average tendency to play office politics
12 and above	Above-average tendency to play office politics; strong need for power

Skill Development: Thinking about your political tendencies in the workplace is important for your career because most successful leaders are moderately political. The ability to use politics effectively and ethically increases with importance in the executive suite. Most top players are effective office politicians. Yet being overly and blatantly political can lead to distrust, thereby damaging your career.

5. *Be politically correct.* Political correctness involves being careful not to offend or slight anyone, and being civil and respectful.[47] An effective use of political correctness would be to say that "We need a ladder in our department because all workers must access the top shelves." It would be politically incorrect to say, "We need ladders because we have short workers working here who cannot reach the top shelves." Carried too far, political correctness can push a person in the direction of being too bland and imprecise in language. The ultra-politically correct person, for example, will almost never mention a person's race, sex, ethnicity, or health status when referring to another worker. Ultra-political correctness also involves using supposedly correct terms to describe people even if a given individual rejects the label. For example, many black people are incorrectly referred to as "African American" when in fact they are citizens of Africa, Haiti, England, or another country. These people are Africans, Haitians, or English, they are not African American.

6. *Send thank-you notes to large numbers of people.* One of the most basic political tactics, sending thank-you notes is simply an application of sound human relations. Many successful people take the time to send handwritten notes to employees and customers. Handwritten notes are warmer than e-mail messages, but both help create bonds with their recipients.

Relatively Unethical Political Tactics

In the ideal organization, each employee works harmoniously with work associates, all focused on achieving organizational goals rather than pursuing self-interest. Everyone trusts each other. In reality, not all organizations are ideal and many people use negative political tactics to fight for political advantage. Negative politics, including attempts to discredit other people, are more likely to take place when the job market is bad and there are fewer jobs available within a company and more people competing for them.[48] Here we describe four unethical political tactics.

1. *Backstabbing.* The despised yet widely practiced backstab requires that you pretend to be nice even while planning someone's demise. A frequent form of backstabbing is to initiate a conversation with a rival or someone you dislike about the weaknesses of a common boss. You encourage negative commentary and make careful mental notes of what the person says. When these comments are passed along to the manager, the other person appears disloyal and foolish.

E-mail provides a medium for backstabbing. The sender of the message documents a mistake made by another individual and includes key

---

[47]Robin J. Ely, Debra Meyerson, and Martin N. Davidson, "Rethinking Political Correctness," *Harvard Business Review*, September 2006, p. 80.

[48]Sarah E. Needleman, "Defending Yourself Against Career Saboteurs," *The Wall Street Journal*, November 11, 2008, p. D4.

people on the distribution list. A sample message sent by one manager to a rival began as follows: "Hi Ruth. Thanks for being so candid about why you think our corporate strategy is defective. I was wondering if you had any additional suggestions that you think would help the company compete successfully...."

A useful counterattack to the backstab is to ask an open-ended question such as, "I'm not sure I understand why you sent that e-mail about my not supporting the corporate strategy. Can you explain why you did that, and what made you think I do not support corporate strategy?" You might also add, "Do you think this situation is serious enough to discuss with the boss?"

2. *Setting up someone to fail.* A highly devious and deceptive practice is to give someone an assignment with the hopes that he or she will fail and therefore be discredited. The person is usually told that he or she is being chosen to tackle this important assignment because of a proven capability to manage difficult tasks. (If the person does perform well, the "set-up" will backfire on the manager.) A typical example of setting a person up to fail is to assign a supervisor to a low-performing unit staffed mostly with problem employees who distrust management.

3. *Playing territorial games.* Also referred to as *turf wars*, territorial games involve protecting and hoarding resources that give one power, such as information, the authority to make decisions, and relationships with key people. Organization members also become territorial over physical spaces and ideas ("That was my idea"). A relationship is "hoarded" in such ways as not encouraging others to visit a key customer, or blocking a high performer from a promotion or transfer. For example, the manager might tell others that his star performer is mediocre to prevent the person from being considered a valuable transfer possibility. Other examples of territorial games include monopolizing time with clients, scheduling meetings so someone cannot attend, and shutting out coworkers from joining you on an important assignment. Not allowing group members to speak directly with your boss is another example of a territorial game because you are hoarding contacts with your boss.[49]

4. *Being unpredictable.* Some particularly devious executives behave unpredictably by design to keep people off guard. People are easier to control when they do not know whether you will be nice or nasty. In the words of business commentator Stanley Bing, "This quality of rampaging unpredictability is a well-known tool used by terrorists, authoritarian brainwashers, and those who wish to command and dominate others. It's used because it works better than straight-out intimidation, which can be anticipated and psychologically prepared for."[50]

---

[49]Annette Simmons, *Territorial Games: Understanding and Ending Turf Wars at Work* (New York: AMACOM, 1998); Graham Brown, Thomas B. Lawrence, and Sandra L. Robinson, "Territoriality in Organizations," *Academy of Management Review*, July 2005, pp. 577–594.

[50]Stanley Bing, "What Would Machiavelli Do?" *Fortune*, December 5, 1999, pp. 222–223.

Any political tactic can be considered unethical if it is used to advance oneself at the severe expense of others.

Exercising Control of Negative Organizational Politics

Carried to excess, organizational politics can damage productivity and morale and hurt the careers of innocent people. The productivity loss stems from managers and others devoting too much time to politics and not enough time to useful work. When workers perceive the presence of too much office politics, their performance may suffer. This tendency is noticeable for older workers.[51] A number of studies have related the perception of politics in the organization to psychological strain, to the intention to leave the employer, and to a weaker commitment (or engagement) while on the job.[52]

Just *being aware of the presence of organizational politics* can help a manager stay alert for backstabbing and other negative manifestations. The politically aware manager carefully evaluates negative statements made by one group member about another.

Open communication can also constrain the impact of political behavior. For instance, open communication lets everyone know the basis for allocating resources, thus reducing the amount of politicking. If people know in advance how resources will be allocated, the effectiveness of kissing up to the boss will be reduced. *Avoiding favoritism* (giving the best rewards to the group member you like the most) is a powerful way of minimizing politics within a work group. If trying to be the boss's pet is not effective, people are more likely to focus on good job performance to get ahead. Annette Simmons recommends that managers *find a way to talk about territorial games.* Addressing the issues and bringing them out in the open might make group members aware that their territorial behavior is under close observation.[53]

---

[51]Darren C. Treadway et al., "The Role of Age in Perceptions of Politics—Job Performance Relationships: A Three-Study Constructive Replication," *Journal of Applied Psychology,* September 2005, pp. 872–881.

[52]Chu-Hsiang Chang, Christopher C. Rosen, and Paul E. Levy, "The Relationships between Perceptions of Organizational Politics and Employee Attitudes, Strain, and Behavior: A Meta-Analytic Examination," *Academy of Management Journal,* August 2009, pp. 770–801.

[53]Simmons, *Territorial Games,* p. 218.

Summary of Key Points

1 Describe the steps in the communication process.

The communication process involves four basic elements, all of which are subject to interference, or noise. The process begins with a sender encoding a message and then transmitting it over a channel to a receiver, who decodes it. Feedback from receiver to sender is essential. In successful communication, the receiver decodes the message, understands it, and then acts on it.

2 Recognize the major types of nonverbal communication in the workplace.

Six major modes of transmitting nonverbal messages are hand and body gestures; facial expressions and movements; posture; body placement; voice quality; and clothing, dress, and appearance. Nonverbal communication has been applied to help screen airline passengers as security risks.

3 Explain and illustrate the difference between formal and informal communication channels.

Formal channels follow the organization chart. Formal channels include media such as intranets, e-mail, videoconferences, Web conferences, physical meetings, and the company blog. Social media Web sites such as Facebook can be used as a formal channel. Web conferences are particularly useful when employees are geographically dispersed. Management by walking around can be considered both a formal and an informal communication channel.

Informal channels are the unofficial networks of communication that supplement the formal pathways. Leaders often use informal networks to accomplish goals. Informal networks, or communities of practice, can help attain important organizational goals. Chance encounters with employees are useful for communication. The grapevine is the major informal communication pathway; it often transmits rumors. Management can take steps to neutralize negative rumors by enhancing formal channels. Messages are transmitted in four directions: upward, downward, sideways, and diagonally. Upward communication program and policies include the open-door policy and town hall meetings.

An important output of both formal and informal communication channels is the transmission of information to other workers to advance knowledge and learning throughout the organization. The learning organization creates and transfers knowledge, and knowledge management leverages knowledge to generate business value.

4 Identify major communication barriers in organizations.

Barriers exist at every step in the communication process. Among them are (1) low motivation and interest, (2) inappropriate language, (3) defensive communication, (4) insufficient nonverbal communication, (5) information overload, (6) poor communication skills, and (7) electronic communication problems.

5 Develop tactics for overcoming communication barriers.

To overcome communication barriers, you must (1) understand the receiver, (2) communicate assertively and directly, (3) use two-way communication and ask for clarification, (4) elicit verbal and nonverbal feedback, (5) enhance listening skills, (6) unite with a common vocabulary, (7) be sensitive to cultural differences, and (8) engage in metacommunication (communicate about the communications).

6 Describe how to conduct more effective meetings.

To improve communication effectiveness and the decision-making quality of meetings, follow these suggestions: (1) meet only for valid reasons; (2) start and stop on time, and offer refreshments, (3) keep comments brief and to the point; (4) avoid electronic distractions, (5) capitalize on technology when appropriate, (6) encourage critical feedback and commentary, (7) strive for wide participation; (8) solve small issues ahead of time with e-mail; (9) consider "huddling" when quick action is needed; and (10) ensure that follow-up action is assigned and recorded.

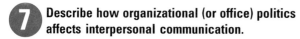

7 **Describe how organizational (or office) politics affects interpersonal communication.**

Politics is related to communication because so much interpersonal communication in organizations is politically motivated. Relatively ethical political tactics include (a) developing power contacts, (b) being courteous, pleasant, and positive, (c) creating a positive image, (d) asking satisfied customers to contact your boss, (e) being politically correct, and (f) sending thank-you notes to people when appropriate. Four relatively unethical political tactics are (a) backstabbing, (b) setting up someone to fail, (c) playing territorial games, and (d) being unpredictable. Used for a negative purpose, any political tactic can be unethical. Managers must take steps to control excessive negative politics. Open communication and avoiding favoritism can help.

Key Terms and Phrases

Communication, 429
Encoding, 430
Decoding, 430
Feedback, 430
Noise, 431
Nonverbal communication, 431
Formal communication channels, 434
Informal communication channel, 436
Grapevine, 439

Communication network, 441
Learning organization, 443
Knowledge management, 443
Defensive communication, 445
Information overload, 445
Informative confrontation, 449
Active listening, 451
Metacommunicate, 454
Organizational politics, 456

Questions

1. Employers continue to emphasize good communication skills as one of the most important qualifications for screening career-school and business graduates. What are some of the reasons for this requirement?
2. How might understanding the steps in the communication process help managers and professionals do a better job?
3. What kind of facial expression do you think might make a person appear intelligent?
4. Some managers send text messages instead of telephoning or sending e-mails to employees and potential job candidates because they think this is how younger workers prefer to communicate. What do you see as the advantages and disadvantages of using text messages to communicate in the workplace?
5. How could employees sending messages to each other on Twitter and Facebook during working hours improve organizational communications?
6. To what extent do you think communication technologies such as GoToMeeting.com (an online meeting tool) will ever virtually eliminate face-to-face meetings in the workplace?
7. Many workers who have been laid off contend that if they had possessed better political skills they could have avoided losing their job. What are they talking about?

Skill-Building Exercise 12-A: Practicing Your Active Listening Skills

Before conducting the following role plays, review the suggestions for active listening in this chapter. The suggestion about reflecting the message back to the sender is particularly relevant because the role plays involve emotional topics.

The Elated Coworker. One student plays the role of a worker who has just been offered a promotion to supervisor of another department. She will be receiving 10 percent higher pay and be able to travel overseas twice a year for the company. She is eager to describe full details of her good fortune. Another student plays the role of the coworker to whom the first worker wants to describe her good fortune. The second worker decides to listen intently to the first worker. Other class members will rate the second student on his or her listening ability.

The Discouraged Coworker. One student plays the role of a worker who has just been placed on probation for poor performance. His boss thinks that his performance is below standard and that his attendance and punctuality are poor. He is afraid that if he tells his girlfriend, she will leave him. He is eager to tell his tale of woe. Another student plays the role of a coworker he corners to discuss his problems. The second worker would like to listen intently to his problems but is pressed for time. Other class members will rate the second student on his or her listening ability.

When evaluating the active listening skills of the role players, consider using the following evaluating factors, on a scale of 1 (low) to 5 (high):

Evaluation Factor	Rating				
	1	2	3	4	5
1. Maintained eye contact					
2. Showed empathy					
3. Reflected back what the other person said					
4. Focused on other person instead of being distracted					
5. Asked questions					
6. Let other person speak until he or she was finished					

Total Points: _____

Skill-Building Exercise 12-B: Cross-Cultural Communication Skills

The information presented in the chapter about overcoming cross-cultural communication barriers will lead to cross-cultural skills development if practiced in the right setting. During the next 30 days, look for an opportunity to relate to a person from another culture in the way described in this chapter. Observe the reaction of the other person to provide feedback on your cross-cultural effectiveness.

Management Now: Online Skill-Building Exercise:
The Communication Component of Jobs

Search the Internet for a description of any three jobs that might interest you now or in the future. The job must mention some type of communication component, such as "good presentation skills." Based on this brief sample of three jobs, reach a conclusion about the communication requirements of the type of work that interests you. An easy starting point might be to visit the "hotjobs" section of Yahoo! Restrict your analysis to jobs that appear to have been posted within the last sixty days. If you are currently working, you might use a job description for that position.

12-A # Case Problem

Do We Need This Blogger?

Genève Ltd. is a manufacturer of upscale clothing and accessories for men and women. The company is headquartered in New York and has worldwide distribution. Manufacturing is carried out in the United States, Italy, Spain, Lithuania, and most recently, China. Genève was founded in 1925 and has remained in business as an independent company.

As the demand for formal business attire diminished during the 1990s, Genève suffered a 35 percent decrease in sales. However, as the demand for formal business attire rebounded from 2002 forward, Genève reestablished its sales volume. A few late-night shows featured guests who mentioned they were wearing suits with the Genève label and this resulted in a surge in sales.

CEO Pauline Matthieu holds a 10 a.m. staff meeting most Monday mornings. Although she would like to have the meetings at 8 a.m., Matthieu recognizes that the commuters on the top executive team can rarely get to the office before 9:30 a.m. On this particular Monday, Matthieu is visibly upset. She tells her staff:

It's not my pattern to dig too deeply into operational matters. As you know, I'm interested primarily in strategy and merchandising. Yet, I'm ticked off today. You probably all know about Jimmy Kincaid, the production planner from our Vermont plant who has set up a blog on http://Blogger.com to host his personal forum about Genève. What he has to say about our fashions and our company usually isn't too negative, but he has become an embarrassment.

In his latest blog, Jimmy has superimposed the faces of apes on the models featured in a current ad. The male ape says that Genève fashions will never be sold at Wal-Mart or Target, and the female ape responds, 'Are you sure?'

"I guess that is a little edgy," said Harry Overstreet, vice president of operations. "Can you give us another recent example of Jimmy's blogs that should be a concern to the company?"

"I have a print copy in my briefcase," replied Matthieu. "I will read it to you:"

> *The Genève label is still tops, but we're slipping into some of the offshoring excesses of other companies. I saw a few undercover photos taken in one of our China factories, and the image does not do us proud. There are loads of Chinese women working in cramped quarters, the lighting is poor, and some of the girls working the cutting tools look to be adolescents.*
>
> *Maybe the cool Genève image has an ugly underbelly at times.*

Georgia Santelli, vice president of merchandising, commented, "Has any manager in our Vermont operation attempted to shut down this clown? I mean, he is a corporate menace."

Overstreet chimed in, "Wait a minute. Jimmy Kincaid may be a clown at times, yet he also says a lot of good things about Genève. He drops a lot of hints that create a buzz for our next season's offerings. One time he mentioned something about seeing a new handbag in the design stages that will make thousands of women switch from Coach bags."

Sam Cohen, the director of marketing, said the company is contemplating a policy on blogging, and that it has been discussed internally. He said, "Let me dredge up the preliminary policy from my laptop. Pauline was in on one of the preliminary discussions, but we didn't do much with it."

Cohen projected the slides, containing some bulleted points, on the conference room screen:

- At work, employees can use their blogs only for work-related matters.
- Employees cannot disclose confidential or proprietary information.
- Private issues must be kept private.
- Public statements cannot be defamatory, profane, libelous, harassing, or abusive.
- Employees can form links for their blogs to Genève only with permission from executive-level management.
- An employee's blog must contain the following disclaimer: "The views expressed on this blog are mine alone and do not necessarily reflect the views of Genève Ltd."
- A breach of the above blogging policy could result in discipline up to and including termination.

"I'm still ticked off at Jimmy, but before we take action, let's think through whether he has done something drastically wrong. We have to protect Genève brand equity, but we must be fair. Let's talk."

Discussion Questions

1. Even though the blogging policy has not yet been implemented, how well have Kincaid's actions conformed to the tentative policy?
2. What steps, if any, do you think top management should take to control Kincaid's blogs?
3. What relevance does this case have for the subject of interpersonal communication?

Source: The blogging policy ideas are adapted from "Myemployersucks.com: Why You Need a Blogging Policy," *Virginia Employment Law Letter*, http://www.HRhero.com.

12-B Case Problem

Networking Megan

Megan Lopez worked for several years as an accounts payable supervisor at a hospital. She enjoyed the work, the group she supervised, and the hospital setting. Yet Megan craved a more adventuresome career, work with more flexible hours, and the opportunity to earn a higher income. In her words, "Carter, my husband, and I both work, but we are struggling to break even. We need to build up an investment portfolio so we can send our children to college. Shauna, our oldest, starts college in three years."

While searching job boards on the Internet, Megan saw an opening for a mortgage broker in White Plains, N.Y., the same town in which she and her family lived. Shortly after sending a résumé and cover letter to Regency Brokers, Megan received a phone call from Ken Demster, the Regency owner. She agreed to an interview, and was made a job offer during her second interview. The job offer meant that Megan would represent Regency in obtaining contracts for residential and commercial mortgages. Megan would work on commission only, receiving 50 percent of the value of the contract. The borrowers would pay Regency a fee of about $250 for helping them find a suitable mortgage. Ashley would receive about 25 percent of the fee the mortgage holder paid Regency.

Before agreeing to quit her job at the hospital and sign up with Regency, Megan asked what it would take for her to be successful as a mortgage broker. Ken replied, "I have a single answer for you. Network like crazy. There are hundreds of people out there who need a mortgage now or in the future, or who would like to refinance. You just have to find them before another mortgage broker does or they go directly to their bank or credit union."

"A few years back, some mortgage brokers in our office were making over $300,000 per year. The business has cooled down somewhat, but there is still lots of opportunity. Residential and small business sales are not going away. You create your own destiny in this business."

With some trepidation, Megan accepted the position. She and Carter agreed that she already had a lot of contacts, and that she could add all of Carter's contacts to her network. Megan became a certified representative for Regency on March 1, just before the peak home-buying season. She maintained a Word diary of her networking activities; nine of her entries follow:

March 8: While getting my hair done at Chez Louise, I gave out my card to all nine women at the salon and to the owner and two other stylists. I explained to them that if any of them needed a new mortgage, or wanted to refinance, just contact me. I also told them to please refer to me anybody they heard of who wanted an original mortgage or to refinance.

March 19: I sent e-mail messages to the 50 people I knew best in my graduating class at college, informing them of my new position and explaining how I could help in finding the best mortgage for them.

April 1: I went to a large home furnishing store and started up conversations with several of the shoppers. I gave each one a card, with the same pitch about their own needs or referring to me anybody mortgage shopping.

April 17: While taking a break at Starbuck's, I overheard a couple talking about their plans for home ownership. I quickly introduced myself and gave the couple my business card. Unfortunately, I happened to splatter my coffee on the man's shirt.

May 3: We had a plumbing problem with the air-conditioning unit dumping water all over the floor. The plumber was a friendly guy, so I popped him my business card just in case he was looking for a mortgage. I asked him to tell others in his plumbing company about me also.

June 25: I attended a 10-year high-school reunion and gave about 50 people my card after striking up a conversation with them.

July 1: I hit five garage sales in one day. I struck up conversations with as many people as I could and gave them my card. One lady seemed interested.

July 15: I asked dear old mom and dad to give me the names, e-mail addresses, and phone numbers of their ten closest friends. I contacted every one explaining how I might be able to obtain the best possible mortgage for them.

August 16: I attended the White Plains chapter of Finance Women in Business and gave my card out to 26 members. Most of the women said they were not looking for a mortgage.

After seven months of searching for sales leads through networking and some random telephone calls, Megan had earned a total of $1,850 in commissions. Feeling discouraged and beaten down, she asked Ken for advice. Ken replied, "You are doing a good job of networking. But remember you are just planting seeds. It will take time for you to develop a successful mortgage broker business. Just dig into your savings to tide you over until you are making as much money as you want.

"Also, have you and Carter or your parents thought about refinancing your mortgage? You would get credit for those fees."

Discussions Questions

1. What is your evaluation of Megan's networking technique and skills?
2. What suggestions can you offer Megan so she can develop a more useful set of leads?
3. What is your evaluation of Megan's political skill?
4. What is your evaluation of Ken's political skill?
5. What does this case have to do with communication in organizations?

Teams, Groups, and Teamwork

Kristy Barnes became the Chief of Police in a small town where the crime rate had been higher than average for the region. Within two years after her appointment, the overall crime rate in the town had dropped 24 percent, and complaints about the police had dropped 39 percent. When Kristy was asked to explain the drop in crime and complaints about the police department, she attributed much of the success to improved teamwork. In her words:

"Our police team can't take credit for the total drop in crime. Our community has fewer jobs, and the average age of our population has increased. As you know, there is a statistical connection between youth and crime, with older people committing fewer crimes.

"I'm also not saying that the Chief of Police who just retired wasn't a team builder. I am saying that I have been fortunate to assemble a great team. We all have key roles to play, and we cooperate totally with each other. For example, our police officers feed any relevant information they have on a crime to the investigator. Nobody is jealous because another member of the police force has higher rank.

"Let me give you an example of the team spirit we have on our force. Jeff, a rookie cop, broke his ankle while trying to apprehend a burglar. Jeff had scaled a fence and took too big a jump. The next day three of our members visited Jeff during their off-duty hours to cheer him up and congratulate him for trying so hard.

"One of the most gratifying parts of my work as Chief of Police is the feedback we get from other departments. For example, the school superintendent and the head of the fire department have thanked our police department for how smoothly we work with them. My reaction is that cooperation is natural because all the town workers should have one goal in mind—serve the public to the best of our abilities."[1]

The story about the police chief presents a common theme in organizations. Teamwork, team leadership, and team play are major contributors to organizational performance. The heavy emphasis on teams and group decision making in the workplace increases the importance of understanding teams and other types of groups. (You will recall the discussion of group decision making in Chapter 5 and the mention of teams throughout the book.) We approach an additional understanding of teams, groups, and teamwork here by presenting a handful of key topics: types of groups and teams, characteristics of effective work groups, stages in the development of groups, building teamwork, and becoming a team player. We also describe the manager's role in resolving conflict that takes place within groups and between groups.

LEARNING OBJECTIVE 1

Identify various types of teams and groups, including self-managed work teams and project groups.

group

A collection of people who interact with one another, are working toward some common purpose, and perceive themselves to be a group.

TYPES OF TEAMS AND GROUPS

A **group** is a collection of people who interact with each other, are working toward some common purpose, and perceive themselves to be a group. The head of a customer service team and her staff would be a group. In contrast, 12 people in an office elevator would not be a group because they are not engaged in collective effort. A **team** is a special type of group. Team members have complementary skills and are committed to a common purpose, a set of performance goals, and an approach to the task. **Teamwork** is characterized by understanding and commitment to group goals on the part of all team members.[2]

Some groups are formally sanctioned by management and the organization itself, while others are not. A **formal group** is deliberately formed by the organization to accomplish specific tasks and achieve goals. Examples of formal groups include departments, project groups, task forces, committees, and Six Sigma teams. In contrast, **informal groups** emerge over time through the interaction of workers. Although the goals of these groups are not explicitly

---

[1]Case history collected in Rochester, New York, May 2010.

[2]Jon R. Katzenbach and Douglas K. Smith, "The Discipline of Teams," *Harvard Business Review*, March–April 1993, p. 113.

team
A special type of group in which members have complementary skills and are committed to a common purpose, a set of performance goals, and an approach to the task.

teamwork
A situation characterized by understanding and commitment to group goals on the part of all team members.

formal group
A group deliberately formed by the organization to accomplish specific tasks and achieve goals.

informal group
A group that emerges over time through the interaction of workers.

 PLAY VIDEO

Go to www.cengage. com/management/ dubrin and view the video for Chapter 13. How does Numi Teas approach working in teams? What did you learn about teams from this video?

self-managed work team
A formally recognized group of employees who are responsible for an entire work process or segment that delivers a product or service to an internal or external customer.

stated, informal groups typically satisfy a social or recreational purpose. Members of a department who dine together occasionally constitute an informal group, and the group might also meet an important work purpose by discussing technical problems of mutual interest. A collection of workers who decide to interact on a company social networking site might also be considered an informal group.

All workplace teams share the common element of people who possess a mix of skills working together cooperatively. No matter what label the team carries, its broad purpose is to contribute to a collaborative workplace in which people help each other achieve constructive goals. Here we describe five distinct types of work groups that have many similarities. The groups are self-managing work teams, project teams and task forces, cross-functional teams, top management teams, and virtual teams.

Because of the widespread use of teams, it is helpful for you to be aware of the skills and knowledge needed to function effectively on a team, particularly a self-managing work team. Exhibit 13-1 presents a representative listing of team skills as perceived by employers.

Self-Managed Work Teams

Almost all organizations have some form of team structure, often a type of self-managed team. A **self-managed work team** is a formally recognized group of employees who are responsible for an entire work process or segment that delivers a product or service to an internal or external customer.[3] Two other terms for self-managed work are *self-directed work team*, and *work team*. Self-managed work groups originated as an outgrowth of job enrichment. Working in teams broadens the responsibility of team members.

Self-managed work teams usually have a member who is designated team leader. At the same time, the team is likely to have an external leader, often a middle manager, to whom the team reports.[4] The self-managing work team is not totally independent.

The key purposes for establishing self-managed teams are to increase productivity, enhance quality, reduce cycle time (the amount of time required to complete a transaction), and respond more rapidly to a changing workplace. Self-managed work teams also present an opportunity to empower employees.

Members of the self-managed work team typically work together on an ongoing, day-by-day basis, thus differentiating it from a task force or committee. The work team often assumes total responsibility or "ownership" of a

---

[3]Richard S. Wellings, William C. Byham, and Jeanne M. Wilson, *Empowered Teams: Creating Self-Directed Work Groups That Improve Quality, Productivity, and Participation* (San Francisco: Jossey-Bass, 1991), p. 3.

[4]Frederick P. Morgeson, "The External Leadership of Self-Managing Teams: Intervening in the Context of Novel and Disruptive Events," *Journal of Applied Psychology*, May 2005, p. 497.

EXHIBIT 13-1　**Team Skills**

A variety of skills are required to be an effective member of various types of teams. Several differ-ent business firms use a skill inventory to help guide team members toward the competencies they need to become high-performing team members. Review each team skill listed and rate your skill level using the following classification:

S = strong (capable and comfortable with effectively implementing the skill)
M = moderate (demonstrated skill in the past)
B = basic (minimum ability in this area)
N = not applicable (not relevant to the type of work I do or plan to do)

	Skill Level (S, M, B, or N)		Skill Level (S, M, B, or N)
Communication Skills		**Thought Process Skills**	
Speak effectively	_____	Use sound judgment	_____
Foster open communications	_____	Analyze issues	_____
Listen to others	_____	Think "outside the box"	_____
Deliver presentations	_____	**Organizational Skills**	
Prepare written communication including PowerPoint	_____	Know the business	_____
		Use technical/functional expertise	_____
Self-Management Skills		Use financial/quantitative data	_____
Act with integrity	_____		
Demonstrate adaptability	_____	**Strategic Skills**	
Engage in personal development	_____	Recognize big picture impact	_____
		Promote corporate citizenship	_____
Strive for results	_____	Focus on customer needs	_____
Commitment to work	_____	Commit to quality	_____
Thought Process Skills		Manage profitability	_____
Innovate solutions to problems	_____		

---

product or service. A work team might be assigned the responsibility for pre-paring a social networking Web site for a search engine company. At other times, the team takes on responsibility for a major chunk of a job, such as build-ing a truck engine (but not the entire truck). The self-managed work team is taught to think in terms of customer requirements. The team member might ask, "How easy would it be for a left-handed person to use this tire jack?"

To promote the sense of ownership, management encourages workers to be generalists rather than specialists. Each team member learns a broad range of skills and switches job assignments periodically. Members of the self-directed work team frequently receive training in team skills. Cross train-ing in different organizational functions helps members develop an overall perspective of how the firm operates. Exhibit 13-2 presents the distinguishing

EXHIBIT 13-2	Characteristics of a Self-Managed Work Team

1. Through empowerment, team members share many management and leadership functions, such as making job assignments and giving pep talks.
2. Members plan, control, and improve their own work processes.
3. Members set their own goals and inspect their own work.
4. Members create their own schedules and review their group performance.

5. Members often prepare their own budgets and coordinate their work with other departments.
6. Members typically order materials, keep inventories, and deal with suppliers.
7. Members hire their own replacements or assume responsibility for disciplining their own members.
8. Members assume responsibility for the quality of their products and services, whether provided to internal or external customers.

Source: Adapted from Richard S. Wellings, William C. Byham, and Jeanne M. Wilson, *Empowered Teams: Creating Self-Directed Work Groups That Improve Quality, Productivity, and Participation* (San Francisco: Jossey-Bass, 1991), p. 3.

characteristics of a self-managing work team. Studying these characteristics will provide insight into work teams.

The level of responsibility for a product or service contributes to team members' pride in their work and team. At best, the team members feel as if they operate a small business, with the profits (or losses) directly attributable to their efforts. An entry-level worker, such as a data-entry clerk in a government agency, is less likely to experience such feelings.

Project Teams and Task Forces

Project teams comprise the basic component of the matrix structure described in Chapter 8. A **project team** is a small group of employees working on a temporary basis in order to accomplish a particular goal. Being able to manage a project is a core competence for most managers.[5] One reason is that projects are so frequently used to manage change, such as launching a new product, introducing a new method of delivering service, or manufacturing a large product including a new vehicle launch. Here we present additional details about project teams to help you understand this important type of work group.

project team
A small group of employees working on a temporary basis in order to accomplish a particular goal.

1. Project managers operate independently of the normal chain of command. They usually report to a member of top-level management, often an executive in charge of projects. This reporting relationship gives project members a feeling of being part of an elite group.
2. Project managers negotiate directly for resources with the heads of the line and staff departments whose members are assigned to a given project. For example, a project manager might borrow an architectural technician from the building design department. For the team member who likes job rotation, project teams offer the opportunity for different exciting projects from time to time.

[5]Robert Buttrick, "Project Management," in Perseus Publishing's *Business: The Ultimate Resource* (Cambridge, MA: Perseus, 2002), p. 165.

3. Project managers act as coordinators of the people and material needed to complete the project's mission, making them accountable for the performance of the people assigned to the project. Project members therefore feel a sense of responsibility to their project leader and their team.

4. Members of the project team might be from the same functional area or from different areas, depending on the needs of the project. The members of a new-product development team, for example, are usually from different areas. A cross-functional team might therefore be regarded as a special type of project team. An example of a project team with members from the same functional area would be a group of financial specialists on assignment to revise the company pension program.

5. The life of the project ends when its objectives are accomplished, such as adding a wing to a hospital or building a prototype for a new sports car. In contrast, most departments are considered relatively stable.

Project teams are found in almost every large company. Being part of a project encourages identification with the project, which often leads to high morale and productivity. A frequently observed attitude is "we can get this important job done." From the standpoint of the organization, a project team offers flexibility. If the project proves not to be worthwhile, the project can be disbanded quickly without having committed enormous resources to renting a separate building or hiring a large staff. If the project is a big success, it can become the nucleus of a new division of the company or a major new product line.

One problem with project teams, as well as other temporary teams, is that people assigned to the project may be underutilized after the project is completed. Unless another project requires staffing, some of the project members may be laid off.

task force
A problem-solving group of a temporary nature, usually working against a deadline.

A **task force** is a problem-solving group of a temporary nature, usually working against a deadline. It functions much like a project team, but it is usually of smaller size and more focused on studying a particular problem or opportunity. The task force is often used to study a problem and then make recommendations to higher management. Representative task-force assignments include: investigating whether stock options are being used illegally and unethically in the company; finding a potential buyer for the company; making recommendations about improved promotional opportunities for minorities and women; and investigating whether the number of suppliers can be reduced. Being a member of a task force is good for your career because you are likely to make good contacts and be noticed if the task force produces useful results.

cross-functional team
A group composed of workers from different specialties at the same organizational level who come together to accomplish a task.

Cross-Functional Teams

A **cross-functional team** is a group composed of workers from different specialties, at the same organizational level, who come together to accomplish a task. (A cross-functional team might be considered a type of project team or

MANAGEMENT IN ACTION

Hypertherm Chief Executive Organizes for Teamwork

Richard Couch is the chief executive of Hypertherm Inc., a closely held maker of metal-cutting equipment in Hanover, New Hampshire, with annual revenues of approximately $200 million. He has long promoted cooperation with a company-wide profit-sharing plan that pays the same percent of salary to each employee.

As Hypertherm grew in the 1990s, Couch saw increasing friction between departments such as engineering and marketing. In 1997, he reorganized the company into cross-functional teams based on Hypertherm's five product lines. He forced the teams of researchers, engineers, marketers, and salespeople to sit together in closely bunched circles. He wanted the teams close to the shop floor, but retreated in the face of safety rules requiring that manufacturing be shielded by a wall.

The plan met resistance at first. One engineer complained about "sitting next to this marketing guy. I don't have anything to say to him," Couch recalls. "I thought, precisely my point. Maybe you will actually say something to him." Some employees quit, he says, although the once-unhappy engineer is still at Hypertherm.

Today, Couch credits the reorganization with helping Hypertherm grow faster and more profitably. Instead of having only one product-development team, Hypertherm has five, which helps the company introduce new products faster. Couch says the new organization is also more efficient, because salespeople and marketers, who know customers best, are more involved in product development. The company heavily emphasizes technical training to develop the workforce it needs. Toward this end, the Hypertherm Technical Training Institute was opened in 2007 to train future machinists and employees.

The company recently paid $6.7 million in profit-sharing, equivalent to 26 percent of salaries, to its 612 employees. Couch acknowledges that the team approach doesn't appeal to everyone. "The star can make more money going somewhere else," he says. But with attrition below 5 percent annually, Couch believes Hypertherm is doing a good job screening out non-team players before they are hired.

Case Questions

1. In what way did cross-functional teams fit the purposes of Hypertherm?
2. How do you think the company screens out non-team players before they are hired?
3. What is the difference between a star and a team player?

Source: Scott Thurm, "Teamwork Raises Everyone's Game," *The Wall Street Journal,* November 7, 2005, p. B8; "Hypertherm Named September 'Innovation Rocks!' Award Winner," www.nheconomy.com/innovation-rocks/Hypertherm.aspx, September 2007.

even a task force.) A cross functional team blends the talents of team members from different specialties as they work on a task that requires such a mix. To perform well on a cross-functional team, a person must think in terms of the good of the larger organization rather than in terms of his or her own specialty. A typical application of a cross-functional team would be to develop a new product such as a video mobile phone. Among the specialties needed on such a team would be computer science, engineering, manufacturing, industrial design, marketing, and finance. (The finance person would help guide the team toward producing a video mobile phone that could be sold at a profit.)

When members from different specialties work together, they take into account each other's perspectives when making their contribution. For example, if the manufacturing representative knows that a video mobile phone must sell for about one-fourth the price of a plasma screen TV, then he or she will have to build the device inexpensively. Using a cross-functional team for product development enhances communication across groups, thus saving time.

In addition to product development, cross-functional teams might be used to improve customer service, reduce costs, and improve the workings of a system such as online sales. Cross-functional teams are used widely in conglomerates such as Siemens and Tyco. They often include representatives from different companies within the larger organization.

A key success factor for cross-functional teams is that the team leader has both technical and process skills. The leader needs the technical background to understand the group task and to recognize the potential contribution of members from diverse specialties. At the same time, the leader must have the interpersonal skills to facilitate a diverse group of people with limited or even negative experience in working collectively.[6] The success of a cross-functional team requires collaboration among its members.

A major advantage of cross-functional teams is that they enhance communication across groups, thereby saving time. The cross-functional team also offers the advantage of a strong customer focus because the team orients itself toward satisfying a specific internal or external customer or group of customers. A challenge with these teams, however, is that they often breed conflict because of the different points of view.

The accompanying Management in Action illustrates how a cross-functional team can be used to develop products and enhance cooperation.

Top-Management Teams

The group of managers at the top of most organizations is referred to as the management team or the top-management team. Yet as consultant Jon R. Katzenbach observes, few groups of top-level managers function as a team in the sense of the definition presented earlier in this chapter.[7] The CEO gets most of the publicity, along with credit and blame for what goes wrong. Nevertheless, groups of top-level managers are teams in the sense that they make most major decisions collaboratively with all members of the top-management group included. Michael Dell (Dell Computers) exemplifies

---

[6]Glenn Parker, "Team with Strangers: Success Strategies for Cross-Functional Teams," http://www.glennparker.com/Freebees/teaming-with-strangers.html. Material copyright © 1998 Glenn Parker.

[7]Jon R. Katzenbach, "The Myth of the Top Management Team," *Harvard Business Review*, November–December 1997, pp. 82–99.

a highly visible chairman and CEO who regularly consults with trusted advisors before making major decisions.

The term top-management team has another less frequently used meaning. A handful of companies are actually run by a committee of two or more top executives who claim to share power equally, as described in Chapter 8. In this way they are similar to a husband-and-wife team running a household. The co-CEO arrangement fits here, where two executives become a CEO team.

Quite often the egos of the power-sharers are too big for the team arrangement to work well. Some observers are skeptical that a company can really be run well without one key executive having the final decision. Can you imagine your favorite athletic team having two head coaches, or your favorite band having two leaders?

Virtual Teams

virtual team

A small group of people who conduct almost all of their collaborative work by electronic communication rather than in face-to-face meetings.

Workplace teams are no longer tied to a physical location. A **virtual team** is a small group of people who conduct almost all of their collaborative work by electronic communication rather than in face-to-face meetings. E-mail, including IM, is the usual medium for sharing information and conducting meetings. Collaborative software (or groupware) is another widely used approach to conducting an electronic meeting. Using collaborative software, several people can edit a document at the same time, or in sequence, and also have access to a shared database. Videoconferencing is another technological advance that facilitates the virtual team.

A more advanced approach is to have a company Website (intranet) dedicated to the shared project. Members can update other members, and the status of the project is posted daily. A "virtual work space" of this type was shown at Shell Chemical to be more effective than sending hundreds of e-mail messages back and forth to each other.[8]

The trend toward forming cross-cultural teams from geographically dispersed units of a firm increases the application of virtual teams. Strategic alliances in which geographically dispersed companies work with each other depend on virtual teams in many regards. The field technician in Iceland who holds an electronic conference with her counterparts in South Africa, Mexico, and California realizes a significant cost savings over bringing them all together in one physical location. IBM makes some use of virtual teams in selling information technology systems, partially because so many IBM field personnel work from their homes, vehicles, and hotel rooms. Meeting electronically does not cure all the problems of geographically dispersed teams from different cultures. For example, the manager or team leader must often confront the problem of different attitudes toward

---

[8]Ann Majchrak, Avrind Malhotra, Jeffrey Stamps, and Jessical Lipnack, "Can Absence Make a Team Grow Stronger?" *Harvard Business Review,* May 2004, pp. 134–135.

hierarchy and authority. For example, workers from many cultures don't feel comfortable with the flat structure of a team.[9]

Virtual teams are sometimes the answer to the challenge of hiring workers with essential skills who do not want to relocate. The company can accommodate these workers by creating virtual teams, with perhaps one or two members working in company headquarters. A similar application of virtual teams is to integrate employees after a merger. Instead of relocating several employees from the acquired company, a virtual team is formed. In one merger, the company's legal division became virtual teams.

Trust is a crucial component of virtual teams. Managers must trust people to perform well without direct supervision. Team members develop trust in their coworkers without the benefit of face-to-face meetings. Managers face the same challenge as that for assembling self-managed work teams: self-reliant and talented employees must be selected for the team. Getting team members to feel that they are part of a team is another challenge that can sometimes be met by the occasional face-to-face meeting.

Importance of Good Leader-Member Relationships. As with teams that work together in physical proximity, good relationships between the leaders of virtual teams and the team members enhances team member satisfaction. The quality of the relationship between leaders and team members is often referred to as LMX (leader-member exchange). A study was conducted with 375 workers who volunteered to engage in virtual work. Virtual workers who have a high quality relationship with their supervisors (as measured by the LMX questionnaire) are likely to be more committed to the organization. In contrast, virtual workers with a low quality relationship with the leader had a significant reduction in commitment. High-quality relationships with the leader were strongly related to job satisfaction of team members. The presence of a high-quality leader-member exchange was related to job performance mostly for those workers who spent a lot of time working virtually.[10]

Importance of Ample Communication. High-performing virtual teams typically have ample communication among members. One study showed that members of successful virtual design teams send significantly more and longer messages to each other than low-performing teams. A key part of these messages was updating each other on the transition of their projects from one phase to another. Another aspect of ample communication was that the leaders of the high-performing teams took responsibility for making summaries of the team's work and sending messages throughout the project.[11]

---

[9]Jeanne Brett, Kristin Behfar, and Mary C. Kern, "Managing Multicultural Teams," *Harvard Business Review*, November 2006, pp. 87–88.

[10]Timothy D. Golden and John F. Veiga, "The Impact of Superior–Subordinate Relationships on the Commitment, Job Satisfaction, and Performance of Virtual Workers," *Leadership Quarterly*, February 2008, pp. 77–88.

[11]"Ramp Up for Virtual Teams," *Manager's Edge*, August 2009; Jerry Fjermestad, *Chief Learning Officer*, www.clomedia.com.

Virtual teams are inadvisable in industries such as manufacturing, health care, and restaurants. Any type of work that is sequential or integrated would create problems for a virtual team, including project work that emphasizes face-to-face interaction.[12]

LEARNING
OBJECTIVE **2**
Describe the
characteristics of
effective groups
and teams.

CHARACTERISTICS OF EFFECTIVE WORK GROUPS

Groups, like individuals, possess characteristics that contribute to their uniqueness and effectiveness. As shown in Exhibit 13-3, these characteristics can be grouped into eight categories. Our description of work group effectiveness follows this framework.[13]

1. *Enriched job design.* Effective work groups follow the principles of job design embodied in job enrichment and the job characteristics model described in Chapter 7. For example, task significance and task identity are both strong. Group members therefore perceive their work as having high intrinsic motivation. In short, exciting, challenging work contributes to group effectiveness.

2. *Empowerment and shared leadership.* An effective group or team believes in its authority to solve a variety of problems without first obtaining approval from management. An important modern perspective is that effective leaders require leadership from all team members, not just the team leader. As described in Chapter 7, group members take turns exerting leadership when the task at hand fits their expertise. Taking turns exerting leadership energizes group members.

3. *Interdependent tasks, information sharing, and rewards.* Effective work groups are characterized by several types of group member dependencies on one another. Such groups show task interdependence in the sense that members interact and depend on one another to accomplish work. Goal interdependence refers to the linking of individual goals to the group's

---

[12]Carla Johnson, "Managing Virtual Teams," *HR Magazine*, June 2002, p. 70; Cristina B. Gibson and Susan G. Cohen (eds.), *Virtual Teams That Work: Creating Conditions for Virtual Team Effectiveness* (San Francisco: Jossey-Bass, 2003).

[13]Vanessa Urch Druskat and Steven B. Wolff, "Building the Emotional Intelligence of Groups," *Harvard Business Review*, March 2001, pp. 80–90; Claus W. Langred, "Too Much of a Good Thing? Negative Effects of High Trust and Individual Autonomy in Self-Managing Work Teams," *Academy of Management Journal*, June 2004, pp. 385–399; Aparna Joshi and Huntak Roh, "The Role of Context in Work Team Diversity Research: A Meta-analytic Review," *Academy of Management Journal*, June 2009, pp. 599–627; Jessica R. Messner-Magnus and Leslie A. DeChurch, "Information Sharing and Team Performance: A Meta-Analysis," *Journal of Applied Psychology*, March 2009, pp. 535–546; Jeffrey A. LePine et al, "A Meta-Analysis of Teamwork Processes: Tests of a Multidimensional Model and Relationships with Team Effectiveness Criteria," *Personnel Psychology*, Summer 2008, pp. 273–307; Craig L. Pearce, Charles C. Manz, and Henry P. Sims Jr., *Organizational Dynamics*, July–September 2009, pp. 234–237.

EXHIBIT 13-3	**Work-Group Characteristics Related to Effectiveness**

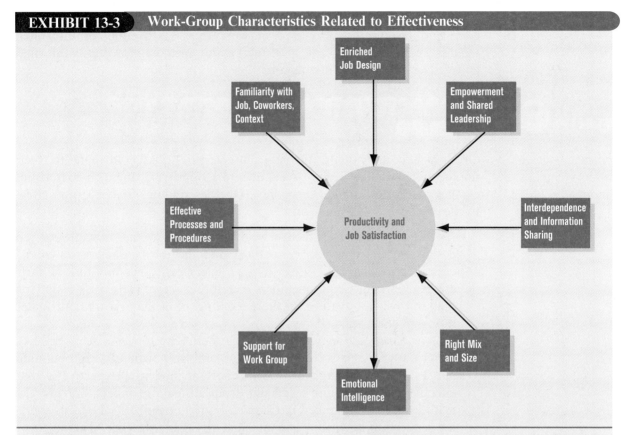

Sources: Michael A. Campion, Ellen M. Papper, and Gina Medsker, "Relations between Work Team Characteristics and Effectiveness: A Replication and Extension," *Personnel Psychology,* Summer 1996, p. 431; Stanley M. Gulley, Kara A. Incalcaterra, Aparna Joshi, and J. Matthew Beaubien, "A Meta-Analysis of Team Efficacy, Potency, and Performance: Interdependence and Level of Analysis as Moderators of Observed Relationships," *Journal of Applied Psychology,* October 2002, pp. 819–832; Vanessa Urch Druskat and Steven B. Wolff, "Building the Emotional Intelligence of Groups," *Harvard Business Review,* March 2001, pp. 80–90; Claus W. Langred, "Too Much of a Good Thing? Negative Effects of High Trust and Individual Autonomy in Self-Managing Work Teams," *Academy of Management Journal,* June 2004, pp. 385–399.

goals. Unless the task requires interdependence, such as building a motorcycle, a team is not needed. A member of a sales team might establish a compensation goal for herself, but she can realize this goal only if the other team members achieve similar success. For interdependence to work well, group members must share information. An integration of 72 studies involving more than 4,500 groups and 17,000 group members demonstrated that information sharing is associated with team performance. The clearer the task, the more likely that information will be shared. Information sharing was also associated with group cohesiveness and job satisfaction.[14]

4. *Right mix and size.* A variety of factors relating to the mix of group members are associated with effective work groups. The diversity of

---

[14]Jessica R. Messner-Magnus and Leslie A. DeChurch, "Information Sharing and Team Performance: A Meta-Analysis," *Journal of Applied Psychology*, March 2009, pp. 535–546.

group members' experience, knowledge, and education generally improves problem solving. Teams with members who have diverse educational backgrounds are likely to benefit from the breadth of information that stems from the diversity. For example, a person who majored in fine arts could make a design suggestion that engineers and business specialists might overlook. In general, functional (work specialty) diversity tends to enhance performance. Cultural diversity includes attributes such as gender, race, ethnicity, and age. These factors tend to have a small negative effect on group performance, but the relationship is complex. Cultural diversity tends to enhance creativity by bringing various viewpoints into play. However, only when team members enjoy high quality interactions can the full benefits of diversity be realized. The interactions relate to both the task itself (such as talking about improving a motorcycle starter) and social interactions (such as chatting about children during a break).[15] A curious finding is that cultural diversity has positive effects on performance in the service industry, but negative effects in manufacturing.[16] (A possible explanation here is that service settings required more interaction with diverse customers and clients, so diversity is an advantage.)

Groups should be large enough to accomplish the work, but when groups become too large, confusion and poor coordination may result. Larger groups tend to be less cohesive. Cross-functional teams, work teams, committees, and task forces tend to be most productive with seven to ten members. The rule of thumb at Amazon is that product development teams should be small enough to be fed on two large pizzas.[17] (We assume no team members are super-size or super-hungry.)

Another important composition factor is the quality of the group or team members. Bright people with constructive personality characteristics contribute the most to team effectiveness. A study involving 652 employees composing 51 work teams found that teams with members higher in mental ability, conscientiousness, extraversion, and emotional stability received higher supervisor ratings for team performance.[18] (Put winners on your team and you are more likely to have a winning team.)

5. *Emotional intelligence.* The group itself should have high emotional intelligence; they should be able to build relationships both inside and outside the team and make constructive use of its emotion. Norms that establish

---

[15]Priscilla M. Ellsass and Laura M. Graves, "Demographic Diversity in Decision-Making Group: The Experience of Women and People of Color," *Academy of Management Review*, October 1997, p. 968.

[16]Aparna Joshi and Huntak Roh, "The Role of Context in Work Team Diversity Research: A Meta-analytic Review," *Academy of Management Journal*, June 2009, pp. 618–619.

[17]Robert D. Hof, "Jeff Bezos' Risky Bet," *Business Week*, November 13, 2006, p. 58.

[18]Murray R. Barrick et al., "Relating Member Ability and Personality to Work-Team Processes and Team Effectiveness," *Journal of Applied Psychology*, June 1998, pp. 377–391; Leslie DeChurch and Jessica R. Mesmer-Magnus, "The Cognitive Underpinnings of Effective Teamwork: A Meta-Analysis," *Journal of Applied Psychology*, January 2010, pp. 32–53.

mutual trust among group members contribute to an emotionally intelligent group.[19] A potential problem, however, is that when group members trust each other too much, they neglect to monitor each others' work and may not catch errors and unethical behavior.[20]

6. *Support for the work group.* One of the most important characteristics of an effective work group is the support it receives from the organization. Key support factors include giving the group the information it needs, coaching group members, providing the right technology, and providing recognition and other rewards. Training quite often facilitates work group effectiveness. The training content typically includes group decision making, interpersonal skills, technical knowledge, and the team philosophy. Managerial support in the form of resources and confidence in group effort fosters effectiveness.

7. *Effective processes within the group.* Many processes (activities) take place within the group and influence effectiveness. One is the belief that the group can do the job, reflecting high team spirit and potency. Effectiveness is also enhanced when workers provide social support to each other through such means as helping each other have positive interactions. Workload sharing is another process characteristic related to effectiveness. Communication and cooperation within the work group also contribute to effectiveness. Collectively, the right amount of these process characteristics contributes to cohesiveness, or a group that pulls together. Without cohesiveness, a group will fail to achieve synergy.

   Teams that can be trusted to follow work processes and procedures tend to perform better. Adhering to such processes and procedures is also associated with high-quality output. Although following processes and procedures might appear to be a routine expectation, many problems are created by workers who fail to do so. For example, a group might show a productivity dip if workers on a project fail to back up computer files and a computer virus or worm attacks.

8. *Familiarity with jobs, coworkers, and the environment.* Another important set of factors related to work group effectiveness is familiarity. It refers to the specific knowledge group members have of their jobs, coworkers, and the environment. Familiarity essentially refers to experience. For many jobs, experience—at least to the point of proficiency—is an asset. The contribution of familiarity is evident when new members join an athletic team. Quite often the team loses momentum during the adjustment period.

   Teams and groups with all or most of these characteristics develop a feeling of **collective efficacy,** a group's shared belief in its combined capabilities

---

[19]Vanessa Urch Druskat and Steven B. Wolff, "Building the Emotional Intelligence of Groups," *Harvard Business Review*, March 2001, pp. 80–90.

[20]Claus W. Langred, "Too Much of a Good Thing? Negative Effects of High Trust and Individual Autonomy in Self-Managing Work Teams," *Academy of Management Journal*, June 2004, pp. 385–399.

to organize and execute the courses of action required for certain outcomes. Collective efficacy is a factor of substantial impact. Results based on more than 6,000 groups and 31,000 individuals showed that collective efficacy was significantly related to group performance.[21] A manager is therefore well advised to help the group or team develop some of the above eight characteristics. Successful organizations are characterized by the presence of many effective work groups and teams.

Effective leadership should supplement the characteristics of an effective work group. Team leaders must emphasize coaching more than controlling. The group as an entity should be coached, not only individual members. An example would be talking with the group about communicating more freely with each other. Frederick P. Morgeson, in a study conducted in three organizations, found that supportive coaching was associated with being perceived as effective by team members. Coaching in the form of the manager jumping in with suggestions was associated with effectiveness when the team was facing an urgent problem.[22]

LEARNING
OBJECTIVE **3**
Describe the
stages of group
development.

STAGES OF GROUP DEVELOPMENT

To understand the nature of work groups, one must understand what the group is doing (the content) and how it proceeds (the process). A key group process is how a group develops over time. To make this information meaningful, relate it to any group to which you belonged for at least one month. Understanding the stages of group development can lead to more effective group leadership or membership. We describe the five group stages next.[23] (See Exhibit 13-4.)

Stage 1: Forming. At the outset, members are eager to learn what tasks they will be performing, how they can benefit from group membership, and what constitutes acceptable behavior. Members often inquire about rules they must follow. Confusion, caution, and cordiality typically characterize the initial phase of group development.

Stage 2: Storming. During this "shakedown" period, individual styles often come into conflict. Hostility, infighting, tension, and confrontation occur at this stage. Members may argue to clarify expectations about their contributions. Coalitions and cliques may form within the group, and one

---

[21]Alexander D. Stajkovic, Dongseop Lee, and Anthony J. Nyberg, "Collective Efficacy, Group Potency, and Group Performance: Meta-Analyses of Their Relationships, and Test of a Mediation Model," *Journal of Applied Psychology*, May 2009, pp. 814–828. The definition of collective efficacy is based on Albert Bandura, *Self-Efficacy: The Exercise of Control* (Englewood Cliffs, N.J.: Prentice Hall, 1997).

[22]Frederick P. Morgeson, "The External Leadership of Self-Managing Teams: Intervening in the Context of Novel and Disruptive Events," *Journal of Applied Psychology*, May 2005, pp. 497–508.

[23]J. Steven Heinen and Eugene Jacobsen, "A Model of Task Group Development in Complex Organizations and a Strategy for Implementation," *Academy of Management Review*, October 1976, pp. 98–111.

EXHIBIT 13-4	The Stages of Group Development

Most groups follow a predictable sequence of stages.

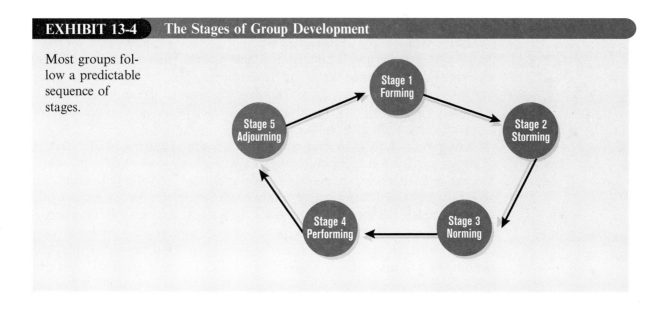

or two members may be targeted for exclusion. Subgroups may form to push an agenda. (Despite the frequency of storming, many workplace groups work willingly with one another from the outset, thus skipping Stage 2.)

Stage 3: Norming. Overcoming resistance and establishing group norms (standards of conduct) follow the storm. Cohesiveness and commitment begin to develop. The group starts to come together as a coordinated unit, and harmony prevails. Norms stem from three sources: The group itself quickly establishes limits for members, often by effective use of glares and nods. For example, the team member who responds sarcastically to the group leader's suggestions might receive disapproving glances from other members. Norms may also be imposed that are derived from the larger organization and professional codes, such as that used by accountants and financial planners. A third source of norms might be an influential team member who inspires the group to elevate its performance or behavior. A team member might say, "Why stop at having the best safety record in this division? Let's be number one in the entire company."

Stage 4: Performing. When the group reaches the performing stage, it is ready to focus on accomplishing its key tasks. Issues concerning interpersonal relations and task assignment are put aside as the group becomes a well-functioning unit. Internal motivation and creativity are likely to emerge as the group performs. At their best, members feel they are working "for the cause," much like a political campaign team or a team bringing a breakthrough product to market.

Stage 5: Adjourning. Temporary work groups disband after accomplishing their task. Those same group members, however, develop important relationships and understandings they can take with them. These will be valuable should they be part of a similar team in the future. The link between adjourning and forming shown in Exhibit 13-4 indicates that many groups do reassemble after one project is completed. The link between Stages 4 and 5 would not apply for a group that disbanded and never worked together again.

Helping the group move past the first three stages into performing poses a key managerial challenge. At times, leaders may need to challenge group members to spend less time on process issues and more time on task—getting the job done!

MANAGERIAL ACTIONS FOR BUILDING TEAMWORK

Given the importance of teams, managers may need to invest time in building teamwork. Here we highlight managerial actions and organizational practices that facilitate teamwork.[24] We use the term *managerial practices* to include team leader practices because many groups and teams do not use the title team leader for the person in charge. A department manager, for example, might be able to build teamwork. Good teamwork enhances, but does not guarantee, a successful team. For example, a group with excellent teamwork might be working on improving a service no longer valued by the company or its customers. No matter what the output of the team, it will probably be ignored.

1. *Begin with a mission and an agreement on the meaning of success.* A natural starting point in developing teamwork is to have a mission that is accepted by the team, such as one that relates to providing an outstanding experience for customers. A clearly articulated mission translates into the team having an urgent, constructive purpose. Knowing and accepting the mission includes agreeing on what constitutes success. Gordon Bethune, the CEO who helped rebuild Continental Airlines from "worst to first," maintains that the entire team must agree on what constitutes success. Every team member must say: "Yes, that's it."[25]

2. *Help the group focus on its strengths.* Teams that experience group efficacy are more likely to be cohesive and work together smoothly. A useful subject for at least a portion of a team meeting is to respond to the question, "What are our team's strengths?" and "What do we do well?" Articulating these positive points might help the team feel stronger.[26] An example of both a team strength and doing something well might be on-time delivery of high-priority projects.

---

[24]Some of the key research support for this section stems from Katzenbach and Smith, "The Discipline of Teams," p. 112; "Build Teamwork by Showing Employees You Respect Them," *Manager's Edge*, April 2002, p. 1; DeChurch and Mesmer-Magnus, "The Cognitive Underpinnings of Effective Teamwork: A Meta-Analysis," pp. 32–53.

[25]Shelia M. Puffer, "Continental Airlines' CEO Gordon Bethune on Teams and New Product Development," *Academy of Management Executive*, August 1999, p. 30.

[26]"Ask Positive Questions," *Manager's Edge*, March 2010, p. 1.

3. *Compete against a common enemy.* Competing against a common enemy often builds team spirit. It is preferable that the adversary be external, such as an independent diner competing against franchised family restaurants.

4. *Make teamwork the norm.* A primary strategy for teamwork promotes the attitude that working together effectively is an expected norm. The team leader can communicate the norm of teamwork by making frequent use of words and phrases that support teamwork. Emphasizing the words *team members* or *teammates*, and deemphasizing the words *subordinates* and *employees*, helps communicate the teamwork norm.

5. *Use consensus decision making and provide information.* Using the consensus decision-making style provides another way to reinforce teamwork. A sophisticated approach to enhancing teamwork, it feeds team members valid facts and information that motivate them to work together. New information prompts the team to redefine and enrich its understanding of the challenge it is facing, thereby focusing on a common purpose.

6. *Use teamwork language.* A subtle yet potent method of building teamwork emphasizes the use of language that fosters cohesion and commitment. In-group jargon bonds a team and sets the group apart from others. For example, a team of computer experts says "Give me a core dump" to mean "Tell me your thoughts."

micromanagement
Supervising group members too closely and second-guessing their decisions.

7. *Minimize micromanagement.* To foster teamwork, the manager should minimize **micromanagement**, or supervising group members too closely and second-guessing their decisions. Micromanagement can hamper a spirit of teamwork because team members do not feel in control of their own work. Morale suffers when the manager is more concerned about the format of a document than its purpose.[27]

8. *Reward the team and individuals.* A high-impact strategy for encouraging teamwork rewards the team as well as individuals. The most convincing team incentive is to calculate compensation partially on the basis of team results. Managers might also apply positive reinforcement whenever the group or individuals engage in behavior that supports teamwork. For example, team members who took the initiative to have an information-sharing session can be singled out and praised for this activity. Research supports the practical idea that individual team members should be rewarded for their individual contributions as well as their contribution to the team effort. These are referred to as hybrid rewards.[28]

9. *Encourage face-to-face communication.* An emerging approach to enhancing teamwork is to encourage team members to supplement

---

[27]Jared Sandberg, "Bosses Who Fiddle With Employees' Work Risk Ire, Low Morale," *The Wall Street Journal*, April 25, 2006, p. B1.

[28]Matthew J. Pearsall, Michael S. Christian, and Aleksander P. J. Ellis, "Motivating Independent Teams: Individual Rewards, Shared Rewards, or Something in Between?" *Journal of Applied Psychology*, January 2010, pp. 184–185.

e-mail communication and text messaging with phone calls and face-to-face meetings. The old fashioned method of humans interacting with one another in person has proven to be of value in the era of communication technology.

10. *Show respect for team members.* Showing respect for team members is a general technique for building teamwork. Respect can be demonstrated in such ways as asking rather than demanding something be done. For example, say "Jeremy, could you investigate our developing a Facebook page for the team?" Giving team members your undivided attention when they come to you with a problem is another demonstration of respect. Making positive comments about team members, and not talking behind their backs, is another way of showing respect. An indirect way of respecting all members is to lead them all in approximately the same manner. According to leader–member exchange theory, the successful leader has different relationships with each group member. New research suggests, however, that the leader should avoid a high level of differentiation in working with team members. Members should be treated essentially alike to help build teamwork.[29] There will always be some need for differentiated leadership, such as providing more coaching to a less-skilled team member.

11. *Participate in offsite teamwork training.* Another option available to organizations for enhancing teamwork comes through experiential learning such as sending members to offsite (or outdoor) training. Because accomplishing the mission and astronaut surviving depends on high-level teamwork, NASA invests two weeks every several years in wilderness training to develop teamwork among astronauts.[30] In outdoor training, participants acquire leadership and teamwork skills by confronting physical challenges and exceeding their self-imposed limitations. In rope activities, which are typical of outdoor training, participants attached to a secure pulley with ropes climb ladders and jump off to another spot. A day at an auto-racing track, another form of outdoor training for elite teams, provides team members with an opportunity to drive at racecar speeds in some kind of cooperative venture. Yet another approach to team building requires the group to prepare a seven-course meal. All of these challenges require teamwork rather than individual effort, hence their contribution to team development.

Outdoor training generally offers the most favorable outcomes when the trainer helps the team members comprehend the link between such training and on-the-job behavior. Reviewing what has been learned is a key step in this direction. Still, the manager should not impose outdoor training on the growing number of workers who dislike the idea or fear bodily damage. Dissent is growing about outdoor activities that require

[29]Joshua R. Wu, Anne S. Tsui, and Angelo J. Kinicki, "Consequences of Differentiated Leadership in Groups," *Academy of Management Journal*, February 2010, pp. 90–106.

[30]Robert Levine, "The New Right Stuff," *Fortune*, June 12, 2006, pp. 116–118.

athletic ability because less physically capable team members feel disadvantaged.[31]

12. *Rise to the challenge of teamwork for virtual teams.* Building teamwork within a virtual team creates additional challenges because members rarely meet face-to-face and have less opportunity to build the chemistry often found within traditional teams. A study involving 15 European and U.S. multinational companies observed that certain factors helped build teamwork in virtual teams. Several of the success factors are as follows: First, invest in an online resource where team members can readily learn about each other. Second, to capitalize on familiarity, choose a few team members who have worked together previously. Third, create an online site where team members can exchange ideas, collaborate, and encourage and inspire each other. Fourth, when establishing the team, rely on volunteers as much as possible. Volunteers are more likely to enjoy being virtual team members and will therefore be willing to cooperate with each other.[32]

Effective managers pick and choose from strategies as appropriate to build teamwork. Relying too heavily on one tactic, such as establishing a mission statement or outdoor training, limits the development of sustained teamwork.

LEARNING OBJECTIVE 5

Explain the actions and attitudes of effective team players.

BEING AN EFFECTIVE TEAM PLAYER

Being an effective team player makes collaborative effort possible. Being an effective team player also affects managerial perceptions because managers value such behavior among employees and job applicants. Here we describe a number of skills, actions, and attitudes contributing to effective team play. For convenience, five are classified as task-related and five as people-related. In reviewing these attributes, remember that all team situations do not have identical requirements.

Task-Related Actions and Attitudes

Task-related actions and attitudes focus on group or teamwork goals rather than on interpersonal relationships. An effective team player is likely to behave and think in the following ways:

1. *Possesses and shares technical expertise.* Most people are chosen to join a particular work team on the basis of their technical or functional expertise. Glenn Parker believes that using technical expertise to outstanding advantage requires a willingness and ability to share that expertise. It is

[31]Duff McDonald, "Why We All Hate Offsites," *Business 2.0*, May 2006, p. 79; Jared Sandberg, "Can Spending a Day Stuck to a Velcro Wall Help Build a Team?" *The Wall Street Journal*, December 26, 2006, p. B1.

[32]Lynda Gratton, "Working Together...When Apart," *The Wall Street Journal*, June 16–17, 2007, p. R4.

also necessary for the technical expert to be able to communicate with team members in other disciplines who lack the same technical background.[33]

2. *Assumes responsibility for problems.* The outstanding team player assumes responsibility for problems. If he or she notices a free-floating problem (not yet assigned to a specific person), the team member says, "I'll do it." The task should be one suited for independent rather than coordinated activity, such as conducting research.

3. *Is willing to commit to team goals.* The exceptional team player will commit to team goals even if his or her personal goals cannot be achieved for now. For instance, the team member seeking visibility will be enthusiastic about pursuing team goals even if not much visibility will be gained.

4. *Is able to see the big picture.* As described in Chapter 1, a basic management skill is to think conceptually. Exceptionally good team players exhibit this same skill. In team efforts, discussion can get bogged down in small details. As a result, the team might temporarily lose sight of what it is trying to accomplish. The team player (or team leader) who can help the group focus on its broader purpose plays a vital role.

5. *Is willing to ask tough questions.* A **tough question** helps the group achieve insight into the nature of the problem it faces, what it might be doing wrong, and whether progress is sufficient. Tough questions can also be asked to help the group see the big picture. Asking tough questions helps the group avoid groupthink. Here is a representative tough question asked by a team member: "I've been to all our meetings so far. What specifically have we accomplished?"

6. *Is willing to try something new.* An effective team player experiments with new ideas even if the old method works relatively well. Trying something new leads to a spirit of inventiveness that helps keep the group vibrant. In a Harley-Davidson manufacturing team, several of the workers designed a device to guide the brush in painting Harley's trademark striping. Although the more experienced manufacturing technicians had been successful with the hand-painting method, in the spirit of teamwork they were willing to try the new technique.

tough question
A question that helps the group achieve insight into the nature of the problem, what it might be doing wrong, and whether progress is sufficient.

People-Related Actions and Attitudes

Outstanding team players cultivate a conscious awareness of their interpersonal relations within the group. They recognize that effective interpersonal relationships are important for task accomplishment. An outstanding team player is likely to do or think the following:

1. *Trust team members.* The cornerstone attitude of the outstanding team player is to trust team members. If you do not believe that the other team members have your best interests at heart, it will be difficult to

---

[33]Glenn M. Parker, *Cross-Functional Teams: Working with Allies, Enemies, & Other Strangers* (San Francisco: Jossey-Bass Publishers, 1994), p. 3.

share opinions and ideas. Trusting team members includes believing that their ideas are technically sound and rational until proven otherwise. Another manifestation of trust is taking a risk by trying out a team member's unproven ideas. (As cautioned above, however, do not trust teammates to the point that you never monitor their work.)

2. *Share credit.* A not-to-be-overlooked tactic for emphasizing teamwork is to share credit for your accomplishments with the team. Sharing credit is authentic because other members of the team usually have contributed to the success of a project. Stephen Covey, best-selling author and consultant, says that teamwork is fostered when you don't worry about who gets the credit.[34] To the strong team player, getting the group task accomplished is more important than receiving individual recognition.

3. *Recognize the interests and achievements of others.* A fundamental tactic for establishing yourself as a solid team player is to recognize the interests and achievements of others. Let others know that you care about their interests by such means as asking, "How do my ideas fit into what you have planned?" Recognizing the achievements of others can be done by complimenting their tangible accomplishments.

4. *Listen actively and share information.* The skilled team player listens actively both inside and outside of meetings. An active listener strives to grasp both the facts and feelings behind what is being said. Information sharing helps other team members do their job well and communicates concern for their welfare. Information sharing can take many forms, such as sending links to useful Web sites, news clips, and magazine articles and recommending relevant books.

5. *Give and receive criticism.* The strong team player offers constructive criticism when needed, but does so diplomatically. A high-performance team demands sincere and tactful criticism among members. In addition to criticizing others in a helpful manner, the strong team player benefits from criticism directed toward him or her. A high-performing team involves give and take, including criticism of each other's ideas. The willingness to accept constructive criticism is often referred to as self-awareness. The self-aware team player insightfully processes personal feedback to improve effectiveness.

6. *Don't rain on another team member's parade.* Pointing out the flaws in another person's accomplishments, or drawing attention to your own achievements when somebody else is receiving credit, creates disharmony within the group. When a teammate is in the spotlight, allow him or her to enjoy the moment without displaying petty jealousy.

---

[34]Steven Covey, "Team Up for a Superstar Office," *USA Weekend*, September 4–6, 1998, p. 10.

LEARNING
OBJECTIVE
Point to the
potential
contributions and
problems of teams
and groups.

POTENTIAL CONTRIBUTIONS AND PROBLEMS OF TEAMS AND GROUPS

Given that teams and groups are such an integral part of how organizations function, it is easy not to look critically at their contribution. However, researchers, writers, and managerial workers themselves assess the contributions of groups, both the upside and downside, especially with teams.

Potential Contributions of Teams and Groups

Teams and groups make a contribution to the extent that they produce results beyond what could be achieved without a high degree of collaboration among workers. Considerable case history evidence supports the contribution of teams over independent effort. The previous discussion of self-managed work teams presented examples of this evidence. Another perspective on the importance of teams is **lift-outs**—the practice of recruiting an entire high-functioning team from another organization. The company doing the recruiting believes that the team is more important for attaining its goals than an individual star. It is also believed that the recruited team can get up to speed rapidly in the new setting. An imported team might also help the company enter a new market or line of business quickly.[35]

lift-outs (in relation to teams)

The practice of recruiting an entire high-functioning team from another organization.

Lift-outs have been frequent in such industries as financial services, law, and information technology. Now professional services firms, such as management consulting and accounting, are hiring more teams. Despite the increase in lift-outs, the concept can raise legal issues and might be considered unethical. Is it fair to decimate a competitor by hiring one of its key teams? Or is it just part of competitive business?

Teams tend to be most useful as a form of organization under the following conditions:[36]

- When work processes cut across functional lines (as in new-product development)
- When speed is important (keeping the number of team meetings to a minimum)
- When the organization faces a complex and rapidly changing environment (as in developing toys and video games for the next holiday season)
- When innovation and learning have high priority (entering a new market or field)
- When the tasks to be accomplished require integration of highly interdependent performers (gathering inputs for a strategic plan)

---

[35]Boris Groysberg and Robin Abrahams, "Lift Outs: How to Acquire a High-Functioning Team," *Harvard Business Review*, December 2006, pp. 133–140; Jena McGregor, "I Can't Believe They Took the Whole Team," *Business Week*, December 18, 2006, pp. 120–122.

[36]Russ Forrester and Allan B. Drexler, "A Model for Team-Based Performance," *Academy of Management Executive*, August 1999, p. 47.

When these conditions do not exist, the organization is better off assigning the task to more traditional groups or to individuals working alone. Remember that a team is essentially a supergroup.

Potential Problems of Teams and Groups

Although the collaborative workplace enjoys popularity, many concerns accompany the use of teams and groups. In Chapter 5, discussing problem solving and decision making, we described two problems with groups: time wasting and groupthink. Here we look at other problems: group polarization, social loafing, limited accountability, ostracism of a member, and career retardation.

Group Polarization

group polarization
A situation in which post-discussion attitudes tend to be more extreme than pre-discussion attitudes.

During group problem solving or group discussion in general, members often shift their attitudes. Sometimes the group moves toward taking greater risks, called the risky shift. At other times the group moves toward a more conservative position. The general term for moving in either direction is **group polarization**, a situation in which post-discussion attitudes tend to be more extreme than pre-discussion attitudes.[37] For example, members of an executive team become more cautious about entering a new market following a group discussion.

Group discussion facilitates polarization for several reasons. Discovering that others share our opinions may reinforce and strengthen our position. Listening to persuasive arguments may also strengthen our convictions. The "devil-made-me-do-it" attitude is another contributor to polarization. If responsibility is diffused, a person will feel less responsible—and less guilty—about taking an extreme position.

Group polarization has a practical implication for managers who rely on group decision making. Workers who enter into group decision making with a stand on an issue may develop more extreme post-decision positions. For example, a team of employees who were seeking more generous benefits may decide as a group that the company should become an industry leader in employee benefits.

Social Loafing

social loafing
Freeloading, or shirking individual responsibility, when a person is placed in a group setting and removed from individual accountability.

An unfortunate by-product of group and team effort happens when an under-motivated person squeezes by without contributing a fair share. **Social loafing** is freeloading, or shirking individual responsibility, when a person is placed in a group setting and removed from individual accountability. The concept is said to have been first described by a sociologist who was studying group behavior among people playing tug-of-war with a rope. Readers who have worked on group projects for courses may have encountered this widely observed dysfunction of collective effort.

---

[37]Gregory Moorhead and Ricky W. Griffin, *Organizational Behavior: Managing People and Organizations*, 4th ed. (Boston: Houghton Mifflin, 1995), pp. 52–62.

Two motivational explanations of social loafing have been offered. First, some people believe that because they are part of a team, they can "hide in the crowd." Second, group members typically believe that others are likely to withhold effort when working in a group. As a consequence, they withhold effort themselves to avoid being played for a sucker.

As one approach to minimizing the effects of social loafing, a manager may ask group members to contribute to the evaluation of each other. Concerns about being evaluated as a freeloader by peers prompt some people to work harder.

Limited Accountability

A curious problem about workplace teams is that they are often given credit for accomplishment but rarely blamed for failures. Instead, individual team members are blamed for team failures and the group escapes blame. Support for this argument comes from two complicated studies involving graduate business students who were assigned to a variety of group tasks and who had the opportunity to assign credit and blame after the tasks were completed. Another way of interpreting these results is that teams develop a positive halo and are perceived as able to attain high performance.[38] When the team does fail, observers (including the manager) look for individuals to blame.

Ostracism of Unwanted Group Member

ostracism

The extent to which an individual group member perceives that he or she is being ignored by the other group members.

Despite team spirit, groups can be cruel in ostracizing an unwanted or unpopular member. **Ostracism** is the extent to which an individual group member perceives that he or she is being ignored by the other group members. Several surveys have suggested that many employees feel they have been given the silent treatment by other members of the workgroup. Sometimes the ostracism is a form of discrimination based on gender, age, race, ethnicity, or sexual orientation.[39]

At other times, ostracism is based on an individual's personality or low work performance. Being ostracized has a strong negative impact on a group member's well being. Even when ostracism is warranted, it is dysfunctional. It would be better for the other group members to work with the individual to help him or her be welcomed into the group. Or, the group might ask the manager to get help for the unwanted worker if he or she has a personality or performance problem.

Career Retardation

A final concern about teams arises from focusing too much on group or team effort, rather than individual effort, which can retard a person's career.

---

[38]Charles E. Naquin and Renee O. Tynan, "The Team Halo Effect: Why Teams Are Not Blamed for Their Failures," *Journal of Applied Psychology*, April 2003, pp. 332–340.

[39]D. Lance Ferris et al, "The Development and Validation of the Workplace Ostracism Scale," *Journal of Applied Psychology*, November 2008, pp. 1348–1366.

Some managers classify workers as team players versus leaders. (The perception is somewhat misleading because most effective leaders and managers are also good team players.) Yet it is true that a person who tries too hard to be a good team player might become a conformist and not seek individual recognition. People who do break away from the team and become higher-level managers are typically those known for independent thought and outstanding accomplishment.

For those who want to advance beyond team member or team leader, it is important to be recognized for outstanding performance. As a team member, volunteer to take on leadership roles such as chairing a meeting or coordinating a special project. Bring a dossier of your individual accomplishments to your performance review. Every team has a most valuable player (MVP) who is still a good team player.

LEARNING OBJECTIVE **7**

Describe the positive and negative aspects of conflict and how team leaders and managers can resolve conflict.

conflict
The simultaneous arousal of two or more incompatible motives.

RESOLVING CONFLICT WITHIN TEAMS AND GROUPS

Although harmony and collaboration are an important goal of groups and teams, some disagreement and dispute is inevitable. **Conflict** is the simultaneous arousal of two or more incompatible motives. It is often accompanied by tension and frustration. Whenever two or more people in the group compete for the same resource, conflict occurs. Two team members, for example, might both want to take the team's one allotted seat on the corporate jet on business trips they are taking the same day. Conflict can also be considered a hostile or antagonistic relationship between two people.

Another reason conflict often occurs is because of the existence of factions within a group, often because group members are from different units within the company. After a merger or acquisition, groups may form made up of people from the two companies.[40] A positive purpose of such groups might be to help smooth the integration of two large firms such as Chrysler and Fiat.

Here we look at three aspects of conflict particularly relevant to managers and team leaders of small groups: task versus relationship conflict, consequences of conflict, and methods of conflict resolution.

Task versus Relationship Conflict

Some conflicts within a group deal mostly with disagreements over how work should be done. They are referred to as task or *cognitive* conflicts because they deal mostly with the work itself rather than emotions and relationships. Two group members, for example, might argue over whether it is better to use their limited advertising budget to buy space on the outside of a bus or on the Internet. **Task conflict** focuses on substantive, issue-related

task conflict
Conflict that focuses on substantive, issue-related differences related to the work itself.

---

[40]Jiato Li and Donald C. Hambrick, "Factional Groups: A New Vantage on Demographic Faultlines, Conflict, and Disintegration in Work Teams," *Academy of Management Journal*, October 2005, p. 794.

differences related to the work itself. These issues are tangible and concrete and can be dealt with more intellectually than emotionally.

Other conflicts within the group are more people-oriented. They occur because people have personality clashes, are rude to each other, or simply view problems and situations from a different frame of reference. **Relationship conflict** focuses on personalized, individually oriented issues. The conflict relates to subjective issues that are dealt with more emotionally than intellectually.[41] One symptom that relationship conflict exists within the group is when, during a meeting, two people say to each other frequently, "Please let me finish. I'm still speaking." Relationship conflict might also take place based on generational differences such as young people disliking the fact that older workers prefer e-mail over text message for most communication.

Task conflict in moderate doses can be functional because it requires teams to engage in activities that foster team effectiveness. Team members engaged in moderate task conflict critically examine alternative solutions and incorporate different points of view into their goals or mission statement. Because frank communication and different points of view are encouraged, task conflict can encourage innovative thinking. In contrast, relationship (or affective) conflict undermines group effectiveness by blocking constructive activities and processes. By such means as directing anger toward individuals and blaming each other for mistakes, relationship conflict leads to cynicism and distrust.

An analysis of many studies cautions that both task conflict and relationship conflict can be equally disruptive. A little conflict may be beneficial, but this advantage quickly breaks down as conflict intensifies.[42] The underlying explanation is that most people take differences of opinion personally, regardless of whether the issue is strictly the task or their personal characteristics.

relationship conflict
Conflict that focuses on personalized, individually oriented issues.

Consequences of Conflict

Conflict results in both positive and negative consequences. The right amount of conflict may enhance job performance, but too much or too little conflict lowers performance. If the manager observes that job performance is suffering because of too much conflict, he or she should reduce it. If performance is low because employees are too placid, the manager might profitably increase conflict. For example, the manager might establish a prize for top performance in the group.

Positive Consequences of Conflict

Many managers and scholars believe that job conflict can have positive consequences. The right amount of conflict is usually quite low—somewhat like

---

[41]Carsten K. W. De Dreu and Laurie R. Weingart, "Task versus Relationship Conflict, Team Performance, and Team Member Satisfaction: A Meta-Analysis," *Journal of Applied Psychology*, August 2003, pp. 741–749.

[42]De Dreu and Weingart, "Task Versus Relationship Conflict," p. 746.

fat in your diet. Because a touch of conflict is beneficial, it is dysfunctional for a team to fear conflict.[43] With the right amount of conflict in the workplace, one or more of the following outcomes can be anticipated.

1. *Increased creativity.* Talents and abilities surface in response to conflict. People become inventive when they are placed in intense competition with others.
2. *Increased effort.* Constructive amounts of conflict spur people to new heights of performance. People become so motivated to win the conflict that they may surprise themselves and their superiors with their work output.
3. *Increased diagnostic information.* Conflict can provide valuable information about problem areas in the department or organization. When leaders learn of conflict, they may conduct investigations that will lead to the prevention of similar problems.
4. *Increased group cohesion.* When one group in a firm is in conflict with another, group members may become more cohesive. They perceive themselves to be facing a common enemy.

Negative Consequences of Conflict

When the wrong amount or type of conflict exists, job performance may suffer. Some types of conflict have worse consequences than others. A particularly bad form of conflict is one that forces a person to choose between two undesirable alternatives. Negative consequences of conflict include the following:

1. *Poor physical and mental health.* Intense conflict is a source of stress. A person under prolonged and intense conflict may suffer stress-related disorders. Many acts of workplace violence stem from highly stressed employees or former employees who experienced conflict with supervisors or coworkers. Many of the people who return to the workplace to shoot former coworkers and the manager were dismissed for poor performance.
2. *Wasted resources.* Employees and groups in conflict frequently waste time, money, and other resources while fighting their battles. One executive took a personal dislike to one of his managers and ignored his cost-saving recommendations.
3. *Sidetracked goals.* In extreme forms of conflict, the parties involved may neglect the pursuit of important goals. Instead, they focus on winning their conflicts. A goal displacement of this type took place within an information technology group. The rival factions spent so much time squabbling over which new hardware and software to purchase that they neglected some of their tasks.
4. *Heightened self-interest.* Conflict within the group often results in extreme demonstrations of self-interest at the expense of the group and the larger organization. Individuals or groups place their personal

---

[43]Patrick M. Lencioni, *The Five Dysfunctions of a Team* (San Francisco: Jossey-Bass, 2002).

interests over those of the rest of the firm or customers. One common result of this type of self-interest is hogging resources. A team member might attempt to convince the team leader to place him on an important customer troubleshooting assignment even though he knows his rival on the team is better qualified.

Methods of Conflict Resolution

Managers spend as much as 20 percent of their work time dealing with conflict. A leader who learns to manage conflict effectively can increase his or her productivity. In addition, being able to resolve conflict enhances one's stature as a leader. Employees expect their boss to be able to resolve conflicts. Here we describe the five basic styles or methods of resolving conflict: forcing, accommodating, sharing, collaborating, and avoiding. An effective manager will choose the best approach for the situation.

Forcing

The forcing, or competitive, style is based on the desire to win one's own concerns at the expense of the other party, or to dominate. A person with a forcing style is likely to engage in win-lose ("I win, you lose") power struggles, resulting in poor teamwork. Steve Jobs, the legendary leader of Apple Inc., relies on forcing to resolve conflict such as in questions about design issues. Because of his stature and power, subordinates are usually willing to accept the forcing style of Jobs.

Accommodating

The accommodative style favors appeasement, or satisfying the other's concerns without taking care of one's own. People with this orientation may be generous or self-sacrificing just to maintain a relationship. An irate customer might be accommodated with a full refund "just to shut him (or her) up." The intent of such accommodation might also be to retain the customer's loyalty.

Sharing

The sharing style is midway between domination and appeasement. Sharers prefer moderate but incomplete satisfaction for both parties. The result is compromise. The term *splitting the difference* reflects this orientation. The sharing style of conflict resolution is commonly used in such activities as purchasing a house or car. Within the work group, sharing might take the form of each team member receiving the same percentage salary increase rather than haggling over dividing the pool of money available for increases.

Collaborating

In contrast to the sharing style, collaboration reflects an interest in fully satisfying the desire of both parties. It is based on an underlying win-win philosophy, the belief that after conflict has been resolved both sides should gain something of value. For example, a small-company president might offer the management team more stock options if they are willing to take a pay cut to help the firm through rough times. If the firm succeeds, both parties have scored a victory. All parties benefit from collaboration, a win-win approach to resolving conflict. Compliance with the solution occurs readily, and the relationship between those in conflict improves.

A conflict-resolution technique built into the collaboration style is *confrontation and problem solving.* Its purpose is to identify the real problem and then arrive at a solution that genuinely solves it. First the parties are brought together and the real problem is confronted.

Another collaborative approach involves asking what action can break an impasse. When a conflict reaches a point where progress is at a standstill, one of the parties asks, "What would you like me to do?" The other side often reacts with astonishment and then the first party asks, "If I could do anything to make this situation okay in your eyes, what would that be?"[44] Frequently the desired action—such as "Treat me with more respect"—can be implemented.

An example of win-win conflict resolution took place between PN Hoffman, a condominium developer, and the First Congregational Church of Christ in Washington DC. The developer planned to build 140 condominiums on a street where one of Washington's oldest churches had existed since the end of the Civil War. As part of the deal, PN Hoffman agreed to build a $17 million sanctuary for the church with eight floors of apartments above, along with balconies, a swimming pool, and a fitness center. The church planned to occupy the first two floors and continue serving breakfast and dinner to several hundred homeless people. A PN manager said he recognized that some home buyers might not care to live above a homeless service center, but other potential buyers would be "fully aware of the urban lifestyle."[45] PN Hoffman won because they could go ahead with their development; the Church won because it could continue to function intact and add a new sanctuary. Was this an example of conflict resolution made in heaven?

Avoiding

The avoider combines uncooperativeness and unassertiveness. He or she is indifferent to the concerns of either party. The person may actually be withdrawing from conflict or relying upon fate. Managers sometimes use the avoiding style to stay out of a conflict between team members. The members are left to resolve their own differences.

Experience and research suggest that the cooperative approaches to resolving conflict (sharing and collaboration) work more effectively than the competitive approaches (forcing and accommodation). For example, a study conducted with 61 self-managing teams involved 489 employees from the production department of a leading electronics manufacturer. A cooperative

---

[44]James A. Autry, *Love & Profit* (New York: Morrow, 1991).

[45]Paul Schwartzman, "Million-Dollar Condos with a Soup Kitchen Below," *Washington Post*, (http://www.washingtonpost.com), December 27, 2006.

(focus on mutual benefits or win-win) approach to conflict resolution led to confidence in skills for dealing with conflict. The heightened confidence in dealing with conflict, in turn, led to more effective performance as evaluated by managers.[46]

Resolving Conflicts Between Two Group Members

A high-level managerial skill is to help two or more group members resolve conflict between or among them. Much of the time a manager invests in conflict resolution is geared toward assisting others to resolve their conflict. The most useful approach is to get the parties in conflict to engage in confrontation and problem solving. The manager sits down with the two sides and encourages them to talk to each other about the problem, not to the manager. This approach is preferable to inviting each side to speak with the manager alone, which encourages each side to attempt to convince the manager that he or she is right. An abbreviated example follows:

> Manager: *I've brought you two together to see if you can overcome the problems you have about sharing the workload during a period in which one of you is overloaded.*
>
> Melissa: *I'm glad you did. Luke never wants to help me, even when I'm drowning in customer requests.*
>
> Luke: *I would be glad to help Melissa if she ever agreed to help me. If she has any downtime, she runs to the break room so she can chat on her cell phone.*
>
> Melissa: *Look who's talking. I have seen you napping in your SUV when you have a little down time.*
>
> Manager: *I'm beginning to see what's going on here. You are antagonistic toward each other and you're looking for little faults to pick. With a little more respect on both sides, I think you would be more willing to help each other.*
>
> Luke: *Actually, Melissa's not too bad. And I know she can perform well when she wants to. Next time I see her needing help, I'll pitch in.*
>
> Melissa: *I know that the name "Luke" can sound like a tough guy, but our Luke really has a warm heart. I'm open to starting with a fresh slate. Maybe Luke can ask me politely the next time he needs help.*

Conflict specialist Patrick S. Nugent believes that being able to intervene in the conflicts of group members is a management skill that grows in importance. Such competencies are useful in an emerging form of management based less on traditional hierarchy and more on developing self-managing subordinates and teams.[47]

---

[46]Steve Alper, Dean Tjosvold, and Kenneth S. Law, "Conflict Management, Efficacy, and Performance in Organizational Teams," *Personnel Psychology*, Autumn 2000, pp. 625–642.

[47]Patrick S. Nugent, "Managing Conflict: Third-Party Interventions for Managers," *Academy of Management Executive*, February 2002, p. 152.

Summary of Key Points

① **Identify various types of teams and groups, including self-managed work teams and project groups.**

Formal groups are deliberately formed by the organization, whereas informal groups emerge over time through worker interaction. Representative types of work teams include self-managed work teams, project teams, task forces, cross-functional teams, top-management teams, and virtual teams.

② **Describe the characteristics of effective groups and teams.**

Effective work group characteristics are well documented. Member jobs are enriched, and workers feel empowered to solve problems including sharing leadership. Group members operate interdependently in terms of tasks and rewards. Culturally diverse members enjoy task and social interaction. The right size of the group, the intelligence and personality of group members, and the emotional intelligence of the group as a whole are all crucial factors. The work group requires good support from management. Effective group processes include team spirit, workload sharing, and communication and cooperation. Following work processes and procedures also aids effectiveness, as does familiarity with jobs and coworkers.

③ **Describe the stages of group development.**

Groups usually go through predictable stages: forming, storming, norming, performing, and adjourning. A key managerial challenge is to get the group to the performing stage.

④ **Summarize managerial actions for building teamwork.**

Managers and leaders can enhance teamwork through many behaviors, attitudes, and organizational actions including the following: begin with a mission statement and an agreement on the meaning of success; help the group focus on its strengths; compete against a common adversary; make teamwork the norm; use a consensus decision-making style, and provide information; use teamwork language; minimize micromanagement; reward the team and individuals; encourage some face-to-face communication; show respect for team members; participate in offsite teamwork training; and rise to the challenge of teamwork for virtual teams.

⑤ **Explain the actions and attitudes of an effective team player.**

Task-related actions and attitudes of effective team players include: sharing technical expertise; assuming responsibility for problems; committing to team goals; seeing the big picture; asking tough questions; and trying something new. People-related actions and attitudes include trusting team members; sharing credit; recognizing others; listening and information sharing; giving and receiving criticism; and not downplaying the success of others.

⑥ **Point to the potential contributions and problems of teams and groups.**

Teams and groups make a contribution when they lead to results that could not be achieved without collaboration. Evidence indicates that collective effort leads to enhanced productivity. Lift-outs of competitive teams suggest that teams are productive. Groups and teams also have potential problems. Group polarization (taking extreme positions) may occur, and members may engage in social loafing (freeloading). Groups too often escape blame for their mistakes, with individuals being blamed instead. Unwanted group members may be ostracized. Focusing too much on group or team effort instead of on attaining individual recognition can retard a person's career.

⑦ **Describe the positive and negative aspects of conflict and how team leaders and managers can resolve conflict.**

Although harmony and collaboration are important goals of groups and teams, some conflict is inevitable. Task or cognitive conflict focuses on substantive, issue-related differences. Relationship or affective conflict focuses on personalized, individually oriented issues that are dealt with more emotionally than intellectually. Task conflict in small doses leads to such positive outcomes as creative problem solving. Positive consequences of conflict also include increased effort, obtaining diagnostic information, and increased group cohesion. Negative consequences of conflict include wasted resources and heightened self-interest.

Five major modes of conflict management have been identified: forcing, accommodating, sharing, collaborating, and avoiding. Each style is based on a combination of satisfying one's own concerns (assertiveness) and satisfying the concerns of others (cooperativeness). Confrontation and problem solving is a widely applicable collaborative technique of resolving conflict. Managers often must resolve conflict between and among group members, and confrontation and problem-solving skills are useful.

Key Terms and Phrases

Group, 470
Team, 470
Teamwork, 470
Formal group, 470
Informal group, 470
Self-managed work team, 471
Project team, 473
Task force, 474
Cross-functional team, 474
Virtual team, 477

Micromanagement, 486
Tough question, 489
Lift-outs (in relation to teams), 491
Group polarization, 492
Social loafing, 492
Ostracism, 493
Conflict, 494
Task conflict, 494
Relationship conflict, 495

Questions

1. In what way is participating on a sports team, musical band, or orchestra good preparation for being a member of a work group on the job?
2. Why is experience working on a cross-functional team particularly valuable for a person who aspires to a career in management?
3. To what extent are you concerned that your individual talents will go unnoticed if you are a strong team player?
4. What do you think explains the fact that the role of project manager continues to grow in importance?
5. Give an example of a tough question a manager might ask a team.
6. Provide two examples of interdependent (or collaborative) tasks in the workplace for which teams are well suited.
7. Describe an example of conflict you have witnessed as a team member, at work, for a class project, or a sports team. How might this conflict have been resolved?

Skill-Building Exercise 13-A: Housing for the Homeless

Organize the class into teams of about six people. Each team takes on the assignment of formulating plans for building temporary shelters for the homeless. The task will take about one hour and can be done inside or outside of class. The dwellings you plan to build might be two-room cottages with electricity and indoor plumbing. During the time allotted to the task, formulate plans for going ahead with Housing for the Homeless. Consider dividing up work by assigning certain tasks or roles to each team member. Sketch out tentative answers to the following questions:

1. How will you obtain funding for your venture?
2. Which homeless people will you help?
3. Where will your shelters be located?
4. Who will do the actual construction?

After your plan is completed, evaluate the quality of the teamwork that took place within the group. Specify which teamwork skills were evident and which ones did not surface. Search the chapter for techniques you might use to improve teamwork. The skills used to accomplish the housing-for-the-homeless task could relate to the team skills presented in Self-Assessment Quiz 13–1 or some team skill not mentioned in this chapter. Here is a sampling of the many different skills that might be relevant in this exercise:

□ Speaks effectively
□ Listens to others
□ Innovates solutions to problems
□ Thinks outside the box
□ Displays a high level of cooperation and collaboration
□ Provides knowledge of the task
□ Sees the big picture
□ Focuses on deadlines

Skill-Building Exercise 13-B: The Scavenger Hunt

The class organizes into groups to conduct a 35-minute scavenger hunt on school premises. Your instructor might give you five items to scavenge or you might use the following list. The group must return in 35 minutes with as much of the task accomplished as possible. All groups that return with the five items are winners. During a debriefing session, answer these two questions: (1) What did we learn about teamwork? (2) Which personal characteristics of the team members contributed to the success, or failure, of the group.

Possible Items for Your Scavenger Hunt

1. A container of motor oil.
2. A fountain pen.
3. A man's necktie.
4. A book with "group" or "teamwork" in the title.
5. A piece of wood (not a piece of furniture).

Management Now: Online Skill-Building Exercise: Productivity of Teams and Groups

The U.S. Department of Labor regularly publishes information about the productivity of workers, but there is much less information published about the productivity of teams and work groups. Conduct an Internet search to find two sources of information on team or workgroup productivity that have been published within the last six months. See whether you can find information other than that provided by consulting and training firms that specialize in teambuilding. Compare your findings with those of a few classmates. If you cannot find any evidence about group productivity in general, at least find a case history of any successful work group posted within the last year.

13-A Case Problem

Team Player Jessica

Jessica was happy to find a position as a scanning technician at a business process outsourcing company, Specialist Resource Inc. A major part of the Specialist's business was converting paperwork related to human resource management into digital form. Clients would mail their forms, such as medical claims, to Specialist. Scanning technicians would then insert the claim forms into large scanning machines to make the conversion to digital. Clients would then have digital instead of paper documents for health claims and other human resource records.

The scanning technicians interacted with other employees in several ways. Because many of the claims received contained illegible identifying information, they were sent to a security department that attempted to obtain the proper identification for the forms. The scanning technicians were expected to help level the workload among the technicians. For example, if one of the technicians was overwhelmed, someone who was caught up was supposed to help. The company frequently held small celebrations in the office such as a brunch in honor of a new employee.

Jessica believed that if she performed well in her position as scanning technician she would be eligible for promotion to the information technology department. Eventually being promoted to a supervisor position was also within the realm of possibility. Jessica recognized that having good skills and speed in scanning documents were not sufficient. Her size-up of the situation was that being a good team player would be required if she wanted to be considered for promotion. Jessica then set out to develop a reputation.

The next Monday morning Jessica arrived at the office with a box of donuts and bagels, which she placed in the break room with a note that said, "Enjoy your coffee or tea this morning with a treat from your coworker Jessica." Several of the other scanning technicians thanked Jessica but one technician said, "Why did you bring us donuts and bagels? You're not our supervisor."

A week later, Jessica implemented another tactic designed to boost her reputation as a team player. She sent an e-mail to the other technicians informing them that they were free to send her an e-mail or an IM anytime they were overloaded with documents to scan. Jessica said that she would help the over-loaded coworker so long as she was caught up on her own work.

A week later Jessica reflected, "I think am developing a reputation as a good team player, but I can't give up yet. I think there's something else I should try." Jessica then wrote an e-mail to the other scanning technicians, as well as her supervisor. The e-mail read in part:

"We all know that it takes a village to raise a child. Did you also know that it takes a group of friendly and cooperative coworkers to get a scanning technician up to speed? I want to thank you all for your cooperation and friendliness. You have been very helpful to me."

Discussion Questions

1. How effective do you think Jessica's initiatives are in helping her develop a reputation as a strong team player?
2. If you were Jessica's supervisor, how would you react to the e-mails she sent to the group?
3. What advice might you offer Jessica to help her advance her reputation as a team player?

13-B Case Problem

Home Rehab Day at Tymco

Fifteen years ago Maria Cortez was working as a freelance writer of technical manuals for a variety of companies. The manuals supported a number of products including household appliances, alarm systems, lawnmowers, and tractors. Soon Cortez's freelance activity became more than she could handle, so she subcontracted work to one other freelancer, and then another, and then another. Two years later, Cortez founded Tymco and the firm has grown steadily. The company now provides technical manuals, training and development, and foreign language translation and interpreting.

Tymco now employs 75 full-time employees, as well as about 45 freelancers who help the company with peak loads and specialized services. For example, one freelancer translates software into Japanese. Another freelancer specializes in preparing user guides for digital cameras and digital video cameras.

Cortez recently became concerned that the unit heads and other key personnel in the company were not working particularly well as a team. She explained to Tim Atkins, a training specialist on the staff, "We all work for a company called Tymco, yet we function like independent units and freelancers. I notice that our staff members hardly ever have lunch together. I've arranged a couple of group dinners and we have a nice meal, but no team spirit seems to develop.

"I think that if we had better teamwork, our units could help each other. We might even be able to cross-sell better. I'll give you an example. A person in the technical manual group might have an assignment to prepare a manual for an appliance. He or she should immediately mention that Tymco has another group that could do the foreign language translations for the manual. A lot of manuals for U.S. distribution are written in English, Spanish, and French."

Atkins replied, "Look, I've been eager to run a team development activity that has worked well for dozens of companies. It is so simple. We first designate who you think should be included in the group that requires the most development as a team. You choose one work day for the team-building activity. It involves targeting an old house badly in need of repair in a poor neighborhood. Abandoned houses don't count. We need a house with a family living in it. Working with churches in the neighborhood, it's easy to find a suitable house and a family willing to be helped.

"About a week before the team-building date, a handy person and I visit the house to get some idea of the type of work that needs to be done. We then purchase paint, roofing shingles, wood, and other needed supplies. We also round up the ladders, paint brushes, and tools. Our team descends on the house about 7:00 a.m. the morning of the rehabilitation.

"On team building day, the group descends on the house and starts the rehab process. Two days is usually needed. If we start the job on Friday, it could be finished on Saturday. In this way the group would receive one day off from work and the members would contribute one day of their time."

Maria was so enthusiastic about Atkins' idea that she agreed on the spot that Friday, May 19 would be the team-building day. She suggested that the day be called Tymco Home Rehab. Cortez made up a list of ten key employees, including her, to participate in the team-building activity.

Friday morning five cars and trucks arrived at 47 Blodgett Street filled with Tymco staff members, ladders, tools, and home-building supplies. Teena Jones, supervisor of technical manuals, shouted to the group, "We can't get anywhere until we start getting rid of the debris around the house and in the hallway. So let's get shovelling. The dumpster is on the way."

"Grab a few people and do what you want," said Larry Boudreau, supervisor of technical documentation. "If we don't patch up that roof first, nothing else will matter. I need two warm bodies who aren't acrophobic [afraid of heights] to help me." Two staffers agreed to work with Larry, while the seven other staff members including Cortez formed the clean-up brigade.

"Carpentry is my thing," said Mary Benito from translations services. "Let's get out the hammers, saws, nails, and screws and start repairing this broken porch first. I want us to be ready for painting the house by noon tomorrow."

"Do what you want, Mary," said Dale Jenkins, a technical training team leader. "I'm good at home plumbing, and the toilets and sinks here are leaking more than the Titanic. I need a skilled pair of hands to help me. Any volunteer?"

Maria said, "While you folks are shovelling debris and fixing, I'll run out and get us the food for snacks and lunch and I'll order pizza for a supper break."

"That's the most sensible idea I've heard today," commented Larry.

The Tymco team-building participants had supper together at 5:00 that evening and went home at 8:00, planning to return at 7:00 the next morning. By 1:00 Saturday painting had begun, with all ten people on the team participating. By 7:30, the house at 47 Blodgett Street was painted. The family, who were staying with neighbors, came by to cheer and weep with joy.

The Tymco team members exchanged smiles, hi-fives, and hugs. "We can all go home now feeling that we've accomplished something really important as a team. And we can come back to the office on Monday morning knowing that we can work well as a team despite a few bumps and bruises."

"Good comment, Mary," said Ian Graham from the technical manual group. "Yet, I'm not so sure that replacing shingles on an old roof has made me a better team player."

Discussion Questions

1. What evidence was presented in this case that the staff members from different units at Tymco might have become better acquainted.
2. What should Maria do next to improve the chances that the home rehab day results in genuine team development?
3. What evidence is presented in this case that the home rehab day did give a boost to team spirit?
4. How valid is Ian's comment about replacing shingles having no particular impact on becoming a better team player?

CHAPTER 14

Information Technology and e-Commerce

FourSquares Labs Inc. is a company in the forefront of mobile advertising by integrating social media with marketing. "Foursquare" itself is a game for the mobile phone that provides players incentives to check it at restaurants, bars, and retailers—broadcasting the location of players to friends and potential advertisers. Jessica Green, the owner of a Pita Pit franchise in Brookline, Massachusetts, said she brought in customers as her own special offer popped up on mobile phone screens as users checked in from nearby competitors.

Participating merchants are able to reward consumers who use the service to promote their establishment. Users visit the FourSquare Web site to download a free mobile-phone application for a participating merchant. When customers visit the participating establishment, such as a restaurant, they can "check-in" via the mobile application, letting their friends know where they are and racking up possible points with the merchant. (Tipping off friends is a key part of the marketing.) Another example of the user obtaining an incentive is that some restaurants and hotels advertise special offers to the Foursquare user who checks in most often.

OBJECTIVES

After studying this chapter and doing the exercises, you should be able to:

1. Summarize the demands information technology places on the manager's job.

2. Describe positive and negative consequences of information technology for the manager.

3. Discuss the impact of the Internet and social media sites on customer and other external relationships.

4. Explain the effects of the Internet on internal company operations.

5. Pinpoint factors associated with success in e-commerce.

The application uses global-positioning technology so that consumers need to be at a business to get credit for checking in—though technically they could just be close by. It also offers consumers the option to notify members of the Twitter and Facebook networks whenever they check in. "It's a mini sales pitch from the users to their friends," says co-founder Dennis Crowley.

AJ Bombers, a burger joint in Milwaukee, joined up with FourSquare by promising a free burger and fries to anyone who dethroned its "mayor"—a title FourSquare bestows on the person who "checks in" to an establishment the most via the mobile application. The restaurant also ran a promotion where customers could get a free cookie by posting a recommendation to their FourSquare profiles of a menu item or something to do while they're at the eatery, such as play a board game. AJ co-owner Joe Sorge says sales of menu items promoted on FourSquare have risen roughly 30% since the restaurant began using the service.

FourSquare can be used by businesses of all sizes in any location, although Crowley says its key draw are small U.S. establishments where consumers hang out, such as coffee shops and clubs. A key feature of FourSquare is that it enables business owners to engage with customers in an ultra-targeted way. FourSquare is free for both businesses and consumers. To generate revenue, FourSquare is working to develop partnerships with various consumer brands and outlets for a fee.[1]

The story about the company that helps other companies use social media (or social networking) to assist with marketing illustrates that managers must understand the ways in which new technologies can influence their business. Perhaps managers do not need to have the technical knowledge to link a Web site to a global positioning device, but they do need to know how such technology could affect the business. This chapter highlights how information technology, including e-commerce, influences the manager's job. Although e-commerce is part of information technology, it is described separately here because of its profound impact on both the manager's job and the conduct of the business. Your present

---

[1]Sarah E. Needleman, "Services Combine Social Media, Marketing," *The Wall Street Journal*, February 23, 2010, p. B7; Galen Moore, "Foursquare Leads New Advertising Model," *Mass High Tech* (www.masshightech.com), April 26, 2010; Zachary Wilson, "Foursquare Offers Analytics to Businesses, Enables Easy Customer Stalkin…" *www.fastcompany.com*, March 9, 2010.

knowledge of information technology, including computers, provides the necessary technical background for understanding this chapter.

LEARNING OBJECTIVE

Summarize the demands information technology places on the manager's job.

INFORMATION TECHNOLOGY AND THE MANAGER'S JOB

Information technology changes the work methods of workers in a wide variety of jobs. For example, office workers are rarely out of touch with their computers, and associates in auto supply stores use computerized databases to search for the availability of replacement parts. Managerial workers also feel the profound influence of information technology. In this section we look at the heavy demand information technology places on managers, as well as the specific impact of wireless devices.

Increased Demands Placed on Managers

From the perspective of work methods, the landscape of a manager's job looks substantially different. Instead of handing work to an office assistant, the manager now types, sends, and receives his or her own messages and makes appointments on a personal digital assistant or smart phone. Our concern here, however, is with the broader implications of the changes created by information technology. Management today must build an organization that constantly transforms itself as information technology increases competition. For instance, Mark Kolko, the CEO of a supplier of industrial motors, said there is no such thing as a loyal customer anymore because other vendors can be found so readily through the Internet.[2]

Managers must develop and respond continuously to new technologies, new types of businesses, and new people in the form of employees and customers. Information technology itself changes so rapidly that managers must adapt themselves to the changes and help others adapt. For example, managers expect and prepare for productivity dips while workers adapt to a new companywide software system.

Another general issue with technology, including information technology, is how the development and spread of the new technology increases the importance of innovating to remain competitive. The continuous development of technology decreases product life cycles, creating more pressure on managers and workers involved in the development and manufacture of products. Quite often products in traditional industries now promote their features linked to information technology. In bragging about the new generation of Ford automobiles, CEO Alan Mulally said, "It's cool to connect. But it's past cool. It's a reason to buy. We're going to be the coolest, most

Go to www.cengage.com/management/dubrin and view the video for Chapter 14. Why is technology and e-commerce important at Evo Gear? What are some of the challenges and limitations they face?

---

[2]Interview with Mark Kolko, CEO of Power Equipment Co., Rochester, New York, October 14, 2006, and updated March 22, 2010.

useful app you've ever had."[3] As Ford Motor Company sees it, an automobile is now an "app" (computer application).

Information and communications technology is at the center of the technological revolution. This technology is used in most business firms and provides an integral part of many systems, such as inventory control. Information technology makes globalization more practical because it allows ready access to employees all over the world at nominal cost. The same technology makes it feasible to customize many industrial products by combining special features with standard features, such as a Dell computer to meet your personal preferences.

The sampling of technological changes just mentioned illustrates why information technology pushes managers into a continuous learning mode. Even if the manager is not an expert on how to use information technology to customize mass-produced products, the manager still must have a working understanding of the process. Otherwise, he or she will seem foolish when asked questions.

The Wireless Environment, Including Wi-Fi

A specific, direct consequence of information technology comes from managers' use of wireless communication devices to facilitate their work from different locations. For almost a century, managers used wired telephones to stay in touch with the office. In the modern environment, rapidly evolving devices give managers more constant access to the office and to customers. Smart phones, including the ever present BlackBerry and iPhone, and laptop computers are standard in the manager's tool kit.

Many managers use laptop computers away from the office for the same purposes they would use a desktop computer when in the office. Managers who travel find laptops particularly convenient for preparing daily reports as well as processing e-mail and conducting Internet searches while on the road. The growing availability of Wi-Fi has enhanced the value of laptop computers because the Internet can be accessed even when an electrical outlet is not available. (*Wi-Fi* refers to wireless fidelity, a high-speed, high-capacity network built on radio signals.) Most business-oriented hotels and restaurants now offer Wi-Fi networks, as do Internet cafés.

To use most mobile devices effectively, the manager must be able to tolerate a miniaturized keyboard and have sharp vision. Not every manager finds these devices comfortable or productive. For example, many managers and professionals still prefer paper-based desk planners over personal digital assistants. Some managers prefer to wait until they return to the office to obtain information through e-mail and the Internet so they can enjoy the comforts of a large monitor.

---

[3]Quoted in Paul Hochman, "Ford's Big Reveal," *Fast Company*, April 2010, p. 93.

THE POSITIVE AND NEGATIVE CONSEQUENCES OF INFORMATION TECHNOLOGY

Information technology is integrated into the everyday work of first-level and middle-level managers and staff professionals. Top-level managers also rely on PCs, laptops, and smart phones to conduct their work. Executives who still depend on office assistants to access their e-mail or open Web pages are extremely rare. The vast majority of executives are information tech-savvy. Here we look at both the advantages and disadvantages of information technology as part of the manager's job. Many of the outstanding advantages of information technology for the manager stem from Web 2.0. The term refers to an emphasis on the interactive use of the Internet, such as blogging back and forth with customers and employees, as well as on workers collaborating with each other electronically.

Positive Consequences of Information Technology for the Manager

An information technology revolution that did not help managers, other workers, and organizations perform better would not last. The following description of the positive consequences of IT emphasizes its benefits to managerial work. Exhibit 14-1 outlines these potential advantages.

Improved Productivity and Teamwork

A major justification for installing information technology is its capability for improving productivity. Information technology facilitated much of the slimming down of organizations. A reduction in staffing leads to increased productivity, providing that the sales volume remains constant or improves. For example, most banks found they could reduce the number of branches and consolidate customer service into centralized customer support (call) centers. From the perspective of the job seeker, a negative side to improved productivity has been slow job growth.

EXHIBIT 14-1 **Positive Consequences of Information Technology for the Manager**

Information technology can help the manager work smarter.

1. Improved productivity and teamwork
2. Increased competitive advantage
3. Enhanced business models
4. Improved customer service and supplier relationships
5. Enhanced communication and coordination, including the Virtual Office
6. Quick access to vast information (e.g. dashboard)
7. Enhanced analysis of data and decision making
8. Greater empowerment and flatter organizations
9. Time-saving through employee self-service
10. Monitoring work and employee surveillance

Small business owners can increase their productivity in many ways by exploiting information technology. An advanced application of IT is using online services to find sources of investment capital. The business owner posts a message to which potential investors (venture capitalists) respond. Finding investors online can be quicker than extensive letter writing and telephone campaigns.

Information technology enhances teamwork by allowing team members to maintain frequent contact with each other through e-mail, cell phones, and text messaging. Even if the group cannot hold an in-person meeting, team members can give electronic feedback to each other's ideas. Furthermore, with extensive use of IT, teammates can work in geographically dispersed locations. (The virtual office will be described later.)

Increased Competitive Advantage (or Avoiding Competitive Disadvantage)

Effective use of information technology can give a firm a competitive advantage. Information technology enables companies to conduct business in ways that would be impossible without such technology. For example, it would be difficult to buy and sell used cars throughout the country without using the Internet, such as is done through eBay. The alternative would be to use toll-free telephone numbers for faxing photos of the vehicles. Today, not using modern information technology makes a company noncompetitive. Imagine how embarrassing it would be for a company to have neither a Web site nor e-mail for interacting with customers and suppliers. Today, even low-tech establishments such as restaurants and sub shops often have Web sites and e-mail addresses.

Enhanced Business Models

A *business model* refers to a company's general plan for earning money. For example, Victoria's Secret sells merchandise through toll-free telephone numbers, by mail, in physical stores, and online. By using information technology, Victoria's Secret has expanded its method of distribution. Information technology assists not only in direct selling but also in maintaining inventory and targeting expensive catalogs to the right potential buyers. The Dell model is dependent on information technology: build to order while reducing costs substantially and creating a direct path to the consumer. This model would not work without information technology. The Internet enables a tech-savvy company like Dell to extend the model even further, smoothly interacting with suppliers and providing new channels to customers.[4] Dell has lost some of its competitive advantage in recent years to Acer and Hewlett-Packard, yet its enhanced business model has kept it a strong competitor in the market for computers and related services. Note

---

[4]James Champy, "Technology Doesn't Matter—but Only at Harvard," *Fast Company*, December 2003, p. 119.

that an enhanced business model is another way of gaining competitive advantage.

Improved Customer Service and Supplier Relationships

Advances in information technology, including networking, can lead to improved customer service and smoother working relationships with suppliers. Customer service improves when service representatives can immediately access information to resolve a customer problem. USAA, a large financial services firm, provides a model for the industry in terms of prompt service. The company sells insurance directly to the public, without the use of external sales representatives or insurance agents. Policyholders can call an 800 number to receive immediate answers to complex questions such as how much rates will increase if a 16-year-old family member becomes a licensed driver. The USAA Web site also has a customer service option, but it contributes less to high-quality customer service than do the phone conversations with a live person.

Supplier relationships can be more productive when suppliers and purchasers are part of the same network. Large retailers such as Wal-Mart authorize some of their suppliers to ship and stock goods based on electronic messages sent from point of purchase to the suppliers' computers. When inventory gets low on a fast-moving item, supplies are replenished automatically without a retail store official having to make a phone call or send a letter.

extranet
A secure section of a Web site that only visitors with a password can enter.

Another development to improve customer services is the **extranet**, a secure section of a Web site that only visitors with a password can enter. Many financial services firms use an extranet to allow customers to manage accounts and trade stocks online. The extranet is also used to share inventory or customer information with suppliers, send information to vendors, and sell products and services.

Enhanced Communication and Coordination, Including the Virtual Office

Nowhere is the impact of information technology on the manager's job more visible than in communication and coordination. By relying on information technology, managers can be in frequent contact with group members without being physically present. They can also be part of the **virtual office**, in which employees work together as if they were part of a single office despite being physically separated. Highly coordinated virtual office members form a virtual team, as described in Chapter 13. Such teams are groups of geographically separated coworkers who are assembled using information technology to accomplish a task.

virtual office
Employees who work together as if they were part of a single office despite being physically separated.

The virtual office and virtual teams conduct much of the work through virtual meetings, a gathering of participants in scattered locations using videoconferencing or e-mail. A videoconference enables people to see and hear each other through real-time video. Virtual meetings can accommodate from

4 to 200 people. Large firms often establish their own videoconferencing centers, whereas smaller firms typically rent a center as needed. Videoconferencing can enhance productivity by reducing travel costs and time, and it appeals to workers who fear flying and dislike going through airport security.

Frequent electronic contact with company employees, customers, and suppliers enhances coordination. The alternative is for the manager to communicate primarily when back at the office. A high-tech manager is never away from the office—even if he or she would like to be!

microblogging
Sending brief updates about work activities to employees.

A major development in the managerial application of communication technology is **microblogging**, or sending brief updates online about work activities to employees. Microblogs are also used socially, such as with Twitter. Managers and other workers can post or read messages on several electronic devices including computers and mobile phones. To avoid some of the clutter on social networking sites, many companies now use closed networks on platforms such as Yammer and Presently.[5] Because so many workers today prefer brief messages, microblogging fits their attention span. Also, microblogs are effective because they can serve as headline reminders, such as "Need your budget input by tomorrow at 4 p.m." In days of old, managers sent paper memos and phone messages for the same purpose. A major customer or supplier might have even received a telegram.

e-leadership
Providing leadership to people when their work is mediated by information technology.

Virtual teams, virtual meetings, and other means of communicating via information technology have created the necessity for **e-leadership**, or providing leadership to people when their work is mediated by information technology. Instead of a warm smile and a handshake, the leader might send a congratulatory note by e-mail. Or the leader might set up an internal Web site to obtain input from workers about a controversial or complex issue. The general idea is that the e-leader relies heavily on information technology to build and maintain relationships with group members.[6]

Quick Access to Vast Information

Information technology gives managers quick access to vast amounts of information. A careful library researcher could always access vast amounts of business-related information. Advances in information technology, however, allow for fingertip access if the manager has the right computer search skills. For example, a sales manager might want a targeted list of prospects for her company's new pool tables. She uses an electronic database to locate sporting goods stores in her region, ranking them by revenue and zip code to streamline her sales strategy.

Intranet (or company intranet)
A Web site for company use only.

A major contributor to accessing information quickly is the company **intranet**, a Web site for company use only. Workers at all levels can use the intranet for critical information such as inventory levels, new product

---

[5]"Mtg @ 4: Microblogging Goes to Work," *Manager's Edge*, May 2009, p. 7.

[6]Bruce J. Avolio and Surinder S. Kahai, "Adding the 'E' to E-Leadership: How It May Impact Your Leadership," *Organizational Dynamics*, No. 4, 2003, pp. 325–326.

development, and sales. Executives make regular use of an intranet for accessing bottom-line information such as quarterly profit/loss reports, company stock reports, profiles of key employees and customers, and meeting minutes. Google uses an intranet to collect employee suggestions for improving the company's products and services. Employees from all departments are expected to regularly submit ideas to advance the company.

Another way for managers to be constantly informed is through a dashboard. The essential idea behind a dashboard is that it places all the computerized data the manager, business owner, or corporate professional might need in one place. Instead of a batch of reports to integrate, the dashboard generates key data in an easy-to-read, constantly updated dashboard-style readout. For a dashboard to be highly valuable, the manager must first identify the company's critical drivers (or success factors). These typically include revenue and sales data and marketing data such as new sales leads. Other drivers include customer satisfaction and worker productivity and satisfaction. The dashboard can emit signals about where improvement is needed, such as inventory getting too low or too high.[7]

Lewis Farsedakis, the owner of the successful cosmetics firm Blinc Inc., says, "The dashboard enables me to measure the business results on a daily basis. It also enables me to catch business problems as they emerge, as opposed to later."[8]

Although dashboards have a scientific, slick appearance, they provide useful readouts only if they are based on accurate data. For example, is someone who clicked on your Web site to receive product information truly a sales lead? Or is a sales lead someone who has received the product information and has requested that a representative visit his or her company?

Enhanced Analysis of Data and Decision Making

Closely related to gathering a wider array of information, information technology allows for better analysis of data and decision making. Managers at business firms of all sizes now analyze data better to improve efficiency. A before-and-after example follows:

The office manager of a large medical practice in Birmingham, Michigan, observed that during December, January, February, and the first half of March many patients cancelled their appointments. As a result, revenue for the medical group was down during these months. The medical staff and the office manager accepted these cancellations as a reality of medical practice. The office manager then decided to conduct a computerized statistical analysis of which patients in particular had the most cancellations. It was found that, in general, older patients and others with mobility problems had the highest number of cancellations during the most severe part of

---

[7]Mark Henricks, "Dashing Looks," *Entrepreneur*, August 2006, p. 60; Bill Schaefer, "Digital Dashboards," *HR Magazine*, May 2008, p. 35

[8]Quoted in Henricks, "Dashing Looks," *Entrepreneur*, p. 60.

winter. The partial solution to the cancellation problem was as follows: A member of the office staff would telephone older patients and those with mobility problems in advance of the scheduled appointment and suggest they ask a family member or friend to drive them to the office. The outreach program, based on an analysis of patient data, reduced wintertime cancellations 40 percent.

Another way in which information technology helps managers make better decisions is through gathering multiple inputs on an online document before taking action. A **wiki** is a password-protected Web page that allows for the collaboration of multiple users. Each contributor can add ideas to the document or plan and suggest improvements to the suggestions of other contributors. Visualize a manager posting on the company wiki a proposal for reducing retirement costs. He suggests reducing the pension of every retiree by $100 per month. One of the collaborators on the document writes, "You better not rush into this. The negative publicity for our company could be enormous." Several other collaborators agree with the comment about the bad publicity, so the manager decides to look for another way to reduce costs.

wiki
A password-protected Web page that allows for collaboration of multiple users.

Greater Empowerment and Flatter Organizations

The widespread use of information technology gives more workers access to information they need for decision making. As a result, more workers can be empowered to make decisions. Fewer layers of management are needed to act as information conduits. Instead, workers at lower levels access information directly through computer networks. Information technology therefore provides line employees with the documents they need to perform their jobs more effectively and make decisions on their own.

Time Saving Through Employee Self-service

Another important way in which information technology benefits managers is by allowing employees to serve themselves in some areas rather than requiring managerial or staff assistance. Managers are freed from the need to supervise routine activities. From the standpoint of top management, fewer managers and staff support are necessary.

A notable example of information technology-based employee self-service is the electronic travel and expense reporting (T&E) system used at Cisco Systems Inc. Employees submit expense reports through an intranet and browser. When an employee logs on to the system, it registers charges from his or her corporate American Express card. The employee then adds out-of-pocket expenses and the system generates a travel and expense report. Within four days, the employee receives the reimbursement by direct deposit to his or her bank. In the past, expense reports submitted by paper took 21 days for reimbursement at Cisco.

Another advantage to the company is that the system can spot discrepancies and send the e-form back to the employee for clarification. A suspicious form can be routed for audit approval. After all the proper information is in place, the system can generate the credit card payments to American Express and cash reimbursements to the employee. By automating the process, Cisco auditors boosted the number of claims they can review annually from 19,000 to 35,000. The firm saves money by paying off credit card debt faster. Additionally, the cost of processing an expense report dropped from more than $25 down to $3.

Cisco now uses many of the same self-service techniques to improve its internal travel reservation system. Jennifer Loftin, now manager of Global Spend Optimization, says, "It's letting managers and employees focus on high-value activities."[9]

Monitoring Work and Employee Surveillance

Automation in the workplace not only changes how employees labor, it changes the ability of management to measure and monitor the work and the workers. In many jobs—especially in manufacturing and the more mechanical service industries—employees are increasingly held to standards derived from metering or measuring the work. Management has new responsibilities and tools to oversee employee behavior in the wired workplace. Closer monitoring of work might be perceived as an advantage of information technology from the perspective of some managers. However, workers and some managers might perceive such surveillance to be a *negative* feature of information technology. The topic of computer-aided monitoring of work will be reintroduced in Chapter 15 about controls. One example of technology-based employee surveillance will suffice for now:

> *An employee called in sick to Scott McDonald, CEO of Monument Security in Sacramento, California. The CEO decided to investigate. He had already informed his staff of 400 security guards and patrol drivers that he was installing Xora, a software program that tracks workers' whereabouts through surveillance technology on their company cell phones. A Web-based "geo-fence" around work territories would alert the boss if workers strayed or even drove too fast. (The technology also enabled McDonald to route workers more efficiently.) So when McDonald logged on, the program told him exactly where the worker was—and it wasn't in bed with the sniffles. "How come you're eastbound on 80 heading to Reno right now if you're sick?" asked the boss. There was a long silence—the sound of a job ending—followed by "You got me."[10]*

What is your opinion of the fairness of using Xora to track the whereabouts of workers? Does a worker have the right for an occasional "mental health day" at Reno, Nevada?

---

[9]Samuel Greengard, "Technology Finally Advances HR," *Workforce*, January 2000, pp. 38–39; New job title from Jigsaw.com, accessed March 25, 2010.

[10]Kristina Dell and Lisa Takeuchi Cullen, "Snooping Bosses," *Time*, September 11, 2006, p. 62.

Negative Consequences of Information Technology

Information technology continues to make extraordinary contributions to organizational productivity. Nevertheless, the same exciting technology produces some unintended negative consequences. Even when these negative consequences do not affect the manager directly, he or she usually plays a major role in dealing with the consequences. For example, if extensive use of information technology deteriorates customer service, the manager faces angry customers and discouraged employees. Awareness of these potential problems can help managers prevent them from occurring.

1. *Wasting time at the computer.* One subtle problem occurs when managers or other employees become **computer goof-offs**. They spend so much time attempting new computer routines and accessing information of questionable value that they neglect key aspects of their jobs. Some managers, for example, would prefer to surf the Internet for low-value information than to confront an employee about a discipline problem. More will be said about time wasting with computers in Chapter 17. The problem at hand is that some managers fall into the trap of thinking that being connected is their most important responsibility. A manager who spends too much time working the Internet and a smart phone might not invest enough time in thinking strategically or interacting personally with employees and customers.

2. *Repetitive-motion disorders.* As was described in Chapter 7, information technology contributes to repetitive motion disorders found in the workplace. In addition to well-designed workplaces, improved technology may decrease repetitive-motion disorders. Voice recognition systems enable computer users to dictate commands into word processors, thereby cutting back on keyboarding. More managers and other workers are now making use of voice recognition software such as Dragon Naturally Speaking. Dictation software now allows for continuous speech, rather than pauses between words as in the past. But watch out for the "Wreck a nice beach" problem. (Repeat "Wreck a nice beach" a few times until you get the joke.) Another problem for many workers is that dictation does not allow for the precision and easy correction of inputting data by keyboard.

3. *Deterioration of customer* service. A problem of considerable magnitude comes from the deterioration in customer service that sometimes accompanies information technology. Many banks, for example, force customers with a service problem to call a toll-free number rather than allowing them to deal with a branch representative. A voice-response system instructs the customer to punch in lengthy account numbers and make choices from a complicated menu. The process is time-consuming and impersonal and difficult for customers unfamiliar with information technology. A related problem occurs when highly automated customer-service operations appear unfriendly and detached. An extensive investigation into self-service technologies uncovered several areas of customer

computer goof-offs
Employees who spend so much time attempting new computer routines and accessing information of questionable value that they neglect key aspects of their job.

discontent. Self-service machines were often broken, Web sites were down, personal identification numbers failed to work, and items were not shipped as promised.[11] (The same study also found many positive features of employee self-service such as being able to order goods 24/7.)

4. *Dealing with baffled consumers.* Another challenge for managers in dealing with consumers in the information age is that some electronic products are baffling to use for many people. As a result, these people become dissatisfied customers and the manager may have to deal with angry customers and poor sales of a particular product. A case in point is the advanced digital camera that comes with a 125-page operator's manual—not including the software guide. Analysts attribute some of the blame to falling electronics prices, which leaves less money to spend on after-sales service.

   The problem for managers is that many consumers may finally be fed up. People are embracing the latest gadgets with less enthusiasm than for previous generations of technology, except for advances in smart phones. Part of the problem is that the new consumer electronics are difficult to comprehend. A small industry of information technology technicians who make house calls has arisen to help baffled consumers. One such national chain is Geeks on Wheels. However, there is a limit to how many baffled customers are willing to pay an outside firm to help them work their information technology gadget.

5. *Wired managerial workers.* As implied in the discussion of wireless communication, information technology results in wired managerial workers. Being electronically connected to the office at all times leads many managers and professionals to complain that their employers expect them to be always available for consultation. Many managers, for example, are expected to bring smart phones and laptop computers on vacation so they can respond to inquiries from the office and customers. The widespread use of Wi-Fi intensifies the problem because there are more opportunities to remain linked to the office. Not only are managers wired themselves, but they often expect workers to be available to receive electronic messages after working hours, including weekends and holidays.

   A problem noted with devices such as a BlackBerry is that managers sometimes make decisions too quickly because instant communication lends itself to superficial thinking. Instead of reflecting on a problem, the manager dashes back an answer to a problem.[12]

6. *The encouragement of nonproductive multitasking.* A major negative consequence of information technology is that it encourages inappropriate

---

[11]Mary Jo Bitner, Amy L. Ostrom, and Matthew L. Meuter, "Implementing Successful Self-Service Technologies," *Academy of Management Executive*, November 2002, p. 110.

[12]Bill Husted, "Execs Embrace, Lament Always Being in Touch," *The Atlanta Journal Constitution*, http://www.ajc.com, June 9, 2006.

multitasking. Using several electronic devices at once often interferes with a person's ability to concentrate carefully on the major problem at hand. Computerized information encourages multitasking to the point that many managers feel they are wasting time unless they are attempting two tasks at once, such as talking on a cell phone and accessing e-mail. The problem is that diminished concentration often leads to poorer-quality work. "Multitasking doesn't look to be one of the great strengths of human cognition," according to James C. Johnston, a research psychologist at NASA. "It's almost inevitable that each individual task will be slower and of lower quality."[13] Another problem with multitasking is its inherent rudeness, such as when a manager peeks at his or her smart phone while talking to a subordinate about a problem. Accidents, such as car crashes while talking on a cell phone or sending a text message, are another serious problem.

Another way to understand the potential hazards of multitasking is to personalize the problem. If you were a passenger in an airplane going through a storm, would you want the pilot to be chatting on the cell phone or reading e-mail while commandeering the plane?

7. *Excessive requirements to learn and adapt to new communication technologies.* For the techno savvy, learning new communication technologies frequently is a welcome challenge. Each new app learned is a source of joy. For many managers, however, the constant demand to learn new technologies and procedures is frustrating because productivity and concentration can suffer while a person is learning something new and complex. If the manager does not understand how to use a new technology, he or she might feel embarrassed and not sufficiently skilled in communication technology.

One of hundreds of possible examples would be when a company requires managers to learn Kluster, a group decision-making tool. The developer of the software describes it as "a Web-based platform where companies can come on and run projects for any decision-making activity that could be better served by asking a group of people." By using Kluster, business firms can take advantage of bringing the public, their customers, and their own employers in on interactive and user-friendly projects.[14] However, complicated decision-making software is not so user-friendly when the manager is trying to learn how to use it the morning before a meeting with a major customer who is threatening to change suppliers.

---

[13]Quoted in Jared Sandberg, "Cubicle Culture: Yes, Sell All my Stocks. No, the 3:15 from JFK. And Get Me Mr. Sister," *The Wall Street Journal*, September 12, 2006, p. B1.

[14]Quoted in Amanda Kooser, "Work Smarter," *Entrepreneur*, April 2008, p. 73; www. Kluster.com, accessed March 27, 2010.

THE IMPACT OF THE INTERNET ON CUSTOMERS AND OTHER EXTERNAL RELATIONSHIPS

The Internet profoundly affects how business is conducted. Developments of similar magnitude include electricity, the railroad, and the interstate highway system. As a consequence, the Internet also influences managerial work, especially the technical problem-solver role of a manager who might be contributing ideas about such work as marketing, purchasing, and information systems. Even when managers are not directly involved in such specialized activities, they are still concerned with making decisions about the Internet. Here we look at eight ways in which the Internet affects external relationships: e-commerce marketing, social media and customer relationships, e-commerce purchasing, changing of intermediaries, enhanced globalization, integrating the old and new economies, living with increased visibility, and integrating the crowd into decision making.

The Marketing Side of e-Commerce

The biggest impact on business from the Internet comes from selling many goods and services to other businesses and consumers online. Seventy-five percent of business conducted on the Internet today takes place between firms (B2B, or business-to-business) rather than with individual consumers. Forrester Research predicts that online retail sales in the United States are predicted to reach $249 billion by 2014, and will constitute about 8 percent of U.S. retail sales by then. About 52 percent of computer product sales are made online.[15]

Because many consumers first research a product online and then make a purchase at a store, the influence of the Internet on marketing is far greater than is reflected by actual sales conducted online. A specific example of the interrelationship between online and offline selling might occur in this manner: A person reads a print ad that includes a Web site address, visits the Web site to learn about a specific product, and then visits the store to make the purchase.

E-commerce affects managerial work in four major ways. First, the manager must be familiar with e-commerce to suggest strategies for marketing over the Internet and resolving problems. Second, managers who formerly worked directly with salespeople (such as coaching and motivating) may have fewer subordinates. One Web specialist might replace 50 face-to-face salespeople. The manager, with fewer people to supervise, would spend more time developing business strategy and perhaps interacting with a few major customers.

Third, e-commerce can bring about a challenge to sales volume even more quickly than with traditional marketing. A powerful example occurred when Google announced a few years ago that it would offer free turn-by-turn navigation software; the sales of Garmin and other navigation devices were

---

[15]"US Web Retail Sales to Reach $249 Billion by '14–Study," *Reuters.com*, March 8, 2010.

negatively affected.[16] The ready availability of directory information on the Internet has made it more difficult for the Yellow Pages to sell space. When the new product is given away, the obsolescence of the competitor's product is a possibility.

Fourth, by use of the Internet many more customers and consumers are brought into decisions about product development, an activity referred to as *crowdsourcing*. The basic idea is that consumers provide input potentially useful to marketers through Internet platforms such as blogs, wikis, and company Web sites that allow for input. A large number of parents, for example, might explain to a crib manufacturer through the manufacturer's interactive Web site that they need a crib that makes it difficult for toddlers to jump over the rail. The blueprint for crowdsourcing is the open source software developers use to work collaboratively to develop software alternatives to Microsoft products.[17] (The crowdcasting mentioned in Chapter 4 in reference to strategy formulation is an application of crowdsourcing.)

The Social Media and Customer Relationships

A substantial change in managing customer relationships in recent years has been contacting them through social networking Web sites, now usually referred to as the social media. Small businesses appear to make more extensive use of sites such as Facebook and Twitter to find and interact with customers. Vast numbers of managers already use social networking sites for personal and professional life, and they must now understand how to squeeze marketing advantage from the social media.

Obtaining this advantage is more complex than simply posting a brief comment on a social networking site. Special expertise is required to know how to reach customers and effectively utilize the hundreds of apps available for social networking. For example, Facebook recommends a number of preferred developer consultants to businesses and individuals looking to build applications. FourSquare Labs Inc., described at the outset of this chapter, is an example of a firm that helps other companies use social media effectively.

A major purpose of social networking for business is to establish a means for people to connect to the company's brand. Making this connection is often difficult because, as with e-mail, most people's social networking pages are bombarded with messages from people who are in reality sending you an advertisement. You may have noticed, for example, that hundreds of people who are now "following you" on Twitter are companies or individuals offering a product or service.

---

[16]Jeremy Philips, "The Great Disruption," *The Wall Street Journal*, November 5, 2009, p. A17; Book review of Ken Auletta, *Googled: The End of the World as We Know It* (New York: Penguin, 2009).

[17]Jeff Howe, *Crowdsourcing: Why the Power of the Crowd is Driving the Future of Business* (New York: Crown Business, 2008).

To gain positive results from social media advertising, business owners and other managers must regularly interact with consumers and not simply create static profiles.[18] The interaction might involve getting back quickly to anyone who responded to your posting, rather than using your posting as a straightforward advertisement. When a social media site includes fans and lists, the interaction with one person might have a multiplier effect because the individual's "fans" might also be informed of the interaction.

D-D Flannery, the CEO of a public relations firm, has developed a list of suggestions for managers who want to make effective use of social networking sites and related media. Her suggestions, as adapted next, integrate a good deal of wisdom on the subject of social media and business.[19] We also include an additional suggestion from another online image specialist.

- Be present on many different social platforms appropriate to your line of business, such as video/photo sharing, blogging, micro-blogging, RSS feeds, and more. An example here is that many executives place statements about themselves and their companies on YouTube to help humanize their company.
- Interact with your visitors and engage in online conversations. Without the interaction, your pages lose an edge over pop-up ads and other advertisements.
- Stay informed about the comments people are making about your brand, the company, and its managers.
- Keep your pages updated with fresh and interesting content. Many company pages provide useful consumer information not directly linked to their brand, such as how to reduce utility bills and keep the air fresh in your home at the same time.
- Let site or page visitors know how to stay informed and connect with you.
- The most essential component of successful online branding is the human touch, according to Mary van de Weil. "People are craving a story. They want to know something about who they're buying from, and feel like they need to like and trust you. You've got to shout what it is that makes you special and different. Our personalities are what drive our brands."[20]

To repeat, managers may not need to be specialists in social media, but they have to be aware of its possibilities and pitfalls. A manager would be naïve to believe that with the advent of social media, all problems of marketing and public relations have been resolved.

---

[18]Sarah E. Needleman, "Entrepreneurs Question Value of Social Media," *The Wall Street Journal*, March 16, 2010, p. B7; Alexia Nielsen, "Facebook Pages and Business: How to Promote Your Company on the World's Largest Media Network," *TriplePoint Company News & Commentary* (www.triplepointpr.com), December 27, 2009.

[19]Adapted and expanded from D-D Flannery, "Use Social Networking to Connect with Consumers," Rochester, New York, *Democrat and Chronicle*, February 21, 2010, p. 3E.

[20]Quoted in Jason Ankeny, "Building a Brand on a Budget," *Entrepreneur*, May 2010, p. 50.

The Purchasing Side of e-Commerce

An important consequence of e-commerce is that it sometimes enables companies to purchase more efficiently than they could by speaking to sales representatives or purchasing through catalogs over the telephone. Many companies assume that both customers and suppliers prefer to conduct business with them over the Internet. For example, a company cannot stay on the General Electric-approved supplier list unless the company is willing to accept orders and inquiries online.

Companies realize smaller transaction costs and a time saving by purchasing over the Web. As a result, product prices tend to be lower than when purchasing through sales representatives or catalogs. The purchaser can ask questions online about products and services. A good starting point for any company wanting to purchase over the Internet would be to visit http://www.yahoo.com/business. The manager or professional can quickly locate companies that offer the product or service he or she needs, and then make inquiries.

Purchasing over the Internet saves time because purchasing agents spend less time talking to and being entertained by sales representatives. Nevertheless, e-commerce has not completely eliminated the human touch in business. Many big deals are still made over lunch and on the golf course, and executives tend to purchase from people they like. Furthermore, many well-established companies that have worked hard to develop their brand names refuse to join buyer exchanges. The established companies are concerned that online buying through an exchange or open market often results in the lowest bidder (sometimes an unknown supplier) getting the sale. Business is conducted with customers online, but not through the medium of a large buyer exchange. A company with a good reputation would prefer that customers stay loyal to them based on high product quality and after-sale service.

Changing of Intermediaries

The Internet has made it easier for buyers and sellers to deal directly with each other. As a result, many business firms that acted as intermediaries between buyers and sellers have been forced out of business or have had to redefine themselves. Among those affected are travel agents, many retailers, food brokers, and independent sales representatives. For example, airlines are now selling only about 50 percent of their tickets through outside agents. Included in this figure are online travel agencies not directly owned by airlines, further reducing the share of sales for the traditional agent. Most travel agencies that have survived offer services such as arranging complex business trips and vacations, where knowledge of the hotels and best airline service is important.

The Internet has badly squeezed music retailers in terms of both paid legal purchases such as iTunes and illegal downloading or file sharing. Of enormous significance to music publishers, the popular social network MySpace began a program several years ago to enable its members to sell their own tunes directly on the site, circumventing music publishers entirely. MySpace says it hosts Web pages for more than 3 million recording artists with bands of many different sizes.[21]

Despite many intermediaries being forced out of business, many others, including supply companies, are still in business. The supply companies themselves are engaged in e-commerce because they sell over the Internet as well as by phone and in-person. And although the Internet may be forcing out some intermediaries, others have been created, such as a broker that promises to obtain you the best price for airline tickets.

An example of a Web-based intermediary is an online auction for business that locates suppliers who are willing to supply what a company needs at the price the company is willing to pay. Many companies now sell through eBay as well as Amazon.com Inc. and Yahoo Inc. Another Internet-based intermediary is an eBay store that takes care of preparing your offerings for sale on eBay and also handles the shipping. The influence of these stores has diminished recently, as more people have learned to navigate eBay on their own.

The Enhancement of Globalization

The Internet is a driving force in globalization for several reasons. E-mail and Web sites allow for rapid communication with business partners throughout the world. Being in rapid contact with partners in other countries, such as a company's customer service center in a country 7,000 miles away, helps bring about a feeling of closeness. Companies throughout the world can trade more readily with each other because so much buying and selling takes place over the Internet.

The Internet facilitates globalization in part because more and more countries throughout the world have developed their telecommunications infrastructure. A case in point is China, which has surpassed the United States in Internet use. According to research conducted by Internet World Stats, Chinese Internet users number about 360 million, or about 27 percent of the population. The United States had 228 million active Internet users in 2009—about 74 percent of the population.[22] The vast majority of Web users in China are individuals, not companies. However, plenty of business firms are included among the online Chinese, thereby contributing to globalization. It is therefore easier for a company like Hewlett-Packard to be in frequent contact with its Chinese subcontractors to review such issues as delivery dates and product quality.

---

[21]Alex Veiga, "MySpace Intrudes on Music's Middlemen: Website to Enable Members to Sell Own Tunes Directly," The Associated Press, September 4, 2006.

[22]"Top 20 Countries with the Highest Number of Internet Users," *Internet World Stats* (www.internetsorldstats.com), accessed March 25, 2010.

Integrating the New Economy with the Old Economy

Managers at all levels face the challenge of how to integrate the traditional way of doing business (the old economy) with e-business (the new economy), sometimes referred to as the difference between bricks and clicks. During the initial surge of e-businesses, many Internet-based companies regarded traditional business firms as virtually obsolete. Many predicted that establishments such as shopping malls, automobile dealers, and companies that sold hard-copy greeting cards would soon go the way of the dinosaurs. They thought companies that acted as brokers between business firms and suppliers would soon be vaporized (tough talk for being run out of business).

Well-established companies that integrated e-commerce into their marketing and internal operations became the biggest beneficiaries of the Internet revolution. These same companies suffer from less business swings. Traditional retailers such as Wal-Mart, Target, Best Buy, Macy's, and Sears are attracting more shoppers with enhanced Web sites including easy-to-use search capabilities. Also, virtually every large industrial firm has its own Web site.

At Staples, customers can purchase from its catalog, retail stores, or Web site. Each of these channels is designed to serve as a sales pitch and backup for the others. In terms of channels, there is no effort to sway the customers one way or another. "Whatever makes their life easier," comments Paul Gaffney, the company's chief information officer.[23]

Living with Increased Visibility

An unanticipated consequence of the Internet is a different kind of visibility than in the past to which companies must adjust. People who like or dislike the organization can disseminate this information over the Internet by using personal blogs and the mini-blogs found on social networking sites. You-Tube is a specific vehicle for posting emotionally laden gripes. Several Web sites encourage consumers to voice their complaints. The general principle is that when a company slips up in terms of customer service, the snafu becomes a tale consumers will often broadcast widely.[24] An example of a slip up might be a luxury hotel chain not having made appropriate accommodations for a wheel-chair user.

Negative comments on the Web can be dismissed as the work of jealous people or kooks, but the exposure carries the potential to badly hurt the corporate image. At times company employees will post negative comments about their own organization. Employees sometimes create a Facebook page to make nasty comments about their own employer. At a retirement community in Philadelphia, a Facebook page was started by teenagers who worked in the kitchen. The young workers thought it was funny to share

---

[23]Tim Hanrahan, "When Worlds Collide," *The Wall Street Journal*, April 28, 2003, p. R4. The comment is still relevant as shown on www.Staples.com, as accessed March 29, 2010.

[24]Jena McGregor, "Customer Service Champs," *Business Week*, March 2, 2008, p. 37.

MANAGEMENT IN ACTION

Companies Combat Online Insults

In recent years, disgruntled consumers have launched hundreds of Web sites to air their grievances—from starbucked.com and ihatestarbucks.com to boycottwalmart.com and againstthewal.com. A study by FairWinds shows that some companies have been more aggressive than others in fighting back. Xerox, for example, has bought or reregistered about 20 unflattering domain names, including xeroxstinks.com, xerox corporationsucks.com, and ihatexerox.net.

Xerox says it is selective in deciding which pejorative domain names to buy. The names it now owns make up less than half a percent of the company's domain portfolio. But the company has a watch list of domains it would like to buy: While it owns ihatexerox.net and ihatexerox.org, someone else owns ihatexerox.com. If that domain became available, Xerox would likely buy it, says Rebecca Berkich, the manager of Search Marketing and Domains for Xerox.

In its study, FairWinds looked at a subset of the so-called gripe sites: those that end in the phrase "sucks.com" There are some 20,000 domains on the Internet that fit that description, according to FairWinds. (Only 2,000 domains end in the phrase "stinks.com.") The use of sucks.com has become frequent enough to lead to the creation of a Web site with the same name.

Of the companies surveyed, 35 percent own the domain name for their brand including the word "sucks." They include Wal-Mart Stores, Coca-Cola, Toys "R" Us, Target, and Whole Foods Market. Some 45 percent of these domains have yet to be registered by anyone.

Starbucks says that for all the gripe sites that exist, it has just as many fan sites. "We appreciate that our customers and partners (employees) take the time to share their thoughts about Starbucks. This feedback—good and bad—ultimately makes us a better company," a spokeswoman said in a statement.

Case Questions

1. How ethical is it for a company to purchase a negative domain name so as to prevent a complainer from getting rights to it?
2. To what extent might it be a good investment of company funds to purchase negative domain names that could be used to complain about the company?

Source: Excerpted from Emily Steel, "How to Handle 'IHateYourCompany.com'," *The Wall Street Journal*, September 5, 2008, p. B5; www.sucks.com, 2010.

stories about what they did in the kitchen with the equipment and food when a supervisor was not present.[25]

Companies recognize the need for risk and damage control in a variety of scenarios. For example, management at several large companies purchases a set of potential negative domain names, such as http://www.companyname.sucks.org. In this way, the critics will not be able to launch such a site. The accompanying Management in Action provides more details about this preemptive maneuver against online critics.

---

[25]Sandy Miller, "Employees Building Unauthorized Social Sites," *examiner.com*, April 15, 2010.

To counteract the downside of increased visibility, management must work extra hard to create fans and to deal openly with the issues that make people dislike you. Suppose a company subcontracts the manufacture of a clothing line to a company that hires prison labor working at low wages under punitive working conditions. The company addresses the issue by setting higher standards for subcontractors to minimize negative publicity over the Internet.[26] Another hope is that only a handful of consumers with an ax to grind will bother visiting a negative Web site about your company.

LEARNING OBJECTIVE **4**
Explain the effects of the Internet on internal company operations.

THE EFFECTS OF THE INTERNET ON INTERNAL OPERATIONS

Working in an Internet environment affects internal operations as well as relationships with outsiders. Doing business on the Internet is far more complicated than simply taking orders by means of an electronic catalog. E-commerce often brings about changes in the way in which a company operates. Here we look at several issues influenced by the Internet environment: more effective work processes, a squeeze on profits and pressure toward cost control, dealing with instability and chaos, data mining, and cloud computing.

More Effective Work Processes

The Internet ushered in a new era and transformed the way in which businesses operate internally. Using the Internet, many companies changed their methods of distributing goods, of collaborating inside the company, and of dealing with suppliers. Technology companies pioneered this use of the Internet to develop more effective work processes and overhaul their operations. In general, the flattening of the business playing field (see the section in Chapter 2 about the *flat world*) has encouraged more effective work processes for companies to stay competitive in a global economy. Information technology makes it easier to send work offshore and keep a project going 24/7. The Internet and workflow software have reduced the negative aspects of geographic distances. For example, radiologists in Los Angeles might send CAT-scans of the brain to Barcelona, Spain, for diagnosis and interpretation of images.[27]

Here we look at several examples of how the impact of information technology, including the Internet, has improved work processes and operations.

The Ordering and Production of PCs

Ingram Micro, the biggest PC distributor, teamed up with Solectron, a major contract manufacturer of high-technology equipment. Ingram custom makes PCs inexpensively for brand-name computer companies. Instead of the PC companies handling orders and manufacturing, Ingram and Solectron

---

[26]Esther Dyson, "Mirror, Mirror, on the Wall," *Harvard Business Review*, September–October 1997, pp. 24–25.

[27]Silviya Svejenova, "Quo Vadis, Europe?" *Academy of Management Perspectives*, May 2006, p. 83.

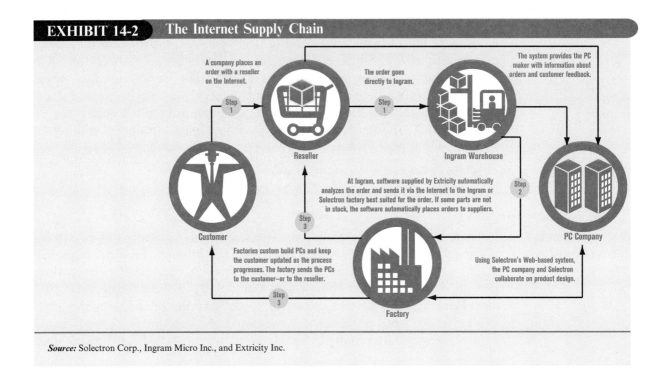

EXHIBIT 14-2 The Internet Supply Chain

A company places an order with a reseller on the Internet.

The order goes directly to Ingram.

The system provides the PC maker with information about orders and customer feedback.

Step 1

Step 1

Reseller

Ingram Warehouse

Customer

At Ingram, software supplied by Extricity automatically analyzes the order and sends it via the Internet to the Ingram or Solectron factory best suited for the order. If some parts are not in stock, the software automatically places orders to suppliers.

Step 2

PC Company

Step 3

Factories custom build PCs and keep the customer updated as the process progresses. The factory sends the PCs to the customer—or to the reseller.

Using Solectron's Web-based system, the PC company and Solectron collaborate on product design.

Step 3

Factory

Source: Solectron Corp., Ingram Micro Inc., and Extricity Inc.

perform the task for them. The Web-based system speeds up communication and decreases assembly times. The PC companies continue to design and market their products and handle quality assurance. The difference in operations comes from their alliance with Ingram, which functions as a virtual company.[28] The Web-based system enhances productivity because products are shipped more rapidly.

Exhibit 14-2 presents a step-by-step analysis of the Web-based process for customizing an order for a PC.

Work Streamlining for a Wine Maker

work streamlining
Eliminating as much low-value work as possible and concentrating on activities that add value for customers or clients.

A major contribution of information technology has been **work streamlining**, the elimination of as much low-value work as possible replaced by concentration on activities that add value for customers or clients. Streamlining thus minimizes waste and helps perform work more efficiently. You are probably quite familiar with the concept of streamlining research by accessing databases from your computer rather than visiting a physical library. An industrial example took place at Trinchero Family Estates, the winery that produces Sutter Hill and other popular brands of wines. Because the wine is low priced, production efficiency receives high priority.

Company management wanted to track the processing of grapes from harvesting to bottling to selling. Trinchero specialists set up an online system

---

[28]Steve Hamm and Marcia Stepanek, "From Reengineering to E-Engineering," *Business Week e.biz*, March 22, 1999, p. 16; www.ingrammicro.com, accessed April 1, 2010.

fed by bar codes on everything from barrels of grapes to bottles of wine. The payoff was a reduction in the cost of handling raw materials by 3 percent. Furthermore, the company avoided spending $100,000 on a system to comply with new bioterrorism rules.[29] It could now document when the grapes were handled and who was handling them. According to the Bioterrorism Response Act of 2002, every U.S. food processing company except farms and restaurants must be able to account for every link in the supply chain.

Squeeze on Profits and Pressure toward Cost Control

The changing flow of information created by the Internet tipped the balance of power from sellers to buyers. In the past, sellers had almost all the information about profit margins and manufacturer's true costs. Industrial buyers and individual consumers can now use the Web to uncover information about costs that puts them on the same level as professionals. Many prospective car purchasers today walk into dealers' offices with copies of factory invoices showing the true dealer cost of a given car model. The dealer is no longer able to claim, "We are giving you this car at $50 over dealer cost" unless it is true.

Given that the buyer knows so much about costs, the seller must offer products with lower profit margins than in the past. The manager is therefore responsible for controlling costs in any sensible way possible including reducing turnover, minimizing expenditures, and using the Internet for purchasing.

Data Mining

data mining

The extraction of useful analyses from the raw mass of business transactions and other information.

The term **data mining** describes the extraction of useful analyses from the raw mass of business transactions and other information. Through data mining, you extract patterns from data. Data mining derives its name from the similarities between searching for valuable business information in a large database and mining a mountain to find valuable ore.[30] Data mining is yet another useful application of information technology to business, linked to the Internet because some of the databases are accessed over the Internet. Data about what consumers are searching for on the Web can help with product research and decision making. For example, consumers who search for food supplements on the Internet might be good prospects for books about natural healing. The topic of data mining might therefore also fit the section in this book about marketing uses of the Internet.

Insurance companies use data mining to help price insurance policies, particularly automobile policies. For example, a revamped pricing model used by Allstate Corp. considers data such as the driver's credit history, allowing the company to predict more accurately how many claims a driver

---

[29]Heather Green, "The Web Smart 50," *Business Week*, November 21, 2005, p. 94.

[30]This section is based closely on Kurt Thearling, "An Introduction to Data Mining," http://www.thearling.com/text/dmwhite/dmwhite.htm, accessed April 2, 2004.

is likely to file. The underlying human factor here might be that someone with a good credit record tends to be responsible about paying bills on time and driving safely. Data mining by an insurance company can lead to lower premiums for some drivers and higher premiums for others.

Data mining helps deliver answers to such questions as "Which customers are most likely to respond to my next promotional mailing, and why?" and "Which job candidates are likely to stay with the company a long time, and why?" Two major outputs of data mining are as follows:

- *Automated prediction of trends and behavior.* Questions that traditionally required extensive hands-on analysis can now be answered directly from the data in rapid fashion. Predictive marketing is a key example. Data on previous promotional mailings can be used to identify the targets most likely to maximize return on investment in future mailings. A certain age group within a particular zip code, for example, might be the most receptive to purchasing smoked meats through the mail.
- *Automated discovery of previously unknown patterns.* Data mining tools rifle through databases and identify previously hidden patterns. An example of pattern discovery is the analysis of retail sales data to identify seemingly unrelated products that are often purchased together, such as laser cartridges and video games.

The technique underlying data mining is modeling. In brief, modeling refers to building a model (or general framework) in one situation where you know the answer and then applying the model to a situation where the answer is yet unknown. You might know how your customers behaved in one situation—such as whether they were receptive to HDTV—and use that model to estimate who might purchase a satellite radio service.

Cloud Computing

Cloud computing
(a) moving data and software from computer hard drives to the virtual storage space on the Internet and (b) the vast array of interconnected machines managing the data and software that were formerly run on desktop computers.

A final major impact of the Internet on internal operations to be described here is **cloud computing**, a term that has two related meanings. First, cloud computing refers to moving data and software from computer hard drives to the virtual storage space on the Internet. Instead of owning software and storing your own data, the Internet takes over these functions. Software is located on the vendor's servers running on the Internet or "in the cloud."[31] Second, cloud computing refers to the vast array of interconnected machines managing the data and software that were formerly run on desktop computers.[32] Both definitions point to the fact that vital activities related to computer use have now shifted from inside the organization to an external organization via the Internet.

[31]Dave Zielinski, "Be Clear on Cloud Computing Contracts," *HR Magazine*, November 2009, p. 63.
[32]Steve Hamm, "Cloud Computing's Big Bang for Business," *Business Week*, June 15, 2009. p. 42.

The major point of cloud computing is for all data-handling to take place on remote servers accessed by the Internet. Using such a model, business firms and other organizations could move their information technology operations off premises. Cost savings would accrue from paying for only the storage and data processing they use and not maintaining an internal IT staff.[33]

Avon is an example of a company making extensive use of cloud computing. One hundred and fifty thousand sales leaders are equipped with a cloud-based computing system accessible with smart phones and PCs. The technology keeps the leaders up to date on the sales of each rep, alerting them when the reps have not placed an order recently or when they are late on payments to Avon. The purpose of the cloud-computing system is to increase the sales volume and efficiency of Avon's distribution system.[34]

A manager should carefully think through the implications of having complete trust in cloud computing. Imagine that you have worked 25 days developing strategy for your company and that your report includes considerable data analysis and carefully worded plans. As you have gone through several versions of your plan, you have stored it on somebody's "cloud" without having printed a copy. Come the morning of your presentation you attempt to access your document. You find that (a) the Web site you need is not in service, and (b) the vendor is out of business. Another grim possibility is that a hacker from a country 7,000 miles away has stolen your strategic plan and sold it to a competitor.

For the prudent manager, cyberspace is probably too fragile to be your sole resource for storing valuable information. Using the Internet for software delivery is probably a safer bet than using the Internet for both software delivery and the sole method of data storage without your own backup. When using cloud computing, be sure you use a highly reliable vendor that uses a backup system for data storage.

LEARNING OBJECTIVE **5**
Pinpoint factors associated with success in e-business.

SUCCESS FACTORS IN E-COMMERCE

To help synthesize the vast amounts of information about the impact of the Internet, here we list six factors that contribute to success in e-business. Factors that contribute to success in any type of business, such as offering high-quality products customers want, also apply.[35]

---

[33]Analysis by Jessica Hodgson, "Selling and Software," *The Wall Street Journal*, December 17, 2009, p. A25, made in book review of Marc Benioff, *Behind the Cloud* (San Francisco: Jossey-Bass, 2009).

[34]Hamm, "Cloud Computing's Big Bang for Business," p. 43.

[35]Andrea J. Cullen and Margaret Taylor, "Critical Success Factors for B2B E-Commerce Use within the UK NHS Pharmaceutical Supply Chain, *International Journal of Operations & Production Management*, Number 11, 2009, pp. 1156–1185; Jennifer Reingold, "What We Have Learned in the New Economy," *Fast Company*, March 2004, pp. 57–58; Beckey Bright, "How Do You Say 'Web'," *The Wall Street Journal*, May 23, 2005, p. R11; Brian Gow and Ben Elgin, "Click Fraud: The Dark Side of Online Advertising," *Business Week*, October 2, 2006, pp. 46–56; Loretta Chao, "What Happens When an e-Bay Steal Is a Fake?" *The Wall Street Journal*, June 26, 2006, p. D1; Joël-Denis Bellavance, 'Les Criminels Menacent la Cyberéconomie,' [Criminals Threaten the Cybereconomy] http://www.cyberpress.ca, le 16 October, 2006.

1. *Develop an excellent call center to allow for the human touch.* Despite conducting business over the Internet, many customers want to follow up with telephone calls. Several online investment brokers found that telephone traffic actually increases after online trading is initiated. Many customers want to follow up online inquiries with human beings. Customers often seek the type of clarification that is difficult to obtain by asking questions online.

2. *Keep customers informed about order progress.* The online transaction is not completed until the customer receives the order and is satisfied. If the company experiences shipping delays, it should notify the customer. The problem of delays is especially relevant for complex products such as industrial machinery or custom-made computer servers.

3. *Constantly monitor and update the e-business system.* Many order systems turn out to be much more complex than their developers realize, and executing an order can be complicated and time-consuming. For example, the icon for executing the sale should be clearly visible. At one of the major airlines, the icon for "online boarding" can only be found by digging into an option under "customer service." It is also important to monitor the quality of the information on the Web site, such as accurately reporting any possible negative side effects of a food supplement or vitamin.

4. *Mix bricks and clicks.* The most successful players in e-tailing give customers the opportunity to purchase online, in stores, and by telephone. Among the many successful companies that offer multiple channels for customer purchases are Acer Computer, Macy's, Panasonic, and Lands End (now a division of Sears).

5. *Develop a global presence.* Customers throughout the world like to shop on American Web sites and this provides a unique opportunity for U.S. companies. Although the U.S. firm must adapt to local tastes and laws, back-office, distribution, and marketing functions translate well overseas. Web veterans suggest that the best way to perform well in foreign markets is to bring in experienced local partners who know the nuances of the market and can work through local rules and regulations. One key regulation is to obtain a local domain name, such as one ending in ".co.uk" for Britain. Several surveys indicate that up to 80 percent of Europeans shop first at Web sites with local domains. How about CarloRossi.co.fr for selling low-price California wine in France?

6. *Protect customers against fraud.* At the retail level in particular, crime and fraud are rampant on the Internet. In business-to-business transactions also, trusting the vendor is essential. To maintain a good reputation and to prevent the loss of valuable customers, companies must protect their customers against identity threat. A given customer may know which Web site led to identify theft, but might become discouraged about making any future purchases on the Web. As a consequence, all companies engaged in e-commerce must protect customers as much as possible through secure Web sites.

Another common type of fraud found on the Internet is the sale of counterfeits (or knockoffs) of luxury brands. The problem is more pronounced on the Internet because prospective purchasers see only a photograph of the merchandise, and the photo might not be of the product being sold. Auction sites such as eBay, Yahoo!, and Amazon cannot be blamed for fake merchandise offered on their sites because they only put buyers and sellers together. However, a person who learns he or she has purchased a fake Gucci wallet on eBay may not want to make another purchase on that site. (eBay and other auction sites are aware of this fraud, and try hard to screen out criminals.)

Despite the many positive changes brought about by the Internet revolution, some of its promises fell short. The vast majority of consumers prefer to shop in stores, most automobile dealers don't pay much attention to auto prices listed on the Internet, and personal contacts still dominate high-level business. The Internet supplements and enhances traditional business activity but does not replace the practice of management and personal relationships.

Summary of Key Points

1 **Summarize the demands information technology places on the manager's job.**

Management must build an organization that constantly transforms itself as information technology increases competition. To remain competitive requires innovation. Information and communications technology are at the center of the technological revolution and make globalization more practical because of ready access to employees everywhere. In general, information technology places managers in a continuous learning mode. Wireless communication devices facilitate work from different locations.

2 **Describe the positive and negative consequences of information technology for the manager.**

Information technology helps the manager work smarter in such ways as improved productivity and teamwork, competitive advantage (or avoiding competitive disadvantage), enhanced business models, improved customer service and supplier relationships, enhanced communication including the virtual office, quick access to vast information, enhanced analysis of data and decision making, greater empowerment and flatter organizations, time saved through employee self-service, and monitoring work and employee surveillance.

Negative consequences of information technology include wasting time at the computer, repetitive-motion disorder, deterioration of customer service, dealing with baffled customers, wired managerial workers, the encouragement of nonproductive multitasking, and excessive requirements to learn and adapt to new communication technologies.

3 **Discuss the impact of the Internet on customer and other external relationships.**

The biggest impact of the Internet on business comes from selling many goods and services to other businesses over the Internet. Seventy-five percent of business conducted on the Net today occurs between firms (B2B). The manager must be familiar with e-commerce to help develop strategy, and the manager may work with a reduced staff because of online selling. A substantial change in managing customer relationships in recent years has been contacting them through the social media, with customer interaction being highly important.

E-commerce sometimes enables companies to purchase more efficiently than they could through other channels. Managers face the major challenge of how to integrate the traditional way of doing business (the old economy) with e-business (the new economy). Relying strictly on Internet sales is rarely profitable. Well-established companies that integrate e-commerce into their marketing and internal operations have benefited the most from the Internet revolution.

Using the Internet, many companies changed their methods of distributing goods, of collaborating inside the company, and of dealing with suppliers. Buyers' power makes it more difficult to charge higher prices, forcing companies to more carefully control costs. Some intermediaries, such as travel agents, have changed because of the Internet. Globalization is enhanced because of the Internet. Companies also experience increased visibility, particularly from angry consumers.

4 **Explain the effects of the Internet on internal company operations.**

The Internet affects companies in a number of ways, beginning with more effective work processes as encouraged by the flattening of the business playing field through global competition. Information technology facilitates changing the method of distributing goods, and work streamlining. The Internet also squeezes profits and exerts pressure toward cost control and facilitates data mining. Two outputs of data mining are automated prediction of trends and behavior and automated discovery of unknown patterns. The Internet has led to cloud computing, which relies on the software and data handling of computer systems external to the company.

5 **Pinpoint factors associated with success in e-commerce.**

Successful e-businesses provide an excellent call center to allow for the human touch and keep customers informed about order progress. The e-business system requires constant monitoring and updating. Other strategies e-businesses can employ include mixing bricks and clicks, developing a global perspective, and protecting customers against fraud.

Key Terms and Phrases

Extranet, 512
Virtual office, 512
Microblogging, 513
E-leadership, 513
Intranet (or company intranet), 513

Wiki, 515
Computer goof-offs, 517
Work streamlining, 528
Data mining, 529
Cloud computing, 530

Questions

1. What do you regard as the most important way in which a manager can use information technology?
2. What is it about using a personal digital assistant or smart phone that so many managers believe increases their productivity?
3. The criticism is often heard that managers spend too much time working with their computers and smart phones. What else should they be doing?
4. Propose a new model for restaurants (other than the quick service type) that will capitalize on automation and information technology.
5. When you log into Twitter, how much attention do you pay the tweets from advertisers? How would your answer to this question influence your decision as to how much effort your company should invest in attempting to communicate with customers and clients through Twitter?
6. Many retailing experts predict that retail stores will never die because online shopping cannot replace the experience of visiting a store. What aspects of visiting a store make it preferable to shopping online for so many people?
7. You may have noticed that one of the most frequently offered product categories online is pharmaceuticals. However, the number of physical pharmacies, such as CVS, Rite Aid, and Target, continue to grow. Why do so many consumers continue to choose to purchase pharmaceuticals offline?

Skill-Building Exercise 14-A: Cost Reduction through Information Technology

Work in small groups to identify ten tangible ways that a manager can use information technology to reduce costs. For each item on your list, explain precisely the way in which information technology will reduce costs. Take into account all types of information technology, from a desktop printer to the Internet. A team leader from each group might present the team's findings to the rest of the class.

Skill-Building Exercise 14-B: Thinking about Data Mining

As implied in the text, data mining boils down to making sense of bits of information embedded in a large mass of information. No matter how exquisite the software performing the data mining, the manager or professional must have good intuition about the potential value of information or patterns of information. To get you in the right mind-set for data mining, do the following puzzlers.

- You are a manager in an insurance company. Your data mining software notes that people under 30 purchase less sun-blocking lotion, buy more cigarettes, and are more likely to let their auto inspection stickers expire. What sense do you make of these data that could help your insurance company?

- You are a human resources professional. Your data mining software indicates that employees who purchase American flags, watch professional football on TV, and own an SUV tend to stay longer with the company. What implications might this information have for staffing your company?

- You are a marketing specialist at a music company. Your data mining software indicates that people who purchase toothpaste with fluoride, own an umbrella, and give money to charity are more likely to pay to download music. What value for your company might you extract from this information?

Management Now: Online Skill-Building Exercise: Sizing up an Executive on YouTube

Many CEOs and other high-level executives send messages to the public and employees by uploading a personal video statement onto YouTube. (An assistant may do the technical work.) Search for an executive video presentation recorded during the last sixty days. You might use the search word of a company that interests you, or the name of the executive. Evaluate the impact the executive's YouTube message makes in terms of such factors as (a) the importance of the message, (b) the credibility of the message, and (c) the executive's verbal and nonverbal communication skills.

14-A Case Problem

How Far Can MyGofer Go?

Sears Holding Corporation was recently searching for ways to revitalize its Sears stores and Kmart stores. Among its objectives were finding fresh ways to sell Kenmore appliances and Craftsman tools in an age of smart phones and social networking sites. Many years ago, shoppers would place orders using the venerable Sears catalog and then pick up their orders at a nearby Sears store. Sears Holding assembled a team of 180 e-commerce specialists to find fresh, online, and smart-phone ways of selling its products. The new marketing strategy is dubbed, "Shop Your Way." Management at Sears Holding presents MyGofer, one component of the strategy, as a fundamental change in the way a retail store operates.

The new marketing experiment to supplement traditional store shopping is for customers to place orders on MyGofer.com and then visit a nearby store and pick up their merchandise. The customer swipes a credit card at a kiosk and then waits while employees, who wear uniforms resembling fast-service food servers, bring out the merchandise.

The MyGofer experiment began with a single pickup center in Joliet, Illinois, at a converted Kmart store. Consumers seemed to react positively to the new shopping method, according to Imran Jooma, a vice president of e-commerce for Sears Holding. Part of the experiment included the old-fashioned layaway program, which helped boost holiday sales during its first trial period. Online business for Sears has been increasing steadily, while in-store sales have been declining steadily.

The MyGofer program is part of the marketing strategy of Sears Holding chairman Edward S. Lampert, who has tried to stop the sales decline ever since he merged Sears with Kmart in 2005. Lampert and his advisors thought there would be a bigger payoff in Web ventures, which they preferred to heavy investment in refurbishing existing Sears and Kmart stores.

Another Internet marketing initiative is an iPhone app called Sears Personal Shopper, which enables shoppers to photograph products they might want, such as someone else's handbag or mountain climbing shoes. The person who took the photo sends the images to workers who can track them down at Sears or Kmart and offer them for sale. Sears Holding has also established two social networking sites, MySears.com and MyKmart.com, that also function as online shopping sites.

Discussion Questions

1. How effective do you think MyGofer will be as a retail venture?
2. In what way is Sears Holding a combination of the old economy and the new economy?
3. What advice can you offer Sears to make MyGofer even more successful?
4. How is MyGofer doing recently?

Sources: Tim Manners, "MyGofer," *www.reveries.com/mygofer*, January 20, 2010; Miguel Bustillo and Geoffrey A. Fowler, "Sears Scrambles Online for a Lifeline," *The Wall Street Journal*, January 19, 2010; "Mygofer," *www.searsholding.com*, accessed March 23, 2010.

14-B Case Problem

The Adoring Bloggers

Kathy is the managing director of the Center City Athletic Club, a chain of twenty-six athletic clubs. Although the club is sufficient for generating a profit, Kathy and her management staff believe that the club could do better with the right type of advertising and publicity.

Derek, the club director of marketing and sales, explained that a couple of marketing efforts have not been successful in generating new members. One approach was to invest in a program of newspaper advertising that consisted of a decal lightly glued to the front page of the Sunday edition of the local newspaper. The decals did not bring in even one new member. Radio advertising brought in a few inquiries and two new family memberships. Billboard advertising on a major highway in the outskirts of the city brought in apparently no new members.

During a meeting with Derek, Kathy suggested that a better way to create a buzz about the club would be to get bloggers to say nice things about the club, including comments on Facebook and Twitter. Derek said in a somber tone, "Hold on, Kathy. The Federal Trade Commission says anybody who is paid to blog must admit that fact on the blog site."

Kathy replied, "I'm not talking about paying anybody to say nice things about Center City. And it would also be silly for staff members to post favorable comments about our club on social networking sites or on personal blogs. If anybody figured out what we are doing, it could lead to negative publicity for the club.

"What I have in mind is for about a dozen Center City Athletic Club staff members to get a friend or relative to say something positive about our club on a social networking site or personal blog. We just hand out some useful things to say, even with a little goofy talk to

make the blogs sound authentic. I'll send you an e-mail later with what I have in mind."

That night Derek received an e-mail from Kathy with four sample blog statements that staff members would be encouraged to get friends and family to send, as follows:

- Followed my chiropractor's advice about getting a personal trainer at Center City Athletic Club. Best health move I've made in a decade.
- Luv those friendly folks @Center City Athletic Club. They treat me like a prince.
- I'm shaping up really good at Center City. I will look dynamite by spring.
- No day would be complete for me without my workout at Center City Athletic Club. The training equipment is great, and the trainers are even better.

After studying the four sample messages, Derek had some concerns. He thought, "I'm wondering whether this blog campaign idea could backfire. It seems a little hokey, and it would be embarrassing if we got caught. I'll sleep on this idea and get back to Kathy tomorrow morning."

Discussion Questions

1. What do you advise Derek, as the director of market and sales, to tell Kathy?
2. What ethical concerns do you have about the proposed blogs?
3. How effective do you think favorable comments on social networking sites and personal blogs would be in enhancing enrollment at the Center City Athletic Club?
4. How effective do you think "goofy talk" would be to help the blogs seem more authentic?

CHAPTER 15

Essentials of Control

OBJECTIVES

After studying this chapter and doing the exercises, you should be able to:

1. Explain how controlling relates to the other management functions.

2. Understand the different types and strategies of controls.

3. Describe the steps in the control process.

4. Explain the use of nonbudgetary control techniques.

5. Have an awareness of the various types of budgets and the use of budgets and financial ratios for control.

6. Explain how managers and business owners manage cash flow and control costs and use nontraditional measures of financial performance.

7. Describe how an information system contributes to control.

8. Specify several characteristics of effective controls.

Four years ago, executives of Burgerville, a regional restaurant chain, agreed to pay at least 90 percent of health-care premiums for hourly employees who work at least 20 hours a week. Today, the executives say the unusual move has saved money by cutting turnover, boosting sales, and improving productivity. Burgerville's experience is notable for the food-service industry, where turnover is high and fewer than half of chains offer health insurance for part-time hourly employees, according to People Report, a research firm.

Burgerville, a 39-restaurant chain based in Vancouver, Washington, has long followed a distinctive path. It offers hormone-free meat, uses wind energy to power its stores, and prints nutritional information on its receipts. Its move to pay more health-care costs began with a 2005 employee survey, in which health costs unexpectedly registered as the top concern. At the time, Burgerville offered limited coverage to hourly employees, who had to pay premiums of roughly $42 a month for a family plus annual deductibles of up to $1,000. Only about 3 percent of Burgerville's hourly workers were enrolled, said Chief Executive Jeff Harvey.

In absorbing more of the costs, Burgerville's annual health-care bill nearly doubled, to $4.1 million from $2.1 million, but company leaders figured the move would boost recruiting and retention. Executives say the plan paid for itself, and more. Turnover plunged in one year to 54 percent from 128 percent in the previous year. That's a big deal when it costs an average of $1,700 to replace and train a restaurant worker, according to People Report.

Harvey believes that part-time hourly employees work harder to qualify for more hours, which are assigned on a priority system based on performance. Employees work 20 hours a week to qualify for the health plan. "As soon as employees realized the value of the health-care benefit, they started to work [hard] to win the 20 hours," Harvey said.

Burgerville managers say that work ethic translates into higher revenue. Sales rose 11 percent after the plan was implemented, with the average customer check rising to $7.41 from $6.90. In a recent year, the average check reached $8.50 and employee turnover fell to 52 percent. Annual revenue of the chain is about $70 million.[1]

The story about the hamburger chain illustrates, among other managerial practices, that a successful enterprise stays on top of financial measures such as turnover data and average sales per customer. Even more important, the Burgerville experience illustrates that investing money in a positive way can sometimes help control costs. The control function of management involves measuring performance and then taking corrective action if goals are not being achieved.

Controls make many positive contributions to the organization. Controlling aligns the actions of workers with the interests of the firm. Without the controlling functions, managers cannot know whether people are carrying out their jobs properly. Controls enable managers to gauge whether the firm is attaining its goals. Controls often make an important contribution to employee motivation. Achieving the performance standards set in a control system leads to recognition and other deserved rewards. Accurate control measurements give the well-motivated, competent worker an opportunity to be noticed for good work.

In this chapter, we emphasize the types and strategies of controls, the control process, budgets and controls, how managers manage cash flow and cut costs, and the use of information systems in control. Finally, we describe characteristics of effective controls.

---

[1]Sarah E. Needleman, "Burger Chain's Health-Care Recipe," *The Wall Street Journal*, August 31, 2009, p. B4.

CONTROLLING AND THE OTHER MANAGEMENT FUNCTIONS

LEARNING OBJECTIVE ①
Explain how controlling relates to the other management functions.

Controlling, sometimes referred to as the *terminal management function*, takes place after other functions have been completed. Controlling is most closely associated with planning, because planning establishes goals and the methods for achieving them. Controlling investigates whether planning was successful.

The links between controlling and other major management functions are illustrated in Exhibit 15-1. Controlling helps measure how well planning, organizing, and leading have been performed. The controlling function also measures the effectiveness of the control system. On occasion, the control measures are inappropriate. For example, suppose one measure of sales performance is the volume of sales. Such a measure might encourage a sales representative to push easier-to-sell products instead of helping the company establish a few new products. Spending more time developing a market for the new products would probably boost the sales representative's effectiveness. More will be said about effective control measures later.

▶ **PLAY VIDEO**

Go to www.cengage. com/management / dubrin and view the video for Chapter 15. What types of controls are used at Recycline? How are these important to their business?

The planning and decision-making tools and techniques described in Chapter 6 can be used as tools and techniques of control as well. For example, a Gantt chart keeps track of how well target dates for a project are being met. Keeping track is a control activity. If an event falls behind schedule, a project manager usually takes corrective action.

TYPES AND STRATEGIES OF CONTROLS

LEARNING OBJECTIVE ②
Understand the different types and strategies of controls.

Controls can be classified according to the time at which the control is applied to the activity—before, during, or after. Another way of describing controls relates to the source of the control—external versus internal.

The Time Element in Controls

A **preventive control** takes place prior to the performance of an activity. A preventive control prevents problems that result from deviation from

---

EXHIBIT 15-1   **The Links Between Controlling and the Other Management Functions**

The control function is extremely important because it helps managers evaluate whether all four major management functions have been implemented.

preventive control
A control that takes place prior to the performance of an activity.

concurrent control
A type of control that monitors activities while they are carried out.

feedback control
A control that evaluates an activity after it is performed.

external control strategy
An approach to control based on the belief that employees are motivated primarily by external rewards and must be controlled by their managers.

performance standards. Preventive controls are generally the most cost-effective. A manufacturer that specifies quality standards for purchased parts establishes a preventive control. By purchasing high-quality parts, the manufacturer prevents many instances of machine failure. Preventive controls are also used in human-resource management. Standards for hiring employees are preventive controls. For example, a company may require that all job candidates be nonsmokers. This preventive control helps decrease lost productivity due to smoking breaks outside the building and smoking-related illnesses. The company might also save some money on health insurance premiums because smokers are likely to have a high number of health claims, leading to high premiums based on claims experience.

Concurrent controls monitor activities while they are carried out. A typical concurrent control takes place when a supervisor observes performance, spots a deviation from standard, and immediately makes a constructive suggestion. For example, suppose a telemarketing manager overhears a telemarketing specialist fail to ask a customer for an order. On the spot, the manager would coach the telemarketer about how to close an order.

Feedback controls evaluate an activity after it is performed. Feedback controls measure history by pointing out what went wrong in the past. The process of applying the control may provide guidelines for future corrective action. Financial statements are a form of feedback control. If a financial report indicates that one company in a conglomerate lost money, top-level managers can then confer with company (or division) managers to see how to improve the situation.

Exhibit 15-2 summarizes the three types of time-based controls. Most firms use a combination of preventive, concurrent, and feedback controls. An important part of a manager's job is choosing controls appropriate to the situation.

External versus Internal Controls

Controls can be classified according to their underlying strategy. **External control strategy** is based on the belief that employees are primarily motivated by external rewards and must be controlled by their managers. An effective external control system involves three steps. First, the objectives and performance standards must be relatively difficult in order to gain optimum effort of team members and leave little leeway in performance. Second, the objectives and measures must be set in such a way that people cannot manipulate or distort them. For instance, top-level management should make its own investigation of customer satisfaction rather than take the word of field personnel. Third, rewards must be directly and openly tied to performance.

An external control strategy produces several different effects. On the positive side, employees may channel considerable energy into achieving objectives. Employees do so because they know that good performance leads to a reward. A tightly structured control system translates into a high degree of control over employee behavior.

| EXHIBIT 15-2 | Three Types of Time-Based Controls |

Controlling can take place before, during, or after an event or process. Preventive controls usually offer the biggest payoff to the organization.

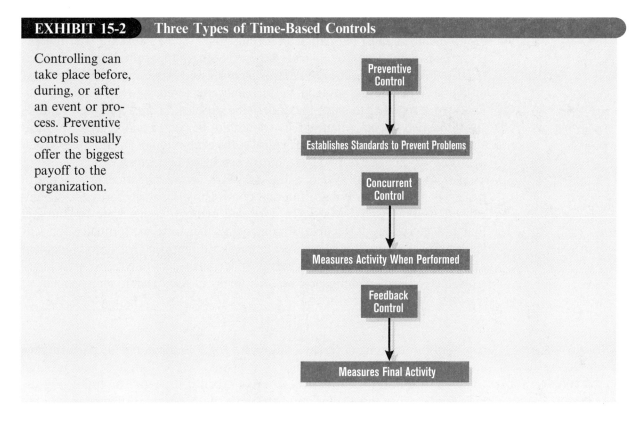

External control can create problems, however. Employees may work toward achieving performance standards, but they may not develop a commitment to the firm. They may reach standards but not be truly productive. Reaching standards without being productive is sometimes referred to as "looking good on paper" or "looking good digitally." Suppose the marketing and sales director of a telecommunications company establishes as a performance standard a high number of customers processed. To achieve this standard, the customer-service manager instructs the customer-service representatives, "Take care of as many calls as you can. And minimize the time customers are kept on hold." As a result, the customer-service reps spend brief amounts of time on the phone attempting to resolve problems with most customers. Instead of customers being happy with customer service, many of them are dissatisfied with the abrupt treatment. The standard of taking care of more customers is met, yet at the same time customer service deteriorates.

internal control strategy

An approach to control based on the belief that employees can be motivated by building their commitment to organizational goals.

Internal control strategy is based on the belief that employees can be motivated by building their commitment to organizational goals. Empowerment of individuals and teams relies on an internal control strategy. Management may impose the controls, but employees are committed to them. Hyundai Corp. provides an instructive example of employees being committed to controls, especially in the form of high quality and cleanliness. Adhering to high quality is part of the Hyundai culture, so the majority of Hyundai manufacturing workers enjoy meeting the quality standards imposed by management.

Building an effective internal control system requires three steps. First, group members must participate in setting goals. These goals are later used as performance standards for control purposes. Second, the performance standards (control measures) must be used for problem solving rather than for punishment or blame. When deviations from performance are noted, superiors and subordinates work together to solve the underlying problem. Third, although rewards should be tied to performance, they should not be tied to only one or two measures. An internal control strategy calls for the evaluation of an employee's total contribution, not one or two quantitative aspects of performance.

An internal control system is not necessarily good, and an external control system is not necessarily bad. Internal controls work satisfactorily for a high-caliber, well-motivated workforce. External controls compensate for the fact that not everybody is capable of controlling their own performance (or self-leadership) or committed to organizational goals. If applied with good judgment and sensitivity, external control systems work quite well. The effective use of controls thus follows a contingency, or "if…, then…," approach to management.

STEPS IN THE CONTROL PROCESS

LEARNING
OBJECTIVE 3
Describe the steps
in the control
process.

The steps in the control process follow the logic of planning: (1) performance standards are set, (2) performance is measured, (3) performance is compared to standards, and (4) corrective action is taken if needed. The following discussion describes these steps and highlights the potential problems associated with each one. Exhibit 15-3 presents an overview of controlling.

Setting Appropriate Performance Standards

A control system begins with a set of performance standards that are realistic and acceptable to the people involved. A **standard** is a unit of measurement used to evaluate results. Standards can be quantitative, such as cost of sales,

EXHIBIT 15-3   Steps in the Controlling Process

Controlling begins with setting meaningful standards that are accepted by the people doing the measuring and those being measured.

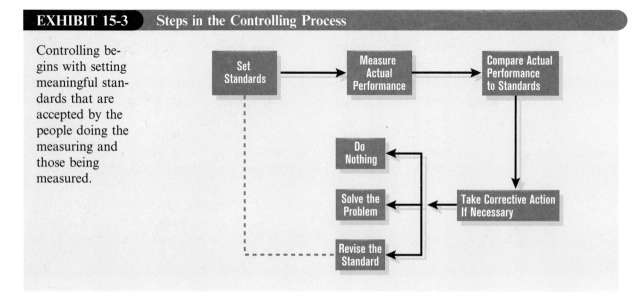

standard
A unit of measurement used to evaluate results.

profits, or time to complete an activity. Standards can also be qualitative, such as a viewer's perception of the visual appeal of an advertisement. Laws are often the basis for standards because performance must comply with laws and regulations, such as those relating to the disposal of toxins, fair employment practices, and safety. An effective standard shares the same characteristics as an effective objective (see Chapter 4). Exhibit 15-4 presents two of the performance standards established for a customer-service representative unit within a telecommunications company.

Historical information about comparable situations often provides the basis for setting initial standards. Assume a manufacturer wants to establish a standard for the percentage of machines returned to the dealer for repair. If the return rate for other machines with similar components is 3 percent, then the new standard might be a return rate of no more than 3 percent.

At times, profit-and-loss considerations dictate performance standards. A case in point is the occupancy-rate standard for a hotel. Assume a break-even analysis reveals that the average occupancy rate must be 75 percent for the hotel to cover costs. Hotel management must then set an occupancy rate of at least 75 percent as a standard.

Measuring Actual Performance

To implement the control system, performance must be measured. Performance evaluations are one of the major ways of measuring performance. Supervisors often make direct observations of performance to implement a control system. A simple example would be observing to make sure a sales associate always asks a customer, "What else could I show you now?" A more elaborate performance measure would be a ten-page report on the

---

EXHIBIT 15-4	Two Performance Standards Established for a Customer-Service Operation

The performance standards shown here give customer-service representatives precise targets for meeting organizational objectives. Performance evaluation is based on how well customer-service representatives, individually and as a group, meet these standards.

CSR Objectives	Distinguished Performance (4 points)	Above-Standard Performance (3 points)	Standard Performance (2 points)	Below-Standard Performance (1 point)
Customer Satisfaction	89% or higher overall customer satisfaction	86%–88% overall customer satisfaction	83%–85% overall customer satisfaction	<83% overall customer satisfaction
Calls Answered in 30 Seconds	Group consistently answers 80% or more of calls within 30 seconds.	Group consistently answers 75%–79% of calls within 30 seconds.	Group consistently answers 70%–74% of calls within 30 seconds.	Group consistently answers <70% of calls within 30 seconds.

status of a major project submitted to top-level management. The aspects of performance that accountants measure include manufacturing costs, profits, and cash flow (available cash on hand). Measurement of performance is much more complex than it would seem on the surface. The list that follows presents three important conditions for effective performance measurement:[2]

1. *Agree on the specific aspects of performance to be measured.* Top-level managers in a hotel chain might think that occupancy rate is the best measure of performance. Middle-level managers might disagree by saying, "Don't place so much emphasis on occupancy rate. If we try to give good customer service, the occupancy rate will take care of itself. Instead, let's try to measure customer service."

2. *Agree on the accuracy of measurement needed.* In some instances, precise measurement of performance is possible. Sales volume, for example, can be measured in terms of customer billing and accounts paid. The absolute number or percentage of customer returns is another precise measurement. In other instances, precise measurement of performance may not be possible. Assume top-level managers of the hotel chain buy the idea of measuring customer service. Quantitative measures of customer satisfaction—including ratings that guests submit on questionnaires and the number of formal complaints—are available. However, many measurements would have to be subjective, such as the observation of the behavior of guests, including their spontaneous comments about service. These qualitative measures of performance might be more relevant than the quantitative measures.

3. *Agree on who will use the measurements.* In most firms, managers at higher levels have the authority to review performance measures of people below them in the hierarchy. Few people at lower levels object to this practice. In a team-based organization, peers might be allowed to see each other's performance measurements. Anther issue centers on the level of staff access to control reports. Line managers sometimes believe that too many staff members make judgments about their performance.

Comparing Actual Performance to Standards

After establishing standards and taking performance measurements, the next step is to actually compare performance to standards. Key aspects of comparing performance to standards include measuring the deviation and communicating information about it.

deviation
In a control system, the size of the discrepancy between performance standards and actual results.

Deviation in a control system indicates the size of the discrepancy between performance standards and actual results. It is important to agree beforehand how much deviation from the standard is a basis for corrective action. When using quantitative measures, statistical analysis can determine

---

[2]Richard O. Mason and E. Burton Swanson, "Measurement for Management Decision: A Perspective," *California Management Review,* Spring 1979, pp. 70–81.

how much of a deviation is significant. Recall the 75 percent occupancy rate standard in the hotel example. A deviation of plus or minus 3 percent may not be considered meaningful but rather caused by random events. Deviations of 4 percent or more, however, would be considered significant. Taking corrective action only in the case of significant deviations applies the exception principle.

Sometimes a deviation as small as 1 percent from the standard can have a big influence on company welfare. If a business unit fails by 1 percent to reach $100 million in sales, the firm has $1 million less money than anticipated. At other times, deviations as high as 10 percent might not be significant. A claims department might be 10 percent behind schedule in processing insurance claims because of an unanticipated event such as a hurricane. However, the claims manager might not be upset, knowing that all the claims will eventually be processed.

When statistical limits are not available, it takes wisdom and experience to diagnose a random deviation. Sometimes factors beyond a person's influence lead to a one-time deviation from performance. In such a case, the manager might ignore the deviation. For example, a person might turn in poor performance one month because he or she faced a family crisis.

For the control system to work, the results of the comparison between actual performance and standards must be communicated to the right people. These people include the employees themselves and their immediate managers. At times, the results should also be communicated to top-level managers and selected staff specialists. They need to know about events such as exceptional deviations from safety and health standards. For example, nuclear power plants are equipped with elaborate devices to measure radiation levels. When a specified radiation level is reached or exceeded, key people are automatically notified.

Taking Corrective Action

An evaluation of the discrepancy between actual performance and a standard presents a manager with three courses of action: do nothing, solve the problem, or revise the standard. Each of these alternatives may be appropriate, depending on the results of the evaluation.

Do Nothing

The purpose of the control system is to determine whether plans are working. No corrective action is required if the evaluation reveals that events are proceeding according to plan. Doing nothing, however, does not mean abdicating, or giving up, responsibility. A manager might take the opportunity to compliment employees for having achieved their objectives (thus increasing employee motivation) but do nothing about their approach to reaching objectives because performance measurements show it to be effective.

Solve the Problem

The big payoff from the controlling process concerns the correction of deviations from standard performance. If a manager decides that a deviation is significant (nonrandom), he or she starts problem solving. Typically the manager meets with the team member to discuss the nature of the problem. Other knowledgeable parties might participate in the problem-solving process. At times, a significant deviation from a performance standard demands a drastic solution. A severe shortfall in cash, for example, might force a retailer to sell existing inventory at a loss.

Sometimes a manager can correct the deviation from a performance standard without overhauling current operations. An office manager in a group dental practice used a control model to measure the percentage of professional time allotted to patient care. The analysis revealed that non-billed time exceeded 10 percent—an unacceptable deviation. The corrective action involved two steps. First, workers scanned dental records to find patients overdue for cleaning and checkups. Second, the office manager sent e-mail messages or phoned these people and asked whether they would like to schedule an appointment for cleaning and a checkup. The successful e-mail and telemarketing campaign virtually filled all the slack time within ten days.

Revise the Standard

Deviations from standard are sometimes attributable to errors in planning rather than to performance problems. Corrective action is thus not warranted because the true problem is an unrealistic performance standard. Consider an analogy to the classroom: If 90 percent of students fail a test, the real problem could be an unrealistically difficult test.

Standards often must be revised because of changes in the external environment. For example, as more and more companies shifted to e-commerce, standards of hotel occupancy rates had to be lowered. The reason is that business travel decreased as more business was conducted over the Internet rather than in person. The use of videoconferences to substitute for in-person meetings also bit into hotel occupancy. Planning for a new task can also create a need for revised standards. Performance quotas may be based on "guesstimates" that prove to be unrealistically difficult or overly easy to reach. A performance standard is too difficult if no employee can meet it. A performance standard may be too easy if all employees can exceed it. As Exhibit 15-3 shows, revising standards means repeating the control cycle.

NONBUDGETARY CONTROL TECHNIQUES

LEARNING OBJECTIVE 4
Explain the use of nonbudgetary control techniques.

One way of classifying control techniques is to divide them into two categories: those based on budgets and those not based on budgets. In this section, we describe nonbudgetary techniques and classify them into two types. **Qualitative control techniques** are methods based on human judgments about performance that result in a verbal rather than a numerical evaluation. For example, customer service might be rated as "outstanding." Even using a 1-to-5 rating scale could be interpreted as a qualitative technique because the rating is based on an overall human judgment. **Quantitative control techniques** are methods based on numerical measures of performance, such as number of orders processed per hour.

Exhibits 15-5 and 15-6 summarize qualitative and quantitative control techniques, respectively. The purpose in listing them is primarily to alert you to their existence. Chapter 6 provided details about four of the quantitative control techniques described in Exhibit 15-6. When interpreting the results of an audit, it is necessary to carefully evaluate the processes used to provide the information. A key factor to investigate is the political motivation of the people conducting the audit. Are the auditors going out of their way to please management? Are they out to make management look bad? Or are they motivated only to be objective and professional?

The auditing process has come under considerable scrutiny in recent years because of many reported cases of unethical and illegal reporting of financial information by business firms. Auditors are dependent on the client for their fees, and the same firm that audits a company's books might be selling consulting services to them. Auditors, being human, suffer from an unconscious bias to see what they want to see and not displease the clients

qualitative control technique
A method of controlling based on human judgments about performance that results in a verbal rather than numerical evaluation.

quantitative control technique
A method of controlling based on numerical measures of performance.

EXHIBIT 15-5	Qualitative Control Techniques

The competence and ethics of people collecting information for qualitative controls influence the effectiveness of these controls.

Technique	Definition	Key Features
External audit	Verification of financial records by an external agency or individual	Conducted by an outside agency, such as a CPA firm
Internal audit	Verification of financial records by an internal group of personnel	Wide in scope, including evaluation of control system
Management audit	Use of auditing techniques to evaluate the overall effectiveness of management	Examines a wide range of management practices, policies, and procedures
Personal observation	Manager's firsthand observations of how the well plans are carried out	Natural part of a manager's job
Performance appraisal	Formal method or system of measuring, evaluating, and reviewing employee performance	Points out areas of deficiency and areas for corrective action; manager and group member jointly solve the problem

EXHIBIT 15-6	Quantitative Control Techniques Used in Production and Operations

Quantitative control techniques are widely accepted because they appear precise and objective.

Technique	Definition	Key Features
Gantt chart	Chart depicting planned and actual progress of work on a project	Describes progress on a project
PERT	Method of scheduling activities and events using time estimates	Measures how well the project is meeting the schedule
Break-even analysis	Ratio of fixed costs to price minus variable scosts	Measures an organization's performance and gives basis for corrective action
Economic-order quantity (EOQ)	Inventory level that minimizes ordering and carrying costs	Avoids having too much or too little inventory
Variance analysis	Major control device in manufacturing	Establishes standard costs for materials, labor, and overhead, and then measures deviations from these costs

they serve.[3] It is sometimes difficult to be objective because of our unconscious tendencies to survive by not biting the hand that feeds us. As they say, "Whose bread I eat, whose song I sing."

Another problem is that sometimes auditors ask managers whose books they are investigating whether they (the managers) suspect fraud. If the managers say no, the auditors are less likely to dig deeply because there is less apparent risk.[4] The Sarbanes-Oxley Act of 2002 includes provisions for making auditors more independent and puts the accounting industry under tightened federal oversight.

BUDGETS AND BUDGETARY CONTROL TECHNIQUES

LEARNING OBJECTIVE **5**

Have an awareness of the various types of budgets and the use of budgets and financial ratios for control.

When people hear the word *budget,* they typically think of tight restrictions placed on the use of money. The car-rental agency name Budget Rent-A-Car was chosen because of popular thinking that the adjective *budget* means conservative spending. In management, a budget does place restrictions on the use of money, but the allotted amounts can be quite generous. A **budget** is a plan, expressed in numerical terms, for allocating resources. The numerical

---

[3]Jonathan Weil, "Behind Wave of Corporate Fraud, A Change in How Auditors Work," *The Wall Street Journal*, March 25, 2004, p. A1.

[4]Max H. Bazerman, George Lowenstein, and Don A. Moore, "Why Good Accountants Do Bad Audits," *Harvard Business Review,* November 2002, pp. 96–102.

budget
A spending plan expressed in numerical terms for a future period of time.

terms typically refer to money, but they could also refer to such things as the amount of energy or the number of laser cartridges used. A budget typically involves cash outflow and inflow.

Because a budget outlines a plan for allocating resources, virtually every manager assumes some budget responsibility. Without budgets, keeping track of how much money is spent in comparison to how much money is available would be nearly impossible. Here we look at different types of budgets and how to use budgets for control. Readers familiar with accounting and finance will find much of this information a review.

Types of Budgets

Budgets can be classified in many ways. For example, budgets are sometimes described as either fixed or flexible. A *fixed budget* allocates expenditures based on a one-time allocation of resources. The organizational unit receives a fixed sum of money that must last for the budget period. A *flexible budget* allows for variation in the use of resources on the basis of activity. Under a flexible budget, for example, an e-commerce department would receive an increased information technology budget if the department increased the scope of its program. Any type of budget can be classified as fixed or flexible.

Many different types of budgets help control costs in profit and nonprofit firms. Exhibit 15-7 presents a tabular summary of eight commonly used budgets. Most other budgets are variations of these basic types. Exhibit 15-8 provides an example of one of the revenue-and-expense budgets.

Suggestions for Preparing a Budget

Although budgets give the appearance of being factual, objective documents, judgment, and political tactics enter into budget preparation. When preparing a budget, a manager can impress higher-ups if he or she tracks variables with care and makes sound assumptions. In contrast, if the manager allocates resources poorly or permits too much flab, he or she will lose credibility. Here are several recommendations for preparing a sensible budget:[5]

- *Leave wiggle room.* Optimistic projections with little basis in reality will come back to haunt you. Budget conservatively for income and liberally for expenses. Using this approach, you will be impressive if you constrain costs and generate more revenue than you anticipated.
- *Research the competition.* Do some fact-finding to determine how your competitors at other firms arrive at their budget estimates. For example, find out how others adjust for inflation or an industry slump. Managers

---

[5]The first three suggestions are from "Master the Art of Budget Projection," *Working SMART*, March 1999, p. 6; the last one is from Edward Low Foundation, "How to Prepare a Cash Budget," *eSmallOffice* (http://www.esmalloffice.com/), Copyright © 1999–2006.

EXHIBIT 15-7   Budgets Commonly Used in Organizations

Type of Budget and Definition	Notable Characteristic
Master budget—consolidates budgets of various units.	Purpose is to forecast financial statements for entire company.
Cash budget—forecast of cash receipts and payments.	Important control measure because it reflects a firm's ability to meet cash obligations and to invest in new opportunities.
Cash flow budget—prediction of a business firm's cash inflow and outflow over a specified time.	Primary purpose is to predict the firm's capacity to take in more cash than it dispenses.
Revenue-and-expense budget—describes in currency amounts plan for revenues and operating expenses.	Most widely used budget, such as a sales budget to forecast sales and estimate expenses.
Production budget—a detailed plan that identifies the products and services needed to match sales forecast and inventory requirements.	Follows the sales forecast and can be considered a production schedule.
Materials purchase/usage budget—identifies the raw materials and parts that must be purchased to meet production demands.	When accurate, leads to smooth production. Can be used in retailing to purchase merchandise.
Human-resource budget—provides a schedule to identify human-resource needs for future and the compensation requirements.	Needed to satisfy sales and production demands, and predicts whether hiring or layoffs will be required.
Capital expenditure budget—a plan for spending money on assets used to produce goods or services.	Are usually regarded as major expenditures and are tied to long-range plans.

who submit the best budgets show comparisons to the competition and explain how they can outperform and why.

- *Embrace reality.* Study the facts carefully, and take a historical perspective in arriving at the correct estimates for any given financial period. For example, if your industry traditionally experiences high turnover, factor high turnover costs into your budget forecast.
- *Do not neglect intuition.* Future sales are contingent on many factors including the competition, the local economic climates, and your own internal operations and capacity. Past experience is important, but so is intuition. Estimates must be based on reality and yet contain a little creativity and optimism, if warranted.

EXHIBIT 15-8	March Revenue-and-Expense Budget for Nightclub and Restaurant			

Item	Budget	Actual	Over	Under
Revenues	$40,000	$42,500	$2,500	
Beginning inventory	3,500	3,500		
Purchases	19,250	19,000		$250
End inventory	3,000	3,000		
Cost of goods sold	19,750	19,500		
Gross profit	20,250	23,000	2,750	
Salaries expense	10,500	10,500		
Rent and utilities expense	1,500	1,500		
Miscellaneous expense	100	250	150	
Maintenance expense	650	650		
Total operating expenses	12,750	12,900	150	
Net income before tax	7,500	10,100	2,600	
Taxes (40%)	3,000	4,040		1,040
Net income	$4,500	$6,060		

Budget summary: Revenues and net income exceed budget by $2,500 and $1,560, respectively.
Note: Data analyzed according to Generally Accepted Accounting Principles by Jose L. Cruzet of Florida National College.

Budgets and Financial Ratios as Control Devices

The control process relies on the use of budgets and financial ratios as measures of performance. To the extent that managers stay within budget or meet their financial ratios, they perform according to standard.

Budgets and the Control Process

Budgets are a natural part of controlling. Planned expenditures are compared to actual expenditures, and corrective action is taken if the deviation is significant. Exhibit 15-8 shows a budget used as a control device. The nightclub and restaurant owner operates with a monthly budget. The owner planned for revenues of $40,000 in March. Actual revenues were $42,500, a positive deviation. The discrepancy is not large enough, however, for the owner to change the anticipated revenues for April. Expenses were $150 over budget, a negative deviation the owner regards as insignificant. In short, the performance against budget looks good. The owner will take no corrective action on the basis of March performance.

Financial Ratios and the Control Process

A more advanced method of using budgets for control is to use financial ratio guidelines for performance. Four such ratios are presented here.

gross profit margin
A financial ratio expressed as the difference between sales and the cost of goods sold, divided by sales.

Gross profit margin. One commonly used ratio is **gross profit margin**, expressed as the difference between sales and the cost of goods sold, divided by sales:

$$\text{Gross profit margin} = \frac{\text{Sales} - \text{Cost of goods sold}}{\text{Sales}}$$

This ratio measures the total money available to cover operating expenses and to make a profit. If performance deviates significantly from a predetermined performance standard, corrective action must be taken. Gross profit margins are highly regarded by many managers. Seven months after Julian Day was appointed CEO of RadioShack a few years ago, sales had declined but profits had increased. Day said on a conference call with investors, "Even though sales are very important, sales themselves are not the goal. Gross profit dollars are."[6]

Assume the nightclub owner needs to earn a 30 percent gross profit margin. For March, the figures are as follows:

$$\text{Gross profit margin} = \frac{\$42,500 - 19,500}{\$42,500} = \frac{\$23,000}{\$42,500} = 0.54 \text{ or } 54\%$$

The night club owner is quite pleased with the gross profit margin of 54 percent, and will take no corrective action. However, for the next budgeting cycle, the owner might raise expectations.

profit margin
A financial ratio measuring return on sales, or net income divided by sales.

Profit margin. One could argue that the gross profit margin presents an overly optimistic picture of how well the business is performing. Another widely used financial ratio is the **profit margin**, or return on sales. Profit margin measures profits earned per dollar of sales as well as the efficiency of the operation. In the business press, the profit margin is usually referred to as simply the margin; it is calculated as profits divided by sales.

$$\text{Profit margin} = \frac{\text{Net income}}{\text{Sales}} = \frac{\$6,060}{\$42,500} = 0.14 \text{ or } 14\%$$

A profit margin of 14 percent would be healthy for most businesses. It also appears to present a more realistic assessment of how well the nightclub in question performs as a business.

---

[6]Quoted in Mary Ellen Lloyd and Kris Hudson, "New CEO's Cost Cuts Pay Off for Radio Shack," *The Wall Street Journal*, February 28, 2007, p. C10.

return on equity
A financial ratio measuring how much a firm is earning on its investment, expressed as net income divided by owner's equity.

Return on equity. The **return on equity** is an indicator of how much a firm is earning on its investment. It is the ratio of net income to the owner's equity, or

$$\text{Return on equity} = \frac{\text{Net income}}{\text{Owner's equity}}$$

Assume that the owner of the nightclub and restaurant invested $400,000 in the restaurant and that the net income for the year is $72,500. The return on equity is $72,500/$400,000 = 0.181, or 18.1 percent. The owner should be satisfied, because few investments offer such a high return on equity.

revenue per employee
A financial ratio measuring how much revenue is generated by each employee, expressed as total revenues divided by the number of employees.

Revenue per employee. A simple financial ratio that is widely used by business managers is **revenue per employee**, expressed as

$$\text{Revenue per employee} = \frac{\text{Total revenues}}{\text{Number of employees}}$$

A company that generated $40 million in sales with 100 employees would have revenue per employee of $400,000, a reasonably representative figure. Three examples of revenue per employee are as follows: Apple, Inc., $1,014,969 (exceptional); DISH Network Corp, $482,190 (healthy); Flextronics International Ltd., $170,112 (toward the low end).[7] Revenue per employee is often used to measure the productivity of the firm. Top management at Cisco Systems, for example, uses revenue per employee as its primary productivity measure.

The ratios presented above offer a traditional view of the financial health of an organization because they emphasize earning a profit. Many start-ups in the telecommunications, information technology, and biotechnology fields with revenues far below their expenses pay salaries and other expenses out of investor capital. Dozens of other companies do not pay their bills at all because they lack the necessary cash. Without cash to pay bills and profits to pay investors, most companies eventually fail. Ratios such as profit margin and return on equity are still relevant in today's economy.

Other Measures of Financial Health

Several other measures of financial success in addition to financial ratios are widely used by managers. The purpose of most of these measures is to portray the company in a favorable light, so as to impress investors. Economic value added, however, is a conservative measure of a company's financial performance.

economic value added (EVA)
Measures how much more (or less) a company earns in profits than the minimum amount its investors expect it to earn.

Economic value added (EVA). A measure of financial health that works much like a financial ratio is **economic value added (EVA)**. EVA refers to

[7]J. Bryan Scott, "NASDAQ-100 Revenue per Employee," *www.jbryanscott.com*, February 7, 2009.

how much more (or less) the company earns in profits than the minimum amount its investors expect it to earn. The index can also be regarded as a measure of the company's efficiency in using resources, or its true economic profit. The minimum amount, also known as the *cost of capital*, represents what the company must pay the investors to use their capital. Cost of capital is calculated as the overall percentage cost of the funds used to finance a firm's assets. If the sole source of financing were junk (high risk) bonds that paid investors 7 percent, the cost of capital would be 7 percent. All earnings beyond the minimum are regarded as excess earnings.

For example, assume that investors give their company $2 million to invest and the investor's minimum desired return is 7 percent, or $140,000 per year. The company earns $300,000 per year. The EVA is $160,000, calculated as follows:

Earnings:	$300,000
− Cost of capital:	$140,000 (7% × $2 million capital)
Excess earnings:	$160,000

To put the matter quite simply, if you could earn 3 percent on your investment just by purchasing CDs in a bank, why invest that money in a business that does not return much more than 3 percent? Investors expect higher excess earnings when they invest in a risky venture, such as a company with unproven technology entering a new industry. An example might be manufacturing electronic communication systems for space stations. Investors willing to settle for lower excess earnings usually invest in a company with proven technology in a stable industry, such as construction supplies. EVA is a frequently used control measure because it focuses on creating shareholder value.

Earnings before interest, taxes, depreciation, and amortization (EBITDA). A rough measure of the success of a company is how much it earns after deducting all expenses but interest, taxes, depreciation, and amortization. **EBITDA is earnings before interest, taxes, depreciation, and amortization.** Capital-intensive business firms often report EBITDA to give investors an inkling of available cash before debt payments, taxes, depreciation, and amortization charges.[8] EBITDA has become a well-established measure of the financial success of telecommunications, cable, and media companies.[9] Companies in other fields, including retailing, have begun reporting EBITDA. Dollar General, one of the most expanding retailers in recent years, had a 35 percent increase in EBITDA during the 2008 recession.[10] (Many upscale shoppers went downscale during the Great Recession.)

EBITDA paints an optimistic picture of a company's financial health because it excludes important costs. For example, the United Refining

EBITDA = revenue − expenses (excluding interest, tax and depreciation, amortization)

---

[8]Richard McCaffrey, "The Limits of EBITDA (News—Telecom Sector)," *The Motley Fool* (http://www.fool.com), Copyright © 1995–2006.

[9]"Calculating EBITDA," in Perseus Publishing's *Business: The Ultimate Resource* (Cambridge, MA: Perseus, 2002), p. 677.

[10]Peter Lattman, "Dollar General Is Paying Off for KKR Fund," *The Wall Street Journal*, March 24, 2009, p. B1.

Company at one time reported quarterly net income of $6.1 million and EBITDA of $20.1 million. Imagine how profitable many businesses would be if they did not have to pay taxes.

Pro forma earnings. Another way of "putting lipstick on a pig" is to report earnings that exclude nonrecurring items such as restructuring and merger costs. **Pro forma** is a financial statement that excludes write-downs for goodwill and other one-time charges not relevant to future earnings. A large depreciation cost might also be excluded, such as a computer company downgrading the value of a warehouse full of desktops that are not powerful enough to run Microsoft's latest operating system.

Pro forma is also referred to as "earnings excluding bad-stuff." The use of pro forma earnings has been criticized because it does not follow Generally Accepted Accounting Principles (GAAP). In Amazon.com's early days, when it was struggling to produce a profit, company management published pro forma earnings. Eventually Amazon.com became a highly profitable company and management no longer emphasized pro forma earnings; in this case, the pro forma statement made sense.

Net debt. Yet another measure of the financial health of an organization is how much money it owes after taking into account how much money is on hand to eliminate the debt if necessary. **Net debt** refers to a company's debt minus the cash and cash equivalents it has on hand. The net debt calculation might be considered a cosmetic device to make corporate debt appear slimmer. Yet informing the public that debt could be lowered immediately, if necessary, seems like a reasonable assertion.

pro forma
A financial statement that excludes write-downs or goodwill and other one-time charges not relevant to future earnings.

net debt
A company's debt minus the cash and cash equivalents it has on hand.

MANAGING CASH FLOW AND COST CUTTING

In addition to developing and monitoring the cash budget, many managers pay special attention to keeping cash on hand to prevent overreliance on borrowing and being perceived by investors as a firm in financial trouble. Both cash flow and controlling, or cutting, costs help meet these objectives. We look at these two major business processes separately.

Managing Cash Flow

Cash is so vital to keep almost any type of organization running that it has been analyzed in many ways. **Cash flow** is the amount of net cash generated by a business during a specific period. Although this definition appears straightforward, many other definitions of cash flow add to its complexity. For example, cash flow can also be described as the excess of cash revenues over cash outlays. Another complexity is that cash flow is calculated in many ways. A useful and readily understandable approach is to divide a corporation's cash flow statement into four sections. Three specify different sources of cash; a fourth section combines the first three.[11]

LEARNING OBJECTIVE 6
Explain how managers and business owners manage cash flow and control costs, and use nontraditional measures of financial performance.

cash flow
Amount of net cash generated by a business during a specific period.

---

[11]Anne Tergesen, "The Ins and Outs of Cash Flow," *Business Week,* January 22, 2001.

1. *Cash provided by (or used in) operating activities.* This section indicates how much cash a business uses (a loss), thereby containing clues to the health of earnings. Cash from operating activities is the heart of cash flow and includes subsections: net income, provision for uncollectible money owed to the company, tax benefit from stock options, receivables, inventories, and accounts payable. When most people think of cash flow, they are referring to cash generated by earnings.
2. *Cash provided by (or used in) financing activities.* This section records cash from or paid to outsiders such as banks or stockholders.
3. *Cash provided by (or used in) investing activities.* Recorded here is the cash used to buy or received from selling stock, assets, and businesses, plus capital expenditures.
4. *Summary.* This revealing section lists cash at the beginning and end of the specific period, plus the change in cash position.

A subtle problem with the four types of cash flow listed above is that accounting firms do not always agree with managers as to the definition of *cash.* Of course, money deposited in a bank or in the cash registers or safes is cash, but what about money invested in short-term money market funds, certificates of deposit, or bonds? Are these investments really the equivalent of cash? The Big Four accounting firms are strict about what they count as cash equivalents. Short-term or highly liquid investments are generally classified as cash.[12]

Firms with large cash flows make attractive takeover targets because acquiring firms are likely to use the cash to pay off the cost of the acquisition. A company that does not want to be taken over might deliberately lower its cash flow by taking on a lot of debt. A large cash flow for a business owner contributes to peace of mind because the owner can keep operating without borrowing during a business downturn. During turbulent times, having cash in the bank gives managers a feeling of tranquility. With stocks and other investments being so volatile in recent years, "cash is royalty" is truer than ever. Cash on hand is a key measure of financial well-being. For large companies, having abundant cash available makes purchasing another company at a bargain much more feasible and the acquiring company can act quickly.

Cash flow analysis is well accepted because it provides a more accurate picture of financial health than sales volume. A company frequently makes a sale but then does not receive payment for more than 30 days. Cash flow analysis provides an important tool because it is less subject to distortion than is a statement of revenues. Many managers use the questionable accounting practice of classifying as "revenue" goods in the hands of distributors, which have not yet been sold, and contracts for which no money has yet been exchanged.

---

[12]Steven D. Jones, "Firms Ponder What Constitutes Cash," *The Wall Street Journal*, July 27, 2006, p. C3.

MANAGEMENT IN ACTION

Cash Doesn't Lie

Martin D. Sass, age 67, is chairman of MD Sass, which invests $7 billion mostly via separately managed accounts. He analyzes stocks as if every company could be adding water to its oil tanks. (The analogy relates to a notorious salad oil scandal in 1963 when a company was found storing water in a New Jersey tank farm that supposedly housed soybean oil.) We're not talking about fraud but the difference between reported earnings and cash generation. Investors, he says, get too fixated on the reported earnings. Sometimes, the cash generation is worse than the earnings. Sometimes it's better.

Case in point: Computer game firm Activision Blizzard reported a net of $113 million in one year. But it did better than that. It took in an additional $300 million, mostly for subscriptions to online multiplayer games. It gets the cash now but records the revenue only over time, as the subscriptions run out. Sass owns $40 million of this stock.

"I am religious about cash flow," says Sass, who worked in his father's Brooklyn hardware store as a kid. "To me, it's the most important number." Sass likes companies trading at low multiples of their free cash flow—low, that is, in relation to rivals or to the same company in past years.

Sass is hoping to cash in on the ongoing deterioration of municipal finances. He owns Penn National Gaming and International Gaming Technology, both of which he figures will see increasing orders as state and local governments look to casinos to raise revenue. Penn National trades at eight times free cash flow.

Case Questions
1. What useful message might Sass's investment strategy of looking at cash flow have for practicing managers?
2. When Activision Blizzard receives a payment for a subscription, why shouldn't management report that subscription fee as income right away?
3. What do you think of the ethics of Sass investing in casinos?

Source: Daniel Fisher, "Cash Doesn't Lie," *Forbes*, April 12, 2010, pp. 52, 55.

Cash flow analysis helps keep managers focused on the importance of managing cash. Paying suppliers too quickly wastes money, as does paying too slowly. The latter may lead to penalties or higher prices because the supplier must compensate for late payments. Taking steps to receive prompt payment from customers is an essential part of cash management.

free cash flow

A refinement of cash flow that measures the cash from operations minus capital expenditures.

A refinement of cash flow is **free cash flow**, or the cash from operations minus capital expenditures. The capital expenditures in this context are investments necessary to maintain or expand the company's fixed assets. Free cash flow takes into account the idea that managers should be thinking of needed expenditures, such as purchasing a modern call center, before they brag about how much cash is on hand. Similarly, before calculating how much cash is available, homeowners must set aside a reserve for the inevitable replacement of the roof or the furnace.

A heavy concern with cash flow, or preserving cash, can lead to business practices that some people might consider unsavory, such as the delay of paying bills in order to keep cash on hands as long as possible. Part of the success of Amazon.com has been attributed to its ability to take in money for selling merchandise before paying suppliers. A couple of years, ago Amazon built up cash flow by steadily lengthening the time it consumes before paying suppliers. At one point, the company extended its bill payments to an average of 72 days, up from 63 days a year before. As a result, free cash flow elevated by 116 percent.[13]

The accompanying Management in Action illustrates the importance of a company's cash flow from the standpoint of a financial manager.

Cost Cutting to Improve Financial Health

The ideal way to improve cash flow is to generate more revenue than expenses. However, generating more revenue can be an enormous challenge. For example, additional advertising might not pay off, a new product might flop, and offering huge discounts may evaporate profits. Many companies therefore trim costs to improve cash flow. Even when revenues are increasing, some firms reduce costs to remain more competitive. As you may have noticed, the less cash you spend, the more you have on hand. How do managers know when it is time to cut costs? Obviously, when a firm has low cash flow or is losing money, costs must be cut pronto. In addition, managers can use ratios as rules of thumb. For example, a company might want to keep sales expenses at or below 10 percent of sales.

Here we look at how making the right type of investment can reduce costs and at the potential hazards of cost reduction. Exhibit 15-9 presents a broad sampling of cost-cutting measures.

Investing in Positive Approaches to Cost Reduction

Investing money in the right process or equipment can often lead to useful cost reductions. A small example: If a company invests in a new printer that consumes fewer inkjet or laser cartridges, the company might start saving money within a few months. A bigger example: More than 50 airlines have hired the Pratt & Whitney unit of United Technologies Corp. to wash their engines with a machine that can deep clean while simultaneously collecting and purifying the hazardous runoff. Clean engines burn less fuel, and fuel is the largest component of operating costs.[14]

Investing money in videoconferencing equipment is a widespread practice for reducing travel expenses. At Newell Rubbermaid, Inc., many staff members are encouraged to skip airplanes entirely and use videoconferencing in place of the trips. A company spokesman said, "Employees have realized they don't always need to run off to Europe or wherever to get business done

---

[13]Martin Peers, "Amazon's Astute Timing," *The Wall Street Journal*, October 30, 2009, p. C10.

[14]J. Lynn Lunsford, "Engine Washing Cuts Airline Fuel Costs," *The Wall Street Journal*, June 11, 2008, p. B1.

EXHIBIT 15-9   **A Variety of Ways to Cut Costs**

Saving money can greatly affect profit levels, so managers look for ways to trim costs that do not damage productivity or morale. Annual savings range from a few hundred dollars to millions, depending on the measures used. As noted, cost cutting carried to the extreme can backfire in terms of product quality and morale.

Techniques Focused Mostly on People

- Trim salaries and bonuses by up to 10 percent and ask employees to take one week of unpaid leave during the holiday season. Eliminate cost-of-living allowances. Cut back on health-care insurance for retirees, and freeze their annual pensions. Reduce the number of paid holidays for current employees.
- Include higher-paid workers in a layoff because layoffs focused only on low-wage workers result in less dramatic savings.
- Lay off low–performing workers and hire back sparingly after the layoff; many workers will have adapted their work pace to handle the increased workload. Consider voluntary buyouts, such as giving six months of severance pay, to reduce the headcount.
- Minimize business travel by using e-mail, phone, company Web sites, or videoconferencing when possible. Have business travelers fly coach instead of first class, and stay at budget hotels and motels. Establish per diem rates for meal allowances instead of an open-ended travel account substantiated by receipts.
- Keep offices, factories, and laboratories at the coolest or warmest temperature that does not lower morale or productivity or damage equipment. Encourage employees to wear warm clothing in cold months and light clothing in warm months.
- Establish a telecommuting program to reduce the demand for office space. Use

virtual teams when workers are geographically dispersed.
- Place frequent business travelers on hoteling status, whereby they do not have a permanent office or cubicle when in the office.
- Ask employees to conduct bimonthly brainstorming sessions to find ways to reduce costs. Offer rewards for the best savings.
- Keep on the payroll only those employees who contribute to the goals of the firm. Hire consultants and subcontractors instead of keeping on the payroll employees whose skills are needed only occasionally. Establish a cadre of retired employees who can serve as temporary workers during peak periods.
- Relocate some operations from higher to lower cost-of-living areas, such as from New York to Mississippi or from Ireland to Poland.
- Drop customers who cost you money because of their constant demands for service despite modest purchases.
- Eliminate free coffee and food except for special occasions such as training or Saturday morning meetings.
- Automate wherever possible to reduce payroll costs so long as the automation does not drive away business (such as in many call centers that rely heavily on menus driven by voice recognition).

Techniques Focused Mostly on Material and Equipment

- Use remanufactured parts wherever feasible. As a general rule, 70 percent of the cost to build something new is in the materials, and 30 percent in the labor. Salvaging and rebuilding typically get the material costs down to 40 spercent.[15]

---

[15]Brian Hindo, "Everything Old is New Again," *Business Week*, September 25, 2006, p. 65.

- Compare prices on the Internet before committing to a purchase. Use lower-price office and factory supplies such as less expensive pencils, ball point pens, and latex gloves. Make two-sided photocopies. Save on office expenses by having employees maintain the lawn and carry out refuse to the dumpsters. Eliminate battery-operated office clocks and other battery-operated electronic devices whenever feasible.
- Substitute e-mail messages for postal mail whenever possible. To save on telephone bills, use Internet phones.
- Instead of owning advanced hardware and software, use information technology on demand (cloud computing) to provide for information technology requirements.
- Lease equipment when it is less expensive than owning.
- Demand an immediate 5 percent price cut from all suppliers. (Asking for more is likely to lead to resistance and lower-quality supplies.)
- Hold a sale of surplus and obsolete equipment. At the same time, sell equipment over an Internet auction site.
- Centralize buying for a multilocation company, and ask managers to cart some supplies with them after a visit to headquarters.
- Subcontract manufacturing and services that can be done less expensively by other firms.
- Sell the corporate jet and limousines, and ask executives to fly on commercial airlines and drive their own vehicles for business (or take the bus or train). When it is more economical, have company representatives use their own vehicles at IRS mileage rates instead of renting vehicles.
- Trim box sizes for USPS shipments to save on postage costs and for FedEx and UPS.

- Close unprofitable retail stores, and relocate from shopping malls to areas of lower rent (if the relocation does not drive away customers).
- Introduce only those new products or services that appear to have a high probability of success.

Techniques Focused Mostly on Money Management

- Centralize purchasing to obtain better prices on bulk purchases, as done by Home Depot and many other large, geographically dispersed firms. At the same time, reduce the number of suppliers to obtain volume discounts (each surviving vendor will get more business).
- Try eBay and other auction sites when making purchases, or use a reverse auction in which suppliers bid on providing you the equipment or supplies you need.
- Ask suppliers for discounts on early payments. If the discounts are not granted, pay all bills including taxes, utilities, and suppliers as late as possible without incurring a fee. In this way, you earn a return on the money rather than someone else.
- Share office expenses and support services with other small businesses. Rent a large office space together, and divide it into offices for each firm.
- Use activity-based costing to help trim costs that do not add value for customers.
- Consolidate advertising and marketing with one agency to earn volume discounts.
- Use a "sweep" checking account that places your unused balances in a relatively high-paying money market account overnight.

effectively."[16] Nevertheless, there are times when an in-person meeting with an out-of-town customer is a good investment, because the human touch is needed to close a deal or resolve a problem.

The story at the outset of the chapter about how investing in health-care benefits saved the restaurant chain money is another illustration of a positive approach to cost reduction. Many human-resource managers believe that an investment in the physical and mental health of employees saves money in the long run. Experience with wellness programs has convinced many business leaders that investing in disease prevention and wellness programs reduces costs associated with health problems.[17]

Automation in general is a positive investment that often reduces costs, such as the reduction in the number of store associates required with automated, self-service checkout counters. The lean manufacturing movement exemplifies how investing in automation can reduce costs. For example, many manufacturing plants operated by Parker Hannifin Corp require only a handful of workers or only a single highly trained worker. As a result, revenue per employee has moved up from $125,000 to $200,000 during a nine-year period.[18]

Potential Hazards of Cost Reduction

A caution about cost cutting is that it can lead to low morale and lower-quality goods and services. It can also foster the image of a cheap company. For example, using old newspapers as packing material is environmentally friendly and saves money, but this practice does not fit with a high-quality image.

A dramatic example of the possible negative side effects of cost cutting took place at Toyota during 2010. Eight million automobiles were recalled due to mechanical failures associated by U.S. regulators with 51 deaths. Previous to Toyota officials knowing that runaway acceleration was causing the crashes, a company executive said that a simple manufacturing process would sometimes ignite small fires in a component as a direct result of cost cutting. The fire was just one sign that the cost cutting that had squeezed more than $10 billion from global operating costs in six years had gone too far. At one point, Jim Press, the top Toyota executive in the United States, warned his superiors in Japan that vehicle quality was slipping.[19]

In fairness to Toyota, the company still has millions of satisfied customers and some of the accidents involving stuck accelerators were attributed to driver error (such as placing the right foot on the accelerator instead of the brake pedal while in a state of panic).

---

[16]Mike Esterl, "More Lucrative Business Travelers Now Teleconference, Fly Coach," *The Wall Street Journal*, February 18, 2010, p. B1.

[17]Jennifer Schramm, "Wellness: Health's Keystone," *HR Magazine*, January 2010, p. 68.

[18]Timothy Aeppl and Justin Lahart, "Lean Factories Find It Hard to Cut Jobs Even in a Slump," *The Wall Street Journal*, March 9, 2009, p. A1.

[19]Alan Ohnsman, Jeff Green, and Kae Inoue, "The Humbling of Toyota," *Bloomberg Business Week*, March 22 and 29, 2010, pp. 33–34.

Another classic case of cost cutting gone too far was Circuit City, now bankrupt. Its brand name was bought by an online retailer. The company laid off 3,400 experienced workers and replaced them with new hires at lower pay. Company executives were so focused on cutting costs that they underestimated the real value of effective store associates. Shoppers quickly noticed the deterioration in customer service and stopped patronizing Circuit City.[20]

Yet another example here of the potential unintended dysfunctional consequences of cost cutting apparently took place at BP, leading up to the fatal April 20, 2010 blowout of the Deepwater Horizon oil rig in the Gulf of Mexico. The explosion killed eleven people and triggered the biggest offshore oil spill in U.S. history and shortly became one of the worst environmental disasters in recorded history. The House Energy and Commerce Committee concluded that BP PLC engineers made a series of cost-savings decisions that ran counter to the advice of contractors in the days before the explosion.

"Time after time, it appears that BP made decisions that increased the risk of a blowout to save the company time or expense," stated the Committee report. Specific cost-savings that backfired included the company's uncommon well design and its fatal decision not to fully circulate drilling mud (which could have cleared out pockets of gas). Furthermore, BP personnel skipped critical testing, which could have pinpointed problems with the well's cementing.[21]

We caution about managers resorting to cost-cutting measures that make the company appear cheap. The situation is worsened when everybody but top-level managers and selected professionals is expected to trim costs. Cynicism can mount, as illustrated by the following fictitious lodging standard for business travel:[22]

> *All employees are encouraged to stay with relatives and friends while on business travel. If weather permits, public areas such as parks should be used as temporary lodging sites. Bus terminals, train stations, and office lobbies may provide shelter in periods of inclement weather.*

NONTRADITIONAL MEASURES OF FINANCIAL PERFORMANCE

As managers continue to look for ways to measure the financial performance of the companies or units they manage, several nontraditional measures of

---

[20]Rachel Beck, "Slash and Burn Backfires for Circuit City," Associate Press, January 14, 2008.

[21]Erika Bolstad, "BP Note: Rig was 'Nightmare Well,'" McClatchy Newspapers, June 15, 201; Neil King Jr., and Russell Gold, "BP Crew Focused On Costs: Congress," *The Wall Street Journal*, June 15, 2010, p. A1.

[22]"Work Place Notices: New Corporate Cost-Cutting Policy," http://www.home.att.net/~angry_old_man/, accessed January 14, 2007.

financial performance have emerged. Four such indicators are the balanced scorecard, activity-based costing, the measurement of intellectual capital, and relative standing against the competition.

The Balanced Scorecard

balanced scorecard
A set of measures to provide a quick but comprehensive view of the business.

Many researchers and managers have abandoned their exclusive reliance on financial ratios and related indices to measure the health of a firm. Managers continue to look for ways to overcome the limited view of performance sometimes created by budgets. An accounting professor and a technology consultant worked with hundreds of companies to devise a **balanced scorecard**—a management system that enables organizations to clarify their vision and strategy and translate them into action.[23] Managers using the balanced scorecard do not rely on short-term financial measures as the only indicators of a company's performance. The balanced scorecard is a strategic approach and performance management system that helps an organization set goals and measure performance from four perspectives that are vital to all businesses, as outlined in Exhibit 15-10.

The balanced scorecard continues to help companies widen their horizon about what constitutes success. A recent application of the scorecard is to help alliances work more effectively. Only about 50 percent of alliances are successful. Most are defined by service level agreements that identify what each side agrees to deliver rather than what each hopes to gain from the partnership. The balanced scorecard helps the partners in the alliance evolve their focus from contributions and operations to strategy and commitment. For example, building a strategy map can help a company see how attaining objectives at department levels helps the firm achieve business-process, customer, and ultimately financial objectives.[24] (Refer again to Exhibit 15-10.)

The balanced scorecard supports a strategy to the extent that it directs the company effort toward achieving the four goals of financial health, customer satisfaction, business processes, and learning and growth. Internal business processes are the mechanisms through which performance expectations are achieved. An example of an internal business process would be building products and services to meet customer requirements. Compensation is based on achieving all the factors included in the balanced scorecard. Many managers attend seminars given by the Balanced Scorecard Institute to guide them in using the balanced scorecard approach.

---

[23]Robert S. Kaplan and David P. Norton, "Using the Balanced Scorecard as a Strategic Management System," *Harvard Business Review*, January–February 1996, pp. 75–77; Kaplan and Norton, "Clarifying and Communicating Vision and Strategy into Action: The BSC Framework," http://www.valuebasedmanagement.net, September 27, 2006.

[24]Kaplan, Norton, and Bjarne Rugelsjoen, "Managing Alliances with the Balanced Scoreboard, *Harvard Business Review*, January–February 2010, pp. 114–120.

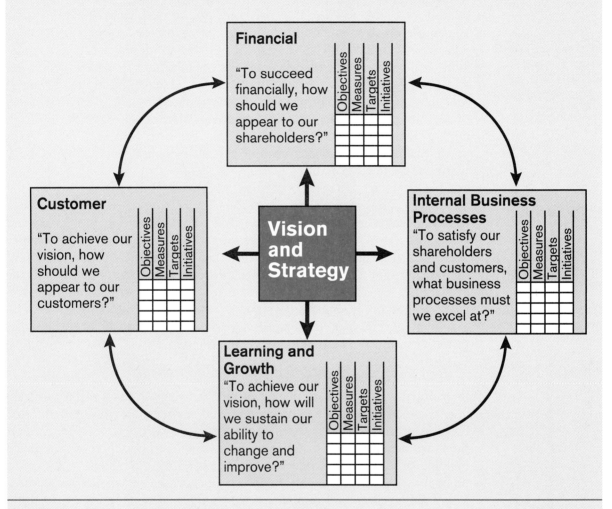

EXHIBIT 15-10   The Official Model for the Balanced Scorecard

The balanced scorecard suggests that we view the organization from *four* perspectives and that we develop metrics, collect data, and analyze it relative to each of these perspectives:

- The Learning and Growth Perspective
- The Business Process Perspective
- The Customer Perspective
- The Financial Perspective

Source: "The Balanced Scorecard Institute," http://www.balancedscorecard.org.

---

activity-based costing (ABC)

An accounting procedure that allocates the costs of producing a product or service to the activities performed and the resources used.

Activity-Based Costing

Concerns that conventional methods of measuring financial performance may be misleading prompt the use of another approach to understanding the true costs involved in conducting business. **Activity-based costing (ABC)** is an accounting procedure that allocates the costs of producing a product or service to the activities performed and the resources used. An activity-based costing system offers managers a more strategic approach to their business because it presents a comprehensive view of all the costs involved in making a product or service and getting it to market.[25]

Among these costs would be research and development, marketing, and delivery. In contrast, a more traditional cost system might focus most on costs such as labor, parts, and administrative overhead. Some ABC systems rank activities by the degree to which they add value to the organization or its outputs. For example, at UPS the truck driver might add more value to the service than the fuel, truck maintenance, or human-resource support.

Activity-based costing is used in both the public and the private sectors. For example, many combat activities within the Department of Defense have been using cost-per-unit measures for a long time. Among these applications are Air Force units that manage with the measure *cost per flying hour*. The Navy manages in *cost per streaming hour* and the Army in *cost per tank mile*.[26] All three measures involve costs such as research and development time, salaries, deterioration of equipment, and support workers back at the base. Treating military personnel for stress disorders might be part of *cost per tank mile*.

By using activity-based costing, managers can assess the productivity of products and business units by assigning costs based on the use of company-wide resources. The profitability of customers can also be assessed: Some customers use up so many resources that they are not profitable. Is it worth selling a $45 pair of shoes to a customer who tries on 20 pairs before making a decision? Similarly, an industrial customer might be unprofitable because he or she requires too much service.

How does activity-based costing work in practice? Let's assume a company introduces two new cell phone models. One phone is used for general purposes, including photos and video clips. The other phone is a waterproof model targeted at people who are so attached to technology, or are in such demand, that they want a cell phone that works in the shower or in a swimming pool. The manufacturing cost is $100 for the conventional model and $130 for the shower model. However, the activity-based cost is $125 for the conventional model and $400 for the shower model. The difference represents the resources used and the people consulted in order to make the shower model as safe as possible for its intended use. The wet-look model also requires extensive consultation with the legal staff to iron out any possible product liability claims.

The calculations in activity-based costing follow the calculations in traditional accounting, except that ABC might take into account more materials and processes in determining costs. As shown in Exhibit 15-11, the average unit cost is calculated by dividing the total cost of production by the total

---

[25]Robin Cooper and Robert S. Kaplan, "The Promise—and Peril—of Integrated Cost Systems," *Harvard Business Review*, July–August 1998, p. 111.

[26]"Activity-Based Costing Concept Paper: Accounting for Operational Readiness," http://www.dod.mil/comptroller/icenter, accessed January 15, 2007.

EXHIBIT 15-11   Measuring Unit Costs with Activity-Based Costing

Unit Cost: Aligning costs to outputs and increasing cost visibility

Identify Cost of Inputs

Labor + Machinery + Raw Materials

Process

Determine Cost per Unit of Output

Total Output
Determine Total Cost

$$\frac{\text{Total Cost}}{\text{Total Output}}$$

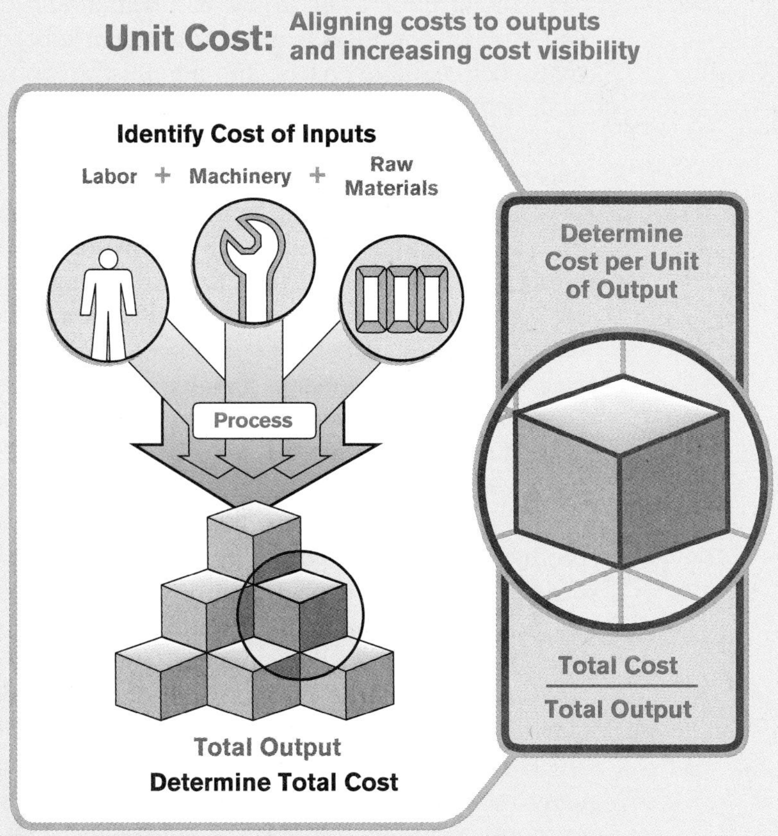

Source: "Accounting for Operational Readiness," http://www.dod.mil/comptroller/icenter/learn/abconcept.htm, accessed January 15, 2007.

number of units of output produced. You will find many good uses in your career for this handy formula.

Measurement of Intellectual Capital

Activity-based costing is but one advance in measuring the financial performance of a firm. A more radical approach regards employee brainpower as a major contributor to the wealth of an organization. This approach makes some attempt to measure **intellectual capital**, which is the value of useful ideas and the people who generate them. In brief, intellectual capital is knowledge and the basis for knowledge management. If you are smart and talented, you are probably worth more to a company than its new business jet. Components of intellectual capital include employee knowledge, patents, and research.

intellectual capital
The value of useful ideas and the people who generate them.

A Columbia University study estimates that investing in intangible assets such as research and development and employee education and training yields a return eight times greater than an equal investment in new plants and equipment. The reason is that new machinery only allows for incremental improvements. Research and development and employee education lead to innovations that bring competitive advantage.[27]

The difficult part of using intellectual capital to measure value comes in trying to attach a reliable value to a group of programmers, for example, and the software they produce. In traditional accounting methods, a fleet of company trucks would receive a higher valuation than the company's software. Intellectual assets are found throughout a firm. An office assistant who has a good feel for customer preference is also a valuable asset, even if this value is difficult to measure. Setting such valuation raises a number of issues because the company does not own the office assistant who can leave at will.

Robert Howell, a professor of finance and accounting, believes that the real assets of a knowledge-intensive company are the know-how of its workforce, intellectual property (such as its patents), brand equity, and relationships with employees, customers, and suppliers. As a starting point as to how these might be valued, Howell says, "At a minimum, I would book as assets such costs as recruitment and training and development and amortize them over some sort of employment life. Why aren't they as much of an asset as some piece of machinery?"[28]

If you are a manager and you want to help your company preserve intellectual capital, it is important to keep smart people happy and satisfied. The many human-resource initiatives described in Chapter 9 would be helpful, as well as day-by-day effective leadership.

Relative Standing against the Competition

Performance success is often measured by comparing this year's results with those attained the previous years, such as sales increase or decrease in operating costs. Andrew Likierman, the dean of London Business School, suggests that comparing one's performance against the competition is more meaningful. For example, if your sales decreased 5 percent this year, you might be doing quite well if your two biggest competitors experienced decreases of 9 percent and 8 percent.

Likierman also suggests that measuring performance in terms of anticipated market share is a valuable performance metric. One way to obtain

---

[27]"Intellectual Capital: How Top Performing Companies are Measuring the Intangible," http://www.best-in-class.com/research/bestpracticespotlights/intellectual_capital_20.htm, accessed July 9, 2004.

[28]Quoted in Thomas A. Stewart, "Accounting Gets Radical," *Fortune*, April 16, 2001, p. 192. Much of the discussion of intellectual capital is based on the entire article, pp. 184–194.

such information is to ask customers. Enterprise, the car-rental company, relies on the Enterprise Service Quality Index, which measures the intention of customers to return. An employee at each Enterprise branch phones a random sample of customers and asks whether they plan to use Enterprise again. When the index rises, the company is gaining market share; when it falls, other rental companies will be getting a piece of the Enterprise business. Branch managers place the results next to profitability numbers on monthly financial statements and factor them into criteria for promotion.[29] (We caution here that customer surveys should not be taken too frequently because they can be annoying.)

LEARNING OBJECTIVE 7
Describe how an information system contributes to control.

information system (or management information system)
A formal system for providing management with information useful or necessary for making decisions.

INFORMATION SYSTEMS AND CONTROL

An **information system (IS)**, or **management information system (MIS)**, is a formal system for providing management with information useful or necessary for making decisions. A managerial control based on valid information makes an effective IS an indispensable part of any control system. The next sections describe how an information system can be used to control and monitor work electronically.

EXHIBIT 15-12 Examples of Control Information Supplied by Information Systems

Information systems can:

- Report on sales of products by territory, sales representative, and customer category
- Supply inventory-level information by region, plant, and department
- Describe magazine subscribers by age, income, occupational level, and ZIP code
- Report turnover rates by age, sex, job title, and salary level
- Supply information about budget deviations by location, department, and manager
- Automatically compile financial ratios and compare them to industry standards
- Automatically compile production and operation control indexes and compare them from plant to plant
- Print out a summary of overdue accounts according to customers, and goods or services purchased
- Report hospital-bed occupancy rates according to diagnosis, sex, and age of patients
- Report when sudden increases in absenteeism occur, suggesting that employee stress levels are unacceptably high
- Calculate, by subsidiary, the return on investment of cash surpluses
- Make, using the Internet, price comparisons for goods and services
- Estimate how baby boomers are likely to retire within the next five years, thereby providing clues to upcoming recruiting needs

---

[29]Andrew Likierman, "The Five Traps of Performance Measurement," *Harvard Business Review*, October 2009, p. 98.

Control Information Supplied by an Information System

The control information that can be generated by an information system is virtually unlimited. Exhibit 15-12 shows a sampling of what an IS keeps track of. A company-specific example is Southland Corp., which owns and franchises the 7-Eleven convenience stores. Its computerized information system tracks inventory and forecasts sales. The system can precisely track 2,300 items and help individual stores stock the right number of items such as Slurpees and low-fat turkey breast on pita. Another advantage of the information system is that it can help analyze sales trends on such factors as time of day, weather, and socioeconomic level of the neighborhood. A computer information system of this type can help the individual store manager and owner cope with the major problems of overstocking perishable items and understocking hot items—such as beer, soft drinks, and snacks in response to a major sports event on television.

Computer-Aided Monitoring of Work

computer-aided monitoring of work

A computer-based system to monitor the work habits and productivity of employees.

Information systems are widely used for **computer-aided monitoring of work**. In this type of monitoring, a computer-based system gathers data about the work habits and productivity of employees. The content of electronic messages is also frequently monitored. Employee monitoring systems capitalize on the networking of computer terminals to monitor the work of employees who use computer terminals in their jobs or who operate complex machine tools. Once the monitoring software is installed, the central computer processes information from each terminal and records the employee's efficiency and effectiveness.

A factor contributing to electronic monitoring of work is that an increasing number of employees conduct their work far from their manager's gaze, including at home and in hotel rooms. In the face of global competition and tight budgets, managers are forced to boost worker productivity. Another argument in favor of the use of electronic monitoring is that electronic evidence plays an important role in lawsuits and regulator investigations including insider trading.

Workers Most Likely to Be Monitored

Office workers, including those in frequent telephone contact with the public, are the most likely to be monitored. Word-processing specialists are measured by such factors as words keyed per minute, the number of breaks taken, and the duration of each break. The reservation center for JetBlue Airways consists of 700 reservation agents who work from home using computers and phone systems provided by the company. JetBlue management is able to attain exceptional productivity with the assistance of software that enables it to track each agent's telephone activity. When an agent receives a call, the telephone system logs data such as the duration of the call, who hangs up first, and whether the agent is immediately available to answer another call. To monitor quality, every month a supervisor listens to about ten calls, recorded at random, for each worker supervised.[30]

Computer-aided monitoring is also used for purposes of data-loss prevention—the unauthorized transmission of sensitive data to company outsiders. Leaks are a major concern in health care and law, and also in product development and marketing. Software such as SecureCare keeps track of all computer activities, including the use of detachable devices such as USB flash drives. The software can be set to automatically enforce security policies, including the blocking of certain phrases.[31] An example of a phrase that might be blocked would be "Great new product coming down the pike."

A general guideline is that high-technology monitoring tools can be applied best with workers who perform discrete, measurable tasks during prescribed hours, such as employees in call centers, finance departments, and insurance claims. Monitoring workers whose jobs primarily involve thinking is much more difficult. For example, a chemist might be looking out the window with his feet on the desk—yet at the same time developing an idea for a drug that will prevent high blood pressure. When monitoring is used for purposes of data-loss prevention, whether work is measurable is irrelevant.

Concerns about Electronic Monitoring Systems

The major advantage of an electronic monitoring system is the close supervision it allows managers. Some employees welcome computerized monitoring because it supplements arbitrary judgments by supervisors about their productivity. Computerized work-monitoring systems have substantial disadvantages, however. Many argue that these systems invade employee privacy and violate their dignity. As a result, lawsuits are being filed against companies. Electronic monitoring often contributes to low levels of job satisfaction, absenteeism, high turnover, and job stress.

As the technology of computer-aided monitoring of work becomes more advanced, it raises concerns about privacy issues. Many employees object to being monitored on password-protected sites when they are using nonwork computers and smart phones.[32] For example, a worker might think he has the right to express his frustration with his job and supervisor by posting a Tweet via his BlackBerry during a rest break. The company might think otherwise.

Another concern about electronic monitoring is that executives are usually not monitored even though they are in a better position than other

---

[30]The information about JetBlue and the few preceding statements are from Riva Richmond, "It's 10 a.m. Do You Know Where Your Workers Are?" *The Wall Street Journal*, January 12, 2004, pp. R1, R4.

[31]Amanda C. Kooser, "On Watch," *Entrepreneur*, September 8, 2008, p. 31.

[32]Dionne Searcey, "Employers Watching Workers Online Spurs Privacy Debate," *The Wall Street Journal*, April 27, 2009, p. A13.

workers to commit fraud such as stealing company money and selling trade secrets. Finally, some people are concerned that members of the IT group involved in security have too much power to monitor the electronic communications of other workers. For example, a worker shopping for lingerie on the Internet during the workday could be accused of accessing pornography by a vindictive information technology specialist.

The results of computer-aided monitoring of work are often used to take action that seems unduly harsh against employees who violate company rules. A survey about electronic monitoring and surveillance involving 526 companies indicated that 25 percent of the organizations surveyed fired workers for misusing the Internet, 25 percent terminated employees for e-mail abuse, and 6 percent were fired for misusing office phones. Over 80 percent of the companies surveyed inform employees that the surveillance will take place and post policies about e-mail and Internet use.[33]

Gaining Acceptance for Computer-Aided Monitoring

A study with young workers provides some understanding of when electronic monitoring will be the best accepted. Seasonal high school and college students were surveyed about their reaction to being monitored in their work at a summer amusement water park. In one condition of the study, lifeguards were told in advance that they would be monitored to maintain safety standards and to reduce insurance costs. The lifeguards were even told when the detectives with their video cameras would be on the scene. In the other condition, a group of private detectives posed as customers of the water park and surreptitiously videotaped ticket agents, food service, and gift shop employees. The workers had more favorable attitudes toward the surveillance when they were given advance notice of the system.[34] (Would you have predicted these results?)

An important recommendation to managers about electronic monitoring of workers is to establish an Acceptable Usage Policy and an employee monitoring policy. The usage policy defines appropriate as well as inappropriate use of corporate resources, including the use of telecommunication devices. For example, setting up an eBay business with your employer's desktop is out of bounds. The monitoring policy explains exactly where and when inappropriate Internet access is blocked and when the company monitors telephone, computer, and Internet usage.[35]

---

[33]Survey results reported in Javad Heydary, "Companies Step Up Electronic Monitoring of Employees," *Ecommerce Times* (http://www.ecommercetimes.com), July 21, 2005.

[34]Audra D. Hovorka-Mead, William H. Ross Jr., Tracy Whipple, and Michella B. Renchin, "Watching the Detectives: Seasonal Student Employee Reactions to Electronic Monitoring With and Without Advance Notification," *Personnel Psychology*, Summer 2002, pp. 329–362.

[35]Gary S. Millefsky, "Employee Monitoring Facts Every CIO Should Know," *http://www. SearchCIO.com,* July 25, 2006, p. 3.

CHARACTERISTICS OF EFFECTIVE CONTROLS

An effective control system improves job performance and productivity by helping workers correct problems. A system that achieves these outcomes possesses distinct characteristics. The greater the number of the following characteristics a given control system contains, the better the system will be at providing management with useful information and improved performance:

1. *The controls must be accepted.* For control systems to increase productivity, employees must cooperate with the system. If employees are more intent on beating the system than on improving performance, controls will not achieve their ultimate purpose. For example, the true purpose of a time-recording system is to ensure that employees work a full day. If workers are intent on circumventing the system through such means as having friends punch in and out for them, the time-recording system will not increase productivity.

2. *The control measures must be appropriate and meaningful.* People tend to resist control measures that they believe do not relate to performance in a meaningful way. The number of visitors to a Web site is sometimes used as a performance measure for the developers of the site. A glitzy Web site might attract a lot of traffic because it is recommended by network members to each other, yet the visitors may not necessarily purchase from the merchants advertising on the site. For the Web site to continue to generate ad revenues, a more meaningful performance measure is the number of visitors who click on the advertisers' links and make a purchase. A less glitzy site that attracts fewer but more serious buyers would indicate that the Web site developer is doing a better job.

3. *An effective control measure provides diagnostic information.* If controls are to improve performance, they must help people correct deviations from performance. A sales manager might be told that he or she was performing well in all categories except selling to small-business owners. This information might prompt the manager to determine and emphasize services the company sells that have more appeal to small businesses.

4. *Effective controls allow for self-feedback and self-control.* A self-administering control system saves considerable time. Employees can do much of their own controlling if the system permits them access to their own feedback. An example is a system whereby clients complain directly to the employee instead of going to management.

5. *Effective control systems provide timely information.* Controls lead to positive changes in behavior if the control information is available quickly. It is more helpful to give workers daily rather than monthly estimates of their performance against quota. Given day-by-day feedback, an employee can make quick adjustments. If feedback is withheld until the end of a month or a quarter, the employee may be too discouraged to make improvements.

6. *Control measures are more effective when employees have control over the results measured.* People rebel when held responsible for performance deviations beyond their control. For example, a resort hotel manager's profits might fall below expectations because of a factor beyond his or her control such as a sudden shift in weather that results in cancellations.

7. *Effective control measures do not contradict each other.* Employees are sometimes asked to achieve two contradictory sets of standards. As a result, they resist the control system. Employees told to increase both quantity and quality, for example, may experience confusion and chaos. A compromise approach would be to improve quality with the aim of increasing net quantity in the long run. Care taken in doing something right the first time results in less rework. With less time spent on error correction, eventually the quantity of goods produced increases.

8. *Effective controls allow for random variations from standard.* If a control allows for random variations that do not differ significantly from the standard, then it is more effective. An ineffective way of using a control system is to quickly take action at the first deviation from acceptable performance. A one-time deviation may not indicate a genuine problem. It could simply be a random or insignificant variation that may not be repeated for years. For example, would you take action if a team member exceeded a $3,000 travel expense allowance by $2.78?

9. *Effective controls are cost-effective.* Control systems should result in satisfactory returns on investment. In many instances they don't because the costs of control are too high. Having recognized this fact, some fast-service restaurants allow employees to eat all the food they want during working hours. The cost of trying to control illicit eating is simply too high. (This policy provides the added benefit of building worker morale.)

10. *The controls do not limit innovation.* Controls aimed at the executive level can sometimes restrict innovation because they emphasize short-term profit at the expense of investing money in ways that might pay off in the future. The emphasis on short-term earnings per share helps boost the stock price but may restrict investments in long-term growth opportunities.[36] A CEO whose success is measured by this quarter's profits might think, "Why spend $4 million on research and development that might never pay off when I can look good by reporting the $4 million as profit for this quarter?"

In short, the intelligent and sensible use of controls enhances organizational and individual effectiveness without creating morale problems and resentment. Managers must control and lead at the same time.

---

[36]Clayton M. Christensen, Stephen P. Kaufman, and Wily C. Shih, "Innovation Killers: How Financial Tools Destroy Your Capacity to Do New Things," *Harvard Business Review*, January 2008, pp. 98–105.

Summary of Key Points

1 **Explain how controlling relates to the other management functions.**

Controlling is used to evaluate whether the manager is effective in job planning, organizing, and leading. Controls can also be used to evaluate control systems.

2 **Understand the different types and strategies of controls.**

Controls can be classified according to when they are applied. Preventive controls are applied prior to the performance of an activity. Concurrent controls monitor activities while they are being carried out. Feedback controls evaluate and prompt corrective action after activity performance.

Controls can also be classified according to their underlying strategy. An external control strategy is based on the assumption that employees are primarily motivated by external rewards and must be controlled by their managers. An internal control strategy assumes that managers can motivate employees by building commitment to organizational goals.

3 **Describe the steps in the control process.**

The steps in the controlling process include setting standards, measuring actual performance, comparing actual performance to standards, and taking corrective action if necessary. Before measuring performance, agreement must be reached on the aspects of performance to be measured, the degree of accuracy needed, and who will use the measurements.

The three courses of action open to a manager are to do nothing, to solve the problem, or to revise the standard. Taking corrective action only on significant deviations is called the *exception principle*.

4 **Explain the use of nonbudgetary control techniques.**

Nonbudgetary control techniques can be qualitative or quantitative. Qualitative techniques include audits, personal observation, and performance evaluation. The auditing process has come under considerable scrutiny in recent years because of many cases of unethical and illegal reporting of financial information by business firms. Quantitative techniques include Gantt charts, PERT, and economic-order quantity.

5 **Have an awareness of the various types of budgets and the use of budgets and financial ratios for control.**

A budget is a spending plan for a future period of time, expressed in numerical terms. A fixed budget allocates expenditures based on a one-time allocation of resources. A flexible budget allows variation in the use of resources based on the level of activity. Eight types of budgets are summarized in Exhibit 15-7 for reference purposes. Budgets function as a natural part of controlling. Managers use budgets to compare planned expenditures to actual expenditures, and they take corrective action if the deviation is significant.

Four key financial ratios are gross profit margin, profit margin, return on equity, and revenue per employee. Other ways of measuring financial performance are economic value added (EVA); EBITDA, revenue – expenses (interest, taxes, depreciation, and amortization); pro forma earnings; and net debt.

6 **Explain how managers and business owners manage cash flow and control costs and use nontraditional measures of financial performance.**

Closely tied in with the cash budget is the special attention managers pay to cash flow. Cash flow measures how much actual cash is available for conducting business. The three sections of a cash-flow statement are cash provided by (or used in) operating activities, financing activities, and investing activities. A firm that writes off many income deductions will have a bigger cash flow. Many companies trim costs to improve cash flow. Too much cost cutting can lead to low morale, low quality, and a company image of cheapness.

Many researchers and managers no longer rely exclusively on financial ratios and related indices to measure the health of a firm. Instead, they use a balanced scorecard that measures the various aspects of an organization's performance and is also a management system for implementing vision and strategy. Activity-based costing offers another approach to measuring financial performance that goes beyond traditional measures. The method focuses on the activities performed and the resources used to deliver a product or service. Two other approaches to determining a firm's wealth measure intellectual capital, or the brainpower of a firm, and relative standing against the competition.

 Describe how an information system contributes to control.

An information system (IS), or management information system (MIS), is a formal system for providing management with information useful or necessary for making decisions. The IS provides considerable information used for control. Information systems are also used for the electronic monitoring of the work habits and productivity of employees and the content of electronic messages

(such as data retention by the company). Although the method helps managers monitor employee performance and protect secrecy, it has met with considerable criticism. An effective monitoring policy explains exactly where and when inappropriate Internet access is blocked and when the company monitors telephone, computer, and Internet usage.

 Specify several characteristics of effective controls.

An effective control system results in improved job performance and productivity because it helps people correct problems. An effective control measure is accepted by workers, is considered appropriate, provides diagnostic information, allows for self-feedback and self-control, and provides timely information. It also allows employees some control over the behavior measured, does not embody contradictory measures, allows for random variation, is cost-effective, and does not limit innovation.

Key Terms and Phrases

Questions

1. Provide an example of how feedback from customers can be used as part of a control system.
2. Tony works full-time as a computer-repair technician who makes onsite repairs for individuals and small businesses. He says his gross profit margin is 94 percent because last year his total revenues were $100,000 and his expenses were $6,000. "I'm actually doing better than Microsoft. They talk about gross profit margins of 80

percent," says Tony. What is wrong with Tony's estimate of his gross profit margin?

3. How does EVA give a company a more accurate picture of its profitability than does profit margin?

4. Prominent CEOs and management scholars have often said, "You can't achieve greatness by cutting costs." What are these people talking about?

5. Managers of some small businesses save costs by eliminating most of the land-line telephones and require that employees use their personal cell phones to make most business calls. What do you see as the advantages and disadvantages of this approach to cost cutting?

6. What type of intellectual capital do you think you provide, or will be providing, an employer?

7. In several companies, a performance standard for maintenance technicians is to have relatively few demands for service from the manufacturing department. Explain the logic behind this performance standard.

Skill-Building Exercise 15-A: Constructive and Destructive Cost Cutting

Using in-person interviews, phone conversations, e-mail, blogs, or social networking sites, do some live research on cost cutting with several individuals. Ask your respondents for examples of useful, or constructive, cost cutting they have observed on the job. You might include yourself as an interviewee for this exercise. Do the same for useless, or destructive, cost cutting. Look for patterns. What type of cost-cutting measure is likely to be well accepted by workers? What type of cost-cutting measure is likely to be resisted by workers?

Skill-Building Exercise 15-B: Financial Ratios

Jessica Albanese invested a $50,000 inheritance as equity in a franchise print and copy shop. Similar to well-established national franchises, the shop also offers desktop publishing, digital printing, and

ITEM	FINANCIAL RESULT
Revenues	$255,675
Beginning inventory	15,500
Purchases	88,000
End inventory	14,200
Cost of goods sold	89,300
Gross profit	166,375
Salaries expense	47,000
Rents and utilities expense	6,500
Miscellaneous expense	1,100
Maintenance expense	750
Total operating expenses	55,350
Net income before taxes	111,025
Taxes (40 percent)	44,410
Net income	66,615

computer graphics services. Jessica's revenue-and-expense statement for her first year of operation is in the previous page.

Working individually or in small groups, compute the following ratios: gross profit margin, profit margin (return on sales), and return on equity. Groups might compare answers. Discuss whether you think that Jessica is operating a worthwhile business.

Management Now: Online Skill-Building Exercise: Computing Financial Ratios of Public Companies

Here is an opportunity to analyze the finances of one of your favorite companies. Go to http://www. hoovers.com and search for your favorite brand of clothing or car or another interesting company. Use the most current financial information given in Hoover's, including the section on additional financial information. Compute as many of the financial ratios presented in this chapter as you can with the information available. Based on your analyses, what is your opinion of the financial health of the company that you researched? What recommendations can you make to management?

15-A Case Problem

Mr. Potato Head Visits Starbucks

Starbucks Corp. built its business as the anti-fast food café. The Great Recession and growing competition a few years ago forced the coffeehouse giant to see the virtues of behaving like its streamlined competitors. Under an initiative put into practice at its U.S. stores, there would be no more bending over to scoop coffee from below the counter, no more idle moments waiting for expired coffee to drain, and no more dillydallying at the pastry case.

Pushing the Starbucks's drive is Scott Heydon, the company's "vice president of lean thinking." He and a 10-person "lean team" were going from region to region armed with a stopwatch and a Mr. Potato Head toy that they challenge managers to put together and re-box in less than 45 seconds.

Heydon says reducing waste will free up times for baristas—or "partners"—to interact with customers and improve the Starbucks experience. "Motion and work are two different things. Thirty percent of the partners' time is motion; the walking, the talking, reaching, bending," he says. He wants to lower that. If Starbucks can reduce the time each employee spends making a drink, he says, the company could make more drinks with the same number of workers or have fewer workers. One of Starbucks' biggest expenses is store labor, which costs about 24 percent of revenue annually.

The company began testing lean methods in Oregon. One of the first stores was managed by Tara Jordan, in Oregon City. "In my eyes, we couldn't get better," says Jordan. Her store boasts one of the fastest Starbucks drive-through windows in the company, with an average time per order of 25 seconds. To help her understand how work can be done more efficiently, Kim Landreth, a member of the lean team, brought a Mr. Potato Head to Jordan's store and sprinkled the ears, nose, lips, and other accessories across several tables.

Using a stop watch, Landreth timed how long it took Jordan to assemble the toy and place it in its box. It took more than a minute. Landreth than asked her to think about how she could complete the task faster. Moving items closer together shaved time, as did altering the order of assembly. Over the course of two hours, Jordan amended the time: about 16 seconds. "That really opened my eyes," she says.

The next project: observing the area where blended drinks, such as frappuccinos, are made. "I thought it was going to be the best station in my store," Jordan said. "What I saw was how much my partners were moving and reaching for things that were never made in the same place. It took way too long to make one beverage," she says.

They moved all but the most commonly ordered syrup flavors and store pitchers closer to where drinks are made. After learning that topping the drinks with whipped cream and chocolate or caramel drizzle at the drink station was slowing down production, they moved those items closer to where drinks are handed to customers. The changes shaved eight seconds off the 45-second process. "Just to top the beverage with whipped cream and drizzle took six seconds," Jordan says. In all, new methods have cut two seconds off the store's drive-through time—to an average of 23 seconds. Between September 2008 and June 2009, her store experienced a 10 percent increase in transactions. The company says that having food and drinks ready to go quickly can boost traffic because that keeps people from leaving stores.

At a lot of stores, Starbucks baristas used to grind all of the day's coffee in the morning and keep it under a counter. They had to bend over and scoop the grounds each time they made a new batch. The absence of grinding sounds and the fresh coffee aroma were among the things Howard Schultz criticized before he returned to the company as chief executive in January 2008 to try to turn things around.

Now baristas are required to grind beans for each batch and timers buzz every eight minutes to signal when it's time to make new coffee. At a busy downtown Chicago Starbucks, store manager Ryan Dobbertin says bins of beans are kept under the counter so barristas can find a particular roast without having to pause and read the label. They quickly differentiate between pitchers of soy, nonfat, and low-fat milk.

At the beginning of an April day a few years ago, Dobbertin's store had a customer-satisfaction score of 56 percent; by June it had jumped to 76 percent. His store has seen a 9 percent increase in transactions between April and June. Not all stores are as far along. At a different downtown Chicago store, baristas one morning temporarily ran out of coffee around 7:45 a.m. Heydon observed two workers at the espresso machine and traced their movements on what's been called a "spaghetti map" because of all the lines.

Starbucks has faced some resistance to the program. "They're trying to turn workers into robots," says Erik Forman, a barista in Minneapolis. "It's going to essentially turn the café into a factory. They want to control our every move in order to pinch every possible penny."

Discussion Questions

1. To what extent has Starbucks caught on to a cost-effective way of reducing labor expenses in their stores (cafés)?
2. How should Starbucks managers deal with baristas who do not like the lean methods of working?
3. What would you think of Starbucks using in-store coffee vending machines to save even more money?
4. What effect would the amount of store traffic at Starbucks stores have on the true cost savings derived from lean techniques?
5. If you have visited a Starbucks store recently, can you suggest how the baristas can be even more productive, thereby earning or saving the company more money? Maybe you can patronize a Starbucks café just to complete this assignment. (The expense could be tax deductible!)

Source: Julie Jargon, "Latest Starbucks Buzzword: 'Lean' Japanese Techniques," *The Wall Street Journal*, August 4, 2009, pp. A1, A10; "Recession Forces Starbucks to Think Lean," *MSN Money*, August 6, 2009, pp. 1–4.

15-B Case Problem

MySpace is Our Place

A case is brewing in federal court in New Jersey that pits bosses against two employees who were complaining about their workplace on an invite-only discussion group on MySpace.com. The case tests whether a supervisor who managed to log into the forum—and then fired employees who bad-mouthed supervisors and customers there—had the right to do so.

The case has some legal and privacy experts concerned that companies are intruding into areas that their employees had considered off limits. The question is whether employees have a right to privacy in their non-work-created communications with each other.

The case centers on two employees of Houston's restaurant in Hackensack, New Jersey: bartender Brian Pietrylo and waitress Doreen Marino. In 2006, the two workers created and contributed to a forum about their workplace on MySpace.com. Pietrylo e-mailed invitations to coworkers, who then had to log on using a personal e-mail address and a password.

"I thought this would be a nice way to vent ... without any outside eyes spying on us. This group is entirely private," Pietrylo wrote in his introduction to the forum, according to court filings.

In the forum, Pietrylo and Marino, who was his girlfriend, made fun of Houston's décor and patrons and made sexual jokes. They also made negative comments about their supervisors. The supervisors were tipped off to the forum by Karen St. Jean, a restaurant hostess, who logged into her account at an after-hours gathering with a Houston's manager to show him the site. They all had a laugh, St. Jean said in a court deposition, and she didn't think about any more about it.

But later, another supervisor called St. Jean into his office and asked her for her e-mail and password to the forum. Then login information was passed up the supervisory chain, where restaurant managers viewed the comments.

The following week, Pietrylo and Marino were fired. Houston's managers have said in court filings that the pair's online posts violated policies set out in an employee handbook, which includes professionalism and a positive attitude.

In their lawsuit, Marino and Pietrylo claim that their managers illegally accessed their online communication in violation of federal wiretapping statutes. They also claimed that the managers violated their privacy under New Jersey law.

St. Jean said in a deposition that she feared she would be fired if she didn't give up her password, a twist in the case that could sway a jury against the company.

Discussion Questions

1. You be the judge. Who is right in this case, the company or the two employees?
2. You be the manager. What should the managers at Houston's have done when they learned about the negative comments on MySpace?
3. You be the ethics specialist. How ethical were the managers in looking in the MySpace comments? How ethical were the employees in posting negative comments about their employer and its patrons on MySpace?
4. You be the Internet researcher. What was the eventual outcome of this case?
5. To what extent is Karen St. Jean a backstabber?

Source: Dionne Searcey, "Employers Watching Workers Online Spurs Privacy Debate," *The Wall Street Journal*, April 23, 2009, p. A13.

Managing Ineffective Performers

V alerie Frederickson, a human-resources consultant in Silicon Valley, had a delicate problem: Her office administrator was smart and well-spoken, but after two months on the job, she didn't seem to like the work. "We needed to have her do things like data entry and cleaning the refrigerator, and she wanted to plan events for us," Frederickson says.

So Frederickson decided to let the administrator go— gently. She gave the woman a small amount of severance pay, helped her get a new job, and assured her that the firing wasn't personal. "I told her, 'I like you a lot, and I think of you like a little sister, but I don't want you working here any more. I would like to give you the type of work you seem to want. But we just don't have what you are looking for in our department. The job we have requires the most basic type of help, like data entry and tidying up the place.'"

Frederickson went on to explain to the office administrator that she had many skills and talents that were not being used effectively on the job. "You want to do more higher level work than the position calls for. You want to plan events, yet we have lots of basic work that needs to be performed regularly. I hope we didn't oversell you on the job when you were hired."

The office administrator thought over Frederickson's comment and admitted that the job was a poor fit for her needs. "I thought maybe I could grow the job into something that fit my needs, but I guess I was wrong. I never had a chance to be a true office administrator. Instead, the job calls for someone who does grunt work every day.

"I'll try to find a better fit for me in my next job."[1]

The incident about the office administrator who wasn't a good fit for the job illustrates how dealing with substandard performance is another key part of a manager's job, even if it might be the most uncomfortable. The human resources manager in question handled the situation well, even though terminating an employee is the last resort in managing poor performance.

ineffective job performance

Job performance that lowers productivity below an acceptable standard.

Managerial control requires dealing constructively with **ineffective job performance**, defined as performance that does not meet standards for the position. Ineffective performers are also referred to as *problem employees* because they create problems for management.

Ineffective performers lower organizational performance directly by not accomplishing their fair share of work. They also lower organizational productivity indirectly. Poor performers decrease the productivity of their superiors by consuming managerial time. Additionally, the productivity of coworkers is often decreased because coworkers must take over some of the ineffective performer's tasks. In this chapter, we address ineffective performance as a control problem for which the manager can take corrective actions. However, control of performance might also involve effective leading, motivating, and staffing.

LEARNING OBJECTIVE **1**

Identify factors contributing to poor performance.

FACTORS CONTRIBUTING TO INEFFECTIVE PERFORMANCE

Employees are or become ineffective performers for many different reasons. The cause of poor performance can be rooted in the person, the job, the manager, or the company. At times, the employee's personal traits and behaviors create so much disturbance that he or she is perceived as ineffective. Performance is sometimes classified as ineffective, or substandard, because of an arbitrary standard set by management, such as the rank-and-yank system mentioned in Chapter 9.

Exhibit 16-1 lists a variety of factors that can contribute to ineffective performance. These are divided into four categories related to the employee, the job, the manager, or the organization. The true cause of ineffective performance is usually a combination of several factors. Assume that an

---

[1]The first two paragraphs are from Phred Dvorak, "Firing Good Workers Who Are a Bad Fit," *The Wall Street Journal*, May 1, 2006, p. B5.

PLAY VIDEO

Go to www.cengage
.com/management/
dubrin and view the
video for Chapter 16.
What did you learn
about human-resource
management from
this video?

employee is late for work so frequently that his or her performance becomes substandard. The contributing factors in this situation could be the worker's disrespect for work rules, an unchallenging job, and an unduly harsh supervisor. One factor may be more important than others, but they are all contributors.

The following list expands on how the factors described in Exhibit 16-1 are related to ineffective performance:

The Employee

* *Insufficient mental ability and education.* The employee lacks the problem-solving ability necessary to do the job. For example, the employee is not able to understand the software used to run a machine. Poor communication skills are included here, such as inability to listen carefully to instructions or speak clearly to customers and coworkers. Insufficient mental ability and education of the U.S. workforce available for basic jobs have become a major challenge for managers.

EXHIBIT 16-1   Factors Contributing to Ineffective Performance

Dozens of factors can lower job performance. The factors listed constitute the majority of the reasons for ineffective performance.

Factors Related to the Employee
Insufficient mental ability and education
Insufficient job knowledge
Job stress or burnout
Low motivation and loafing
Excessive absenteeism and tardiness
Emotional problems or personality disorder
Alcoholism and drug addiction
Tobacco addiction or withdrawal
  symptoms
Conducting outside business on the job
Family, personal, and financial problems
Physical limitations
Preoccupying office romance
Fear of traveling, especially flying
Poor organizational citizenship behavior

Factors Related to the Job
Ergonomics problems and repetitive
  motion disorder
Repetitive, physically demanding job
Built-in conflict
Night-shift work assignments

Substandard industrial hygiene
A "sick" building

Factors Related to the Manager
Inadequate communication about job
  responsibilities
Inadequate feedback about job performance
Inappropriate leadership style
Negative and untrusting attitude
Bullying or intimidating manager

Factors Related to the Organization
Organizational culture that tolerates poor
  performance
Poor ethical climate
Counterproductive work environment
Negative work-group influences
Intentional threats to job security
Violence or threats of violence
Sexual harassment
Workplace harassment in general
A compensation/reward structure that
  encourages deviant behavior

* *Insufficient job knowledge.* The employee is a substandard performer because he or she comes to the job with insufficient training or experience. The employee might be smart enough to learn but lacks the skills to perform the job today. Insufficient job knowledge includes technological obsolescence, meaning the employee has not kept up with the state of the art in his or her field. He or she avoids using new ideas and techniques and becomes ineffective.

* *Job stress and burnout.* Severe short-term stress leads to errors in concentration and judgment. As a result of prolonged job stress, an employee may become apathetic, negative, and impatient. He or she can no longer generate the energy to perform effectively.

* *Low motivation and loafing.* An employee who is poorly motivated will often not sustain enough effort to accomplish the amount of work required to meet standards. Closely related to low motivation is goofing off and loafing. Many employees spend too much time surfing the Internet or engaging in other diversionary activities such as making personal phone calls and running personal errands during working hours.

* *Excessive absenteeism and tardiness.* The employee is often not at work for a variety of personal or health reasons. Lost time leads to low productivity, costing employers an estimated 15 percent of payroll expenses.[2]

* *Emotional problems or personality disorder.* The employee may have emotional outbursts, periods of depression, or other abnormal behaviors that interfere with human relationships and work concentration. A government study indicated that 3.2 percent of full-time American workers suffered from depression in one year. Personal care and food and beverage workers were the most likely to be depressed.[3] Even without a certifiable emotional problem, workers experiencing strongly negative emotions, such as anger, may become counterproductive.[4] Cynical behavior may lower the performance of an entire work group if the negative attitude spreads to others.

* *Alcoholism and drug addiction.* The employee cannot think clearly because his or her mental or physical condition has been temporarily or permanently impaired by alcohol or other drugs. Attendance is also likely to suffer. A national U.S. survey indicated that 3.1 percent of employed adults use illicit drugs on the job and that 14.1 percent of workforce members are illicit drug users off the job.[5] (Illicit drugs in

---

[2]Sarah Fister Gale, "Sickened by the Cost of Absenteeism, Companies Look for Solutions," *Workforce Management*, September 2003, p. 72.

[3]"SAMSHA's 2008 National Survey on Drug Use and Health," *oas.samhsa.gov/nsduhLatest. htm,* Updated September 12, 2009, p. 94.

[4]Jixia Yang and James Diefendorf, "The Relations of Daily Counterproductive Workplace Behavior with Emotions, Situational Antecedents, and Personality Moderators: A Diary Study in Hong Kong," *Personnel Psychology*, Summer 2009, p. 286.

[5]Michael R. Frone, "Prevalence and Distribution of Illicit Drug Use in the Workforce and in the Workplace: Findings and Implications from a U.S. National Survey," *Journal of Applied Psychology*, July 2006, pp. 856–869.

this study included marijuana, cocaine, and four psychotherapeutic drugs.) Managers must be aware that not every drug user is impaired; many develop tolerance to drugs, including prescription drugs.

- *Tobacco addiction or withdrawal symptoms.* The employee who smokes is often fatigued and takes so many cigarette breaks that his or her work is disrupted. Sick leave may also increase. Even workers who stop smoking may suffer performance problems for a while. However, when smokers drop the habit, they may become more productive. According to one estimate, the cumulative lost time due to smoking breaks can add up to one day per week.[6]

- *Conducting outside business on the job.* The employee may be an "office entrepreneur" who sells merchandise to coworkers or spends time on the phone and e-mail, working on investments or other outside interests. Operating an eBay business or other online auction site during working hours is a notable distraction. Time spent on these activities lowers productivity.

- *Family, personal, and financial problems.* The employee is unable to work at full capacity because of preoccupation with an off-the-job problem such as a marital dispute, conflict with children, a broken romance, or indebtedness. In reference to financially troubled employees, E. Thomas Gorman, professor emeritus at Virginia Tech, says, "They are absent more frequently and waste time at work dealing with financial matters—on the telephone with creditors, trying to get a loan from their 401(k)."[7]

- *Physical limitations.* Job performance decreases as a result of injury or illness. For example, according to the American Council on Exercise, low-back pain is a leading cause of job-related disability and absenteeism in the United States.[8] Many problems of physical limitations are self-imposed, such as obesity or high blood pressure due to limited physical exercise and poor eating habits.

- *Preoccupying office romance.* For many people, a new romance is an energizing force that creates positive stress and results in a surge in energy directed toward work. For others, an office romance becomes a preoccupation that detracts from concentration. Time spent together in conversation and long lunch breaks can lower productivity.

- *Fear of traveling, especially flying.* In an era of worldwide terrorism, some employees refuse to travel for business, particularly by airplane, because of their perception of the potential danger. Others are hesitant to visit tall office towers. During a disease epidemic, some workers refuse

---

[6]Mark Schoeff Jr., "Smoke-Free Marriott Moves to Help Workers Kick Habit," *Workforce Management*, January 15, 2007, p. 6.

[7]Quoted in Eilene Zimmerman, "Financial Education Courses Can Be a Valuable Asset in Employers' EAP Portfolios," *Workforce Management*, May 8, 2006, p. 52.

[8]"Protecting Your Back at Work," *Fit Facts* (American Council on Exercise), www.acefitness.org, accessed April 6, 2010.

to travel out of fear of germs. Yet to meet the full requirements of the job, many employees are required to visit remote locations.[9]

- *Poor organizational citizenship behavior.* A subtle cause of low performance is that some employees will not inconvenience themselves to provide assistance not strictly related to their job descriptions. Therefore, they are poor organizational citizens. **Organizational citizenship behavior** is employee behavior that is discretionary and typically not recognized or rewarded but which nevertheless helps the organization. A small example would be taking it on your own initiative to repair a broken chair that might create an accident. An analysis of 49 different groups found that workers low on organizational citizenship behavior were more likely to engage in counterproductive workplace behaviors.[10] The counterproductive behaviors include any activities that harm the organization, such as wasting resources and stealing money.

organizational citizenship behavior

Employee behavior that is discretionary and typically not recognized or rewarded but that nevertheless helps the organization.

The Job

- *Ergonomics problems and repetitive motion disorder.* If equipment or furniture used on the job contributes to fatigue, discomfort, or injury, performance problems result. For example, if an employee develops neck pain and eyestrain from working with a poorly designed computer configuration, performance will suffer. As described in Chapter 7 about job design, repetitive motion disorder, including carpal tunnel syndrome, is a major problem that stems from poorly designed or poorly utilized computer equipment.

- *Repetitive, physically demanding job.* A repetitive, physically demanding job can cause the employee to become bored and fatigued, leading to lowered performance. Many workers report feeling burned out from working for package-delivery services because of the constant heavy physical demands, leading to mental stress. The problem has become more acute as online shopping increases, particularly during the holiday season.

- *Built-in conflict.* The nature of the job involves so much conflict that job stress lowers performance. The position of collection agent for a consumer-loan company might fit this category. So would a telemarketer who receives a high percentage of rejections, including slammed-down telephone receivers.

- *Night-shift work assignments.* Employees assigned to all-night shifts suffer many more mental lapses and productivity losses than those assigned to daytime or evening shifts. A major problem is that night-shift work interrupts the natural rhythms of the body.

---

[9]Clarence T. Pollard, "Fear of Flying," *HR Magazine*, January 2002, pp. 81–84.

[10]Reeshad S. Dalal, "A Meta-Analysis of the Relationship Between Organizational Citizenship Behavior and Counterproductive Work Behavior," *Journal of Applied Psychology*, November 2005, pp. 1241–1255.

- *Substandard industrial hygiene*. Excessive noise, fumes, uncomfortable temperatures, inadequate lighting, high humidity, and fear of injury or contamination engender poor performance.
- *A "sick" building*. In some office buildings, a diverse range of airborne particles, vapors, and gases pollute the indoor environment. As described on the Web site "Doctor Fungus," the problems include the transmission of standard infectious diseases such as tuberculosis and carbon monoxide poisoning related to recirculation of exhaust fumes. The result can be headaches, nausea, and respiratory infections. Performance suffers and absenteeism increases.[11]

The Manager

- *Inadequate communication about job responsibilities*. The employee performs poorly because he or she lacks a clear picture of what the manager expects. For example, a worker might spend the entire day defragging the hard drive on her desktop computer because the manager did not explain that he really wanted her to consolidate a few suppliers. As a result, the worker is accused of wasting time.
- *Inadequate feedback about job performance*. The employee makes a large number of errors because he or she does not receive the feedback—early enough or at all—to prevent them.
- *Inappropriate leadership style*. The employee performs poorly because the manager's leadership style is inappropriate to the employee's needs. For example, an immature employee's manager gives him or her too much freedom and the result is poor performance. This employee needs closer supervision. Related to leadership style is the problem of some managers unwittingly setting up a group member to fail. The manager perceives a given group member as mediocre, and that person lives down to the manager's expectations, perhaps because the group member loses some self-confidence.[12]
- *Negative and untrusting attitude*. Some managers believe that employees cannot be trusted to behave ethically or in the best interest of the company. As a result, these managers will often exert too much control, leading some employees to retaliate by such means as personally slowing down production. When managers expect the worst from employees, the employees often live down to the managers' expectations.[13]
- *Bullying or intimidating manager*. Many employees are intimidated and bullied by a manager to the point that they cannot work effectively.

[11]"Sick Building Syndrome," http://www.doctorfungus.org, January 22, 2007, p. 1.

[12]Barrie E. Litzky, Kimberly A. Eddleston, and Deborah L. Kidder, "The Good, the Bad, and the Misguided: How Managers Inadvertently Encourage Deviant Behaviors," *Academy of Management Perspectives*, February 2006, p. 95.

[13]Jean-François Manzoni and Jean-Louis Barsoux, "The Set-Up-to-Fail Syndrome," *Harvard Business Review*, March–April 1998, pp. 101–113.

Bullying and intimidation go far beyond being firm and setting high standards. They include such behaviors as publicly insulting group members, yelling, and responding with insensitivity toward personal requests such as time off to handle a severe personal problem.

The Organization

* *Organizational culture that tolerates poor performance.* An organization culture that has low expectations creates an atmosphere conducive to substandard performance. A closely related problem occurs when an organization has a history of not imposing sanctions on employees who perform poorly. When managers demand better performance, many employees may not respond to the new challenge.

* *Poor ethical climate.* An unethical climate sets the tone for employees engaging in deviant behavior that can produce poor performance, as suggested by a study of working business graduates. Among these behaviors are working on personal matters during work time and intentionally slowing down the work pace.[14]

* *Counterproductive work environment.* The employee lacks the proper tools, support, budget, or authority to accomplish the job. An example would be a telecommuter whose company-provided computer is plagued with viruses, and the company hesitates taking care of the problem.

* *Negative work-group influences.* Group pressures restrain good performance or the work group penalizes a high-performance worker. Similarly, peer-group social pressure may cause an employee to take overly long lunch breaks, neglecting job responsibilities. A study conducted in 20 organizations showed that antisocial behaviors such as lying, spreading rumors, loafing, and absenteeism were more frequent when coworkers exhibited the same behavior.[15]

* *Intentional threats to job security.* A company might make excessive work demands on an employee in the form of veiled threats that the job will be eliminated unless the extra work is done. Performance suffers as the worker becomes fearful and anxious.

* *Violence or threats of violence.* Employees may witness violent behavior in the workplace, such as physical assaults, knifings, shootings, or threats of violence. Many employees not directly affected are nevertheless distracted and fearful, leading to lowered productivity.

* *Sexual harassment.* The employee who is sexually harassed usually experiences enough stress to decrease concentration and performance in general. Both men and women are sexually harassed, with about

---

[14]Dane K. Peterson, "Deviant Workplace Behavior and the Organization's Ethical Climate," *Journal of Business and Psychology*, Fall 2002, pp. 47–61.

[15]Sandra L. Robinson and Anne M. O'Leary-Kelly, "Monkey See, Monkey Do: The Influence of Work Groups on the Antisocial Behavior of Employees," *Academy of Management Journal*, December 1998, pp. 658–672.

16 percent of sexual-harassment complaints being filed by men.[16] *Textual harassment* is a new form of sexual harassment that consists of inappropriate, and sexually toned, text messages on the job.[17]

- Sometimes an employee who files a sexual-harassment complaint is retaliated against in the form of exclusion from meetings he or she previously attended. The consequent feelings of alienation might lower job performance. In situations where the manager is the harasser, resentment toward the manager may lead to lowered performance. The person who commits sexual harassment and is under investigation for or charged with the act is likely to experience stress and preoccupation about the charges. One consultant observes that the gossip and distraction stemming from an explosive sexual-harassment case can cause a temporary 20 percent dip in productivity.[18]

- *Workplace harassment in general.* A continuing problem in the workplace is that some people (black, female, Latino, gay, young, or old) are harassed or verbally and physically attacked because of membership in a group. Workplace harassment is distinct from sexual harassment because the bothersome behavior is not sexually toned. All types of harassment can lower job performance if the harassed worker becomes overly stressed and distracted. Two studies showed that when workers are subjected to more than one form of harassment, such as gender and age, the negative effects on their well-being are even stronger.[19]

- *A compensation/reward structure that encourages deviant behavior.* An ineffective compensation/reward structure, similar to an ineffective control standard, might encourage workers to perform in counterproductive ways. Too much compensation based on commissions might encourage some sales workers to engage in counterproductive practices. Studies of sales representatives in a variety of industries whose income was over 80 percent based on commissions found evidence of workplace deviance, including undercharging for services, lying about meeting quotas, and padding expense accounts. For example, automobile service technicians who work on commission might be encouraged to recommend unnecessary repairs; this practice ultimately leads to a poor reputation for the service center.[20]

You are invited to take the self-quiz in Exhibit 16-2 to ponder tendencies of your own that could ultimately contribute to substandard performance. Many sports figures, elected officials, and business executives experience the problems pinpointed in the questionnaire.

---

[16]Data from the EEOC reported in Dana Mattioli, "More Men Make Harassment Claims," *The Wall Street Journal*, March 23, 2010, p. D4.

[17]"Textual Harassment," *www.shrm.org/hrmmagazine*, November 2009.

[18]Cited in Sheila Anne Feeney, "Love Hurts," *Workforce Management*, February 2004, p. 37.

[19]Jana L. Raver and Lisa H. Nishii, "Once, Twice, or Three Times as Harmful? Ethnic Harassment, Gender Harassment, and Generalized Workplace Harassment," *Journal of Applied Psychology*, March 2010, pp. 236–254.

[20]Litzky, Eddleston, and Kidder, "The Good, the Bad, and the Misguided," pp. 93–94.

EXHIBIT 16-2   **The Self-Sabotage Questionnaire**

Directions: Indicate how accurately each of the following statements describes or characterizes you, using a five-point scale: (0) very inaccurately, (1) inaccurately, (2) midway between inaccurately and accurately, (3) accurately, (4) very accurately. Consider discussing some of the questions with a family member, close friend, or work associate. Another person's feedback may prove helpful in providing accurate answers to some of the questions.

1. Other people have said that I am my worst enemy.   _____
2. If I don't do a perfect job, I feel worthless.   _____
3. I am my own harshest critic.   _____
4. When engaged in a sport or other competitive activity, I find a way to blow a substantial lead right near the end.   _____
5. When I make a mistake, I can usually identify another person to blame.   _____
6. I have a strong tendency to procrastinate.   _____
7. I have trouble focusing on what is really important to me.   _____
8. I have trouble taking criticism, even from friends.   _____
9. My fear of seeming stupid often prevents me from asking questions or offering my opinion.   _____
10. I tend to expect the worst in most situations.   _____
11. Many times I have rejected people who treat me well.   _____
12. When I have an important project to complete, I usually get sidetracked and then miss the deadline.   _____
13. I choose work assignments that lead to disappointments even when better options are clearly available.   _____
14. I frequently misplace things such as my keys and then get very angry at myself.   _____
15. I am concerned that if I take on much more responsibility, people will expect too much from me.   _____
16. I avoid situations, such as competitive sports, where people can find out how good or bad I really am.   _____
17. People describe me as the "office (or class) clown."   _____
18. I have an insatiable demand for money and power.   _____
19. When negotiating with others, I hate to grant any concessions.   _____
20. I seek revenge for even the smallest hurts.   _____
21. I have a giant-size ego.   _____
22. When I receive a compliment or other form of recognition, I usually feel I don't deserve it.   _____
23. To be honest, I choose to suffer.   _____
24. I regularly enter into conflict with people who try to help me.   _____
25. I'm a loser.   _____

Total score   _____

Scoring and interpretation: Add your answers to all the questions to obtain your total score. Your total score provides an approximate index of your tendencies toward being self-sabotaging or self-defeating.

0–25:   You appear to have few tendencies toward self-sabotage. If this interpretation is supported by your own positive feelings toward your life and yourself, you are in good shape with respect to self-defeating behavior tendencies. However, stay alert to potential self-sabotaging tendencies that could develop at later stages in your career.

26–50:   You may have some mild tendencies toward self-sabotage. It could be that you do things occasionally that defeat your own purposes. A person in this category, for example, might write an angry e-mail memo to an executive, expressing disagreement with a decision that adversely affects his or her operation. Review actions you have taken during the past six months to decide if any of them have been self-sabotaging.

51–75:   You show signs of engaging in self-sabotage. You probably have thoughts, and carry out actions, that could be blocking you from achieving important work and personal goals. People whose scores place them in this category characteristically engage in negative self-talk that lowers their self-confidence and makes them appear weak and indecisive to others. For example, "I'm usually not good at learning new things." People in this range frequently experience another problem. They sometimes sabotage their chances of succeeding on a project just to prove that their negative self-assessment is correct.

76–100:   You most likely have a strong tendency toward self-sabotage. (Sometimes it is possible to obtain a high score on a test like this because you are going through an unusually stressful period in your life.) You might discuss your tendencies toward undermining your own achievements with a mental health professional.

LEARNING OBJECTIVE ❷
Describe the control model for managing ineffective performers.

THE CONTROL MODEL FOR MANAGING INEFFECTIVE PERFORMERS

The approach to improving ineffective performance presented here follows the logic of the control process shown in Exhibit 16-3. Problem identification and problem solving lie at the core of this approach. The control process for managing ineffective performers is divided into the eight steps illustrated in Exhibit 16-3; these should usually be followed in sequence. This section will describe each of the steps in detail. Another key method of improving ineffective performance—employee discipline—receives separate attention later in the chapter.

Two cautions are in order for those using the control model for improving ineffective performance. First, the model may need slight modification to follow company procedures. Company policy, for example, might establish certain procedures about documenting poor performance and reporting it immediately to higher levels of management. Second, the control process is not designed to deal with mental illness. An employee who begins to neglect the job because of a sudden change in personality should be immediately referred to a human-resource specialist. The specialist, in turn, will make an appropriate referral to a mental-health professional.

EXHIBIT 16-3   The Control Model for Managing Ineffective Performers

The most systematic and effective method for bringing ineffective performance up to standard is to follow the control process, referred to in this application as the control model.

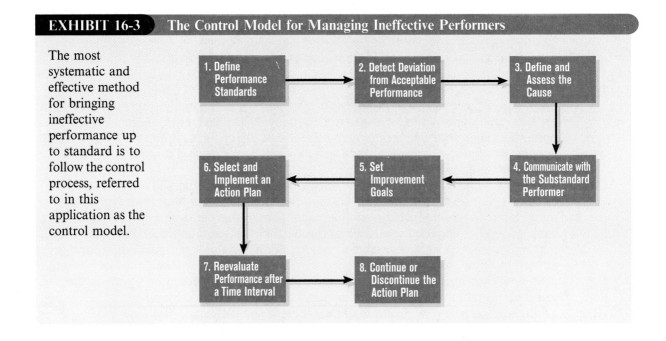

Define Performance Standards

Penalizing employees for not achieving performance standards without first carefully communicating those standards is unfair. Therefore, the first step in the control model for managing ineffective performers is to clearly define what is expected of employees. Performance standards are commonly established by such means as job descriptions, work goals, production quotas, and formal discussions of what is to be accomplished in a position.

Detect Deviation from Acceptable Performance

Detection is the process of noting when an employee's performance deviates from an acceptable standard. Managers use the various control measures described in Chapter 15 to detect deviations from acceptable performance. For performance to be considered ineffective or poor, it must deviate significantly from the norm.

At times, quantitative measures can be used to define ineffective performance. For some jobs, ineffective performance might begin at 30 percent below standard. For other jobs, the cutoff point could be 20 or 50 percent, or any other percentage of deviation that fits the situation. What percentage of deviation from standard do you think would be acceptable for a commercial airline pilot? For a bank teller?

Personal observation plays a key role in detecting ineffective performance. One reason that observation is so important is that it is a concurrent control. By the time quantitative indicators of poor performance have been collected, substantial damage may have been done. Assume a bank manager observes that one of the mortgage loan officers is taking unduly long lunch hours on Fridays. Upon return, the officer appears to be under the influence of alcohol. Eventually, this unacceptable behavior will show up in quantitative indicators of performance. However, it might take a year to collect these data.

Define and Assess the Cause

At this stage, the manager attempts to diagnose the real cause of the problem. Following the logic of Exhibit 16-1, the primary contributor to the problem could be a personal factor or a factor related to the job, the manager, or the organization. A discussion with the employee (the next step in the control model) may be necessary to reveal the major cause of the problem. For example, an office assistant was absent so frequently that her performance suffered. She claimed that photocopying made her sick. The supervisor investigated further and called in the company health and safety expert. A medical examination confirmed that the office assistant was allergic to the trace fumes from the toner in the large-volume photocopier. After the office assistant was reassigned, her attendance became satisfactory.

Communicate with the Substandard Performer

After detecting unacceptable performance or behavior, the manager must communicate concern to the worker. At times, a simple discussion will suffice. At other times, a more sensitive form of feedback may be necessary. **Confrontation** means dealing with a controversial or emotional topic directly. Confrontation is necessary whenever the employee does not readily admit to experiencing a problem.

> **confrontation**
> Dealing with a controversial or emotional topic directly.

Managers often avoid confrontation for several reasons. They may have limited skill in criticizing employees. Or, they may prefer not to deal with the anger and resentment that confrontation is likely to trigger. A third reason is the manager not wanting to make the employee feel uncomfortable. Another concern about confrontation is that the rights of the employee might be violated if he or she is suffering from alcoholism or another problem covered by the Americans with Disabilities Act. In reality, the law allows employers to confront employees with disabilities and to hold those with an alcohol problem to the same performance standards of other employees.[21]

A recommended confrontation technique is to communicate an attitude of concern about the employee's welfare. To use this technique, confront the person in a sincere and thoughtful manner. Using the words *care* and *concern* can be helpful. For instance, a manager might begin by saying: "The reason I'm bringing up this problem is that I care about your work. You have a good record with the company, and I'm concerned that your performance has slipped way below its former level."

---

[21]Saundra Jackson, Ruhal Dooley, and Diance Lacy, "Substance Abuse, Ethics, Intermittent Leave," *HR Magazine*, July 2003, p. 41.

Another confrontation approach that might be helpful is to pose questions about poor performance so that the worker is more involved in the process.[22] Asking the worker to furnish information rather than to simply respond yes or no is better for encouraging dialog. Two examples follow:

- "How many days have you showed up late in the last six months?"
- "How do you think your error rate compares to other workers in our unit?"

Set Improvement Goals

improvement goal
A goal that, if attained, will correct unacceptable deviation from a performance standard.

The fifth step in the control model is to set improvement goals. An **improvement goal** is one that, if attained, will correct an unacceptable deviation from a performance standard. The goals should be documented on paper or electronically. Improvement goals should have the same characteristics as other objectives (see Chapter 4). Above all, improvement goals should specify the behavior or result that is required. Vague improvement goals are not likely to cause changes in performance.

An example of a specific improvement goal is, "During this month, nine of your ten customer service reports must be in on time." This specific goal is likely to be more effective than a general improvement goal such as, "Become more prompt in submitting customer service reports."

If the ineffective performer expresses an interest in improvement, joint goal setting is advisable. By providing input into goal setting, the substandard performer stands a good chance of becoming committed to improvement. At times, managers must impose improvement goals on substandard performers, especially in cases involving a motivation problem. If substandard employees were interested in setting their own improvement goals, they would not have a motivation problem.

Select and Implement an Action Plan

The setting of improvement goals leads logically to the selection and implementation of action plans to attain those goals. Much of the art of remedying ineffective performance is contained in this step. Unless appropriate action plans are developed, no real improvement is likely to take place. Many attempts at improving substandard performance fail because the problem is discussed and then dropped. Thus the employee has no concrete method of making the necessary improvements.

Types of Action Plans

An action plan for improvement can include almost any sensible approach tailored to the specific problem. An action plan could be formulated to deal with every cause of ineffective performance listed in Exhibit 16-1.

---

[22]"Confronting Poor Performers," *Team Briefings*, Preview Issue, 2007.

Action plans for improving ineffective performance can be divided into two types. One type is within the power of the manager to develop and implement. Plans of this type include coaching, encouraging, and offering small incentives for improvement. The other type of action plan is offered by the organization or purchased on the outside. It includes training programs, stress-management programs, and stays at alcoholism-treatment centers. Exhibit 16-4 lists a selection of feasible corrective actions.

When attempting to improve ineffective performance resulting from a variety of personal problems, the preferred action plan for many managers is to refer the troubled worker to an **employee assistance program (EAP)**. The EAP is an organization-sponsored service that helps employees deal with personal and job-related problems that interfere with job performance. Professionals who specialize in dealing with particular problems staff an employee assistance program. Many companies that do not have an EAP of their own refer employees to such a program that serves firms in the area. Employee assistance programs offer extensive services to employees. For example, three of the services offered by the EAP associated with the Federal Occupational Health are as follows:

- Seven-day, 24-hour telephone access for employees and family members to professional counselors for assessment, consultation, referral, and crisis management.
- Professional assessment of issues related to mental health, substance abuse, and workplace and other challenges in living.
- Face-to-face short-term, focused counseling for individuals, couples, and families.[23]

Employees and their families use assistance programs to cope with a variety of personal and family problems and illnesses. Among them are alcoholism and other substance abuse, financial and legal difficulties, emotional problems, chronic illnesses such as AIDS or cancer, compulsive gambling, and weight control. Employees also use EAPs to deal with job-related concerns such as work stress, chronic job dissatisfaction, and sexual harassment.

When supervisors refer employees to the EAP, workplace problems should be the focus. The supervisor should not say, "I am encouraging you to go to the EAP. The EAP can help you with any personal problems you may have." Say instead, "I encourage you to go to the EAP. The EAP may be able to help you solve your workplace problems."[24] The second approach usually creates less defensiveness than the first.

employee assistance program (EAP)

An organization-sponsored service to help employees deal with personal and job-related problems that hinder performance.

---

[23]"Documenting the Value of Employee Assistance Programs," *Federal Occupational Health Program Support Center*, http://www.foh.dhhs.gov, April 2010.

[24]Jonathan A. Segal, "I'm Depressed—Accommodate Me!" *HR Magazine*, February 2001, p. 148.

EXHIBIT 16-4   Corrective Actions for Ineffective Performers

When attempting to bring ineffective performers up to standard or beyond, managers can either take action by themselves or refer employees to a company program designed to help them with performance problems.

Managerial Actions and Techniques

- **Coaching**. The manager points out specifically what the performer could be doing better or should stop doing. In daily interaction with the team members, the manager makes suggestions for improvement. Coaching is the most widely used technique for performance improvement.
- **Closer supervision**. The manager works more closely with the subordinate, offering frequent guidance and feedback.
- **Reassignment or transfer**. The manager reassigns the ineffective performer to a position that he or she can handle better. An emerging approach is to assign a low-performing worker to a group of high-performing workers. Quite often the low performer will rise to the expectations of the high-performing environment. The former low performer recognizes that the group needs him or her to perform well.[25]
- **Motivational techniques**. The manager attempts to improve employee motivation by using positive reinforcement or some other motivational technique.
- **Corrective discipline**. The manager informs the employee that his or her behavior is unacceptable and that corrections must be made if the worker is to remain employed by the firm. The employee is counseled as part of corrective discipline.
- **Lower performance standards**. If performance standards have been too high, the manager lowers expectations of the team member. Consultation with higher management would probably be necessary before implementing this step.
- **Job rotation**. If ineffective performance results from staleness or burnout, changing to a different job of comparable responsibility may prove helpful.

Organizational Programs

- **Employee assistance programs (EAPs)**. The employee is referred to a counseling service specializing in rehabilitating employees whose personal problems interfere with work.
- **Wellness programs**. The organization encourages employees to participate in specialized programs that help them stay physically and mentally healthy. Physical exercise and nutrition instruction are typically included. By focusing on wellness, employees may prevent or cope with health problems—such as heart disease or an eating disorder—that interfere with job performance or lead to absenteeism. The wellness program usually includes stress management.
- **Career counseling and outplacement**. The employee receives professional assistance in solving a career problem, including being counseled on finding a job outside the firm.
- **Job redesign**. Specialists in human-resource management and industrial engineering redesign job elements that could be causing poor performance. For example, the job is changed so that the employee has less direct contact with others and this leads to reduced conflict.

---

[25]Bernhard Weber and Guido Hertel, "Motivation Gains of Inferior Group Members: A Meta-Analytical Review, *Journal of Personality and Social Psychology*, June 2007, pp. 973–993.

- **Training and development programs.** The employee is assigned to a training or development program linked directly to his or her performance deficiency. For example, a reserved sales representative receives assertiveness training.
- **Executive or personal coaching.** The company hires a personal coach who helps the professional or managerial worker with such problems as poor interpersonal relationships, difficulty in resolving conflict, and ineffective approach to problem solving.
- **Anger-management program.** The company sends a worker whose anger results in poor performance to an anger-management workshop, where he or she learns how to control anger and express it in constructive ways. The problem is that anger creates a less cohesive workplace and damages morale. Anger also interferes with focused attention, therefore impairing judgment and decreasing reaction time.[26]

Implementation of the Action Plan

After the action plan is chosen, it must be implemented. As shown in Exhibit 16-3, implementation begins in Step 6 and continues through Step 8. The manager utilizes the approaches listed under "Managerial Actions and Techniques" in Exhibit 16-4. Human-resources specialists outside the manager's department usually implement organizational programs.

An important part of effective implementation is the continuation of the remedial program. Given the many pressures facing a manager, it is easy to forget the substandard performer who needs close supervision or a motivational boost. Often, a brief conversation is all that is needed.

Reevaluate Performance after a Time Interval

Step 7 in the controlling process helps ensure that the process is working. In this step, the manager measures the employee's current performance. If the remedial process is working, the team member's performance will move up toward standard. The greater the performance problem, the more frequent the reevaluations of performance should be. In instances of behavior problems such as alcoholism, weekly performance checks are advisable.

Formal and Informal Reviews

A reevaluation of performance can be formal or informal. A formal progress review takes the form of a performance-evaluation session. It might include written documentation of the employee's progress and samples of his or her work. Formal reviews are particularly important when the employee has been advised that dismissal is pending unless improvements are made. Reviews are critical to avoid lawsuits over a dismissal.

---

[26]Linda Wasmer Andrews, "When It's Time for Anger Management," *HR Magazine*, June 2005, p. 132.

The first level of informal review consists of checking on whether the employee has started the action plan. For example, suppose a reserved sales representative agreed to attend an assertiveness-training program. One week later, the manager could ask the rep, "Have you signed up for or started the training program yet?"

The next level of informal review is a discussion of the employee's progress. The manager can ask casual questions such as, "How much progress have you made in accounting for the missing inventory?" Or the manager might ask, "Have you learned how to use the new diagnostic equipment yet?"

Positive Reinforcement and Punishment

If the employee makes progress toward reaching the improvement goal, positive reinforcement is appropriate. Rewarding an employee for progress is the most effective way of sustaining that progress. The reward might be praise, encouragement, or longer intervals between review sessions. The longer time between reviews may be rewarding because the employee will feel that he or she is "back to normal."

Giving rewards for improvement generally proves more effective than giving punishments for lack of improvement. Yet if the problem employee does not respond to positive motivators, some form of organizational punishment is necessary. More will be said about punishment in the discussion about employee discipline.

Continue or Discontinue the Action Plan

Step 8 in the control model for managing ineffective performers is making the decision whether to continue or discontinue the action plan. This step can be considered the feedback component of the control process. If the performance review indicates the employee is not meeting improvement goals, the action plan is continued. If the review indicates goal achievement, the action plan is discontinued.

An important part of using the control model to manage ineffective performers is realizing that positive changes may not be permanent. Performance is most likely to revert to an unacceptable level when the employee is faced with heavy job pressures. For instance, suppose an employee and a manager formulated an action plan to improve the employee's work habits. The employee's performance improved as a result. When the employee is under pressure, however, his or her work may once again become badly disorganized. The manager should then repeat the last five steps of the process, beginning with confrontation.

COACHING AND CONSTRUCTIVE CRITICISM

Most performance improvement takes place as a result of a manager dealing directly with the worker not meeting standards. The usual vehicle for bringing about this improvement is **coaching**. It is a method for helping employees perform better, which usually occurs on the spot and involves informal discussions and suggestions. Workplace coaching is much like coaching on the

---

LEARNING OBJECTIVE **3**

Know what is required to coach and constructively criticize employees.

coaching
A method for helping employees perform better, which usually occurs on the spot and involves informal discussion and suggestions.

constructive criticism

A form of criticism designed to help improve performance or behavior.

athletic field or in the performing arts. Coaching involves considerable **constructive criticism**, a form of criticism designed to help people improve. To be a good coach, and to criticize constructively, requires considerable skill.

Business psychologists James Waldroop and Timothy Butler point out that good coaching is simply good management. Coaching requires the same skills that contribute to effective management, such as keen observation, sound judgment, and an ability to take appropriate action. Coaching and effective management share the goal of making the most of human resources.[27] The following suggestions will help you improve your coaching skill if practiced carefully:

1. *Focus feedback on what is wrong with the work and behavior rather than the employee's attitude and personality.* When the feedback attacks a person's self-image, he or she is likely to become hostile. A defensive person is more likely to focus on getting even rather than getting better. Another way to upset the person being coached is to exaggerate the nature of the poor performance, such as saying, "You've committed the same mistake 100 times," when you have only observed the mistake four times.

2. *Be timely with negative feedback.* Negative feedback should be given close in time to the incident of poor performance. If you observe a worker being rude to a customer, do not wait until the annual performance evaluation to share your observation. Schedule a coaching session as soon as feasible. The worker might be rude to many more customers before he or she receives your criticism.

3. *Listen actively and empathize.* An essential component of coaching employees requires careful listening to their presentation of both facts and feelings. Your active listening will encourage the employee to talk. As the employee talks about his or her problem, you may develop a better understanding of how to improve performance. As you listen actively, the opportunity to show empathy will arise naturally. Suppose the employee blames being behind schedule on the servers being down so frequently. You might show empathy by saying, "Yes, I know it is frustrating to have a computer breakdown when faced with a deadline. Yet we all have to deal with this problem."

4. *Ask good questions.* An effective workplace coach asks questions that help people understand their needs for improvement. Start the coaching session by asking a question, thereby encouraging the person being coached to be an active participant immediately. Consultant Marilyn J. Darling says that effective coaching is based on asking good questions. She notes that the simpler the question, the better. (Notice that the questions are open-ended, as described earlier in the chapter.)

   - "What are you trying to accomplish?"
   - "How will you know if you have succeeded?"

---

[27]James Waldroop and Timothy Butler, "The Executive as Coach," *Harvard Business Review*, November–December 1996, p. 111.

- "What obstacles do you believe are stopping you?"
- "How can I help you succeed?"[28]

5. *Engage in joint problem solving.* Work together to resolve the performance problem. One reason joint problem solving is effective is that it conveys a helpful and constructive attitude on the part of the manager. Another is that the employee often needs the superior's assistance in overcoming work problems. The manager is in a better position to address certain problems than is the employee.

6. *Offer constructive advice.* Constructive advice can be useful to the employee with performance problems. A recommended way of giving advice is first to ask an insightful question. You might ask the employee, "Could the real cause of your problem be poor work habits?" If the employee agrees, you can then offer some specific advice about improving work habits. As part of giving advice, it is more effective to suggest that a person do something rather than try to do something. For example, it is more persuasive to say, "Be at our staff meetings on time," than to say, "Try to be at our staff meetings on time." "Trying" something gives a person an excuse not to succeed.

   An especially effective aspect of constructive advice is to help the person who is performing poorly understand the link between the negative act and attaining key goals such as increased revenue and productivity.[29] Suppose a store manager typically neglects to respond to questions asked by customers using the "Contact Us" function. His or her manager/coach might point out, "Customers who are ignored will soon ignore us, leading to the loss of some important customers, along with some important sales. We need every customer we can get or keep."

7. *Give the poor performer an opportunity to observe and model someone who exhibits acceptable performance.* A simple example of modeling would be for the manager to show the employee how to operate a piece of equipment properly. A more complex example of modeling would be to have the poor performer observe an effective employee making a sale or conducting a job interview. In each case, the ineffective performer should be given opportunities to repeat the activity.

8. *Obtain a commitment to change.* Ineffective performers frequently agree to make improvements but are not really committed to change. At the end of a session, discuss the employee's true interest in changing. One clue that commitment may be lacking is when the employee too readily accepts everything you say about the need for change. Another clue is agreement about the need for change but with no display of emotion. In either case, further discussion is warranted.

---

[28]Marilyn J. Darling, "Coaching Helps People through Difficult Times," *HR Magazine*, November 1994, p. 72.

[29]Gary P. Latham, Joan Almost, Sara Mann, and Celia Moore, "New Developments in Performance Management," *Organizational Dynamics*, Vol. 34, No. 1 (2005), p. 85.

9. *When feasible, conduct some coaching sessions outside of the performance evaluation.* The coaching experience should focus on development and improvement. The performance review is likely to be perceived by the ineffective performer as a time for judging his or her performance. Despite this perception, performance evaluations should include an *aspect* of development.

10. *Applaud good results.* Effective coaches on the playing field and in the workplace are cheerleaders. They give encouragement and positive reinforcement by applauding good results. Some effective coaches shout in joy when a poor performer achieves standard performance; others clap their hands in applause.

EMPLOYEE DISCIPLINE

LEARNING OBJECTIVE **4**
Understand how to discipline employees.

discipline
Punishment used to correct or train.

summary discipline
The immediate discharge of an employee because of a serious offense.

corrective discipline
A type of discipline that allows employees to correct their behavior before punishment is applied.

Up to this point, the chapter emphasized positive approaches to improving substandard performance. At times, however, using the control model requires a manager to discipline employees in an attempt to keep performance at an acceptable level. It is also part of an effective manager's role to be willing to take harsh and unpopular action when the situation requires such behavior. **Discipline**, in a general sense, is punishment used to correct or train. In organizations, discipline can be divided into two types.

Summary discipline is the immediate discharge of an employee because of a serious offense. The employee is fired on the spot for rule violations such as stealing, fighting, selling illegal drugs on company premises, or hacking into confidential computer files. In unionized firms, the company and the union have a written agreement specifying which offenses are subject to summary discipline.

Corrective discipline allows employees to correct their behavior before punishment is applied. Employees are told that their behavior is unacceptable and that they must make corrections if they want to remain with the firm. The manager and the employee share the responsibility for solving the performance problem. The controlling process for managing ineffective performers includes corrective discipline. Steps 4 through 7 in Exhibit 16-3 are based on corrective discipline. Corrective discipline sometimes includes a written letter to an employee summarizing what has taken place so far. The letter is similar to the written warning aspect of progressive discipline (described in the following section), but the letter is less explicit about the consequences of no improvement by the employee. A sample counseling letter is shown in the accompanying Management in Action.

Taking disciplinary action is often thought of in relation to lower-ranking employees. Managers, professionals, and other salaried employees, however, may also need to be disciplined for behaviors such as in backdating stock options for themselves and harassing employees.

The paragraphs that follow describe three other aspects of discipline. First, we describe the most widely used type of corrective discipline,

MANAGEMENT IN ACTION

A Counseling Letter Sent to an Underperforming Employee

To: Employee's Name

From: Supervisor's Name

Subject: Counseling Session

Date: Memo written and distributed

On (date of session), we met to discuss your work performance and specifically your low productivity. This memorandum is intended to serve as a summary of our discussion.

We began the meeting by reviewing a summary of your work during the four months that I have been your supervisor. I stated that I had to reassign an ongoing system test that had been assigned to you because you were not making any progress. I also noted that you had been assigned to develop a simple tracking system for the Office of Internal Audit (OIA) three months ago. I stated that I had accompanied you to the initial meeting with the customer and I noted that you did a good job with the systems analysis work and completed it in a timely fashion. I pointed out, however, that you completed the systems analysis for the OIA system two months ago, and it appears that you have done virtually no work on it since.

I reminded you that you had contracted with the customer to complete the system within 90 days, and now you have missed that deadline. I said that there was very little output to show for the time you had spent in the unit. I explained that during the same time period, the other Senior Programmer Analysts who had similar assignments were extremely productive and the work unit as a whole had completed many projects. I noted that you were assigned a similar amount of work as your co-workers. I further noted that when you were assigned to work on projects with other Programmer Analysts, you frequently arrived late to meetings or missed them altogether, which has had a negative

impact on your co-workers' ability to get the work done on time.

I explained that this level of productivity was unacceptable and was having a negative impact on overall office productivity and morale. I stated that some of your co-workers have requested not to be assigned to work with you because you frequently arrive late to meetings or miss them entirely and do not complete assigned tasks.

In response, you stated that you haven't had a performance evaluation, good or bad, in a few years and you felt that no one cared whether you "coasted" or not. You also asked whether this meant that management was now implementing production quotas.

I acknowledged that it is not appropriate that you have not had an evaluation in the last few years and I assured you that I would evaluate you in a timely manner in the future. I pointed out that although your job assignment has changed, your basic tasks have not substantially changed since the last time you did receive a written evaluation. I reminded you that since I have been assigned as your supervisor, I have provided you with both verbal and written feedback. I stated that while management was not setting quotas, you are still expected to perform an acceptable amount of work and at this time your level of productivity is unacceptable.

I then asked you what you perceived to be the cause of this problem. You acknowledged that you have been very unhappy about your work and your attitude has not been the greatest, but stated that there was no incentive to be more productive. You stated that you were only a Grade 18, that you had been passed over twice for promotion, and that you were paid the same whether you wrote 10 lines of code or 100,000. You stated that you had not intentionally failed to complete your assignments, you just lacked motivation. You also stated that management has had a grudge against you since you filed a grievance against a former supervisor a few years ago.

In response, I reiterated that as a senior programmer analyst, you must meet minimally acceptable performance standards to keep a satisfactory performance rating and that while it is true that high productivity does not directly translate into higher pay, your performance as a programmer analyst is a primary consideration when promotional opportunities arise. I pointed out that if you really wished to be considered for promotion, you should not only improve your production but also set a better example for less experienced programmer analysts by completing tasks on time.

I further explained that when I was assigned to be your supervisor, I approached the task with an open mind. In evaluating your performance, I am only addressing work deficiencies I have observed in the last four months. I stated that when I accompanied you to a customer meeting, you had no problems and showed yourself to be a skilled and competent programmer analyst. I told you that I am still open minded and that it is my hope and expectation that you will apply greater effort to your job. You acknowledged that maybe you were "in a slump" and that you would make a greater

effort to improve your work and your performance in general.

I informed you that your continued poor performance would be reflected in your Annual Performance Evaluation and could result in a referral to Labor Relations for possible disciplinary action. I stated that it was my hope you would take the necessary steps to improve. We agreed to meet in two months to review your progress. In closing, I informed you that a copy of this memorandum would be placed in your personal history folder.

Employee's Signature _____

Supervisor's Signature _____

Copy: Personal History Folder

Case Questions

1. Does it appear that the supervisor was sufficiently clear about the disciplinary problem?
2. What impact do you think this letter might have had upon the employee in question?
3. Why didn't the supervisor simply send a brief e-mail or text message to the employee about the performance problem?

Source: http://www.goer.state.ny.us/train/onlinelearning/EC/SampleMemo.html

progressive discipline. Second, we explain the rules for applying discipline. Third, we examine the positive consequences of punishment to the organization.

Progressive Discipline

progressive discipline

The step-by-step application of corrective discipline.

Progressive discipline is the step-by-step application of corrective discipline, as shown in Exhibit 16-5. Progressive discipline alerts the employee that a performance problem exists, such as not properly documenting claims on an expense report. The manager confronts and then coaches the poor performer about the performance problem. If the employee's performance does not improve, the employee is informed in writing that improvements must be made. The written warning contains more specific information than the oral warning. Some of this specific information might be documentation of the problem, much like the letter contained in the accompanying Management in Action. The written notice often includes a clear statement of what will

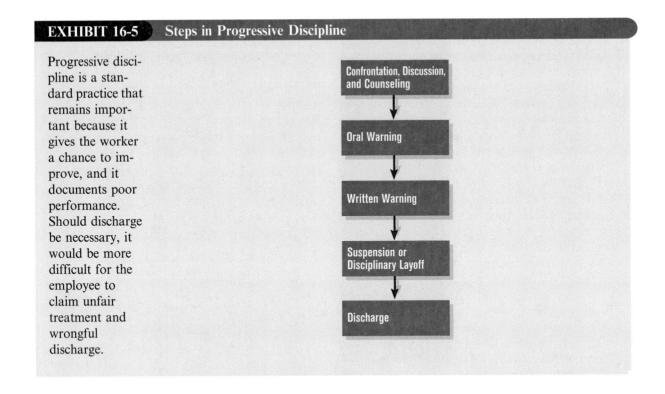

EXHIBIT 16-5 **Steps in Progressive Discipline**

Progressive discipline is a standard practice that remains important because it gives the worker a chance to improve, and it documents poor performance. Should discharge be necessary, it would be more difficult for the employee to claim unfair treatment and wrongful discharge.

Confrontation, Discussion, and Counseling

Oral Warning

Written Warning

Suspension or Disciplinary Layoff

Discharge

happen if performance does not improve. The "or else" could be a disciplinary layoff or suspension. If the notice is ignored and the disciplinary action does not lead to improvement, the employee may be discharged.

Progressive discipline, an old concept, continues to be widely used for two key reasons. First, it provides the documentation necessary to avoid legal liability for firing poorly performing employees. Second, many labor-management agreements require progressive discipline because of the inherent fairness of the step-by-step procedure. Employees are not harshly punished for first offenses that fall outside the realm of summary discipline.

Rules for Applying Discipline

This chapter discussed discipline as it relates to the correction of ineffective performance. However, discipline is more frequently used to deal with infractions of policy and rules. The employee in these situations may not necessarily be a poor performer. The administration of discipline, whether for poor performance or infractions, should adhere to certain time-tested rules. Before applying these rules, a manager in a unionized firm must make sure they are compatible with the employee discipline clauses in the written union agreement.

The red-hot-stove rule offers an old-fashioned but still valid principle in administering discipline. According to the *red-hot-stove rule*, employee discipline should be the immediate result of inappropriate behavior, just as a burn is the result of touching a very hot stove. The employee should receive a warning (the red metal), and the punishment should be immediate, consistent, and impersonal. A manager should keep this rule and those that follow in mind when disciplining employees. Several of these suggestions incorporate the red-hot-stove rule.

1. *All employees should be notified of what punishments will be applied for what infractions.* For example, paralegals might be told that discussing the details of client cases with outsiders, a violation of company policy, will result in discharge.

2. *Discipline should be applied immediately after the infraction is committed.* As soon as is practical after learning of a rule violation, the manager should confront the employee and apply discipline.

3. *The punishment should fit the undesirable behavior.* If the punishment is too light, the offender will not take it seriously. If, on the other hand, it is too severe, it may create anxiety and actually diminish performance.

4. *Managers should be consistent in the application of discipline for each infraction.* Every employee who violates a certain rule should receive the same punishment. Managers throughout the organization should impose the same punishment for the same rule violation. An employment law newsletter advises that the key to a sound discipline policy is equal treatment for all who commit equal offenses.[30]

5. *Disciplinary remedies should be applied impersonally to offenders.* "Impersonal" in this context implies that everybody who is a known rule violator should be punished. Managers should not play favorites.

6. *Documentation of the performance or behavior that led to punishment is required.* Justification for the discipline must be documented in substantial detail. Documentation is essential for defending the company's action in the event of an appeal by the employee or the union or in the case of a lawsuit.

7. *When the discipline is over, return to usual work relations.* The manager should not hold a grudge or treat the rule violator as an outcast. How the person who violated the rule is treated could become a self-fulfilling prophecy. Treating the person who was disciplined as an outcast may make that person feel alienated, causing his or her performance to deteriorate. If the person is treated as someone who is expected not to commit mistakes, he or she will most likely try to live up to that expectation.

You will know that the effort you invest in corrective or progressive discipline is successful when the worker you have disciplined has returned to acceptable performance. In contrast, your efforts in progressive discipline have not been successful when the worker does not improve or his or her performance deteriorates. If progressive discipline proceeds in the spirit of coaching, it is more likely to be successful. In contrast, if progressive

---

[30]"Track All Discipline to Show Unbiased Process," *HR Specialist: New York Employment Law*, March 2010 Special Issue, p. 1.

discipline results in a legalistic battle with each side fighting for its rights, changes in performance are unlikely.

Positive Consequences of Punishment

Conventional wisdom is that punishment should be avoided in the workplace or used only as a last resort because of its negative side effects. Workers who are punished may become anxious, fearful, revengeful, and even violent. Evidence, however, suggests that punishment perceived in certain ways can actually benefit the organization.[31]

A key factor in whether punishment is beneficial is the employee's *belief in a just world,* belief that people get the rewards and punishments they deserve. Employees who believe in a just world are likely to accept punishment when they violate rules or perform poorly because they believe they deserve to be punished. As a consequence, they do not complain about punishment and might even spread the word that the organization is fair.

When employees observe that another employee has been punished justly (fairly), they will often rally on the side of management. The employees may think that the offending employee deserved the punishment. In some instances, other employees may desire that a rule violator be punished because it fits their sense of justice.

Just punishment also informs employees that certain types of misconduct will not be tolerated, as documented in an interview study conducted with 77 managers from different organizations. Many managers regard punishment as an opportunity to promote vicarious learning (in this sense, learning through others).[32] For example, if one employee receives a ten-day suspension for racial harassment, other employees learn that the organization takes racial harassment seriously.

LEARNING OBJECTIVE **5**

Develop an approach to dealing with difficult people, including cynics.

difficult person
An individual whose personal characteristics disturb other people.

DEALING WITH DIFFICULT PEOPLE, INCLUDING CYNICS

Although to this point the chapter focused on dealing with substandard performers, another group of employees may perform adequately yet be annoying and waste managers' time as well as that of coworkers. At times their performance slips below standard because they divert their energy from accomplishing work. A person in this category is often referred to as a **difficult person**, an individual whose personal characteristics disturb other people. Difficult people are such a drain on productivity and personal well-being that they are the subject of study in both the business press and

---

[31]Gail A. Ball, Linda Klebe Treviño, and Harry P. Sims Jr., "Just and Unjust Punishment: Influence on Subordinate Performance and Citizenship," *Academy of Management Journal,* April 1994, pp. 300–301.

[32]Kenneth B. Butterfield, Linda Klebe Treviño, and Gail A. Ball, "Punishment from the Manager's Perspective: A Grounded Investigation and Inductive Model," *Academy of Management Journal,* December 1996, p. 1493.

research journals. Approximately 10 percent of the workforce can be classified as difficult people, a statistic that highlights the importance of this topic.[33]

Four Types of Difficult People

Difficult people have been placed into many different categories or types. Among them are whiners and complainers, know-it-alls, office bullies, pessimists, poor team players, back stabbers, and saboteurs. People who whistle in the office are considered difficult by many, yet some people find the whistling to be soothing. A common feature of difficult people is that they focus on their own needs and agendas, such as wanting to control and manipulate others. For example, the office bully who insults and intimidates others is attempting to control them. Here we focus on four of the most frequently found types of difficult employees: the disgruntled, the passive-aggressive, the uncivil, and change resisters. Later we highlight cynics because of their unusual nature.

Disgruntled workers are angry and often see themselves as victims. They justify their feelings by blaming work associates, including supervisors, coworkers, and customers. Typically, they isolate themselves from those around them.[34] Extremely disgruntled employees with low emotional stability may engage in workplace violence. The *passive-aggressive worker*, on the other hand, expresses anger and hostility by such means as neglecting to take care of an emergency or sitting silently in a meeting without making a contribution.

Uncivil workers are becoming more common as standards for civility in society continue to lower. A survey of 2,000 respondents indicated that nearly four out of five people believe that lack of respect and courtesy is a serious problem that appears to be getting worse. Representative examples of uncivil behavior include dealing with your request while talking on the phone with another person, processing e-mail while talking to you, insulting you in public, and barging past you from the other direction as you exit a door. According to workplace-behavior researchers, many workers who have been treated uncivilly decrease work effort, time on the job, productivity, and performance.[35]

---

[33]Tim McClintock, "Dealing with Difficult People," *Projects@Work* (www.projectsatwork.com), November 17, 2008, p. 1.

[34]Paul Falcone, "Welcome Back Disgruntled Workers," *HR Magazine*, February 2001, p. 133.

[35]Except for the examples, the information about incivility is from Christine Pearson and Christine L. Porath, "On the Nature, Consequences and Remedies of Workplace Incivility: No Time for 'Nice'? Think Again," *Academy of Management Executive*, February 2005, pp. 7–18; Brad Estes and Jia Wang, "Integrative Literature Review: Workplace Incivility: Impacts on Individual and Organizational Performance," *Human Resource Development Review*, 2008, pp. 218–240.

Change resisters tend to live in the past and have difficulty learning new procedures and adjusting to new initiatives.[36] They will often cling to old technologies when the rest of the unit or organization is immersed in a newer version of the technology. Years ago, change resisters might have been the last to accept direct deposit of their paychecks. In the present, they might resist communicating with work associates through social media. Instead, they cling to e-mail and the telephone.

Tactics for Dealing with Difficult People

Much of the advice about dealing with difficult people centers on certain tactics, as described next. It will often be necessary to use a combination of these tactics to help a difficult person become more cooperative. The more the difficult behavior is an ingrained personality pattern, the more difficult it will be to change. In contrast, it is easier to change difficult behavior that stems from the pressures of a given situation. For example, a worker who is sulking because he was not appointed as team leader might not be a long-term passive-aggressive personality.

The list that follows describes a variety of tactics for dealing with difficult people. Pick and choose from them as needed to fit the situation. Despite the many categories of difficult people, the approach to dealing with them is about the same for each type. The medical analogy is that the same antibiotic works successfully for a wide variety of infections.

- *Give feedback about the difficult behavior and stay focused on the issues at hand.* To bring about change, it's essential to provide timely feedback about the problems the difficult person is creating. Do not react specifically to the problem-maker's antics, but instead stay focused on work issues. Describe the behavior you want changed and explain why the behavior is disruptive. Be clear in your communication. Pause for a moment and wait for a response. Acknowledge what the person says, and then state what must be changed, such as "Please stop giving customers an exasperated look and a loud exhale when they make a special request." Ask how the difficult person will make the change, and then get a commitment to change. (Notice the good coaching technique.)
- *Use tact and diplomacy.* Team members who irritate you rarely do annoying things on purpose. Tactful actions on your part can sometimes take care of these problems without your having to go through the controlling process. For example, if a coworker is engaging in a tirade about the company, you might say, "I am really interested in your observations, but I will not reach my goals today if I don't get these e-mails out by 5:00 this afternoon." (Notice the use of "I" statements instead of "you" statements. In this way you are focusing on the problem being created rather than on the individual's character.[37]) When subtlety does not

---

[36]"Tame Team Tigers: How to Handle Difficult Personalities," *Manager's Edge*, Special Issue 2008, p. 8.

[37]"Keep Conflicts from Festering," *Manager's Edge*, August 2009, p. 5.

work, you may have to confront the person. Incorporate tact and diplomacy into the confrontation. For example, as you confront a team member, point out one of his or her strengths.

- *Use humor.* Nonhostile humor can often be used to help a difficult person understand how his or her behavior annoys or blocks others. The humor should point to the person's unacceptable behavior but not belittle him or her. You might say to a subordinate who is overdue on a report: "I know we are striving for zero defects in our company. But if you wait until your report is perfect before submitting it, we may not need it anymore." Your humor may help the team member realize that timeliness is an important factor in the quality of a report.

- *Give recognition and attention.* Difficult people, like misbehaving children, are sometimes crying out for attention. Give them recognition and attention and their difficult behavior will sometimes cease. For example, in a staff meeting, mention the person's recent contributions to the department. If the negative behavior is a product of a deeper-rooted problem, recognition and attention by themselves will not work. It may be necessary to refer the employee for professional counseling.

- *Listen and then confront or respond.* When discussing the problem with the difficult person, allow the individual a full expression of feelings. Next, acknowledge your awareness of the situation and confront the person about how you size up the situation. Finally, specify what you would like to see changed. For example, say: "Please stop complaining so much about factors beyond our control." Avoid judging the person ("You shouldn't be like that") or generalizing ("You always act this way").[38] Part of confrontation includes standing up to a difficult person, especially a bully. Include a statement such as, "I've listened to you, now I have something to say."[39]

- *Stand fast and do not make unwarranted concessions.* A variety of difficult people, particularly bullies, expect you to sacrifice your position or standards, such as breaking the rules just for them. If a person insults you, don't laugh it off or sidestep the remarks. Instead, say, "That's not called for. I cannot let your lack of professionalism pass unnoticed." If you are not intimidated and do not appear insecure, the difficult person is less likely to keep pushing for the advantage.[40]

- *Boost the difficult worker's self-confidence.* Many workers who complain and make excuses frequently or exhibit other forms of difficult behavior are suffering from low self-confidence. They may not stay focused on work because of fear of failure. Assign these employees an easy task so they can succeed and begin to build self-confidence. Then move up the

---

[38]Sam Deep and Lyle Sussman, *What to Say to Get What You Want* (Reading, MA: Addison-Wesley, 1991).

[39]"Fighting off Bullies," WorkingSMART, September 1997, p. 1; http://www.kickbully.com/ 2004.

[40]"How to Deal with 'Problem' Workers," *Positive Leadership*, Sample Issue 2004, p. 6.

scale with a more difficult task. Administer praise and recognition after each success.[41]

- *If the difficult person is your boss, defend yourself without a defensive tone.* A difficult person with formal authority over you will sometimes attack you in a mean-spirited way. Imagine that your boss finds a mistake in your work and then says to you, "You're totally screwing up." You can defend yourself without a defensive tone by saying, "It is true that I made a mistake, and I appreciate constructive feedback to minimize errors in the future." Acknowledge the error, but defend yourself by refusing to be incorrectly labeled as a screw-up.[42]

Dealing with Cynical Behavior

Many employees carry extremely negative attitudes toward their employers, and these negative attitudes often take the form of cynicism. Much of the cynicism appears to be a reaction to top-level management actions, such as boosting their own compensation while laying off lower-ranking workers to save money. Hiring contract and temporary workers at the expense of offering full-time employment also leads to cynicism. Global outsourcing creates cynicism because executive positions are rarely sent overseas. Cynics are classified as difficult people because they express their cynicism more negatively and persistently than do others.

Cynicism is usually expressed by finding something negative about even the best intentions of others. An investigation into the topic concludes that workplace cynicism is shown on any of three dimensions:

- *A belief that the organization lacks integrity* (The cynic might say, "Our advertising is a pack of lies.")
- *A negative affect toward the organization* (Cynics frequently make such comments as "This company is the pits" or "Who in his right mind would join this company today?")
- *Tendencies toward disparaging and critical behaviors directed at the organization that are consistent with these beliefs* (The cynic might use a competitor's consumer product and brag about it.)[43]

Managers may not want to suppress dissent, but too much cynicism in the workplace can lower the morale of others and interfere with recruiting positive people. Cynicism can also be distracting enough to harm productivity. One promising approach to dealing with cynics is to ignore cynical comments and move on to another subject. If the cynic is seeking attention by being cynical, the lack of response will defeat the purpose of the sarcastic comments.

---

[41]McClintock, "Dealing with Difficult People," p. 3.

[42]Nando Pelusi, "Dealing with Difficult People," *Psychology Today*, September/October 2006, p. 69.

[43]James W. Dean Jr., Pamela Brandes, and Ravi Dharwadkar, "Organizational Cynicism," *Academy of Management Review*, April 1998, pp. 341–352.

Cynical commentary can sometimes be reduced by demanding evidence to support harsh comments. Ask for the facts behind the opinion. A cynic might say, "I doubt there will be any money in the bonus pool this year. As usual, top management is taking care of itself first and leaving little money for the rest of us." You might respond, "I seriously doubt top management is going to deny us raises. Where did you get your information?" As in dealing with most difficult people, it's unlikely you will be able to change the individual substantially. However, you can work toward enough improvement to bring about a more positive working relationship.

LEARNING OBJECTIVE 6

Explain the recommended approach to terminating employees.

termination
The process of firing an employee because of poor job performance, unacceptable behavior, or interpersonal problems.

good cause
A legally justifiable or good business reason for firing an employee.

wrongful discharge
The firing of an employee for arbitrary or unfair reasons.

TERMINATION

When corrective actions fail to improve ineffective performance, an employee is likely to be terminated. The company may also assist the person in finding new employment. Termination is considered part of the control process because it is a corrective action. It can also be considered part of the organizing function because it involves managing talent in terms of replacing an untalented person.

Termination is the process of firing an employee because of poor job performance, unacceptable behavior, or interpersonal problems. Termination is regarded as the last alternative. It represents a failure in staffing and in managing ineffective performers. Nevertheless, to maintain discipline and control costs, a firm is often forced to terminate nonproductive employees. When substandard performers are discharged, it communicates the message that adequate performance must be maintained. Thus, a firing can be valuable because it may increase the productivity of employees who are not fired.

Termination usually takes place only after the substandard performer has been offered the types of help described throughout this chapter. In general, every feasible alternative—such as retraining and counseling—should be attempted before termination. A manager must also accumulate substantial written documentation of substandard performance. Appropriate documentation includes performance evaluations, special memos to the file about performance problems, e-mail messages written to the employee about his or her performance, and statements describing the help offered the employee.

Employees must be fired for **good cause**, a legally justifiable or good business reason. For example, it is easy to fire an employee who is caught taking bribes from a vendor or because management decides to close a unit of the company. Without documenting substandard performance, the employer can be accused of **wrongful discharge**, the firing of an employee for arbitrary or unfair reasons, such as age. Many employers face wrongful discharge suits. Court rulings in the last 25 years increasingly prohibited the termination of employees when good faith, fair dealing, and implied contracts were at issue. When a termination is mismanaged, the employer may be subject to a lawsuit even though the reasons for termination were well-founded.[44] To minimize major errors in firing an employee, follow these guidelines:

* *Document carefully the substandard performance that led to the termination.* This is the most fundamental rule for avoiding retaliation, including a lawsuit, by the fired employee. Adequate documentation would include a series of below-average performance appraisals and such objective data as a series of missed financial targets.
* *Never fire an employee when you are angry.* Words said in anger may be too harsh and could reveal a prejudice. For example, an angry manager might say, "I'm getting rid of you, Harry, because we need some fresh young thinkers in this department."
* *Never fire anyone based on second-party information.* For your own legal protection, you should have first-hand knowledge and evidence of the employee's unsatisfactory, immoral, or illegal behavior. For example, a frequent reason for firing a worker today is based on *accusations* of sexual harassment by one person. Managers must collect solid evidence before firing an employee based solely on accusations.
* *Be direct and clear in your language.* Inform the employee explicitly that he or she is being fired and why. Yet ease the blow with a few reassuring phrases such as, "I am sorry this job did not work out for you. Good luck in your next job."
* *Avoid surprises.* Employees should never be totally surprised by being terminated for poor performance. They should receive regular feedback on their performance, as well as suggestions for improvement. Poor performance reviews help take the surprise element out of being terminated.[45] (Good management counts even when terminating workers.)

---

[44]Margaret Fiester, "Terminating Employees, Fostering Culture, Paying for Training Time," *HR Magazine*, August 2009, p. 25.

[45]"How to Avoid the 5 Classic Firing Mistakes," *The HR Specialist*, March 2008, p. 6.

Summary of Key Points

1 **Identify factors contributing to poor performance.**

Job performance is ineffective when productivity falls below a standard considered acceptable at a given time. Ineffective performers consume considerable managerial time. The causes of poor job performance can be rooted in the employee, the job, the manager, or the organization. Usually, ineffective performance is caused by a combination of several factors.

2 **Describe the control model for managing ineffective performers.**

The approach to improving ineffective performance presented in this chapter is a controlling process. It consists of eight steps that should be followed in sequence: (1) define performance standards, (2) detect deviation from acceptable performance, (3) define and assess the cause, (4) communicate with the substandard performer, (5) set improvement goals, (6) select and implement an action plan, (7) reevaluate performance after a time interval, and (8) continue or discontinue the action plan.

Corrective actions for ineffective performers are divided into managerial actions and techniques and organizational programs. Managerial actions include coaching, close supervision, and corrective discipline. Organizational programs include employee assistance programs (EAPs), counseling, outplacement, job redesign, and anger-management programs.

3 **Know what is required to coach and constructively criticize employees.**

Coaching and constructive criticism are useful approaches to managing poor performers. Coaching consists of giving advice and encouragement. Most coaching includes constructive criticism. Skill is required to coach ineffective performers and criticize them constructively. Among the components of good coaching are advice and applause for good results.

4 **Understand how to discipline employees.**

The controlling process may call for discipline. Summary discipline is the immediate discharge of an employee who commits a serious offense. Corrective discipline gives employees a chance to correct their behavior before punishment is applied. The manager and the employee share responsibility for solving the performance problem. Corrective discipline involves counseling.

The major type of corrective discipline is progressive discipline. It represents a step-by-step application of corrective discipline. The manager confronts the ineffective performer about the problem and then coaches him or her. If the employee's performance does not improve, the employee is given a written warning. If this process fails, the employee is suspended or given a disciplinary layoff. The next step is discharge.

The red-hot-stove rule refers to administering discipline right away. The situation should include a warning; consistent, impersonal punishment should be administered immediately following an infraction.

Punishment can help an organization because many employees believe that a rule violator should be punished. Punishment emphasizes that certain types of misconduct will not be tolerated.

5 **Develop an approach to dealing with difficult people, including cynics.**

Difficult people exist in many different types, including the disgruntled, passive-aggressive workers, uncivil people, change resisters, and cynics. When dealing with difficult people, give feedback about the behavior and stay focused on the issue at hand. Use tact and diplomacy, and humor, while giving recognition and attention. Listen to the difficult person, and confront the person about your evaluation of the situation. Do not make unwarranted concessions. Boost the difficult person's self-confidence by starting with an easy task to perform. If your boss is the difficult person, defend yourself without using a defensive tone. One approach to dealing with cynics is to ignore cynical comments. Another approach is to challenge the cynic to support the basis for his or her cynicism.

6 **Explain the recommended approach to terminating employees.**

Termination should take place only after the substandard performer has been offered the type of help built into the control model. Documentation of poor performance is required. Coworkers should be offered a performance-based explanation of why the substandard performer was terminated. Never fire anyone based on second-hand information. Employees should never be totally surprised by being terminated for poor performance.

Key Terms and Phrases

Ineffective job performance, 588
Organizational citizenship behavior, 592
Confrontation, 599
Improvement goal, 600
Employee assistance program (EAP), 601
Coaching, 604
Constructive criticism, 605
Discipline, 607

Summary discipline, 607
Corrective discipline, 607
Progressive discipline, 609
Difficult person, 612
Termination, 617
Good cause, 617
Wrongful discharge, 617

Questions

1. What is a potential fallacy behind the idea that workers in the bottom 10 percent or 5 percent of the workforce are substandard performers?
2. What is the link between managing ineffective performers and organizational productivity?
3. Why is it that first-level supervisors usually spend more time managing ineffective performance than do C-level executives?
4. How might an athletic coach apply the control model for managing ineffective performers to improve team performance?
5. Why should management be willing to rehabilitate employees through an employee assistance program when so many workers have been downsized in recent years?
6. In what type of job might being a difficult person not be much of a liability?
7. What is your opinion of the merits of using an outside consultant to terminate substandard performers?

Skill-Building Exercise 16-A: Managing Ineffective Performance Role-Play

Imagine that you are the team leader, and one of the team members frequently fails to show up when a critical task must be performed. He or she usually has an excuse, such as another assignment from upper management, a funeral, or a medical appointment. You and the other team members are concerned that this person is a social loafer. One person plays the role of the teammate with excuses; one person plays the role of the team leader; and three or four other students play the role of the team members. At your meeting today, you intend to confront the errant team member and you have developed a plan for improvement. Being a true team, all team members will contribute to dealing with the problem member. Run the session for about 10 to 15 minutes.

Skill-Building Exercise 16-B: Bully Busting

Workplace bullying continues to receive attention as a serious workplace problem. In this role-play, one student plays the role of an abusive, intimidating bully who likes to damage the self-esteem of coworkers. Today the bully is particularly upset because his or her long overdue cell phone account has been turned over to a collection agency. During the rest break, this bully decides it is time to initiate bullying with a coworker seated at the table. Another student plays the role of the worker who is the bully's target. After receiving about four minutes of abuse, the second role player gets into the bully busting mode. Observers will judge both the acting ability of the role players, and the effectiveness of the bully buster.

Management Now: Online Skill-Building Exercise:
Finding a C-Level Manager Worthy of Being Terminated

It is easy to talk in the abstract about what type of behavior by a high-level manager warrants the manager being fired. Your assignment is to search the Internet for a story published within the last three months of a specific C-level executive who you think should be fired from his or her position. Document in about 50 words why you think the executive should be terminated. Also, estimate what you think adequate severance pay should be for the executive in question.

16-A Case Problem

"It Takes Me a Long Time to Get Here"

Mark works as a cost estimator for a commercial construction company in Denver, Colorado. He reports to Tanya, the manager of cost estimating. Tanya regards Mark as a satisfactory performer, but she disapproves strongly of his frequent tardiness. During a snowfall, Mark is often over 90 minutes late for work.

One Thursday morning, Tanya sent Mark an e-mail requesting that he meet with her at 3 that afternoon. Mark responded immediately and said that he would have up to one hour for the meeting because he had to leave promptly at 4 p.m. to deal with a family emergency.

Tanya began the meeting by saying, "Mark, as I have mentioned before, your lateness is getting out of hand. You are too late for work too often. Sometimes I am looking around for you at 10 in the morning, and you are nowhere to be found. A few times your coworkers have asked me where you are because they need your input. What is your problem, Mark?"

"Tanya, you might be judging me a little too harshly. I have a valid excuse. I live 65 miles away, and that is a long commute. It is hard to estimate the traffic. And during the snow season, it is difficult to judge the road conditions. It takes me a long time to get here."

"So why do you live 65 miles from our office?" responded Tanya. "Can't you work out a better living arrangement so you can be closer to work?"

"I've got two problems that I respectfully would like you to understand. First, my father has M.S. (multiple sclerosis), and he needs me to live with him to help out. He's a widow, and he doesn't have the money to hire a home health aide.

"My second problem is that rents are sky high in this mile high city. I would need a 50 percent raise to live in an apartment near here. Do you see my predicament now?"

"I sympathize with your challenges, Mark, but I need you to report to work on time. I can accept the fact that you might face an occasional emergency, but you need to be more prompt about reporting to work.

"Let me think about the problem a little more, and get back to you."

Discussion Questions

1. What recommendations can you offer Tanya to be more effective in dealing with Mark's tardiness problem?
2. To what extent do you think Tanya should be more tolerant with respect to Mark's problem of being tardy?
3. What advice can you offer Mark with respect to his arriving to work late?

16-B Case Problem

Coach Fred Zweiger

Fred Zweiger is a vice president and investment consultant at a large branch of a leading financial services firm. Zweiger's main responsibility is managing the portfolios of clients with over $300,000 in assets. Reporting to Zweiger are two office assistants, and his administrative assistant Maria Mehani. Maria's main responsibilities are taking care of administrative tasks in relation to clients, such as making sure they complete the correct paperwork or computer forms, and arranging meetings between clients and Fred.

Each client is supposed to have one face-to-face meeting with Fred each year to discuss his or her investment portfolio. Maria telephones the clients to encourage them to visit the office for the meetings. Relatively little contact with clients is conducted over e-mail, to minimize the security risk of account numbers or social security numbers beings stolen by hackers.

Maria has worked as Fred's assistant for three years. He has been generally satisfied with her performance yet believes that if Maria reached out more to clients she would help establish better client relationships, thus encouraging more investments by clients. Fred has also noticed that several clients have mentioned that Maria continues to spell their names incorrectly and needs several reminders on address changes. As a result of these needs for improvement, Fred decides to hold a coaching session with Maria.

Later that afternoon, Fred drops by Maria's desk about 25 feet outside his office. He explains that he would like to have a staff-development meeting with her on Thursday at 4 p.m., right after the U.S. stock markets close. Maria responds with a smile, "Are you going to develop me to become a financial consultant? Or are you going to fire me?"

"Somewhere in between," responded Fred with a smile. "I'll see you Thursday." A partial transcript of the meeting is presented next.

Fred: Thanks for being here on time. It was a great day on Wall Street, so I'm in a good mood to talk about your development. Specifically I want to talk about your development into a more helpful administrative assistant to me.

Maria: I thought that I was already pretty helpful. I do whatever is required in my job description. Also, I stay late many times without overtime pay just to take care of office details.

Fred: Maria, I am not accusing you of doing a poor job. I just think you could do a better job. You need more oomph, more push, more caring, and more warmth in what you are doing.

Maria: More oomph, push, caring, and warmth. I don't know what you're talking about. I like my job but I wasn't hired to be a cheerleader.

Fred: If you don't know what I'm talking about, it only proves that I'm right. You're missing out on the subtle things needed to be an outstanding administrative assistant to an investment consultant.

Maria: I feel like I'm being accused of not doing things that are not even in my job description. I was never told this job required oomph and warmth toward clients.

Fred: But it is part of your job to serve our clients in the best way you can. You need to show them more concern and interest when they telephone you, or come into the office to see me. You should act like everyone is our most important client. To make matters worse, I've heard lots of complaints that you don't spell some of the clients' names correctly on the envelopes you mail them.

16-B Case Problem

Maria: What do you mean by "lots of complaints"? Is that two, three, four, or one hundred?

Fred: I haven't kept a log, but I think you are making way too many mistakes with our clients' names. A few of our clients with long Indian last names have complained the most. Just be a little more careful with the names. The big change I want is for you to make more of an impact on our clients. Form stronger bonds with them.

Maria: How do you recommend I make that big change with all the other responsibilities I have?

Fred: You figure it out. Maybe study a book about charisma or go to a human relations seminar. I'll pay for it. That's all I have to say on the subject for now.

Maria: I'll talk to you later, Fred. I am not very happy about our meeting today.

Discussion Questions

1. What is Fred doing wrong from a coaching standpoint?
2. What is Fred doing right from a coaching standpoint?
3. What suggestions would you offer Maria so she can develop warmer and closer relationships with clients?
4. What is your evaluation of Maria's willingness to develop her job-relevant skills?

CHAPTER 17

Enhancing Personal Productivity and Managing Stress

OBJECTIVES

After studying this chapter and doing the exercises, you should be able to:

1 Identify techniques for improving work habits and time management.

2 Explain why people procrastinate, and identify techniques for reducing procrastination.

3 Understand the nature of stress and burnout, including their consequences.

4 Explain how stress can be managed effectively.

Primary Freight Services, Inc., an international shipping company headquartered in Rancho Dominguez, California, introduced a three-month stress management program for its 70 employees in a January during the Great Recession, six weeks before shortening the workweek to four days and cutting everyone's pay 29 percent. The program is aimed at teaching employees how to take care of themselves physically, mentally, and emotionally. It offers counseling on productive ways to use their extra day at home—whether spending more time with family, pursuing a hobby, or finding a second job or a work-from-home situation.

As a result of the program, the mood at Primary Freight's three offices in Southern California, Chicago, and New Jersey remains "remarkably upbeat," reports Carl Schwarm, vice president of sales and marketing. "In our industry, so many companies are going through layoffs and furloughs that I think people are very happy to have a job and to know that they're working for a company that is looking forward and finding ways to make a bad situation a manageable situation."[1]

---

[1]Pamela Babcock, "Workplace Stress? Deal with It!" *HR Magazine*, May 2009, p. 70.

The anecdote about the shipping company taking positive steps to help employees cope with a potentially negative situation illustrates how managers understand the importance of stress in the workplace. The managers wanted to help employees cope with the stress of job insecurity and, at the same time, keep worry from interfering with job productivity. In this chapter, we describe methods for both improving productivity and managing stress, which are as interlocked as nutrition and health. If you are well organized, you will avoid much of the negative stress that stems from feeling that your work and life are out of control. If your level of stress is about right, you will be able to concentrate better on your work and be more productive.

The emphasis in this final chapter of the book is on managing yourself rather than managing other people or managing a business. Unless you have your work under control and effectively manage stress, it is unlikely you can be an effective manager or leader.

LEARNING OBJECTIVE ❶

Identify techniques for improving work habits and time management.

productivity
How effectively you use your resources to achieve your goals.

IMPROVING YOUR WORK HABITS AND TIME MANAGEMENT

High personal productivity leads to positive outcomes such as higher income, more responsibility, and recognition. **Productivity** in this sense is how effectively you use your resources to achieve your goals.[2] In an era of work streamlining and downsizings based on company consolidations, the demand for high productivity among managerial workers has never been higher. Managers, as well as other workers, pressure themselves to produce more for every hour of work. Productivity enhancers, such as daily planners, sell at record rates. High job productivity also allows you to devote more worry-free time to your personal life. In addition, high productivity helps reduce the stress experienced when a person's job is out of control. The present thrust in time management is to help people lead a better life. Don Wetmore, president of The Productivity Institute, says, "Time management is the foundation for creating balance in our lives in vital areas, such as health and family."[3]

Here we describe improving productivity by improving work habits and time management. In the next section, we approach productivity improvement from the perspective of reducing procrastination. Improving your work habits and time management is much like applying scientific management to boost personal productivity.

---

[2]Adaptation of a definition presented in Robert D. Pritchard et al., "The Productivity Measurement and Enhancement System: A Meta-Analysis, *Journal of Applied Psychology*, May 2008, p. 540.

[3]Quoted in Kathryn Tyler, "Beat the Clock," *HR Magazine*, November 2003, p. 103.

Go to www.cengage
.com/management/
dubrin and view the
video for Chapter 17.
How do the people
in this video manage
stress on the job?
How do you think
stress affects their
work and personal
lives?

work ethic
A firm belief in the
dignity and value of
work.

Develop a Mission, Goals, and a Strong Work Ethic

A major starting point in becoming a better organized and more productive person is to have a purpose and values that propel you toward being productive. In the words of Stephen Covey, "without a Personal Mission Statement, you have nothing to plan and act for."[4] Assume that a person says, "My mission in life is to become an outstanding office supervisor and a caring, constructive spouse and parent." The mission serves as a compass to direct that person's activities and assist with developing a reputation that will lead to promotion. Goals are more specific than mission statements; they support the mission statement and contribute to the same effect. For example, the person in question might one day set a goal to respond by the end of the day to 75 customer inquiries that have accumulated on the company Web site. Accomplishing that amount of work would be one more step toward being promoted to supervisor.

Closely related to establishing goals is to have a strong **work ethic**—a firm belief in the dignity and value of work. Developing a strong work ethic may lead to even higher productivity than goal-setting alone. For example, one might set the goal of earning a high income. This practice would lead to some good work habits, but not necessarily to a high commitment to quality. A person with a strong work ethic believes in producing work or service of high quality, is highly motivated, and minimizes time-wasting activities. Having a strong work ethic also implies that you are an engaged worker, committed to your employer and willing to put in extra effort on the job.[5]

Clean Up Your Work Area and Sort Out Your Tasks

People sometimes become inefficient because their work area is messy. They waste time looking for things and neglect important papers. Electronic documents can also be lost, though not as readily. The chance of losing or misplacing electronic documents increases monthly because many people create so many different files and documents. It is best to store never-used or rarely used files in a place other than your hard drive. To get started on improving personal productivity, clean up your work area and sort out what tasks you need to accomplish.

Most documents are stored on computers, on external drives, or on the servers of cloud computing services. Yet most companies still have many paper documents that must be carefully filed so they can be retrieved on demand. Some types of financial and medical records are legally required to include paper copies. Having well-organized physical files remains an important part of cleaning up your work area.

Getting Things Done is a popular system for improving productivity that touches on many of the principles described in this chapter. The starting

---

[4]Cited in Ed Brown, "The 'Natural Laws' of Saving Time," *Fortune*, February 1, 1999, p. 138.

[5]Ed Frauenheim, "Commitment Issues," *Workforce Management*, November 16, 2009, p. 20.

point for uncluttering your life is to collect everything you must do that is unfinished or undecided. After that, you begin sorting out the tasks and assigning priorities in terms of their accomplishment[6] (as described below).

Get rid of as much clutter as possible, including personal souvenirs, and clean up your work area. Work area includes your briefcase, your file of phone numbers, your hard drive, and your e-mail files. Having loads of e-mail messages stacked in your Inbox, Sent Items, and Deleted Items can make it difficult to notice and pay attention to important new messages. Weeding out your mailing list is also important. Ask to be removed from the distribution of paper and e-mail messages that are of no value. Rebel against being spammed. Many people begin the workday by immediately deleting unwanted e-mail messages. Deleting these messages is a bigger task for people who work at home or at smaller firms that lack elaborate protections against spam.

Recognize that the issue of avoiding clutter is controversial. Many workers believe that working in the midst of a mess is effective so long as you are able to find what you need within the mess. One book, *A Perfect Mess,* advises people not to be too organized. According to the book, being super-organized restricts flexibility and your ability to respond to spur-of-the-moment opportunities.[7] Recent research suggests that the amount of clutter might simply reflect differences in cognitive mental style; achieving a clutter-free environment might mean fighting against a natural tendency.[8] Another problem with avoiding clutter by filing away papers is that many people work by the "out of sight, out of mind" principle. If something is put into a drawer or other file, it will be neglected.

Prepare a To-Do List and Assign Priorities

A to-do list lies at the heart of every time-management system and is a building block for planning because it records what needs to be accomplished. A survey of small-company executives revealed that about 95 percent keep a list of things to do. Most of them have between 6 and 20 items on their list, and few accomplish everything on the list every day.[9] The accompanying Management in Action illustrates how a top-level executive relies on a to-do list to accomplish work. Another example is Mark Hurd, the co-president and member of the board of Oracle Corporation. He personally maintains a spreadsheet that tracks and analyzes his daily to-do items.[10]

In addition to writing down tasks you must do, assign priorities to them. A simple categorization, such as top priority versus low priority, works well for most people. In general, take care of top-priority tasks before

---

[6]Paul Keegan, "The Master of Getting Things Done," *Business 2.0,* July 2007, p. 77.

[7]Eric Abrahamson and David H. Freedman, *A Perfect Mess: The Hidden Benefits of Disorder* (Little Brown and Company, 2006).

[8]Research cited in Jay Dixit, "Office Spaces," *Psychology Today,* March/April 2010, p. 49.

[9]Mark Hendricks, "Just 'To-Do' It," *Entrepreneur,* August 2004, p. 71.

[10]Adam Lashinsky, "Mark Hurds' Moment," *Fortune,* March 16, 2009, p. 94.

low-priority ones. There are so many things to do on any job that some very low-priority items may never get done. Keep your to-do list on a desk calendar or a large tablet or in your computer. Setting deadlines for accomplishment is helpful in directing your efforts, so long as the deadlines are real rather than arbitrary. A real deadline would be one imposed by your boss or by law, or one that you must attain so you can start on another project by a particular date.

A word-processing file may suffice, but more advanced software for work scheduling is also available, such as Microsoft Outlook. Small slips of paper in various locations tend to be distracting and are often misplaced. Plan the next day's activities at the end of each work day, including discharging today's unfinished work. This will give you a fresh plan of attack for the next day.

Many workers use daily or weekly planners to serve as a to-do list. A planner typically divides the day into 15-minute chunks and leaves room for the daily to-do list. Some planning systems are linked to a person's mission, thus giving an extra impetus to accomplishing tasks. No matter how elaborate the system that incorporates the humble to-do list, it will not boost productivity unless the items are referred to frequently, perhaps daily. Some well-organized people plan their to-do list in their head. As they move through the day, they keep working the list.

Taking care of a small, easy-to-do task first—such as sharpening pencils—has a hidden value. It tends to be relaxing and gives you the emotional lift of having accomplished at least one item on your list. Accomplishing small tasks helps reduce stress.

A variation on the to-do list with enormous consequences for productivity and safety is the checklist. The checklist prescribes steps that must be taken while executing a procedure when a deviation from this procedure could have strong negative consequences. According to Dan Heath and Chip Heath, checklists are effective because they inform workers about the best course of action, showing them the ironclad way to do something.[11] In a hospital, a valid checklist would help prevent infections in surgical patients and eliminate the risk of cutting off the wrong limb during surgery. In a retail store, a checklist would help prevent accepting a bogus check. In a factory, a checklist would help prevent shipping a defective product. Of course, all of these checklists must contain valid entries to be effective.

Streamline Your Work

A work habit and time-management principle essential today is work streamlining—eliminating as much low-value work as possible and concentrating on activities that add value for customers or clients. To streamline work, justify whether every work procedure, e-mail message, report, meeting, or ceremonial activity contributes value to the firm. The number of group luncheon

---

[11]Dan Heath and Chip Heath, "The Heroic Checklist," *Fast Company*, March 2008, pp. 66, 68.

MANAGEMENT IN ACTION

Leading Banker Uses To-Do List to Keep Organized

James (Jamie) Dimon, chairman and chief executive of JPMorgan Chase & Co., has become Wall Street's banker of last resort. A decade after Dimon's career seemed shattered by his notorious ouster from Citigroup, Inc., he was playing a critical role in the global crunch at a time when rival firms were on their knees. For example, in 2008, J.P. Morgan had agreed to buy Bear Stearns Cos.

From helping to salvage a Home Depot transaction to rallying other banks to heed the Federal Reserve's attempt to provide market relief, Dimon has emerged as one of Wall Street's most powerful players at a time when many firms were scrambling for leadership.

J.P. Morgan "stands behind Bear Stearns," Dimon said in a news release. "Bear Stearns' clients and counterparties should feel secure that J.P. Morgan is guaranteeing Bear Stearns' counterparty risk. We welcome their clients, counterparties and employees to our firm, and we are glad to be their partner."

All weekend, Dimon was locked in negotiations to buy the 85-year-old institution. If he had balked, government officials and others worried that Bear would be forced to file for bankruptcy protection, causing ripple effects throughout the global financial system. Nevertheless, two years later, Dimon balked at the government's attempts to restrict executive pay and force banks to increase lending. He organized an aggressive lobbying effort to combat regulation that would curb the bank's profits.

Dimon's intense involvement is typical of the hands-on boss and detail-oriented New Yorker who places a hand-written to-do list in his breast pocket each morning. On the left side is a list of items that must be addressed. On the lower right quadrant is a list of what Dimon refers to as "people who owe me stuff"—responses to unanswered questions, return phone calls, and the like.

Case Questions

1. James Dimon is one of the mostly highly paid bankers in the world. Why doesn't he use something fancier than a hand-written to-do list to help keep him organized?
2. In what way might being well organized contribute to the success of a high-level banker like Dimon?

Sources: Robin Sidel, "In a Crisis, It's Dimon Once Again," *The Wall Street Journal*, March 17, 2008, pp. C1, C2; Grace Kiser, "J.P. Morgan CEO Jamie Dimon Takes on Washington," *The Huffington Post* (www.huffingtonpost.com), April 7, 2010.

meetings away from the office might be cut in half, giving staff members more time during the day to conduct urgent work. A basic example of work streamlining would be to take advantage of the United States Postal Service package pick-up service instead of visiting the post office to ship packages.

Masterfoods analyzed who was communicating with whom in order to understand how its product-development, packaging, and process-development staff spent their time. A surprising finding was that too much time was being spent in collaboration. The manager of research and development said, "When we looked at the data, it turned out it was hard to do business internally. People had to talk to 30 or 40 other people just to get their jobs done, which took away from their time to work on new ideas." Masterfoods then redesigned the workflow of the packaging group to eliminate many of the extraneous steps that consumed so much time.[12]

Work at a Steady, Rapid Pace

Although a dramatic show of energy (as in "pulling an all-nighter") is impressive, the steady worker tends to be more productive in the long run. The spurt employee creates many problems for management; the student who works in spurts is in turmoil at examination time or when papers are due. Managers who expend the same amount of effort day by day tend to stay in control of their jobs. When a sudden problem or a good opportunity comes to their attention, they can fit it into their schedule. Working at a steady pace often means always working rapidly. To be competitive, most organizations require that work be accomplished rapidly.

An important exception about working rapidly all the time is that some decisions require careful deliberation and should not be rushed. A team of researchers studied for 19 months the decision making of an Internet start-up. Making decisions too rapidly resulted in many errors in purchasing software and hiring people.[13]

The recommendations about working rapidly yet making major decisions deliberately are compatible. After you take enough time to make a major decision, work rapidly to accomplish the tasks necessary to implement the decision. A manager might carefully weigh the evidence about the value of outsourcing some call center operations to Africa. After the decision is made, the manager and his or her staff work rapidly to make the outsourcing a reality.

Minimize Time Wasters and Interruptions

An important strategy for improving personal productivity is to minimize time wasters. Each minute invested in productive work can save you from working extra hours. A major time waster is interruptions from others. One of the benefits of telecommuting is that interruptions from other workers are minimized. When doing intellectually demanding work, getting the appropriate flow of thought is difficult. When interrupted, people lose momentum and must launch themselves again. The definition of what constitutes an *interruption* is tricky. A coworker asking you to participate in a basketball pool is certainly an interruption, but socializing with him or her might strengthen your network. Some executives feel that a demand from a

---

[12]Michael Mandel, "The Real Reasons You're Working So Hard ... and What You Can Do About It," *Business Week*, October 3, 2005, p. 66.

[13]Leslie A. Perlow, Gerardo A. Okhuysen, and Nelson P. Repenning, "The Speed Trap: Exploring the Relationship between Decision Making and Temporal Context," *Academy of Management Journal*, October 2002, pp. 931–955.

EXHIBIT 17-1	Four Types of Interruptions and their Positive and Negative Consequences	
Type of Interruption	**Negative Consequences for Person Being Interrupted**	**Positive Consequences for Person Being Interrupted**
Intrusion (unexpected encounter)	Not enough time to accomplish the task leading to stress; disruption in concentration	Informal feedback and information sharing that otherwise might not be available
Break (planned or spontaneous recess from work)	Procrastination and/or significant amounts of time spent relearning essential details of work being performed	Alleviation of fatigue or distress; more job satisfaction; time for ideas to incubate; refreshed approach to task
Distraction (secondary activity that disrupts concentration)	Mediocre performance when work is complex and demanding, and requires full attention	Enhanced performance when the distraction increases stimulation levels on routine tasks
Discrepancy (inconsistency between what you expected and what is really happening)	Strong negative emotional reaction (such as from finding out that you have been working on improving a product that management has decided to drop)	Recognition of the need for change and triggering person into action

Source: Adapted and abridged from Quintus R. Jett and Jennifer M. George, "Work Interrupted: A Closer Look at the Role of Interruptions in Organizational Life," *Academy of Management Review*, July 2003, p. 497.

customer should never be classified as an interruption. A sudden demand from a boss might also not be classified as an interruption.

A contingency perspective on interruptions is that most of them are harmful to work, but some are helpful. For example, if somebody walks into your cubicle while you are attempting to calculate a gross profit margin—that your boss wants in ten minutes—the interruption is dysfunctional. Yet at another time, chatting with an intruder could result in some useful information sharing; that interruption is functional. A scientific analysis of the positive and negative consequences of four different types of interruptions is presented in Exhibit 17-1.

A time waster of considerable magnitude is searching the Internet for information not strictly related to work, or Internet surfing. Lost productivity is a major problem as workers surf the Internet for nonwork reasons. A widely quoted survey of 2,000 workers by Salary.com found that Americans waste about 20 percent of their time at work, 34.7 percent indicating that surfing the Internet is the biggest distraction.[14]

---

[14]"Employees Waste 20% of Their Work Day According to Salary.com Survey," Salary.com, 2007.

A related problem is bandwidth waste, as workers download complex graphics and videos (especially with the popularity of YouTube). Legal liability may surface when workers transfer or display sexually explicit content because such material may be interpreted as creating a hostile work environment. E-mail and Internet-borne viruses may work their way into the company's information technology system as a by-product of surfing.

Another computer-related drain on productivity is the frequent shifting from one computer-related task to another. A contributing factor is that it takes time to refocus on the next task because most activities have a start-up phase. Constant jumping from one task to another or attempting to do two tasks at once, also referred to as *multitasking*, can be a time waster.[15]

Exhibit 17-2 presents a list of significant ways to reduce wasted time. Many of the other suggestions in this chapter can help you save time directly or indirectly.

Concentrate on One Task at a Time

Productive managers develop their capacity to concentrate on the problem facing them at the moment, no matter how engulfed they are with other obligations. Intense concentration leads to sharpened judgment and analysis and decreases the chance of major errors. Another useful by-product of concentration is reduced absentmindedness. The person who concentrates on the task at hand allows less chance of forgetting what he or she intended.

Multitasking has become a typical mode of operation for many workers. However, multitasking is best reserved for routine tasks such as discarding unwanted e-mail messages and cleaning your desk at the same time. As described in Chapter 14, multitasking on important tasks may lead to serious errors, and many forms of multitasking may be perceived as rude by other workers who do not engage in the same behavior. *Surfer's voice* is a term used to describe the habit of half-heartedly conversing with someone on the telephone while simultaneously surfing the Web, reading e-mail messages, or exchanging instant messages.[16]

A major problem with multitasking is that it can lead to accidents and death both on and off the job. If you are driving your car for company business and talking on your cell phone at the same time, your employer is liable if you get into an accident. One estimate is that drivers using cell phones cause about 3,000 fatal crashes a year in the United States and 570,000 accidents. A driver talking on a cell phone is four times more likely to crash than a person not talking, and a hands-free device does not reduce the risk substantially.[17] Sending text messages while driving is an even more hazardous form of multitasking.

---

[15]Alina Dizik, "Services to Help Us Stop Dawdling Online," *The Wall Street Journal*, January 28, 2010, p. D2.

[16]Dennis K. Berman, "Technology Has Us So Plugged into Data, We Have Turned Off," *The Wall Street Journal*, November 10, 2003, p. B1.

[17]Studies cited in Matt Richtel, "Promoting the Car Phone, Despite Risks," *The New York Times* (www.nytimes.com), December 27, 2009, pp. 1, 2.

EXHIBIT 17-2 **Ways to Prevent and Overcome Time Wasting**

Wasted time is a major productivity drain, so it pays to search for time wasters in your work activities. The following list suggests remedies for some of the major time wasters in the workplace.

1. Use a time log for two weeks to track time wasters.
2. Minimize daydreaming on the job by forcing yourself to concentrate.
3. Avoid using the computer as a diversion from work; resist sending jokes back and forth to network members, friends, and followers; avoid playing video games; and resist checking out recreational and shopping Web sites during working hours.
4. Batch similar tasks such as responding to e-mail messages or returning phone calls. For example, in most jobs, it is possible to be productive by reserving two or three 15-minute periods each day for taking care of e-mail correspondence. Checking e-mail too frequently is a major time waster unless it's necessary for your job.
5. Socialize on the job just enough to build your network. Chatting with coworkers is a major productivity drain and one of the reasons so many managers work at home part of the time when they have analytical work that must be done.
6. Be prepared for meetings; have a clear agenda and sort through the documents you will be referring to. Make sure electronic equipment is in working order before attempting to use it during the meeting.
7. Keep track of important names, places, and things to avoid wasting time searching for them. For example, designate a place for your keys and flash drive both at home and at work. Visualize where you place items; say to yourself, "I am putting my sunglasses over the visor on the driver's side of my car."
8. Set a time limit for repetitive tasks after you have done them once or twice.
9. Prepare a computer template for letters and documents that you send frequently. (The template is essentially a form letter, especially with respect to the salutation and return address.)
10. Avoid perfectionism, which leads you to redo a project "just a little bit more." Let go and move on to another project.
11. Make use of bits of time between appointments. Use those minutes to send a business e-mail or revise your to-do list. (Note the exception to the batch principle.)
12. Sort out your mail over a wastebasket or recycling bin. Immediately dispose of mail you have no need to open now or later. You save time by having less accumulated mail to sort through a second time.
13. Resist grabbing for your cell phone or smart phone at every conceivable moment, such as when you exit the building. Some of the time devoted to chatting on the cell phone could be invested in planning your work or searching for creative ideas. Many managers and corporate professionals consult their personal digital assistant for business instead of social purposes on the way to or back from lunch.
14. Minimize procrastination, the number-one time waster for most people.

Source: Suggestions 4, 5, and 6 are based on Stephen R. Covey with Hyrum Smith, "What If You Could Chop an Hour from Your Day for Things That Matter Most?" *USA Weekend*, January 22–24, 1999, pp. 4–5. Suggestion 7 is based partly on "How to Boost Your Brainpower," *TopHealth*, October, 2009, p. 2.

Notice the important difference between multitasking, which refers to doing two or more tasks at the same time, and working on multiple tasks in sequence. For example, it is the usual case for a manager or corporate professional to be assigned to two different projects, such as one for product development and another for environmental protection. Multitasking would be doing a spreadsheet on product development while talking on the phone to a coworker about carbon footprints. Working on multiple projects would include spending the morning on product development and the afternoon on environmental protection.

The case for concentrating on one important task at a time is strongly stated by time-management guru Stephanie Winston: "Successful CEOs do not multitask … They concentrate intensely on one thing at a time … [H]ow can you do your best work if you're constantly distracted?"[18] An exception is that there are some successful CEOs who routinely consult their BlackBerrys while talking to employees or customers. People of this nature are often referred to as "CrackBerrys." (The analogy refers to addiction to crack cocaine.)

In contrast to the problems just stated, multitasking for routine tasks can lead to productivity gain. A growing form of multitasking involves working with two computer monitors. You use one monitor to go about your regular work and the other monitor for e-mail. In this way, you need not constantly minimize and maximize your document to access e-mail. However, if you are working on a document that requires full attention, it is hazardous to continually glance at the e-mail monitor. For example, if you are analyzing tax data for the company, resist looking at your second monitor.

Concentrate on High-Output Tasks

Many people interpret time-management techniques as a way of becoming a tidy perfectionist who never lets a detail slip by. In contrast, a major time-management principle is that to become more productive on the job or in school, concentrate on tasks in which superior performance could have a large payoff. For a manager, a high-output task would be to develop a strategic plan for the department or find ways to obtain a high return on investment for surplus cash. For a student, a high-output task would be to think of a creative idea for an independent study project. Expending your work effort on high-output items is analogous to looking for a good return on investment for your money. The high-output strategy also follows the Pareto principle, described in Chapter 6.

A new twist on high-output tasks is that they usually involve some risk because they are a departure from the typical way of doing business. The risk taker may work fewer hours than other workers but courageously pushes for new ideas. For example, someone working for Dell or Hewlett-Packard might develop a replacement for the standard desktop computer. Many people are hesitant to take such risks because they fear failure, standing out, or being rejected.[19]

---

[18]Quoted in Anne Fisher, "Get Organized at Work—Painlessly," *Fortune*, January 10, 2005, p. 30.

[19]Seth Godin, "A Brief History of Hard Work, Adjusted for Risk," *Fast Company*, April 2003, p. 64.

Do Creative and Routine Tasks at Different Times

Another way to improve productivity is to organize your work so you are not constantly shifting between creative and routine tasks. The desired pay-off of this is similar to concentrating on high-output tasks. For many people, it is best to work first on creative tasks because they require more mental energy than routine tasks. A few people prefer to get minor paperwork and e-mail chores out of the way so they can get to the pleasure of creative tasks. Whichever order you choose, it is important not to interrupt creative (or high-output) tasks with routine activities such as deleting spam or rearranging the desk.

It is also helpful to tackle creative tasks when you are typically at your best. For many people, morning is the best time; for others, afternoon is best. The reason for selecting your high-energy time for creative work is that creativity requires considerable mental energy. Routine work can be performed when you are not at your best mentally.

Stay in Control of Paperwork, E-Mail, and Voice Mail

No organization today can accomplish its mission unless paperwork, including the electronic variety, receives appropriate attention. If you handle paperwork improperly, your job may spiral out of control. Once your job is out of control, the stress level will increase. Invest a small amount of time in paperwork and electronic mail every day. Avoid becoming a paper shuffler or frequently rereading e-mail messages. Handle a piece of paper or an e-mail message only once. When you pick up a hard-copy memo or read an electronic one, take some action: throw it away or delete it, route it to someone else, write a short response to the sender, or flag it for action later. Loose ends of time can be used to take care of the flagged memos.

A recommended method for efficiently dealing with paper memos and letters is to place them into stacking bins on the floor labeled "To Read," "To File," and "To Do."[20] E-mail messages could be placed into folders with the same labels.

Staying in control of voice-mail messages is also important for productivity. Stacked-up voice-mail messages will often detract from your ability to concentrate on other work. Not promptly returning voice-mail messages creates the problem of perceived rudeness and poor customer service. Disciplining yourself to answer voice-mail messages in batches, as mentioned in Exhibit 17-2, will help you manage these messages productively.

Make Effective Use of Office Technology

Many managerial workers boost their productivity by making effective use of office technology. Yet the productivity gains are not inevitable. A person may be able to receive rapidly transmitted e-mail messages from all over the world, search the Internet on a smart phone, and produce exquisite pie

---

[20]Lisa Kanarek, "Clean Sweep," *Entrepreneur*, June 2006, p. 44.

charts, but increased sales and decreased costs do not always follow. Boosting your personal productivity is contingent upon choosing equipment that truly adds to productivity. Productivity suffers when you must spend time learning the technology, consulting with the tech center, or transporting equipment to the repair shop. The situation of Brandon Hunt, a 28-year-old who specializes in rehabilitating distressed real estate and then selling it for a profit, illustrates the positive impact of technology on productivity.

> *For Hunt, "flipping" is a high-speed, high-tech process. The morning after buying a house in need of repair, he visits with a locksmith to secure the property. He decides on how many fans, light fixtures, window panes, and cans of paint will be needed and estimates needed flooring supplies. He enters the information into a spreadsheet on his BlackBerry. Next, he e-mails the order to the local Lowe's home improvement store with an address and a delivery date. The contractor arrives on the same day as the delivery by Lowe's, and the houses are typically ready for listing within two weeks.*[21]

A major reason many workers do not achieve productivity gains with information technology is that they do not invest the time saved in other productive activity. If sending a batch of e-mail messages instead of postal mail saves you two hours, you will only experience a productivity gain if the two hours are then invested in a task with a tangible output, such as searching for a lower-cost supplier. Another problem is that electronic communication systems such as IM divert your attention from the task at hand. A major problem with using social media rather than e-mail to communicate with coworkers is that visiting a social networking site diverts attention from work.

Office technology devices are attractive and intriguing, but sometimes simple mechanical or handwritten procedures are faster than office technology. For example, the simple 3 × 5 index card remains a powerful low-technology way of preparing and executing a to-do list. Managers and professionals who move from one location to another may find it a time waster to access a computer just to check their daily list. Even a palm-size computer can be more disruptive than simply glancing at an index card attached to a pocket calendar. A complaint some people have about large 8½ × 11 planners is they are cumbersome to lug around unless you are carrying an attaché case.

Practice the Mental State of Peak Performance

peak performance
A mental state in which maximum results are achieved with minimum effort.

To achieve maximum potential productivity, one must transcend ordinary levels of concentration and devotion to duty. That occurs in **peak performance**, a mental state in which maximum results are achieved with minimum effort. People who achieve peak performance typically have an important mission in life—such as building a top-quality company.[22]

---

[21]Prashant Gopal, "Flipper, Come Home. All Is Forgiven," *Bloomberg Business Week*, April 10, 2010, p. 26.

[22]Ingrid Lorch-Bacci, "Achieving Peak Performance: The Hidden Dimension," *Executive Management Forum*, January 1991, pp. 1–4; Don Straits, "Peak Performers: In Search of the Best," pp. 1–2, http://www.careerbuilder.com, accessed March 10, 2006.

Peak performers remain mentally calm and physically at ease when challenged by difficult problems. They focus intensely and stay involved, much as they would in playing the best tennis games of their lives. Peak performance also involves careful planning for the task to be accomplished, including obtaining input from others. For example, if you had an upcoming meeting with a major customer, you might research the type of information important to that customer. You may have experienced the state of peak performance when totally involved with a problem or task. At that moment, nothing else seems to exist.

To achieve peak performance, you must continually work toward being mentally calm and physically at ease. Concentrate intensely, but not so much that you choke. In addition to frequent practice, peak performance can be achieved through visualization. In visualization, you develop a mental image of how you would act and feel at the point of peak performance. For example, imagine yourself making a flawless presentation to top-level management about the contributions of your department.

Take Naps or Meditate

Many people believe that a 15-minute or 30-minute nap recharges workers and boosts productivity. Productivity-enhancing naps are important because so many workers, including managers, are sleep deprived.[23] Naps of 30 minutes or more may create grogginess and lower productivity. Well-placed naps actually enhance rather than diminish productivity, and they are an excellent stress reducer. A report published in the *Proceedings of the National Academy of Sciences* showed that a nap with REM (or "dream") sleep improves the ability of people to integrate unassociated information for creative problem solving, as well as boosting memory.[24]

Naps can also prevent industrial disasters by overcoming grogginess before it leads to an accident such as the *Exxon Valdez* oil spill. Naps are an effective way of decreasing incidences of driving while drowsy.

The organizational nap taker must use discretion in napping so as not to be perceived as sleeping on the job. Toward this end, some workers nap in their cars or in a storeroom during lunch break. In companies where the organization accepts such behavior, some employees nap with their heads resting on their desks or worktables during breaks. Many workers continue to nap under their desks. Some companies offer nap rooms or other nap-friendly devices. For example, Google offers nap pods that block out light and sound. This is an extension of its flexible work policy, which says that employees have different styles of work that should be accommodated.[25]

---

[23]Charles A. Czeisler, "Sleep Deficit: The Performance Killer," *Harvard Business Review*, October 2006, pp. 53–59.

[24]Study cited in Robert Stickgold, "The Simplest Way to Reboot Your Brain," *Harvard Business Review*, October 2008, p. 36.

[25]Stickgold, "The Simplest Way to Reboot," p. 36.

Closely related to the productivity-boosting value of napping is *transcendental meditation*, or simply *meditation.* The process physically changes neurological connections between parts of the brain and allows for a deep state of relaxation. Workers who meditate before and after work often find that they can think more clearly about job challenges. A frequently used form of meditation is to position the body in a physically relaxed state and repeat a word, or mantra. Yoga is essentially another form of meditation. Meditation, like striving for peak performance and napping, helps you concentrate and focus, thereby boosting productivity (assuming that you have the right talent and skills to perform well).

Work Smarter, Not Harder

A comprehensive time-management principle is to plan your activities carefully and discharge them in an imaginative way rather than simply working furiously. Several of the time-management suggestions already presented facilitate working smarter, not harder, such as streamlining your work and concentrating on high-output tasks. A working-smart approach requires that you spend a few minutes carefully planning how to implement your task. An example of working smarter would be the placement of an online or newspaper ad to fill a job vacancy. If you list the qualifications precisely, you can significantly decrease the flood of completely unqualified candidates.

Another example of working smarter, not harder, is to use communication technology that fosters collaboration. (As pointed out earlier, however, too much collaboration can slow you down.) A company intranet that allows you to learn what colleagues in other parts of the company are working on will enable you to spend less time in duplicated effort. For example, if you are developing a list of cost-savings suggestions for customer service, and you learn that Kim in Portland, Oregon, is also developing such a list, you can share suggestions.

Build Flexibility into Your System

A time-management system must allow some room for flexibility. How else could you handle unanticipated problems? If you work 50 hours per week, build in a few hours for taking care of emergencies. If your plan is too tight, delegate some tasks to others or work more hours. Perhaps you can find a quicker way to accomplish several of your tasks. As with other forms of planning, do not let your to-do list become a straightjacket that prevents you from capitalizing on new opportunities. Marissa Mayer, vice president search products and user experience at Google, notes that her workday changes so rapidly that she sometimes must revamp the to-do list she prepared the night before. She once said, "This morning I had my list of what I thought I was going to do today, but now I'm doing entirely different things."[26] Mayer would then rapidly develop a new to-do list to take care of tasks for the changed day.

Suppose an item on today's to-do list is to download the latest antivirus program. A customer calls unexpectedly and wants to place a $150,000

---

[26]Quoted in "How I Work," *Fortune*, March 20, 2006, p. 68.

order. Do not reply, "Let me call you back after I have finished checking for new antivirus programs." Finally, to avoid staleness and stress, your schedule must allow sufficient time for rest and relaxation.

LEARNING OBJECTIVE **2**
Explain why people procrastinate, and identify techniques for reducing procrastination.

procrastination
The delaying of action for no good reason.

UNDERSTANDING AND REDUCING PROCRASTINATION

The number-one time waster for most people is **procrastination**, the delaying of action for no good reason. When we procrastinate, there is a gap between intention and action.[27] Reducing procrastination pays substantial dividends in increased productivity, especially because speed can give a company a competitive advantage. Procrastination must be taken seriously because such tendencies can doom a person to low performance. Exhibit 17-3 gives you an opportunity to think about your own tendencies toward

EXHIBIT 17-3	**Procrastination Tendencies**

Circle *Yes* or *No* for each item:

1. I usually do my best work under the pressure of deadlines.	Yes	No
2. Before starting a project, I go through such rituals as sharpening every pencil, straightening up my desk more than once, and discarding bent paper clips.	Yes	No
3. I crave the excitement of the "last-minute rush."	Yes	No
4. I often think that if I delay something, it will go away, or the person who asked for it will forget about it.	Yes	No
5. I extensively research something before taking action, such as obtaining five different estimates before getting the brakes repaired on my car.	Yes	No
6. I have a great deal of difficulty getting started on most projects, even those I enjoy.	Yes	No
7. I keep waiting for the right time to do something, such as getting started on an important report.	Yes	No
8. I often underestimate the time needed to do a project, and say to myself, "I can do this quickly, so I'll wait until next week."	Yes	No
9. It is difficult for me to finish most projects or activities.	Yes	No
10. I have several favorite diversions or distractions that I use to keep me from doing something unpleasant.	Yes	No

Total yes responses ___

The more *yes* responses, the more likely it is that you have a serious procrastination problem. A score of 8, 9, or 10 strongly suggests that procrastination lowers your productivity.

procrastination, so get to it without delay. Here we consider why people procrastinate and what can be done about the problem.

Why People Procrastinate

People procrastinate for many different reasons. Some of them are deeprooted emotional problems, and others are more superficial and directly related to the work. Here we look at seven major reasons for procrastination.

1. Some people fear failure or other negative consequences. As long as a person delays doing something of significance, he or she cannot be regarded as having performed poorly on the project. Other negative consequences include looking foolish in the eyes of others or developing a bad reputation. For instance, if a manager delays making an oral presentation, nobody will know whether he or she is an ineffective speaker. Fear of failure can be—but is not always—a deep-rooted personality problem that makes it difficult to overcome procrastination by following the suggestions presented in the next section. To use a baseball analogy, "If I don't get up to bat, I can't strike out."[27]

2. Procrastination may stem from a desire to avoid uncomfortable, overwhelming, or tedious tasks. Many people delay preparing their income tax forms for this reason.

3. People frequently put off tasks that do not appear to offer a meaningful reward. Suppose you decide that your computer files must be thoroughly updated. Even though you know it should be done, having a completely updated directory might not be a particularly meaningful reward to you. A related reason for procrastination is that impulsivity drives the problem. We can receive an immediate reward right now by delaying a task, such as taking the time to get a refreshment or receive a tweet. The reward for completing a project is far into the future.[28]

4. Some people dislike being controlled. When a procrastinator does not do things on time, he or she has successfully rebelled against being controlled by another person's time schedule.

5. People sometimes are assigned tasks they perceive to be useless or needless, such as checking someone else's work. Rather than proceed with the trivial task, the individual procrastinates.

6. A curious reason for procrastination is to achieve the stimulation and excitement that stems from rushing to meet a deadline. For example, some people enjoy fighting their way through traffic or running through an airline terminal so they can make an appointment or airplane flight barely on time. They appear to enjoy the rush of adrenaline, endorphins, and other hormones associated with hurrying.

7. Procrastination is sometimes a symptom of a negative emotional state such as self-defeating behavior (see Exhibit 16-2 about self-sabotage) or

---

[27]Steven Berglas, "Chronic Time Abuse," *Harvard Business Review*, June 2004, pp. 96–97.

[28]Steven Kotler, "Escape Artists," *Psychology Today*, September/October 2009, p. 73.

depression. The procrastinator may want to fail as a form of self-punishment or may be so depressed that he or she just cannot get started on an important task. In such cases, mental-health counseling may be required. Procrastination can also result from a negative form of perfectionism in which a person believes the project at hand has not been polished enough to deliver to another person. A deadline might be missed as the person thinks, "With just a little more work, my report will be perfect."

Approaches to Reducing and Controlling Procrastination

Procrastination often becomes a strong habit that is difficult to change. Nevertheless, the following strategies and tactics can be helpful in overcoming procrastination:

1. *Break the task down into smaller units.* By splitting a large task into smaller units, you can make a job appear less overwhelming. This approach is useful, of course, only if the task can be done in small pieces, such as a small-business owner preparing tax returns by working on one category of expenses at a time: "Friday I document telephone and Internet expenses; Saturday I'll work on travel and entertainment."

2. *Make a commitment to others.* Your tendency to procrastinate on an important assignment may be reduced if you publicly state that you will get the job done by a certain time. You might feel embarrassed if you fail to meet your deadline.

3. *Reward yourself for achieving milestones.* A potent technique for overcoming any counterproductive behavior pattern is to give yourself a reward for progress toward overcoming the problem. Make your reward commensurate with the magnitude of the accomplishment.

4. *Calculate the cost of procrastination.* You can sometimes reduce procrastination by calculating its cost. Remind yourself, for example, that you might lose out on obtaining a high-paying job you really want if your résumé and cover letter are not ready on time. The cost of procrastination would include the difference in the salary between the job you do find and the one you really wanted. Another cost would be the loss of potential job satisfaction.

5. *Post encouraging notes in your work and living areas.* Encourage yourself to get something done by a particular time via small notes left on your desk or attached to your computer monitor, or perhaps written on your computer's screensaver. For example, "The plan for recycling laser print cartridges is due September 15, and YOU CAN DO IT!!!!!"

6. *Counterattack.* Another way of combating procrastination is to force yourself to do something uncomfortable or frightening. After you begin, you are likely to find that the task is not as onerous as you thought. Assume you have been delaying learning a foreign language even though you know it will help your career. You remember how burdensome it was studying another language in school. You grit your teeth and

| EXHIBIT 17-4 | A Time and Activity Chart to Combat Procrastination |

Charting key tasks and their deadlines, along with your performance in meeting the deadlines, can sometimes help overcome procrastination.

Tasks to Be Accomplished	Deadlines for Task Accomplishment					
	Jan 1	**Jan 31**	**Feb 15**	**Feb 28**	**Mar 15**	**Mar 31**
Expense reports	Did it					
Real-estate estimates		Blew it				
Web site installed			One day late			
Replace broken furniture				Made it		
Plan office picnic					On time	
Collect delinquent account						Blew it

remove the cellophane from the CD for the target language. After listening for five minutes, you discover that beginning to study a foreign language again is not nearly as bad as you imagined.

7. *Post a progress chart in your work area.* The time and activity charts presented in Chapter 6 can be used to combat procrastination. As you chart your progress in achieving the steps in a large project, each on-time accomplishment will serve as a reward and each missed deadline will be self-punishing. The constant reminder of what must be accomplished by what date will sometimes prod you to minimize delays. Exhibit 17-4 presents a basic version of a chart for combating procrastination. The time and activity chart is helpful because it fits into the more general solution to procrastination—getting organized.

LEARNING OBJECTIVE 3
Understand the nature of stress and burnout, including their consequences.

THE NATURE OF STRESS AND BURNOUT

Job stress and its related condition, job burnout, contribute to poor physical and mental health. Employee stress is a source of discomfort and a major concern to managers and stockholders. According to one estimate, worker stress costs $300 billion annually due to lost productivity, increased workers' compensation claims, and health-care costs. Also, 16 percent of health-care costs are attributed to job stress.[29]

In order to effectively prevent and control stress, you first must understand the nature and cause of these conditions. A good starting point in understanding stress symptoms is to take the self-quiz presented in Exhibit 17-5.

[29]Survey results presented in "Stress Costs," *Changing Minds.org* (www.changingminds.org), Syque 2002–2010.

EXHIBIT 17-5	The Stress Questionnaire

Here is a brief questionnaire to give a rough estimate of whether you are facing too much stress. Apply each question to the last six months of your life. Check the appropriate column.

Mostly Yes	Mostly No	
☐	☐	1. Have you been feeling uncomfortably tense lately?
☐	☐	2. Do you frequently argue with people close to you?
☐	☐	3. Is your romantic life very unsatisfactory?
☐	☐	4. Do you have trouble sleeping?
☐	☐	5. Do you feel lethargic about life?
☐	☐	6. Do many people annoy or irritate you?
☐	☐	7. Do you have constant cravings for candy and other sweets?
☐	☐	8. Is your consumption of cigarettes or alcohol way up?
☐	☐	9. Are you becoming addicted to soft drinks, coffee, or tea?
☐	☐	10. Do you find it difficult to concentrate on your work?
☐	☐	11. Do you frequently grind your teeth?
☐	☐	12. Are you increasingly forgetful about little things, such as answering e-mail or mailing a letter?
☐	☐	13. Are you increasingly forgetful about big things, such as appointments and major errands?
☐	☐	14. Are you making far too many trips to the lavatory?
☐	☐	15. Have people commented lately that you do not look well?
☐	☐	16. Do you get into verbal fights with others too frequently?
☐	☐	17. Have you been involved in more than one breakup with a friend lately?
☐	☐	18. Do you have more than your share of tension headaches?
☐	☐	19. Do you feel nauseated much too often?
☐	☐	20. Do you feel light-headed or dizzy almost every day?
☐	☐	21. Do you have churning sensations in your stomach far too often?
☐	☐	22. Are you in a big hurry all the time?
☐	☐	23. Are far too many things bothering you these days?
☐	☐	24. Do you hurry through activities even when you are not rushed for time?
☐	☐	25. Do you often feel that you are in the panic mode?

Scoring

0–6	Mostly Yes answers: You seem to be experiencing a normal amount of stress.
7–16	Mostly Yes answers: Your stress level seems high. Become involved in some kind of stress-management activity, such as the activities described in this chapter.
17–25	Mostly Yes answers: Your stress level appears to be much too high. Seek the help of a mental-health professional or visit your family physician (or do both).

stress

The mental and physical condition that results from a perceived threat that cannot be dealt with readily.

As used here, **stress** is the mental and physical condition that results from a perceived threat that cannot be dealt with readily. Stress is therefore an internal response to a state of activation. The stressed person is physically and mentally aroused. Stress ordinarily occurs in a threatening or negative situation, such as being fired. However, stress can also be caused by a positive situation, such as receiving a major promotion or bonus.

Symptoms of Stress

A person experiencing stress displays certain symptoms indicating that he or she is trying to cope with a stressor (any force creating the stress reaction). These symptoms can include a host of physiological, emotional, and behavioral reactions.

Physiological symptoms of stress include increased heart rate, blood pressure, breathing rate, pupil size, and perspiration. These symptoms surface because of chemical changes in the body that ultimately produce the hormones cortisol and adrenaline and activate the body's fight-or-flight response. If these physiological symptoms are severe or persist over a prolonged period, the result can be a stress-related disorder such as a heart attack, hypertension, migraine headache, ulcer, colitis, or allergy. The underlying problem is that under chronic stress, cortisol weakens muscles, suppresses the immune system, and elevates the risk of high blood pressure.[30] Because of the weakened immune system, people may experience difficulty shaking a common cold or recovering from a sexually transmitted disease. In general, any disorder classified as psychosomatic is precipitated by emotional stress.

Emotional symptoms of stress include anxiety, tension, depression, discouragement, boredom, prolonged fatigue, feelings of hopelessness, and various kinds of defensive thinking. Note that anxiety is a general sense of dread, fear, or worry for no immediate reason and is a symptom of stress. Behavioral symptoms include nervous habits such as facial twitching and sudden decreases in job performance due to forgetfulness and errors in concentration or judgment. Increased use of alcohol and other drugs may also occur. A study with Chinese workers indicated that job stress was associated with increased consumption of alcohol. Less emotionally involved workers drank the most, but so did workers with high involvement.[31] It is possible that workers who take their job quite seriously are more prone to drinking when they face job problems. Procrastination is another potential symptom of negative stress.

Job Performance Consequences of Stress

Stress has both negative and positive job consequences, and these consequences are closely related to symptoms. For example, if a worker concentrates poorly or consumes too much alcohol as a result of stress, his or her job performance will suffer. **Hindrance stressors** are those stressful events and thoughts that have a negative effect on motivation and performance.

hindrance stressors
Stress events and thoughts that have a negative effect on motivation and performance.

---

[30]Laboratory findings reported in Shirley S. Wang, "Stress Hormone's Surprise Powers," *The Wall Street Journal*, February 2, 2010, p. D2.

[31]Songqi Liu, Mo Wang, YuJie Zhan, and Junqi Shi, "Daily Work Stress and Alcohol Use: Testing the Cross-Level Moderation Effects of Neuroticism and Job Involvement," *Personnel Psychology*, Autumn 2009, pp. 575–597.

challenge stressors
Sources of stress that have a positive direct effect on motivation and performance.

In contrast, **challenge stressors** have a positive direct effect on motivation and performance.[32] A study showed that hindrance stressors will often decrease organizational citizenship behavior and increase counterproductive (poor performance) behaviors.[33]

People require the right amount of stress to keep them mentally and physically alert. Managers create challenge stressors by challenging workers and being passionate about work.[34] If the stress is particularly uncomfortable or distasteful, however, it will lower job performance—particularly on complex, demanding jobs. An example of a stressor that will lower job performance for most people is a bullying, abrasive manager who wants to see the employee fail.

A person's perception of something (or somebody) usually determines whether that something or somebody acts as a challenge or hindrance stressor. For example, one person might perceive an inspection by top-level managers to be so frightening that he is irritable toward team members. Another manager might welcome the visit as a chance to proudly display her department's high-quality performance. An extensive review of research about job stress concludes that stress is less likely to lower performance when employees have high levels of self-esteem and commitment to the organization (are engaged).[35]

job burnout
A pattern of emotional, physical, and mental exhaustion in response to chronic job stressors.

After prolonged exposure to job stress, a person runs the risk of feeling burned out—a drained, used-up feeling. **Job burnout** is a pattern of emotional, physical, and mental exhaustion in response to chronic job stressors. Cynicism, apathy, and indifference are the major behavioral symptoms of the burned-out worker. Hopelessness is another key symptom of burnout; workers often feel that nothing they do makes a difference and that they are not accomplishing much of value. Correspondingly, burnout involves losing a sense of the basic purpose and fulfillment of your work.[36] Supervisors are more at risk of burnout than other workers because they deal primarily with the demands of other people.

Two studies conducted in a variety of organizations showed that burnout in the form of emotional exhaustion leads to lowered job performance, less organizational citizenship behavior, and an intention to quit.[37] Have you

---

[32]Jeffery A. Lepine, Nathan P. Podsakoff, and Marcie A. Lepine, "A Meta-Analytic Test of the Challenge-Stressor-Hindrance Stressor Framework: An Explanation for Inconsistent Relationships among Stressors and Performance," *Academy of Management Journal*, October 2005, pp. 764–775.

[33]Jessica B. Rodell and Timothy A. Judge, "Can 'Good' Stressors Spark 'Bad' Behaviors? The Mediating Role of Emotions in Links of Challenge and Hindrance Stressors with Citizenship and Counterproductive Behaviors," *Journal of Applied Psychology*, November 2009, pp. 1438–1451.

[34]Peg Gamse, "Stress for Success," *HR Magazine*, July 2003, p. 102.

[35]Steve M. Jex, *Stress and Job Performance: Theory, Research, and Implications for Managerial Practice* (Thousand Oaks, CA: Sage, 1998).

[36]Lin Grensing-Pophal, "HR, Heal Thyself," *HR Magazine*, March 1999, p. 84.

[37]Russell Cropanzano, Deborah E. Rupp, and Zinta S. Byrne, "The Relationship of Emotional Exhaustion to Work Attitudes, Job Performance, and Organizational Citizenship Behaviors," *Journal of Applied Psychology*, February 2003, pp. 160–169.

ever experienced the phenomenon of being so exhausted that your motivation suffered?

Absence of ample positive feedback and other rewards is strongly associated with job burnout. As a consequence of not knowing how well they are doing and not receiving recognition, employees often become discouraged and emotionally exhausted. The result is often—but certainly not always—job burnout. The right type of leader/manager can help prevent the problems of burnout. For example, a study with two different samples of workers suggested that workers who perceived their leaders to be charismatic were less likely to suffer from burnout. Workers who do not feel in control of their own fate were more likely to avoid burnout if they have a charismatic leader.[38]

Factors Contributing to Stress and Burnout

Factors within a person, as well as adverse organizational conditions, can cause or contribute to stress and burnout. Personal-life stress and work stress also influence each other. Work stress can create problems—and therefore stress—at home. And stress that stems from personal problems can lead to problems—and therefore stress—at work. Because stress is additive, if you have considerable personal stress, you will be more susceptible to job stress, and vice versa.

Factors within the Individual

Hostile, aggressive, and impatient people find ways of turning almost any job into a stressful experience. Such individuals are labeled *Type A*. Their more easygoing counterparts are labeled *Type B*. In addition to anger, the outstanding trait of Type A people is their strong sense of time urgency, known as "hurry sickness." This sense of urgency compels them to achieve more and more in less and less time. Angry, aggressive (usually male) Type A people are more likely than Type Bs to experience cardiovascular disorders.

Although Type A behavior is associated with coronary heart disease, only a few features of the Type A personality pattern may be related to cardiac disorders. The adverse health effects generally stem from hostility, anger, cynicism, and suspiciousness in contrast to impatience, ambition, and drive. Recognize also that not every hard-driving, impatient person is correctly classified as Type A. Managers who enjoy working with other people are not particularly prone to heart disease. An example follows, describing a 30-year-old Type A manager loaded with hostility and at high risk for heart attack:

> *When business associates fail to follow straightforward directions or miss deadlines on projects, Matt Sicinski gets angry, really angry. "My feet get cold, and I get a throbbing in my head," says Mr. Sicinski, who works for a company that runs drug studies for the pharmaceutical industry. "I can feel*

---

[38]Annebel H. B. De Hoogh and Deanne N. Den Hartog, "Neuroticism and Locus of Control as Moderators of the Relationships of Charismatic and Autocratic Leadership with Burnout," *Journal of Applied Psychology*, July 2009, pp. 1058–1067.

every muscle in my body tense up." Sometimes in the middle of a conversation, he puts the phone on mute, he says, and starts "cursing somebody up one side and down the other." He is on a combination of drugs to control his blood pressure, with limited success, he says.[39]

locus of control

The way in which people look at causation in their lives.

Another notable personality characteristic related to job stress is **locus of control**, the way in which people look at causation in their lives. People who believe that they have more control over their actions than do external events are less stress prone. For example, a 50-year-old person with an internal locus of control might lose his job and say, "I don't care if a lot of age discrimination in business exists. I have many needed skills and many employers will want me. Age will not be an issue for me in finding suitable employment." This man's internal locus of control will help him ward off stress related to job loss. A 50-year-old with an external locus of control will experience high stress because that person believes that he or she is helpless in the face of job discrimination.

A study with 5,185 managers from 24 geopolitical entities around the world found a strong association between having an internal locus of control and both psychological and physical well-being. In this study, having low well-being was the same as having stress symptoms.[40]

People who have high expectations are likely to experience job burnout at some point in their careers, because they may not receive as many rewards as they are seeking. People who need constant excitement also face a high risk of job burnout, because they bore easily and quickly.

Related to factors within the individual that contribute to stress are personal problems and worries. For example, workers who worry about housing costs bring considerable stress with them into the workplace. Exhibit 17-6 reports the results of a stress survey of 2,000 adults conducted as part of Mind/Body Health education campaign of the American Psychological Association. These causes of stress stem from both work and personal life. Three of these causes are directly related to worries about finances.

Adverse Organizational Conditions

Under ideal conditions, workers experience just enough stress to prompt them to respond creatively and energetically to their jobs. Unfortunately, high stress levels created by adverse organizational conditions lead to many negative symptoms.

Work and Information Overload. A major contributor to job stress is work overload. Demands on white-collar workers appear to be at an all-time high, as companies attempt to increase work output and decrease staffing at the same time. In Japan, many incidents have been reported of managers and

---

[39]Ron Winslow, "Choose Your Neurosis: Some Type A Traits are Riskier than Others," *The Wall Street Journal*, October 22, 2003, p. D1.

[40]Paul E. Spector and 29 other contributors, "Locus of Control, and Well-Being at Work: How Generalizable are Western Findings?" *Academy of Management Journal*, April 2002, pp. 453–466.

EXHIBIT 17-6	Causes of Stress among the General Population

Causes of Stress	Percent of Respondents Experiencing the Stressor
Work	67
Money	78
The economy	75
Relationships (spouse, children, girl/boyfriend)	59
Family responsibilities	58
Personal health concerns	58
Health problems affecting my family	61
Housing costs (mortgage or rent)	59
Job stability	58
Personal safety	42

Source: APA Stress in America Survey, reported in Michael Price, "The Recession is Stressing Men More than Women," *Monitor on Psychology*, July/August 2009, p. 10.

corporate professionals who work so many hours that they die from over-work, a condition referred to as *karoshi*. In one instance, a 41-year-old man-ager of a McDonald's restaurant worked more than 80 hours of overtime per month for six months before dying of a cerebral hemorrhage.[41]

A specific overload demand relates to information overload, as many managers and professionals are so bombarded with simultaneous and com-peting messages that they suffer from *attention deficit trait*. The sheer volume of information, combined with the many different ways of accessing informa-tion, makes many workers deficient in their ability to pay attention.[42] The brain becomes overloaded, and this leads to symptoms of distractibility, inner frenzy, and impatience. According to Edward M. Hallowell, people with this trait struggle to stay organized, set priorities, and manage time.[43] In short, their brains are so loaded they become spastic. (If you are suffering from attention deficit trait, follow the suggestions about personal productiv-ity and stress management presented in this chapter.)

Extreme Interpersonal Conflict. Extreme conflict with coworkers, including office politics or conflict with managers, is also a stressor. Another annoy-ance is short lead times—too little notice to get complex assignments accom-plished. A powerful stressor today is job insecurity due to the many mergers and downsizings. Worrying about having one's job outsourced to another region or country or to a subcontractor is also a stressor.

---

[41]La Gérante Meurt de Surmenage au Japon, *Journal de Montréal*, October 29, 2009, p. 11. ("The Manager Dies of Overwork in Japan," Montreal Journal, October 29, 2009.)

[42]Maggie Jackson, "Quelling Distraction," *HR Magazine*, August 2008, p. 44.

[43]Edward M. Hallowell, "Why Smart People Underperform," *Harvard Business Review*, January 2005, pp. 54–62.

EXHIBIT 17-7	The Job Demand–Job Control Model

A worker is likely to experience the most job stress when he or she exercises low control over a job with high demands.

	Low Job Demands	High Job Demands
Low Control	Passive Job	High-Strain Job
High Control	Low-Strain Job	Active Job

role ambiguity
A condition in which the job holder receives confusing or poorly defined expectations.

Role Ambiguity. Not knowing what is expected of you has been long observed as a major job stressor. **Role ambiguity** is a condition in which the job holder receives confusing or poorly defined expectations. The person facing extreme role ambiguity proclaims, "I don't know what I'm supposed to be doing or what will happen to me if I do it." A synthesis of many studies involving more than 35,000 employees found that role ambiguity is one of the two job stressors most strongly related to negative job performance. The other is situational constraints, factors in the work setting that limit the worker's ability to accomplish the job. These could be improper machinery or inadequate supplies.[44]

Limited Control Over Work. According to the **job demand–job control model**, workers experience the most stress when the demands of the job are high and they have little control over the activity.[45] (See Exhibit 17-7.) A customer-service representative with limited authority who has to deal with a major error by the firm would fit this category. In contrast, when job demands are high and the worker has high control, the worker will be energized, motivated, and creative. A branch manager in a successful business might fit this scenario.

job demand–job control model
A model that shows that workers experience the most stress when the demands of the job are high and they have little control over the activity.

Adverse Customer Interaction and Emotional Labor. Interactions with customers can be a major stressor. Stressful events include customers losing control, using profanity, badgering employees, harassing employees, and lying. Part of the problem is that the sales associate often feels helpless when placed in conflict with a customer. The sales associate is told that "the customer is always right." Furthermore, the store manager usually sides with the customer in a dispute with the sales associate.

[44]Simona Gilboa, Arie Shirom, Yitzhak Fried, and Cary Cooper, "A Meta-Analysis of Work Demand Stress and Job Performance: Examining Main and Moderating Effects," *Personnel Psychology*, Summer 2008, pp. 227–271.

[45]Marilyn L. Fox, Deborah J. Dwyer, and Daniel C. Ganster, "Effects of Stressful Job Demands and Control on Physiological and Attitudinal Outcomes in a Hospital Setting," *Academy of Management Journal*, April 1993, pp. 290–292.

Another aspect of adverse customer interaction is the stressor of having to control the expression of emotion to please or avoid displeasing a customer. Imagine having to smile at a customer who belittles you or makes unwanted sexual advances. **Emotional labor** is the process of regulating both feelings and expressions to meet organizational goals.[46] Regulation involves both surface acting and deep acting. Surface acting means faking expressions such as smiling; deep acting involves controlling feelings such as suppressing anger toward a customer you perceive to be annoying or hostile. Faking feelings often leads to the emotional exhaustion component of burnout.

Sales workers and customer-service representatives experience considerable emotional labor among all workers because so often they must fake facial expressions and feelings so as to please customers. The supervisor often dictates the type of emotional display permitted (or display rules). Call center workers are expected to calm angry callers—a behavior that often requires the suppression of negative feelings. In addition, they are supposed to end calls on a positive note, perhaps with a sale.[47]

Work–family Conflict. Work–family conflict is a major stressor that represents a combination of individual and organizational factors contributing to stress. This conflict occurs when the individual must perform multiple roles: worker, spouse, and, often, parent. The stress comes about because of the difficulty of attempting to fill two roles at the same time. For example, having to manage a restaurant on New Year's Eve while your spouse insists you celebrate the event together could cause work–family conflict. Dual-earner couples are particularly susceptible to work–family conflict because of the demands on their time.

Another major contributor to work–family conflict is the blurring of boundaries between work and family life caused by information technology. A Lexmark study of knowledge workers found that 92 percent of respondents admit they initiate or receive work-related communications outside of work. Another information technology–based source of work–family conflict is that people bring home into work, such as shopping online during working hours and sending e-mail to family and friends. In the words of Jared Sandberg of *The Wall Street Journal*, "Work and life aren't so much balanced as they are stirred into a stew that often satisfies neither quarter."[48]

The more time invested in the job, the greater the exposure to work–family conflict and the greater the stress. A confusing aspect of work–family conflict is that it works in both directions. Work responsibilities can

---

emotional labor
The process of regulating both feelings and expressions to meet organizational goals.

work–family conflict
A major stressor that represents a combination of individual and organizational factors contributing to stress.

---

[46]Alicia A. Grandey, "Emotion Regulation in the Workplace: A New Way to Conceptualize Emotional Labor," *Journal of Occupational Health Psychology*, Vol. 5, No. 1 (2000), pp. 95–110.

[47]Steffanie L. Wilk and Lisa M. Moynihan, "Display Rule 'Regulators': The Relationship between Supervisors and Worker Emotional Exhaustion," *Journal of Applied Psychology*, September 2005, pp. 917–927.

[48]The survey results and the quote are from Jared Sandberg, "Back to the Future: Mixing Work, Home Is a Very Old Dilemma," *The Wall Street Journal*, December 12, 2006, p. B1.

create conflict with home responsibilities, and family responsibilities can create conflict with work. The conflict in both directions creates stress.[49] Imagine yourself as a marathon runner who runs a weekend marathon. You are too exhausted to go on a business trip on Monday, so you become stressed about dealing with this conflict.

Although work–family conflict is widespread, current research suggests that being committed to the marital and parental role might actually enhance the work performance of managers. The study was conducted with 346 managers from 314 organizations throughout the United States who attended a leadership development program. Using both questionnaires and ratings of work performance, the researchers found that family commitment and marital commitment did not interfere with work. Furthermore, being committed to the parental role was associated with improved work performance. One explanation for the findings offered by the researchers is that when you have a committed marital partner, he or she helps you in your work. Another possibility is that being committed to marriage and family is a motivational force for performing well.[50]

Many companies have implemented programs, such as flexible working hours and telecommuting, to help employees deal with work–family conflict. However, during the Great Recession, less interest was focused on work–family conflict. A contributing factor was that many workers fearful of job security did not want to place extra demands on managers.

STRESS-MANAGEMENT TECHNIQUES

LEARNING OBJECTIVE **4**
Explain how stress can be managed effectively.

Everybody experiences stress, so how you manage stress can be the key to your well-being. Constructive techniques for managing job stress on your own can be divided into three categories: control, symptom management, and escape. Companies often provide services, such as wellness programs, that give you the opportunity to implement some of these techniques. A major role for managers in dealing with the stress of workers is to encourage them to pursue stress-management techniques on their own or rely on company programs. When choosing methods of stress reduction, it is useful to select methods you truly enjoy so they won't feel like chores, explains Susie Mantell, a stress-management specialist.[51]

---

[49]Leslie B. Hammer, Talya N. Bauer, and Alicia A. Grandey, "Work–Family Conflict and Work-Related Withdrawal Behaviors," *Journal of Business and Psychology*, Spring 2003, pp. 419–434.

[50]Laura M. Graves, Patricia J. Ohlott, and Marion N. Ruderman, "Commitment to Family Roles: Effects on Managers' Attitudes and Performance," *Journal of Applied Psychology*, January 2007, pp. 44–56.

[51]Cited in Teri Evans, "Toxic Avoiders," *Business Week Small Biz*, December 2008/January 2009, p. 33.

Methods for Control and Reduction of Stress

The six control techniques described below consist of both actions and mental evaluations that help people take charge in stressful situations.

1. *Get social support.* Few people can go it alone when experiencing prolonged stress. Receiving social support—encouragement, understanding, and friendship—from other people is an important strategy for coping successfully with job stress.

2. *Improve your work habits.* You can use the techniques described for improving your personal productivity to reduce stress. People typically experience stress when they feel themselves losing control of their work assignments. Conscientious employees are especially prone to negative stress when they cannot get their work under control.

3. *Develop positive self-talk.* Stress-resistant people are basically optimistic and cheerful. This kind of positivism can be learned by switching to positive self-talk instead of thinking negative thoughts.

4. *Hug the right people.* Hugging is seriously regarded as vital for physical and mental well-being. People who do not receive enough quality touching may suffer from low self-esteem, ill health, depression, and loneliness. Conversely, quality touching may help people cope better with job stress. The hugging, however, must represent loving and caring.

5. *Demand less than perfection from yourself.* By demanding less than 100 percent performance from yourself, you will fail less frequently in your own perceptions. Not measuring up to one's own unrealistically high standards creates a considerable amount of stress. Few humans can operate with zero defects or ever achieve Six Sigma perfection!

6. *Strive not to neglect aspects of life outside of work.* There is a big difference between a negative workaholic and a person who simply works hard and long to attain constructive goals. A negative workaholic usually becomes anxious when not working.[52] When a person neglects other aspects of life outside of work, such as physical exercise and spending time with family and friends, the person is more likely to suffer from stress symptoms such as irritability and lack of focus.

Symptom Management

This category of stress management refers to tactics that address the symptoms related to job stress. Dozens of symptom-management techniques have been developed, including the following:

1. Make frequent use of relaxation techniques, including meditation. Learning to relax reduces the adverse effects of stress. The **relaxation response** is a general-purpose method of learning to relax; it is a form of meditation. The key ingredient of this technique is to make yourself quiet and comfortable. At the same time, think of the word *one* (or any simple chant or prayer)

relaxation response
A general-purpose method of learning to relax by yourself.

---

[52]Dana Mattioli, "When Devotion to Work Becomes Job Obsession," *The Wall Street Journal*, January 23, 2007, p. B8.

with every breath for about ten minutes. The technique slows you down both physiologically and emotionally and at the same time reduces the adverse effects of stress. The relaxation response is a physical state of deep rest that counteracts the harmful effects of fighting stressors.[53]

2. *Get appropriate physical exercise.* Physical exercise helps dissipate some of the tension created by job stress and also helps the body ward off future stress-related disorders. A physically fit, well-rested person can usually tolerate more frustration than can a physically run-down, tired person. One way in which exercise helps combat stress is that it releases endorphins. These morphine-like chemicals are produced in the brain and act as painkillers and antidepressants. Workers who travel frequently particularly need physical exercise because travel can damage the body, producing such symptoms as muscle cramps and even blood clots from long airplane trips. More information about the benefits of physical exercise is presented in Exhibit 17-8.

3. *Try to cure hurry sickness.* People with hurry sickness should learn how to relax and enjoy the present for its own sake. Specific tactics include having at least one idle period every day; eating nutritious, not overly seasoned, foods to help decrease nervousness; and finding enrichment in an area of life not related to work.

Removal of the Stressor

Methods of removing the stressor are actions and reappraisals of situations that provide the stressed individual some escape from the stressor. Eliminating the stressor is the most effective escape technique. For example, if a manager is experiencing stress because of serious understaffing in his or her department, that manager should negotiate to receive authorization to hire additional help. Mentally blocking out a stressful thought is another escape technique, but it may not work in the long run.

A strategic method of escaping stress is to first identify your work skills and then find work to match those skills. Assessing your skills and preferences can help you understand why you find some tasks or roles more stressful than others.[54] For example, many people enter the computer or information technology field without having appropriate skills and interest for that type of work. When they are asked to perform such tasks as coding for nine hours in one day, they become stressed because they lack the right aptitude and interest for such work.

Given that you could probably locate five million articles, books, and Internet comments on the subject of job stress, we have not mentioned every possible approach to managing stress. To prevent information overload, study Exhibit 17-9 for more ideas on reducing stress and reinforce a few suggestions made already.

---

[53]Reported in "A Conversation with Mind/Body Researcher Herbert Benson," *Harvard Business Review*, November 2005, p. 54.

[54]William Atkinson, "When Stress Won't Go Away," *HR Magazine*, December 2000, pp. 108–109.

EXHIBIT 17-8 The Benefits of Physical Exercise

- Increases energy and reduces frequent feelings of fatigue
- Reduces feelings of tension, anxiety, and depression
- Improves sleep
- Improves concentration
- Enhances self-esteem and self-confidence
- Helps you lose weight or maintain a healthy weight providing you do not consume more food because you have exercised
- Reduces the risk of heart disease or improves cardiac function if you have had a heart attack or bypass; reduces harmful cholesterol and raises the level of HDL (good) cholesterol in as little as eight weeks. Good results are most likely to occur when combined with moderate alcohol consumption (two glasses per day for adult males, one for adult females).
- Reduces the risk of colon cancer
- Lowers pulse rate, thereby decreasing high blood pressure and the risk of stroke
- Controls blood sugar levels if you have, or are at risk for, diabetes
- Improves bone density and lowers the risk of osteoporosis and fractures as you get older
- Improves muscle tone so you feel better and look better
- Slows the effects of aging, such as physical and mental decline, and increases longevity

Source: The American Heart Association, the American College of Sports Medicine, Shape Up America!, The American Academy of Family Physicians, and National Cattlemen's Beef Association. As compiled by Shari Roan, "The Theory of Inactivity," The Los Angeles Times, March 9, 1998; Tara Parker-Pope, "Doctors' Orders: Ways to Work Exercise Into a Busy Day," *The Wall Street Journal,* January 9, 2007, p. D1; Tedd Mitchell, "To Balance Cholesterol: Exercise," *USA Weekend,* February 17–19, 2006, p. 10.

EXHIBIT 17-9 Stress Busters

- Take a nap when facing heavy pressures. Napping is regarded as one of the most effective techniques for reducing and preventing stress (as well as enhancing personal productivity). Rest helps because negative events tend to be perceived as less frustrating when you have enough sleep.
- Give in to your emotions. If you are angry, disgusted, or confused, admit your feelings to yourself. Suppressing your emotions adds to stress.
- Take a brief break from the stressful situation and do something small and constructive like washing your car, emptying a wastebasket, or getting a haircut.
- Get a massage because it can loosen tight muscles, improve your blood circulation, and calm you down.
- Get help with a stressful task from a coworker, boss, or friend.
- Concentrate on reading, surfing the Internet, a sport, or a hobby. Contrary to common sense, concentration is at the heart of stress reduction.
- Have a quiet place at home and have a brief idle period there every day.
- Take a leisurely day off from your routine.
- Finish something you have started, however small. Accomplishing almost anything reduces some stress.
- Stop to smell the flowers, make friends with a young child or elderly person, or play with a kitten or puppy.
- Strive to do a good job, but not a perfect job.
- Work with your hands, doing a pleasant task.
- Find somebody or something that makes you laugh, and have a good laugh.
- Minimize drinking caffeinated or alcoholic beverages. Drink fruit juice or water instead.
- Simplify your life by getting rid of unessential activities and possessions. Less mental and physical clutter will help you gain more control of your life, leading to less stress. But don't cut back so much that an impoverished life creates new stress.

Summary of Key Points

1 Identify techniques for improving work habits and time management.

One way of increasing your personal productivity is to improve your work habits and time-management skills: Develop a mission, goals, and a strong work ethic. Clean up your work area, and sort out your tasks. Prepare a to-do list, and assign priorities. Streamline your work. Work at a steady, rapid pace; minimize time wasters and interruptions; and concentrate on one task at a time. Concentrate on high-output tasks; do creative and routine work at different times; and stay in control of paperwork, e-mail, and voice mail. Making effective use of office technology is essential. Practice the mental state of peak performance, take naps, or meditate; work smarter, not harder; and build flexibility into your system.

2 Explain why people procrastinate, and identify techniques for reducing procrastination.

Avoid procrastinating by understanding why you procrastinate and taking remedial action, including the following: break the task down into smaller units, make a commitment to others, reward yourself for achieving milestones, calculate the cost of procrastination, post encouraging notes in your work and living areas, counterattack against an uncomfortable task, and post a progress chart.

3 Understand the nature of stress and burnout, including their consequences.

Stress is the mental and physical condition that results from a perceived threat that cannot be dealt with readily. Symptoms of stress can be physiological, emotional, and behavioral. Stress has job performance consequences. Hindrance stressors are negative, whereas challenge stressors are positive. Job burnout is a pattern of emotional, physical, and mental exhaustion in response to chronic job stressors. Hopelessness is another key symptom of burnout.

Job stress is caused by factors within the individual such as Type A behavior and an external locus of control. A variety of adverse organizational conditions, including work overload, role ambiguity, low control over a demanding job, and work–family conflict, contribute to stress. People with high expectations are candidates for burnout. Limited rewards and lack of feedback from the organization contribute to burnout.

4 Explain how stress can be managed effectively.

Methods of preventing and controlling stress and burnout can be divided into three categories: attempts to control stressful situations, symptom management, and removal of the stressor. Specific tactics include getting social support, improving your work habits, using relaxation techniques, getting appropriate physical exercise, eliminating the stressor, and using the freeze-frame technique.

Key Terms and Phrases

Productivity, 626
Work ethic, 627
Peak performance, 637
Procrastination, 640
Stress, 644
Hindrance stressors, 645
Challenge stressors, 646

Job burnout, 646
Locus of control, 648
Role ambiguity, 650
Job demand–job control model, 650
Emotional labor, 651
Work-family conflict, 651
Relaxation response, 653

Questions

1. What is your mission in life? If you do not have a mission, how might you develop one?

2. Have you noticed the frequent errors in dealing with business firms, such as billing errors, names spelled incorrectly, and customer problems that were not fixed? What work-habit explanation can you offer for all these errors?

3. With so many tasks being computerized, why bother studying about improving personal productivity?

4. Assume that it is possible to be highly productive even if your work area is cluttered and littered. Why might having an uncluttered, tidy work area still help you in your career?

5. Why might interacting with coworkers, bosses, and customers through social-networking sites result in a productivity drain?

6. Why are good work habits and time management so effective in reducing job stress?

7. Assume you are the human-resource director for a large, diversified company and you want to develop a policy about employee napping to boost productivity and reduce stress. Perhaps you might want to call in a few other managers to help you refine the policy. Plan for several possibilities: (a) how many members of a department or team are allowed to nap at the same time, (b) if you have a formal napping room, who is allowed to use the room at the same time, and (c) what priority will napping have in relation to taking care of urgent tasks.

Skill-Building Exercise 17-A: Getting Uncluttered

Many time-management experts believe that a major contributor to low productivity is a life cluttered with material possessions. If you have less clutter around you, your concentration and focus will improve. A specific recommendation is to make it a habit to throw out one object every day, including old newspapers, magazines, and e-mail messages. (Selling some of your clutter in a garage sale or on eBay or donating to Goodwill or another charity might be an extra incentive.) Beginning today, throw out something every day from your living quarters or work area. Anything you discard counts, from a few pencils stubs to an obsolete computer tower. By the end of two weeks, see how much progress you have made in reducing clutter. Of more significance, analyze whether your efforts at becoming uncluttered are enhancing your ability to accomplish work. Has this exercise reduced stress and made you feel better?

Skill-Building Exercise 17-B: Good and Bad Ways to Reduce Stress

The purpose of this exercise is to help participants understand the difference between constructive and less constructive ways of reducing stress. Needed for the exercise is a whiteboard, a blackboard, an overhead projector, or a computerized method of projecting information on a screen.

For ten minutes, participants suggest as many techniques as possible for managing or reducing stress that they are willing to share with class members. (Some class members might have ways of reducing stress they would prefer to keep private.)

Participants speak one at a time. As each new technique is suggested, the audience shouts either "good" or "bad." Based on majority opinion, the moderator places the technique in the good or bad column.

A good technique is defined roughly as one that produces almost all benefits. A bad technique is one that produces short-lived benefits such as a "high" followed by negative side effects. (An example would be getting drunk to escape a major problem.) For some or all of the techniques, people should justify their classifications as good or bad.

After the techniques are listed for all to see, the class discusses any conclusions about the difference between good and bad techniques. The group also discusses why knowing the difference is important.

Source: The idea for part of this exercise is from Robert E. Epstein, "Stress Busters: 11 Quick, Fun Games to Tame the Beast," *Psychology Today*, March/April 2000, p. 34.

Management Now: Online Skill-Building Exercise: Boosting and Lowering Productivity on the Internet

Gather into small teams or work individually to identify ten ways in which the Internet can increase personal productivity either on the job or at home. Include at least two ideas on your list that have been posted within the last 12 months. Also identify several ways in which the Internet can decrease personal productivity. To supplement your own thinking, you might search for ideas on how the Internet is supposed to boost productivity. Also, look for negative comments about the ability of the Internet to boost productivity. Based on your experience with using the Internet, comment on whether you think the Internet is becoming a more useful productivity tool or method.

17-A Case Problem

Sean Struggles to Get Started

Sean is the customer-service supervisor at an office-supply business located in Indianapolis. His boss Peg, the director of sales and marketing, assigned him the task of preparing an indepth report as to why the firm has been steadily losing customers. When he first received the assignment, Sean replied, "Give me a break, Peg. We're losing customers simply because many of our customers are shifting to e-commerce. They buy online directly from the manufacturers, or from the major supply companies such as Staples, Office Depot, and OfficeMax."

Peg retorted in a stern tone, "Sean, you are oversimplifying the problem. There are still office supply companies in every city. Most manufacturers do not want to deal with small orders, and companies like Staples have not created a monopoly. Please have that report to me in ten days."

"I've got a lot on my plate, but I will get to it," said Sean. "I'll do what I can to make your deadline."

Sean did not welcome preparing the report. He felt that he was already overloaded with work and that a report would not reveal much that he did not already know. He thought, "Maybe I'll start the report late this Sunday afternoon, right after the Colts have finished playing. That should give me an hour and a half."

The Colts game went quickly, ending just a couple of minutes after 4 p.m. that Sunday. Sean reflected, "What kind of crazy workaholic am I? Why start collecting data on a report now, when I could take Lisa (his daughter) and Max (his Labrador) for a walk. It's a beautiful fall day."

Sean then decided to begin the report Monday morning at 11, sharp. "I'll be in a heavy work mode on Monday." At 10:45 that morning, one of the distribution specialists sent Sean an e-mail message requesting that Sean meet with him ASAP to discuss pricing errors he had found on the company Web site. Sean decided to meet right away because in his mind dealing with an immediate operational problem was more important than writing a report.

Sean then decided to begin working on the customer-loss project at 3 p.m. Wednesday because his schedule was usually light on Wednesday afternoon. When the time came, Sean began to feel nervous. "What should I do to get started? Maybe I'll look on the Internet for some ideas." After inserting the search phrase "Customer loss prevention" into Bing.com, Sean found more than nine million listings. He thought, "Maybe I will read a few dozen of these articles before getting started. Why re-invent the wheel?"

Sean then printed the first ten articles he found and thought, "I will take these home and read them after Lisa is sleeping, and Jan (his wife) has started watching her TV tonight. Besides, the report is not due for another six days. I have plenty of time."

That night Sean fell asleep on the couch before he took the reports from his case.

Discussion Questions

1. To what extent does it appear that Sean has a procrastination problem?
2. What advice can you offer Sean to help him get started on the report about losing customers?
3. What should Peg do to help Sean accomplish his assignment of preparing the report?

17-B Case Problem

Brittany Faces Reality

One year ago, Brittany returned enthusiastically to the work force after 12 years of being a full-time homemaker and a part-time direct sales representative for beauty products. Brittany's major motive for finding a full-time professional job was to work toward her career goal of becoming marketing manager in a medium-size or large company. To help prepare for this career, Brittany completed a business administration degree over a five-year period.

Another compelling reason for returning to full-time employment was financial need. Brittany's husband owned and operated an appliance and electronics store that was becoming less profitable each year. Several large appliance stores had moved into the area, resulting in fewer customers for Suburban Appliances (the name of the family business). Brittany and her husband Maurice concluded that the family could not cover its bills unless Brittany earned the equivalent of a full-time income.

After three months of searching for full-time employment, Brittany responded to a job board ad for a marketing assistant position. The ad described the position as part of a management training program with an excellent future. Ten days after submitting her cover letter and résumé, Brittany was invited for an interview. The company proved to be a national provider of automobile and homeowner insurance. The human-resources interviewer and hiring manager both explained that Brittany's initial assignment would be to work as a telemarketer. Both advised Brittany that many people were applying for these telemarketing positions.

Brittany would be required to telephone individual consumers and small-business owners and make a sales pitch that would motivate them to transfer their automobile or homeowner insurance to her company. The company supplied a computerized list of names and telephone numbers across the country. Using this list, Brittany could take advantage of time-zone differences to telephone people during their dinner times as well as at other times. Brittany would receive a small commission for each customer who made the switch to her company. Her major responsibility in addition to telephone soliciting would be to enter the results of her conversations into a computer and prepare summaries.

One week after the interview, Brittany was extended a job offer. She accepted the offer despite some concern that the position was a little too far removed from the professional marketing position she sought. Brittany was assigned to a small cubicle in a large room with about 25 other telemarketers. She found the training program exciting, particularly with respect to techniques for overcoming customer resistance. Brittany reasoned that this experience, combined with her direct selling of beauty products, would give her excellent insights into how consumers think and behave. For the first two weeks, Brittany found the calls to be uplifting. She experienced a surge of excitement when a customer agreed to switch to her company. As was the custom in the office, she shouted "Yes" after concluding each customer conversion to her company.

As the weeks moved slowly on, Brittany became increasingly restless and concerned about the job. Her success ratio was falling below the company standard of a 3 percent success rate on the cold calls. A thought kept running through Brittany's mind: "Even if I'm doing well at this job, 97 percent of people I call will practically hang up on me. And I can't stand keyboarding all these worthless

17-B Case Problem

reports explaining what happened as a result of my calls. It's a horrible waste of time."

Brittany soon found it difficult to sleep peacefully, often pacing the apartment after Maurice had fallen asleep. She noticed that she was arguing much more with Maurice and the two children. Brittany's stomach churned so much that she found eating uncomfortable. She often poked at her food, but drank coffee and diet soft drinks much more than previously. After six months of working at the insurance company her weight plunged from 135 pounds to 123 pounds. Brittany's left thumb and wrists were constantly sore. One night when Maurice asked her why she was rubbing the region below her thumb, Brittany said, "I push the mouse around so much during the day that my thumb feels like it's falling off."

During the next several months, Brittany spoke with her supervisor twice about her future in the company. Both times the supervisor explained that the best telemarketers become eligible for supervisory positions, providing they have proved themselves for at least three years. The supervisor also cautioned Brittany that her performance was adequate, but not exceptional. Brittany thought to herself, "I'm banging my head against the wall and I'm considered just average."

As Brittany approached a full six months in her position, she and Maurice reviewed the family finances. He said, "Sales at the store are getting worse and worse. I predict that this year your salary will be higher than profits from the store. It's great that we can count on at least one stable salary in the family. The kids and I really appreciate it."

Brittany thought, "Now is the worst time to tell Maurice how I really feel about my job. I'm falling apart inside and the family needs my salary. What a mess."

Discussion Questions

1. What aspects of work stress are revealed in this case?
2. What suggestions can you make to the company for decreasing the stressors in the position of telemarketer?
3. What advice can you offer Brittany to help her reduce her stress?

Glossary

360-degree feedback A performance evaluation (or appraisal) in which a person is evaluated by a sampling of all the people with whom he or she interacts.

A

achievement need The need that refers to finding joy in accomplishment for its own sake.

action plan The specific steps necessary to achieve a goal or an objective.

active listening Listening for full meaning, without making premature judgments or interpretations.

activity In the PERT method, the physical and mental effort required to complete an event.

activity-based costing (ABC) An accounting procedure that allocates the costs of producing a product or service to the activities performed and the resources used.

administrative management The use of management principles in the structuring and managing of an organization.

affiliation need A desire to have close relationships with others and to be a loyal employee or friend.

affirmative action An employment practice that complies with antidiscrimination law and corrects past discriminatory practices.

anchoring In the decision making process, placing too much value on the first information received and ignoring later information.

authority The formal right to get people to do things or the formal right to control resources.

autocratic leader A task-oriented leader who retains most of the authority for himself or herself and is not generally concerned with group members' attitudes toward decisions.

B

balance of trade The difference between exports and imports in both goods and services.

balanced scorecard A management system that enables organizations to clarify their vision and strategy and translate them into action. Also, a set of measures to provide a quick but comprehensive view of the business.

behavior modification A way of changing behavior by rewarding the right responses and punishing or ignoring the wrong responses.

behavior In performance evaluation, what people actually do on the job.

behavioral approach to management An approach to management that emphasizes improving management through an understanding of the psychological makeup of people.

behavioral interviewing A style of interviewing in which the interviewer asks questions whose answers reveal behaviors that would be either strengths or weaknesses in a given position.

bounded rationality The observation that people's limited mental abilities, combined with external influences over which they have little or no control, prevent them from making entirely rational decisions.

brainstorming A group method of solving problems, gathering information, and stimulating creative thinking. The basic technique is to generate numerous ideas through unrestrained and spontaneous participation by group members.

break-even analysis A method of determining the relationship between total costs and total revenues at various levels of production or sales activity.

budget A spending plan expressed in numerical terms for a future period of time.

bureaucracy A rational, systematic, and precise form of organization in which rules, regulations, and techniques of control are specifically defined.

C

carpal tunnel syndrome The most frequent cumulative trauma disorder that occurs when frequent wrist bending results in swelling, leading to a pinched nerve.

cash flow The amount of net cash generated by a business during a specific period.

centralization The extent to which authority is retained at the top of the organization.

challenge stressors Sources of stress that have a positive direct effect on motivation and performance.

charisma The ability to lead or influence others based on personal charm, magnetism, inspiration, and emotion.

c-level manager A recent term to describe top-level managers who usually have the word *chief* as part of their title.

cloud computing Moving data and software from computer hard drives to virtual storage space on the Internet.

Also, the vast array of interconnected machines managing the data and software that were formerly run on desktop computers.

coaching A method for helping employees perform better, which usually occurs on the spot and involves informal discussion and suggestions.

coalition A specific arrangement of parties working together to combine their power, thus exerting influence on another individual or group.

collective efficacy A group's shared belief in its combined capabilities to organize and execute the courses of action required for certain outcomes.

communication The process of exchanging information by the use of words, letters, symbols, or nonverbal behavior.

communication network A pattern or flow of messages that traces the communication from start to finish.

compressed workweek A full-time work schedule that allows 40 hours of work in less than five days.

computer-aided monitoring of work A computer-based system to monitor the work habits and productivity of employees. The content of electronic messages also may be monitored.

computer goof-off Employees who spend so much time attempting new computer routines and accessing information of questionable value that they neglect key aspects of their job.

concurrent control A type of control that monitors activities while they are carried out.

conflict The simultaneous arousal of two or more incompatible motives.

conflict of interest A situation that occurs when one's judgment or objective is compromised.

confrontation Dealing with a controversial or emotional topic directly.

constructive criticism A form of criticism designed to help improve performance or behavior.

contingency approach to management A perspective on management that emphasizes that no single way to manage people or work is best in every situation. It encourages managers to study individual and situational differences before deciding on a course of action.

contingency plan An alternative plan to be used if the original plan cannot be implemented or a crisis develops.

contingent workers Part-time or temporary employees who are not members of the employer's permanent workforce.

corporate social performance The extent to which a firm responds to the demands of its stakeholders for behaving in a socially responsible manner.

corporate social responsibility The idea that firms have an obligation to society beyond their economic obligations to owners or stockholders and beyond those prescribed by law or contract.

corrective discipline A type of discipline that allows employees to correct their behavior before punishment is applied.

creativity The process of developing novel ideas that can be put into action.

critical path The path through the PERT network that includes the most time-consuming sequence of events and activities.

cross-functional team A group composed of workers from different specialties at the same organizational level who come together to accomplish a task.

cultural sensitivity Awareness of local and national customs and their importance in effective interpersonal relationships.

culture shock A group of physical and psychological symptoms that may develop when a person is abruptly placed in a foreign culture.

cumulative trauma disorders Injuries caused by repetitive motions over prolonged periods of time.

D

data mining The extraction of useful analyses from the raw mass of business transactions and other information.

data-driven management The idea that decisions are based on facts rather than impressions or guesses.

decentralization The extent to which authority is passed down to lower levels in an organization.

decision A choice among alternatives.

decision tree A graphic illustration of the alternative solutions available to solve a problem.

decision-making style A manager's typical pattern of making decisions.

decisiveness The extent to which a person makes up his or her mind promptly and prudently.

decoding The communication stage in which the receiver interprets the message and translates it into meaningful information.

defensive communication The tendency to receive messages in a way that protects self-esteem.

deficiency needs Lower-order needs that must be satisfied to ensure a person's existence, security, and requirements for human contact.

delegation Assigning formal authority and responsibility for accomplishing a specific task to another person.

Delphi Technique In relation to forecasting, the process of a facilitator gathering the forecasts, well as the reasons for them, from the specialists in the panel.

departmentalization The process of subdividing work into departments.

development A form of personal improvement that usually consists of enhancing knowledge and skills of a complex and unstructured nature.

deviation In a control system, the size of the discrepancy between performance standards and actual results.

difficult person An individual whose personal characteristics disturb other people.

discipline Punishment used to correct or train.

diversity training Training that attempts to bring about workplace harmony by teaching people how to get along better with diverse work associates.

diversity A mixture of people with different group identities within the same work environment.

downsizing The slimming down of operations to focus resources and boost profits or decrease expenses.

E

earnings before interest, taxes, depreciation, and amortization (EBITDA) A well-established formula to measure the financial success of telecommunications, cable, and media companies.

economic order quantity (EOQ) The inventory level that minimizes both administrative costs and carrying costs.

economic value added (EVA) The measure of how much more (or less) a company earns in profits than the minimum amount its investors expect it to earn.

e-leadership Leadership provided to people whose work is mediated by information technology.

e-learning A Web-based form of training.

emotional intelligence Qualities such as understanding one's feelings, empathy for others, and the regulation of emotion to enhance living.

emotional labor The process of regulating both feelings and expressions to meet organizational goals.

emotional tagging The process by which emotional information attaches itself to the thoughts and experiences shared in our memories.

employee assistance program (EAP) An organization-sponsored service to help employees deal with personal and job-related problems that hinder performance.

employee benefit Any noncash payment given to workers as part of compensation for their employment.

employee network groups A group composed of employees throughout the company who affiliate on the basis of group characteristics such as race, ethnicity, gender, sexual orientation, or physical ability status.

employee orientation program A formal activity designed to acquaint new employees with the organization.

empowerment The process by which managers share power with group members, thereby enhancing employees' feelings of personal effectiveness.

encoding The process of organizing ideas into a series of symbols designed to communicate with the receiver.

engagement The level of commitment workers make to their employer.

entrepreneur A person who founds and operates an innovative business.

entropy A concept of the systems approach to management that states that an organization will die without continuous input from the outside environment.

ergonomics The science of fitting the worker to the job.

ethically centered management An approach to management that emphasizes that the high quality of an end product takes precedence over its scheduled completion.

ethics The study of moral obligation, or separating right from wrong.

event In the PERT method, a point of decision or the accomplishment of a task.

evidence-based management The systematic use of the best available evidence to improve management practice.

expectancy theory of motivation The belief that people will expend effort if they expect the effort to lead to performance and the performance to lead to a reward.

expected time The time that will be used on the PERT diagram as the needed period for the completion of an activity.

expected value The average return on a particular decision being made a large number of times.

external control strategy An approach to control based on the belief that employees are motivated primarily by external rewards and must be controlled by their managers.

extranet A secure section of a Web site that only visitors with a password can enter.

F

feedback The communication stage in which the receiver responds to the sender's message.

feedback control A control that evaluates an activity after it is performed.

first in, first out (FIFO) Selling an item first that has been in inventory the longest.

first-level managers Managers who supervise operatives (also known as first-line managers or supervisors).

flat organization structure A form of organization with relatively few layers of management, making it less bureaucratic.

flow experience The ultimate involvement in work or a condition of heightened focus, productivity, and happiness.

forced rankings An offshoot of evaluating employees against a performance standard in which employees are measured against one another.

formal communication channel The official pathways for sending information inside and outside an organization.

formal group A group deliberately formed by the organization to accomplish specific tasks and achieve goals.

free cash flow A refinement of cash flow that measures the cash from operations minus capital expenditures.

functional departmentalization An arrangement that defines departments by the function each one performs, such as accounting or purchasing.

G

gainsharing A formal program allowing employees to participate financially in the productivity gains they have achieved.

gantt chart A chart that depicts the planned and actual progress of work over the period of time encompassed by the project.

geographic departmentalization An arrangement of departments according to the geographic area or territory served.

global leadership skills The ability to effectively lead people from other cultures.

global start-up A small firm that comes into existence by serving an international market.

goal An overall condition one is trying to achieve, or a conscious intention to act.

good cause A legally justifiable or good business reason for firing an employee.

grapevine The informal means by which information is transmitted in organizations.

gross profit margin A financial ratio expressed as the difference between sales and the cost of goods sold, divided by sales.

group decision The process of several people contributing to a final decision.

group polarization A situation in which post-discussion attitudes tend to be more extreme than pre-discussion attitudes.

group A collection of people who interact with one another, are working toward some common purpose, and perceive themselves to be a group.

groupthink A psychological drive for consensus at any cost.

growth needs Higher-order needs that are concerned with personal development and reaching one's potential.

H

hawthorne effect The phenomenon in which people behave differently in response to perceived attention from evaluators.

heuristics A rule of thumb used in decision making.

high-performance work system A way of organizing work so that front-line workers participate in decisions that have an impact on their jobs and the wider organization.

hindrance stressors Stressful events and thoughts that have a negative effect on motivation and performance.

homeshoring Moving customer service into workers' homes as a form of telecommuting.

horizontal structure The arrangement of work by teams that are responsible for accomplishing a process.

I

improvement goal A goal that, if attained, will correct unacceptable deviation from a performance standard.

ineffective job performance Job performance that lowers productivity below an acceptable standard.

informal communication channel An unofficial network that supplements the formal channels in an organization.

informal group A group that emerges over time through the interaction of workers.

informal learning Any learning in which the learning process is not determined or designed by the organization.

informal organization structure A set of unofficial relationships that emerge to take care of events and transactions not covered by the formal structure.

information overload A condition in which an individual receives so much information that he or she becomes overwhelmed.

information system (or management information system) A formal system for providing management with information useful or necessary for making decisions.

informative confrontation A technique of inquiring about discrepancies, conflicts, and mixed messages.

intellectual capital The value of useful ideas and the people who generate them.

internal control strategy An approach to control based on the belief that employees can be motivated by building their commitment to organizational goals.

intranet (or company intranet) A Web site for company use only.

intuition An experience-based way of knowing or reasoning in which the weighing and balancing evidence is done unconsciously and automatically.

J

job burnout A pattern of emotional, physical, and mental exhaustion in response to chronic job stressors.

job characteristics model A method of job enrichment that focuses on the task and interpersonal dimensions of a job.

job crafting The physical and mental changes individuals make in the task or relationship aspects of their job.

job demand–job control model A model demonstrating the relationship between high or low job demands and high or low job control. It shows that workers experience the most stress when the demands of the job are high and they have little control over the activity.

job description A written statement of the key features of a job and the activities required to perform it effectively.

job design The process of laying out job responsibilities and duties and describing how they are to be performed.

job embeddedness The array of forces attaching people to their jobs.

job enlargement Increasing the number and variety of tasks within a job.

job enrichment An approach to including more challenge and responsibility in jobs to make them more appealing to employees.

job evaluation The process of rank-ordering jobs based on job content, to demonstrate the worth of one job in comparison to another.

job involvement The degree to which individuals identify psychologically with their work.

job rotation A temporary switching of job assignments.

job sharing A work arrangement in which two people who work part-time share one job.

job specialization The degree to which a job holder performs only a limited number of tasks.

job specification A statement of the personal characteristics needed to perform the job.

judgmental forecast A qualitative forecasting method based on a collection of subjective opinions.

just-in-time (JIT) system A system to minimize inventory and move it into the plant exactly when needed.

K

knowledge management The ways and means by which a company leverages its knowledge resources to generate business value.

L

last in, first out (LIFO) Selling an item first that was received last in inventory.

lateral thinking A thinking process that spreads out to find many alternative solutions to a problem.

leadership The ability to inspire confidence and support among the people who are needed to achieve organizational goals.

leadership efficacy A specific form of efficacy (or feeling effective) associated with the level of confidence in the knowledge, skills, and abilities associated with leading others.

leadership grid An approach to classifying leadership style based on different integrations of the leader's concern for production (results) and people (relationships).

leadership style The typical pattern of behavior that a leader uses to influence his or her employees to achieve organizational goals.

learning organization An organization that is skilled at creating, acquiring, and transferring knowledge.

lift-outs (in relation to teams) The practice of recruiting an entire high-functioning team from another organization.

locus of control The way in which people look at causation in their lives.

M

management by objectives (MBO) A systematic application of goal setting and planning to help individuals and firms be more productive.

management The process of using organizational resources to achieve organizational objectives through planning, organizing and staffing, leading, and controlling.

manager A person responsible for the work performance of group members.

maslow's need hierarchy The motivation theory that arranges human needs into a pyramid-shaped model with basic physiological needs at the bottom and self-actualizing needs at the top.

matrix organization A project structure superimposed on a functional structure.

mentor A more experienced person who develops a protégé's abilities through tutoring, coaching, guidance, and emotional support.

metacommunicate To communicate about a communication to help overcome barriers or resolve a problem.

microblogging Sending brief updates about work activities to employees online.

micromanagement Supervising group members too closely and second-guessing their decisions.

middle-level managers Managers who are neither executives nor first-level supervisors, but who serve as a link between the two groups.

milestone chart An extension of the Gantt chart that provides a listing of the subactivities that must be completed to accomplish the major activities listed on the vertical axis.

mission The firm's purpose and where it fits into the world.

modified work schedule Any formal departure from the traditional hours of work, excluding shift work and staggered work hours.

moral intensity The magnitude of an unethical act.

moral laxity A slippage in moral behavior because other issues seem more important at the time.

motivation The expenditure of effort to accomplish results.

multicultural worker An individual who is convinced that all cultures are equally good and who enjoys learning about other cultures.

multiculturalism The ability to work effectively and conduct business with people from different cultures.

multinational corporation (MNC) A firm with operating units in two or more countries in addition to its own.

N

need A deficit within an individual, such as a craving for water or affection.

net debt A company's debt minus the cash and cash equivalents it has on hand.

noise In communication, unwanted interference that can distort or block a message.

nominal group technique (NGT) A group decision making technique that follows a highly structured format.

nonprogrammed decision A decision that is difficult because of its complexity and the fact that the person faces it infrequently.

nonverbal communication The transmission of messages by means other than words.

O

offshoring Global outsourcing.

open-book company A firm in which every employee is trained, empowered, and motivated to understand and pursue the company's business goals.

operating plans The means through which strategic plans alter the destiny of the firm.

operational planning Planning that requires specific procedures and actions at lower levels in an organization.

organization structure The arrangement of people and tasks to accomplish organizational goals.

organizational citizenship behavior Employee behavior that is discretionary and typically not recognized or rewarded but that nevertheless helps the organization.

organizational culture (or corporate culture) The system of shared values and beliefs that actively influence the behavior of organization members.

organizational politics Informal approaches to gaining power or other advantage through means other than merit or luck.

ostracism The extent to which an individual group member perceives that he or she is being ignored by other group members.

outsourcing The practice of hiring an individual or another company outside the organization to perform work.

P

$P = M \times A$ An expression of the relationship between motivation and performance, where P refers to performance, M to motivation, and A to ability.

pareto diagram A bar graph that ranks types of output variations by frequency of occurrence.

participative leader A leader who shares decision making with group members.

peak performance A mental state in which maximum results are achieved with minimum effort.

performance evaluation (or appraisal) A formal system for measuring, evaluating, and reviewing performance.

policies General guidelines to follow in making decisions and taking action.

power motivation A strong desire to control others and resources or get them to do things on your behalf.

power The ability or potential to influence decisions and control resources.

preventive control A control that takes place prior to the performance of an activity.

problem A discrepancy between ideal and actual conditions.

procedures A customary method for handling an activity. It guides action rather than thinking.

procrastinate   To delay in taking action without a valid reason.

procrastination   The delaying of action for no good reason. When we procrastinate, there is a gap between intention and action.

productivity   In reference to your work habits, how effectively you use your resources to achieve your goals.

product–service departmentalization   The arrangement of departments according to the products or services they provide.

profit margin   A financial ratio measuring return on sales, or net income divided by sales.

profit-sharing plan   A method of giving workers supplemental income based on the profitability of the entire firm or a selected unit.

pro forma earnings   A financial statement that excludes write-downs or goodwill and other one-time charges not relevant to future earnings.

program evaluation and review technique (PERT)   A network model used to track the planning activities required to complete a large-scale, nonrepetitive project. It depicts all of the interrelated events that must take place.

programmed decision   A decision that is repetitive, or routine, and made according to a specific procedure.

progressive discipline   The step-by-step application of corrective discipline.

project organization   A temporary group of specialists working under one manager to accomplish a fixed objective.

project team   A small group of employees working on a temporary basis in order to accomplish a particular goal.

pygmalion effect   The idea that people live up to the expectations set for them.

Q

qualitative control technique   A method of controlling based on human judgments about performance that result in a verbal rather than numerical evaluation.

quantitative approach to management   A perspective on management that emphasizes use of a group of methods in managerial decision making that are based on the scientific method.

quantitative control technique   A method of controlling based on numerical measures of performance.

R

realistic job preview   A complete disclosure of the potential negative features of a job to a job candidate.

recognition need   The desire to be acknowledged for one's contributions and efforts and to feel important.

recruitment   The process of attracting job candidates with the right characteristics and skills to fill job openings.

reengineering   The radical redesign of work to achieve substantial improvements in performance.

reference check   An inquiry to a third party about a job candidate's suitability for employment.

relationship conflict   Conflict that focuses on personalized, individually oriented issues.

relaxation response   A general-purpose method of learning to relax, a form of meditation.

results   In performance evaluation, what people accomplish, or the objectives they attain.

return on equity   A financial ratio measuring how much a firm is earning on its investment, expressed as net income divided by the owner's equity.

revenue per employee   A financial ratio measuring how much revenue is generated by each employee, expressed as the number of employees divided by total revenues.

role   An expected set of activities or behaviors stemming from a job.

role ambiguity   A condition in which the job holder perceives confusing or poorly defined expectations.

rule   A specific course of action or conduct that must be followed. It is the simplest type of plan.

S

satisficing decision   A decision that meets the minimum standards of satisfaction.

scenario planning   The process of preparing responses to predicted changes in conditions.

scientific management   The application of scientific methods to increase individual workers' productivity.

self-leadership   The process of influencing oneself.

self-managed work team   A formally recognized group of employees who are responsible for an entire work process or segment that delivers a product or service to an internal or external customer.

shadowing   Directly observing the work activities of the mentor by following the manager around for a stated period of time, such as one day per month.

situational leadership II (SLII)   An explanation of leadership that matches leadership style to the capabilities of group members on a given task.

Six Sigma   A data-driven method for achieving near-perfect quality with an emphasis on preventing problems.

Also, a philosophy of driving out waste and improving quality and the cost and time performance of an organization.

small-business owner   An individual who owns and operates a small business.

social loafing   Freeloading, or shirking individual responsibility, when a person is placed in a group setting and removed from individual accountability.

socialization   The process of coming to understand the values, norms, and customs essential for adapting to the organization.

social network analysis   The mapping and measuring of relationships and links between and among people, groups, and the organization.

span of control   The number of workers reporting directly to a manager.

stack-ranking   A ranking system that requires managers to rank each employee within each unit and distribute raises and bonuses accordingly.

stakeholder viewpoint   The viewpoint on social responsibility contending that firms must hold themselves responsible for the quality of life of the many groups affected by the firm's actions.

standard   A unit of measurement used to evaluate results.

stockholder viewpoint   The traditional perspective on social responsibility, believing that a business organization is responsible only to its owners and stockholders.

strategic human resource planning   The process of anticipating and providing for the movement of people into, within, and out of an organization to support the firm's business strategy.

strategic planning   A firm's overall master plan that shapes its destiny.

strategy   The organization's plan, or comprehensive program, for achieving its vision, mission, and goals in its environment.

stress   The mental and physical condition that results from a perceived threat that cannot be dealt with readily.

subculture   A pocket in which the organizational culture differs from the dominant culture, as well as other pockets of the subculture.

summary discipline   The immediate discharge of an employee because of a serious offense.

superordinate goals   An overarching goal that captures the imagination.

SWOT analysis   A method of considering the strengths, weaknesses, opportunities, and threats in a given situation.

synergy   A concept of the systems approach to management that states that the whole organization working together will produce more than the parts working independently.

systems perspective   A way of viewing problems based on the concept that an organization is a system, or an entity, of interrelated parts.

T

tactical planning   Planning that translates a firm's strategic plans into specific goals by organizational unit.

talent management   A deliberate approach to attract, develop, and retain people with the aptitude and abilities to meet future and current organizational needs.

task conflict   Conflict that focuses on substantive, issue-related differences related to the work itself.

task force   A problem-solving group of a temporary nature, usually working against a deadline.

team   A special type of group in which members have complementary skills and are committed to a common purpose, a set of performance goals, and an approach to the task.

team leader   A manager who coordinates the work of a small group of people while acting as a facilitator and catalyst.

teamwork   A situation characterized by understanding and commitment to group goals on the part of all team members.

telecommuting   An arrangement in which employees use computers to perform their regular work responsibilities at home, in a satellite office, or from a remote worksite.

termination   The process of firing an employee because of poor job performance, unacceptable behavior, or interpersonal problems.

time-series analysis   An analysis of a sequence of observations that have taken place at regular intervals over a period of time (hourly, weekly, monthly, and so forth).

top-level managers   Managers at the top one or two levels in an organization.

tough question   A question that helps the group achieve insight into the nature of the problem, what it might be doing wrong, and whether progress is sufficient.

training   Any procedure intended to foster and enhance learning among employees, particularly directed at acquiring job skills.

traits   Stable aspects of people, closely related to personality.

transformational leader   A leader who helps organizations and people make positive changes in the way they do things.

transnational corporation   A special type of MNC that operates worldwide without having one national headquarters.

two-factor theory of work motivation   The theory contending that there are two different sets of job factors. One set can satisfy and motivate people; the other set can only prevent dissatisfaction.

U

unity of command   The classic management principle stating that each subordinate receives assigned duties from one superior only and is accountable to that superior.

V

variable pay   When the amount of money a worker receives is partially dependent on his or her performance.

vertical thinking   An analytical, logical process that results in few answers.

virtual office   Employees who work together as if they were part of a single office despite being physically separated.

virtual team   A small group of people who conduct almost all of their collaborative work by electronic communication rather than in face-to-face meetings.

virtuous circle   The relationship between social and financial performance where corporate social performance and corporate financial performance feed and reinforce each other.

vision   An idealized picture of the future of an organization.

W

whistle blower   An employee who discloses organizational wrongdoing to parties who can take action.

wiki   A password-protected Web page that allows for collaboration of multiple users.

work ethic   A firm belief in the dignity and value of work.

wrongful discharge   The firing of an employee for arbitrary or unfair reasons.

work–family conflict   A major stressor that represents a combination of individual and organizational factors contributing to stress. It occurs when the individual must perform multiple roles: workers, spouse, and often parent.

work streamlining   Eliminating as much low-value work as possible and concentrating on activities that add value for customers or clients.

INDEX